HANDB[OOK OF]
DIVERSITY MANAGEMENT

Beyond Awareness to Competency Based Learning

Edited by
Deborah L. Plummer

University Press of America,® Inc.
Lanham · New York · Oxford

4720 Boston Way
Lanham, Maryland 20706

PO Box 317
Oxford
OX2 9RU, UK

Printed in the United States of America
British Library Cataloging in Publication Information Available

ISBN 0-7618-2458-8 (paperback : alk. ppr.)

™ The paper used in this publication meets the minimum requirements of American National Standard for Information Sciences—Permanence of Paper for Printed Library Materials, ANSI Z39.48—1984

Contents

Section II: Skill-Based Learning

Section III: Professional Issues

Foreword

This handbook comes at a time when the field of work on diversity in organizations is at a critical stage in the life cycle. It is too old to benefit from the latest "buzz"-word phenomenon whereby many organizational change initiatives or academic streams of thought get escalating attention from the sheer fact that they are new. On the other hand, the field is not yet old enough to have a solid track record of proven methodologies to establish it as part of the mainstream of organizational work.

I believe that this in-between status applies to diversity management both as a field of academic inquiry and as a field of organizational practice. It is a precarious position and I am not at all sure where we are going from here. I am clear though about my hopes for the field and about what I believe the field needs at this juncture. One such hope is for better application of existing theory. There is presently a lot of knowledge that is not really being used at a level of purity that gives us a proper opportunity to learn whether or not it is valid theory. For example, screening people for diversity competence as part of hiring and promotion decisions has been predicted to be an important factor for creating an inclusive work environment, but few organizations have actually implemented this idea. Indeed theory about diversity management is inevitably embedded in virtually all diversity action plans. Yet, there is an epidemic of failures to follow through on the implementation of these plans and consequently we have not learned nearly as much as we should have about *effective* diversity management.

A second hope is for a much more serious effort by academics and organizational leaders to partner to conduct empirical research on the most vital questions (e.g. under what circumstances does diversity produce better performance outcomes in work groups than homogeneous groups).

Third, the field would be greatly helped by more attention of national governments to establish diversity management as an integral part of the national agenda for both domestic and foreign policy. In this regard, the effort over the past few years of the Australian government comes to mind as an example worthy of study. Their effort includes the sponsoring of research and of national and international conferences where the results of the research are discussed and translated into action agendas for use in the educational and employment sectors.

Meeting these critical needs requires diligence to continue to develop and disseminate the base of knowledge on diversity management and thus my optimism about the future is enhanced by books like this one. In this volume, Deborah Plummer has assembled a wonderful mix of topics and of well informed authors to write about them. Ed Hubbard's chapter debunks myths that are barriers to measurement for diversity change efforts. Miller & Katz draw on their extensive experience as counselors to organizations to offer two chapters which combine to create a " how to guide" for organization change. Mikchael Brazzel's chapter on conflict demonstrates the range of the book by drawing heavily on academic theory and empirical research. Herb Stevenson's piece on visioning offers a refreshingly different approach by applying principles that he says derive from a Native American visioning process. Sandra Shullman gives us a provocative discussion of possible scenarios of the future of the field and explains criteria for evaluating whether or not diversity management is or is not becoming a "profession". To these Deborah adds contributions from such seminal thinkers in the field as R. Roosevelt Thomas and Marilyn Loden. This is just a sample of the gems of insight to be discovered here.

As we move forward with the work, I hope that the breadth and depth of thought that is represented in this volume will become standard for discourse about diversity. If that happens, our chances of realizing the great potential for diversity to add value to human endeavors will be markedly improved.

Taylor Cox Jr., Ph.D.
August, 2002

Preface

In 1997, the first Master of Arts degree program in Diversity Management began at Cleveland State University in the Department of Psychology. The faculty for this program, comprised of CSU professors, NTL Institute professional members and local diversity consultants, has had the opportunity of working with almost 100 students in this innovative program over the past five years. I have had both the challenge and gift of serving as Director of this program.

Developing the curriculum for this program opened my eyes to the reality that the field of diversity management has burgeoned. The fact that there are now journals, a degree program and a professional organization (Diversity Leadership Forum [DLF]) demonstrates that the roots of the field are beginning to sprout.

As a faculty, we were in a constant search for materials and resources for this program. We have generally provided several notable texts and numerous journal articles for the courses, but still lacked a comprehensive text that students could use for reference after a course. The *Handbook of Diversity Management* is a response to our need; yet, the audience for this handbook is broad — adult learners in human resource management, independent consultants and trainers, school administrators, law enforcement officials, and community leaders. The chapters of the book represent the curriculum of the Diversity Management Program and the field of Diversity Management. They offer something for seasoned and novice diversity practitioners and provide diversity knowledge for general organizational professionals.

For the seasoned professional, the handbook serves as a compendium of information that can support fieldwork. For the novice learner, it offers the theories and frameworks to support understanding the practice side of the field. For organizational professionals, the handbook can be used as a reference to aid in the creation of initiatives and support organizational effectiveness

The content of the *Handbook* is divided into three sections: Theoretical Foundations, Skill-Based Learning, and Professional Issues. The chapters can be read in sequence for a "snapshot" of each of the components of diversity management that together present a comprehensive picture of the field. The *Handbook* can also be read on need-to-know basis by selecting specific chapters. The section entitled "Chapters at a Glance" support the use of the handbook for either a comprehensive overview or specific understanding of a component.

The text has an outstanding outline of professional contributors; thus, the book is easily recognized as valuable reading. Contributors to the book are outstanding scholars in the field of diversity management— R. Roosevelt Thomas, Jr., Taylor Cox, Jr., Edward Hubbard, Judith Katz, Frederick Miller, and Marilyn Loden. They are authors of best-selling books in the field of diversity management. All of the contributors are not only scholars, but also practitioners, which add to the depth and breadth of the chapters. A brief biographical sketch of each contributor is included at the end of the book.

The *Handbook of Diversity Management* makes a valuable contribution to the scholarship of diversity, not only because of its contributors, but because the comprehensive, integrative nature of the presentation. This integrative presentation helps define Diversity Management as a field. The book is not a collection of readings or essays, but a conceptualization of the arena of Diversity Management. The framework of the book builds a strong business case for serious consideration as a professional field of study. From this perspective, the book begins with an overview chapter. Chapter Two is about Diversity Management's historical and theoretical roots. Michael Brazzel, a seasoned diversity consultant and practitioner, writes this second chapter.

In Chapter Three, consistent with his call to move us beyond race and gender, Roosevelt Thomas urges readers to gain conceptual clarity around existing diversity frameworks. New ways of thinking and approaching differences are set forth in Evangelina Holvino's treatise of theories of differences in Chapter Four.

Chapters Five through Eight continue to build conceptual ground. Steve Slane and Donald Seyler provide a concise and practical summary of the application of social psychology to diversity practice. Lalei Gutierrez and Phil Belzunce present a theoretical yet inspirational chapter on developing cultural competence through use of self. Vikki Winbush and Jacquie McLemore offer an integrative presentation that nicely highlights the vast amount of literature on group dynamics and diversity. The section on Theoretical Foundations closes with a synthesis of diversity and change management by diversity consultant and researcher, Beverly Fletcher.

The book proposes that Diversity Management is a field of professional practice as well as an area of systematic study and scientific inquiry. The section on Skill-Based Learning demonstrates this proposal. Writing the chapter on diagnosing provided me with the opportunity to integrate much of what I have done over the past 20 years with organizations. I hope that it proves useful to other practitioners.

Never has the business case for diversity been made stronger than through the professional contributions of Ed Hubbard. His chapter on assessing, measuring, and analyzing the impact of diversity initiatives gives new meaning to the phrase, "what doesn't get measured, doesn't get done." Because of his contributions, the work of diversity gets done.

If when managing a diverse workforce, measurement is a necessity, then building relationships is the key to effectively doing the work. By shifting our focus from facilitating diversity issues and confronting diversity problems to facilitating diversity opportunities, Marilyn Loden offers us new definitions of our roles and approaches to eradicating institutional "isms" as diversity facilitators. Similarly, Leslie Saunders underscores that relationship-building skills are what moves organizations forward on the continuum from exclusion to inclusion. Leslie's chapter is loaded with case presentations from her many years of experience as a diversity consultant to illustrate this point.

Michael Brazzel and Pat Bidol-Padva offer ways to manage diversity conflict that move it out of the realm of confrontation. Michael's chapter lays the theoretical framework, while Pat's chapter stages a system for practice within organizations. Collectively, these chapters suggest approaches and systems to support turning conflict into opportunities for individual, interpersonal and organizational growth.

The final section on Professional Issues brings together the theory and practice aspects of Diversity Management. Judith Katz and Frederick Miller share their expertise as pioneers in Diversity

Management in their two chapters — one on consultation skills, and the other on how to build inclusion and leverage diversity as a way of doing business.

To this point, the book has focused on corporate businesses. Diversity Management is important in service organizations as well. A chapter on diversity work in non-profit, faith-based organizations, schools, and community, and government agencies is included that applies the principles of Diversity Management to these settings. Husband and wife team — Jim Henkelman-Bahn and Jackie Bahn-Henkelman, — draw on their many years of practice in these arenas to tease out the subtle and not-so-subtle differences for how diversity work gets done in these settings.

Diversity consultants have collectively agreed that without leadership support, Diversity Management initiatives in organizations fizzle or remain stagnant. Ollie Malone, in his chapter on Diversity Leadership, simplifies leadership's role for any busy executive and sets a framework that practitioners can use as a guide. Similarly, Herb Stevenson lays the ground for how visioning processes can be used to build inclusion in an organization. Drawing from his Native American traditions, he shows how visioning, when used from an Open-Undirected, approach supports the inclusion of many voices.

In this age of a renewed push toward corporate responsibility, the chapter on diversity ethics could not be timelier. Rev. Joan SalmonCampbell lays the groundwork for the application of diversity to ethical discourse. The reflective tone of the chapter offers the practitioner a way to organize and develop his or her own sense of diversity ethics.

The book ends with a chapter that is reflective of the tone in which it began. Is Diversity Management a profession? A field of study? A discipline? Or a field of practice? What are the benefits of its stabilization as a profession? These are questions deftly raised and addressed by international consultant and psychologist, Sandy Shullman. I believe it is fitting to end this book on this note of inquiry. I trust that it will stimulate much needed discussion, dialogue, and continued research in the area of Diversity Management.

Finally, the subtitle of this book—*Beyond Awareness to Competency Based Learning*—points to the set of skills and competencies provided for the reader. The first section of Theoretical foundations develops the diversity competencies of Creative Management of Differences, Use of

Self as a Tool and Change Management Skills. The second section on Skill Based Learning enhances Cultural-Specific Discernment skills, Effective Communicating Across Differences and Conflict and Collaborative Problem-Solving Skills. The third section which focuses on Professional Issues focuses the practitioner on Self-Education and Collaborative Learning. All of these diversity competencies support the diversity scholar/practitioner in effective diversity work that adds values to all groups, organizations and systems.

Acknowledgements

As a psychologist who began my professional career in clinical work with an emphasis in multicultural counseling, I relied on many of the authors of this text to understand how to apply what I knew about diversity to the organizational level. Many of the contributors to this text have been my teachers as I attended their professional workshops or as I read their writing. I am profoundly grateful to each of the contributors of this book for past and present learning. I am especially grateful to Taylor Cox, Jr. for writing the Foreword.

This book would not be a reality without the expertise, drive, energy and spirit of its Managing Editor, Veronica Cook-Euell. I am eternally grateful for her support of this project.

I gratefully acknowledge permission to reprint or publish adaptations of chapters by Judith H. Katz and Frederick A. Miller, Edward E. Hubbard and R. Roosevelt Thomas, Jr.

Authors Jim Henkelman-Bahn and Jacqueline Bahn-Henkelman wish to acknowledge the contributions of Alexsandra Stewart to their chapter. Alexsandra Steward has worked extensively with government agencies and non-profit organizations and contributed to their chapter from her wealth of experience.

Chapters at a Glance

I Overview of the Field of Diversity Management

This chapter addresses the overarching themes that are present in a study of human differences. It provides an introduction to Diversity Management- exploring its nature and process, assumptions and values, the forces that shape it today, and the professional practice of Diversity Management. A brief glossary of diversity terms are contained in the chapter to assist the reader toward a collaborative understanding of these terms, not only for this chapter and but throughout the book. It engages the reader by providing a Diversity Quiz and the Racial Identity Status for self-assessment to enhance learning and stimulate discussion. The chapter closes with examining Use-of-Self as a tool in Diversity Management.

II The Historical and Theoretical Roots of Diversity Management

As an emerging field of theory, research, teaching and practice, Diversity Management has its historical and theoretical roots in many disciplines. Thus, this chapter begins with a discussion of the defining parameters, the values, and the relationship of Diversity Management to social justice. The chapter then presents a comprehensive examination of the history of Diversity Management, delineating its social and judicial roots. A presentation of demographic and economic changes set the stage for addressing the theoretical roots of this field of study. The categories of levels of human systems – individual, group and organization - frame the exploration of Diversity Management's theoretical roots. Included in this section is a discussion of diversity frames of reference and oppression theory. The chapter concludes with a section on the practice of Diversity Management as it relates to the theoretical base presented earlier in the chapter.

III Approaches to Work Force Mixtures

Conceptual clarity around diversity issues is imperative for meaningful, sustainable progress in the diversity field. This chapter, by a noted diversity practitioner and scholar, presents four approaches to work force mixtures: managing workforce diversity, managing strategic diversity, understanding differences and managing pluralism. The goals and motives of each approach are examined. With this differentiation, a practitioner can use these approaches as analysis tools to sort through the various perspectives and issues in the diversity arena. Choosing the appropriate approach is a dynamic process. Thus, practitioners must consistently assess and change their diversity strategies to reflect shifting organizational realities. A prerequisite for effective strategizing is conceptual clarity around the available options explained in this chapter. The chapter supports practitioners in making quality decisions that will advance the mission and goals of organizations.

IV Theories of Differences: Changing Paradigms for Organizations

This chapter contrasts two approaches to working with differences, the traditional dominant and the feminist - post-colonial and explores their implications for organizational change. The characteristics of the traditional dominant approach to working with differences are described based on psychological theories of difference and functional themes of organizational change. Alternatively, a description of features and examples of a feminist-postcolonial approach is offered. This approach integrates race, ethnicity, class and gender and focuses on social change. Finally, suggestions are made for how human resource professionals; diversity professionals and managers can use a feminist - post-colonial approach to differences to guide organizational change in more complex and dynamic ways.

V Social Psychological Process in Diversity Practice

Not only do the interests of social psychologists and diversity practitioners overlap, but also an understanding of social psychological theory is fundamental to diversity work. This chapter highlights several areas of social psychology research and theory relevant to diversity practice: person perception and impression formation, social cognition, attraction, social influence, attitude and attitude change, and prejudice. Throughout the chapter, the authors present a theoretical concept with its diversity application. This chapter is fundamental to understanding the dynamics of human differences.

VI Developing Cultural Competence Through Use of Self

The self is a psychological construct that describes a person's inner world of experience. As diversity practitioners, the self the most important tool we have. Knowing how to use ourselves as a tool is key to our work. This chapter explores two models of developing cultural competence through use-of-self in the contextual field of diversity: the Being Model and the Ground Sequence Model. In our development as diversity practitioners, we need to realize how we affect our clients through our personal encounters with them - both in how we are and in what we do. Both models presented in this chapter provide practitioners with a guide to understand, support and enhance our use-of-self as a tool in diversity work.

VII Diversity and Group Dynamics

This chapter describes the evolution of group dynamics and diversity, both as separate fields of interest and as they intersected and produced a rich field of empirical and descriptive studies. The studies identified in this chapter support the practitioner in organizations whose work groups have heterogeneous membership. The discussion presented in the chapter is directed at expanding the knowledge and skill repertoires of persons responsible for the function and success of groups within organizations. This includes diversity professionals, those in executive and line management positions and internal or external organizational development consultants. Three key leverage points - Design, Context, and Process -for working with diverse groups are explored.

VIII Diversity: A Strategy for Organizational Change and Success

It has often been noted that managing diversity means organizational culture change. Change leadership necessitates understanding the multiple differences that exist in organizations, and requires the ability to harness the creative potential of those differences. This chapter explores the change competencies necessary for leaders who value diversity as a business strategy. To further explore specific competencies, *The Diversity Competencies Inventory* is offered as a tool for self-exploration.

IX Diagnosing Diversity in Organizations

The aim of this chapter is to help the practitioner understand the process of diagnosing diversity in organizations. It focuses on the process of identifying the current state of an organization and the methods for analysis. Topics explored in this chapter include: the process of organizational diagnosis through the lens of diversity, diagnostic tools that support inclusion, application of the process of data gathering and analysis to diversity, feeding back diagnostic diversity information, and the challenges in diagnosing organizations in a diversity context.

X Assessing, Measuring and Analyzing the Impact of a Diversity Initiative

Diversity is often viewed as a "soft" and sometimes unclear contributor to the organization's performance and bottom-line. In this chapter, one of the foremost diversity researchers and practitioners demonstrates how assessing, measuring and analyzing the impact of a diversity initiative can generate a wealth of resources for improved performance and enhanced productivity. This chapter identifies a brief sample of tools, techniques and procedures to assess, measure, and analyze diversity initiatives in quantitative and qualitative terms. It is designed to help outline methods to tie diversity to the organization's bottom line performance outcomes. Assessing, measuring, and analyzing the impact of diversity initiatives is a critical link for success in diversity management and organizational performance today, and in the future.

XI Facilitating Diversity Issues

Heightening awareness of issues about human differences, particularly race and gender, has been the primary goal of diversity facilitation in the past. Now, with the benefit of this accumulated experience to draw on, the author, a seasoned diversity practitioner, takes stock of the impact of past diversity educational efforts and charts the course for future diversity facilitation. By challenging us to redefine our priorities and arena of diversity work, the author moves the field of diversity management beyond awareness. In addition, concepts and tools that can take facilitation to the next level of work - consolidating support and bridge building - are provided.

XII Momentum and Internal Organizational Relationship Building: On the Road from Exclusion to Inclusion

The collective Diversity Management consulting experience over the past 30 years has demonstrated that an organization's movement from exclusion to inclusion is dependent on a balanced combination of sanctions by top leadership, shared vision and an egalitarian environment. The key to these variables is relationship building - both internally and externally. Building multi-level relationships that support inclusive work environments is the topic of this chapter. Using a road trip analogy, the author takes the reader on a journey to organizational inclusion while offering strategies for making the road trip as trouble-free as possible.

XIII Diversity Conflict and Diversity Conflict Management

This chapter presents a conceptual framework for exploring the conflict that results from diversity. It distinguishes diversity conflict that is based in human differences from diversity conflict that results from a system of oppression. It offers a list of actions that change the nature and intensity of specific conflict situations and it offers strategies to manage conflict. To realize the advantages of diversity conflict, the destructive side of oppression-based diversity conflict must be addressed intentionally and consciously by eradicating racism, sexism, heterosexism and other forms of oppression. Collaborative conflict management processes are useful for resolving diversity conflict based in human differences.

XIV Conflict Resolution Systems for Diversity

Organizational conflict occurs when one or more individuals are dissatisfied. The sources of dissatisfaction in organizations with a diverse workforce often include such factors as unclear communications, the negative impact of policies and procedures, incompatible interests, cultural differences, power discrepancies, and the perception that people are not respected. This chapter builds on the concepts of the previous chapter on diversity conflict and describes a conflict escalation cycle as a framework for differentiating diversity conflict. It further offers a conflict resolution system for diversity initiatives that aids organizations in collaborative resolution of diversity conflict.

XV Diversity Consultation Skills

This chapter describes some of the assumptions on which the work of building inclusion and leveraging diversity is based. It also outlines some of the skills, competencies and behaviors that are essential for individuals involved in creating a culture of inclusion that leverages diversity. When beginning a diversity consultation, it is essential to assemble a team with a diverse range of skills and experiences and a range of viewpoints drawn from inside and outside the organization. That team must model the behaviors of inclusion, the effectiveness of being diverse, and the high performance that results. The key is creating effective partnerships for change. Consultants must gather and develop the fundamental skills demanded by the work. The skills described in the chapter include: Acquiring Vision, Finding the Self-Interest, Positioning and Creating Alignment, Getting Leader Buy-In, Partnering, Managing and Valuing Conflict, Developing Communication Skills, Measuring Results, Honoring the System, Supporting Leaders Without Colluding, Pacing, and Accepting a Continuous Change Process.

XVI Building Inclusion and Leveraging Diversity as a Way of Doing Business

Creating a new organizational culture that is inclusive high performing, and sustainable is not something you can do on paper or overnight. It can only be accomplished by transforming the behavior of *people*. The effort to build inclusion and leverage diversity cannot be achieved by a few isolated programs or one-size-fits-all training packages. It must involve a *total system change*. Policies, practices, and programs that shape people's behavior within the organization must change. It includes teaching leaders, managers, and line workers new skills, creating new ways of defining and measuring success and working comprehensively with people inside and outside the organization. One successful methodology for creating a culture of inclusion that leverages diversity features four key phases of development. These four phases are described the chapter: Building the Platform for Change, Creating

Momentum, Making Diversity and Inclusion a Way of Life, and Leveraging Learning and Challenging the New Status Quo.

XVII Diversity Management in Specialized Settings: Non-Profits, Faith-Based and School Organizations, Community and Government Agencies

The work of the diversity professional in non-profit, faith-based and school organizations and community and government agencies is much like the work of the diversity professional in any organization in our society. All of the basic issues are present. The difference between these organizations is the service orientation and the altruistic motivations of many of the people involved. These differences can either boost diversity goals or act as a barrier to diversity work. Transformation of non-profit organizations and government agencies into truly diverse organizations is critical for their efficacy in the 21st century. This chapter presents the characteristics of these specialized settings and illustrates these points with case studies.

XVIII Diversity Leadership

If organizations are to undertake diversity as a culture change initiative (which is the author's clear bias) then the diversity effort is subject to the learning that has accumulated over more than 50 years of focused attention on the demands of organizational change. The organizational change literature clearly reinforces the mandate for leadership. Diversity is no exception. In this chapter, the author draws from more than 25 years of experience in helping organizations and their leadership change in order to create climates conducive to effective diversity management and organizational success.

XIX Visioning for Inclusive Organizations

Inclusion and inclusiveness are the critical elements of a visioning process that has the power to elicit commitment and inspire individuals.

This chapter examines Open-Undirected visioning methods, offers a correlation between the organizational visioning and vision questing in Native American traditions, and provides a brief case study of the effectiveness of this blended visioning process as a model for organizational work. Open-Undirected methods tend to encourage inclusiveness; both by virtue of including more people in interviewing procedures and by the underlying objectives of the vision itself. Most organizations use Active-Directed methods of visioning that are strategy-oriented, top-down approaches, emphasizing guided questioning and problem solving to produce a constructed picture and achieve a specified outcome. However, recent times have seen the inception of Open-Undirected methods of visioning that are often developed from cross-cultural practices and that are awareness-oriented, bottom-up approaches. Rather than pursuing a preset outcome, these methods wait for a compelling organizational picture to emerge. Whereas both methods can be inclusive, the Active-Directed visioning process will be more reflective of what already exists, including institutionalized forms of exclusion.

XX A Framework for Diversity Ethics

This chapter examines ethics through the lens of Diversity Management. It offers a framework for individuals to use in exploring their own thinking about decision-making and values and practitioners to use in distinguishing between a personal code of conduct and a universal moral mandate. For diversity practitioners working toward an enhanced commitment by organizations to value human differences in the workplace, examination of this topic is critical to the development of their understanding and their standards.

XXI Diversity Management: Its Future as a Profession

This chapter returns to the earlier concepts in the first section to address whether the practice of Diversity Management fits the requirements of a profession. In doing so, the author- a psychologist and organizational consultant- poses questions to practitioners for examination and dialogue. Is movement toward a profession a good idea? What could the professional future hold for the diversity community? Although the author concludes that the field is still being crafted and professional roles and paths are still emerging, she lays a foundation for charting the direction of the future of Diversity Management.

Chapter 1

Overview of the Field of Diversity Management

Deborah L. Plummer

This book is about the field of diversity management — the theory and practice of understanding human differences. Perhaps when you think of diversity you think of programs and initiatives employed in organizations, communities, agencies, and schools rather than an entire discipline of study. You may associate diversity with the principle of respect or simply think of it as race relations. You may broadly define diversity as another name for human differences such as race, ethnicity, gender, age, sexual orientation, religion, occupational role and status, mental and physical ability, and the number of ways in which human beings are different. You would be partially correct with any of these thoughts — the field of diversity management is broad and is most often experienced in practice rather than studied as a discipline. Yet it is a field of professional practice as well as an area of systematic study and scientific inquiry. The field of diversity management is rooted in several disciplines — the behavioral sciences, business, and education. The domain of the field focuses on multiple levels of human systems — the individual, interpersonal, organizational, and societal. For example, on the individual level, such topics as the use of self and racial-identity development are subjects of study. On the interpersonal level, communicating across differences, managing resistance and conflict, and collaborative problem-solving skills are important areas of examination. On the organizational level, issues such as creating the business rationale, diversity strategic planning, recruiting and retaining diverse work populations, and measuring and analyzing diversity initiatives come to the forefront. On the societal level, the topics of social justice, building inclusion, eradicating "isms," and creating economic parity are prominent. Thus, in order to grasp the field of diversity management, one has to look through quite a wide lens.

You may feel a bit overwhelmed already by this introduction to the many areas of diversity management. However, the purpose of this text is to present the boundaries for the topic, broad though they be, and to help you to gain a better understanding of diversity management as an area of scholarship and practice.

This book reviews the field of diversity management and examines the theoretical foundations, skill-based learning, and professional issues that encompass the field. This chapter provides an introduction to diversity management, exploring its nature and process, its assumptions and values, the forces that shape diversity management today, and the professional practice of diversity management.

The objectives of this chapter are to raise your awareness of and increase your understanding of the following topics:

- ✓ The language of diversity and its implications for business and personal growth
- ✓ Frameworks for understanding the many aspects of diversity
- ✓ Levels of human systems and how systems thinking helps us to understand diversity
- ✓ Exploration of racial identity development and the cultural pat terns that are part of American society
- ✓ History of the diversity management field
- ✓ Assumptions and values of the field of diversity management
- ✓ The professional practice of diversity management

Defining Diversity

Not long ago, an American in the Midwest might have to travel to the East or West Coasts or across continents to truly witness racial and ethnic diversity. Yet recently, while browsing through the aisles at a newly opened neighborhood bookstore in the Midwest, I was struck by the number of racial/ethnic groups represented by its customers. If I had taken a video of the people that I saw in that Midwest neighborhood bookstore, it would feature:

- A young White male studying the best-seller list
- An Asian female humming softly as she browsed the aisle
- An older African American male in a business suit, headed toward the travel section
- A blonde mom getting her kids settled in the children's-book section
- A middle-aged woman in a wheelchair at the information desk
- A Muslim woman, seated in one of the lounge chairs, reading a book
- A young Jewish male asking a question at the checkout counter
- And probably a host of other folks, whose group membership iden tity was not so visible to me.

Yet I could guess — and be relatively safe in the accuracy of my assumption — that I would also find diversity if I went into a bookstore and saw only White European individuals or only Native Americans or only Asians or only African Americans or only Hispanics. Even within the same racial/ethnic groups, diversity exists. Clearly, diversity is experienced on the individual level as well as on the group and societal levels. Diversity is the hallmark of the American experience.

The changing demographics of the United States, such as I witnessed in that Midwest bookstore, have also influenced the diversity management movement. Workforce 2000 is now more than a reality, and the forecasts of increased diversity expected to occur over the next 20 years have been loudly projected.

How much do you know about the changing demographics that have influenced the diversity management movement? To find out, take the following quiz. Release the need to be right and jot down your first thought as your answer. Your answers will reveal a lot about your perception of the world and your experiences.

DIVERSITY QUIZ

Questions 1-5:

Based on the 2000 census data estimates, what is the percentage (within 3 percentage points) of the total population that each of the following groups represents?

1. Percentage of Asians in the U.S. population.
2. Percentage of Blacks in the U.S. population.
3. Percentage of Hispanics/Latins in the U.S. population.
4. Percentage of American Indians in the U.S. population.
5. Percentage of Whites in the U.S. population.

Questions 6-10:

What percentage of the total world population lives in each of the following geographic areas?

Area	A	B	C	D
	under 10%	10%-30%	30-50%	Over 50%
6. Africa				
7. Asia				
8. Europe				
9. N. America				
10. S. America				

Questions 11-13:

What percentage (within 3 percentage points) of the average U.S. wage paid to White males is earned by the following groups?

11. Average wage for Blacks, as a percentage of average wage for White males.
12. Average wage for Hispanics/Latins, as a percentage of average wage for White males.

13. Average wage for White females, as a percentage of average wage for White males.
14. What percentage of working-age women in the U.S. is presently in the workforce
    a) 50-59%
    b) 60-69%
    c) 70-79%
    d) 80-89%

15. What percentage of U.S. families now fits the profile of *working father, homemaker mother, and two or more children?*
    a) 10%
    b) 15%
    c) 20%
    d) 25%

16. True or False: Federal protection against employment discrimination is provided for gays and lesbians.
17. What percentage of the workforce falls under the definition of "disability" as delineated by the Americans with Disabilities Act?
18. What is the projected percentage of Americans who will be over 65 years of age in the year 2015?
19. Which subgroup has the largest population older than 65 years?

    a) European American Women
    b) European American Men
    c) Asian American Women
    d) Latin American Women

20. By 2010, what is the projected percentage of American children who will be Black, Hispanic/Latin, or Asian?
21. What percentage of the population is estimated to be gay or les bian?
22. What is the number of federally recognized Native American tribal units in the United States?
23. What geographic area is the leading source of new-entry U.S. engineers, doctors, and technical workers?
24. What is the fastest growing religion in the world?

25. What is the largest Hispanic group in the U.S.?

26. True or False: On the 2000 census, mixed-raced Americans were allowed to check off more than one racial category.

Examine your responses and compare them to the answers provided at the end of this chapter. Were there any surprises in what you learned? What was the source of your answers? Was it your educational experience? Your general reading? What you have seen or heard in the media? Your general personal experience?

Often, when we are unaware of factual information about a topic, we rely on our experiential knowledge to provide us with answers. Because our experience is inherently limiting, we can often be wrong about what we have experienced as truth. Social psychologists call this phenomenon the "availability heuristic." We draw on what is readily available as truth and generalize this information as knowledge. A helpful skill for discerning whether information that is readily available to us is based in facts rather than perception is *examining assumptions*.

It is probably obvious to most of us that our assumptions play a large role in how we evaluate our environment. Yet it is this aspect of our thinking that often goes unexamined. Thus, it is imperative that we examine the underlying assumptions behind our beliefs. By learning to identify our assumptions, we can more effectively explore differences with others and work to build common ground and consensus. By examining assumptions, we can more creatively and effectively analyze core misunderstandings and cultural clashes. Go back to your original responses for the quiz and examine the assumptions underlying your thinking that led to your answers. Hopefully, you will have learned more about yourself and your thinking process than you did from whether you were right or wrong in your response. For example, the percentages of People of Color, and the differences in their earned wages from those of White Americans, often surprise people. Think about how People of Color are often portrayed in the media and in our educational system. When race is more often noted when it refers to non-Whites, it leads one to misconceptions about actual numbers and how racial groups are representative of the total population. The number of Native American tribal units also may have surprised you. Again, think about how we might have obtained this information. In most parts of the United States, information about American Indians is limited and unavailable. You may have projected the number of individuals over the age of 65 in 2015 to be much higher than the actual percentage. Again, think about what we hear in the media — especially through advertisements about the growing population of senior citizens and the concerns of the aged. Commercials for products specifically geared toward seniors are now a regular part of our television-viewing experience. All of this information influences how we think about demographic diversity.

Now that we have examined the changing demographics that have influenced the diversity movement, let us turn our attention back to unraveling the meaning of the term diversity. Surely, diversity was with us long before U.S. companies began to prepare for the changing face of the American workforce. As long as there have been human beings, there has been diversity.

The Language of Diversity

What comes to your mind when you think of the word "diversity"? Perhaps you think of differences and of cultural groups getting along better. Maybe your thinking is focused on race and gender issues and the civil rights movement. It could be that for you, the term "diversity" is synonymous with affirmative action. You may think the term is overused and has a negative connotation, that diversity only means that Whites and males will be bashed and held responsible for years of discrimination that individually they had nothing to do with. You may associate it with a company's attempt to avoid a lawsuit or the way it deals with women and People of Color who are complaining. Whether it holds a positive or negative connotation, "diversity" is clearly a loaded term. Its meaning has evolved over the years from its roots in race and gender relations to the building of inclusive environments and the management of basic human differences. The meaning of diversity is largely dependent on its context. The following sections place diversity in context and define it on an individual and personal level and from an organizational perspective.

Individual and Personal Diversity

Diversity, from an individual or personal context, refers to the differences among people, with respect to race, ethnicity, culture, gender, age, class, mental and physical ability, sexual orientation, religion, stature, educational level, job role and function, and personality traits. It embraces all of the many ways in which we are like and not like other human beings. As an individual, I am like some people and unlike others. I am unique and like no one else, yet I am a member of the human race and share a similar genetic and emotional constitution with other human beings. That is the paradox of diversity. We are unique and we are the same.

Traditional approaches to understanding differences are born out of a dominance model. This model says that yes, we are all alike, yet some of our differences are inherently better than others. Males are better than females, white skin is better than dark skin, able bodies are better than disabled bodies, young is better than old, heterosexual orientation is better than homosexual orientation...and the list could go on and on, for every dimension of difference that exists on the human level. You may be reading this and thinking how illogical it sounds even to think that way. Yet we all have a tendency to see differences in a hierarchical manner. That is how the brain works. Unfortunately, this kind of thinking leads us to treat differences as if they were independent variables — as if you could go about your day with only one dimension of your humanity!

Current thinking about differences treats them from a relational model. We, as human beings, are a complex intersection of all the many

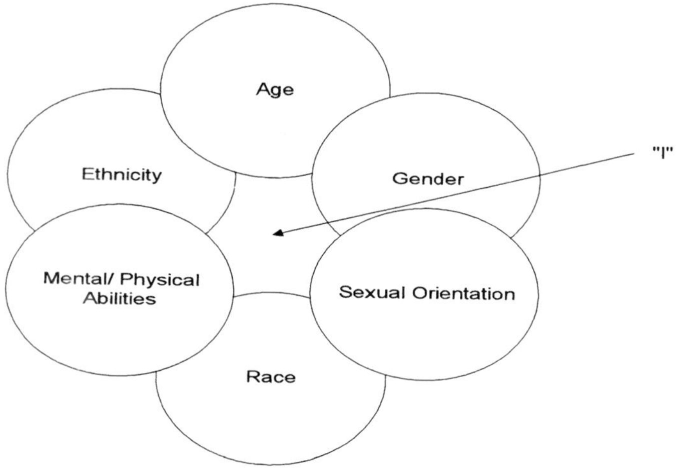

Model 1: Multiple Identities

dimensions of diversity that makes us uniquely us and yet like other people. This kind of thinking supports an understanding of the complex interactions of social relations and fosters the skills necessary to navigate our increasingly multicultural world. I cannot separate my gender from my race or my ethnicity, or separate my mental and physical abilities from my age or sexual orientation. Who I am is a wonderfully made, complex set of variables that makes me uniquely me (see Model 1).

Sometimes the term "diversity" is used interchangeably with other terms such as "multiculturalism" and "race relations." It is sometimes used as a synonym for social justice. Here is a simple glossary of terms that might help you to clarify the meaning of much of the vocabulary in the lexicon of diversity.

Working Definitions

***DIVERSITY*:** Differences among people with respect to age, class, ethnicity, gender, health, physical and mental ability, race, sexual orientation, religion, stature, education level, job level and function, personality traits, and other human differences.

***CULTURAL DIVERSITY*:** The inclusion and acceptance of the unique worldviews, customs, norms, patterns of behavior, and traditions of many groups of people.

***SOCIAL JUSTICE*:** The elimination of oppression and "isms" to create a full and equal participation of all groups in a society where the distribution of resources is equitable and where all members are physically and emotionally safe and secure.

***"ISMS"*:** Destructive attitudes or beliefs, such as racism, sexism, heterosexism, ableism, classism, ageism, and other forms of oppression, which are based in power and prejudice about human differences.

***PREJUDICE*:** Favorable or unfavorable prejudgment of people based on their group membership. A preconceived, unfavorable suspicion, intolerance, or hatred of others because of their group memberships.

PLURALISM: A culture that incorporates mutual respect, acceptance, teamwork, and productivity among people who are diverse.

MULTICULTURALISM: A pluralistic culture that reflects the interests, contributions, and values of members of diverse groups.

You may think that the definition of diversity is too broadly defined and therefore does not hold any real meaning. Everything that comes under the topic of human beings seems to be related to diversity. Yet the key to diversity is the valuing and managing of differences in such a way that the results lead to inclusion. The salient characteristic of multiculturalism is respect and appreciation for differences that lead to added value and representation of all cultures. The essence of social justice is the establishment of a fair and equitable system for multicultural communities and organizations. Here's a simple chart for distinguishing diversity from these related terms:

Diversity: Key is inclusion.
Multiculturalism: Key is appreciation and respect for cultures.
Social Justice: Key is fairness.

Other Relevant Terms

Diversity is often addressed on the interpersonal level when issues of conflict are concerned. We all have grown up embedded in our own culture and believing that our cultural practices are the norm for human behavior. For example, when I was a young child my mother exposed me to the Girl Scouts organization. Mindful of the fact that she was raising me as a Catholic and sending me to a predominantly White Irish Catholic school, my mother intentionally choose a troop for me to join that was made up of all African American girls. It was within this context that I learned Negro spirituals. I never distinguished those songs from the traditional Girl Scout songs I learned in my troop. Because our troop leaders also did not make a distinction, I assumed that all of the songs learned in the context of Girl Scouts were all "Girl Scout songs." Imagine my surprise, when I was attending the county Girl Scout summer camp, to find out that "Woke Up

This Morning" and "Come by Here" were not Girl Scout songs!

We are all ethnocentric and culturally myopic to some extent. We all need to widen the lens through which we see the world — our world-view — and remain culturally sensitive in the process. The following section provides some definitions of the terms discussed in the above example.

***WORLDVIEW*:** The unique perspective, or way of interpreting life's experiences, employed by individuals or groups.

***CULTURAL SENSITIVITY*:** Basic and obvious respect and appreciation for various cultures that may differ from your own.

***ETHNOCENTRISM*:** The tendency to use one's own group as a norm or standard by which to assess other groups.

***CULTURAL MYOPIA*:** The belief that one's particular culture is appropriate to all situations and relevant to all other individuals.

Organizational Diversity

When organizations became aware of the changing numbers and the cultural and gender differences that would be reflected in the workforce during the 21st century, many organizational leaders and managers began to examine their minority representation and company policies and practices for inclusiveness. Against the backdrop of legislation mandating Equal Employment Opportunity and Affirmative Action, the notions of fairness and doing what is right motivated many companies to increase the numbers of their employees who were women and People of Color. Other companies became acutely aware that, unless they matched their demographics to the demographics of the consumers and constituents they wished to serve, their business would suffer. Fully functioning organizations realized that incorporating diversity into the way they did work and including the different perspectives and thinking that human differences bring would give them a competitive advantage.

Fair Organizations → Consumer-Oriented Organizations →
Learning Organizations → Fully Functioning Organizations →
Progressive Organizations

Progressive companies knew that diversity not only made good business sense; it also translated into business cents!

While diversity on the individual and interpersonal levels focuses on respect and honoring of differences to ensure healthy personal and professional relationships and peaceful communities, diversity on the organizational level is tied to organizational effectiveness and economic growth.

It has often been said that employees are an organization's greatest assets. Thus, it makes intellectual sense for dollars to be spent to develop and support human resources. Although a great deal of research dating back to the Elton Mayo and the Hawthorne studies reveals that the noneconomic social processes connected with work are an important contributor to productivity, some organizations disregard or make secondary the social factors in the workplace. From the research on teams and group dynamics, we know that heterogeneous groups often experience decreased cohesion and increased conflict, but once a shared focus is achieved, these groups evidence increased productivity and creativity. This productivity and creativity is further increased if the diverse group has the skills and support systems necessary for its members to coalesce. Organizations that connect diversity to effective practices support their employees with training that will help them to become culturally competent; they also have structures that maintain a diversity-affirming environment.

Fortune magazine reports that minority business enterprises are the fastest-growing business segment in America. African American, Hispanic, and Asian American markets represent an annual spending power of $700 billion dollars. Seventy-five percent of consumers would buy a product from a socially responsible company, or would switch retailers, if cost and quality were equal. Approximately half of all business travelers are now women. The global market now affects most American companies, motivating them to be more competitive in finding and retaining employees. Employees of the new generation bring to the workplace different and expanded expectations, such as the need for spiritual meaning and a sense of making a contribution. With these facts, it is easy to make the case for diversity management in business; it would simply be shortsighted for business not to manage diversity well.

Definition of Organizational Diversity

In an organizational framework, diversity refers to making use of and leveraging human differences toward organizational effectiveness and productive business goals. The foundations of organizational diversity are rooted in a clear understanding of the interplay between individual and interpersonal diversity dynamics as well as the social justice issues that are so much a part of the fabric of our society.

For example, there have been several cases in which the question was raised of the appropriateness for the workplace of an employee's hairstyle (typically the braided styles worn by African American women and the long ponytails of American Indian men), particularly in companies where profits are tied to selling to the mainstream public. Company policies have leaned toward establishing more conservative or conventional styles (typically patterned after those favored by European Americans) as the norm. The business case from this perspective is clear: If customers are affected negatively by the hairstyle, or even are mildly curious, then the issue will distract the buying public from their focus on the product or service and may ultimately result in the loss of a sale. The other side of this issue is equally compelling: A hairstyle is a matter of personal preference, not a requirement for selling a product. Americans represent many different cultures, and no one cultural preference should take precedence over another.

What do you think about this issue? How would you handle this diversity dilemma?

Companies that are culturally competent and are characterized by learning and organizational effectiveness understand the complexity of this issue, and they focus on what will make the business more effective *and* maintain a high-performing workforce that leverages diversity. To give one side of the coin more weight than the other will lead to imbalance. Resolving this issue will mean that employees who choose to wear a culturally-specific hairstyle will need to be supported with the necessary competencies to manage a customer's possible negative reaction (or even mild curiosity) in ways that manage to get the job done without offending the customer. And the organization needs to support the employee and the consumer further, with skills that keep the sales focused on the product or service line. Consumers also need to be educated about the value placed on diversity by an organization. Remember, the majority of Americans support and expect social responsibility from companies. When cultural diversity is affirmed in a manner that makes good business sense, it is hard not to support the company's mission and vision, and ultimately buy the product or use its services.

Hopefully, the interplay between individual, interpersonal, and organizational diversity stood out for you in that example. The employee exercises his/her right to a hairstyle preference (individual level) that affects the employee/client relationship (interpersonal), which in turn may or may not affect a sale and ultimately the bottom line of the company (organizational).

Related Organizational Diversity Terms

In exploring the field of diversity management, there are other frequently used terms that are directly related to organizational effectiveness. Knowing these terms will be useful in your understanding of organizational diversity. Progressive organizations have moved beyond simply meeting Equal Employment Opportunity requirements and matching the demographics of organizations with critical consumers or constituent groups to connecting diversity to organizational effectiveness. Here are some definitions of terms that reflect the circumstances that occur when diversity is incorporated into the organization's culture in a manner that is diversity proficient:

- **INCLUSION:** Embracing and fully involving all people and their diversity in the work and life of organizations, communities, and society.

- **LEVERAGING DIVERSITY:** Enhancing organizational effectiveness and performance by making use of the different perspectives, experiences, and abilities that people bring to the workplace.

- **CULTURAL COMPETENCE:** The capacity to function effectively with all cultures and to successfully navigate a multicultural society.

- **ORGANIZATIONAL CULTURAL COMPETENCE:** The capacity to function effectively with all cultures and to make creative use of a diverse workforce in a way that meets business goals and enhances performance.

These definitions lend clarity to one's understanding of the nature of diversity and the field of diversity management. Now let's turn our attention to examining a framework for categorizing the many aspects of diversity that will help further deepen your understanding of diversity.

Dimensions of Diversity

Marilyn Loden and Judy Rosener use the terms "primary and secondary dimensions" to distinguish between the many aspects of human differences. Primary dimensions are defined as those aspects that contribute to the core of identity and are inborn. Those dimensions typically included as primary are age, ethnicity, gender, race, mental/physical abilities, and sexual orientation. Secondary dimensions are those aspects of our identity that contribute to our core but do not fundamentally change the essence of who we are. Examples of secondary dimensions include education, income, religion, work experience, and family status. If I won a lottery of several million dollars, it would make me significantly richer, but it would not change my race, gender, ethnicity, age, sexual orientation, or physical or mental ability. I would now be a rich Black, Jamaican, middle-aged, able-bodied, heterosexual female, but none of my primary dimensions would change.

Embedded in the core of who we are as individuals are those clusters of behavioral traits and mental sets called personality. Personality is the unique combination of traits that allows a person to express who he or she is as an individual. Even identical twins who share the same genetic makeup have different personalities. So I may share with another person the same race, ethnicity, gender, sexual orientation, defined set of physical/mental abilities, and even age, and I would still be different from that individual because of personality (see Figure 1).

Although the shape of the circle depicted in Figure 1 shows the dimensions of diversity in an even pattern of distribution, the actual visual presentation of any individual's characteristics will be dynamic and ever-changing. For example, earlier in my own life, race and gender would have occupied a very large portion of my circle. As I struggled with issues of racial identity and my place in the world as an African American woman, these dimensions were the looking glass that reflected the way I interacted with the world. Today, as I grow older, age and mental/physical abilities represent a significant portion of the visual representation of my personal diversity identity. Racial identity and gender role have been defined and stabilized, and the developmental tasks of aging have become central to my understanding of the world and my everyday experience.

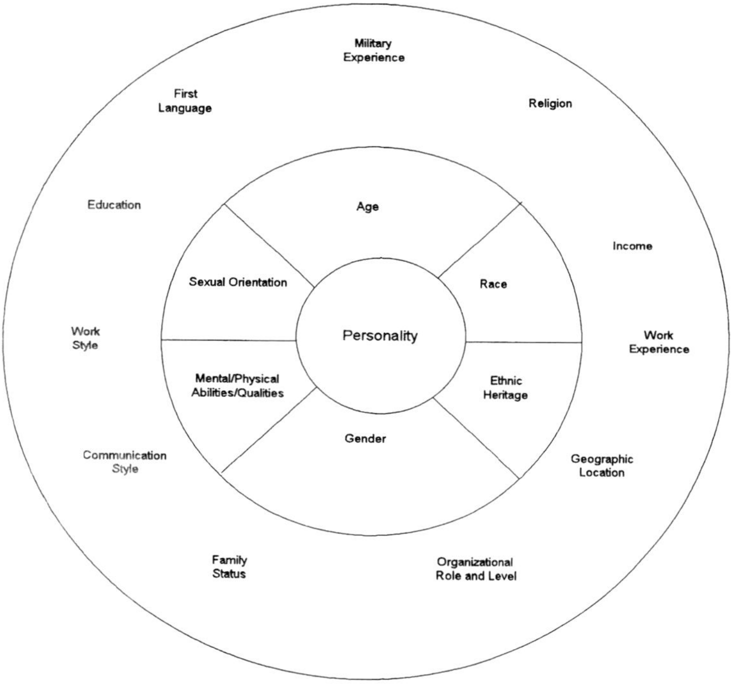

Figure 1. Primary and Secondary Dimensions of Diversity
Loden, M. (1996) *Implementing Diversity.* Chicago, IL: Irwin Publishing Company. Reprinted with permission.

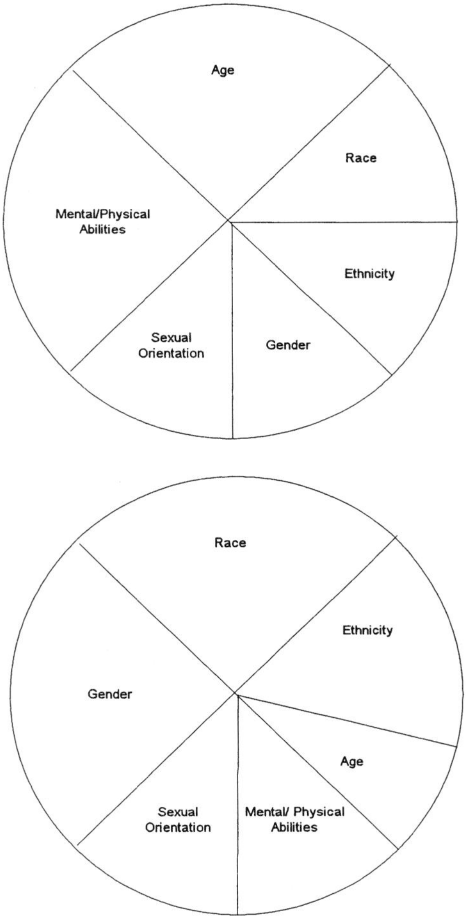

Figure 2. An example of a young adult and middle adult Diversity Circle

The pictures in Figure 2. depict my own circle of diversity in my young adult years paired with my current circle of diversity. Take a few minutes to depict your own representation of the dimensions of diversity in your present life.

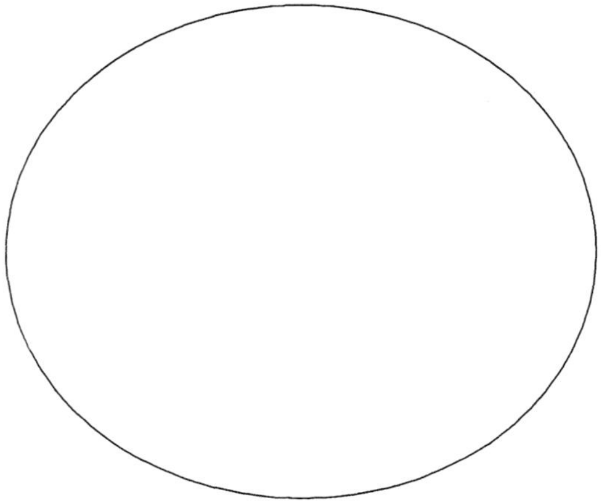

Figure 3. Your Circle of Diversity

Group Membership Identity

As unique as I am as an individual, I also share with others a group member identity. Every person also holds a gender identity, racial-group identity, and ethnic identity. In addition, your sexual orientation, age, and mental/physical ability identify you with a group of people who share similar statuses. Along with our individual and group member identity, we can be identified as members of the particular organization where we work and, in this country, as Americans. We are generally not consciously aware of our group membership identity unless we "bump up" against it in the environment. For example, I am not typically aware of my femaleness unless I find myself in a room with all men. I become aware of race when I find myself, or another member of my race, standing out as "different." Understanding human differences from a systems perspective will help to make this clear. Diversity is not only represented by individual differences; it is also characterized by the level of human system that is shaping one's thinking.

Levels of Human Systems

In the previously cited example of the diversity hairstyle dilemma, we noted the interplay of the various levels of human systems. Understanding this concept is critical to unraveling the complexity of diversity. Here's another example that will illustrate this concept.

During a given day, we might get up in the morning and spend anywhere from a few moments to an hour reflecting on how we are feeling and what our personal goals for the day might be. We may then connect with family members and relay those thoughts and feelings to others, and/or hear about their thoughts and feelings about how the day will turn out. We may notice a difference between what our spouse/partner thinks and what might be on the mind of a teenage son or daughter. Our day continues as we go to work and meet the challenges of project goals and assisting on work teams. Sometime during the day, we might glance at the paper and listen to the news, in order to get in touch with societal and world concerns. We may end the day in a fashion very similar to the way we started it — connecting with family and reviewing the day.

This chronology illustrates the interplay of systems we experience almost unconsciously during our day. A level of system is a way of bounding — or drawing parameters around — an experience (see Figure 4). We choose (sometimes unconsciously) the level to which we will give our attention. For example, you may automatically notice individuals in a group, while a friend only notices people collectively. Our socialization process, educational background, and personality characteristics all play a part in determining the level to which we choose to attend. The levels of human system include:

- Intrapsychic or individual
- Interpersonal
- Group
- Organizational or institutional
- Societal
- Global

The definitions of each level follow, along with a description from theabove example that illustrates how levels of systems are evident in our daily life.

Intrapsychic Level — Boundary is the self system *(reflecting on our thoughts and feelings).*

Interpersonal Level — Boundary is one of the following *(connecting with family at breakfast)*:

- **Individual/Individual** *(connecting with our spouse/partner),*
- **Individual/Group** *(speaking to the kids),*
- **Individual/Subgroup** *(connecting with the adults rather than the kids at breakfast or with the females instead of the males at work).*

Group Level — Boundary is set by the purpose of the group and includes all members of the group (*noticing differences in male/female perspectives or between Whites and People of Color).*

Organizational — Boundary is the systematic set of purposes, rules, practices, and traditions that govern an institution (*working on goals and work products*).

Societal — Boundary is the many facets of culture (language, norms, values, sanctions, family composition and functions, gender identity and roles, politics, religious and spiritual beliefs and practices, degree of ethnic/racial identity and acculturation) that influence and shape people (*connecting with societal news*).

Global — Boundary is worldwide (*connecting with world news).*

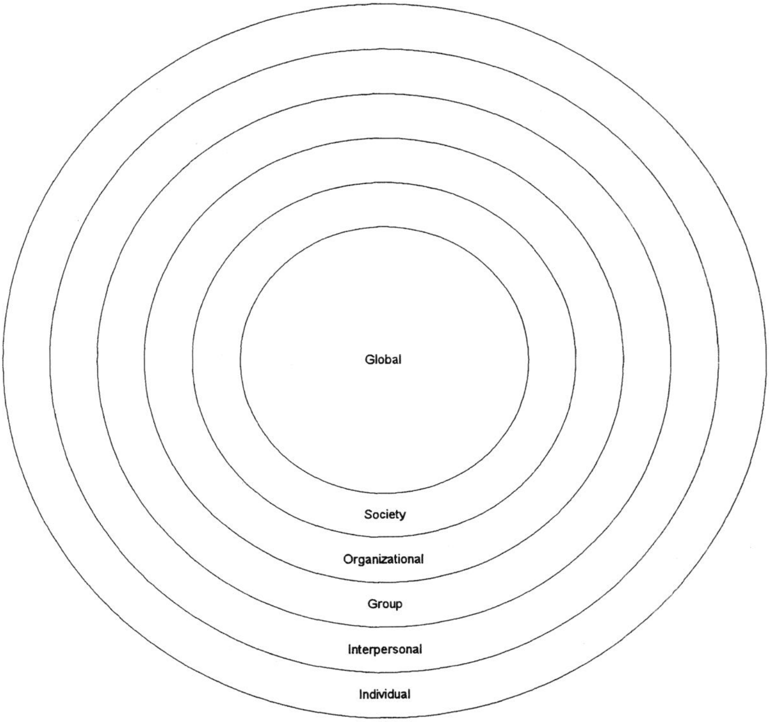

Figure 4. Levels of System

Diversity management cuts across all levels of human system. Our diversity package (the specific race, gender, age, ability, sexual orientation, stature, religion, etc.) determines what level of system we engage in and the lens through we see our world. For example, when I am traveling with a White friend in a predominantly White setting, it is not unusual for another African American to say hello to me or to nod and smile. This sometimes confuses my White friend, who is baffled when she finds out that I am not personally acquainted with this individual. I explain that it is a connection of group member identity that has prompted the greeting. Similarly, if a man finds himself in a room filled with women, when another male enters there is generally an acknowledgment (often a sigh of relief) that someone else is present who shares the same gender (group membership identity). A physically large woman attending a graduate program comments on how happy she is to see other women of her size in the class. Discovering at a workshop other people who share their own religion often brings about a sense of community for the individuals identified with that group.

I am sure that you can think of countless times when you have been more aware of your group membership identity than of your individual personality. You may have experienced this not only on the group level, but on the organizational or societal levels as well. Your identity as an employee of Company X makes you different from employees of Company Y. At a meeting of Companies X and Y, you may be acutely aware of your differences from Company Y employees — and of how similar you are to your Company X coworker in your presentation and communication style. This may not have been in your awareness at all when you were working together at Company X. If you have traveled abroad, you may have been much more aware of your American identity (societal level) than you ever are when you are at home in America. Thus, we experience, routinely and almost unconsciously, diversity interacting with system levels.

The Language of Culture

The terms "culture," "ethnicity," "nationality," and "race" have often been used interchangeably in our everyday speech. Yet learning the distinct meaning of these terms, and using them intentionally in our conversations, can increase the effectiveness of cross-cultural and cross-racial communications. The following paragraphs give us some working definitions of these terms.

- **Culture:** A socially transmitted, shared design for living; patterns for interpreting reality that are based on values and practices of a group of people who interact together over time.

- **Ethnicity:** A group of people related according to a common racial, national, tribal, religious, linguistic, or cultural origin.

- **Nationality:** The status of belonging to a particular territory by origin, birth, or naturalization.

- **Race:** A pseudo-biological system of classifying people based on shared genetic history or physical characteristics.

Examine these definitions and see whether you can determine the many cultural groups to which you belong, as well as your ethnicity, nationality, and race. As a Black (race), Jamaican/Panamanian (ethnicity), American (nationality), I am aware of the many cultural groups of which I find myself a part (Catholic, Educator, Psychologist, Middle Class, etc.).

Culture influences our thinking and behaving in ways that are most likely unconscious. Culture is transmitted through family, educational system, and societal practices. America is host to more than 300 cultures that differ around such issues as control, independence, gender roles, time orientation, and risk behavior. In our society, European American culture dominates and sets the standard for most American norms. Take, for example, time orientation. Diversity scholar Norma Carr-Ruffino (1996) distinguishes between *circular time cultures* — Latino, Middle Eastern, and some Asian and African cultures — that experience time as a circle, with each point in time regarded as sacred and worthy of being experienced fully in the moment, and *step-by-step time cultures* — United States, Euro-American cultures — that experience time as being made up of the past, present, and future, with attention being given to the future. In most African, Cuban, and Mexican cultures, time is determined by repeated cycles of activities, such as the agricultural cycles of planting, cultivating, and harvesting. From this perspective, time is only viewed in the past and present tenses. Thus,, for most People of Color in America, orientation of time is something that is altered or modified in the workplace.

If a meeting is scheduled to start at 9:00 a.m., does that mean we begin the agenda at 9:00, or do we begin to gather in the room and greet one another at 9:00? Is the gathering process as central to a successful meeting as the prompt attention to the agenda?

What do you think? How would you handle time management, in a meeting of culturally diverse employees?

Approaches to Managing Culture

Organizations with diverse work environments struggle with the issue of how to manage cultural diversity successfully. Allowing individuals to fully express who they are maximizes creativity and productivity in organizations and contributes to peaceful, respectful communities. Managing differences evokes a bit of discomfort at the individual and interpersonal levels, and similarly brings discomfort on the organizational level. Most organizations and community agencies solve the cultural dilemma by one of the following approaches.

1. ***Cultural Deficient Approach:*** Popular in the 1960s through the 1970s, this premise considered cultures that were not White European to be lacking in cultural strengths, determining that the best approach to dealing with those who were culturally different was to provide them with opportunities for cultural education and development. This approach is consistent with the melting pot/assimilation model that was (and, some would argue, still is) dominant in America. Minority populations melted into or assimilated with the majority culture. In this case, A (White European Culture) + B (African, Asian, Indian, Hispanic) equaled A (White European). $A + B = A$.

2. ***Culturally Blind Approach:*** Considered by many to be forward-thinking, this approach de-emphasized cultural differences and emphasized cultural similarity. In theory, it appears to be diversity-affirming, but in practice, it demonstrated a hierarchical and superior approach. In other words, in order for me, a White European, to deal with you, a Person of Color, I have to pretend that I see not color, but only the ways in which we are the same. In reality, I see that you are a Person of Color, but I work with you *as if* you were just like *me*.

3. ***Cultural Denial Approach:*** This approach also puts emphasis on cultural sameness, but instead of being blind to color, we deny that differences even exist. We are all human beings. We are all Americans. We all put our pants on the same way. We all have red blood inside. The denial of cultural roots, historical impact, and variance in the experience of American dreams and ideals is strong.

4. ***Cultural Tourist Approach:*** This approach emphasizes the strengths of each culture and celebrates differences by sharing culture. We "visit" each other's cultures and are welcomed as guests. Cultural feasts, where we share foods and traditions (usually in the form of dance and dress), are popular in organizations and educational settings. Simplistic in its orientation, this approach does not deal with the differences in expression of cultural values and norms that often lead to clashes and miscom-

munication.

5. ***Cultural Tapestry Approach:*** This approach recognizes and celebrates the differences that are evident in multicultural environments. As with an exquisite tapestry that holds individual artistic impressions, yet holds a unified piece of art in its totality, organizations that abide by this approach incorporate the various ways of knowing, thinking, and perspective into the very fabric of how business is done.

The "Big 8"

Of the many dimensions of diversity and the varied aspects of culture, diversity-management consultants and researchers have found that, in work environments, the diversity dimensions most often managed for organizational effectiveness are:

1. ***Race***
2. ***Gender***
3. ***Ethnicity/nationality***
4. ***Organizational role/function***
5. ***Age***
6. ***Sexual orientation***
7. ***Mental/physical ability***
8. ***Religion***

Informally called the "Big 8" by diversity consultants, these dimensions have received the most attention, and they may hold the most information about critical issues and suggested interventions for management of those issues. The following Table summarizes these findings.

DIMENSION	CRITICAL ISSUES	INTERVENTION
Race	Communication styles, perceptions/stereotypes, locus of control, career mobility, competitive vs. cooperative behavior, time orientation, partisan politics, philosophical compatibility, loyalty	Diversity-awareness and skill-building training, recruitment and retention of diverse employees, multicultural mentoring, group dynamics and team building sessions, discretionary power mapping
Gender	Communication styles, perceptions/stereotypes, work-life balance, career mobility, competitive vs. cooperative behavior, partisan politics, loyalty	Diversity-awareness and skill-building training, glass-ceiling audits, cross-gender mentoring
Ethnicity/Nationality	Communication styles, assimilation vs. acculturation issues, perceptions/ stereotypes, career mobility	Mentoring, diversity awareness and skill-building training
Sexual Orientation	Homophobia, sexual double	Sexual-orientation education,

	standard, "Don't ask, don't tell," lavender glass ceiling	support and affinity groups, partner benefits
Organizational Role/Function	Us vs. them, communication, values, partisan politics, loyalty	Diversity council/task force, deep-dive sessions, diversity dialogues
Mental/Physical Ability	Socialization, coworker sensitivity, transportation, technical support, career mobility	ADA education, reasonable accommodations, protection from undue hardship
Age	Younger: work ethics, values, work-life balance, creativity and meaning Older: skill obsolescence, retirement, loyalty, recognition, communication styles	Cross-generational work teams, diversity training, diversity dialogue sessions
Religion	Religious practice during the workday, respect, prejudice, perceptions/stereotypes	Diversity-awareness training, reasonable accommodations, case by case evaluation

Table 1. "Big 8" Diversity Dimensions

Understanding Race

Of all of the above dimensions of diversity, arguably the one that is most politically and socially loaded is that of race. Recently, scientists have drawn the conclusion that the racial categories recognized by society are not reflected on the genetic level. Thus, the standard labels used to distinguish people by "race" have little or no biological meaning. Having found that physical features are shaped by environment and nutrition, anthropologists have adopted a "no race" position since 1960, stating that biological variability does not conform to discrete categories labeled as "race." There is only one race — the human race.

Why, then, do these categories persist? Racial categories remain alive as sociopolitical constructs. Our brain is attuned to the packaging of details into categories; it prompts us to exaggerate the significance of human features into what we call racial categories. We are programmed to recognize certain features — such as skin color, hair texture, shape of nose and eyes, and size of lips — and place them into either Caucasian, Native American, African, or Asian groups. (The appellations of Hispanic or Latino designate an identification derived from one or more of the four major races.) We are also socialized to believe that certain characteristics and personality traits belong to individuals who are members of each race. For example, Caucasians have strong work ethics and are rational, Native Americans are spiritual and reserved, African Americans are spontaneous and lazy, Asians are conformist and detached, and Hispanics are emotionally expressive and fatalistic. These stereotypes are part of the fabric of American culture; when left unexamined, they lead to the perpetuation of racism.

Let's take a moment to define stereotypes and to distinguish them from generalizations and cultural patterns.

✦**Stereotype**: A widely held belief, usually oversimplified and based on limited data and perceptions.

✦**Generalization**: An inference or conclusion derived from empirical data

✦**Cultural Patterns**: Behaviors, attitudes, and beliefs practiced and held by a critical mass of a cultural group.

So, the *stereotype* about Asians being conformist may have its roots in the *generalization* of group-over-individual preference that is linked to a *cultural pattern* of valuing harmony. Nevertheless, to attach the label of "conformist" to all Asians would definitely lead to cultural miscommunication and less than satisfactory personal and professional relationships.

Racial Identity Development

Racial identity development is a process that occurs for all people, regardless of ethnicity or culture. Unlike other areas of identity development — social, personality, cognitive, or physical — racial identity received little attention until the late 1960s. Prompted by the civil rights movement, researchers began to examine the process by which we come to understand ourselves as racial beings. Since that time, there has been burgeoning research and discussion about the process by which a person incorporates his/her race.

Racial identity refers to the psychological connection with one's race rather than the mere identification with skin color or demographic category. For example, many racial groups have terms that refer to individuals whose demographic racial identity does not match their psychological or racial identification. In the African American community, one might be referred to as an "Oreo," which connotes a state of being black on the outside and white in the inside. Similarly, "lemon" or "banana" is used to refer to Asians; the term is "apple" for Native Americans. Mexican Americans refer to such an individual as a "Tio Thomas" (Mexican Uncle Tom). Jewish people would refer to that individual as a "WASH" (White Anglo Saxon Hebrew). White adolescents who prefer to act more like African American teens are called "wiggers." All of these terms speak to the essence of racial identity. It is a process of group identity that is distinct from our other identity roles. For many of us, this racial socialization process has been unconscious. To become aware of your own process of racial identity development, take a few minutes and reflect on the following questions.

Reflections on Your Process of Racial Identity Development

- ✦When did your first come to know about your race?
- ✦Describe your racial socialization process:

- ✦What did your parents tell you about your race?
- ✦What did you learn in school about your race?
- ✦What did you learn from the media (TV, newspapers, magazines, radio, Internet) about your race?
- ✦With whom were you taught to associate?
- ✦What did you learn about your race's intellectual capacity?
- ✦What did you learn about your race's pugnaciousness (ten dency tofight)?
- ✦What value was placed on same-race accomplishments and achievements?
- ✦What value was placed on same-race failures and embar rassments?
- ✦What markers tell you about your membership in your race?
- ✦Biological (physical features)?
- ✦Cultural (ways of expression, thinking, and knowing; manner of dress; choice of social activities, language, humor, time orientation)?
  - — Historical (how American customs, norms, and policies affect you)?
  - — Physical environment/space (decor, artwork)?

Describe the racial makeup of your family. Your social group. Your neighborhood. Your political circle.

Have you ever had the experience of racial stress? (Racial stress is the psychological discomfort, based on racial group membership, that is felt in a situation or in a particular setting.)

Your response to these questions tells you something about your racial-identity resolution process. Perhaps you are unresolved about your developmental process, or confused by trying to identify its impact in your life. That is normal. Researchers of racial identity have found that the developmental process is influenced by other dimensions of diversity as well as by our life stage and its associated developmental tasks. For example, a young Asian American male attending graduate school will perhaps experience his Asian identity differently from the way that his Asian-born grandfather would. Or an African American 16-year-old, never having experienced overt racism, would view race relations in America very differently from the way a 50-year-old African

American would. A White American may think of himself only as being "not Black" rather than embracing "Whiteness" as a racial identity.

Styles of racial-identity resolution differ from individual to individual. Yet researchers have found similar progressions in the movement of the process for both People of Color and those who share a White European racial background. The following paragraphs describe the process of racial-identity resolution for each group.

Racial-Identity Resolution Process For People of Color

Identification with Dominant Race or Race Neutrality

For some People of Color, the journey of discovering their racial identity begins with their identifying with those who are White. Historically — and to some extent still today — White Europeans in America have dominated or greatly influenced what is considered the norm in American society. Thus, it would make sense for an individual growing up with minority status to identify with or take cues about behavior and thought from those in the majority. Educational systems and organizational life are designed around the customs and beliefs of majority culture. For those individuals not firmly embedded in their racial-identity group's culture, the racial-socialization process will most likely be that of White culture. Others, aware of their skin-color difference, who yet find their behavior and thought aligned with those of the dominant race, experience what noted scholar Dr. William Cross (1995) calls "race neutrality." For these individuals, their racial identity is not central, or core, to who they are, but is in the background. Such a person's thought might go: "I am a person who happens to be Hispanic, or Black, or Asian, or Native American." In other words, being a person or a human being is primary, and race is a secondary or neutral factor in one's life.

Impact Awakening

At this point in the racial-identity resolution process, the impact of racism on the life of a Person of Color is felt. A young Puerto Rican girl beginning to date encounters attitudes of racial distinction when she discovers that the parents of her white boyfriend object to her simply because she is Puerto Rican. A Native American college student faces the demeaning of his culture by sports mascots. A well qualified African American engineer finds herself unable to get a second interview with companies where her White counterparts easily obtain jobs. A young African American professional male is stopped by the police simply for driving in an affluent White neighborhood. An Asian candidate for an academic position is shut out because his potential colleagues are uncomfortable with his accent and feel he will not fit in. In reaction to such encounters, individuals who have experienced them may feel the need to alter the way they view themselves as racial persons in America. They may then live out an identity based on the perceptions and prejudices of others rather than on the essence of who they are.

Race Immersion

For many People of Color, the response to racism has greatly influenced their racial-identity process, causing them to reject involvement with other groups or simply to have a strong preference for remaining embedded with, or encapsulated in, their own racial group. Their racial-identity resolution process is satisfied by their eliminating or minimizing contact with members of the dominant race. They conduct all their professional and personal activities with members of their own race, thereby limiting or eliminating the influence of White culture. Such individuals see their identity as a Person of Color through the lens of racism and victimization. They identify being White in America through the lens of oppression, entitlement, and privilege. Thus, separatism is valued and deemed the only acceptable way to remain psychologically healthy in America.

Internalization and Integration

This status is categorized by an internalization of a consistent, stable racial identity that is integrated into one's lifestyle. One's racial identity is fully owned and accepted, and thus may not appear to be a salient factor in one's life. Yet it is so seamlessly integrated into the person's being that expressions of racial identity are natural and easily recognizable to others through such indicators as manner of speaking, customs, practices, manner of dress, etc. Racial identity is integrated into not only one's lifestyle but also other aspects of one's personality and other dimensions of diversity.

Multicultural Identity

To recognize and accept the many aspects of culture that have influenced and contributed to one's person is characteristic of a multicultural identity. With this recognition and acceptance, one is able to fully embrace, acknowledge, and appreciate his/her racial identity, and at the same time respect and honor other racial identities.

Racial-Identity Development Process for Whites

Unawareness of Race

For a member of the dominant race, it is easy to conceptualize oneself as the norm. As with a computer system, the default value is set. White European Americans are very much the default value in this country; American cultural norms have been rooted in an amalgamation of European ancestry. History, corporate policies and procedures, and leadership in this country have all been determined and influenced by White culture. Thus, it is easy for White Americans never to have "Whiteness" in their awareness or, perhaps, never to struggle with being different or with seeing themselves represented in certain ways in the world.

Acknowledgment of Whiteness

When consciousness of race is raised, the individual must come to terms with the implications and ramifications of what being White in America is about. This means recognizing the privileges and entitlements afforded to people with white skin in America. As with the encounter experience for People of Color, Whites in this status become aware of how racism operates and are acutely in touch with how they may have unwillingly and unwittingly been a part of a system of oppression based on skin color.

Rejection of Privileged Whiteness

With the awareness of privilege and entitlement, and the acknowledgment that these conditions have been afforded those in this country who have white skin, comes a rejection of covert racist beliefs and the implications and ramifications attached to privileged Whiteness in this country. There is recognition that there is a difference in treatment of Whites and People of Color in this country and a focus on how Whiteness brings privilege. For example, a White male friend told me about a conversation he had with a police officer who pulled him over in traffic for not fully stopping at a stop sign. He argued with the officer about the ridiculous nature of this attempt to ticket him and humorously accused him of being overzealous. When he finished recounting his experience, my friend acknowledged his acute awareness of the fact that, had he been Black, he never could have gotten away with saying what he did. What was in my friend's awareness was privileged Whiteness.

Transcending Privileged Whiteness

Armored by the awareness of privilege and motivated by the energy of enlightenment, Whites who experience this status develop and integrate a new White identity that transcends modern forms of racism, privilege, and entitlement. Like People of Color, as they interact in society, they have an active consciousness of their group member identity as Whites. They are quick to own when "Whiteness" is problematic and are ready to change systems and act out of an unentitled/unprivileged White identity.

Development of a Multicultural Identity

Similar to this status for People of Color, Whites in this status fully embrace White identity and at the same time value and appreciate other races for their contributions and achievements. Whites in this status understand the historical residuals on People of Color and engage in systems thinking when analyzing racial issues. They are quick to challenge any level of system that supports inequality, oppression, and social injustice.

Now that you have read an explanation of each of the statuses of the racial-identity resolution process, take a few minutes to perform the following self-assessment of your own racial-identity status.

Racial-Identity Status Self-Assessment

Directions: Check those statements that apply or that are mostly true for you.

1.		My race does not play a significant role in my everyday life.
2.		I have had the experience of feeling guilty for having denied the significance of race in a situation
3.		I try to learn all I can about my race
4.		I feel a sense of pride about my race
5.		My race has little to do with my sense of happiness and well-being
6.		I can recall receiving some historical information (positive or negative) about my race that had a profound impact on me.
7.		I can name recent incidents or examples of privilege and entitlement that are afforded to White Americans and not to People of Color
8.		I am at peace about my racial identity and do not feel the need to be defensive about racial matters.
9.		I value other aspects of my life such as religion, lifestyle, social status, or career, more than I do my race.
10.		I have been confused, alarmed, or depressed over a racial issue.
11.		I regularly attend political and cultural meetings that focus on racial issues
12.		I believe that racism is part of the American experience, and I work to erase its presence
13.		I have not given much thought to racial issues or concerns
14.		I have been angry at another race for causing social problems
15.		I often read about the history of my race
16.		I insist on being acknowledged as a member of my race
17.		I have at times been acutely aware of the fact that race matters, even in a domestic society.

18.		As a result of a racial incident or information about race that I've acquired, I have felt energized to do something about racial issues on either a societal or personal level
19.		The decore of my home reflects my race
20.		I recognize and appreciate other racial heritages and believe their contributions and achievements are of value to the American experience
21.		My race has been more of a problem to me than a blessing
22.		I feel an overwhelming love for and attachment to my race
23.		I believe we should strive for a "colorblind" or "colorless" society.
24.		I believe that some members of my race are not fully racially identified
25.		I believe we should all consider ourselves American, regardless of race.
26.		I associate primarily with people from my own race
27.		I have often felt pride when someone of my race makes a significant achievement, even when I do not personally know the individual
28.		In today's society, too much is made of racial differences
29.		I have had the experience of being angry about how my race has been represented in the media
30.		I take the opportunity to challenge racial injustice whenever it happens

To score your assessment, refer to the key at the end of this chapter. Once you have scored it, you may note that most likely you have a score for each status. Those results are typical and illustrate the fact that racial-identity status is a dynamic process with many facets of expression. You may, however, have one or two predominant scores that represent your racial-identity resolution status.

In our everyday experience, we are likely to express different aspects of our racial-identity resolution. For example, with my family and in social situations, I may tend to be more unaware of race or place less salience on it. Or, if my family and social interactions are more culturally encapsulated, I may find my racial identity more immersed in my racial heritage. In my professional life, I may display more multicultural attitudes and have work friendships that cross racial lines. When I review my lifespan, I find that my racial-identity status may have changed, depending on what life stage I was in. In my youth I was more encapsulated; as an adolescent and young adult I was more multicultural; as a middle-aged adult I became more encapsulated again; then, as an older adult, I became more reflective of multicultural attitudes.

The racial identity resolution process for most individuals follows varied paths. For some, it might be linear and stable. For others, it may go in stages, like climbing stairs. For yet others, it is more of a spiral pattern, with statuses being cyclical and depending on one's life stage. And for many, racial-identity resolution is often multifaceted, representing the complex nature of human behavior and the dimensions of diversity (see Figure 5).

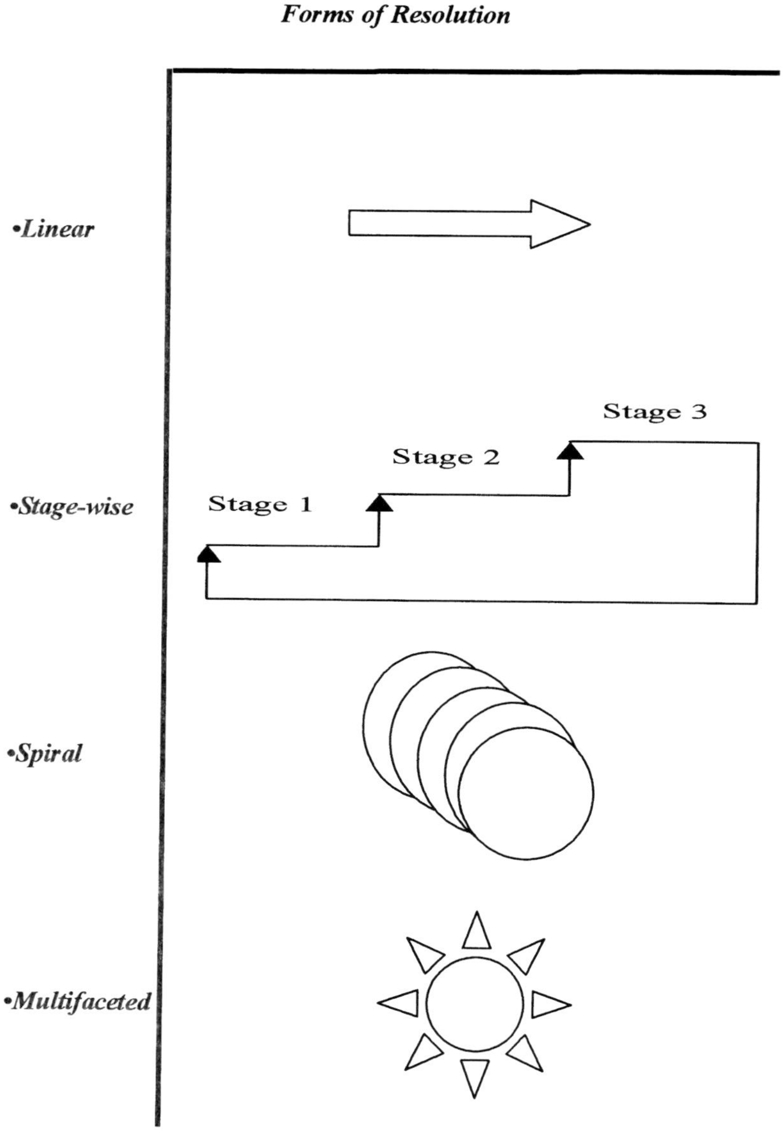

Figure 5. **Racial-Identity Development Resolution Process**

While reading this section on racial-identity development, you may have found yourself thinking about how this information also applies to other dimensions of diversity. Similarly, gender-identity and sexual-orientation development have processes that may mimic racial-identity development. You may want to spend some time researching gender- and/or sexual-orientation developmental processes, as a way to deepen your understanding of the dimensions of diversity.

How does this information on racial-identity development help us to understand others and more effectively manage diversity in our personal and professional lives? Here are some points to consider:

✦No one race is monolithic. Understanding the variance in racial identification helps us to respect individual differences and eliminate stereotypical thinking.

✦Racial identity may be stable but not fixed. Because race is a sociopolitical construct, how I express my racial identity may vary, depending on lifestage and situation.

✦Although there are similarities among races in ways of knowing and expression, intraracial (within race) differences are just as viable as interracial (between races) differences.

✦Understanding my own racial-identity resolution process is one of the most useful tools I can have for interacting with members of my own race and with others of different races.

Managing Diversity in Your Personal and Professional Life

I have often made the statement that, despite the years I have devoted to studying, teaching, and writing about the topic of diversity, the learning will never be completed. Diversity is an endless topic for exploration. We will all probably still be trying to make sense of it six months after we are in the grave! Sometimes I hear people reduce diversity management to an issue of basic respect. It is truly that — and much more. Sometimes people define diversity simply as differences. Diversity is that — and much more. There are those who believe diversity is no more than a passing trend, dreamt up and kept alive by consultants to make money. As an organizational direction/mission, or as a societal movement, the catalyst for diversity's energy is indeed time-bound (we will explore this more in the next section). Yet there is not a consultant alive who could sustain its energy unless it had some reality and meaning in the lives of American workers. As our world and workforce continue to become increasingly diverse, having the skills to navigate our environments becomes a necessity.

Historical Perspectives of Diversity Management

Knowing the past helps us to understand the present and better envision the future. Presented here to aid in understanding the past and present perspectives of diversity management is a brief outline of its historical roots. The theoretical roots of diversity management are in the disciplines of business, psychology, education, and anthropology. Heavily influenced by social processes and the zeitgeist, or spirit of the times, the field of diversity management has burgeoned since its conception in the 1960s. The following timeline depicts, by decades, some of the highlights of the development of diversity management.

Diversity Timeline

1960s

- Origins in civil rights movement
- Overt segregation
- Color/gender blindness was goal
- Social and moral focus
- Researchers noted psychological effects of "isms" on victim
- Racial-identity development theory established
- Assimilation/acculturation were frameworks for managing differences
- Cultural-deficit models represented thinking of the time

1970s

- Dimensions/framework for diversity established
- Racial and gender differences were the primary dimensions explored

- "Quotas" influenced recruitment and retention efforts
- Legal approaches were the drivers for diversity initiatives
- Emphasis on recruitment of women and people of color

1980s

- Values in the workplace began to come under study
- Hiring/performance/retention practices were examined for diversity
- Social justice became the business imperative
- Culturally different models replaced deficit models
- Workforce 2000 demographics made a business impact

1990s

- Theories of difference established
- Pluralistic models dominated thinking
- Communication structures supporting inclusion were researched and practiced
- Retention issues motivated organizations to become the "Employer of Choice"
- Value-added practices were incorporated in organizations
- Learning became the model for progressive organizations
- Global issues influenced business thought and practice
- Organization of diversity professionals began
- Diversity degree programs were established

Where do you see diversity management headed in this millennium? How to do you see yourself in the picture?

Pioneers in the Field of Diversity Management

The field of diversity management has many unsung heroes. In every major and minor organization across the United States — especially during the 1960s and 1970s — there were many diversity champions. The complete list would certainly be extensive; however, this section offers snapshots of a few of the pioneers in the field, for their contributions to the scholarship and practice of diversity management.

Price Cobbs. *Consultant/Psychiatrist, coauthored Black Rage and supported understanding of group-based differences.*

Taylor Cox. *Researcher/Professor/Consultant, systematically and objectively analyzed cultural diversity in organizations, effectively blending theory and practice.*

Elsie Y. Cross. *In the 1970s, inaugurated a workshop on race and men and women in the workplace; coined the term "managing a diverse workforce" and then shortened it to "managing diversity."*

Lee Gardenswartz and Anita Rowe. *Merged diversity with management trends such as team building.*

Lewis Griggs. *Through videos, computer-learning products, and sponsorship of annual diversity conferences, disseminated the message of diversity to millions.*

David Jamieson and Julie O'Mara. *Consultants/Authors of Managing Workforce 2000.*

Judith Katz. *Through writings and research, reframed the system of racism to educate whites on the complicity of the practice.*

Marilyn Loden. *Through extensive research and experience, designed models for full participation of diverse employees.*

Frederick A. Miller. *Pioneered methodology for strategic culture change in major corporations.*

Robert Terry. *Author of For Whites Only, a pioneering examination of racism geared toward White Americans.*

R. Roosevelt Thomas, Jr. *Through writings and research, expanded understanding of diversity and linked diversity management to organizational-culture change.*

Use of Self as a Tool for Managing Diversity

The "self" is a psychological term that refers to one's inner experience. We are free to share what goes on in our inner world with others, or to keep the experience to ourselves. Our inner experience is constantly being affected by what goes on in our environment. It houses all our history as well as our reactions to our world. Thus, the first place that diversity management needs to happen is within ourselves. This is often a harder task than managing diversity for others. Although this section comes last in this chapter on understanding diversity, learning to make use of yourself as a tool for managing personal and professional diversity issues is your greatest asset. The following is a starter list of some prescriptive behaviors for self-management of diversity issues.

Conditions for Self-Management of Diversity Issues

Someone who effectively self-manages diversity issues:

- ✓ Values a variety of opinions and insights.
- ✓ Recognizes the challenges and learning opportunities that new perspectives bring.
- ✓ Bases expectations of others on individual traits and qualities rather than group member identity.
- ✓ Seeks out ways to personally and professionally develop diversity competencies.
- ✓ Encourages and accepts openness in others.
- ✓ Makes people feel valued.
- ✓ Is emotionally resilient when a diversity mistake is made.
- ✓ Spends time with a wide variety of people.
- ✓ Has a clear sense of self as a person of culture.
- ✓ Has a basic understanding of the field of diversity management.

Continued reading, dialogue, and attendance at diversity workshops and classes will further your personal understanding of diversity and enhance your professional skills in the workplace, sharpening such tools as:

- ✦ Collaborative learning

- Creative management of differences
- Conflict and collaborative problem-solving skills
- Communicating across differences
- Cultural-specific discernment skills
- Effective diversity management begins with awareness and development of one's self, in order to experience the positive impact of human diversity.

The Professional Practice of Diversity Management

As you may already have gleaned, the field of diversity management is a practitioner-based field that relies on theory and research to support the interventions that happen on multiple levels of system. In one sense, we are all diversity managers. We engage in personal and professional growth, and we relate to family and friends interpersonally. We manage diverse interactions presented to us in our work environments and in our society. For years, countless individuals have transferred their skills at managing human differences on many levels into professional careers. Many of these individuals have developed models and frameworks. Some have written articles, books, book chapters, essays, and lectures to capture their thinking and share their learning with others. These factors, along with the changing demographics in America and the shift to a global perspective, have set the stage for the science of diversity management to emerge. By the 1990s, it was clear that the field of diversity management warranted consideration as a field of independent study. Characteristic of an independent field, professional organizations emerge and training in the field becomes more structured and systematic. For example, in 1997, the first Master's Degree in Diversity Management was offered at Cleveland State University, in partnership with NTL Institute for Applied Behavioral Science. The Diversity Management Program is an innovative professional-development program of education and training in diversity theory, research, and practice. Active programs of research that further the scholarship in the field are mandatory for its participants. In 1998, the first professional organization devoted solely to diversity professionals — Diversity Leadership Forum (DLF) — was incorporated in Washington, D. C. The mission of the organization is to develop the field of diversity by advocating benefits of an inclusive society, by educating our members and other stakeholders, and by promoting professional standards, competencies, and research.

As a field in its infancy, diversity management struggles with defining its parameters. Paramount in this struggle is the continuous dialogue concerning how much of oppression and social-justice theory "belongs" in the field. In many ways, the field is one of social action and advocacy, and in many ways, it is a field of scientific inquiry into the management of human differences.

Because diversity management is a burgeoning area of interest to many professionals in corporations, nonprofits, social services, faith-based organizations, and government agencies, the discussion of credentials and certification becomes necessary. What kind of training, to what degree of intensity, constitutes a professional diversity practitioner?

As a field that is defined by the interplay of human differences in interpersonal, organizational, community, and societal settings, it is not surprising that the boundaries may appear a bit fuzzy. However, whether the issue is theoretical boundaries or certification, the field of diversity management is a vibrant field of study that enhances the presence and positive impact of human diversity.

Conclusion

This chapter is intended to support your journey of understanding in the field of diversity management and to heighten your awareness of your own identity as a member of this diverse society. Understanding diversity and yourself is key to developing the skills that will enhance your personal and professional life. No matter where you are on your journey into understanding diversity — whether you're just getting started or you're well down the road — hopefully, you have been enlightened by these topics and will be more so by those still to be presented. As our world becomes increasingly diverse, may you find this book a useful navigator for your professional and personal development.

Appendix A

Diversity Quiz Answers

1. 3.6%
2. 12.3%
3. 12.5%
4. .9%
5. 65%
6. B
7. D
8. B
9. A
10. A
11. 72%
12. 57%
13. 74%
14. B
15. A
16. False
17. 25%
18. 17%
19. A
20. 46%
21. 10%
22. 541
23. Asia
24. Islam
25. Mexican
26. True

Appendix B

Racial Identity Self-Assessment Scoring

Directions: Place a mark in the box for the numbers you have checked. After you have completed marking those boxes for the checked items, add the columns for your score. The number represents your endorsement of attitudes represented for the statuses described in the section on racial-identity development, which are briefly summarized below.

Status 1 Attitudes	Status 2 Attitudes	Status 3 Attitudes	Status 4/5 Attitudes
1	2	3	4
5	6	7	8
9	10	11	12
13	14	15	16
21	17	19	17
23	18	22	18
25	27	24	20
28	29	26	30

Status 1: Describes a level of unawareness of self as a racial person, or low importance given to race matters in one's life.

Status 2: Describes a state of awakening as a racial person.

Status 3: Describes a strong identification with one's race and/or a rejection of privileged Whiteness.

Status 4/5: Describes an integration of race in one's life, and multicultural attitudes.

References

Carr-Ruffino, N. (1996). *Managing diversity: People skills for a multi cultural workforce.* San Francisco, CA: Thomson Executive Press.
Cross, W.E. (2000). *The psychology of nigrescence: Revising the cross model.* In Ponterotto, J.G., Casas, J.M., Suzuki, L.A. & Alexander, C.M. (Eds.) *Handbook of Multicultural Counseling.* (pp. 93-122). Thousand Oaks, CA: Sage Publications, Inc.
Loden, M. (1996) *Implementing diversity.* Chicago, IL: Irwin Professional Publishing.

Selected Bibliography

Carr-Ruffino, N. (1999). *Diversity success strategies.* Woburn, MA: Butterworth-Heinemann, 1999.
Carr-Ruffino, N. (1996). *Managing diversity: People skills for a multi cultural workforce.* San Francisco, CA: Thomson Executive Press.
Cox, Jr. T. (1993). *Cultural diversity in organizations: Theory, research and practice.* San Francisco: Berrett-Koehler Publishers, Inc.
Cox, Jr. T. & Beale, R.L. (1997). *Developing competency to manage diversity: Readings, case & activities* San Francisco: Beret Kohler Publishers, Inc.
Cross, E. Y. (2000). *Managing diversity: The courage to lead.* Westport, Connecticut: Quorum Books
Fernandez, J. (1991). *Managing a Diverse workforce: Regaining the competitive edge.* Lexington, MA: Lexington Books.
Garfield, C. (1992). *Second to None: How our smartest companies put people first.* Homewood, IL: Business One Irwin.
Graham, L. O. (1997). *Proversity.* New York, NY: John Wiley & Sons.
Griggs, L. B. & Lente, L. L. (1996). *Valuing diversity: New tools for a new reality.*
Harris, P. R. & Moran, R. T. (1987). *Managing cultural differences. 2nd ed.* Houston, TX: Gulf Publishing.
Hofstede, G. (1991) *Cultures and organizations.* New York, NY: McGraw-Hill.
Jamieson, D. & O'Mara, J. (1991). *Managing workforce 2000: Gaining the diversity advantage.* San Francisco, CA: Jossey Bass.
Johnston, W. B. & Packer, A. E. (1987). *Workforce 2000: Work and*

workers for the twenty-first century. Indianapolis, IN: Hudson Institute, June.

Loden, M. (1996*)* *Implementing diversity*. Chicago, IL: Irwin Professional Publishing.

Loden, M. & Rosener, J. (1991). *Workforce america: Managing employee diversity as a vital resource.* Homewood, IL: Business One Irwin.

Simons, G. F. (1991). *The questions of diversity, 4th edition*. ODT, Inc.

Thiederman, S. (1991). *Bridging cultural barriers for corporate suc cess: How to manage the multicultural workforce.* Lexington, MA: Lexington Books.

Thiederman, S. (1991). *Profiting in america's multicultural market place: How to do business across cultural lines.* Lexington, MA: Lexington Books.

Thomas, Jr. R. R. (1996). *Building a house for diversity*. New York, NY AMACOM.

Thomas, Jr. R. R. (1999*)*. *Redefining diversity*. New York, NY: AMA COM, 1996.

Thomas, Jr., R. (1991). *Beyond race and gender: Unleashing the power of your total work force by managing diversity*. New York, NY: AMACOM.

Chapter 11

Historical and Theoretical Roots of Diversity Management

Michael Brazzel

Diversity Management

Diversity management is an emerging field of theory, research, teaching and practice. While there is no consensus among diversity management practitioners about purpose, methods, outcomes and values, a working definition of the field is:

> **Diversity management uses applied behavioral science methods, research and theory to manage organizational change and stability processes, that support diversity in organizations and eliminate oppression based on race, gender, sexual orientation and other human differences, in order to improve the health and effectiveness of organizations, while affirming the values of respect for human differences, social justice, participation, community, authenticity, compassion, proaction and humility, effectiveness and health, and life-long learning.**

From the perspective of this working definition, the purpose of the diversity management field is to improve the health and effectiveness of organizations. It is a field that uses applied behavioral science methods, research and theory. It is focused on change and stability processes involving diversity and social justice in organizations. Diversity management is a values-based field and values are an integral part of the definition and how practitioners conduct their work.

Diversity management is a cross-disciplinary field that uses applied behavioral theory and methods. The applied behavioral sciences include: anthropology, economics, education, human resource management, organization behavior, organization development, political science, psychology, social work, and sociology.

The applied behavioral sciences address the whole range of human systems: individuals, groups, organizations, communities and societies. Each level of system can be further divided into subsystems and key aspects of the environment for that level of system. Psychologists are likely to be concerned with intra-personal (or intra-psychic), individual and interpersonal levels. Organization behavior practitioners interested in small groups focus on group members, the group, and the intergroup and organizational environment (Gillette and McCollom, 1995, p. 5). Organization development practitioners may subdivide the organization level to include organization subsystems, the organization, and the inter-organization and organization network environment.

The diversity management field focuses on organizations. Organizations are viewed broadly. They can include for-profit businesses and industries; non-profit / non- governmental organizations; prisons, police departments and courts; educational institutions and systems; local, regional, national and global government bodies; labor unions; religious organizations; community organizations; organizations concerned with environmental, consumer safety and civil rights issues; political parties. They include: organizations that are set up on a temporary and on a long-term basis; single organizations and networks of organizations; organizations located in one nation and global organizations.

Diversity management interventions into organizations and organizational change and stability processes can include working inside organizations — with individuals and groups/teams in organizations, parts of the organization, and the whole. Diversity management interventions may also involve changing organizations from outside, rather than from inside organizations, by organizing and working with community and societal groups concerned with diversity and social justice issues in organizations.

Diversity management addresses both diversity and social justice issues. Diversity refers:

1. to the many differences among people, including age, class, ethnicity, gender, health, physical and mental ability, race, sexual/gender orientation, spiritual practice, stature, education level, job level and function;
2. to cultural differences;
3. to levels of system;
4. to different ways diversity and social justice issues are experienced including, cognitive, behavioral, physical, emotional and beliefs/values experiences.

Social justice is defined and used here to mean the elimination of oppression. Human differences provide for the richness of a varied human experience. They are also the basis for defining group identities and memberships which form the foundation for oppression.

Oppression is the systems of inequality, privilege and violence — i.e., racism, sexism, classism, heterosexism and other forms of oppression — that are institutionalized in the cultures, policies and practices of society and organizations and internalized in individuals. Oppression results in privilege for members of dominant groups of people and harm and violence for marginalized group members. The privilege that results from oppression and gives advantages to dominant group members is the unearned, unacknowledged rights, benefits and opportunities that are a form of "affirmative action" for dominant group members. The violence of oppression results from actions, behaviors and practices that are experienced by marginalized group members as life- diminishing, life-deadening, life-threatening and life-ending as opposed to life-enhancing, life-enriching and life-giving experiences.

Diversity and social justice are two sides of the same coin. They can be viewed separately and they cannot be separated. The diversity management field, and its focus on human differences, exists because of the richness and advantages embedded there for humans and because of the ways humans use differences to harm and privilege each other. Human differences are easier to focus on. Because oppression is more difficult, oppression issues are often ignored or avoided. "Social justice issues must be addressed in order to achieve the potential of diversity" (Miller, 1994, p. xxvi).

Value

The diversity management field is based in values. One list of values for the diversity management field is included in the working definition of diversity management. There is no consensus or research about the values held by diversity management practitioners at this early stage in the life of the field. Diversity management is related to the diversity and the organization and human systems development (OHSD) fields, for which lists of values are also available.

Diversity Field. A list of values for the diversity field was developed by the Diversity Collegium (2001), a group of 25 diversity practitioners, who began meeting in the early 1990s to explore and better understand the field and practice of diversity. Their list of values is part of a conceptual framework prepared for discussion at a June 2001, Diversity Symposium at Bentley College to encourage a "universally accepted conceptual framework for the practice of diversity" (p. 5). They divide the diversity field into three branches: individual and group diversity, organizational diversity and societal diversity (pp.3-4). The diversity management field corresponds in part to the Collegium's organizational diversity branch. The Collegium considers social justice issues to be part of the societal branch, whereas they are included as an integral part of the entire diversity management field in the diversity management working definition.

Organization and Human Systems Development Field. A list of values was developed by Gellermann, Frankel, and Ladenson as a part of "A Statement of Values and Ethics by Professionals in Organization and Human Systems Development" (1990, pp. 372-393). The statement and this list of values for the OHSD field resulted from a participative, 1981-1990 research study that involved review and input from individuals and organization development organizations, associations and networks in more than fifteen countries (p. 366). The OHSD field is also referred to as organization development (p. 366). Diversity management overlaps with the OHSD field.

The three lists of values for the diversity management, diversity, and OHSD fields are shown in Table 1. There are substantial overlaps among the lists.

Perspectives and Paradigms

VALUES OF DIVERSITY MANAGEMENT AND RELATED FIELDS		
Diversity Management Field (Working Definition)	**Diversity Field** (Diversity Collegium, 2001)	**Organization and Human Systems Development Field** (Gellermann, Frankel and Ladenson, 1990)
Respect for human differences Social justice Participation Community Authenticity Compassion Proaction and humility Effectiveness and health Life-long learning	***Global Values:*** Justice and fairness Respect Love/caring/empathy/compassion Responsibility Family/community/relationships Integrity/honesty/truth Life/reverence/ preservation Spirituality Learning/knowledge Freedom ***Business Values:*** Innovation Markets/customers Quality/productivity/profitability	Life and the quest for happiness Freedom, responsibility, and self-control Justice Human potential and empowerment Respect, dignity, integrity, worth, and fundamental rights Authenticity, congruence, honesty and openness, understanding and acceptance Flexibility, change and proaction Learning, development, growth, and transformation Whole-win attitudes, trust, cooperation-collaboration, community and diversity Participation, democracy and appropriate decision making Effectiveness, efficiency and alignment

Table 1. Values of Diversity Management

The terms, "diversity management" and "managing diversity," came into use in the United States in the 1980s. The diversity management field emerged in the 1990s. The overall managing diversity "movement" was a response in organizational decision-making and management processes both to:

- the demands raised by the civil-rights and women's liberation movements, Supreme Court rulings, and federal civil rights, equal opportunity and affirmative action legislation and regulation in the 1950s and 1960s and
- the recognition of competitive and economic self-interest by

organizations for effectively managing the differences represented by an increasingly diverse workforce.

Because of these influences, diversity management practitioners and organizations that are addressing diversity and social justice concerns hold a variety of perspectives and paradigms about diversity management. For example, in 1992 Patti DeRosa listed six approaches to diversity training:

- ✦*Affirmative action/equal employment opportunity (AA/EEO)*: providing organizational compliance with laws and regulations,
- ✦*Valuing differences* : supporting greater personal and interpersonal awareness and respect for human differences,
- ✦*Managing diversity* : improving organization productivity and profit out of business necessity,
- ✦*Inter-cultural relations* : improving interpersonal communications and relationships across human differences,
- ✦*Prejudice reduction* : reducing bias and stereotypes in personal and interpersonal awareness and relationships and supporting personal and interpersonal healing and reconciliation, and
- ✦*Anti-racism / anti-oppression, liberation theory* : providing social justice and systemic change at all levels of human system (DeRosa, 1992).

As with diversity management practitioners, organizations also view diversity management in many different ways. The following are different paradigms which organizations use for giving meaning to the concept of diversity management:

Uphold Sameness, Prohibit I Discourage Differences. The purpose of diversity management for this organization is to maintain an organization of sameness by formal or informal policy and include only people in the work of the organization who fit the prescribed organizational culture. Others, who do not have the correct race, gender, educational or geographic background and other qualifications, are excluded. Differences are permitted only within the limits and prohibitions of the organization. This organization intentionally or unintentionally and consciously or unconsciously maintains dominance and oppression that benefits those with the acceptable qualifications and is to the detriment of those who do not.

Appreciate Everyone. The organization strives to treat each person the same and encourages employees to appreciate and get along with each other regardless of cultural differences. It sees everyone as individuals and attempts to be color-blind, gender-blind and blind in general to human differences. Judith Palmer refers to this as "the golden rule" paradigm (Palmer, 1994, pp. 253-254). "Do unto others as you would have them do unto you." The organization strives through diversity management in this paradigm to maintain a culture of sameness, to suppress differences or to deny that they exist.

Compliance. The organization makes good-faith efforts to recruit, hire and retain sufficient numbers of women, people of color and others who are under- represented in its workforce to comply with moral and federal equal opportunity and affirmative action requirements. David Thomas and Robin Ely refer to this approach as the "discrimination-and-fairness" paradigm (Thomas and Ely, 1996, pp. 81-83). Palmer calls it the "right the wrongs" paradigm (Palmer, 1994, pp. 254-256). The purpose of diversity management is to meet employment goals for under-represented groups of employees and insure equality, respect and fair treatment for them.

Assimilation. The organization is clear about employee norms for dress, style, education, how work needs to be performed and other ways of being in the organization's workforce. Employees are asked to accommodate to these norms — to assimilate. Often the norms represent a narrow band-width of thought, appearance and behavior that fits the style and approach of organizational leaders. Some differences are tolerated when the organization works to maintain visual workforce differences — in the sense of "look different, but act and think in ways that fit into the organization's norms." Roosevelt Thomas describes this assimilation or melting pot approach to diversity management as the traditional approach to managing people for U.S. organizations. He contrasts it with an approach that values and empowers all employees for all their differences (Thomas, 1990, pp. 7-15).

Accept and Celebrate Diversity. The organization accepts, celebrates and values diversity because it makes business sense, provides competitive advantage and is a source of creativity, innovation and productivity. Thomas and Ely describe this diversity management approach as the "access and legitimacy" paradigm (Thomas and Ely, 1996, pp. 83-85). The organization is concerned with achieving differentiation, rather than assimilation. All employees are appreciated and valued because of their differences. Marilyn Loden refers to this approach as the "valuing diversity" paradigm (Loden, 1994, pp. 294-300). Palmer calls it the "value all differences" paradigm (Palmer, 1994, pp. 254-256).

Employees from different cultural backgrounds permit the organization to serve its customers better and to create niche markets that would not otherwise be available to it. The organization notices and accommodates differences in employee requirements involving food, dress, religion, holidays, and family / work concerns. With cultural competency by the organization and its employees, attention is paid to leadership, communication and teamwork across cultural differences including race, gender, ethnicity and nationality (Tropenaars and Hampden-Turner, 1998; Kochman, 1981; Gilligan, 1982; Kanter, 1977; Tannen, 1994). Jean Kim refers to this organizational approach of encouraging employees to understand each other's culture as "cultural enlightenment" (Kim, 1994, pp. 130-134).

Organizational Learning. The organization learns from the cultural differences of employees about how to do its work in fundamentally different and more effective ways. The different cultural perspectives and work styles of all employees lead to a widening and reframing of the issues around what work the organization does and how it does that work. Thomas and Ely refer to this way of thinking about diversity management as the "learning and effectiveness" paradigm (Thomas and Ely, 1996, pp. 85-86). The organization leverages diversity by integrating and internalizing differences among employees to support its learning, growth and effectiveness. In this case, the organization is concerned with integration of cultural perspectives, work styles and other differences, rather than the concepts of differentiation or assimilation associated with other differences paradigms.

Social Justice. The organization works to eliminate oppression based on race, gender, sexual orientation and other differences. Racism, sexism, heterosexism and the other "isms" that are institutionalized in organizational policies, programs, norms and structures are barriers to people being able to do their best work. In this context, Elsie Cross defines managing diversity in terms of the amelioration of oppression and concludes that managing diversity efforts focused solely on differences miss the real issue of oppression (Cross, 2000). The benefits of diversity cannot be realized fully until the privilege and harm that result from oppression are addressed.

These paradigms are interrelated. The range of organizational perspectives and paradigms about diversity management are summarized in Chart 1.as continuation of differences and social justice paradigms.

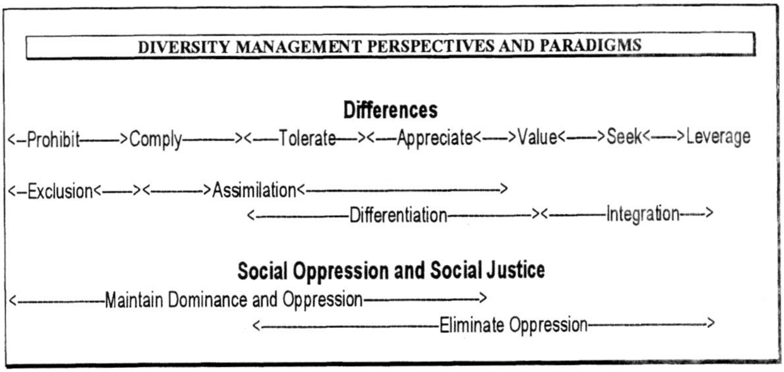

Chart 1. Interrelated Paradigms

Many, if not most, organizations, who are concerned with diversity management, are focused on the management of differences and operate out of one or more of the differences paradigms. They may stand for prohibiting differences and excluding specific groups of people or they may stand for including people. Inclusion can mean different things to different organizations:

- ✦ Compliance with EEO/ AA laws and regulations or tolerating, appreciating, valuing, seeking or leveraging differences and
- ✦ An organizational stance in support of assimilation, of differentiation or of integration of differences.

Organizations may be operating out of several of the differences paradigms at the same time.

Fewer organizations intentionally choose both to manage differences and to address the gains available from the pursuit of social justice — the elimination of institutionalized racism, sexism and other forms of oppression. Organizations that operate out of the left side of the differences continua also operate out of a social injustice or dominance and oppression paradigm, whether intentional or not.

In contrast with the working definition of diversity management described above, the range and variety of these perspectives and paradigms lead to multiple ideas about the purpose of the field of diversity management. In regard to human differences, some consider the purpose of diversity management as the discouragement or prohibition of differences. Others see diversity management's purpose as seeking and leveraging differences for the benefit of organizations. These contrasting views about purpose involve a range of organizational stances toward human differences from exclusion to assimilation, differentiation and integration. The purpose of diversity management may also be defined in relation to the stance of organizations toward social injustice and justice and can range from maintaining dominance and oppression to eliminating oppression within and outside the organization.

The diversity management field, and the managing diversity perspectives and paradigms are based in both the historical and theoretical roots of the field. The historical roots of diversity management are the social unrest of the 1960s and 70s and demographic and economic changes of the 1980s and 90s. These historical events and changes have sometimes resulted in confusion and conflict about whether diversity management should address only diversity or both diversity and social justice. Diversity management's theoretical roots are in the applied behavioral sciences, community organizing and social action. The patterns of theory, research, teaching and practice that have evolved for the field have resulted from the historical and theoretical roots of diversity management.

Historical Roots

Diversity management is rooted in the social protest, civil rights and liberation movements of the 1950s, 60s and 70s; judicial rulings and federal civil rights and equal opportunity legislation in the 1950s and 1960s; and demographic and economic changes in the 1980s and 90s.

Social Protest, Judicial Rulings and Legislation

This section describes some key events and time lines in the history of diversity management and depends on the work of Clare Swanger (1994), Maurianne Adams, Lee Anne Bell and Pat Griffen (1997), and Elsie Y. Cross (2000) and on information from the internet websites of key organizations.

✦ In 1954, *Brown* v. *Board of Education* was argued successfully before the U.S. Supreme Court by Thurgood Marshall, head of the National Association for the Advancement of Colored People's (NAACP) Legal Defense and Educational Fund. In that case, the Supreme Court overturned the 1896 separate-but-equal doctrine in 1954 and in the next year ordered desegregation of public schools.

✦ In 1955 Rosa Parks, a black woman, was arrested for refusing to give up her seat on a Montgomery, Alabama bus to a white man. Dr. Martin Luther King, Jr., organized a year-long boycott of Montgomery buses.

✦ From that time, Dr. King joined with other leaders and freedom workers from the Southern Christian Leadership Council (SCLC), Congress for Racial Equality (CORE), Student Nonviolent Coordinating Committee (SNCC) and other organizations to provide employment and voter education and lead peaceful, non-violent marches, rallies, boycotts, lunch counter sit-ins and strikes for racial equality. These efforts were met with ridicule, threats, beatings, fire hoses, police dogs, arrests, bombings, fires and murder. More than forty people were killed in the struggle for civil rights between 1954 and 1968 (Southern Poverty Law Center, 2000).

✦By the mid 60s, Malcom X, Stokely Carmichael, Eldridge Cleaver and others from the Black Panthers, Nation of Islam, and Black Nationalist Movement advocated retaliatory violence and the separation of the races.

✦President John Kennedy, Dr. Martin Luther King, Jr., Malcom X, Medgar Evers, and Robert Kennedy were assassinated and civil rights leaders and workers murdered.

✦Between 1965 and 1968, protests against racial inequality erupted in more than 160 cities and towns across the country. These protests often involved confrontation with police and local authority and destruction of homes and businesses in black communities.

Other protest, social liberation and civil rights movements began in the 1960s.

✦Anti-Vietnam War protests, draft-card burnings and marches were organized.

✦The counter-culture movement grew among young people.

✦In 1962 Cesar Chavez and Dolores Huerta co-founded the United Farm Workers, a union and civil rights organization for farm and migrant workers. They organized a strike against corporate grape growers and a national grape boycott which lasted from 1965 to 1970.

✦In 1968 the National Council of La Raza was founded as a Latino civil rights advocacy group.

✦The American Citizens for Justice was founded in 1983 to organize for pan-Asian civil rights.

✦The American Arab Anti-Discrimination Committee was formed in 1980 to combat defamation and stereotyping and defend the rights of people of Arab descent.

✦The Anti-Defamation League of B'nai B'rith, working against anti-Semitism, racism and hate crimes and with the Southern Poverty Law Center, which was formed in 1971, provided leadership in tracking and working against racist and neo-Nazi white supremacy groups like the National Alliance, Klan and Patriot militia groups.

✦The Gray Panthers were founded in 1970 by Maggie Kuhn to work against age discrimination and as advocates for the national health care system (Gray Panthers, 2000).

✦Following the lead of the NAACP Legal Defense and Education Fund, legal and civil rights education organizations were formed between 1969 and 1993 to protect the civil rights of Native Americans, Mexican Americans and Latinos, American Arabs, Asian Pacific Americans, women, children, gays and lesbians, people with disabilities and poor people.

✦The American Indian Movement (AIM) was founded in 1968 by Clyde H. Bellecourt and others for the protection of the rights of Native Nations (American Indian Movement, 2000). AIM participated in the 1969, nineteen-month occupation and reclaiming of Alcatraz Island and organized the 1972 Trail of Broken Treaties March on Washington and the 1973 occupation of Wooded Knee. It founded Women of All Red Nations (WARN) in 1978 to address issues facing Indian women and their families. WARN helped expose the U.S. federal program of involuntary sterilization of forty-two percent of the native women of childbearing age during the 1970s (Churchill, 1994).

✦Betty Friedan published The Feminine Mystique in 1963 and raised awareness of abuse, discrimination and violence against women. Women's liberation and consciousness raising groups were formed across the country. The National Organization of Women (NOW) was formed in 1966 and the National Women's Political Caucus followed in 1973. Mass marches, demonstrations, rallies and get-out-the-vote campaigns were organized to focus on increasing the number of women elected officials, support of the *Equal Rights Amendment,* ending sexual harassment and violence against women, reproductive freedom and women's health issues, and opposing racism and bigotry against lesbians and gays.

✦The gay and lesbian rights movement grew out of the Stonewall riots in 1969 — three days of riots in New York City touched off by a police raid of a gay bar in Greenwich Village. The National Gay and Lesbian Task Force was formed. National marches on Washington for lesbian and gay rights were held in 1979 and 1987. Two direct action protest groups, ACT UP and Queer Nation, were organized in 1988 and 1990 to advance gay / lesbian rights.

✦Beginning in 1957 and continuing until the 1990s, Congress passed a series of civil rights laws forbidding discrimination on the basis of gender, color, race, religion, national origin, age or physical disability in areas of employment, education, housing, voting, and public accommodations. The Civil Rights Act of 1964 provided for enforcement of discrimination through private litigation and suits brought by the Equal Employment Opportunity Commission (EEOC). In 1973, AT&T employees won a pay- discrimination class-action lawsuit against AT&T, involving a $50 million consent decree, higher wages and back-pay for women and men of color. As part of the court's decision, AT&T became the first company to engage with the EEOC in an affirmative action agreement.

✦Congress passed the equal rights amendment to the *U. S. Constitution* in 1972 stating that "Equality of rights under the law shall not be denied or abridged by the United States or any state on account of sex." The amendment was ratified by only thirty-five of the necessary thirty-eight states by the 1982 deadline. The Americans with Disabilities Act was passed by the Congress in 1990. In 1994 the Violence Against Women Act became federal law.

In the 1960s, 70s and 80s, organizations addressed diversity issues involving discrimination and racial and gender violence because of:

1. *Fear:* concerns that social and community unrest would move into the workplace,
2. *Law:* compliance with equal employment opportunity and affirmative action laws and regulations and
3. *Values /ethics*: alignment with organizational moral and ethical standards and values — to do the right thing.

The changes that were anticipated from the civil rights actions and accomplishments of the 1960s did not materialize. Women and people of color were hired into entry-level positions and found it difficult to move up in their organizations. White women were able to move into middle management positions, while women and men of color were caught at the lowest levels of management. Few white women and almost no people of color have reached senior management levels (Glass Ceiling Commission, 1995; Fernandez, 1998). In the 1970s, 80s and 90s, the organizational experience of white women and people of color began to be described in terms of glass ceilings, revolving doors, empty pipelines and sticky floors. The salary gaps between white men and women and people of color persist. Employee and consumer discrimination suits against corporate, university and government organizations continue.

Equal employment opportunity and affirmative action began to generate criticism and resistance in the 1970s, especially among white men concerned about the possibility of increased competition for jobs, housing, education and political power by white women and people of color. With the election of Ronald Reagan and then George Bush in the 1980s, the federal government began backing away from enforcement of government EEO and affirmative action programs.

Demographic and Economic Changes

Reasons for Organizational Diversity Initatives

- ✦**Fear:** Avoid workplace unrest
- ✦**Laws:** Comply with EEO/AA; avoid lawsuits
- ✦**Values and Ethics:** Do the right thing
- ✦**Profit:** Enhance effectiveness and competitive advantage

Demographic and economic changes in the 1980s and 90s caused organizations to focus on profit and effectiveness more than fear, law and values/ethics as reasons to address diversity issues They began to see diversity programs as a way to generate greater organizational effectiveness and competitive advantage, even more than as a response to legal and value issues of discrimination and violence toward white women and women and men of color (Baker, 1996).

The 1987 Workforce 2000 report of the Hudson Institute gave new perspective and impetus to organizational efforts to employ women and people of color with forecasts that white women, people of color and immigrants would account for 85 percent of the growth in the U.S. labor force and that those trends would continue into the next century (Johnston and Packer, 1987). In the 1980s many organizations began to find themselves operating increasingly in global markets and challenged to hire a work force capable of operating in the more competitive, international setting. Competitive pressures in the U.S. economy meant searching out and moving into new niche markets with customers from demographic groups not currently being served by organizations — and expanding their labor forces to people who represent those demographic groups. The economic growth, low-unemployment economy of the 1990s caused greater difficulty in hiring and retaining women and people of color.

Because of these changes, the concept of diversity is being talked about and understood in a very different way from the legal, values and fear perspectives of the period before the 1980s. Diversity has become an economic value available to organizations that can be managed for profit, organizational advantage, success and survival (Prasad, 2001, p. 64). As an alternative to investing in diversity programs, some organizations are buying insurance policies to protect against the legal liabilities from lawsuits, mediation results and jury verdicts (Abelson, 2002).

Oppression and social justice concerns are increasingly being seen in organizations and the U.S. as peripheral matters. Some organizations are attempting to move their diversity programs beyond "diversity" — seeing diversity as too linked with EEO/AA, race, racism, gender and sexism. In the place of diversity programs, they are developing programs focused on individual respect, cultural competency, inclusion, and organizational values (Pine, 2001; Wallace, 2001).

Theorectical Roots

The diversity management movement from the 1980s began to emerge in the late 1990s as a field of study, teaching, research and practice. The diversity management field is impacted by its history and based in the applied behavioral sciences, community organizing and social action. The applied behavioral sciences are the social sciences and organization change disciplines with theory and methodology used to explain and bring about organizational change through interventions at the individual, group, organization, community and societal levels of human system. Diversity management interventions can be made at any of the levels of human. The purpose of the interventions is organizational change.

The theoretical roots of the applied behavioral sciences form a foundation for diversity management which can be divided into categories according to level of human system: individual, group, organization, community and society.

Individual Theory and Methods

Kurt Lewin, Karen Horney, Abraham Maslow, Carl Rogers, Carl Jung, Laura and Fritz Perls and other psychologists developed theories for understanding and influencing individual behavior and development (Segal, 1997). Their ideas formed the basis for current thinking about the ways that thoughts, feelings, physical sensations, belief systems, the unconscious and the environment impact individual human behavior in families, groups and organizations. Counseling, coaching and teaching strategies for helping individuals change and develop, for motivating employees, for leadership development, and for the use of one's self as an instrument of change all originate in theories of individual behavior and change.

Group Theory and Methods

Theories for understanding and influencing group behavior, dynamics and development have been heavily impacted by the work of key people in three organizations and the group processes developed in each organization for "here and now," experience-based learning about groups:

The NTL Institute for Applied Behavioral Science. In 1947, NTL Institute was founded by Kenneth Benne, Leland Bradford, and Ronald Lippitt, who were colleagues of Kurt Lewin (Seashore and Katz, 1994, pp. 333-336; Weisbord, 1987, pp. 99-104). NTL is now located in Alexandria, VA. The T-group was developed by Lewin, Benne, Bradford, Lippett and others in 1946 and is offered in programs provided by NTL. The T-group is an unstructured group that provides learning about interpersonal relationships, information about perceptions of one's self and others, and the development and dynamics of groups. NTL Institute offered a program entitled Human Interaction in a Multicultural Context during the early 1980s that used same-culture and cross-culture T-groups to address race, gender and cultural differences and oppression issues (Patricia Bidol-Padva, personal correspondence, February 25, 2002).

The Tavistock Institute of Human Relations. The Tavistock Institute was founded in London, England in 1947. In 1957 Eric Trist and Wilfred Bion introduced the Tavistock or "Tavi" group: a group that has structure, clear boundaries and trainers who are in an leader role and who have very limited interaction with participants. The Tavistock group provides learning about individuals' reactions and relationship with leadership and authority and often unconscious group processes such as pairing, fight-flight, and dependency (Weisbord 1987, pp. 99-104; Segal,1997, pp. 294-295). The A.K. Rice Institute (AKRI) was established in 1970 to provide programs in the U.S. following the Tavistock Institute=s approach to groups. Its national office is in Jupiter, FL. AKRI offers the Diversity Conference and other Tavistock group-based programs that examine the implications of culture, race, gender and other differences for the exercise of leadership and authority (A.K. Rice Institute, 2002).

The Gestalt Institute of Cleveland. In 1954, the Gestalt Institute of Cleveland was established in Cleveland, Ohio by students of Fritz and

Laura Perls, Paul Goodmanand Isadore From. There are other Gestalt Institutes. However, the Gestalt Institute of Cleveland has had the greatest impact on Gestalt therapy (Wheeler, 1998, pp. 84-85), and the applied behavioral sciences. In 1966 the Gestalt Institute began training programs that applied gestalt theory to couples, families, groups and organizations.

The Gestalt group, following the perspectives of the Gestalt Institute of Cleveland, highlights individual learning assisted by a trainer through interactions with the trainer, other participants and experience of the group as a whole (Wheeler, 1998, pp. 84-109; Segal, 1997, pp. 294-295). The Gestalt group serves as a container for individual work with attention paid to thoughts, feelings, physical sensations and values and belief systems of the individual and the group.

The group theories that have evolved from the work and experience of the NTL, Tavistock and Gestalt Institutes and other theorists and practitioners emphasize "here- and-now" experience-based learning, action learning or learning-by-doing. Their ideas form the basis for current understanding of group dynamics and development processes, of how individuals are impacted by group experience, and of leader, trainer and facilitator strategies for group training and education and for helping teams and groups develop and change.

Organizational Theory and Methods

The theories and methods for understanding and influencing organization change and development have also been impacted by the NTL, Tavistock and Gestalt institutes and theorists and practitioners who come from those three schools of thought. Core applied behavioral science approaches for understanding and impacting organizations are:

Action Research. Kurt Lewin, Eric Trist and others developed and used action research (learning by doing and learning through action) as the central applied behavioral science method of organizational inquiry, research and intervention, as the foundation for organization consulting and as a model for organizational change (Weisbord, 1987, pp. 149-152; French and Bell,1995, pp.137-154).

Action research is research "with," rather than research "about", "on" or "for." The concept of cooperation with and participation by the people, who are experiencing the problems/issues and are impacted by actions taken, is as important as the concept of action. Action research is also known as participatory action research, participatory research, cooperative inquiry and collaborative inquiry (Reason and Bradbury, 2001).

The central feature of action research as an organizational methodology and process is organizational practice — participating as a consultant with client organizations in organization change work in order to understand, test and build theory and conduct research. Action research involves joining with the organizational client in contracting, data collection, diagnosis, action, assessment of learnings, identification of next steps and termination of the work.

Open Systems Theory. The systems concepts:

- ✦that organizations impact and are impacted by their environments,
- ✦that characteristics of systems reflect the characteristics of larger systems of which they are a part, and
- ✦that one can intervene at different levels of system to change an organizationare now commonplace in the applied behavioral sciences. Fred Emery brought the open systems theory of Ludwig von Bertalanffy from physics and biology into the organization-focused work of the Tavistock Institute in 1950. Eric Trist and Ken Bamforth used open systems theory in 1951 to view organizations as socio-technical systems in which social systems and technical systems impact on each other (von Bertalanffy, 1950; Weisbord, 1987, pp. 157-178; French and Bell, 1995, pp. 89-94).

Marvin Weisbord broadened the open-systems perspective of organizations to a whole- systems perspective of working for organizational change in the same room with as many key organizational stakeholders as possible (Weisbord, 1987, pp. 237-252).

Traditional Gestalt theories and methods for understanding and influencing individuals, families, and groups were extended and applied to organizations through the Gestalt Institute of Cleveland's Organization and System Development program (Wheeler, 1987, pp. 104-106). That program was organized in 1973 by John Carter, Leonard Hirsch, Elaine Kepner, Carolyn Lukensmeyer, Edwin Nevins, Claire Stratford andJeffrey Voorhees (Nevis, 1987, p. xiii).

Change and Resistance Theory. Kurt Lewin introduced force-field analysis as a way to examine the change and stability forces that operate in organizations (and other human systems) by identifying the driving and restraining forces that lead to change and that maintain the status quo (Ingalls, 1979, pp. 230-231; French and Bell, 1995, pp.191-193). Lewin believed that driving forces (forces for change) attract restraining forces or resistance (forces to keep things the same) — that is, that change and resistance to change are linked. He developed a change model to describe how change takes place, in which there is:

- *unfreezing:* reducing restraining forces;
- *moving:* changing attitudes, beliefs, actions, behaviors, structure; and
- *refreezing:* achieving a new status quo with a balance of driving and restraining forces (Weisbord, 1987, pp. 78, 92-95).

More detailed organizational change models — including the action research process, have evolved from Lewin's initial work. Much of the recent research and applications of the concept of resistance has come from the work and influence of the Gestalt Institute of Cleveland (Wheeler, 1987, pp. 84-132; Mauer, 1996).

Interview and Survey Data Feedback Methods. Action research requires methods for collecting organizational data and for feedback of the data to organization members. In the late 1940s and early 50s, Floyd Mann, Rensis Likert and other staff members of the University of Michigan's Institute for Social Research developed:

- survey methods to systemically collect organizational data and
- employee feedback meetings in which employees worked to analyze and make sense of the data results and identify necessary next steps (French and Bell, 1995, pp.47-49, 219-227; Weisbord, 1987, pp. 192-194).

Data collection methods have evolved to include individual and group interview processes and structured data-development meetings of larger and larger groups of people.

Organization theories and methods have emerged from the organizational work and experience of members of the NTL, Tavistock and Gestalt Institutes and other theorists and practitioners. They developed core theories and methods including, action research, open systems theory, change and resistance theory and interview and survey data feedback methods. Much of the theory that underlies organizational methods is practice theory based in action research. Practice theory and methods often circulate among practitioners through informal, often unpublished, word-of-mouth and practice notes. These ideas and others form the basis for current understanding of organization change, stability and development processes and for consultant theorist strategies for helping organizations develop and change.

Community and Society Theory and Methods: Changing Organizations from the Outside

For the most part, community and society theory in the applied behavioral sciences is an extension and application of organization theory to community and societal organizations. The traditional applied behavioral science perspective about organizational change is that organizations can be changed from the inside through individual, group and organization level interventions. With the exception of a limited, and not very visible, literature on organization stakeholder theory (see e.g., Mitroff, 1983; Frooman, 1999), the applied behavioral sciences have had little to say about changing organizations from the outside — from communities and society.

Some examples of changing organizations from the outside are available from the work of community organizers and socia! activists:

- Saul Alinsky began community organizing in 1938-39 in Chicago's Back of the Yards neighborhood, where he worked with the Congress of Industrial Organizations (CIO) to organize the Packinghouse Workers Union over the opposition of the Chicago stockyard's largest meatpacking companies — Swift, Armour, Wilson and Cudahy (Finks, 1984, pp. 9-18). In 1940 Alinsky established his Industrial Areas Foundation (IAF) to fund community organizing across the country. By the time of his death in 1972, Saul Alinsky had organized several million people in poor neighborhoods and cities across the U.S. and impacted the behaviors and actions of corporations, city governments, churches, universities and other organizations (Finks, 1984, p. 267). Some of his most notable organizing efforts include:

- ✦Chicago's Woodlawn neighborhood in its protest against the University of Chicago's efforts to expand the campus by clearing part of Woodlawn without consulting residents and

- ✦Inner city neighborhoods of Rochester, NY who challenged Kodak employment policies and practices.The IAF continues to train community organizers and support community organizing efforts today.

- ✦Cesar Chavez and Dolores Huerta were early IAF organizers in Latino neighborhoods in California. They moved on to form the United Farm Workers Union to improve working and social conditions for farm worker and Latino communities in California and to organize a nationwide grape boycott.

- ✦Martin Luther King, Jr. organized boycotts, marches, rallies, sit-ins and strikes to improve civil rights, opportunities and access for African-Americans. He was assassinated in Memphis, TN as he began organizing to address the economic inequities of U.S. industry.

- ✦The Highlander Research and Education Center in New Market, Tennessee has been supporting social change and training community organizers and citizens groups since the 1930s when it was founded by Myles Horton and others (Lewis, 2001). Highlander has been involved in the social justice efforts of the Appalachian region and the South: labor organizing, civil rights, environmental safety and community development. The core methodology of the Highlander Center is participatory action research.

- ✦Paulo Friere wrote Pedagogy of the Oppressed (1996) and raised awareness in Brazil, the U.S., and other countries about the use of education systems and institutions to support classism and other forms of oppression and to reinforce the status quo. He initiated a movement to use education to support liberation and freedom for oppressed people.

✦Ralph Nader researched and wrote Unsafe at Any Speed and mobilized theconsumer safety and protection movement.

✦Rachel Carson researched and wrote Silent Spring which was a catalyst for the environmental movement.

✦Betty Friedan was a catalyst for the women's liberation movement with her book, Feminine Mystique.

Community organizers and social activists use a participatory action and learning process very similar to the action research and action learning processes of the applied behavioral sciences. They participate with people in communities and society to identify important and compelling issues, build relationships, community and networks, identify and educate leaders, stand for dissent, act to bring change and learn from results of the change process. The organizing, advocacy, activist and dissent strategies of community organizers and social activists for changing organizations from the outside offer additional perspectives about theory and methods to help organizations develop and change in ways that are healthy and effective for people inside and outside of organizations.

Extensions of Applied Behavioral Science Theory

For the most part, applied behavioral science theorists and practitioners have ignored diversity and oppression in applied behavioral science theories and methods at individual, group, organization, community and society levels of human system. The void around diversity and oppression in applied behavioral science theory and practice occurs:

✦because diversity and oppression is an uncomfortable topic for applied behavioral science theorists, practitioners, and clients,

✦because community organizing and social action, in which diversity and oppression work are more central, are not part of the applied behavioral sciences, and

✦because those action research and practice theories and methods, which do address diversity and oppression issues, are often circulated informally as practice notes and by word-of-mouth and are not readily available in published form.

Nevertheless, this wall of silence by applied behavioral science theorists and practitioners supports and maintains racism, sexism and other forms of oppression. There are a few examples in which applied behavioral theory and methods have been extended to address diversity and oppression:

- ✦Counseling, coaching and teaching methods and strategies for helping individuals change and develop, for motivating employees, for leadership development, and for the use of one's self as an instrument of change depend on theories about individual identity development and change. The concept of individual identity reflects the plurality of social identities — race, gender, age, class, sexual orientation, ability — and the forms of social and internalized oppression based on those and other human differences. Most research has been focused on race and gender identity development. The identity development of white people and people of color is impacted by the racism, privilege and violence of being a part of racist organizations and society (Salett & Koslow, 1994; Helms, 1990). The identity development of men and women is impacted by the sexism, privilege and violence of being a part of sexist organizations and society (Kanter, 1977; Connell, 1999).

- ✦Leader, trainer and facilitator methods and strategies for group training and education processes and helping teams and groups develop and change depend on theories for understanding group / team development processes and how individuals are impacted by group experience. Much of the current theory and methods about the dynamics and development of groups and teams does not consider the impact that oppression can have on groups / teams or the implications of dominant and marginalized group identity and membership. Clayton Alderfer and others associated with the small-group dynamics work at the Yale School of Organization and Management developed embedded intergroup theory to describe how individuals and social identity groups are affected by oppression in organizations and society (Alderfer, 1994, pp. 221-226; Zane, 1994, pp. 340-341; Gillette and McCollom, 1995).

- Consultant strategies and methods for helping organizations manage change, stability and development processes are guided by organization change and development theories and models which, for the most part, do not consider the Implications of diversity and oppression for the health and effectiveness of organizations. Bailey Jackson, Rita Hardiman, Evangelina Holvino and others developed a model that describes stages of an organization's development from a monocultural to a multicultural organization (Jackson & Hardiman, 1981; Jackson & Holvino, 1986 & 1988). Frederick Miller and Judith Katz added to this model by showing it in a diagram, providing new names for the stages and adding to the descriptions for each stage (Miller & Katz, 1995). The monocultural-multicultural organization model provides a diagnostic model that considers:
    - employment / compensation / benefits representation equity,
    - the organization's stance toward differences and the elimination of oppression,
    - individual and organizational actions and behaviors, and
    - interventions and outcomes at each development stage.

Books about the theory and practice of diversity management began being published in the early 1990s. Most of these books are focused on differences. A few books address both differences and social justice. See, for example, the edited books by Cross, Katz, Miller and Seashore (1994); Cross and White (1996); and Adams, Bell and Griffen (1997) and a recent book by Cross (2000). Other diversity books focus on differences, touch lightly on bias, prejudice, stereotyping, discrimination and avoid the issues of oppression.

As the diversity management field has evolved, more attention is being given to diversity and oppression definitions and theory. Action research and practice theories and methods, which do address diversity and oppression concepts and issues, are often circulated informally among diversity management practitioners as unpublished practice notes and by word-of-mouth.

Diversity Frames of Reference. Discussions of diversity can originate from four different frames of reference:

—*Areas of Human Differences.* Human differences are categorized in different ways by various authors. In a framework Marilyn Loden and Judy Rosener call "*dimensions of diversity,*" they identify differences as primary and secondary human differences (Loden & Rosener, 1991, pp. 18-21). Primary differences are in-born and have life-long impact on people's lives. They include race, gender, sexual orientation, physical and mental ability, ethnicity and age. Secondary differences, which are more changeable, less visible and have a less-sustained impact on people's lives, include religion, class, income, education, and other human differences.

—*Aspects of Human Experience.* People are different from each other, as well, in their range of responses about diversity and oppression issues in terms of: ideas, behaviors, attitudes, physical sensations, feelings and core values. These areas of response are the aspects of human experience which define reality. Kate Kirkham refers to the ability to move among these aspects of human experience as "depth of understanding and insight" (Kirkham, 1986). Kirkham also refers to the aspects of human experience, when they are combined with levels of human system, as "*dimensions of diversity.*" These aspects of human experience apply to groups, organizations, communities and society, as well as individuals.

—*Levels of Human System.* Diversity and oppression issues are often addressed at the individual level, involving personal, intrapersonal and interpersonal work on the issues. Diversity and oppression also have consequences for group and inter-group, organization, community and society experience. The experiences of individuals are embedded with their involvement and membership in dominant and marginalized groups, organizations and society. Full consideration of diversity and oppression issues must involve all levels of human system. Kate Kirkham uses the term, "breadth of awareness," to describe the ability to explore and move back and forth across the levels of human sys-

tem (Kirkham, 1986). Kirkham's dimensions of diversity framework is sometimes called the breadth-depth model
—*Elements of Culture.* Different individuals have different cultures. These cultural differences also apply to group cultures, organization cultures (Schein, 1985; Deal and Kennedy, 1982) and societal / national cultures (Hofstede, 2001; Tropensaars and Hampden-Turner, 1998). The building blocks for defining and understanding culture and cultural differences are the elements of culture — cultural differences in, for example, power, status, authority, leadership, language, time, space, intimacy, laws, regulations, rules, norms, standards, structure, values, beliefs, assumptions, ideology and ways of making meaning, rewards and punishments, and spirituality (Brazzel, 2000a, pp. 9-11). Oppression issues come into the picture when the differences between monocultural and multicultural organizations and between dominant and marginalized cultures are considered. At a societal or national level, colonialism is the imposition of the culture of one nation on that of another nation, territory or people. It can involve military invasion; occupation; expropriation of resources, property and land; enslaving people, expelling them and forcing them into prisons, camps, reservations and ghettos; and genocide.

Oppression Theory. The perspective that oppression is a system of inequality that impacts every level of human system is seldom considered in the applied behavioral science or the diversity management literature. Descriptions of oppression theory can be found in edited books by:

—Adams, Bell and Griffen (1997) and Adams, Blumenfeld, Castaneda et al. (2000), which are based in the work of the School of Education's Social Justice Education Program at the University of Massachusetts-Amherst, and

—Cross, Katz, Miller and Seashore (1994), which is sponsored by the NTL Institute for Applied Behavioral Sciences.
The purpose of oppression is supremacy and dominance. Oppression includes racism, sexism and other forms of oppression, all of which are based in human differences. Oppression, and the "isms," are systems of inequality, privilege, and

violence that benefit dominant group members and harm members of marginalized groups. Oppression creates privilege for dominant group members because of their group membership, without regard to personal achievements, contributions, and accomplishments (McIntosh, 1989; Kivel, 1996b, pp. 30-32). Oppression also has costs for dominant group members that are often unacknowledged and unrecognized by them (Kivel, 1996a, pp. 36-39; Brazzel, 1998; Johnson, 2001). The actions, behaviors, and practices of oppression experienced by marginalized group members are life-destroying experiences of violence (Brazzel, 2000b). These experiences range from genocide and slavery — to torture and murder — to discrimination — to denial and silence. The actions, behaviors, and practices of oppression have life-diminishing, life-deadening, life-threatening, and life-ending consequences for marginalized group members because of their group membership, without regard to personal achievements, contributions and accomplishments. The outcomes of oppression for dominant and marginalized group members can be measured in terms of changes in opportunity, access, health, wealth, income, goods and services. In organizations, oppression results in diminished individual and organizational performance.

Oppression rests on a foundation of (1) prejudice and (2) power exercised by dominant groups over marginalized groups. *Prejudice* is favorable or unfavorable prejudgment and categorization of people based on their group membership. When prejudgment is unfavorable, prejudice is a preconceived suspicion, intolerance, or hatred of individuals because of group membership. Prejudices originate and change as a result of life-long social messages, experiences and socialization processes that provide guidelines for appropriate / inappropriate and successful / unsuccessful behaviors. Prejudice forms the basis for seeing dominant group members as "better than," normal, and superior — and marginalized group members as "less than," abnormal, inferior, deficient — even, less than human. Prejudice is incorporated in human processes at all levels of system: individual, group, organization, community and society.

Power exercised by dominant groups over marginalized groups mobilizes and enforces oppression as a system of inequality, privilege and violence. Dominant groups are groups with power to control and use group, organizational and societal resources and to establish sanctions, values, laws, standards, rules, policies, structures, and practices for their benefit and for the disadvantage of marginalized groups and members. The availability of power to support oppression increases with the size and complexity of systems. Individuals have relatively less power than groups, organizations and society.

The concept of dominant and marginalized groups relates to group identity, not individual identity. An individual dominant group member may hold little or no power over organizational and societal resources. Their dominant group identity confers privilege, however, whether chosen or not. In contrast, an individual marginalized group member may have substantial power from position and individual achievement, and because of marginalized group identity, be denied privilege and subjected to harm, without recourse.

Individuals have multiple social-identity group memberships. Most individuals are members of both dominant and marginalized groups.

HUMAN DIFFERENCES	DOMINANT GROUPS	MARGINALIZED GROUPS	FORMS OF OPPRESSION
RACE	White	People of African Heritage, Asian Heritage, Hispanic/ Latino/Latina Heritage Native People. Bi- and Multi-Racial People	Racism, Colorism
ETHNICITY / NATIONALITY	Western European	Arab, Filipino, Haitian, Indian, Jewish, Mexican, Puerto Rican, Roma,	Colorism, Ethnocentrism, Anti-Semitism, Nativism, Nationalism, Xenophobic Oppression, Colonialism
GENDER	Men	Women	Sexism
SEXUAL ORIENTATION	Heterosexual	Bisexual, Gay, Lesbian, Transgender People	Heterosexism
RELIGION	Christian	Agnostic, Atheist, Buddhist, Hindu, Jewish, MuslimY.	Religious Oppression, Anti-Semitism
ABILITY	Able-bodied	People with Disabilities	Ableism
AGE	Adults	Children, Elders	Ageism, Child Abuse, Incest, Elder Abuse
CLASS	Upper, Ruling, Owning Class, Upper Middle Class	Poor, Working Class, Middle Class	Classism

Table 2. Social Identity Groups

Some of the dominant and marginalized groups and the forms of oppression associated with them are shown in Table 2.

The description of dominant and marginalized groups in this chart applies to the United States, particularly for the human differences of race, ethnicity / nationality, and religion. Dominant and marginalized groups in these human differences areas may be different for other nations and regions. The mechanisms used for defining dominant and marginalized groups does not vary among regions and nations.

In the case of race, skin color and other human physical characteristics are used to differentiate dominant and marginalized groups. Arguably, there is no region or nation on Earth where people with darker skin are valued as highly as people with lighter skin. Skin color prejudice is embedded and institutionalized in the laws, regulations, rules, structures, and values of the cultures of organizations and nations to create the system of inequality that is racism.

Skin color and language, religion, dress and other aspects of culture are used to define dominant and marginalized groups in the case of ethnicity and nationality. Economic exploitation by organizations and nations, war, and oppression cause people to migrate and seek refuge from their home regions and nations. Xenophobia and skin color prejudice toward immigrants and refugees are institutionalized in the cultures of organizations and nations. The result is ethnocentrism, xenophobic oppression, nationalism, and racism. When the culture of a dominant organization or nation is imposed on the existing culture of a nation, a region or a people, the resulting system of inequality and oppression is colonialism.

Oppression as a system is maintained and kept in place

—by the actions and support of both dominant and marginalized groups,

—by oppression that is embedded and internalized at multiple levels of system, and

—by multiple forms of oppression that are interdependent and reinforcing.

Dominant groups do not always act alone in support of oppression. Marginalized groups can and do act intentionally, unintentionally, consciously and unconsciously to support racism, ethnocentrism, sexism and other forms of oppression, even when it is to their disadvantage and harm.

Group-Level Interactions of Dominant and Marginalized Groups. Oppression is implemented through actions, behaviors, and practices of inequality, privilege and violence: (1) by the dominant group toward marginalized groups, (2) among marginalized groups, (3) within dominant and marginalized groups, and (4) by collusion of marginalized groups with the dominant group (Hardiman and Jackson, 1997, pp. 20-23). These categories apply to racism and white people and people of color, to sexism and men and women, to heterosexism and heterosexuals, gays, lesbians, bisexuals and transgendered people, and to other forms of oppression.

Institutionalized Oppression. Race, ethnicity, gender, class and other group-based prejudice, that is embedded and internalized in the beliefs, values, policies, laws, structures, practices, and behaviors for all levels of system, is too often seen as "normal." When embedded and internalized prejudice is enforced with dominant group power over marginalized group members, oppression manifests and is internalized as privilege and violence at societal, organizational, and group levels of system. Institutionalized racism, sexism, heterosexism, and other forms of institutionalized oppression contribute to the experience of oppression as out-of-control, unintentional and unconscious, rather than intentional and conscious. Institutionalized oppression is like a computer virus that reproduces itself in other systems and can only be eradicated by searching and rewriting computer programs line-by-line. Individual prejudice-reduction and awareness work can help reduce individual actions that support oppression. And yet without efforts to eliminate prejudice-based values, policies, structures, and practices that empower institutionalized oppression, oppression continues to operate as a system — as if on automatic pilot.

Internalized Oppression. Group-based prejudice from social messages, experience, and socialization processes can also become internalized as privilege and violence in the beliefs, values, and behaviors of individuals who are members of dominant or marginalized groups (Fletcher, 1999, pp. 97-102). Violence as a part of internalized oppression describes the whole range of individual actions, behaviors, and practices that are life-diminishing, life-deadening, life-threatening, and life-ending. Violent actions, behaviors and practices can be self-directed and/or directed toward others. Self-directed violence includes low self-esteem, alcoholism, poor nutrition and health practices, suicide, self-hate. Violent actions, behaviors, and practices toward others include jokes and slurs, silence, avoidance, exclusion, burning, bombing, stalking, lynching and torching (Brazzel, 2000b).

Dominant group members can internalize as justification for violence both:

—group-based privilege as entitlement and

—beliefs about the "abnormality" and "inferiority" of others.

This internalization process can lead to outward-directed actions, practices, and behaviors that support racism, sexism, classism and other forms of oppression for the benefit of dominant group members and the harm of marginalized group members. When internalized expectations of privilege and superiority are not realized, dominant group members can turn inward with violence toward themselves or outward toward family, friends, associates, and strangers.

Marginalized group members can also internalize socially-constructed and prejudice- based views of superiority of dominant groups and inferiority of marginalized groups. Internalized racism, sexism, and other forms of internalized oppression result in self- directed actions, behaviors, and practices of violence and/or outward-directed violence toward family, friends, associates, and strangers.

Multiple, Interdependent and Reinforcing Forms of Oppression. Racism, sexism, and other forms of oppression have interdependent and reinforcing results for the experience of oppression at individual, group, organization, community and societal levels of system. The intersection of multiple forms of oppression have substantive impacts on people's lives (Pharr, 1988, pp. 53-64). White men experience oppression entirely from a perspective of dominant group memberships. They share dominant group experiences of being white with women and of being men with men of color. Women of color experience the inequality, privilege and violence of oppression as members of two marginalized groups. The addition of ethnocentrism, nationalism, heterosexism, classism, ableism, and other forms of oppression multiplies the toll of oppression on people's lives because of group-membership-based prejudice, privilege, and violence.

Global Diversity Management. The diversity management field has evolved from historical and theoretical roots which are heavily grounded with diversity and social justice experiences in the United States. The four diversity frames of reference — areas of human experience, aspects of human experience, levels of human system and elements of culture — and oppression theory have not been applied to the experiences of other nations and regions. That is changing in some areas. Applications in other nations and regions has been encouraged by the documentation of experiences of racism, ethnocentrism, and nationalism by the 2001United Nations World Conference Against Racism, Racial Discrimination, Xenophobia and Related Intolerance and by the work of organizations like United for Intercultural Action: European Network Against Nationalism, Racism and Fascism and in Support of Migrants and Refugees (August 2002).

Theory and Practice

Diversity Management Practitioner Roles by Level of System

✦**Individual:** Counselor, coach, teacher
✦**Group:** Trainer, facilitator, group leader
✦**Organization:** Consultant, practice theorist, researcher, scholar
✦**Community and Society:** Catalyst, organizer, advocate, dissenter, activist

The diversity management field assigns a high value to practice, action research and practice theory because of its roots in the applied behavioral sciences, community organizing, and social action. Members of the field are more likely to describe themselves as practitioners than professionals. Diversity management academics are likely to describe themselves as practice theorists, researchers and scholars. Because of the theoretical roots of the field, other diversity management practitioners are likely to see and describe themselves in one or more roles: counselor, coach, teacher, trainer, facilitator, group leader, consultant, practice theorist / researcher / scholar, catalyst, organizer, advocate, dissenter, and activist .

Diversity-management practice interventions focused on organizational change can be systemic and address the whole organization as a system and they can be at individual, group, organization, community and societal levels. Practice interventions can include a range of activities within the organization and outside in the organization's environment:

—Awareness and skill-building education, training and coaching,

—Development of support structures, positions, mechanisms and networks,
—Leadership and diversity-champion development,
—Organization-change imperative, vision, mission and values statements,
—Team and group building,
—Assessment of and changes in organizational systems, policies and practices,
—Accountability, performance metrics, evaluation and feedback systems,
—Internal and external communication processes,
—Management of, or organization of, relationships with customers, suppliers, partner / competitor organizations, past employees, community / society residents, groups and organizations, and other members of the organization's environment,
—Institutionalization of diversity management program changes in laws, regulations, rules, norms, standards, structure, values, beliefs, assumptions, ideology and ways of making meaning, rewards and punishments and other aspects of the organization=s culture.

Practice interventions can include the organization's stance toward differences, inclusion, differentiation and integration and its stance toward the elimination of racism, sexism and other forms of oppression. Approaches by diversity management practitioners vary in the extent to which they address:

—the individual level of system . . .and not the group, organization, community and society levels,
—the many kinds of human differences, including birth order, geography, personality . . .and not race, gender, sexual orientation and other human differences that underlie the more onerous forms of oppression,
—human differences, inclusion and cultural competency . . .and not oppression,
—prejudice . . .and not oppression, including institutionalized and internalized oppression, and
—awareness and skill-building, through education and training and not structural change.

Descriptions of diversity management practice methods are found, for example, in Baytos (1995), Cox (1993, 2001), Cross (2000), Hayles and Russell (1997), Jackson and Hardiman (1994), Katz and Miller (2001), Loden (1996), Miller and Katz (2002), and Thomas (1990).

Concluding Comments

Diversity management as a field of education, theory, research and practice came into being:

—in the 1960s and 70s out of protest, turbulence and social unrest about oppression,
—organizational hopes in the 1980s and 90s for profit and competitive advantage from diversity,
—the change-from-the-inside perspective of the applied behavioral sciences, and
—the dissent-from-the-outside position of community organizing and social action.
Diversity management stands now in the 2000s with an emerging clarity about theories and methods for supporting organizational change and with an ambivalence about whether to fully address both diversity and the elimination of oppression in this work.

References

Abelson, R. (2002, January 9). Surge in bias cases punishes insurers, and premiums rise. NYTimes.com. Retrieved January 9, 2002 from http://www.nytimes.com.

Adams, M., Bell, L. A., & Griffen, P. (Eds.). (1997). *Teaching for diversity and social justice: A sourcebook.* New York, NY: Routledge.

Adams, M., Blumenfeld, W. J. , Castaneda, R. , et al. (Eds.). (2000). *Readings for diversity and social justice: An anthology on racism, antisemitism, sexism, ableism, and classism.* New York, NY: Routledge.

A. K. Rice Institute (March 2002). Internet website, www.uvm.edu/~mkessler/akrice.

Alderfer, C. P. (1994). A white man=s perspective on the unconscious processes within black-white relations in the United States. In E. J. Trickett, R. J. Watts & D. Birman (Eds.), *Human diversity: Perspectives on people in context* (pp. 201-229). San Francisco: Jossey-Bass Publishers.

American Indian Movement. (June 2000). Internet website, www.aimovement.org.

Baker, O. (1996). The managing diversity movement: Origins, status, and challenges. In B. P. Bowser & R. G. Hunt (Eds.), *Impacts of racism on white Americans* (pp. 139-156). (2nd ed.).Thousand Oaks, CA: Sage Publications.

Baytos, L. M. (1995). *Designing & implementing successful diversity programs.* Englewood Cliffs, NJ: Prentice Hall and the Society for Human Resource Management.

Brazzel, M. (1998, July). *Costs of racism for white people* (unpublished paper).

Brazzel, M. (2000a, October). *Dimensions of diversity frameworks* (unpublished paper).

Brazzel, M. (2000b, August). *Some conscious and unconscious actions, behaviors and practices of oppression* _(unpublished paper).

Churchill, W. (1994). *Indians are us?: Culture and genocide in Native North America.* Monroe, ME: Common Courage Press.

Connell, R. W. (1999). *Making gendered people: Bodies, identities, sexualities.* In M. M. Feree, J. Lorber, & B. B. Hess (Eds.),

Revisioning gender (pp. 449-471). Thousand Oaks, CA: Sage Publications.

Cox, T., Jr. (2001). *Creating the multicultural organization: A strategy for capturing the power of diversity.* San Francisco, CA: Jossey-Bass.

Cox, T., Jr. (1993). *Cultural diversity in organizations: Theory, research & practice.* San Francisco, CA: Berrett-Koehler Publishers.

Cross, E. Y. (2000). *Managing diversity: The courage to lead.* Westport, CT: Quorum Books.

Cross, E. Y., Katz, J. H., Miller, FA., & Seashore E. W. (Eds.). (1994). *The promise of diversity: Over 40 voices discuss strategies for eliminating discrimination in organizations.* Burr Ridge, IL: Irwin Professional Publishing.

Cross, E. Y., & White, M. B. (Eds.). (1996). *The diversity factor: Capturing the competitive advantage of a changing workforce.* Chicago, IL: Irwin Professional Publishing.

Deal, T., & Kennedy, A. A. (1982). *Corporate cultures: The rites and rituals of corporate life.* Reading, MA: Addison-Wesley Publishing Company.

DeRosa, P. (1992). *Six approaches to diversity training in the workplace* (unpublished report). Randolph, MA: Cross-Cultural Consultation.

Diversity Collegium. (2001, June). *Exploring a conceptual framework for the practice of diversity.* Paper presented for collegial review at the Diversity Symposium co-sponsored by Bentley College and the American Institute for Managing Diversity, Waltham, MA.

Fernandez, J. P. (1998). *Race, gender and rhetoric: The true state of race and gender relations in corporate America.* New York, NY: McGraw-Hill.

Finks, P. D. (1984). *The radical vision of Saul Alinsky.* New York, NY: Paulist Press.

Fletcher, B. R. (1999). *Internalized oppression: The enemy within.* In A. L. Cooke, M. Brazzel, A. Craig, & B. Greig (Eds.), *Reading book for human relations training* (8th ed.) (pp. 97-102) . Alexandria, VA: NTL Institute.

Freire, P. (1996). (M. B. Ramos, Trans.). *Pedagogy of the oppressed* (New rev. 20th Anniversary Ed.). New York: Continuum

Publishing Company.

French, W. L., & Bell, C. H., Jr. (1995). *Organization development: Behavioral science interventions for organization improvement* (5th ed). Englewood Cliffs, NJ: Prentice-Hall.

Frooman, J. (1999). Stakeholder influence theories. *Academy of Management Review*, 24 (2), 191-205.

Gellerman, W., Frankel, M. S., & Ladenson, R. F. (1990). *Values and ethics in organization and human system development: Responding to dilemmas in professional life.* San Francisco: Jossey-Bass Publishers.

Gillete, J., & McCollom, M. (Eds.) (1995). *Groups in context: A new perspective on group dynamics.* Lanham, MD: University Press of America Inc.

Glass Ceiling Commission, U.S. Department of Labor. (1995). *Good for business: Making full use of the nation's human capital: The environmental scan.* A Fact-Finding report of the Federal Glass Ceiling Commission. Washington, DC: U.S. Government Printing Office.

Gray Panthers. (June 2000). Internet website, www.graypanthers.org.

Hardiman, R., & Jackson, B. W. (1997). Conceptual foundations for social justice courses. In M. Adams, L. A. Bell, & P. Griffen (Eds.), *Teaching for diversity and social justice: A sourcebook* (pp. 16-29). New York, NY: Routledge.

Hayles, R., & Russell, A. M. (1997). *The diversity directive: Why some initiatives fail & what to do about it.* New York, NY: McGraw-Hill and the American Society for Training and Development.

Helms. J. E. (Ed.). (1990). *Black and white racial identity: Theory. research, and practice.* Westport, CT: Praeger Publishers.

Hofstede, G. (2001). *Culture's consequences: Comparing values, behaviors, institutions, and organization across nations* (2nd ed.). Thousand Oaks, CA: Sage Publications.

hooks, b. (1994). *Teaching to transgress: Education as the practice of freedom.* New York: Routledge.

Ingalls, J. D. (1979). *Human energy: The critical factor for individuals and organizations.* Austin, TX: Learning Concepts.

Jackson, B. W., & Hardiman, R. (1981). *Organizational stages of multicultural awareness* (unpublished paper).

Jackson, B., & Hardiman, R. (1994). *Multicultural organizational development.* In E. Y. Cross, J. H. Katz, F. A. Miller, & E. W. Seashore (Eds.), *The promise of diversity: Over 40 voices discuss strategies for eliminating discrimination in organizations* (pp. 231-239). Burr Ridge, IL: Irwin Professional Publishing.

Jackson, B. W., & Holvino, E. (1988, Fall). Developing multicultural organizations. *Journal of Religion and the Applied Behavioral Sciences,* 14-19.

Jackson, B. W., & Holvino, E. (1986) Working with multicultural organizations: Matching theory and practice. In R. Donleavy (Ed.). *0D Network Conference Proceedings*, 84-96.

Johnson, A. G. (2001). *Privilege, power, and difference.* Boston: McGraw-Hill.

Johnston, W. B., & Packer, A. H. (1987). *Workforce 2000.* Indianapolis, IN: Hudson Institute.

Kanter, R. M. (1977). *Men and women of the corporation*. New York, NY: Basic Books.

Katz, J. H. and Miller, F. A. (2001). Diversity and inclusion as a major culture change intervention: A case study. *0D Practitioner, 33* (3), 30-36.

Kirkham, K. (1986). *Dimensions of diversity: A basic framework* (unpublished paper). Philadelphia, PA: Elsie Y. Cross Associates, Inc.

Kim, J. (1994). *The limits of a cultural enlightenment approach to multiculturalism.* In E. Y. Cross, J. H. Katz, F. A. Miller, & E. W. Seashore (Eds.), *The promise of diversity: Over 40 voices discuss strategies for eliminating discrimination in organizations* (pp. 130-134). Burr Ridge, IL: Irwin Professional Publishing.

Kivel, P. (1992). *Men's work: How to stop violence that tears our lives apart.* Center, MN: Hazeldon.

Kivel, P. (1996a). The costs of racism to white people. In P. Kivel, *Uprooting racism: How white people can work for racial justice* (pp. 36-39). Philadelphia, PA: New Society Publishers.

Kivel, P. (1996b). *Uprooting racism: How white people can work for racial justice*. Philadelphia, PA: New Society Publishers.

Kochman, T. (1981). *Black and white styles in conflict.* Chicago, IL: University of Chicago Press.

Lewis, H. M. (2001). Participatory research and education for social change: Highlander Research and Education Center. In P. Reason & H. Bradbury (Eds.), *Handbook of action research:*

Participative inquiry and practice (pp. 356-362). Thousand Oaks, CA: Sage Publications.

Loden, M. D. (1994). *Diversity management: The challenge of change*. In E. Y. Cross, J. H. Katz, F. A. Miller, & E. W. Seashore (Eds.), *The promise of diversity: Over 40 voices discuss strategies for eliminating discrimination in organizations* (pp. 294-300). Burr Ridge, IL: Irwin Professional Publishing.

Loden, M. (1996). *Implementing Diversity.* Chicago, IL: Irwin Professional Publishing.

Loden, M., & Rosener, J. B. (1991). *Workforce America!: Managing employee diversity as a vital resource.* Homewood, IL: Business One Irwin.

Mauer, R. (1996). *Beyond the wall of resistance: Unconventional strategies that build support for change.* Austin, TX: Bard Books, Inc.

Mcintosh, P. (1989, July/August). White privilege: Unpacking the invisible knapsack. *Peace and Freedom,* 1-4.

Miller, F. A. (1994). Why we choose to address oppression. In E. Y. Cross, J. H. Katz, F. A. Miller, & E. W. Seashore (Eds.), *The promise of diversity: Over 40 voices discuss strategies for eliminating discrimination in organizations* (pp. xxv-xxiv). Burr Ridge, IL: Irwin Professional Publishing.

Miller, F. A., & Katz, J. (1995). Cultural diversity as a developmental process: The path from a monocultural club to an inclusive organization. *The 1995 Annual, Volume 2, Consulting.* J. Pfeiffer & Co.

Miller, F. A., & Katz, J. H. (2002). *The inclusion breakthrough: Unleashing the real power of diversity.* San Francisco: Barrett-Koehler Publishers, Inc.

Mitroff, I. I. (1983). *Stakeholders of the organizational mind: Toward a new view of organizational policy making.* San Francisco, CA: Jossey-Bass Publishers.

Nevis, E. C. (1987). *Organizational consulting: A Gestalt approach.* Cleveland, OH: Gestalt Institute of Cleveland Press.

Judith Palmer. (1994). Diversity: Three paradigms. In E. Y. Cross, J. H. Katz, F. A. Miller, & E. W. Seashore (Eds.), *The promise of diversity: Over 40 voices discuss strategies for eliminating discrimination in organizations* (pp. 252-258). Burr Ridge, IL: Irwin Professional Publishing.

Pharr, S. (1988). The common elements of oppression. In S. Pharr, *Homophobia: A weapon of sexism* (pp.53-64). Inverness, CA: Chardon Press.

Pine, J. T. (2001, December 21). Spreading diversity values without using the "D" word. DiversityInc.com. Retrieved December 22, 2001 from http://www.diversityinc.com.

Prasad, A. (2001, March). Understanding workplace empowerment as inclusion: A historical investigation of the discourse of difference in the United States. *Journal of Applied Behavioral Science, 37* (1), 51-69.

Reason, P., & Bradbury, H. (Eds.). (2001). *Handbook of action research: Participative inquiry and practice.* Thousand Oaks, CA: Sage Publications.

Salett. E. P. , & Koslow, D. R. (Eds.). (1994). *Race, ethnicity and self: Identity in multicultural perspective.* Washington, DC: National MultiCultural Institute Publications.

Schein, E.H. (1985). *Organizational culture and leadership: A dynamic view.* San Francisco, CA: Jossey-Bass Publishers.

Segal, M. (1997). *Points of influence: A Guide to using personality theory at work.* San Francisco, CA: Jossey-Bass Publishers.

Southern Poverty Law Center (June 2000). Internet website, www.spicenter.org.

Seashore, E. W., & Katz, J. H. (1994). NTL's road to multiculturalism: A diverse history. In E. Y. Cross, J. H. Katz, F. A. Miller, & E. W. Seashore (Eds.), *The promise of diversity: Over 40 voices discuss strategies for eliminating discrimination in organizations* (pp. 333-336). Burr Ridge, IL: Irwin Professional Publishing.

Swanger, Clare C. (1994). Perspectives on the history of ameliorating oppression and supporting diversity in United States organizations. In E. Y. Cross, J. H. Katz, F. A. Miller, & E. W. Seashore (Eds.), *The promise of diversity: Over 40 voices discuss strategies for eliminating discrimination in organizations* (pp. 3-21). Burr Ridge, IL: Irwin Professional Publishing.

Tannen, D. (1994). *Talking from 9 to 5: Women and men in the workplace: Language, sex and power.* New York, NY: Avon Books.

Thomas, R. R., Jr. (1990). *Beyond race and gender: Unleashing the power of your total work force by managing diversity.* New York, NY: AMACOM.

Thomas, D. A., & Ely, R. J. (1996, September-October). Making differences matter: A new paradigm for managing diversity, *Harvard Business Review*, 81-83.

Trompenaars. F., & Hampden-Turner, C. (1998). *Riding the waves of culture: Understanding diversity in global business*. New York, NY: McGraw-Hill.

United for Intercultural Action: European Network Against Nationalism, Racism and Facism and in Support of Migrants and Refugees. (August 2002). Internet website, http://www.unitedagainstracism.org.

Von Bertalanffy, L. (1950). The theory of open systems in physics and biology. Science, 3, 23-29.

Wallace, L. (2001, September 20). Race vs. culture: A split decision among the diversity pros. DiversityInc.com. Retrieved September 21, 2001 from http://www.diversityinc.com.

Weisbord, M.R. (1987). *Productive workplaces: Organizing and managing for dignity, meaning, and community*. San Francisco, CA: Jossey-Bass Publishers.

Wheeler, G. (1987). *Gestalt reconsidered: A new approach to contact and resistance* (2nd ed.). Cleveland, OH: Gestalt Institute of Cleveland Press.

Zane, N.C. (1994). Theoretical considerations in organizational diversity. In E. Y. Cross, J. H. Katz, F. A. Miller, & E. W. Seashore (Eds.), *The promise of diversity: Over 40 voices discuss strategies for eliminating discrimination in organizations* (pp. 339-350). Burr Ridge, IL: Irwin Professional Publishing.

Chapter III

Approaches to Work Force Mixtures

R. Roosevelt Thomas, Jr.

Over the past eighteen years, I have advocated the importance of achieving conceptual clarity around diversity issues. I have argued that meaningful, sustainable progress will be difficult to realize without such clarity.

Yet, evidence continues to surface that lack of clarity persists. Consider the following:

✦ Some contend that Managing Work Force Diversity does not constitute a new approach, but rather a continuation of work started over forty-five years ago. If we did not seriously and persistently talk about diversity with respect to the work force until the mid-eighties, how can this contention be true?

✦ I recently heard a speaker comment, "Diversity means *so* many different things to so many different people, but what is important is what it means to you." This perspective implies that any definition is legitimate, as long as it works for you. Also implied is the following sentiment: "Given the nature of diversity, we should be inclusive of all definitions." One can easily imagine the confusion and lack of clarity fostered by this perspective.

✦ Corporate practitioners in global companies increasingly assert that "diversity" does not work abroad, because citizens of other countries tend to see it as an inappropriate effort to export the United States' racial problems. Implied here is that the only critical work force diversity issue is race.

✦ A practitioner recently opined that all "diversity approaches" are the same; therefore, a diversity change agent can embrace any school of diversity thought and achieve her objectives. This, in effect, presents a variation of the "any definition will work" argument.

✦ Several voices in the field now contend that the word "diversity" has lost its utility and has attracted too much negative baggage. Given the comments above, the call for a change in terminology is understandable, albeit premature. Much of the baggage can be traced to a failure to secure conceptual clarity. The challenge, therefore, is not to adopt different terminology and play a semantics game, but rather to pursue conceptual clarity around the existing work force diversity framework.

Toward that end, in this brief chapter, I look at the various approaches to work force mixtures. I wish to foster clarity among practitioners as to their options for addressing work force diversity issues.

Discussion Context

As a framework for our discussion, I offer several contextual propositions. I begin with these framing premises in hopes of establishing a common point of departure and minimizing the probability of our equating apples and oranges.

One basic proposition concerns pluralism. ***Pluralism*** refers to the state of having more than one kind of something; for example, a pluralistic work force with respect to race contains representation from more than one race. Most work force mixture concerns or initiatives revolve around pluralism, most commonly – at least initially in the sixties – with respect to race and/or gender.

A related notion is that **diversity** refers to the mixture of differences and similarities that can exist between and among elements of a pluralistic mixture. So, while a manager may recruit a racially pluralistic work force, she likely will also end up with other variables along which participants are different and similar – that is, along which they are diverse. A pluralistic mixture by definition is a diverse mixture. If this is so, why do we need the concept of pluralism?

Pluralism reflects the reality that when we create mixtures of any kind, we often are focusing on a limited number of diversity dimensions. The emphasis is not on diversity, but on including more than one kind of something – that is, on achieving pluralism.

The manager creating a racially pluralistic work force, for example, focuses only on race with little – if any – cognizance of other diversity dimensions. Only when these other unintentionally included diversity variables present challenges does the manager focus on them. So, Managing Pluralism differs from Managing Diversity.

The **pluralism and diversity questions** constitute another critical contextual premise. As a manager pulls together a work force, he must address these sets of questions. The pluralism questions include the following:

- ✦Do we desire a pluralistic work force?
- ✦If so, with respect to what variables? Race? Gender? Skills? Education?
- ✦If so, how do we achieve the desired pluralism?

Typically, although definitely not always, managers raise the diversity questions after the work force has been assembled. In the set of diversity questions are often the following:

- ✦How much variation with respect to attributes and behavior do we want in our pluralistic work force?
- ✦If we do wish variations, with respect to which attributes and behaviors?
- ✦How do we attain the desired variations?
- ✦If we attain the desired variations, what will be the managerial implications?

In describing how his organization hired a large number of people after a long hiring freeze, one manager provided an example of the pluralistic and diversity questions in action:

> *Not long ago we hired more than we had hired in the last four years. Because of the number of people we were hiring, we were very deliberate about the process. We specifically decided to hire people solely on the basis of the skills we needed. We controlled for no other variable.*
>
> *We did recruit the best class ever, without a doubt! These people are phenomenally qualified. However, there is a lot of diversity!*
>
> *In addition to skills, diversity exists with respect to race, gender, ethnicity, sexual orientation, geographic origin, educational backgrounds, religion, and economic class. I am worried that we are not prepared for this diversity.*

In the language of pluralism and diversity, the manager and his colleagues sought a pluralistic work force with respect to skills. They recruited the necessary skill pluralism along with an enormous range of diversity dimensions they did not consider in the hiring process. The manager appears to be asking the diversity questions. Specifically, he is concerned as to whether he and his colleagues can manage the diversity they attracted unintentionally.

Implicit in the notion of diversity is that of diversity tension. ***Diversity tension*** is the stress and strain that accompanies interactions between pluralistic mixture components that are different and similar in many ways. Tension is not synonymous with conflict. Two people may experience tension between themselves indefinitely without it ever evolving into conflict.

I have come to believe that if you have diversity, you will have diversity tension. The challenge becomes that of working through differences, similarities and tensions in pursuit of shared objectives, as opposed to that of minimizing or eliminating diversity tension.

Diversity Management, then, is the process of making quality decisions in the midst of differences, similarities and tensions. A quality decision is one that advances the organization toward achievement of its mission, vision and bottom-line objectives. This definition of Diversity Management applies for any diversity mixture.

As a manager addresses different pluralistic and diversity mixtures, she can craft from the general definition a more particularized application. For example, ***Managing Work Force Diversity*** can be defined as follows:

> *Managing Work Force Diversity is the process of creating and maintaining an environment that naturally enables all participants to contribute to their full potential in pursuit of organizational objectives.*

A corollary premise is that the Managing Work Force Diversity (MWFD) approach consists of some basic, specific tenets. Stated differently, MWFD possesses substance and concreteness. It is not an abstract, idealistic notion but rather one that can be applied on an everyday basis.

While detailing these tenets would carry us beyond the scope of this essay, a cursory reading of *Beyond Race and Gender: Unleashing the Power of Your Total Work Force* (Thomas, 1991) surfaces some of the crucial ones with respect to the work force:

✦MWFD is first and foremost for the benefit of managers, not for society or the individual contributor.

✦It presumes that managing is a legitimate activity. In some organizations, managers struggle with the word "managing" as much as they do "diversity."

✦MWFD focuses on everyone in the work force and not for certain groups. Managing the diverse work force targets all associates.

✦MWFD's goal is the creation of an environment that enables all individual contributors to contribute to their full potential. This could require changes in organizational culture, systems, policies and practices, not as an accommodation to people who are different, but rather to assure that managers have the wherewithal to access talent however it comes packaged.

✦MWFD is not an end in and of itself, but a means to an end –

namely, the attainment of organizational objectives.

- ✦MWFD recognizes that associates can be different and similar along a number of dimensions, and not just with respect to the traditionally most prominent ones of race and gender.

- ✦MWFD addresses the individual, interpersonal and organizational dimensions. This approach recognizes that change might be required at each of these levels. More specifically, MWFD assumes that both the individual contributor and the company are open to adaptation, as opposed to the burden being primarily that of the associate.

- ✦MWFD requires a business or viability rationale in addition to any moral, social responsibility or legal motives that might exist.

- ✦MWFD requires an in-depth assessment of an organization's culture to determine whether it supports the entity's diversity aspirations. To the extent the culture is not congruent, MWFD calls for corrective modifications.

These tenets either can be found explicitly in *Beyond Race and Gender* or inferred from the text. In any event, they collectively can be viewed as the essence of MWFD, and as such, must provide the context for any application of this approach.

A critical concept with respect to the necessity for Diversity Management is diversity-challenged. ***Diversity-challenged*** refers to the state of having difficulty making quality decisions in the midst of differences, similarities and tension.

With respect to work force differences and similarities, the tendency is to connect the state of being diversity-challenged to that of being biased. This may be a valid connection, as biases still exist and influence behavior.

One can be diversity-challenged, however, because of factors other than bias. For example, the magnitude of complexity may be beyond an individual's cognitive capability. Diversity and complexity mirror each other. If you have pluralism and diversity, you have complexity. If you have complexity, you have diversity. These statements reflect the reality that inclusion of more than one kind of a particular mixture component can generate complexity, even more so when you consider the dimensions along which unintentional and uninvited diversity can emerge.

I am reminded of a high school with over 39 ethnic groups. In a conversation about this school, someone reported that the principal considered a day without violence to be "success." Another observer commented that this was an appallingly low aspiration for the head of an educational enterprise.

Another perspective is that the principal was pioneering in the relatively uncharted waters of managing a multi-ethnic school. No experts for this challenge resided in the principal's "central office," nor did the typical educational administrative texts available to him offer proven prescriptions for such complexities. So, the principal on his own had to muddle through in hopes of keeping peace and achieving some educational objectives where possible. The principal was severely diversity-challenged and needed tools to overcome his limitations.

Diversity Management can be viewed as the antidote for being diversity-challenged. If individuals and organizations were not diversity-challenged, there would not be a need for Diversity Management. Further, if organizations and individual contributors are not clear about their state of being diversity-challenged and related costs, they will have little motivation to become effective in addressing diversity.

Against the backdrop of these contextual propositions, I identify eight approaches to work force mixtures. The approaches, in turn, can be grouped into three categories:

Harmonious Compliance Category

Practitioners in this category emphasize representation, compliance and harmony. They also tend to approach these issues without benefit of MWFD. Stated differently, here Managing Pluralism and Understanding Differences do not reflect the tenets cited above for MWFD. These practitioners utilize paradigms other than those related to diversity to address representation, compliance and harmony, and select as their watchword some variation of "We must create and value a diverse work force."

Managing Pluralism {C}* seeks to assure the desired representation of the targeted groups so that compliance can be achieved with legal, societal and moral requirements. The overall effort stems from moral, social responsibility and/or legal motives and focuses on representation or inclusion for the sake of representation or inclusion. As a consequence, decision paradigms related to these motives are used. No claim is made that pluralism is good for the business or organization.

Understanding Differences {C} pursues harmonious relationships among the pluralistic efforts. As with Managing Pluralism {C}, its motives are moral, social responsibility and /or inclusion.

When observers claim that MWFD dates back thirty to forty years, they are referring to these two compliance-oriented approaches. But since they do not draw on MWFD's tenets, one cannot argue that managers using these options three or four decades ago were managing diversity.

{C} represents Compliance

Even the definition of diversity with its emphasis on similarities and differences does not support this claim. Four decades ago the prevailing focus simply did not target diversity, but rather representation or inclusion. Managers of this era sought to modify the representative profile of their work forces without benefit of an awareness of the diversity that could accompany this inclusion.

Jargonistic Category

In this category, practitioners use the jargon of diversity. While they refer to "Managing Pluralism" and "Understanding Differences" as managing diversity, they have only appropriated the jargon of MWFD and not its substance. The content typically is still that of the "compliance" versions of Managing Pluralism and Understanding Differences.

Practitioners in this category develop elaborate "diversity plans" that look like what they were doing before adopting diversity. Further, they display little awareness and conceptual clarity with respect to MWFD, and likely subscribe to the notion that "diversity" simply represents a change in jargon. They are not cognizant of the differences between MWFD and their past practices.

Why would a manager function in this category? Are their jargonistic efforts in good faith? I think they are.

Action-oriented managers in particular are susceptible to jargonistic traps and the perception that MWFD constitutes nothing new; primarily, because they are unable or unwilling to take the time to become conceptually grounded. Also, given their legal, social responsibility, and moral motivation, these practitioners likely will not see "diversity" as sufficiently important to merit a break from their action-oriented focus. I believe that the failure to gain conceptual clarity is probably the biggest barrier to moving beyond awareness.

Diversity Category

Practitioners do not come voluntarily and enthusiastically to this category, but approach it in pain over not having been able to realize sustainable progress with Managing Pluralism and Understanding Differences. Associates from non-traditional groups would have tended to settle disproportionately in the lower ranks of the practitioners' organizations, plateau prematurely and/or become alienated. The result would have been an inability to maintain the desired level of pluralism. These individuals often leave the organization, and their departure makes it necessary for managers to be in a perpetual recruitment mode. I refer to this dynamic as the frustrating cycle of continuous recruitment.

These managers explore and adopt MWFD as a supplement to their traditional efforts, in hopes of avoiding the frustration of not being able to sustain pluralistic gains. As they become conceptually grounded, they apply MWFD to their Managing Pluralism and Understanding Differences efforts. Familiarity with MWFD also leads to an awareness of Diversity Management - the general model. With this enhanced understanding, managers may begin consideration of addressing mixtures other than the work force as a diversity mixture. This leads to a four-quadrant approach to diversity.

I include the four-quadrant approach as a sub-set of the Diversity Category because it draws from the tenets of MWFD. The four quadrants are described in Figure 1.:

✦ ***Managing Pluralism {D}**** approaches pluralism from the perspective of MWFD's tenets. Consequently, you hear talk about the business rationale for pluralism and the importance of evolving a culture supportive of pluralistic aspirations.

Practitioners here also acquire an awareness of the importance of addressing diversity among the pluralistic elements, if sustainable progress is to be achieved. Here, the practitioner's mindset shifts from pluralism to pluralism and diversity. This does not happen in any of the other categories previously discussed.

✦***Understanding Differences {D}*** approaches relationships from the perspective of MWFD's tenets. In particular, its focus expands to include differences other than the ones used to generate the pluralistic mixture. Also considered are the unanticipated differences contributing to the diversity among the pluralistic elements. As with Managing Pluralism {D}, much greater emphasis is placed on the business or viability rationale and the importance of a supportive culture.

✦***MWFD***, the third quadrant, stresses creating an environment that facilitates accessing the talent of all associates regardless of how similar or different they may be. This approach positions managing diversity as a prerequisite for effective management of pluralism. Familiarity with MWFD concepts lends to a broader understanding of diversity and a desire to address any diversity mixture that is strategic for the corporation.

* ***{D} represents Diversity***

✦***Managing Strategic Diversity*** revolves around the Diversity Management process defined earlier in this chapter. It seeks to create individual and organizational capabilities to surface and address diversity mixtures that are strategic. While the work force may be identified as a strategic mixture, other possibilities include mixtures related to functions, acquisitions and mergers, customers, products, brands or globalism. As practitioners recognize the existence of other diversity mixtures, they seek to become competent in utilizing the general Diversity Management process.

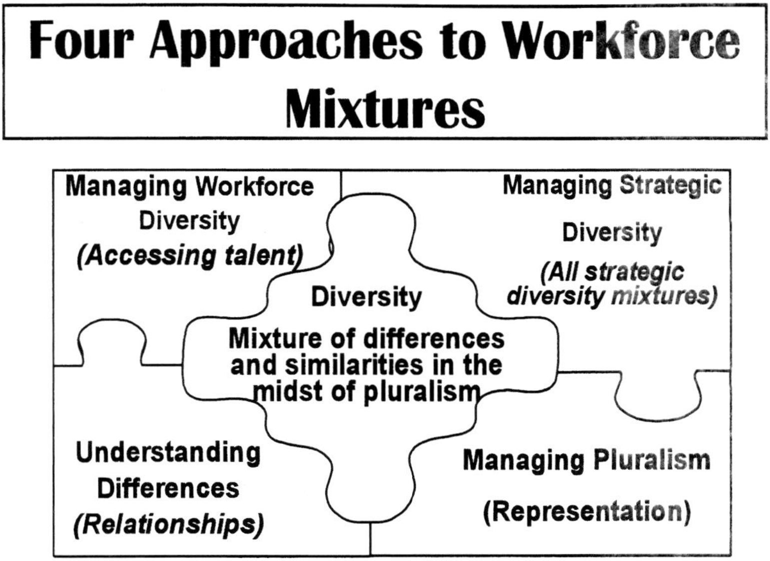

Figure 1. Four Quadrant Approach to Diversity

With respect to the three categories, Harmonious Compliance, Jargonistic and Diversity, I know of several corporations that could be the prototype for each. Some practitioners are in a pure compliance mode and stress pluralistic numerical data without significant reference to "diversity." Others do the same, but with a jargonistic flavor of diversity. My opinion is that the majority of enterprises are active in the Harmonious Compliance and Jargonistic categories.

A significant number, however, have "four quadrant' aspirations (see Figure 1). Of this group the vast majority have applied the MWFD tenets to "Managing Pluralism" and "Understanding Differences." Only a few of this group have progressed significantly with MWFD, and an even fewer (probably count on one hand) have made any gains with "Managing Strategic Diversity."

Approaches to Work Force Mixtures

Approaches	Goal	Motive
Managing Pluralism {Harmonious Compliance}	Representation	Legal, Moral and/or Social Responsibility
Managing Pluralism {Jargonistic}	Representation	Legal, Moral and/or Social Responsibility
Managing Pluralism (Diversity)	Representation	Business (Foremost)
Understanding Differences {Harmonious Compliance}	Harmonious Relationships	Legal, Moral and/or Social Responsibility
Understanding Differences {Jargonistic}	Harmonious Relationships	Legal, Moral and/or Social Responsibility
Understanding Differences (Diversity)	Harmonious Relationships	Viability (Foremost)
Managing Work Force Diversity	Accessing Talent	Viability (Foremost)
Managing Strategic Diversity	Address all strategic diversity mixtures	Strategic Gain

Table 1. Approaches to Workforce Mixtures

Concluding Observations

Two observations readily flow from the discussions in Table 1. One is that practitioners can use the category and approach delineations provided above as analytical tools to sort through the various perspectives and issues in the diversity arena. This type of sorting out will be critical in charting paths for moving beyond awareness.

Consider the statement, "We must create and value a diverse work force." The delineated approaches help us understand when and how this statement can be appropriate or inappropriate. It makes the most sense in the context of Harmonious Compliance's Managing Pluralism and Understanding Differences.

Essentially, in this context it specifically means "We must value being representative (inclusive) with respect to race, gender and other targeted groups, as a vehicle for overcoming the legacy of past enslavement and/or discriminatory practices." So, when the original push for racial and gender pluralism surfaced in the sixties, proponents did not claim the results would be good for organizations, but rather for our society. Also, no claim was made that inclusiveness was inherently good, but specifically that it was desirous with respect to race and gender (later expanded to include other targeted groups). In this context, it makes sense to say we value diversity (defined as race, gender, and other targeted dimensions).

However, in the context of MWFD, it makes less sense to speak of valuing diversity. Here, diversity refers to the pluralistic dimension giving rise to the mixture **and** other unintentional, uninvited, unanticipated attributes and behaviors along which people can be different and similar. How likely is it that a manager will value something that came about unintentionally, some of which may prove valuable and some harmful in terms of the corporation's mission and vision.

The challenge is not that of valuing this unanticipated diversity, but rather that of accepting it as a reality and deciding which aspects to keep, exclude or ignore. In other words, the task becomes managing diversity.

Reflect back on the hiring manager mentioned earlier. After the surge of hiring around the pluralistic dimension of skills only, he feared that unanticipated diversity might overwhelm his company. Although he may come to value the uninvited diversity after he learns how to manage it, he initially did not find it inherently valuable.

Another example is the statement that "we have been utilizing MWFD for thirty-five to forty years." This contention makes sense only in the context of the Harmonious Compliance category.

We have been working on Managing Pluralism {C} and Understanding Differences {C} for roughly forty years. On the other hand, given that MWFD's specifics have evolved over the past twenty years (and are still evolving), one simply cannot say that practitioners were using this option in the sixties and seventies.

Indeed, the notion of work force mixtures did not expand noticeably beyond the designated dimensions of race, gender and other targeted groups until the early eighties. Practitioners until then were preoccupied with racial and gender pluralism.

The sentiment that "all diversity approaches are the same" provides another illustration of where some sorting out would be helpful. It is most valid in the context of the Jargonistic category, where the undergirding assumption is that the conceptual "evolutions" in the diversity field essentially have been semantic in nature.

However, contrasting the "viability" tenets of MWFD and its emphasis on individual and organizational change with the legal, social responsibility and moral motives of Harmonious Compliance makes it difficult to defend the "all approaches are the same" proposition. Managing Pluralism {C} does not equate to Managing Pluralism {D}, nor does Understanding Differences {C} to Understanding Differences {D}. Further, all of these approaches differ significantly from MWFD.

This leads to the second observation: All of these approaches and categories are legitimate. In light of an organization's mission, vision, strategy and external environment, the manager must decide which approach or blend is optimal for his situation. A case can be made for utilizing each approach.

Where management stresses the moral, social responsibility and legal motives for representation, as opposed to the business rationale, MP {C} and UD {C} represent attractive alternatives. Where management wishes eventually to move beyond Harmonious Compliance to MWFD, but judges her organization not to be ready, the Jargonistic category offers a valid transitional choice. For the organization seeking to move to the next level, to escape the frustrating cycle of continuous recruitment, and to advance beyond awareness, MWFD and its four-quadrant option make a lot of sense.

Choosing the appropriate approach is a dynamic process. What constitutes an optimal selection this year may not be three years later. Practitioners must consistently assess and change their diversity strategies to reflect shifting organizational realities. A prerequisite for effective strategizing is conceptual clarity around the available options.

The category and approach dimensions represent a step toward such clarity, and also toward a framework that can be used to assess diversity propositions and issues. Without such a tool, one is reduced to practicing jargonistic and semantic games. Conceptual clarity illuminates the path for moving beyond awareness. Without this clarity we likely will flounder.

Reference

Thomas, Jr., R. Roosevelt, 1991. *Beyond Race and Gender: Unleashing the Power of Your Total Work Force by Managing Diversity.* New York: AMACOM.

Chapter IV

Theories of Differences: Changing Paradigms for Organizations

Evangelina Holvino

The domain of social life is essentially a domain of differences. Mauss[1]

In the diverse and global world of today, differences are part and parcel of everyday life. During the last two decades differences in organizations have become an important area of organizational change under the rubric of "managing diversity," "valuing differences," "diversity management," "multiculturalism," "multicultural organizational development," and "working with diversity" (Cox, 1991; Cross, et al., 1994; Esty, et al., 1995; Jackson and Holvino, 1988; Loden and Rosener, 1996; Merrill-Sands, et al., 2000; Thomas, 1990, 1991, 1995; Thomas and Ely, 1996). Researchers study social identity, identity groups, racial identity development, but it all has to do with differences (Cross, 1995; Ferdman and Gallegos, 2001; Nkomo and Cox,1996). Depending on the context, differences are seen as precious, threatening, denied, valued, appreciated, or tolerated. But it is not differences that are the challenge, but what we do with them.

In this chapter two approaches to working with differences are described and their implications for organizational change explored. One approach to differences, which draws upon psychosocial theories of difference and functional themes of organizational change, underlies the work of most diversity professionals. This approach cannot address the complexity of social relations in today's organizations. Consequently, our visions and ways of implementing diversity change efforts in organizations are limited. In order to more adequately address current social relations in organizations, I draw upon social constructivist theories and feminist and postcolonial writings to develop another approach to differences (Acker, 1992; Holvino, 2000a).

In this chapter, the characteristics of the current dominant approach to working with differences will be described. An explanation of the feminist-postcolonial approach, which integrates race, ethnicity, class and gender into our analyses of organizations, will then be provided. This approach examines the organizational dynamics of differences "differently." Finally, suggestions are made for how human resource, diversity professionals, and managers can use this new perspective on differences to guide organizational change.

The current approach to understanding social differences

Everyday Encounters with Difference

Ever since very early in my life in San Juan when the kindergarten teacher wanted to flunk me because I did not know enough English, I've been dealing with differences. Spanish is my first language, so even to my little girl's mind it seemed a bit unreasonable to demand that I know English at the age of five.

Just a week ago, my partner went to give a talk about our business at the town's Rotary Club. In chatting with people beforehand he mentioned to a member that his partner's name was Evangelina Holvino. To his surprise, the immediate response of the woman to this information, without a hint of self- consciousness was, "Oh, I am glad she was not the one who came to talk about your firm!" Many years later I'm still dealing with differences, and so is everybody else.

The current approach to differences, which draws from psychological and sociological theories of human nature (Billig, 1999), has the following characteristics:

First, it treats differences as *essential* and *inescapable*, because they are considered to derive from the body and/or the psyche. For example, gender (or race) is considered to be the ultimate "*irreducible*" difference (White, 1987).

Loden and Rosener (1991) exemplify this approach by differentiating between "primary differences" - age, sexual orientation, physical abilities, gender, ethnicity, and race - and secondary differences such as religious beliefs, military experience, marital status, income, work background, education, and others (p. 20). Primary differences are seen as the most important type of difference, because persons are born into them and cannot change them at will; differences are innate and unchangeable. Secondary differences are "less important" because they are mutable and able to be changed by circumstances or choice. In this model for example, class is a secondary difference because it is amenable to change. But what this model does not consider is that despite the rhetoric of class mobility, the best predictor of one's socioeconomic class is one's parents' class, suggesting that class may be partly as pre-determined by ones' family as differences such as race are seen to be determined by ones parents' genes.

Second, differences are seen as *isolated* aspects, independent variables, separate from each other. They are studied independently and connected to each other in an additive fashion. Because of this approach to differences the experience of women of color in particular is always misrepresented. For example: Are they women? Or Latinas? Or professionals? Or lesbians? Clearly, it is not sufficient to consider only one of these aspects of a person's complex identity. So, while isolating dimensions of difference and social categories may be a good approach for the purposes of traditional scientific research, it is not the most effective manner to describe an organizational reality, or to design and implement change interventions.

Consider the complex interaction of racism and sexism expressed by Antonia Hernandez, president of MALDEF (the Mexican American Legal Defense and Educational Fund):

> *My experiences with racism and sexism have been, at times, amusing. Once I was refused entry to the lawyers' seating section in court because I was "too young and too pretty." What the white male bailiff meant, of course, was that I was*

> *Mexican. Some might conclude that the bailiff's comment was more sexist than racist, but as a woman of color, I cannot separate my gender from my ethnicity. I cannot report that the comment was less hurtful because it was directed at me as a woman rather than me as a Latina. The result was the same (1994:257)*

Thirdly, the current dominant approach treats differences as if differences were *fixed* and *ahistorical*. From this perspective, gender and racial differences are believed to be universal and constant through time. Race means the same in the United States, China, and Latin America, and what we know about other differences like gender or age applies in all contexts and remains true through time. But even in the United States, during the last three centuries race has not meant the same and racial categories have shifted for specific racial-ethnic groups (Omi and Winant, 1986).

Implications of using the current approach to differences

One of the problems with the current psychosocial-based approach to differences is that it leads to the dilemma that Scott (1988) has aptly named the "equality versus differences conundrum." In other words, if we are truly different, then, no equality is really possible. But, if we are basically and universally the same, differences are ultimately superficial and unimportant; deep inside we are all human and social differences are basically irrelevant. The dilemma plays out in training programs in the dialogue between those who affirm, "You'll never be able to understand my experience," and those who affirm, "Let's focus on similarities, all these talk about differences just makes it so." Neither position helps engage in a dialogue about differences that leads to understanding and change.

A feminist postcolonial approach to differences: An alternative

While many scholars and practitioners refer to "all kinds of dimensions" when they use the term "differences" – dimensions such as function, race, gender, demographics, tenure, age, sexual orientation, cognitive style, occupation, education, family status, culture, ethnicity – as an organizational consultant and educator I am particularly interested in exploring those differences that derive from one's membership in and identification with particular social groups. Differences like class, gender, race, ethnicity, and sexual orientation shape one's social identity at the same time that they form the basis for specific social categorizations of groups of people (Nkomo and Cox, 1996). These categorizations and identities, in turn, impact who we are, how others see us and what they expect of us, and the access and opportunities we have (or not) in organizations. In other words, it is these differences that are deeply tied to systems of inequality.

A feminist postcolonial approach to differences, which draws more from feminist theories and literary, cultural and political studies, works under a different set of premises (Calás and Smircich, 1996; Holvino, 1993).

First, social differences are seen as *relational*. They depend on the formulation of more than one individual and the existence of an "other" without which the first would not make sense. For example, male only exists in relation to female from which it can be differentiated. Thus, there is not a female or a male "gender," but a relation between men and women, which is constructed in terms of a binary opposition between the masculine and the feminine sexes. Gender is the term that refers to this particular relational arrangement that may vary according to the cultural context. From anthropological research in other cultures, one could envision four sets of gender relations: children, females of reproductive age, males of reproductive age, and elders (Gailey, 1987).

In a poignant description of these set of relations as they apply to race in the United States Toni Morrison writes,

> *Africanism is the vehicle by which the American self knows itself as not enslaved, but free; not repulsive, but desirable; not helpless, but licensed and powerful; not history-less, but historical; not damned, but innocent; not a blind accident of evolution, but a progressive fulfillment of destiny. (1992:52)*

Second, differences are seen as *socially constructed*. They reflect the meanings attributed to specific dimensions of human differences that have been signaled as important in a given society. Thus, gender is not an intrinsic characteristic of men and women based on their physical, psychic or socialized attributes, but gender is the meaning attributed to those "differences." These meanings have changed over time and are constantly contested and transformed by academic disciplines, social movements, the state, the media, in everyday interactions, and of course, in organizations.

The differences that are meaningful in any particular moment and society are shaped through time and history and are culture specific. For example, there was a time when Irish immigrants in the United States were considered "nonwhite" (Ignatiev, 1995). Before the 19th century there was no category of "homosexual" and before the last two decades "gay rights" did not exist. Today, after enormous political struggles, civil unions between gays and lesbians, which give them the legal benefits of heterosexual marriages, are legal in the state of Vermont; a set of rights still denied to gays and lesbians in the rest of the USA.

On the Fluidity of Racial Identity

I will never forget how in 1983 a few children in Kano, a northern city in Nigeria where I was working, helped me understand the instability of the category race. I had lived in the USA for a few years after moving from Puerto Rico, and not being white-nor-black I had painfully learned about race relations in this country and its infamous "one-drop rule." (The rule that if you have "one drop" of anything else but white (blood, I guess) you are Black, "less," "other," "breed," "mulatto," "subordinate". But, this is a learning about race that is not universal. In the ancient empires of Africa and many countries in Latin America, "one drop" made you "free" instead of a slave.)

As I walked, the children shouted, "Bature, Bature!" with a mixture of laughter and who knows what else. When I returned to my hotel, I asked, "What does 'Bature' mean?" Much to my surprise, my Nigerian colleague answered, "Bature means 'white'." After years in the USA learning that my racial identity was brown, or black, or Latino, or mixed, anything but white, to those children, in the northern part of Nigeria, I was, once again, white. ("White" was the way I was categorized and learned to see myself in the Puerto Rico I grew up where there has been much racial mixing and everyone is assumed to have some Black ancestry.) Nothing biological or fixed about race, these children proclaimed!

Third, social differences also "construct" who we are and are important elements of our *subjective identity* (Calás and Smircich, 1992). There is not an essential (un-gendered or un-raced) identity that all humans possess, which is then "tarnished" by gender stereotypes as we grow up and become "aware." For example, girls know themselves to be "female" by the age of four.

Instead, subjectivity, how we think of ourselves as social beings, is shaped by gendered beliefs and structures, which are inseparable from our self-identity. Aurora Levins Morales and Rosario Morales, in a call and response mother-daughter dialogue, write about a complex subjectivity shaped by race, gender, ethnicity, language, and nationality, in opposition to uni-dimensional notions of identity:

> *I am what I am.*
> *A child of the Americas.*
> *A light-skinned mestiza of the Caribbean.*
> *A child of many diaspora, born into this continent at the crossroads.*
> *I am Puerto Rican. I am U.S. American.*
> *I am New York Manhattan and the Bronx.*
> *A mountain-born, country-bred, homegrown jibara child,*
> *up from the shtetl, a California Puerto Rican Jew (1986: 212).*

Fourth, differences *signify relations of power*. In our culture, gender reflects the social organization of the relation between the sexes whereas the male is privileged (one-up, desired, better) and women are subordinated (one-down, less, inferior). This privileging process involves both the material – women earn 74 cents compared to a man's dollar - and the symbolic – the color of girls is pink and the color of boys is blue.

When the difference is about class, managers are privileged and workers are not. Latina workers are painfully aware of how power and social differences interact, as the following quote illustrates:

> *The boss tells us not to bring our 'women's problems' with us to work if we want to be treated equal. What does he mean by that? I am working here because of my 'women's problems'-because I am a woman. Working here creates my 'women's problems.' I need this job because I am a woman and have children to feed. And I'll probably get fired because I am a woman and need to spend more time with my children. I am only one person—and I bring my whole self*

> *ably get fired because I am a woman and need to spend more time with my children. I am only one person—and I bring my whole self to work with me. So what does he mean, don't bring my 'women's problem' here? (Hossfeld, 1990:168-9)*

Lastly, differences *intersect with other social processes* like class, race, and ethnicity. They are interdependent or interactive, not "independent variables" which can be understood in isolation of other social differences. For example, while stereotypes of a competent white woman manager are that she is feminine, bright, and driven (Morrison, et al., 1987), Black women managers are perceived as tough, self-sufficient, and caretaking (Dumas, 1985). These different perceptions create different kinds of dilemmas for Black and White women in leadership roles.

The attempt to disconnect gender from race and class, as if being a woman was a universal experience, has been questioned by women of color (Anzaldúa, 1990; Collins, 2000; Hooks, 1984; Hurtado, 1996). They see it as a power move by White affluent feminists to render invisible the situation of women of color and the way in which the experience of being woman is shaped differently by race, ethnicity, class and sexual orientation.

Bell and Nkomo (1992), two African American scholars, have developed a model of social identity that stresses the interrelatedness of social differences by representing race, gender, class and ethnicity as a set of four overlapping circles. For them, identity is at the point where the four circles intersect. But more than intersecting circles, social identity is constructed by a large number of co-existing identity-forming systems in interaction and transaction with each other. The view that social identity is the sum of parts of identities such as race, gender, and class is too simplistic. It misses the dynamic nature of identity formations and manifestations through the human life cycle.

In summary, the model of differences I advocate understands differences to be: 1) *social* (a social relation), 2) signifying *relations of power* (where one aspect of a dichotomy has been privileged), 3) *interactive* with other processes, 4) shaping our *subjective identity*, and 5) useful *categories of analysis*, *historical*, *changing*, and *specific*, not fixed and universal.

Implications of using the feminist postcolonial approach to differences

The feminist postcolonial approach may be more appropriate to help us expand our understanding of organizational dynamics and difference. For example, research on "the glass ceiling" has been an important way of addressing the status of woman in organizations. Women of color, on the other hand, have talked of their ceiling been one of concrete, rather than glass (Catalyst, 1999).

However, research on the glass ceiling for Latino/as[2] suggests that the "glass ceiling" is a very limited metaphor for explaining the situation of Latinos in organizations (Melendez, et al., 1994). Why? One of the key findings was that changes in the labor market and the erosion of traditional sources of organizational advancement like internal job ladders are limiting Latinos' "progress" in organizations. While many of the well-known reasons for the lack of advancement which apply to other groups and which are internal to the organization also apply to Latinas, such as lack of mentoring, culturally-determined models of managerial success, and lack of access to informal networks, these only explain some, but not all of the reasons for Latino's absence and lack of advancement in organizations.

One conclusion from the research is that since the majority of Latina workers are concentrated in the disappearing industries of agriculture and manufacturing, in the lower paid professions or trades, and at entry level jobs, it is less useful to address glass ceiling issues, which imply a managerial or supervisory level in a hierarchical organization, and it is more important to understand the impact of the changing economic and industrial climate on working-class Latinos. In other words, the glass ceiling is revealed as a problem of the middle and affluent classes; what most Latinas need in order to be able to improve their economic position is help in the "pre-organization," for example, educational opportunities and on-the-job training. Their advancement is not so much dependent on the organization itself, but on its environment, which determines what kind of entry opportunities will be available to them in the job market.

The glass ceiling research on Latinos illustrates how a more nuanced approach that considers race, ethnicity, gender, and class with a more complex, feminist postcolonial perspective can generate new insights about differences in organizations. It also helps reveal prior limitations in taken for granted change practices like the glass ceiling, practices which are very much based on current psychosocial approaches to differences.

Using the feminist postcolonial approach as a guide to organizational change

Managers and human resource and diversity professionals need to be aware of how differences are sustained in a variety of ways that relate to and reinforce each other in systemic patterns. One strategy to heighten consciousness of this complexity is to break down the different *levels* and *processes* by which differences and inequality are created and maintained. This makes possible an analysis of differences that goes beyond current dominant approaches and expands choices for designing organizational change interventions.

Levels of system in which differences and inequality occur

One can examine four different levels of system to understand how differences play out in organizations: the individual, the group, the organizational, and the societal levels (Kirkham, 1996; Wells, 1990). In order to understand and intervene effectively to address issues of differences in organizations, an analysis and a balance of interventions at all different levels is needed.

The *individual level* of analysis focuses on the internal dynamics of individuals - their feelings, behaviors, and conceptual frameworks - which support and challenge social differences. For example, theories of socialization that explain how individuals become prejudiced and theories of internalized oppression that explain how people of color contribute to their own oppression are good examples of theories of difference at the individual level.

Typical organization change interventions that address the individual level are coaching and awareness diversity training. The focus on the individual level is a strength of the current psychosocial approach to differences. But if one analyzes and intervenes only at the individual level, the perspective is limited to working one-on-one, missing the larger context in which individuals are embedded, as if individuals existed in a vacuum.

The *group level* of analysis focuses on the power of the group, not just the individuals, to shape behaviors, thoughts and feelings. For example, theories of culture and group identity that explain how group beliefs, norms and interaction patterns shape the behavior of its members are a good example of theories of differences at the group level.

Examples of organizational interventions that focus at the group level are intergroup events and employee support networks. Both types of interventions can generate a great amount of resistance because their focus at the level of the group is contrary to the individualistic ethos of the Euro-American culture in the United States (Alderfer, et al., 1980; Scully and Creed, 1999).

The *organizational level* of analysis focuses on the system-wide processes and structures that shape how differences and inequality are viewed, addressed, reinforced and challenged. Models of multicultural organizational development that explain how organizations manage the incorporation of those who are different than members of the dominant group are a good example of this level of analysis (Chesler, 1994; Jackson and Hardiman, 1994; Jackson and Holvino, 1988; Miller and Katz, 1995).

Examples of organizational interventions at this level are system-wide diversity diagnosis and analysis of discriminatory policies and structures. The limitation of working only at this level is that it does not acknowledge the open system nature of organizations whereas the environment is constantly influencing and influenced by the internal workings of organizations. Thus, there is also a need to look at a next level of analysis; the societal.

The *societal* level of analysis focuses on the institutional influences and the societal processes, symbols, and structures which support and challenge social differences and inequality. For example, the limited portrayal of women, people of color, and working class people in the media is a powerful way in which negative images and beliefs about different groups are shaped. Organizational interventions that address this level of analysis include socially responsible investment, community campus recruitment, and strategic planning processes like the future search conference, which involve community stakeholders in shaping the direction of an organization. Interventions at the societal level are usually perceived to be risky and difficult, thus, most diversity practitioners return to individual levels of analysis in order to feel less anxious about the many forces that need to be considered in the larger context in which organizations are embedded.

But analyzing and intervening at different levels of system is not enough. One must also analyze and intervene in the social processes that create and sustain differences and inequalities in the first place.

Social processes that construct and sustain differences and inequality

Differences are created and sustained through various social processes. Understanding these different processes – symbolic- discursive, structural, and interactive - is also an important task in understanding the interlocking nature of systems of difference and inequality.

Symbolic and discursive processes refer to the ways images, thoughts, and symbols create and maintain (or not) the meaning of differences in an organization. Ideas, mental models, frameworks, norms, and assumptions shape the way we see and behave in the world of work. They get translated into organizational symbols, artifacts and language that reveal, at the same time that they maintain, current arrangements of difference (Weick and Westley, 1996).

Class symbols at work

Class symbols are constructed in many ways and forms in organizations. These symbols, in turn, shape identities and subjectivities that get enacted in daily organizational interactions. In an insurance company I visited, the claims agents worked on the sixth floor of a big gray building. The floor was divided into cubicles, each woman assigned to a small, cramped area. A big monitor located in the middle of the floor flashed the number of calls waiting to be answered. In one corner of the floor was the supervisor's "office," a small space with a metal desk, a couple of chairs, and a few family pictures.

I was then taken to meet the vice president of human resources of the company. We walked a couple of yards to a building with white and black marble floors. A huge chandelier, a wooden staircase, and a bronze sculpture converged in the middle of a magnificent entrance. I was led to a spacious office where an assistant courteously asked me to wait. While I waited I peeked into the VP's office and marveled at the exquisite décor: a large and elaborate mahogany desk with a matching set of period chairs, pink and olive green walls, and soft light illuminating the original paintings. When we met, I could not help but contrast the classic dark wool suit and silk blouse of this well-dressed managerial woman with the pants and casual sweaters of the agents working in the other building. The morning had provided me a tour of the symbols of class in that organization.

How often does this VP visit the agents' cubicles? How many of the agents have been invited to the VP's office? Symbols of class like office space, decoration, dress, and assigned parking spaces forge identities that support class divisions. Managers and workers, even when they are all women, become estranged from each other, less knowledgeable of what each one does, disconnected by their very different work-styles, and less able to communicate and work towards a common goal across these class differences. (Holvino, 2000b)

Structural processes refer to the formal positions and systems that guide and control the work of the organization. Directly or indirectly, organizational structures and systems embody the status of differences in an organization. A classic example of how differences show up in structure is when you observe how an organizational hierarchy is populated in the top positions by white men, in the middle positions by white women, and in the bottom positions by women and men of color.

Rosabeth Moss Kanter's research on women in organizations is an example of the importance of structure in shaping the behavior of individuals and the culture of an organization on the matter of gender differences (1977). Kanter demonstrated how an individual's position in the organizational hierarchy determined the behaviors of power and powerlessness observed in men and women respectively in organizations. She documented four stereotypical roles taken or given to the only "token" woman in organizations where the majority of workers are men: "iron maid," "seductress," "mascot," and "mother," none of which supported women being seen as competent and able to take leadership roles in the organization. In organizations where there was more balance between the numbers of men and women, these dynamics were not observed. What is important to understand is that the stereotypical roles assigned to many women in organizations are not intrinsic to them, but reflect a dynamic of structural dominance in which women, because of their relative low numbers come to be seen and behave in these structurally shaped ways. That is why numbers matter in organizations.

Interactional processes refer to patterns of behavior and interactions between individuals, and among and between work groups that enact and sustain differences in every day organizational life. These behaviors include comments, interpersonal encounters, humor and bantering and other interactions which whether subtle, intentional or not, have the effect of creating a hostile or undermining climate for some and a supportive and favorable climate for others. These behaviors have been called "micro-inequities" because they support invisibility, exclusion, and differential treatment towards people in everyday practices such as feedback, delegation of tasks, peer support, and inclusion in informal social networks (Essed, 1990; Ragins, 1995).

Enacting differences in daily interactions

When people ask me who am I, there are many ways in which I can answer. I am an exile, a woman of color, an immigrant/emigrant, a Puerto Rican, a Latina, I'm Hispanic, mestiza, non-white-non-black, "other." I am boricua. What's in a name? ... Sometimes, I can feel the impatience when someone asks me, "and how do you want to be called, Latino or Hispanic," as if those were my only options. When it matters, I engage in a long explanation. Sometimes I answer, Puerto Rican. Other times, if I'm in the East or New Mexico I answer Hispanic, and if I'm in the Southwest I answer Latina. Or, "where are you from?" is quite a difficult question to answer. "Well...," I mumble, "originally from Puerto Rico. But now I live in Vermont." A Puerto Rican in Vermont, I can hear the question in their minds. When I start by answering that I live in Vermont, they quickly clarify, "but, no, really, where are you from," meaning but not daring to ask, where is your accent from?

Attending to the multiple levels of system and the various complex social processes by which differences are created and sustained is not a matter of either-or, but both/and. For example, the subject created through societal level, media portrayals of people of color is individual *and* collective. In the absence of real experiences with people of color, managers and workers in organizations fill the void in their personal experience with those media stereotypes. The stereotypes in turn, whether consciously or not, are translated into attitudes, interactions, language, and symbols about people of color that permeate all the way through the individual, the group, and the organizational levels.

Understanding and working with these different levels and processes locates each of us in a complex web of social relations, where we are both oppressed and oppressor, agents of change and agents of the status quo, victims and victimizers, hopeful and fearful of differences. With no simple solutions or moral high grounds we must be willing to engage in a constant process of inquiry, learning, and change.

Final Thoughts

In the role of manager, what you pay attention to and how you interpret the differences you encounter reveals your theories of difference in action. For many years, in order to improve the status of women in organizations, managers were trained to ask "How do the differences between men and women manifest themselves in particular behaviors in organizations?" Deborah Tannen's research on the differences between men and women's communication styles is an example of this type of approach (Tannen, 1995). Diversity consultants would then design courses to help women managers change their communication style and speak "more like a man."

The feminist postcolonial question is more like, "How does the way work is organized influence how men and women behave in organizations and what are the limitations and privileges our organization is creating for women and men of different social groups?"

Research at the Simmons School of Management's Center for Gender in Organizations is an example of the second type of question. In their work, everyday practices woven into the fabric of the organization are identified and examined for their potential to disadvantage particular groups. Change experiments are then designed to alter those taken-for-granted practices embedded in the structure, interactions and organizational culture. And the successful experiments that contribute to justice and effectiveness are then institutionalized (Kolb, et al., 1998; Merrill-Sands, et al., 1999; Meyerson and Fletcher, 2000).

In looking towards the future, we need theories of difference that help us change the discourse on differences and change that dominates organizations today. From a discourse where differences are seen as biological, isolated from one another and isolating us from others, to a discourse that reflects the complex dynamics of social differences and social relations in organizations. A feminist postcolonial approach that seeks to understand and advocate for radical change at the various levels and through the different processes that create and sustain differences and inequality is a useful one.

References

Acker, J. (1992). *Gendering organizational theory.* In A.J. Mills and P. Tancred (Eds.), *Gendering Organizational Analysis* (pp. 248-260). Newbury Park: Sage.

Alderfer, C.P. , Alderfer, C.J. , Tucker, L. , and Tucker, R. (1980). *Diagnosing race relations in management.* Journal of Applied Behavioral Science, *16* , 135-166.

Anzaldúa, G. , ed. (1990). *Making face, making soul, Haciendocaras: Creative and critical perspectives by women of color.* San Francisco: Aunt Lute Foundation Books.

Bell, E. L. and Nkomo, S. M. (1992). *Re-visioning women mana er's lives.* In A. J. Mills and P. Tancred, *Gendering Organizational Analysis* (pp 235-247). Newbury Park, CA: Sage.

Billig, M. (1999). *Freudian repression: Conversation creating the unconscious.* Cambridge: Cambridge University Press.

Calás, M.B. , and Smircich, L. (1992). *Re-writing gender into org nizational theorizing: Direction from feminist perspectives.* In M.I. Reed and M.D. Hughes (Eds.), *Re-thinking organization: New dire tions in organizational research and analysis* (pp. 227-253).London: Sage. (1996). *From "the woman's" point of view: Feminist approaches to organization studies.* In S. Clegg, C. Hardy, and W. Nord (Eds.), Handbook of Organization Studies (pp. 212-251). London: Sage.

Catalyst (1999). *Women of Color in Corporate Management: Opportunities and Barriers.* New York: Catalyst.

Chesler, M. (1994). Organization development is not the same as multicultural organizational development. In E. Y. Cross, J. H. Katz, F. A. Miller and E. W. Seashore (Eds.), *The Promise of Diversity* (pp. 240-251). New York: Irwin/NTL.

Collins, P. H. (2000) *Black feminist thought.* (2nd Edition). NY: Routledge.

Cox, T. (1991). The Multicultural Organization, *The Executive, 5,* (2), 34-47. (1993). *Cultural diversity in organizations: Theory, research and practice.* San Francisco: Berrett-Koehler Publishers.

Cross, E., Katz, J., Miller, F. and Seashore, E. (1994). *The promise of diversity: Over 40 voices discuss strategies for eliminating discrimination in organizations.* Burr Ridge, IL: Irwin Professional Publishing.

Cross, W. (1995). The psychology of Nigrescence: Revising the Cross model. In J.G. Ponterotto, J.M. Casas, L. A. Suzuki, and C.M. Alexander, (Eds.), *Handbook of Multicultural Counseling* (pp. 93-122). Thousand Oaks, CA: Sage.

Dumas, R.G. (1985). Dilemmas of Black females in leadership. In A.D. Colman and M. H. Geller (Eds.), *Group Relations Reader 2,* (pp. 323-334). Springfield, VA: Goetz.

Essed, P. (1990). *Understanding Everyday Racism*. Alameda, CA: Hunter House.

Esty, K. , Griffin, R. , and Hirsch, M.S. (1995). *Workplace diversity.* Holbook, MA: Adams Publishing.

Ferdman, B. and Gallegos, P. (2001). Racial identity development and Latinos in the United States. In C. Wijeyesinghe and B. Jackson (Eds.), *New Perspectives on Racial Identity Development*. New York: University Press.

Gailey, C. (1987). Evolutionary perspectives on gender and hierarchy. In B. Hess and M. Ferree (Eds.), *Analyzing gender: A handbook of social science research* (pp. 32-67). Beverley Hills, CA: Sage.

Hernandez, A. (1994). A Latina's experience of the nonprofit sector. In T. Odendahl and M. O'Neill (Eds.), *Woman and Power in the Non Profit Sector* (pp. 255-266). San Francisco: Jossey-Bass.

Holvino, E. (1993) *Organization development, from the margins: Reading class, race, and gender in OD texts*. Unpublished doctoral dissertation. University of Massachusetts, Amherst.

_____.(2000a) Social diversity in social change organizations: Standpoint learnings for organizational consulting. In R. T. Carter (Ed.), *Addressing Cultural Issues in Organizations: Beyond the Corporate Context* (pp. 211- 228). Thousand Oaks, CA: Sage. (2000b)

_____.Class and gender in organ izations: How do we begin to address the intersection. *CGO Insights,* No. 7. Boston, MA: Center for Gender in Organizations, Simmons Graduate School of Management, Simmons College.

Hooks, B., (1984). *Feminist theory: From margin to center*. Boston: South End Press.

Hossfeld, K.J. (1990). "Their logic against them": Contradictions in sex, race, and class in Silicon Valley. In K. Ward (Ed.), Women *workers and global restructuring* (pp. 149-178). Ithaca, NY: ILR

Press, Cornell University.
Hurtado, A. (1996). *The color of privilege: Three blasphemies on race and feminism*. Ann Arbor, MI: The University of Michigan Press.
Ignatiev, N. (1995). *How the Irish became white*. New York: Routledge.
Jackson, B. and Hardiman, R. (1994). *Multicultural organization development*. In E. Cross, J. H. Katz, F. A. Miller and E. W. Seashore (Eds), *The Promise of Diversity* (pp. 221-239). New York: Irwin/NTL.
Jackson, B.W., and Holvino, E. (1988). Developing multicultural organizations. *The Journal of Religion and the Applied Behavioral Sciences*, Fall, 14-19.
Kanter, R.M. (1977). *Men and women of the corporation*. New York: Basic Books.
Kirkham, K. (1996). Managing in a diverse workforce: From incident to 'ism'. In E. Cross, and M. Blackburn White, *The Diversity Factor* (pp 24-46). Chicago: Irwin Professional Publishing.
Kolb, D., Fletcher, J., Meyerson, D., Merrill-Sands, D. and Ely, R. (1998). Making change: A framework for promoting gender equity in organizations. *CGO Insights,* No. 1. Boston, MA: Center for Gender in Organizations, Simmons Graduate School of Management, Simmons College.
Loden, M., and Rosener, J. (1991). *Workforce America! Managing employee diversity as a vital resource*. Homewood, IL: Business One Irwin.
Melendez, E., Carre, F., Holvino, E., and Gomez, C. (1994). Gaston Institute report to the Glass Ceiling Commission, *Barriers to the Employment and Workplace Advancement of Latinos.* Washington DC: U.S. Department of Labor.
Merrill-Sands, D., Fletcher, J. , and Acosta, A. (1999). Engendering organizational change: A case study of strengthening gender-equity and organizational effectiveness in an international agricultural research institute. In A. Rao, R. Stuart, and D. Kelleher, (Eds.), *Gender at Work: Organizational Change for Equality* (pp 77-128). West Hartford, CT: Kumarian Press.
Merrill-Sands, D. and Holvino, E. , with Cumming, J. (2000). Working with diversity: A focus on global organizations. Working Paper No. 11. Center for Gender in Organizations, Simmons School of Management. Boston, MA.

Meyerson, D. and Fletcher, J. (2000). A modest manifesto for shattering the glass ceiling. *Harvard Business Review.* January-February, 127-136.

Miller, F. and Katz, J. (1995). Cultural diversity as a developmental process. In J. Pfeiffer (Ed.), *The 1995 Annual: Volume 2, Consulting* (pp. 267-281). San Diego, CA: Pfeiffer and Company.

orales, A.L. and Morales, R. (1986). *Getting home alive*. Ithaca, NY: Firebrand Books.

Morrison, A. M. (with White, R., and Van Velsor, E.) (1987). *Breaking the Glass Ceiling*. Reading, MA: Addison-Wesley.

Morrison, T. (1992). *Playing in the dark: Whiteness and the literary imagination.* NY: Vintage.

Nkomo, S. and Cox, T. (1996). Diverse identities in organizations. In S. Clegg, C. Hardy and W. Nord (Eds.), *Handbook of Organization Studies* (pp 338-356). London and Thousand Oaks: Sage Publications.

Omi, M. and Winant, H. (1986). *Racial formation in the United States: From the 1960s to the 1980s*. New York: Routledge.

Ragins, B. (1995). *Diversity, power, and mentorship in organizations: A cultural, structural, and behavioral perspective.* In M. M. Chemers, S. Oskamp, and M. A. Costanzo (eds), *Diversity in Organizations: New Perspectives for a Changing Workplace* (pp 91-132). Thousand Oaks, CA: Sage.

Scott, J.W. (1988). Deconstructing equality vs. difference: Or, the uses of post-structuralist theory for feminism. *Feminist Studies, 14* (1), 33-50.

Scully, M. , and Creed, D.W.E. (1999). Restructured families: Issues of equality and need. *The Annals of the American Academy. 562,* 45-65.

Tannen, D. (1995).The power of talk: Who gets heard and why. *Harvard Business Review,* September-October, 139-148.

Thomas, D. and Ely, R. (1996). Making differences matter: A new par adigm for managing diversity. *Harvard Business Review*, September-October, 79-90.

Thomas, R. (1990). From affirmative action to affirming diversity. *Harvard Business Review,* March-April, 107-117.

Thomas, R. (1991). *Beyond race and gender: Unleashing the power of your total workforce.* New York: Amacon.

Thomas, R. (1995). A diversity framework. In M. M. Chemers, S.

Oskamp, and M. A. Costanzo (eds), *Diversity in Organizations: New Perspectives for a Changing Workplace* (pp 245-263). Thousand Oaks, CA: Sage.

Weick, K. and Westley, F. (1996). Organizational learning: Affirming an Oxymoron. In S.R. Clegg, C. Hardy, and W.R. Nord (Eds.), *Managing Organizations: Current Issues*, (pp. 190-208). London: Sage.

Wells, L. (1990). The group as a whole: A systemic socioanalytic per spective on interpersonal and group relations. In J. Gillette and M. McCollom (Eds.), *Groups in Context: A New Perspective on Group Dynamics* (pp. 49-85). Reading: Addison-Wesley.

White, K. (1987). Panel on women and men in organizational life. In J. Krantz (Ed.), *Irrationality in social and organizational life: Proceedings of the 8th A.K. Rice Institute Scientific Meeting* (pp. 91-96). Washington, DC: The A.K. Rice Institute.

Endnotes

[1]In M. Lamont and M. Fournier, Cultivating differences: Symbolic boundaries and the making of inequality, p. 1. Chicago: The University of Chicago Press.

[2]Like many others, I prefer the term "Latino" to "Hispanic," but use both terms to acknowledge the contested nature of the terms and to recognize the preference for the term "Hispanic" in some geographical areas of the United States. I prefer "Latino" because it represents more accurately the U.S. social, political, and cultural phenomena of racialization of a diverse group of people during the last century, and it highlights a mixed-racial composition that recognizes the indigenous and black people of America in our ancestry—not just the white Spanish ancestry. I also alternate between using "Latino," which indicates male, and "Latina," which indicates female, in order to address the gendered nature of the Spanish language.

Chapter V

Social Psychological Processes in Diversity Practice

Steve Slane
Donald J. Seyler

Social Psychological Processes in Diversity Practice Gordon Allport (1968) defined social psychology as "an attempt to understand and explain how the thought, feeling, and behavior of individuals are influenced by the actual, imagined, or implied presence of others" (p.3). From this definition it is clear that the interests of social psychologists and of diversity practitioners overlap.

Social psychology has a long history of involvement in issues of importance to diversity practitioners, such as prejudice and discrimination. Most noteworthy is Gordon Allport's, *Nature of Prejudice,* published in 1954, a book that even today, has much to say about the causes of prejudice. However, there are several other social psychology concepts that are relevant. For example, recent work on social cognition, which examines how we form judgments of others and includes the concept of stereotype, is foundational to diversity work.

This chapter highlights the several areas of social psychology research and theory that we believe are of relevance to diversity practice. It is necessarily a very selective presentation. The topics we have chosen are those we believe actually or potentially are useful to diversity professionals. The chapter does not survey the broad field of social psychology. There are likely social psychological concepts we have omitted that some readers, now or in the future, would find useful in their work. We make no apologies for the omissions. As it stands, the chapter is rather full.

For each topic, we briefly present the basic research and theoretical background of the concept as well as areas of application in diversity practice. For some topics, the diversity application is less obvious, but we include the material because we believe it provides important background for understanding social processes.

The presentation of the material in the chapter progresses from the most molecular, fundamental social processes to the more molar; from person perception to group process. We begin with person perception and impression formation. The most salient and important aspects of our environment are people, and fundamental to all social processes are the impressions we form of the people around us. The impressions we form of people influence our relationships with them. Thus, we will next discuss relationship formation. A number of processes of importance to diversity occur within relationships. The most important of these processes is social influence, the impact we all have on others. An important contributor to social influence is the concept of power. The material that is most relevant to diversity practice, at least historically, is the work on prejudice, discrimination, attitude formation and change, and persuasion. These topics either use or are the result of social influence and group process, and will be considered last.

Person Perception and Impression Formation

An understanding of how people form judgments of other people, is foundational for diversity practice. As diversity professionals, our goal is often to influence, or at least understand the impression formation process. Our interventions are aimed at helping people understand and ameliorate the negative impressions formed about people on the basis of group membership. In order to influence the impression formation process, we must understand it.

Person Perception Accuracy

Historically, American science has been interested in efficiency, getting right answers. Thus, the first person-perception research was concerned with two questions: How accurate is person perception? and, Are some people better at it than others? The goal was to find ways to make people better person-perceivers.

The first step in determining person perception accuracy or who is a good person-perceiver is to decide which characteristics are important. Some attributes are obvious and easily judged; for example, the color of an individual's eyes, or their height. But we are usually not concerned with obvious physical characteristics. Instead, when thinking about person-perception, we are usually interested in aspects of an individual's personality, character, or skill level. These characteristics of an individual are not readily observable. So, how do people judge these attributes? and How do we determine the accuracy of judgments of these traits? Given the difficulties, the interesting observation is not how frequently we make errors, but rather how smoothly different types of people interact over an incredible diversity of situations. The mistakes are significant and interesting but we actually get it right more often than we do not.

One way to determine person perception accuracy is to put people in simple categories. For example, am I an introvert or an extrovert? If you say I'm an introvert and I am, you are accurate; but if I am an extrovert you are inaccurate. Typically, person perception accuracy has been determined by comparing self and other description. The person describes him or herself, then someone else is asked to describe him or her, and the descriptions are compared. There are problems with this approach to determining accuracy. One issue is positive-bias. We are more likely to agree with positive descriptions of us. For example, if you say that I am a nice person or that I am smart, I am more likely to think of you as being accurate, whether or not I am actually smart or nice. Another problem is that the person may not be a good self-perceiver. So his or her self-ratings may not be a valid criterion.

Another way to assess accuracy is to use group judgment as the criterion. I am accurate to the extent that my perception of an individual agrees with the group perception. Finally, objective test data, such as, personality tests can serve as the criterion. The most common method of determining accuracy is to compare a self-description on a series of attributes with another person's rating. The degree of match is the index of accuracy.

Regardless of the ways in which accuracy is assessed, studies show that people can be accurate in their perceptions, so long as they are motivated to be accurate and have access to information through experience with the person. However, people often are not motivated, and they have limited experience with the people about whom they are making judgments. This leads to the use of mental shortcuts, which are more prone to bias, ultimately leading to inaccurate perception. In the context of diversity, one only has to ask the questions, "Who are we more motivated to understand?" and "Who are we likely to have more contact with, people similar to us or people different from us?". Thus, differences on the common diversity dimensions will likely exacerbate differences in person perception accuracy.

Much of the early research on person perception was focused on discovering the characteristics of good person-perceivers. This research has not been successful. Only intelligence and training in the physical sciences (biology, physics, engineering) have been found to be consistently associated with accuracy. At first glance, it seems unreasonable that physical, not social, scientists are more accurate. However, most of this research involved perceptions of people to whom the perceiver had limited exposure. Training in the physical sciences, like chemistry, involves relying on statistical prediction, so they are more likely to guess the average. Psychologists tend to look for the differences in people. In working with someone you don't know well, you're more likely to be wrong if you focus on differences. Psychologists often don't appreciate the baseline information, and don't look for the similarities among people. Nevertheless, if you are in need of counseling, we suggest you see a psychologist instead of an engineer.

Perception of Emotion and Nonverbal Behavior

There are two areas in which people consistently demonstrate accurate person perception: judgment of emotion and nonverbal cues. One of the easiest most accurately perceived person cues is the facial expression of emotion, which appears to be biologically determined and universal. It is the same in a member of a New Guinea tribe as it is in a westerner, and there is very high accuracy in the interpretation of facial expressions at a very young age (Ekman, & Friesen, 1971).

Another area of accuracy is in the understanding of nonverbal behavior. As a part of our socialization we are taught nonverbal behaviors in parallel with our learning of language. Like language, nonverbal behaviors tend to be culture specific. We are accurate so long as we remain within our culture, but have problems when we are required to interpret the nonverbal behavior of members of different cultures.

Mehrabian (1970) has described nonverbal behavior along three dimensions. The first dimension signals positive or negative emotion, liking or disliking, and is called immediacy. Immediacy behaviors include eye-gaze, body orientation, distance, body lean, and other postural clues. Eye gaze is most important, distance is second most important, and so on. The closer you stand to a person, the more you look at them, the more direct and open your posture, the more you convey positive emotion or liking. People enter into an interaction with expectancies about what they should receive in that interaction in terms of immediacy. However, people often have different levels of expected or desired immediacy. In order to maintain this desired level of intimacy or immediacy, the person increases or decreases immediacy behaviors. For example, a person you recently met may stand uncomfortably close to you. If you are unable to move away, you can reestablish a desired level of intimacy by reducing your eye gaze or turning slightly away.

The second dimension that Mehrabian describes is potency, which conveys power and dominance. The nonverbal behaviors indicating dominance are eye gaze, standing closer, and direct and open body posture. These are the same behaviors that indicate immediacy. Whether a particular behavior, such as eye gaze, is interpreted as indicative of liking or dominance/aggression depends on the individual's interpretation of the context. This interpretation is also influenced by culture, gender, and a variety of other factors. In cross-gender situations, these nonverbal behaviors are often misread. Our cultural stereotypes depict women as more affiliative and men as more assertive and lead us to expect certain nonverbal behaviors from members of the other gender. For example, a woman might misread a man's nonverbal expression of liking as "pushy"; and man might misinterpret a woman's nonverbal expression of assertiveness as "coming on". Cross-cultural differences in nonverbal expression are less well understood than gender differences. Thus, the opportunities for confusion and misunderstanding are even greater.

Hall (1966) classified cultures as contact or non-contact based on the level of nonverbal "closeness" or immediacy that was normative. He described southern European and African cultures as being contact, and northern European as non-contact. Members of a contact culture may view members of a non-contact culture as aloof and "standoffish"; while non-contact culture members have difficulty adjusting to the "pushy", aggressive, overly familiar behavior of those from a contact culture.

Mehrabian's third dimension is activity and includes a variety of gestures that control the pace of an interaction, denote points of emphasis, and control turn-taking. For example, in conversation people look at others less when they talk, than when they listen. Looking at an individual while speaking appears to interfere with the flow of speech. This leads to a choreography of eye gaze in conversation. When it is your turn to talk, there is eye-contact, you look away, and begin speaking; when done, you make eye contact, then the other person will begin to talk, will look away, and you continue to look at the person. Eye contact signals "your turn" (Cook, 1977). Continuous eye gaze while the other person is speaking allows the listener to monitor cues to emotional tone and emphasis.

People often think of nonverbal behavior as an avenue to the detection of lying or impression management. Common wisdom is that the key to the detection of lying "is in the eyes"; that people who are lying will have difficulty making eye contact. However, people are well aware that nonverbal and vocal cues may betray their attempt to lie or create a false impression. They therefore make a conscious effort to control their nonverbal behavior. They usually exert this control on nonverbal behaviors in order of most to least important; eye gaze first, then distance, and then posture and position, with gestures last. People who are trying to impression manage will usually be certain to look the person in the eye. However, they forget or fail to manage peripheral, especially gestural cues, such as toe tapping.

Another indicator of lying or impression management is that it is usually exaggerated. Voice volume might seem too high, they might stand too close, or they may maintain unusually high eye gaze. This is the demeanor of high-pressure sales. It produces discomfort because it feels "pushy", too immediate.

People also have a distinct, individual, nonverbal style. In their interactions they tend to maintain a characteristic level of eye gaze, distance, posture, and gestural style. Deviations from this typical style indicate significant shifts in the direction, content, or emotional meaning of the conversation. While these shifts are not always indicative of "impression management", they do usually mean that something significant has occurred, or is about to occur.

Factors Affecting Person Perception

Research on person perception was influenced by the work on object perception conducted in the 1950's and 60's. This work assumed that we perceive people in the same way we perceive bricks or other objects. It attempted to reduce person information to small, easily defined, static chunks. Asch (1946) conducted some of this most influential, early work.

Asch examined the influence of knowledge of specific attributes on the impression one formed of another. In the Asch paradigm, people are presented lists of adjectives describing another person. These adjectives are assumed to have a constant positive or negative valence. The goal was to determine how this information influenced impressions. Two primary findings came out of this work. First, some adjectives took on more importance than others; such as the adjective "warm" and it's opposite "cold". These adjectives had more impact on the overall impression than did other adjectives. Thus, adding "warm" or "cold" to a description of a person may markedly change the overall impression. According to Asch, such information is more central, because it seemed to change the valence or tone of the entire description.

The influence of central traits occurs because these traits are central to our schemas of people. For example, in our mental representations of people, "warm" is linked to many other traits, such as extraversion and fun. When "warm" is activated other traits linked to it in the schema are also activated.

A second outcome of early work on person perception was the description of how different pieces of information about people were combined. Once an impression has been formed, how is new information incorporated? If I have some information about an individual that is highly positive, what happens if I find out something else about the individual that is positive, but not as positive as the initial information? For example, if I know that an individual is hardworking and warm, what happens to my impression if I later find out that the person is also "interesting"? Does this new information make the person more positive or less positive? Most research says that the resulting impression will be less positive.

In dealing with new information, people use an averaging model rather than an additive model. Once you have formed a very positive impression of someone, unless new positive information is at least as positive as the information you already possess, your impression does not become more positive. New information does not simply add incrementally to the existing impression. Furthermore, in the averaging model, early information is more important. It sets the baseline, and new information changes that baseline proportionately less than information received earlier. Thus, the more you already know about a person, the less influential is new information. It also helps account for the widely acknowledged ubiquitousness of first impressions (Asch, 1955).

Identity Negotiation

Early person-perception research was based in object-perception. The goal was to develop accurate understandings of a static object. More recent models of person perception (e.g., Swann 1984, 1987) recognize that people are not static objects, they change, and they also have a vested interest in making you see them as they want to be seen. People are not static, passive, objects, allowing us to impose whatever identity we desire upon them, as the self-fulfilling prophecy assumes. Swann noted that people actively negotiate the view you have of them, based on the sometimes conflicting motives of self-enhancement and self-verification. Sometimes what is negotiated is self-verifying, and sometimes it is self-enhancing. If these two are ever in conflict, self-verification usually wins over self-enhancement.

Swann argues that a dominant motive in interaction is to obtain self-verifying feedback. Typically we want to be seen in a way consistent with the way we see ourselves. We engage in several strategies to insure that we receive self-verification. First of all, we choose the people with whom to interact, who will see us the way we want to be seen. We choose not to interact with people who see us inaccurately. Over a period of time, we are surrounded with people who see us the way we want to be seen. These people become co-conspirators in supporting this negotiated identity. We all act to support each other's identity.

A second self-verifying strategy is to display identity cues. We display ourselves to convey a certain image, and engage in interaction strategies, which promote being seen as one desires to be seen. If a person sees you in a way you don't want to be seen, you are motivated to negotiate. However, the power relationship in the interaction is very important. A less powerful person may be reluctant to negotiate. The person may let the misperception stand, because he or she may not feel in a position to influence the perceiver, may feel negotiation is not legitimate, or may believe it to be too risky to try to influence the misperception. This, of course, is the situation of minority group members in attempting to express, or define, their identity in an environment created by the dominant group.

Social Cognition

Social cognition, broadly defined, is the way we think about social events. It is fundamental to social behavior and includes schemas and stereotypes, and to some extent, attitude. Diversity professionals take into account how people think about others, and they often work to change these views.

Much of social judgment is based on the use of schemas. A schema is a mental representation of an object, event, or group. This representation is usually in the form of a prototype. For example, if you are asked to describe good leaders you call up your schema of a leader and extract attributes from this image to produce your description. These attributes are not stored as abstract lists of traits. For, example, if I am asked to describe a pie, my schema is a pictorial image of the pie, and my description is of the "picture".

One of the characteristics of an impression is that when asked to describe someone, an individual will invariably produce a list of attributes. If we were to ask you to describe a friend, you would produce a list of adjectives. These adjectives can be thought of as nodes in a mental schema. For example, if I activate "leader", elements of the schema might include "decisive" or "thoughtful". But thoughtful might also be part of, or connected to, other concepts and schemas, such as teacher. Thus, activation of a schema, such as leader, may spread to other schemas, such as teacher.

This characteristic of schematic representation is called spreading activation. One of the reasons that adjective descriptions are so powerful is that they are connected to an array of attributes in the schema. Activation of an attribute, spreads to other connected attributes. For example, if a group has been negatively stereotyped as violent, thinking of the negative attribute activates the group as an example. Activating a negative adjective spreads activation to the group, for which the attribute is part of the stereotype. In addition, thinking of the group activates that adjective.

One important aspect of schematic representation is that it links together areas of knowledge. Each time a connection between attributes is activated it is strengthened. If you try to change the negative attributes contained in schemas by convincing people that they're not true, you may inadvertently strengthen the connection between the group and the negative attributes. Contact and interaction in natural settings often work better, because they provide information without directly activating the negative schema.

Functions of Mental Representations

One of the functions of schemas is to direct attention. They act to filter the available stimulation so that only some of it receives attention. A color-blind person doesn't see certain colors. Schemas function in the same way. With a schema activated you are susceptible to information in that category, but less sensitive to information outside the category. For example, you will be more likely to attend to a Utah license plate after a discussion of Utah. You usually don't realize this attention function until a relevant stimulus is encountered.

Schemas also serve an interpretation function. We interpret the behavior of others in terms of the schemas (stereotypes) we apply to them. We expect their behavior to be consistent with the schema. When evaluating a leader, our schema for leaders guides our interpretation of the leader's effectiveness. In this way schema and stereotype are synonymous. Violations of these expectancies, positively or negatively, can strongly affect our judgments of the target person (Vescio & Biernat, 1999).

In general, experience increases the complexity, diversity and differentiation of our schemas. However, there are individual differences in differentiation. Some people are highly differentiated, assimilate new material easily, and others are not. There are both cognitive and personality reasons for this. Some people are not cognitively capable of differentiation; and others are dispositionally unmotivated or resistant to differentiate. Occasionally, adding new pieces to schemas is threatening. Archie Bunker, the T.V. personality known for his bigotry, wanted to stay the way he was; change was threatening to him. Some people are more flexible.

Social cognition involves the development and use of schemas about social information and is expressed in three processes. The first process is attention. Schemas determine the aspects of the environment, which will receive your attention. Second, schemas help us determine what things mean, but what events mean also activate schemas. Third, we use the information in schemas to make judgments. Our mental representations of a person or event become criteria against which we match what we observe.

Social cognition has three goals. The first is to conserve mental energy. It is difficult to begin to understand each new situation or person from the beginning, so people use schemas as mental short cuts. Thus, schemas conserve mental energy by providing pre-existing templates for viewing the world. Expectation-confirmation strategies develop in order to preserve the schema. When we employ the schema we attempt to confirm it. We attend more to expectation-relevant information and we are more attentive to information that confirms the schema than information that disconfirms the schema. We might not attend to a quality in a leader if that quality is not part of our schema about leaders. In addition, a confirmation bias leads us to interpret ambiguous information in a way that supports the schema. One of the functions of the schema is that it helps with memory storage. If "decisive" is part of the schema of leaders, people are more likely to remember instances in which a leader was decisive or not. These processes also create resistance to change in the schema.

The second goal of social cognition is to manage self-image. Social cognition is not a purely objective; information-driven process. People engage in social cognition for a reason; the most important one is enhancing and protecting the self. The self-relevance of the event will change or impact the use of schematic information.

An important self-management technique is social comparison. Social comparison is the tendency to look at other people for information about ourselves, in areas such as ability, emotion, and appropriate behavior (Festinger, 1954). Our choice of person with whom to compare is based on motive. We usually compare ourselves to people who are similar to us. This selectivity of whom we use for comparison serves to further isolate groups. Women tend to "check it out" with other women, men with men, and so on.

We can use downward comparison to make ourselves look and feel good by comparing ourselves to people less able or privileged than us. The comparison makes us feel more important or capable, thus enhancing our self-esteem. This is part of the fabric of prejudice and discrimination. Discriminating against a group not only "keeps them in their place" economically and socially, it enhances the self-view of the oppressor through downward comparison.

The third goal in social cognition is to view the world accurately. The more accurate the perception, the more accurate the understanding of the world, and the more you control that world.

Biases and Distortions in Social Cognition

In understanding behavior, two broad categories of explanations are possible: influences from the setting (e.g., he did it for money) or attributes of the individual (e.g., he was angry). People generally have a correspondence bias in their explanations of social events. This means that people tend to see events as being caused by the individual rather than by the situation, especially if the event is negative, or it is personally relevant.

In America we are more likely to hold people responsible for an event that is not their fault. Part of the reason for this correspondence bias is that people have a tendency to look more at the person when something occurs than at the situation, which surrounds the person. Most of the information processing is about the actor, who is the salient figure against the apparently passive ground of the situation. However, there are motivational reasons as well: it makes life simpler to blame a person. If we blame the situation, we might be at risk to experience the situation ourselves. Negative outcomes enhance the motivational bias and the closer an event is to us, the more likely we are to make a dispositional attribution. As typically used, a stereotype is a dispositional bias; it leads to the perceptions of people as responsible for circumstances, rather than circumstances responsible for people.

Heuristics

We engage in a variety of cognitive shortcuts or heuristics when thinking about social events.

Representativeness. The representativeness heuristic involves the use of a schema about a group. The schema represents a prototype of these activities or people (e.g., police officer, picnic) as the basis of judgment about a particular, often unknown, person or event.

Availability. The availability heuristic is a term describing the tendency to make judgments about events based on their memory impression. In the availability heuristic, we make a subjective probability estimate based on how accessible information is in memory. One of the reasons why people believe air travel is more dangerous than it is actually is the salience of memories involving air travel accidents. There are fewer salient memories of car crashes even though they happen more frequently. Another example is how parents are increasingly afraid for their children in today's society. Parents are less willing now than in earlier years to let their children walk to school; instead, they put their children in the car and drive them. This fear is based on the salience of events presented in the media about children being abducted or murdered while on their way to or from school. However, it is more likely that the child will die in the car on the way to school, than be assaulted while walking to school. In the age group 1 – 4 years, the number one, non-medical, cause of death is by car accident.

The availability heuristic is based in schematic processing. Our schemas are created through our unique experiences. That is, our representations of the world reflect the world with which we have had experience. We frequently see the effect of this in diversity practice. For example, when people in the eastern United States are asked to identify the largest Hispanic minority in America, they usually report Puerto Rican instead of Mexican, which is the correct answer. The reason for the error is that people in the eastern U.S. more frequently encounter Puerto Ricans than Mexicans, so more instances or Puerto Rican are available in the Hispanic schema.

Adjustment. The adjustment heuristic refers to the tendency to use existing schemas to incorporate new information. We don't start a new schema for new information. It is more efficient to adjust the old one.

Attribution

Attribution is historically the term for how individuals engage in assigning a cause for behavior. Kelley (1973) says we have numerous choices available to us in explaining the behavior of others and ourselves. In addition, attribution is an active process of assigning cause and often reflects our personal dispositions as much as the fact pattern available to us.

One of the earliest models of attribution was the theory of correspondent inferences by Jones and Davis (1965). The model explains what kind of information is used, and the way in which a person to comes to a decision about whether a behavior is caused by situational factors or by traits of the person. Correspondence refers to correspondence between the person and cause. If you decide the person caused the event it is described as correspondent. This inference usually has two components, the first being intention. It is assumed that only behavior, which is intended, reflects something dispositional about the person. If we conclude that the behavior was intended, the second component is to decide what it is about the person that caused it.

Jones and Davis describe three factors people use in making correspondent inferences. The first factor is social desirability. Jones and Davis assume that everyone intends to behave in a socially desirable way. Based on that assumption, if the person behaves in a socially desirable way, there is less information that is correspondent about the individual. We are more likely to make a correspondent inference if the individual acts in a counter-normative way. So, when you deal with people who are different than you, a bias is created. You see their non-normative behavior as intentional, and caused by them as individuals, rather than as being part of a normative base from which they come.

The second type of information in Jones and Davis' model is common and non-common effects. A potential explanation of a behavior is present when the behavior is present, and absent when the behavior is absent. In other words, the cause is common to the behavior in situations where the behavior occurs.

The third factor is hedonic relevance. If someone's behavior is personally relevant to you, you are more likely to make a correspondent inference. For example, if someone rear-ends you while driving, you are more likely to conclude the cause was something about the driver instead of the situation than if you witnessed the same driver rear-end someone else.

Kelley (1973, 1979) developed two models of attribution, both of which incorporated ideas contained in Jones and Davis' model. Kelley says that when we make a causal attribution, we look at information concerning consensus, consistency, and distinctiveness or people, time, and objects, respectively. Consensus information is information about other people. Consistency information is about other times, and distinctiveness information is about other objects. Kelley says that in trying to understand the causes of others' behavior, we look for the pattern of information from these three sources. If everyone engages in the behavior, there is little information about a person as an individual. If the individual is the only one engaged in the behavior, (low consensus) it gives you information about the person. For example, if someone reads a book at a rock concert. Consistency information is difficult to gather because it requires observation over time. If the individual always reads at rock concerts (high consistency), we are more likely to make a dispositional attribution than if the individual reads at a rock concert only one time. Kelley calls information about whether the behavior occurs in many situations or only in specific situations, distinctiveness. Does this person read at many events (low distinctiveness), or is this the only situation in which this occurs (high distinctiveness)? If it is not distinctive, then you are more likely to make a dispositional attribution. In general then, we attribute a behavior to personal causes when the behavior has high consistency, low distinctiveness, and low consensus.

Typically, many factors can have some impact on behavior. Kelley states that we look at consensus/consistency/distinctiveness information for one cause, but also for many plausible causes. When we are aware of more than one plausible cause for a behavior, we divide causality among all of these causes. Kelley calls this discounting. If you have two potential causes for an event, you give some causality to each, so it dilutes (discounts) the amount of causality attached to any one cause. To further complicate the picture, these causes may be either facilitative or augmentive. That is, a cause may act to either increase (augment) or decrease (inhibit) the observed behavior. We take this directionality into account when we assign causality. For example, suppose we wish to understand why a student graduates with a 4.0 GPA. If I also know the student has economic privilege, how smart do I consider this individual to be as compared to a student who also earns a 4.0 but comes from a situation that was not privileged? The privilege is augmentative; so I assign some of the performance to the privilege. Therefore, we conclude that the person who overcame adversity (inhibitory effect) is smarter. We make adjustments about the way we understand causality by taking into account inhibitory or augmenting effects.

Fundamental Attribution Error and other Biases

When people engage in attribution their goals are much the same as those of scientists: explanation and prediction. They want to understand the causes of behavior and they use this understanding to form expectations about the behavior of others. However, people are imperfect scientists in that they show bias in their attributions. These biases take a number of related forms.

The most pervasive bias in social cognition is the tendency of an observer to explain an actor's behavior by emphasizing attributes of the actor more than aspects of the situation. This overemphasis on actor causality is referred to as the Fundamental Attribution Error (Ross, 1977). Perceptually and informationally this bias is understandable.

To the observer, the actor is the most salient aspect of the situation. Environmental contingencies are much less obvious. In understanding our own behavior, we tend to do the opposite. We attribute other people's behavior to them, but we attribute our own to the situation. These biases are enhanced when the behavior or the outcome is negative, as in the case of failure. We are much more likely to attribute the failure of others to attributes of them (e.g. laziness), but we are more likely to attribute our own failure to the situation (e.g. task difficulty). Again, one explanation for this bias is perceptual. All of our sensory apparatus is oriented to the environment. We do not see ourselves as figural.

It has also been argued that actor-observer differences in attribution serve an ego-defensive function. Seeing our own failure as influenced by the environment protects our self-esteem. Seeing the failure of others as due to qualities of them reduces our anxiety about failure should we ever find ourselves in a similar situation. Social cognition used in this way is defensive. Blaming individuals for unforeseeable accidental outcomes is another example of this. Homeless people are perceived as having caused their homelessness through their own failure or personal shortcomings. We would be threatened by the view that homelessness might be caused by situational factors. If people are homeless without it being their fault, it means that the same thing could happen to me.

A variation of defensive attribution is the "just world hypothesis". Lerner (1980) observed that in a situation that threatens a person's view of the world as just and reasonable, the person deals with the threat by attributing causality to the individuals who experienced the negative event. The higher the threat, the more people do this. We need to believe that "God doesn't throw dice", and anything that threatens this view increases the tendency to engage in the defensive attribution. This often leads to bizarre outcomes. Sometimes the people least responsible for an event will be blamed most. Who are we more likely to blame for being most responsible for being the victim of rape, a prostitute in a crime filled neighborhood, or a woman raped in her home in a middle class neighborhood. The research shows that the middle class woman challenges our world-view more, and is therefore seen as more personally responsible. This tendency appears counterintuitive, but we must understand that we usually don't have the luxury of making social judgments where two situations can be compared side by side. In order to restore our view of the world, that bad things happen to bad people, we blame the victim.

There are several other biases in social cognition:

Control bias. Most people overestimate their degree of control over events. For example, gamblers believe that they can control games of chance.

Base rate bias. Base rate bias is another example of our poor use of information. We are overly influenced by particulars, ignoring long-term track records. One of the best places to see this in operation is with the way a baseball commentator talks about the players. They often focus on the short term. For example, they describe the player as on a "hot streak" if he is hitting well in the last few games, while seemingly ignoring the player's poor hitting over the rest of his career.

Dilution effect. In the dilution effect, irrelevant information diverts our attention away from relevant information; it causes us to misuse or under-use relevant information. For example, you know that 90% of CEO's of US companies are male. When asked about Company X, you find out the CEO of Company X drives a red sports car, you become uncertain of the CEO's gender. The make and color of the car is irrelivant information, nevertheless it diverts our attention.

Gambler's fallacy. In gambler's fallacy we overestimate the likelihood of an event if it hasn't occurred for some time. For example, we haven't heard from an old friend in a while, so we estimate that we are due for a call sooner than later. People of color, due to past discrimination, often expect discrimination as a result.

Conjunction error. Conjunction error is when we estimate the joint occurrence of two outcomes or events is more likely than the occurrence of either one alone. For example, roughly 10% of the US population is left-handed and 13% is Hispanic. When asked, people typically overestimate the likelihood of left-handed Hispanics in the US population. One form of this error is the illusory correlation.

Illusory correlation. Illusory correlation refers to the observation that groups that are less frequently encountered are seen to have other unusual attributes. For example, even when mental illness has no relationship with crime, the two are seen as going together. We don't say "white national merit scholars" but we do say "black national merit scholars". Similarly, we think of individuals who have suffered a lightning strike as having other odd personal attributes.

False consensus error. The false consensus error assumes that one's experiences and personal qualities are more common in the general population than they actually are. For example, people who don't like broccoli tend to overestimate the number of fellow broccoli haters in the world.

Egocentrism. When we overestimate our contribution to joint outcomes, we are showing egocentrism. For example, when we work on a project as a group, the individuals in the group perceive their contributions to the project as greater than they actually were.

Cognitive conservatism. People also show cognitive conservatism when revising initial judgments. Once you have formed an impression of someone, that impression is slow to change with the addition of new information, which contradicts the first impression. For example, a student in one of my classes was late for several class meetings early in the semester. In spite of the fact that the student has been on time for every class since, I am reluctant to change my judgment of the student as unreliable. This example also illustrates the operation of primary effects. People usually weigh information received early heavier than information received later.

Kelley's (1973) work on judgments of ability is an example of cognitive conservatism. He had people observe others working on tasks. In one situation people started very well then did worse. In another group they started poorly then improved. In the third group, the people did equally throughout. The total number of errors was the same in each group. People perceived the group that started out well and then became less effective as being smarter.

Attributions of success and failure

Weiner (1995) has proposed a model for understanding attributions of success and failure based on two independent dimensions: internal versus external and stable versus unstable. In explaining success and failure, this two-dimensional model yields four combinations of explanations: external, stable (e.g., task difficulty); internal, stable (e.g., ability); external, unstable (e.g., luck); and, internal, unstable (e.g., motivation). Every success or failure of others or ourselves generates causal thinking along these two dimensions. We can think of the self-serving bias in terms of this model (for an example in diversity, see; Imai, 1994; Rice, 1985). In making judgments about our own performance, we tend to see success as due to something internal and/or stable (e.g., ability), and failure as situational and/or unstable (e.g., luck). This bias serves a positive function. If a person attributes success to self, esteem is enhanced.

If I attribute my failure to unstable and/or external factors (e.g., chance), it is self-protective because it justifies continued effort. Attributing failure to changeable outside circumstances allows me to try again. We tend to reverse this pattern of attribution when explaining the behavior of others. I attribute their failures to ability (stable, internal) and their successes to chance (unstable, external). Low self-esteem individuals self-attribute the way we attribute to others. They believe they are a failure due to internal causes, and attribute success to luck.

Attraction

Fundamentally liking or attraction can be thought of as an attitude. Thus, all of the theory and research on the development and change of attitude also applies to attraction. However, there are several additional factors, which are particularly noteworthy in their influence in attraction (see Baumeister & Leary, 1995, for a complete review).

Similarity

The single most important factor in attraction is similarity. We tend to like people who are like us. Similarity is balancing in the sense that it allows me to say "I like me, and if they are similar to me, I must also like them". The problem this effect causes us with regard to differences should be obvious. If liking is so powerfully attached to similarity in our culture, then being dissimilar is a powerful barrier to embracing differences.

Think about the kinds of information you are interested in knowing about people when you first meet them: "where are you from?", "what do you do?". You are listening for a common ground. We gravitate to people who are like us physically, experientially, and attitudinally. We can identify exceptions, but the reason the exceptions are so noticeable is because they are exceptions. For example, we think it is odd when we see a very tall woman with a very short man, no matter how culturally competent we may consider ourselves to be.

Similarity creates balance, but it also produces closeness and contact. People who are similar tend to live and work in proximity, and they are more likely to encounter each other. Research also indicates that the frequency of contact is related to friendship formation. This is one of the important outcomes of diverse living and work environments. They produce contact and a perception of similarity, both of which enhance liking, making it more difficult to maintain a stance of prejudice.

Social Exchange

Social exchange theory is a model developed by Thibaut and Kelley (1959), describing power and satisfaction in a dyadic relationship. It is based on three concepts. It assumes that there is an outcome dimension of exchange or reward in a relationship ranging from no payoff or reward to high payoff or reward. Presumably, you have some expectation of what you should receive in the relationship based on experience. This is called the comparison level; what I expect from the other person. There is also a comparison level for alternatives, which is what I believe I could get from other relationships. By placing actual outcomes into the model in relation to comparison level and comparison level for alternatives, I gain an understanding about the power and satisfaction in a relationship.

Power is the potential for the relationship to impact, or influence me. Satisfaction is the feeling that I experience when I receive what I want. Satisfaction in the relationship is determined by the difference between what I expect (comparison level) and what I actually receive. I am not happy if what I receive is less then what I believe I deserve or expect (comparison level). On the other hand, I am very happy if I receive more than I expect. The power of the relationship is the distance between the outcome and the comparison level for alternatives. You are not going to leave the relationship if you think you won't do better elsewhere. When outcomes are below what you think you deserve (comparison level) but above what you think you will get elsewhere, you are dissatisfied but think you cannot do better. This situation leads you to think you are stuck. This is why people stay in relationships where they are unhappy. According to Thibaut and Kelley the happiness in the relationship is independent of the tendency to stay in that relationship. The tendency to stay in that relationship demonstrates the power of that relationship. Leaving the relationship is not a function of happiness, but rather it is a function of the power of that relationship, which is based on your perception of what else is available.

In long-term relationships, where the outcomes are stable, the satisfaction tends to decrease. This decrease is due to the fact that the expected level of outcomes (comparison level) tends to move upward to match the actual outcomes. We come to feel we deserve those things we are in a habit of receiving. To maintain the same level of satisfaction the outcomes have to be increased. One way to solve this problem is to switch to a different mode of reward. When considering revitalizing a relationship, we often think of finding other means of reward or of relating. One of the implications of the increasing levels of expectations, even in a good relationship is that your ability to reward becomes progressively smaller, and your ability to injure becomes progressively larger. If you fail it is a larger cost, but if you succeed, it is smaller satisfaction.

Social Influence

All social psychology is about social influence, in the sense that influence is a change in a person's thinking, feeling or behaving, as a function of the presence, either implied or real of another individual. However, when discussing social influence, we typically mean direct, obvious influence. Normally, research on social influence occurs under the topics of conformity, obedience, and compliance. These are differentiated in two ways: the obviousness of the social influence attempt and the potential for sanctions. With conformity for instance, the attempt to influence is simply the presence of other people. In conformity situations, an individual matches his or her behavior to what someone else or some other group is doing, without any overt attempt of the group to make the person conform. Usually, the social influences are implied by the relationship among the participants (i.e., peer group conformity).

In compliance the influence attempt is direct but it is informal. There is no overt attempt to manipulate. The individual is asked to comply with a request and any sanctions are implied rather than overt. On the other hand, in obedience the influence attempt is not only direct, but there are potential sanctions involved. When we think of obedience, 'obedience to authority' comes to mind. This is a request with repercussions.

Power

One way to conceptualize social influence is in terms of power. Ordinarily, power is viewed as a negative concept. When thinking of power, dominance, strength, control, and the ability to sanction, come to mind. However, social power is simply the ability to influence or create a change in the way a person thinks, feels, or behaves. Viewed this way, power is not necessarily a negative concept. There are many ways of creating influence involving the use of power. The greatest power, or influence is most often positive. The people you are willingly influenced by, those you love, are the most powerful people in your life. We often don't think of the influence of our loved ones as power, because we willingly change in response to their influence attempts.

Power varies along two important dimensions. One dimension is whether or not power is socially dependent or independent. Some kinds of power depend on people being present to enforce their influence. Other types of power are portable; I can influence someone without actually being there. Socially dependent influence requires surveillance in order to be maintained, such as power using punishment. However, with socially independent power one can have an influence and then leave. Another dimension of power is the extent to which it creates a public or private change. Is there an internalized change in the individual, or are they simply being compliant or obedient?

French and Raven (1959) identified five types of power: reward, coercive, legitimate, referent, and expert. In reward power, social influence is based on the ability of the influence agent to reward the individual for behaving as requested. In reward power, some surveillance is required in order to provide the reward. However, the individual will typically seek out the influence agent in order to obtain the reward. In addition, the influence can become internalized due to the positive value attained by the rewarded behavior. This is a non-avoidant type of influence.

The danger of reward power is overjustification, which can also undermine the internalization of the influence. Overjustification (Deci & Ryan, 1985) is a concept which describes the tendency for overt external rewards to undermine existing intrinsic motivation for the behavior. For example, paying an individual to engage in a behavior he or she already enjoys reduces the likelihood that the individual will engage in the behavior if the reward is later withdrawn.

On the other hand, coercive power is based on punishments or threat, and requires constant surveillance if the influence is to be maintained. The individual experiencing this kind of influence often attempts to avoid the influence. Coercive power also undermines the internalization of the influence and creates public rather than private acceptance. In addition, reactance often occurs when coercive power is used.

Reactance is a concept first described by Brehm and Brehm (1981) referring to a shift in attitude produced when an individual experiences a restriction of freedom. A form of reactance is the 'grass is greener' effect. It describes the tendency to view things that are not available to us as being more attractive. When freedom is restricted, people take steps to restore that freedom. One way to restore perceived freedom is to adopt an attitude in a direction opposite the influence attempt, as in coercive power. Coercive power produces public compliance, but the attitude may become more resistant. We have all heard the comment, "they can't make me do this!" Americans are extremely sensitive to the infringement of personal control, power and autonomy.

In legitimate power, the influence is based on the idea that the power holder has the right, usually due to position or status, to demand performance. Legitimate power can lead to internalization of the influence and usually requires little surveillance.

Referent power is based on the target's identification with the power holder. Someone who is a role model (e.g., Michael Jordan) holds this kind of power. Influence based on referent power can be internalized and surveillance is unnecessary. A negative form of referent power has also been identified. For example, some people may not want to be seen as similar to certain members of their group.

Expert power is influence based on the perceived knowledge held by the power holder (e.g., teacher). It leads to internalized change and doesn't require surveillance.

Self-esteem

When we engage in diversity work, one of our goals is often to change people's view of differences. For some people this can offer a profound challenge to their self-view. The part of the self, which dictates their perception and acceptance of differences, must be changed. This requires that they come to view themselves differently in order to be willing to accept and embrace differences in others, usually involving a dramatic change of self. This falls under what Swann (1997) describes as crisis self-verification.

Swann discusses the cognitive affective crossfire. We possess a cognitive system and an affective system, and they tend to operate separately. When there is conflict between the systems, the cognitive usually wins. A good example of how this works is when self-relevant feedback is received. The cognitive system evaluates it in terms of information content and the accuracy of the feedback. On the other hand, the affective system evaluates feedback based on its emotional valence; how it feels.

People seek out self-confirming information, which is consistent with their definition or expectation of who they are. People also seek out information that is positive in emotional tone, such as feedback from friends.

When you give positive feedback to someone with high self-esteem, the affective and cognitive line up. If you have a good opinion of yourself (high self-esteem), the feedback is viewed as both positive and accurate. The case is very different for people with low self-esteem. Positive feedback is received as positive by the affective system, but as inaccurate or untrue by the cognitive system. The reaction of the low self-esteem individual might be, "thank you, but it is not true."

Most of the time the systems do no appear to be separate because information is consistent across the systems. However, occasionally, as in the case of low self-esteem, the systems come into conflict, resulting in the cognitive-affective crossfire. In these situations research indicates that the cognitive side prevails. People seek information, which is consistent with their self-view, even if that information is negative. This helps explain the resistance of low self-esteem to attempts to increase it.

Programs, which focus on building self-esteem, emphasize positive feedback. The problem is that the recipient does not believe the positive feedback. Furthermore, the person providing the "inaccurate" feedback loses credibility, because he or she constantly "lies" by giving positive feedback.

Swann's viewpoint also helps us understand the tendency of low self-esteem people to seek out failure; it is self-confirming. Internalized oppression can be conceptualized in a similar fashion. Once the oppressed individual has internalized the negative view of the oppressor, the oppressed individual will seek out situations and information, which will confirm the negative identity. This is one of the particularly insidious aspects of oppression, the person "self-oppresses".

In diversity work, it is important to remember that the cognitive and the emotional systems connect, but they function in very different ways. The emotional system is slow and persistent; the cognitive system is quick and facile. It is inefficient to attempt to change one system indirectly by accessing the other. Often, we try to change behavior that has an emotional basis, by providing information. This is a very inefficient way of proceeding. It is very difficult to reason people out of behaviors that are created and supported emotionally.

In our culture and in the field of diversity, we value reason and information. But the distinction between the cognitive and affective systems highlights the potential one-sidedness of our work. We often emphasize teaching and knowledge, but we must recognize that these cognitively based interventions will not work well with emotionally based behaviors.

As change agents, we are involved in placing people in a condition of crisis self-verification. We challenge how people view themselves and others. Swann provides an excellent description of the conditions necessary to produce and to support the change. One of the most important factors in supporting the change is self-concept.

According to Swann, we can create a change in self, but if the community doesn't support the change it is unlikely to last. We can create experiences for people, that change them, but we also need to create organizational change that will confirm the individual change. This change can be viewed as a transition point in a person's life. In the growth and development of the individual, cultures have rituals, which support certain changes in identity, such as graduation, marriage, etc.

These symbolic events celebrate change in people and symbolize societal support for the change. In diversity work, this is an untapped area; finding ways to ritualize transition of self that occurs when people embrace differences. The ritual step is a way of legitimizing something that wouldn't be legitimate without the ritual.

Foot in the Door

The foot in the door phenomenon was first described by Freedman and Fraser (1966). Freedman and Fraser observed that when an individual complied with a small request, they were more likely to comply with a larger request later on. Even sitting and talking is a small compliance and enhances the foot in the door effect. The underlying mechanism for why the foot in the door effect works is not very well understood. The most widely accepted explanation is that the first request creates a changed self-image, making the individual more susceptible to the second, later request.

Door in the Face

The door in the face phenomenon is the opposite of the foot in the door phenomenon, but creates the same outcome (Cialdini, Vincent, Lewis, Catalani, Wheeler, & Darby, 1975). If someone is asked for a large favor first, which they refuse, they are then more likely to comply with a small request. The explanation is based on equity. We feel we have injured the person, so we recompense, restore the balance, by complying with the small request.

Attitude and Attitude Change

Functions of Attitudes

Attitudes are learned and, once learned, attitudes remain and change because they serve certain functions (Katz, 1960). Some attitudes serve an instrumental function, that is, we like the people and things that usually result in reward for us. On the other hand, we have negative attitudes toward objects or events we believe, make our lives more difficult.

Another function of attitude is ego-defense or self-protection. Ego-defensive attitudes are often implicated in prejudice and discrimination. A good example of ego-defensive attitudes is in scapegoating. Rather than acknowledge a shortcoming in ourselves we project it onto a weaker or less advantaged group. By seeing the shortcomings or negative impulse in others, we can also justify behaving negatively toward the scapegoated group. This neatly expresses the very impulse we are unable to admit in ourselves. The self and self-concept is inseparable from the attitude that helps to protect it.

A third function of attitudes is expressive. We have positive attitudes about objects that fit with our worldview, and value systems. For example, a person may view him or herself as a socially enlightened liberal. Certain attitudes about gender and race follow from and support this self-view.

Attitudes also serve a knowledge function. One way to measure attitude is by what you do or do not know, or the way in which you know something. Knowledge is an expression of the attitude and the attitude supports that knowledge. Attitudes protect and preserve certain kinds of knowledge we possess. If I hold a negative attitude about a group, and I have knowledge about that group, that knowledge would not be preserved or maintained without maintaining the attitude. Given the negative attitude, I am likely to know mostly negative information about the group and to resist knowing positive facts about the group. My attitude creates selective knowledge, which, in turn supports the attitude. If I did not have that attitude it would be simple to attack the knowledge, because there would not be a motivational basis for protecting the knowledge.

The implication of a functional view of attitudes is that in order to change attitudes it is important to think about what function they serve. For a given person, a negative racial attitude might be ego-defensive, or instrumental, or identity expressive. When trying to create change, we must consider the functions served by the attitude, so that change efforts can be tailored to the function. With people for whom prejudice serves an ego-protective function, attacking the prejudice through education will likely be ineffective. Instead, the most effective intervention would focus on reducing the fear and anxiety experienced by the individual.

Persuasion

The early work on attitude focused on persuasion. The American way is to approach issues in a practical or functional manner; "how can I fix it or change it?". A team of social psychologists at Yale University conducted some of the most noteworthy research in the 1940's through the 1960's (Hovland, Lumsdaine, & Sheffield, 1949). This group took a functional approach to understanding persuasion, by finding those factors that influence it. They organized these factors into three categories: attributes of the communicator or persuader, elements of the message, and traits of the recipient.

With regard to communicator characteristics, they found that persuasion was influenced most by credibility. We are more persuaded by communicators who are knowledgeable, expert, and whose motives for trying to influence us are legitimate. Making judgments about communicator expertise and motivation involve the attribution processes described earlier.

The second factor outlined by the Yale group is the structure of the message, in terms of its logic and its evaluative elements. In trying to convince someone to vote for the partner benefits for city employees, how do you structure the message and what is the valence or evaluative level of the message? One of the factors to consider is the discrepancy between the current position of the audience and where we want them to be. For a particular attitude or issue, each of us holds a position that is most comfortable and most reflective of our opinion. On either side of that preferred position are positions, not preferred, but which are still agreeable to us. Sherif (1937) calls this range of attitude, the latitude of acceptance. We disagree with positions falling outside the latitude of acceptance, and these positions are called latitude of rejection. People with very strong attitudes have very narrow latitudes of acceptance. There are only certain, limited positions that are agreeable to them. Sherif found that persuasive attempts that fall into the latitude of rejection are likely to boomerang. That is, they move the audience attitude away from, not toward, the persuasive attempt. Maximum attitude change is created when the message is tailored to fall at the edge of the latitude of acceptance. Of course latitude of acceptance and rejection refer to characteristics of the audience as well.

The structure of the message is also important. Should we make a message one-sided or two-sided? Using a two-sided argument is one way of moderating your argument you are trying to position yourself at the edge of the audience's latitude of acceptance. By including some of the other points of view in the message, your message appears balanced. A two-sided argument makes you seem reasonable, credible, and fair. It also helps you inoculate the audience against rebuttal. A two-sided argument contains the inoculation, so it is more resistant to change, than a one-sided argument. If you use a two-sided argument or message, primacy is most influential. It is better to put first the position you wish to be most influential. One-sided messages work better with people who are already supportive of position.

What should be the emotional tone of the argument? Ordinarily, persuasion attempts that make people feel good are most effective. However, fear appeals work under some circumstances. First, the individual must be able to reduce the fear. If people cannot do something about the fear, it will create a change in an opposite direction. Further, the audience could label the persuader negatively, as a person who scares people. Second, the fear should not be so extreme as to cause the audience to avoid the messenger.

Cacciopo and Petty (1986) have identified two routes to persuasion: a peripheral route and a central route. The peripheral route involves superficial processing. Attitude change results from emotional and superficial elements of the message. Persuasion, which employs the central route, relies on deep thinking and the information content of the message.

People engage in central or peripheral processing at different times. When we are not involved in a product or issue, we are more likely to process peripherally, and, thus are more influenced by the emotional tone, image, or irrelevant structural features of the argument. For example, research has shown that during peripheral processing, dividing a message into discrete arguments and emphasizing the number (e.g., "there are four good reasons to buy...") is more effective than the same information presented as a single argument. The tendency to process peripherally or centrally varies from person to person. People who have high needs for cognition are more likely to process centrally, and people low in need for cognition are more likely to process peripherally.

Inoculation

McGuire (1964) first presented the concept of inoculation in reaction to the observation that social psychologists had focused exclusively on how to change attitude, on persuasion. Very little work in social psychology deals with producing attitude stability, or creating a resistance to change. It has concentrated on finding ways to change people, not finding ways to keep people from changing. McGuire argues that we should also study how to produce stability, such as helping children resist peer pressure. McGuire describes beliefs that are "germ-free"; beliefs that have rarely, if ever, been challenged. A culture provides a set of assumptions, values and beliefs about the world some of which are rarely challenged. These "germ-free" beliefs, which we accept in an unquestioning way, are susceptible to manipulation. McGuire found that these beliefs could be easily attacked by a logical argument. To create resistance to attitude change, McGuire describes a process he called inoculation. You inoculate attitude by considering a weaker version of the persuasion, or weaker counter-arguments. It is analogous to injection of a weaker version of a disease to create later resistance to the disease.

McGuire's concepts of "germ-free" attitude and inoculation are strong arguments for diversity. Unchallenged, untested views are vulnerable to persuasion. Experience with diverse ideas and opinions creates resistance. Yet our impulse is often to resist such exposure. Parents are particularly prone to this error with their children. In trying to protect their children, they often shield the children from different viewpoints and experiences. This simply creates a vulnerability to these views at a later time. Good parenting would involve controlled exposure, in small doses, to the alternative view.

Attitudes and Behavior

The common assumption is that people's attitudes are expressed in behavior. If we want to change the behavior, we must attack the attitude; if we want to eliminate discrimination we must attack prejudice. This is based on the assumption that there is a causal connection between attitude and behavior, and that behavior flows from inside to outside, from the personality trait, or from the knowledge to the behavior. If we want to change behavior, we must first change the attitude or knowledge that is causing it. However, a long history of research has failed to find a strong connection between attitude and behavior.

An early study by LaPierre (1934) is an excellent example. In the 1930's, there was a high level of anti-Chinese prejudice in this country. Operating in the context of this prejudice, LaPierre asked hotel and restaurant proprietors by letter if they would be willing to accommodate or serve a Chinese couple visiting the United States. A large majority responded that they would refuse service. Subsequently, LaPierre visited these businesses with a Chinese couple and found that, when actually faced with the Chinese couple, most proprietors were willing to serve them. This study is often used as evidence of the uselessness of attitude in predicting behavior.

Research indicates that the correlation between a particular index of behavior and an expressed attitude is often low. For example, if you ask people about their racial attitudes then you measure their willingness to work on a PTA committee with members of other racial groups, you will likely discover that even racially prejudiced people are willing to work on the committee. On the surface, the behavior would appear to contradict the attitude.

Why are the data so weak for the relationship between behavior and attitude? One hypothesis is that behavior is not connected to traits or attitudes: people hold attitudes, but they do not affect their behavior. Another is a methodological issue, which centers on how attitude and behavior are measured. The tendency is to measure the attitude very generally but the behavior very specifically: whether or not this couple gets served at the restaurant, at this time of day, at this location, by these people. However, specific behavior can be influenced by numerous contextual factors: time of day, location, mood, etc. So, a particular behavior might be connected to the attitude, but it may be influenced by other factors as well. The attitude might not be the dominant influence on that behavior at the point in time, in that situation.

Fishbein and his colleagues (Fishbein & Ajzen, 1974) have demonstrated better consistency between attitude and behavior if they are measured at the same level of generality. If you connect a specific attitude with a specific behavior or a general attitude with a general behavior you usually observe a strong relationship. But if there is a mismatch between attitude and behavior in terms of specificity/generality, the relationship is reduced. General behavior is behavior across many situations, an aggregate. Racial or gender attitudes are usually an aggregate. To properly measure these attitudes they must be examined across multiple situations. It would be important to measure how an individual relates to the group members in many different situations. When attitude and behavior are measured as aggregates, attitude shows good predictiveness of behavior.

What are the implications for diversity practice of the relationship between attitude and behavior? In practice, we often mismatch the level of specificity of attitude and behavior. We often approach a group from the stance of their general attitudes, but the behavior we are trying to change is very specific. In addition, interventions tailored to change general attitudes are not likely to be very effective with specific behaviors. It is also important to recognize that behavior is multiply determined; other factors often support the behavior even if the attitude is changed. The social structure of the organization might maintain the behavior even after attitude change. There are many reasons why a behavior that is discriminatory might persist after a prejudiced attitude is reduced, or that a person might not discriminate even while holding highly prejudiced attitudes.

We must also consider contextual factors, that support the attitude. Our tendency is to focus on the attitude, and we might be successful in initiating attitude change. However, if the individual returns to an organizational or familial situation, which does not support the change, the change is likely to be short-lived.

One important individual difference that relates to attitude-behavior consistency is the concept of self-monitoring (Snyder, 1987). High self-monitors are attentive to situational cues and adjust their behavior accordingly. They often appear to be different people in different situations. Low self-monitors, on the other hand, look internally for the determination of appropriate behavior. In short, the low self-monitor shows more attitude behavior congruence than does the high self-monitor.

Influence is different in high and low self-monitors. Low self-monitors internalize change and are situation resistant. They are less likely to be susceptible to the counter-influences that they will inevitably face in the organization. Ehen working in organizations, it would be useful to identify the low self-monitors and use them as a resource to affect the rest of the group.

Attitude Follows Behavior

One of the lessons of early attitude research is that while behavior is caused by attitude, it is also true that attitude is caused by behavior. Often, the best way to change attitude is by changing the behavior. Our culture believes that behavior is a result of an attitude or belief, out of which comes the behavior. One of the reasons that our culture is so concerned with the concept of stereotype is that we believe people's behavior flows out of belief. In order to change the behavior (discrimination) we must change the belief (stereotype). What we don't understand is that causality goes in the opposite direction as well; belief, attitude, and skill, also result from behavior. One of the best ways to change attitude is by changing the behavior. If I can change your behavior, perhaps through the use of power, I can change your attitude. However, since we want the change to be internalized, the application of power should be minimally constraining.

When changing the behavior we want the least force possible to produce the desired behavior. The more obvious the external constraint, the more the behavior is attributed to external force and not to oneself, and it may produce reactance. Cognitive dissonance includes the concept of minimally sufficient force; just enough force to get people to do something. People will believe they have more control than in actuality and attribute the change to themselves. Over time, people forget the external force and the change accelerates.

The first theory to explicitly describe the conditions under which this occurs and provide a theoretical structure for it was Festinger's (1957) theory of cognitive dissonance. Dissonance theory assumes that people are motivated to have balance or consistency among their various cognitions. These cognitions include beliefs, attitudes, and knowledge about behavior. Inconsistency produces a feeling of dissonance, which, in turn, produces a motivation to re-establish balance. In order to do this, the individual must change some cognitive elements, usually the cognitions that are easiest to change. Most often this is observed when an attitude and a behavior are inconsistent.

Dissonance is created by the knowledge that you have a certain belief, but the additional knowledge that your behavior disconfirms the belief. Usually it is harder to deny what has been done (the behavior) than it is to adjust our attitude, so it is the attitude that we shift in the direction of the behavior, thus reducing the dissonance. In the area of interpersonal attraction, for example, we come to like the people we help, and we come to devalue the people we hurt. If you do something beneficial for someone toward whom you have a neutral attitude, you come to see that person as deserving of your help. What makes them deserve it is that they are likable; they are a good person. Similarly, for those people that you hurt, even by accident, you come to believe that they are deserving of the damage. Your attitude about those people follows your behavior, "I hurt them so they must have deserved it".

The behavior-attitude relationship is captured by the statement, "If I can get you to behave as if, I can get you to believe as if." There is one strong qualifier to this process; the individual must perceive freedom in choosing or engaging in the behavior. If he or she is forced or constrained to behave in a certain way the individual will not see the attitude as relevant to the behavior and no attitude change will occur. In fact, with strong salient force, reactance may result.

The applications to diversity work are obvious. We often concentrate on attitude assuming that changing a person's attitudes and beliefs will lead to changed behavior. However, reversing the sequence offers an approach that may be more efficient. This is one of the reasons initiatives, laws, and programs, which produce positive multicultural behavior, are so important. Given the behavior, we can expect some positive attitude change to result, so long as the individual does not feel forced to engage in the behavior. The message to program developers is to downplay the force. Use the minimum force necessary to produce compliance. One saving element is the American cultural belief in freedom. While we are very sensitive to threats to freedom, Americans tend to believe they have some choice, no matter how constraining the circumstances. Over time, the perception of constraint declines, perceived freedom increases, and the attitude change accelerates.

Prejudice

Prejudice is a particular type of attitude and discrimination is the behavior we expect to follow from or express the prejudice. We usually think of prejudice as a negative attitude toward a group, which is based simply on group membership. It is not based on an actual and factual understanding of the group, and it is overgeneralized by being applied to all members of the group. This is the type of prejudice we discuss here, but it is worth noting that prejudice can be positive (e.g., I enjoy all kinds of cross-cultural events regardless of the culture). There are several sources and functions of prejudice.

Usually the groups that have the most conflict with each other have the most negative attitudes about each other. These are often groups located closest together in terms of economic status such that they are competing for the same resources. In fact, as discussed below, establishing a situation where resources are scarce and groups must compete for them, can easily create prejudice.

There is also a social approval function of prejudice. Some people hold a prejudiced attitude because it is socially acceptable or desirable. The groups with which they identify support those attitudes and professing negative attitudes gain one approval in the group. Other belief systems also support prejudice. There is a strong positive correlation between prejudice and religiosity, and the more politically conservative, the more likely someone is to be prejudiced. Religion, for example, often produces conservatism, which is correlated with strong in-group/out-group boundaries, which enhance prejudice.

People who are most concerned about their position in a group, are the people who are most threatened by people outside the group, and thus, are most likely to be prejudiced. Those with low self-esteem issues, or are authoritarian are individuals who get the most benefit out of an oppressive, homogenous in-group. High self-esteem people don't need to be defensive. They are not dependent on others for their self-love.

Intergroup Conflict

Sherif's (1966) experiments on intergroup conflict illustrate the development and treatment of prejudice. Sherif was interested in the conditions of relationships between in-groups and out-groups and how they tended to promote or support conflict (in behavior) as well as prejudice (i.e., negative attitudes about out-groups). Are there certain conditions, which can produce the intergroup negative attitudes (or a narrowly defined prejudice)? Sherif conducted a study at a summer camp for boys, called Robber's Cave. He created two groups: the Eagles and the Rattlers. Then, he created artificial conflict between the groups by arranging competitions for prizes and privileges in the camp. One group always won and one group always lost. The competition became intense, and the level of hostility between the groups was dramatic. The groups became verbally and physically abusive with each other. A feedback loop exists in this kind of situation. Hostile, discriminatory behavior reinforces out-group negative attitudes, which feeds back and justifies the behavior.

Part of the impact of this research is in demonstrating how quickly and easily prejudice can be created in groups in close proximity, competing for scarce resources. Subsequently, Sherif investigated ways to reduce this prejudice. He created a superordinate goal, one that could only be reached by cooperation between the groups. They faked a broken water line to the camp. It was an emergency situation, which could only be remedied by the groups working together. They discovered that through creating cooperation in working toward a common goal prejudice was reduced. There was friendship formation across group boundaries and the interpersonal dynamics of the camp were changed. Sherif found that when conditions are right, the dynamics of interdependence and superordinate goals create contact between groups, which reduces prejudice.

Stereotypes

The concept of stereotype is central to our understanding of prejudice and discrimination. Both professionals and laypeople view stereotyping as a fundamental cause of prejudice. In fact the concepts are so bound together in our thinking that when we observe prejudice we often assume that it has resulted from a negative stereotype.

One of the sources of this understanding (or actually a stereotype) of stereotype was an early study by Katz and Braly (1935). They gave undergraduates a list of positive and negative adjectives, and a list of nationalities. They asked the students to attach the adjectives to the nationalities. People associated negative adjectives with nationalities they had never encountered. For example, Turks were described as hostile aggressors. This study is frequently used to justify our negative conception of stereotype. It seems to support the view that stereotypes are negative generalizations based on little, if any, experience.

Recently conceptual and research work (Lee, Jussim, & McCauley, 1995) on the concept challenges this view of stereotype. This recent work recognizes that stereotyping is an inevitable outcome of cognition. A stereotype is simply a schema; it is a form of mental categorization that is essential for understanding our world. Basically, schemas (stereotypes) are summaries of our experience. To say that using stereotypes (schemas) is wrong, or to say that we should "avoid stereotyping", is to say that we should not learn from experience; we should not think.

The recent work also points out that not all stereotypes are negative. Many stereotypes are positive (e.g., nurses are caring) or neutral (e.g., basketball players are tall).

The more current also challenges the negative implication that stereotypes are overgeneralized and inaccurate. All categorizations are generalizations in the sense that they are abstractions from experience. As generalizations, they are probabilistic; they apply to most, but not all events or instances in the category. It is overgeneral only if applied in an all-or-none fashion. For example, to say "nurses are caring" is a positive stereotype that is accurate in the sense that is applies to most nurses. The fact that we occasionally encounter an uncaring nurse does not invalidate the stereotype. The stereotype serves a positive function, saving us the effort and time of re-initiating the impression formation process each and every time we encounter a nurse.

The more recent view, to which we subscribe, places stereotype in the category of schema or belief. Beliefs can be positive or negative and accurate or inaccurate. Certainly, as diversity practitioners, we should be concerned with addressing negative and inaccurate stereotypes. However, the prevailing stereotype of stereotypes as invariably negative and inaccurate is in itself inaccurate and overgeneral. We cannot address the category of stereotypes, which are negative and inaccurate by attacking all stereotypes.

There is also a growing body of research on stereotype that addresses the view that stereotypes are applied to (imposed on) others in an invariant fashion. An accumulating body of work (e.g., Eagly, Ashmore, Makhijani, & Longo, 1991) indicates that regardless of group membership, if individuating information is or becomes available the perceiver will take that information into account. In other words, we take into account specific information about individuals, even when it contradicts our stereotype. The stereotype, accurate or not, guides our thinking and behavior mostly at times when we are not in contact with individual members of the stereotyped group. Of course, one implication of this is that individuals who challenge the stereotype become special cases;

they do not result in a change in the stereotype.

One area in which stereotyping has often been implicated as having negative effects is in the educational system. In particular teachers have been accused of treating students according to stereotypes, creating a self-fulfilling prophecy. The self-fulfilling prophecy, first described by Rosenthal and Jacobsen (1966) refers to the observation that teacher expectations cause them to treat students differently, resulting in student behavior that confirms the stereotype. However, numerous studies have failed to replicate the self-fulfilling prophecy effect. A recent, very comprehensive study (Jussim, & Eccles, 1995) of teacher stereotypes, using multiple teachers, classrooms, and spanning a considerable time, found teacher perceptions to be highly accurate. There was no consistent evidence of self-fulfilling prophecy or stereotype. Since the status of the self-fulfilling prophecy is unclear at this time, we will not consider it further.

Our definition of the concept of stereotype will require revision and updating if we are to continue to become better diversity practitioners. But first we must be willing to consider the function that stereotype serves in our own view of prejudice and discrimination.

Contact Hypothesis

A long-standing idea in prejudice reduction is that if we can produce contact between groups we can reduce prejudice and discrimination. Sherif's (1966) work supports the contact hypothesis, but the contact must occur in the right circumstances. Most contact among groups is ineffectual. For example, in many high schools, which are highly diverse, students remain racially and ethnically segregated. The key is to create situations, which increase meaningful contact between groups. Some of this meaningful contact includes interdependence, such as producing common goals. In addition, in order for contact to be successful, there has to be equal status among members of the group. True interdependence insures that equal status is created. Contact works best when it is frequent and lengthy, and schools and work places often provide the best opportunities. For example, Diamond (2001) has found that contact in the classroom with children with disabilities greatly improves attitudes of young children toward children with disabilities.

Jigsaw Classroom

Aronson and his colleagues (Aronson, *et. al.*, 1978) developed an approach to working with prejudice in the classroom that involved creating an environment promotive of positive interpersonal, interracial, and intergender attitudes. He called this cooperative learning arrangement the jigsaw classroom. In the jigsaw classroom, children are divided into subgroups of five to six individuals. They are set to work on a task, or asked to solve a problem or question. Each child is given a different portion of the material or information required to solve the problem or complete the task. This task arrangement requires the children to work cooperatively in order to integrate the information. Since each child has some of the information, they are interdependent, and of equal status. It creates a problem-solving environment that cuts across ability, because each child, regardless of ability, has a necessary piece of the information. It is important to compose groups skillfully across gender, race, ability, and other important dimensions.

Aronson discovered that this process was beneficial in improving attitudes about gender, race, and ability. "Smarter kids" don't view the "not-so-smart kids" as negatively, and vice-versa. Also, there are significant self-esteem benefits for the children and the social relations in the classroom improve (Slavin & Cooper, 1999). Through this approach the teacher is less linear and controlling, and achieves better results than in more controlling classrooms. The educational benefits are better as compared to normal classrooms, and there is less stress and conflict. This jigsaw arrangement is difficult to produce, and it requires a creative, committed teaching staff. However, it doesn't require increased resources. Even when instituted on a small scale, there are benefits. The same effects could be produced in the work place, where tasks can be constructed to equalize impact and contributions of workers. Several studies, in a variety of school conditions have demonstrated the effectiveness of the jigsaw arrangement (e.g., Walker & Crogen, 1998).

Conclusion

It is appropriate to end our discussion with a consideration of jigsaw groups, because most of the concepts considered in the chapter are represented in the jigsaw arrangement. There is evidence that the impressions and attitudes formed during the experience are more positive. The arrangement also demonstrates the importance of power, interdependence, and contact. It is a metaphor for the type of social environment we, as diversity professionals are trying to create.

References

Allport, G. W. (1954). *The nature of prejudice.* Cambridge, MA: Addison – Wesley.

Allport, G. W. (1968). The historical background of modern social psy chology. In G. Lindzey & E. Aronson (Eds.), *Handbood of social psychology.* Vol. 7, 1 – 80. Cambridge, MA: Addison – Wesley.

Aronson, E., Stephen, C. , Sikes, J. , Blaney, N. , & Snapp, M. (1978). *The jigsaw classroom.* Beverly Hills: Sage Publications.

Asch, S. E. (1946). Forming impressions of personality. *Journal of Abnormal and Social Psychology, 41*, 258 – 290.

Asch, S. E. (1955). Opinions and social pressures. *Scientific American, 193*, 31 –35.

Baumeister, R. F. , & Leary, M.R. (1995). The need to belong and desire of interpersonal attachment as a fundamental human motivation. *Psychological Bulletin, 117*, 497 – 529.

Brehm, S. , & Brehm, J. W. (1981). *Psychological reactance: A theory of freedom and control.* New York: Academic Press.

Caciappo, J. T. , & Petty, R. E. (1986). Social processes. In G. H.

Coles , E. Dunchin , & S.W. Porgus (Eds.). *Psychophysiology.* New York: Guilford Press.

Cialdini, R. B., Vincent, J.E., Lewis, S.K., Cataliani, J., Wheeler, D., & Darby, B.L.(1975). Reciprical concessions procedure for inducing compliance: The door-in-the-face technique. *Journal of Personality and Social Psychology, 31*, 206 – 215.

Cook, M. (1977). Gaze and mutual gaze in social encounters. *American Scientist,* 65, 328 – 333.

Diamond, K. E. (2001). Relationships among young children's ideas, emotional understanding, and social contact with classmates with disabilities. *Topics in Early Childhood Special Education, 21* (2), 104 – 113.

Deci, E .L. , & Ryan, R. M. (1985). *Intrinsic motivation and self-deter mination in human behavior.* New York: Plenum.

Eagly, A. H. , Ashmore, R. D. , Makhijani, M. G. , & Longo, L. (1991). What is beautiful is good, but...: A meta-analytic review of research on the physical attractiveness stereotype. *Psychological Bulletin, 110,* 109 – 128.

Ekman, P., & Friesen, W.V. (1971). Constants across cultures in the face and emotion. *Journal of Personality and Social Psychology, 17*, 124 - 129.

Festinger, L. (1954). A theory of social comparison processes. *Human Relations*, 7, 117 – 140.
Festinger, L. (1957). *A theory of cognitive dissonance*. Stanford: Stanford University Press.
Fishbein, M. , & Ajzen, I. (1974). Attitudes toward objects as predictive of single and multiple behavioral criteria. *Psychological Review, 81*, 59 – 74.
Freedman, J. L. , & Fraser, S. C. (1966). Compliance without pressure. The foot-in-the-door technique. *Journal of Personality and Social P sychology*, 4, 195 – 202.
French, J. R. P. , & Raven, B. (1959). *The bases of social power.* Oxford, England: University of Michigan.
Hall, E.T. (1966). *The hidden dimension*. New York: Doubleday.
Hovland, C.I. , Lumsdaine, A.A., & Sheffield, F.D. (1949). *Experiments on mass communication. Studies in social psychology in World War II* (Vol. III). Princeton, N.J.: Princeton University Press.
Imai, Y. (1994). Effects of influencing attempts on the perceptions of powerholders and the powerless. *Journal of Social Behavior and Personality, 9*, 455 – 468.
Jones, E. E. , & Davis, K.E. (1965). From acts to dispositions: the attit bution process in person perception. In L. Berkowitz (Ed.). *Advances in experimental social psychology* (Vol. 2). New York: Academic Press.
Jussim, L.J. , & Eccles, J. (1995). Are teacher expectations biased by students' gender, social class, or ethnicity? In Y. Lee, L. Jussim, & C. McCauley (Eds.). *Stereotype accuracy*, (pp. 245 – 271). Washington, D.C.: American Psychological Association.
Katz, D. (1960). The functional approach to the study of attitudes. *Public Opinion Quarterly, 24,* 163 – 204.
Katz, D. , & Braly, K. W. (1935). Racial prejudice and racial stereotypes. *Journal of Abnormal and Social Psychology*, *30*, 175 – 193.
Kelley, H.H. (1973). The process of causal attribution. *American Psychologist*, 28, 107 – 128.
Kelley, H.H. (1979). *Pesonal relationships: Their structures and processes*. Hillsdale, NJ: Lawrence Erlbaum.
Lerner, M.J. (1980). *The belief in a just world: A fundamental delusion.* New York: Plenum.
LaPierre, R.T. (1934). Attitudes versus actions. *Social Forces, 13,* 230 – 237.

Lee, Y. , Jussim, L.J. , & McCauley, C.R. (1995). *Stereotype accuracy: Toward appreciating group differences*. Washington, D.C.: American Psychological Association.

McGuire, W.J. (1964). Inducing resistance to persuasion: Some con temporary approaches. In L. Berkowitz (Ed.) *Advances in experi mental social psychology*. (Vol. 1). San Diego: Academic Press.

Mehrabian, A. (1970). A semantic spare for nonverbal behavior. *Journal of Consulting and Clinical Psychology*, *35*, 248 – 257.

Rice, B. (1985, September). Performance review: The job nobody likes. *Psychology Today*, 30 – 36. Rosenthal, R., & Jacobson, L. (1966). Teachers' expectancies: Determinants of pupil IQ gains. *Psychological Reports*, *19* (1), 115 – 118.

Ross, L. (1977). The intuitive psychologist and his shortcomings: Distortions in the attribution process. In L. Berkowitz (Ed.). *Advances in experimental social psychology*. (Vol. 10) New York: Academic Press.

Sherif, M. (1937). An experimental approach to the study of attitudes. *Sociometry*, *1*, 90 – 98.

Sherif, M. (1966). *In common predicament. Social psychology of inter group conflict and comparison*. Boston: Houghton Mifflin.

Slavin, R.E. , & Cooper, R. (1999). Improving intergroup relations: Lessons learned from cooperative learning programs. *Journal of Social Issues*, *55* (4), 647 – 663.

Snyder, M. (1987). *Public appearances / private realities: The psychol ogy of self-monitoring*. New York: Freeman.

Swann, W. B., Jr. (1984). Quest for accuracy in person perception: A matter of pragmatics. *Psychological Review*, *91*, 457 – 475.

Swann, W.B., Jr. (1987). Identify negotiation: Where two roads meet. *Journal of Personality and Social Psychology*, *53*, 1038 – 1051.

Swann, W.B., Jr. (1997). The trouble with change: Self-verification and allegiance to the self. *Psychological Science*, *8*, 177 – 180.

Thibaut, J.W., & Kelley, H.H. (1959). *The social psychology of groups*. Oxford, England: John Wiley.

Vescio, T.K. , & Biernat, M. (1999). When stereotype-based expectan cies impair performance: The effect of prejudice, race, and target quality on judgments and perceiver performance. *European Journal of Social Psychology*, *29*, 961 – 969.

Walker, I., & Crogan, M. (1998). Academic performance, prejudice, and the jigsaw classroom: New pieces to the puzzle. *Journal of*

Community & Applied Social Psychology, 8, 381 – 393.

Weiner, B. (1995). *Judgments of responsibility: A foundation for theory of social conduct.* New York: Guilford.

Chapter VI

Developing Cultural Competence Through Use of Self

Lalei Gutierrez
Philip Belzunce

Introduction

An important aspect of developing cultural competence involves increasing one's awareness of self as a cultural being. In this chapter, we will discuss models of developing cultural competence through the use of self in the contextual field of diversity. The self is a psychological construct that refers to the inner, private world of experience or one's inner landscape. Each person has his/her own personal boundaries for the self and has a sense when one is out of his/her comfort zone. Thus, the term, use of self, refers to experiencing the present environment in relationship to the self. Terms such as self-responsible, self-challenging and fully present characterize use-of-self. When we experience the relationship of self and environment (use of self) with awareness and intention, we can use ourselves as tools for behavioral change — others, as well as our own (Plummer, 1999).

In this chapter we will first explore the concept of holism as described by scholar, Ken Wilbur. This concept lays the conceptual groundwork for understanding the Being and Ground Sequences Models. Both of these models illustrate the concept of use of self and have particular application to diversity work.

Holism and Use of Self

We are not born on this earth in a vacuum. No one goes through life always and absolutely alone. In order to survive, we need others, whether we connect through persons, family, society, or culture. The starting point of the paradigm considered in this chapter, the holism paradigm, is to realize that everything is connected to everything else and that all reality, all living beings and things are interconnected (Wilbur, 1996). According to this holographic view, an experience, an event, an interaction, whether political, cultural, social, familial, psychological, or physical, is not an isolated occurrence, affecting only the immediate surroundings, but has reverberations elsewhere, and replications of these patterns can be observed in other levels of system.

Let us begin by acknowledging that you are reading this chapter. How you are approaching this reading material may vary. You may be reading each word, skimming through the material, jotting down notes to yourself that may come in the form of questions, associations, memories, thoughts, and feelings. You may be eating or drinking as you read. However you are proceeding, this pattern has been replicated numerous times, in many different contexts, and by others who approach reading similarly.

Another principle of Holism asserts that we are also more than just a collection of parts, for each part/piece of us contains our whole. This is expressed in the physical world in our genes, wherein each cell contains our whole genetic makeup. Another way of putting it is that all that there was, is, and will be is within each of us. Our personal his/her story contains multitudes of interactions transmitted to us by culture, religion, school, family, society, community, and world events, all affecting how we view life, our values, prejudices, biases, and beliefs about God, our world, and ourselves.

Since time is holographic, each aspect exists everywhere, all the time and in all times. We know that an event in the past can be threaded through the tapestry of our present world experience. These many replications of patterns of interaction become our very own "dance," encoded in the many replications of familial and cultural patterns of interaction. Each of us in this "now" has access to all other moments.

Whoever we are, we bring these personalized, aware or unaware patterns — "the dance" — wherever we go. Many of these patterns have a mythology or values transmitted to us — multigenerationally and culturally — by our environment. These may now be our daily, unquestioned reality, taken as truth, defining how we live our lives, how we make meaning of what we see, hear and do, and how we relate to one another and to people of other cultures.

In the holographic view, connecting with our "parts" or "selves" is embedded in connections to our greater, whole Self, which has more power, creativity, love, and wisdom than do any of our separate parts. Likewise, any group of people together create a greater whole that has more power, love, creativity, and wisdom than each of those people could generate, taken separately, or than the sum of their individual efforts could provide.

The brief explanations above have significant implications as we embark on a course of exploring our inner landscape (i.e. the self). In discovering our diversity within, we open ourselves to an enlightening and coming-to-consciousness process; we allow possibilities and shifts in perception and understanding; and we heal ourselves from the stuckness of frozen patterns of relating to ourselves and others. In taking the journey into ourselves, we are exploring the ground-contexts of the diversities in culture and family that we carry within, and open to choices that contribute to healing our relations to self, to our significant relations, to others, to our earth, and to our world.

In our development as diversity consultants, we need to realize that we affect our clients through our personal encounters with them —both in how we are and what we do. As we become conscious of our beliefs, world view, guiding life metaphors, values, needs, fantasies, fears, moods, thoughts, wishes, and feelings, and as we become more embodied in our experience, we are aware of our presence, as well as what our presence evokes in others. The more we are committed to our process of embracing our diverse parts — not only our strengths but also our shadow — the more we connect with the essence of our beingness, and the more we can use ourselves authentically as instruments in the work of diversity.

We hold that the basic reality in the universe is essence, or "energy," the universal life force. This includes our personal essence (our Thou-ness) and the essence of everything else combined, called universal essence. We believe that all creation comes out of that essence: our consciousness, sensations, being-ness, feelings, mind, and matter, including our physical body. Our interest is not in imposing "correct" wholeness, but to support diversity professionals in:

*(1)*heightening their awareness of their creative adjustments to the external environment through the Ground Sequences and the development of racial/cultural identity;

*(2)*experiencing an embodied connection with him/herSELF (physically, emotionally, mentally, spiritually);

*(3)*accessing and developing internal supports and a larger repertoire of skills and stances from which to choose in any given environment, as they authentically embody their use of self as instrument in the work.

Since, for a diversity professional, our main tool is our **self**, it is of utmost importance that we continually attend to our **use of self as instrument**. The challenge is to continuously participate in our life — integration of our intellectual, emotional, cultural, physical, and spiritual dimensions. Healthy passion is working on becoming more aware and bringing balance to the many aspects of our being. Healthy passion propels us to be a *presence*, a *witness*, a *facilitator*, a *role model*, a **being** that evokes hope, interest, energy, aspiration, positive expectation, appreciation of difference, self-caring, and dialogue. As diversity professionals continue to attend to their growth, development and transformation, what they have to offer their clients will change. For example, in the practice of grounding and rooting in Chi-Kung meditation exercises, we support ourselves in energetically developing our physical self to hold the wide range of human emotions/reactions, and through our grounded trust in the process of transformation, we can be a presence as intervener to groups/facilitator of organizational changes. As we become at home within ourselves, our essence radiates and touches the other's Thou-ness, thus providing the climate for exploration, growth, and transformation.

On a more pragmatic and whole-health level, one of the challenges for the diversity professional is the importance of self-care. This is particularly important because of the intensity, the complexity, and the maximal capacity for this work to trigger survival "trauma trances" encountered in the "isms" or destructive beliefs and attitudes, embedded in multigenerational cultural conditioning. The diversity professional will need to have support systems in place for physical, emotional, mental, and spiritual well-being such as physical exercise, meditation, energetic healing and massage, and a multicultural, collegial team support. Without these, diversity professionals render themselves vulnerable to the stress of the profession: imbalance, burnout, and health problems. The Being Model and Ground Sequence Model explained in the following sections are frameworks for enriching our understanding of the dynamic interplay of environment and use of self.

Being Model

There were seven adults in the room. We had been discussing the agenda for forty-five minutes when the wife of one of the members walked in carrying a six-month-old baby girl in her arms. Immediately, we seven participants shifted our attention to this small, smiling person — and for the next hour, we serious adults were transformed into gurgling, cooing beings, spontaneously inventing hilariously childish gestures and expressions with our hands, faces, and bodies — entertaining ourselves along with the baby.

What makes these little beings so attractive, so compelling, that their presence can turn almost any serious event into an amusing and jovial occasion? Babies are precious, complex, vital, full of life — vessels of spontaneity. Babies — no matter what their shapes, sizes, or colors — captivate us. They are irresistible. We love to observe them and have fun with them. Babies are very real, natural, free, unconstrained, and spontaneous beings.

When babies are hungry, they let us know by crying. When they are happy, they tell us with their smiles. Babies are pure sensation and feelings. We get what we see, and, see what we get — they are pure beings. They respond in an effortless way, spontaneously and transparently.

With babies, we forget our past and our future. In their presence, we are in the present moment. They are pure beauty, and their beauty is not hidden. In communion with the beauty of their essence, one "is". Being in contact with their beingness in the present can change us. The contact can restore our own inner balance and beauty.

In their presence, we experience the mysteries of the spectacular glow of a sunset, the discovery of a truth, the incredible structure of a beautiful flower, the realization of harmony, the astonishment that comes from observing the perfection of a tree or a plant. Babies are the epitome of loveliness, gracefulness, elegance, delicacy, aliveness, freedom, and unadulterated sensitivity. Their very sensitivity is what makes them authentically alive.

Because of the aliveness and pureness of their beings, we see in babies our unrestrained and unmasked, sensitive selves. We can identify with their genuine beingness because we, too, are genuine beings.

Beingness cannot be demonstrated, or explained, or offered. Beingness is simply there, in all its immensity. We cannot touch it or see it. We can only look into its depths — and be aware.

Babies bring us back to a state of awareness of immensity, depths, vulnerability, innocence, and abandon. It is the state of awareness in which we are taken by a loving hand to discover the kingdom of wonders and marvels. It is the state of awareness in which we are placed in touch with our beingness — where the miracle of existence is renewed every day. Babies can bring us back to that blessed state of awareness and receptivity, a state from which we can start to learn, a place T.S. Eliot describes as "the still point" where we can truly dance.

The Environment and the External Self: Creative Adjustment

The baby's being is utterly open, free, and limitless. The baby's beingness is fundamentally simple — and so natural that it can never be complicated, corrupted, or stained. It is so pure that it is beyond even the concepts of purity and impurity.

As we grow up, whatever our lives are like, our beingness is always present. And it is always perfect, always untouched by change. It is pure, intelligent, radiant — an always awake, cognizant, and pristine awareness.

This inner core is the birthright of every human being. But as we become adults, this inner being becomes hidden, enveloped, and obscured by our process of growing up, a product of our interaction with our environment and our culture. Many times it is hard to recognize our beingness because it has become so encased, so wrapped up.

Our omnipresent being could be compared to the sun in the sky. Some days, especially in winter, we may see only the dark clouds and believe with conviction in the delusion that the sun is not present. But just because the bright sun is entirely obscured by the dark clouds, it does not mean the sun is not there, shining.

Why is it so difficult even to conceive of the depth and glory of our beingness? Why is it so hard — even in our best moments — to remember that the dark clouds are not the sun — that the sun is omnipresent?

Why is it so hard to recognize that these dark clouds can never stain nor diminish the sun in any way? Why does this seem such an outlandish and improbable idea?

In our daily lives, we seem to be always busying ourselves, grinding, grasping, running, hurrying up in order to be able to achieve, to obtain, to get, to have. Our environment has taught us to spend our lives reacting, instead of acting from our beingness. Our socialization experiences have emphasized our human *doingness* at the expense of our human *beingness*.

How did we become this way?

There are no quick and easy answers or solutions to this question. We must "come home" to the start of life in order to understand our process of growth and development in the context of our environment and culture. We all have to look back into the past in order to shed light on the origins of our ways of living in the present.

To understand our patterns of living, we need to be cognizant of the creative ways we, as helpless children, adapted to our environment and our culture in order to survive. The process of adapting to our childhood environment, of adjusting to either nurturing or problematic situations, was our way of being alive.

As children, we did whatever we had to do to create conditions of emotional safety — although sometimes these efforts were not sufficient to counter our problematic environment. The way we define and experience ourselves in the present is colored by — and an outgrowth of — our past interactions with our parents, relatives, teachers, etc. How we interact with others and define ourselves in our current lives is based not only in the reality we experience at the moment, but also the accumulated subjective and constructive lenses from which we draw our meanings.

The External Self

Notwithstanding the fact that we all regularly distinguish between the inner being and the external self, it is important to realize that these two selves are aspects of a single self. The inner being is what we were born with — it existed before we had to adjust to our healthy or harsh environments.

The external self is the product of how we as growing children reacted creatively to the environment. As human beings, we were born with not-too-many needs — to be held and caressed, to be fed, to be kept warm and dry, to be stimulated, to develop, and to grow up.

The child will do everything possible to have his/her needs recognized and fulfilled: crying when hungry, reaching out or kicking when needing to be touched, and so on.

If the child's needs to be changed, fed, or held go continuously unsatisfied, the baby will agonize until the parents are effectively aroused to address the situation and/or the baby shuts off the pain by shutting off the needs of the moment.

Since infants are helpless in satisfying their needs (for example, they cannot cook for themselves, cannot change themselves, etc.), they begin to develop ways of coping. One of these ways of coping may be to separate themselves from their sensations, from their consciousness.

This does not mean that these unanswered needs vanish into thin air. The reality is that while these needs may be buried, they will incessantly exert pressures, and the ways that children respond to these pressures become varied. Children's instinctive adjustment — that of separating their being from their needs and feelings — is the start of the stages of development of their external self. For some people, the genesis of separating their being from the external self may spring forth from one crucial or traumatic event; for most human beings, there may had been a slow process of seemingly insignificant or small omissions or commissions, which gradually could build into a major shattering. Sometimes the single crucial event may not necessarily be traumatic from an objective point of reality, while to the child's subjective perspective, it is.

The emergence of the development of a child's external self is not a conscious process. Rather, the growing child begins to react around the parents, and eventually with others, in the fashion expected by everybody.

Over time, as the child continues in the process of reacting this way, the behaviors become fixed, habituated, and automatic. These reactions are no longer at the command of the center of self, but become involuntary, unconscious, and thus automatic. They arise from the terrible feeling of powerlessness that comes when children feel that they will not be seen as themselves, no matter what they do. To realize that there is no way for them to be who they really are is intolerable to children. The only way open for them seems to be to develop a substitute self.

When infants' needs are not progressively met, children's connection with their inner self shuts down in stages. As these denials and deterrence of needs accumulate, critical shifts happen to children. These critical shifts hasten the development of the gap whereby individuals operate in a dual process involving both the inner being and the external self.

The external self is the mask for those feelings. It becomes the child's survival tool. It is important for children to develop this coping or external self, in order to survive and live in a situation where they can grow up. This may mean that children cannot be who they are. The demands of the environment may become the child's explicit and implicit command.

In order to survive, children begin to respond to their parents' needs and begin to struggle to fulfill them. As children grow up, the requirements for them to meet their environment's needs become greater and more complex.

A lamentable and extreme example of excessive parental demands was provided by a patient who came to psychotherapy sometime ago. Albert recalled that his parents — in order to boast to their neighbors and friends that they had a gifted child — pushed him to walk ahead of his time (among other unrealistic developmental demands). As a result, he suffered an irreparable and chronic problem with his legs. Albert also recalled that his parents' demands became more irrational and complex: they required him to get all A's in school, in spite of the fact that his IQ tests showed him to be a C student. They also pushed him to be the star player of the high school basketball team — even though he was physically handicapped.

In developing this external self, we generate different ways of coping, of reacting to external stimuli. The gap that has developed between the inner being and the external self may create a continuous state of emergency alert or tension. This alert tension may drive the child and eventually the adult toward seeking the satisfaction of his/her needs in any way possible.

Until they are fulfilled, continuously unanswered needs subvert any other human ventures. When these needs are not fulfilled, infants experience tension, a feeling of being disconnected from their beingness. Without that essential connection, children feel not their beingness, but their tension.

If the environment is good enough to support wholesome development, where the nurturing people involved allow infants to be healthily spontaneous in their feelings, the external self and the inner being have a semblance of integration. When children's needs are fulfilled by their natural ways of bidding, the pain of their needs is decreased, because the gap between their inner self and their ways of adjusting to their environment is minimal. The closer the relationship of the external self and the beingness, the healthier the individual is and becomes.

On the other hand, the greater the gap between the external self and the inner being, the greater the tendency for the individual to be unhealthy. The gap holds the message: "I am not worthy when I am me; I am not loved when I am really myself; and I am only loved when I lose me."

The gap between the inner being and external self comes about either when the environment is insensitive to the expressed needs of the child or when the child encounters frequently repeated negative responses.

As human beings we are extremely flexible and resilient toward the external demands imposed on us as children; nonetheless, children who undergo, day after day, the imposition of denial or disregard for what is going on inside them experience damaging effects.

Young people begin to mistrust their sensations and feelings; thus arise the beginnings of the disowning and shaming process. Children begin to focus their attention on their external self as a way of adjusting to and surviving an inadequately nurturing external reality. In order to survive, young children start to please the environment by thwarting their own needs.

The baby learns to react to the external reality by acquiescing to, warding off, combating against, and/or performing for that reality. The pattern becomes a matter of reacting for survival rather than responding to one's intrinsic needs, capacities, or behaviors.

As adults, such individuals would carry the same patterns of living and may continue to relate to their environment in the ways they developed in early childhood. Individuals with these patterns of relating are generally out of touch with these parts of themselves.

In other words, the being becomes the "passenger" and the external, reactive self becomes the "driver." As long as there is no sense of beingness available to the person, the environment is valued as an approving function. To a healthy individual, the reverse is true: the being is the driver and the external self is the passenger. The patterns of the healthy individual are based upon that which is intrinsic to the self, to the core being.

No one is exempt from having some parts of our inner self disowned. No one is exempt from creating unhealthy ways of coping with the not-so-completely-healthy environment. Obviously, no one is so totally whole as to have survived to adulthood without developing patterns or creative ways of contacting the environment that may have been functional when they emerged in childhood, but now may or may not be so beneficial in the context of the present grown-up lives.

These patterns in themselves are neutral. They have their own upsides and downsides. One upside to these patterns is that the person involved does not have to think or struggle to find a way to react in given situations. The person involved does not have pre-planned ways of reacting to these circumstances.

Different schools of psychological and psychiatric thought, and various religious persuasions have named these inner "automatic pilots" as shadows, id, devils, dark sides, resistances, demons, monsters, and so on. Whatever we choose to call these repetitive patterns, the bottom line is that these habituated ways of behaving and responding have lives of their own and thus are not governed by our own inner self.

The struggle of these habituated ways of living against our own beingness becomes endless while the gap, the chasm that was earlier developed, remains unresolved.

Paradoxically, it is that constant struggle that continually drives us to seek temporary antidotes that will prevent us from feeling the pain. Yet those struggles have lives of their own, and they drive us away from truly resolving the great pain. In this process of struggling, the inner self loses the most fundamental and intrinsic value of being able to choose in order to be a healthy human being.

The Gap

If we happen to see that the tail is wagging the dog, then we know we have a big problem. Indeed, we do have a big problem when the external self drives the inner being. It may seem outlandish, but for many, this is the reality we are confronted with, every day of our lives.

Sometimes we wake up sweating from our nightmares and fearfully wonder, "Who am I?" Before we could even consider answering this most important and fundamental question, we have finished eating our breakfast and have gone back to our blind, hurrying lives as if nothing had happened — like a gerbil running endlessly in a circular cage, we are a prisoner of our own vicious circle.

Perhaps we keep telling ourselves that we need to stop and look and change our lives by examining and reflecting into the meaning of life. But we seem to be afraid to pause and give ourselves the time to do just that. We seem to be afraid to face the inner unknowns, to begin an inward journey through the dark tunnels of our souls. If we can tolerate the darkness, we may have a chance to look inward — toward a being that we might experience as both pristine and surprisingly wonderful.

But our lives seem to be possessed and swept by a certain momentum that carries us away; we experience ourselves as having no choice or control over it. Knowingly or unknowingly we turn away, run away, or go away.

Our modern culture triumphs in leading our external selves to its own ends — and celebrates the fact — thus discouraging people from realizing that there is more to life than its barren distractions.

And we allow this supposedly modern and sophisticated culture-machine to continually condition us, to assault us from every angle, and to lead us to distraction from our inner beings. We may turn on the television or the radio or read the newspaper just to deflect ourselves from grappling with our own private wars. And so the gap between the external self and our inner beings continues to widen.

Working and accompanying people on their journeys as a psychologist and consultant for more than twenty-seven years, I have been privileged to hear and experience people's deepest pains. I experienced my own inner wounds and theirs as I heard, saw and felt them struggling, avoiding, fumbling, grappling, searching for an oasis of comfort greater than the pain they encounter daily in their lives.

Hundreds of people — in their forties, fifties, sixties, and, even seventies — have confided to me, in different voices and words, the eternal gap, the infinite void they experience, asking the same and most basic question: "Who am I?"

In their voices, they declare:

(1)"I really do not know who I am. I don't feel I exist, but I try to go on living. It is a rat race and I am a prisoner of this race because I just don't know how to get out of it."

(2)"I hide me from me, from other people. I have no respect for myself; I hate myself and I hate those who treat me as a cripple, a sickie — even though I set myself up to be treated that way."

(3)"I try to follow what everybody tells me, hoping that I will be happy. I am confused because I thought if I did what everyone wants me to do, I would be happy. I knew I would not be happy, but I just keep trying to please everybody — even though it destroys me inside. I have no way off this merry-go-round."

(4)"I have a glimpse of me only when I get angry. Even getting angry is a struggle, because afterward I feel so guilty. When I fight with my husband, that means I have for a moment not given in, I've said no, and I feel my deep pain. Then I try to soothe him so that I soothe my own pain. Actually, I fall back on making him happy again because I am so afraid of the pain of him rejecting me, and of feeling my guilt at letting myself get angry."

(5)"I constantly fight with my partner so that I can avoid intimacy. I do not know how to be intimate. I am afraid of it, I run away from it. I feel a deep pain, because I want to love and be loved — but the pain of warding off closeness with someone is easier for me because it is familiar."

(6)"I try my best to get approval from everybody, but no one seems to see me or understand me. There is something wrong with everybody. Why can't they love me? If only someone will love me, I will love myself."

(7)"I am fifty-three years old and when my mother died recently,

I fell into the abyss. All my life, she had been continuously filling this deep hole — and now that she is gone, I do not know what to do."

(8)"I have tried alcohol, cocaine, marijuana, and LSD to avoid my emptiness. I feel high, but after a while ... I am lost."

(9)"All my life I have been running after money. Now I am filthy rich, and I am still unhappy. I knew then and I know now that money can never make anybody happy, but I had no choice; that is the only way I know to run from my demons."

(10) "Please help me to find me."

Let us summarize these different voices and sort out what they are saying. Because of the gap that exists between the external self and the inner being, we can categorize their voices in three areas:

(a)The parts of us that we had to repress because of the insensitiveness of our environment and our culture to our intrinsic and basic needs as a person;

(b)The parts of us that erected a façade in order to respond "adequately" to an inadequately nurturing environment and culture;

(c)The parts of us that disowned our beingness, so that we learned to focus externally in order to survive.

These unrecognized decisions and elements, which we erected as children in order to cope with our outer realities, formed the "personalities" we present to the world.

Though we may feel in our guts that "something" seems to be missing, that there seems to be a "hole" inside, the full realization of our inner beingness seems to be totally outside our awareness, outside our grasp. When we feel empty, confused, aimless, and heavy, the problem may not rest in our genes or chemistries. The problem may be that our environment and our culture have colluded, intentionally or unintentionally, to ensure that we continue to be out of touch with our inner core.

Ground Sequence Model

Figure/Ground

The concept of figure/ground provides a unique and relevant tool for conceptualizing issues of ethnicity and culture and the use of self in diverse contexts. We developed the Ground Sequence Model (see Figure 1.) when we served as faculty at the Gestalt Institute of Cleveland, practicing Couples and Family Therapy and leading the Small Systems Training Program. It was the culmination of our own experiences as Filipinos encountering our training as Gestalt therapists, our explorations of different models of family therapy, our education as psychologists, our training as diversity consultants, and our perceptions about the culture of counseling in the context of "American" culture.

This model provides a perspective that enlarges the possibilities of our gaining awareness of our use of self and opens those possibilities for assessment and intervention.

The present embodies both figure and ground. We may put our attention to *what stands out* for us in the moment, the *figure* (be that an issue, dilemma, feeling, behavior, sensation etc.), while the *ground* is *everything else* (the "given" context, structure, time, pattern etc.) that holds and frames the figure for each person in the interaction. The *ground of culture* is the "invisible present" for those who are immersed in the dominant culture; it can be taken as the implicit standard by which to view and compare self and (different) other. Ground is what is taken for granted, unnoticed or out of awareness. It embodies world-view, the acculturated, adaptive, and habitual styles of interaction with the environment. Ground influences the way we make meaning of experiences of communication, decision-making, implementation of action, and satisfaction/dissatisfaction.

For example, a committee is given the task of designing and implementing a closing activity for a physician who is leaving the medical team. The situation is seen as having the potential to be politically critical by the management of the hospital, which is working on creating an environment appreciative of diversity. There are a variety of feelings — ranging from relief to fear to anger to sadness to shame to guilt — that

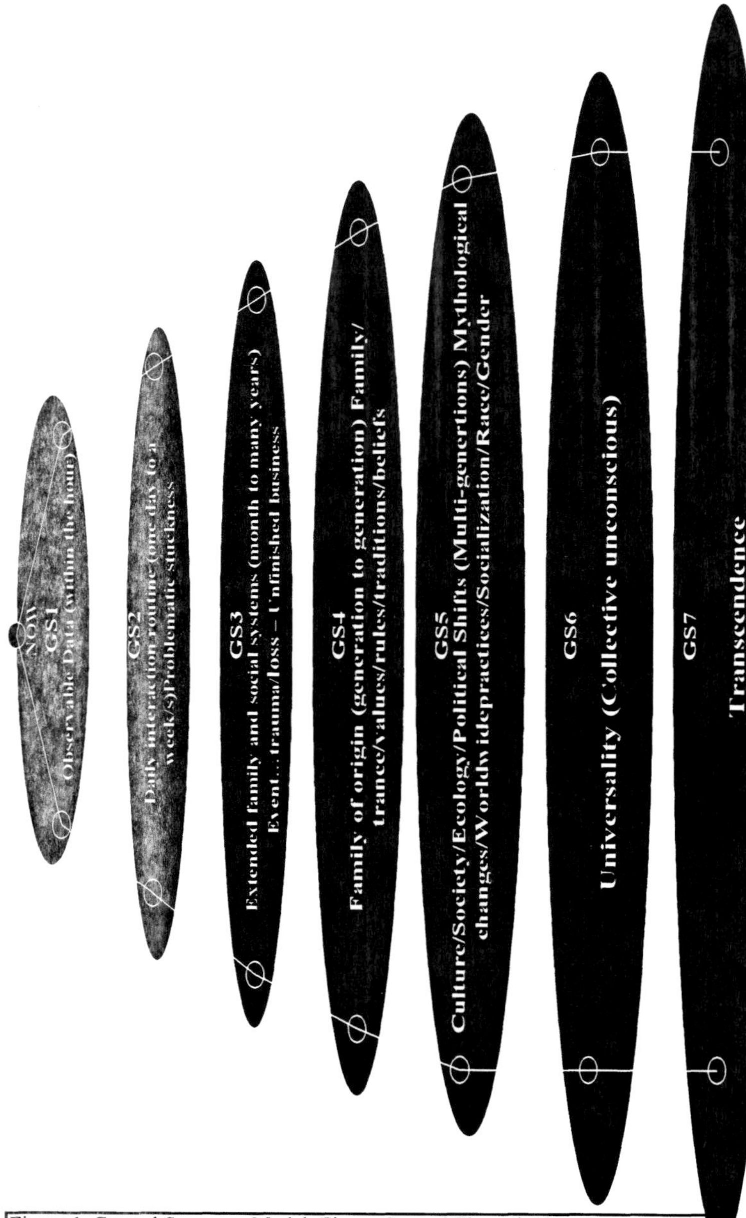

Figure 1. Ground Sequence Model: Figure Ground Through Time Sequence

are not being shared. The task is also complicated by the fact that this physician is a controversial black man — the only black physician in the department — whose competence is respected, envied, and questioned, who holds considerable power over the direction of the team, and whose terminal illness is known to a few, but not to all.

Projections are floating around and the atmosphere is tense. What is figural for the committee is the task. What is figural for the facilitator is the intensified arguing, which seems incongruous to the task on hand. What is not in the awareness of the committee is the ground (i.e., what is this event of departure evoking in all the members? What is being re-enacted, recreated? What is the hidden agenda? What is the pattern, the unfinished business being replayed in the different levels of ground? What assumptions, rules, values are operating?)

While it may appear that the committee is talking about the "same" task, their subjective figures (where they are focusing) may differ. Similarly, the impact of their shared and/or unshared ground is influencing the process of their current interactions and is hindering the committee in its effort to accomplish a satisfactory agreement concerning the plan and implementation of a closing event.

Even as persons of the same culture and ethnic background (with many aspects of shared ground, i.e. cultural values, common history, life experiences, and structures of relationships influenced by economic, ecological, social, and political realities in the larger society) may differ, cross-cultural encounters bring greater complexity in considerations of diversity because issues and themes that grow out of the other's ground may not easily become accessible, understood, or appreciated. When this diversity goes unacknowledged, unappreciated, unknown, the task is even made harder, particularly when there is the assumption that "for us to get along, for things to be right, we should all be feeling, thinking, doing in the same way."

In using the Ground Sequence (GS) model and the Being model as lenses by which to frame perceptions, the facilitator intervenes to engage the committee's participation through listening/hearing and being curious about each other's ground, as it is constituted in the present circumstances or as it is being evoked by the task and the situation that they, as a committee, are dealing with.

This approach helps the committee face the task of taking the large and complex field of perceptions and rendering from it something meaningful, so that they can interact in the current context in some useful and satisfying way, thereby supporting the committee in the accomplishment of their task.

More specifically, the field/ground consists of:

(1) *Inner sensations, feelings, and urges* (what is inside our organism), and *outer sensations* (comprised of our five senses and the environment of people, objects, and social systems).

(2) Our metaphors, meanings, and larger frames of experience are all shaped by our structures of ground, as culture, ethnicity, and religion. What we draw on, in order for us to attend to or to create new figures, is dependent on the richness or the diversity of our ground.

In the beginning phases of this consultation, we found it valuable to attend to the committee/client system's ground, in order to achieve a fuller appreciation of the contextual field affecting the task at hand (goal, objectives, action plans, strategy, etc.). Their experience of having their diversity heard, seen, acknowledged, and understood supported their rising to an energized common focus that honored their diversity. In the middle phases, we worked collaboratively with the committee on the task (closure program for the departing physician) and process figure (honoring their diversity). In the ending phases of consultation, the committee debriefed their work together, expressing their appreciation of having learned from their diversity and of having gained a stimulating, energizing, working team that was different from what it had been when they started.

Ground Sequence Levels

Experiences are embedded in one's own ground, in the constructs one makes of one's perceptual field (Constructivism). Using the GS Levels as a lens, we get a view of the client system's self (mapper) and their relevant ground (their pre-given world) as they exist in context, together, in history, and in development of background, through:

(1) Exploring/assessing the level of embeddedness of a present-

ing issue, dilemma, or theme, and examining how data is organized (narrative/story) for their unique experience of the issue.

(2) Noticing/selecting the GS Level that seems energized and available as a fruitful point of entry for collaborative work.

(3) Reading/assessing feedback from interventions in that GS Level with an openness to information regarding other GS Levels.

(4) Allowing for shifts, when necessary, to other GS Levels — with appropriate interventions.

(5) Assessing in the context of culturally responsive intervention.

(6) Developing a thematic metaphor to hold the complex phenomena/dynamics of figure and ground/field in diversity assessment and intervention.

(7) Attending to differentiation between process (observable and inferred HOW) and content (WHAT).

(8) Appreciating "sacred" ground evoked from GS Levels work.

Ground Sequence Levels Exercise

We offer two exercises to illustrate the model. We suggest that you put everything aside and find a quiet place for reflection. Take a comfortable position. Have before you your GS Levels Diagram (see Figure 1), paper, and a pen, pencil, or crayon. You may also choose to play some reflective music in the background.

GROUND SEQUENCES EXERCISE 1: Reflection

Let us start this presentation with a reflection exercise. You can color, doodle, or write on paper or a flip chart. Follow this exercise step by step.

I. Identify a behavior of yours that has occurred within the past hour. Give this behavior a color, a melody, or a movement. For our purposes, we shall call it Behavior X. Notice what you are saying to yourself about Behavior X. Notice what was going on around you during this hour, and to whom Behavior X is responding or reacting. Notice what need(s) you have that Behavior X is meeting. Describe how Behavior X is helping/benefiting you at this moment. Notice how Behavior X is hindering you at this moment. (See Fig. 1, GS Level 1.)

GS1 — Observations of phenomenological data in the present (within the last hour).

- *Observe present behavior, how the content of conversation is being portrayed in present behavior or in the current interactional pattern.*
- *Observe strengths — what is working well?*
- *Watch for stuckness, for what is not working.*
- *Be aware of present observable ground: ethnic origin, race, cultural characteristics, language, and communication process*

II. Now, let yourself go through your daily or weekly routine. Notice when Behavior X occurs. Describe the context. Notice who is there. What are you saying to yourself? What is the interaction? What are you trying to accomplish (goal) or what need are you meeting? Who is Behavior X helping/hindering? Who is benefiting? (GS2.)

GS2 — Routine, rituals of day/week, repetitive pattern/sequence, or problematic stuckness that has built up over time.

Frequently, when GS1 is addressed, the client will spontaneously reveal how that issue, experience, interaction is calibrated and embedded in a GS2 sequence (which is played out over one day to a week, often depending on daily routines of the client couple/family).

III. Now, let yourself go to a time in a month or year — perhaps when certain events tend to occur: i.e., anniversaries (birthdays, death, divorce, trauma, loss, etc.), monthly or annual meetings, reunions, holidays, etc. What is the event? Describe the context in which Behavior X occurs. Who are the players in this event, and who is Behavior X helping/hindering? Notice repetitive patterns of interactions. What need is Behavior X meeting? (GS3.)

GS3 — Extended family/social systems (e.g., educational, legal, medical) that are part of the repetitive, replicating patterns of interaction or problematic interaction over a period of years.

✦ *Stories of personal trauma, loss, death — where stuckness occurred: how family/system/community responded to the trauma.*

✦ *Unfinished business (heightened in anniversary days). Attempts to finish, showing replications in GS2 and GS1.*

✦ *Economic status, educational status, occupational, and social networks.*

✦ *Family as supportive group.*

✦ *Supportive institutions in ethnic/cultural community.*

IV. Now, as you revisit your family of origin, perhaps choosing a particular time when you were a child and living at home or with your caretakers, what scenario do you see? Notice whose behavior in your family of origin Behavior X mirrors. Assign a color to designate Mirrored Behavior X (MBX). What is the context of MBX? Who is benefiting or being helped with MBX? What values, beliefs, or stories did you hear or experience about MBX? Were there stories of immigration, relocation, translocation, and acculturation? (GS4.)

GS4 — Family of Origin: sequences of patterns from generation to generation.

✦ *Process/variables, structures.*

✦ *Family stories, myths, roles, rules, encoded values, beliefs, religious/spiritual influences/practices on psychological effects of health/illness.*

✦ *Worldview of family group.*

(May calibrate/embed shorter GS3, GS2, and GS1 sequence/patterns. Events in one generation mirror events and processes in previous generations.)

✦ *Immigration, relocation, translocation, acculturation, dislocation.*

V. Take a look at the culture(s) in which your family of origin lived. Which groups of people's habits, customs, practices, and socio-political roles did MBX replicate, and is Behavior X representing? If members of your family of origin's cultural group were to comment on value(s) that MBX and Behavior X uphold, what would they say? Is MBX and Behavior X acceptable behavior in your cultural group? Who is benefiting or being helped? (GS5.)

GS5 — Transcultural generations: culture, race, nationality, gender, ethnicity, language, religion, socio-political, ecological, "isms."

✦ *Primarily in awareness — surface and folk culture: fine arts, literature, drama, classical music, popular music, folk dancing, games, cooking, dress.*

✦ *Primarily out of awareness — deep culture: mental/behavioral process of ethnic/cultural group; healing/health practices, customs, ideals governing child-raising, patterns of superior/subordinate relations, definition of sin, courtship practices, conception of justice, incentives to work, notions of leadership, relationships to time, tempo of work, patterns of group decision-making, conception of cleanliness, attitudes toward the dependent, theory of disease, approaches to problem-solving, conception of status mobility, eye behavior, roles in relation to status, age, sex, class, occupation, kinship, conversational patterns in various social contexts, conception of past and future, definition of insanity, nature of friendship, conception of "self," patterns of visual perception, preference for competition or cooperation, body language, social interaction rate, notions of adolescence, notions about logic and validity, patterns of handling emotions, facial expressions, arrangements of physical space.*

(May calibrate/embed shorter GS4, GS3, GS2, and GS1 patterns.)

VI. Now, take a moment and notice your breathing, your body sensations as you went through steps I to V. As you scan your experience, notice which level holds the most energy (has the most interest) for you. Which level has the least energy? Which level do you want to avoid? Where do you feel stuck? Where do you feel excited? Write down your experience.

If you wish, you may focus on the level that stands out for you. Notice where in your body you are experiencing feeling sensations. Describe your sensations; write or draw them.

Sharing with a Partner

Share with your partner what you experienced through the different GS Levels of this exercise. What awarenesses are you having about the ground of Behavior X? As you share with each other, be aware of your experience in your dyad.

Group Processing

Hear from each dyad about their experience, awareness, and learning. Draw from their experience to inform teaching on GS levels in the concept of figure/ground, systems intervention, holistic assessment/intervention, and multicultural perspectives.

Conclusion

In closing this chapter, we are reminded of Wilber's (1996) examination, in a work of unparalleled scope and originality, the course of evolution as the unfolding manifestation of Spirit, a Tao, a Way, a Current of the Cosmos. His, integrative vision of diverse domains points to the direction we take if we are to participate is allowing "global transformation" to become reality. In moving through the diverse manifestations of the Present Current, we find that richer and "deeper level, a Tao, a Way, a Current of the Cosmos, from which we have not and could never deviate." As diversity consultants we see our work , centered in the Use of Self , as being present to this deeper Current, this Tao. Our work is to allow the appreciation of Beingness and Wholeness to manifest, as that "there are more things in heaven and earth than are dreamt of in one's worldview." Herein lies the possibility of global transformation.

REFERENCES

Plummer, D. L. (1999). Lecture notes for *Diversity Theories Workshop.*

Wilber, K. , (1996). *A brief history of everything,* Boston, MA: Shambhala Publications, Inc.

Chapter VII

Diversity and Group Dynamics

Victoria Winbush
Jacqueline McLemore

Introduction

This chapter describes the evolution of group dynamics and diversity as separate fields of interest, which ultimately intersected in the production of a rich field of empirical and descriptive studies. Drawing upon these studies, key considerations are identified for effectively engaging organizational work groups who have heterogeneous memberships. This discussion is directed at expanding the knowledge and skill repertoires of persons responsible for the functioning and success of groups within organizations. These persons include but may not be limited to those with the role and title of diversity professional, those in executive and line management positions, as well as internal and external organizational development consultants.

Definitions of Group Dynamics, Work Group and Diversity

Group dynamics is here defined as "the field of inquiry dedicated to advancing knowledge about the nature of group life" (Cartwright & Zander, 1968). The terms work group and team are used here interchangeably to describe groups operating within the organizational setting. Specifically, these terms are used to describe a collection of individuals who possess the following characteristics (Guzzo & Dickson, 1996, p. 308):

- ✦See themselves and are seen by others as a social entity
- ✦Are interdependent because of the tasks they perform
- ✦Are embedded in one or more larger social systems within the organization
- ✦Perform a task that affects others

There are many types of teams that operate concurrently within organizations. For example, Gross and Wagner (Gross, 1995; Wagner, 1995) use the categories of parallel team, process team and project team. Parallel teams are those where individuals typically have other duties that impact their performance on the team. Process teams are charged with completing a process as opposed to producing a product. Project teams are charged with completing all the steps in a specific task from start to finish. In terms of duration, teams can be ongoing or time limited in nature.

When examining the interplay of diversity and group dynamics a broad definition of diversity is viewed as most useful. The definition of diversity presented by Larkey (1996) is sufficiently inclusive to account for the many dimensions of diversity, which can be present in a group. Larkey defines diversity as "the differences in worldviews or subjective culture, resulting in potential behavioral differences among cultural groups and differences in identity among group members in relation to other groups". Based on this definition individual work group members can span the continuum from homogeneity to heterogeneity on the following elements of diversity (McGrath, Berdahl, & Arrow, 1995, p. 22):

- ✦Demographic attributes that are socially meaningful in the larger context in which the organization exists (e.g., race, ethnicity, gender, sexual orientation, physical status, religion and education)
- ✦Task-related knowledge, skills and abilities
- ✦Values, beliefs and attitudes
- ✦Personality and cognitive and behavioral styles
- ✦Status in the organization in which the work group is located (e.g., organizational rank, occupational specialty, departmental affiliation, tenure)

Understandably, this chapter cannot address all forms of diversity, which operate in work groups. The primary, though not exclusive, focus taken here is on the various dimensions of demographic diversity and their interaction with group dynamics. This is not to diminish the importance and impact of other aspects of diversity, but more in recognition that demographic differences have been a central focus of more recent research on group dynamics in organizations. This is not surprising given how the demographic landscape of organizations dramatically shifted in the later decades of the 20th century.

The Emergence of Group Dynamics and Diversity as Fields of Study

The development of group dynamics as a field of study emerged in the United States toward the end of the 1930's and began to blossom following World War II. Social scientists were beginning to produce empirical research studies to document the realities and functioning of group life. Factors such as the impact of group norms and the consequences of different leadership styles could now be objectively measured. (Cartwright & Zander, 1968)

The study of group dynamics was embraced by not only the business sector of society, but by government, military and education as well. Business had a particular interest in examining how to make improvements in the productivity of groups. (Cartwright & Zander, 1968) Thus, the use of group dynamics to improve individual functioning within organizations became a reality of organizational life. Illustrations of this are plentiful. For example, in commemorating the 50th anniversary of the Hawthorne studies at Western Electric, Harold Leavitt wrote an essay, "Suppose We Took Groups Seriously..." in which he noted the importance of groups in fostering creativity, innovations and improved decision making (Hackman, 1987). J. Richard Hackman wrote that groups had become the way to get things done in organizations. It was equally important for the field of group dynamics to continue to expand what is known "...about how to design, manage and consult to work groups in organizations" (p. 315).

In the 1990s, diversity emerged as an issue with significant economic implications for American business. It was in this decade that a company's participation in the global market became increasingly necessary to maintain competitive advantage; the prediction of Johnston and Packer (1987) that that the majority of new entrants into the workforce would be composed of women, minorities and immigrants was becoming reality; and individuals were less willing to submerge their own uniqueness in order to "fit in" (Ely & Thomas, 2001). In addition, advanced technology spawned a growth in target marketing that relied on companies having employees who understood the needs of the specific population groups being targeted. The U.S. Department of Labor's "The Glass Ceiling Report" had already documented the fact that discrimination was a critical barrier that impeded the performance and advancement of women and people of color in organizations (Swanger, 1994, p. 19).

While the end of the 1980s had seen a decline in legal incentives for organizations to promote diversity, the five forces identified above began to converge to favor a business rationale for supporting diversity. Elsie Cross (2000) suggests that the basis for understanding how diversity unfolded in organizations was fueled by several major social movements: The civil rights movement, the feminist movement, the growth of organization development as a field of practice, and the development of the group process and personal growth movement. Each of these forces contributed to the creation of a growing body of knowledge and theory that had important implications for understanding the impact of diversity on organizations.

With the advent of the 1980's, the leaders of organizations were beginning to realize that diversity could not be limited to improving the working relationships and performance of individuals considered to be diverse, namely women and people of color. Rather, diversity had to be addressed through the implementation of system-wide interventions, which required changing norms, structures, belief system, policies and procedures. Basically, the new realities of organization life required new ways of thinking about organizations.

Three Key Leverage Points for Working with Groups

While organizations were realizing the productivity advantages of using groups to get the job done, their memberships were becoming more demographically diverse. The co-mingling of group dynamics and diversity has become an everyday occurrence in many organizations. Experience verifies that diversity has a powerful influence on

how groups work. There is increased potential
by higher productivity, creativity and problen
increased potential for failure as exhibited b
thereby impeding productivity, poor decision
the development of destructive conflict wi
(Hackman, 1990; 2002). Perhaps by making the
and field studies on the interaction of group dynamics and diversity more readily available to person(s) charged with maximizing the performance of heterogeneous work groups, it may help tip the balance in favor of success.

In reviewing studies on group dynamics and diversity, three key leverage points emerge for serious consideration by the professional charged with responsibility for an organizational work group. These three key leverage points are design, *context and process.* Design includes the purpose and direction along with group composition. Context refers to the environmental conditions (both internal and external to the organization), that affect how members function as a group. Process focuses on issues of inclusion and exclusion, conflict, communication, and the developmental phases of groups.

Leverage Point One: Design

Purpose

A group performs best when it has a clear, energized sense of where it is going and what it needs to accomplish. Purpose, goals and direction work in concert to provide this energized sense of where the group is going and why. This clarity of purpose and direction may come from anyone having legitimate authority to set the course for the group. This may be the organization's top leader or the person who charters and provides resources for the team.

There is deep theoretical support for the importance of purpose (Bion, 1974; Hackman, 2002; Katzenbach, 1998). In Katzenbach's work on top teams (1998), he emphasizes the criticality and elusiveness of purpose, noting the strengthening and honing quality of purpose. Similarly, J. Richard Hackman (2002), upon completing an updated analysis of what makes for a high performing team, again affirms that team performance is dependent on good, compelling direction. Direction provides energy for the group to move closer its goals.

ckman (2002) identifies three benefits of a team having good ction: (1) improved motivation; (2) easier alignment between perormance strategy and purpose; (3) fuller utilization of team members' skills, resources and knowledge (p. 73). These are important benefits to any work group but even more so for heterogeneous work groups who usually have a longer, steeper learning curve for orienting themselves to each other and to the work they are to perform. Ambiguous direction adds to the uncertainty of the group situation and can contribute to a group having an even longer and steeper learning curve.

Once the group's purpose is clear, there is strong evidence that specific and challenging goals can strengthen a team's performance even more (Knight, Durham, & Locke, 2001; Rosen, 1989) . There are many potential concerns when a work group's goals are neither specific nor challenging. Goals that are too general with ambiguous outcomes and timelines can be under-stimulating. In these situations, members are likely to seek arousing experiences, which can frequently take the form of conflict that is based on background differences. While conflict in and of itself can be useful, it is more productive if it is focused on the task rather than on demographic and other background differences. Because purpose is dynamic and broader than the defined set of tasks, as the context affecting the group changes, the purpose may need to be reshaped, sharpened, or at minimum restated. In this way purpose, direction and goals can help leverage success. An example that illustrates the necessity of purpose follows.

A CEO created a diversity council for a major teaching hospital. He stated that due to his unfamiliarity with the topic area, he was not able to define what he wanted the group to do. However, he thought it was a good idea to have a council in place. His hope was that the group would help him define the purpose. The group met for many months. They had interesting discussions but never seemed to make any headway. Some interesting ideas were brought to the table for discussion, along with some curious, ill-conceived ideas. As a result, members began to lose interest as reflected in declining attendance at the meetings. Even worse, the council developed a reputation as a "do nothing" group that was wasting time and money.

Composition

When diversity is present in an organization, an important consideration in formulating a team is representational diversity. It is important to first determine what "representational" means to the organization in question, as the definition across organizations will vary. In addition to the demographic attributes of diversity, groups can be heterogeneous based on personality, attitudes, background and experience.

There is ample group research that positively relates group heterogeneity to organizational innovations, creativity and decision making effectiveness (Bantel & Jackson, 1989). The value of heterogeneity in completing team tasks is clearest for creative and intellective tasks, which again underscore the value of a group, having a clear sense of purpose (Guzzo & Dickson, 1996). Heterogeneity has been positively correlated with turnover suggesting that care must be taken in developing the group so members can successfully engage with each other and the organization. In most studies, culturally heterogeneous groups eventually perform as well as culturally homogeneous groups, but the culturally diverse groups require time and patience with early phases of the work.

Functional diversity of team members, for example, the kind of work done and the specific skills utilized, adds another important level of complexity. Studies have found that functionally diverse teams can deliver better technical quality, faster schedule performance and better budget performance but specifically by utilizing indirect external communication (Guzzo & Dickson, 1996; Hackman, 2002).

By itself, functional diversity has no direct effects on technical quality, a rather strong negative effect on budget performance, and no direct effect on meeting deadlines. Cross-functional groups also have lower cohesiveness than single function groups and members report increased job stress. The key is to build in opportunities for members to communicate with external sources and to bring information from these external sources back to the team or group as a legitimate part of the group's structure and process. The important reminder is that leveraging the diversity of a demographically and functionally heterogeneous work group requires coaching of leaders, strong team processes and other sources of support for team members.

Size is another important aspect of composition. Size is connected to complexity since the possible combinations of alliances and relationships among and between group members multiplies logarithmically with each additional person. A general guideline is that smaller is better when it comes to member satisfaction and group performance.

However, much of the research on size appears to have been done with groups who were homogeneous in their racial and ethnic makeup, or for whom information about race and ethnicity is not included (Devine, Clayton, Philips, Dunford, & Melner, 1999; Hackman & Vidmar, 1970).

McLeod and Lobel (1992) studied the effects of ethnic diversity on idea generation in small groups where the group size was three or four persons. Hackman (Hackman, 2002, p. 62) (slightly tongue-in-cheek) states that 4.6 is the optimum size, but also adds that teams may function better when there are slightly fewer members than the task requires. When the team focus is related to diversity, there is more likelihood that these groups will need to be larger than what is considered "optimum". It is important to keep the size manageable while continually clarifying the purpose of the group and designing effective communication processes so that even those who are not being selected as team members will not feel excluded. The guideline is to keep the team smaller and to connect the size with the work to be done, remembering that having slightly fewer people than the task requires has been shown to support team effectiveness. An example of a design that uses both clear purpose and effective composition is as follows.

The management team of a mental health agency decided to bring interested staff together to have a series of dialogue sessions about diversity. Some front-end design time resulted in establishing important parameters for the dialogue sessions. First, the group would meet for a set number of sessions. Membership would be closed after the first official session. The group would have an outside facilitator and would come together to explore and discuss topics were of interest to them. The basics of dialogue would be taught in the first session so that members would have the skills to participate effectively. The result was that a consistent group of staff participated in all the sessions. The conversations started with polite exchanges and graduated into dialogues in which members revealed information containing very personal and sensitive content about their diversity related experiences and how it affected their roles in the organization and community. The group maintained a boundary of confidentiality and had a very satisfying experience, creating strong interpersonal connections among the group's members. The existence of these relationships, along with the development of trust and empathy within this small group made a positive contribution to the overall work environment.

Leverage Point Two

Context

Assessing and understanding the context in which a group operates is critical to effectively supporting a group's functioning (Guzzo & Dickson, 1996). Increasing awareness and understanding of context is an important way to "troubleshoot" issues that affect a group's functioning.

Groups within organizations are embedded in larger social systems (e.g. communities, schools, and business organizations). These social systems comprise a major part of the context in which team members perform. For theorists such as McGrath (1991), a fundamental assumption about the nature of groups is that they are partially nested within, and loosely coupled to, a surrounding social system. "Partially nested" refers to the fact that individuals often have social identities with more than one group, and that groups may be parts of more than one social system. "Loosely coupled" refers to the fact that there are few clear, mechanistic-like connections either between groups and surrounding systems or within groups. Rather the systemic connections are less direct and more layered.

A consequence of the embeddedness of teams in organizations is that team performance and effectiveness are tied to the realities that exist within organizations themselves, as well as those that exist in the external environments in which organizations are located. The effectiveness or ineffectiveness of a team can have a significant impact on the larger organization, and changes that occur in the larger organization can influence a team's performance and effectiveness. The teams-in-organizational-context perspective is complex because it implies that the effects of interventions made at one level (individual, group, and organization) may be experienced at other levels.

A study done by Ely and Thomas (2001) may help clarify the importance of context for the work of groups within organizations. Ely and Thomas (2001) gathered data from individuals within three organizations in an effort to identify how members defined the value of diversity based on the work they performed, and the level and quality of interactions, which took place between them and their co-workers. Using this information they identified three specific diversity perspectives, each one drawing significantly from aspects of the particular organizational context and having a strong shaping effect on how members and groups within the each organization performed.

The first is the "integration-and-learning" perspective. In this perspective, diversity is broadly viewed by members of the organization as a resource for learning and change. Holding this perspective shaped how the members viewed the organization's mission, the value of their own heterogeneity, the nature of the work being done, as well as the power and influence of persons inside and outside of the organization.

The second is the "access and legitimacy" perspective. In this perspective, the orienting premise is that since key markets or constituent groups for the organization are racially diverse, the organization needs to be aligned in its own composition with the cultural make-up of these markets. With this perspective the power and influence held by the key market groups significantly influenced how teams within the organization were organized, and the nature of the relationship between the teams and between each team and the organization's executive leadership.

The third perspective is the "discrimination and fairness" perspective. This perspective was built on a value premise regarding what is right or wrong, moral and immoral. The emphasis is on eliminating sexism and racism and on providing equal opportunity for hiring, development and promotion. This emphasis is focused on what is "right". It is not directly connected to the work of the organization or team. Ely and Thomas note that organizations using a "discrimination and fairness" template will measure progress by how well a work group achieves its recruitment and retention goals (Ely & Thomas, 2001).

Ely and Thomas' findings, though based on a limited sample of three organizations, indicated that while all three diversity perspectives led to more highly motivated managers, only the integration and learning perspective provided the kind of rationale and guidance people needed to achieve sustained benefits from diversity. (Ely & Thomas, 2001) They proposed that work groups who evidenced or were successful in creating an integration-and-learning perspective would be more highly functioning than who reflected one of the other two perspectives.

Cox and Blake (1991) offer a different and useful typology for understanding the context for work teams. They identify a monolithic organization as being mostly homogeneous in terms of the majority culture demographics. In the monolithic organization, there will be requisite affirmative action plans but not much in terms of systemic processes and structures to address multiculturalism. Expressions of prejudice through jokes and direct comments are fairly typical. It would be unlikely to find a diversity council or specifically diversity-focused team in this organization except as a reaction to a problem or crises. The second organizational form in this typology is the plural organization where minority culture employees are present, but in smaller numbers and generally at entry or lower levels of the hierarchy. In the plural organization, there are likely to be some policies and practices to deal with diversity. It is also likely that these policies and practices are not systemic and integrated with the daily functioning of the organization. It is in this type of organization that you are likely to hear complaints of "not walking the talk". Because the organization has noticeable heterogeneity, diverse work teams are more likely. Clarity of purpose, goals and directions are especially critical to effective functioning of teams in this environment. The third organization form in this typology is the multicultural organization. There is demographic diversity of many types at all levels of the organization. Overt expressions of prejudice are not supported in the culture of the organization. It is in multicultural types of organizations that diversity and inclusive strategic planning is more likely to occur. There will be more systemic and integrated efforts to effect change in the culture. This typology directly supports understanding contextual variables likely to impact the work of a diverse work team.

Leadership has an important role in the context for a group. Leaders are an obvious and important influence team effectiveness (Guzzo & Dickson, 1996; Hackman, 2002; Katzenbach, 1998). Key leverage points in improving the effectiveness of these teams is coaching of team leaders as well as those who "sponsor" the team in the larger organization. An initial task is assessing the team oriented skill strengths and deficits of the leader. The group dynamics theory and practice directs us to some of the requisite skills: communication, negotiation and influence, creative problem solving and conflict management. Core areas of interpersonal competence, such as those described in the work on emotional intelligence components of leadership by Goleman, Boyatzis and McKee (2002), are other important examples of skill areas important for leaders to develop. An example that illustrates the importance of leadership skills and competence follows.

The director of Brand Marketing for a national snack company wanted to increase the sensitivity of her marketing staff to cultural differences within the team and customer groupings. She decided to create a planning committee to explore and implement strategies to increase the sensitivity within the staff overall. The committee was formed, a facilitator was identified from the Organizational Development and Training staff, and the first meeting was scheduled to get the process started. It was apparent to the facilitator that group members were reluctant to talk. The Director offered the group reassurance and support for the importance of talking openly about issues that might affect strategies for improving sensitivity. At the next meeting, as members began to open up and share their ideas and perceptions, it was clear that they were carrying a lot of concern and in some cases anger about how company management interacted with employees. There were examples offered of inequities, poor communication and insensitivity that members believed needed to be addressed before they could engage around the expressed purpose of the group, which was to examine ways of increasing staff sensitivity to client cultural differences. The Director was concerned because she wanted to keep the focus of the group on improving cultural sensitivity. Their responses seemed to her to take the group off task. The facilitator spent some time coaching the Director on the impact of leadership on group process. The coaching increased the leader's understanding of expanded context of the group. The group was then able to move forward with the process.

Leverage Point Three

Process

The area of process is broad and multifaceted, and therefore only selected aspects determined to be most critical will be highlighted here.

Stages of Group Development

Tuckman (1965) has secured a permanent home in the annals of group dynamics history with his easily remembered stages of group development: forming, norming, storming and performing. Significant research since Tuckman introduced his model now indicates that work groups do not follow a single sequence of developmental stages (Gersick & Hackman, 1990). In fact, group development is an iterative process, that is, phases of work are often repeated many times as internal and external factors shift. Thus, the broader categories of orienting, performing and closing may offer a more useful way of examining and guiding a group's process.

Orienting includes the behaviors and activities designed to familiarize a group's members with each other and the task(s). Orienting occurs at the beginning of a group, and can reoccur at different phases of the work such as when new members or new leadership arrives. It also happens when there is a significant change in the external environment - a case in point is the events of September 11th.

Creation of group norms is a primary activity. This starts at the first meeting of the group and begins to set the tone, framework and structure for how work flows in the team (Gersick, 1990). Group norms are formed very early, whether done consciously, such as an explicit activity to articulate and agree upon norms, or unconsciously, via tacit agreement as the group interacts. Early in a work group, members are doing a considerable amount of meaning making about "Who Am I? Who are we together? What really is our work? How can I 'be' in this group? How will our history/lack of history affect our work?"

Theory and personal experience strongly support consciously working on and articulating norms as a way of managing the work of orienting. Norms are the outcome and norming is the process. Developing norms that can guide and support the group through making decisions, addressing expectations including those about internal and external communication and managing conflicts are critical for effective group performance. The norms also partly comprise the foundation for developing safety for individual members within the group. As safety develops, participants are more willing to raise questions, provide different perspectives, and bring their resources to the table. This is obviously very important in a heterogeneous group where the risks and stakes may be higher than in a homogeneous group.

The exchange of interpersonal information between group members is integral to creating safety. The exchange of interpersonal information increases familiarity, which is central to orienting. Shaw and Barrett-Power (1998) note that diverse work groups have to develop the kind of familiarity that enables them to problem solve, complete their frequently complex tasks and to "hang in there" with each other long enough to establish the group's overall purpose.

Performing is described from Tuckman (1965) to Hackman (2002), as a key element of group life. Shaw and Barrett-Power (1998) describe performing as activities focused on the work of accomplishing the task. One of the key aspects of performing in a diverse work group is conflict management. We know from experience and research that conflict is likely to occur when groups and teams are heterogeneous. "The greater conflict in heterogeneous, rather than homogeneous groups is often due to the difficulty that people have in understanding each other when their backgrounds are diverse" (Lovelace, Shapiro, Weingart, Woodman, Cameron, Ibarra, & Pettigrew, 2001, p. 780). One way of sorting conflict is to recognize the difference between task conflict and emotional conflict. Task conflict is generally driven by functional background differences. It is often focused on interpretation of task related data, distribution of resources or procedures and policies. Emotional or relationship conflict is driven by dissimilarity in race and tenure (Pelled, Eisenhardt, & Xin, 1999) .This form of conflict frequently involves unfavorable attributions, issues of social identity and feelings of self-worth (De Dreu & Van Vianen, 2001). One implication is that close attention is required to the group's process when there is significant racial and ethnic diversity along with tenure and functional diversity. This particular range of diversity is especially common in diversity councils or other representative teams where leaders strive for a "max-mix" of the organizational demography as illustrated in the following example.

A group of professionals from a number of different non-profit agencies came together as a training group over an extended period (up to one year) to learn about cultural diversity in non-profit service delivery. The focus of the training was on the delivery of specific curriculum content to provide participants with an in-depth understanding of the impact of cultural diversity on treatment modalities and program development decisions. Unfortunately the facilitators for the training program had not taken into account the fact that they were bringing together a heterogeneous group of professionals (different educational backgrounds, different professional positions within their respective organizations, significant demographic differences including gender, race/ethnicity, age and sexual orientation) and had not adequately prepared themselves or the participants to deal with the real potential for conflict within the group. Little if any attention was paid to the establishment of group norms. When the conflict did erupt, there were few supports in place to help manage it. Consequently, a great deal of the time was used processing the conflict at the expense of teaching the content of the curriculum.

It is important that persons responsible for a group's performance understand that conflict may be integral to effective task accomplishment. In Pelled, Eisenhardt & Xin's (Pelled et al., 1999) study of 45 teams from three major corporations, task conflict tended to have more favorable performance consequences than emotional conflict. Task conflict was found to support deeper understanding of task issues and it tended to drive the quality of information exchange that benefited problem solving and idea generation. Constructive norms, formed in the orienting phase of a work group's life, help keep task conflict on track and avoid the trust degenerating quality of too much emotional conflict. Also important are basic conflict management skills. These skills enable the group to effectively work through likely differentiation and conflict and ensure that tasks, and the more encompassing purpose, are achieved.

Overall, performance of work groups is strengthened by strong team management skills. The purpose and tasks of the group determine which sets of skills must be acquired and sharpened. Examples include effective skills and processes for creative problem solving and idea generation, communication and project management skills.

Finally, another aspect of performing is that it encompasses the "midpoint" of the group's work. Gersick (1990) has noted that "it may be more difficult than we think to educate a team at the beginning of a project - and more important than we realize to clarify project requirements at the project's midpoint" (Gersick, 1990, p. 110). We emphasize that purpose is dynamic and needs to be revisited at the midpoint of the work team's life.

Closing

Insufficient attention is given to closing or ending a group. We did not find significant research that adequately informed us on the dynamics of ending or closing a group. Gersick (1990) noted that the quality of how a group closed was directly shaped by how they moved through the beginning and midpoint phases of work. For example, in early stages of group development, members "open" up to each other. Personal information is shared and members begin to trust each other with opinions and ideas that may be high stakes and high risk. A certain degree of vulnerability may become part of the interaction dynamics of members. The degree to which members work through these issues to develop trust and do their work affects attitudes towards each other and the group at closing.

Care must be taken to formally close the work group so that learning from the process is articulated and to ensure that the work gets integrated individually and organizationally. Given the context issues, there may be a need to take what has been learned or accomplished to the external environment. Thus, attention to proper closing of a group experience supports learning and ultimately organizational change.

Summary

This discussion has focused on expanding the knowledge and skill repertoires of professionals responsible for the functioning and success of groups within organizations. These groups or teams may be focused on diversity because of their purpose and goals or because of their composition or context—or both. We offer key leverage points from the vast tomes of group dynamics theory and research:

First

Work teams and groups must have clear, energized purpose, goals and direction to be effective.

Second

Composition matters. Keeping size a bit smaller than the task requires and negotiating definitions of what representational means is a lever for success.

Third

Work teams are embedded in large social systems. Members bring their take on the social system "in" with them when they join a team. Also, the context can support or obstruct the team's work. Rarely is the context neutral.

Fourth

> Attention is needed in the orienting and performing phases of group work. There are especially critical tasks to be accomplished and important skills to be used in the process when the group and/or its purpose are diverse. Effectiveness is enhanced when norms and expectations are worked early in the process. Also, leaders and facilitators need strong conflict management, communication and interpersonal skills regardless of the group's specific purpose and tasks.

For diversity professionals, those in executive and line management positions or internal and external organizational development consultants, the leverage points presented offer heightened awareness of diversity management considerations and group dynamics.

References

Bantel, K. A., & Jackson, S. E. (1989). *Top management and innovations in banking: Does the composition of the top team make a difference?* Strategic Management Journal, 10, 107-124.

Bion, W. R. (1974). *Experiences in groups-and other papers.* Oxford: Ballantine.

Cartwright, D., & Zander, A. (1968). *Group dynamics* (3rd ed.). Oxford: Harper & Row.

Cox, T., & Blake, S. (1991). *Managing cultural diversity: Implications for organizational competitiveness.* Academy of Management Executive, 5, 45-56.

Cross, E. Y. (2000). Managing diversity —*The courage to lead.* Westport: Quorom Books.

De Dreu, C. K. W. , & Van Vianen, A. E. M. (2001). *Managing relationship conflict and the effectiveness of organizational teams.* Journal of Organizational Behavior, 22(3), 309-328.

Devine, D. J. , Clayton, L. D. , Philips, J. L. , Dunford, B. B. , & Melner, S. B. (1999). T*eams in organizations: Prevalence, characteristics, and effectiveness.* Small Group Research, 30(6), 678-711.

Ely, R. J., & Thomas, D. A. (2001). *Cultural Diversity at Work: The Effects of Diversity Perspectives on Work Group Processes and Outcomes.* Administrative Science Quarterly, 46, 229-274.

Gersick, C. J. (1990). *The students.* In J. R. Hackman (Ed.), *Groups that work (and those that don't) : Creating conditions for effective teamwork* (pp. 89-111). San Francisco: Jossey-Bass.

Gersick, C. J. , & Hackman, J. R. (1990). *Habitual routines in task-performing groups.* Organizational Behavior & Human Decision Processes, 47(1), 65-97.

Goleman, D. , Boyatzis, R. , & A., M. (2002). *Primal leadership : Realizing the power of emotional intelligence.* Boston: Harvard Business School Press.

Gross, S. E. (1995). *Compensation for teams: How to design and implement team-based reward systems.* 25-38.

Guzzo, R. A., & Dickson, M. W. (1996). *Teams in organizations: Recent Research on Performance and Effectiveness.* Annual Review of Psychology, 47, 307-341.

Hackman, J. R. (1987). *The design of work teams.* In J. W. Lorsch (Ed.), *Handbook of organizational behavior* (pp. 315-342). Englewood Cliffs: Prentice-Hall.

Hackman, J. R. (2002). *Leading teams : Setting the stage for great performances.* Boston: Harvard Business School Press.

Hackman, J. R. (Ed.). (1990). *Groups that work (and those that don't) : Creating conditions for effective teamwork* (1st ed.). San Francisco: Jossey-Bass.

Hackman, J. R., & Vidmar, N. (1970). *Effects of size and task type on group performance and member reactions.* Sociometry, 33(1), 37-54.

Johnston, W. B., & Packer, A. H. (1987). *Workforce 2000.* Indianapolis: Hudson Institute.

Katzenbach, J. R. (1998). *Teams at the top: Unleashing the potential of both teams and individual leaders.* Boston: Harvard University Press.

Knight, D., Durham, C. C., & Locke, E. A. (2001). *The Relationship of Team Goals, Incentives, and Efficacy to Strategic Risk, Tactical Implementation, and Performance.* Academy of Management Journal, 44(2), 326-340.

Larkey, L. K. (1996). *Toward a theory of communicative interactions in culturally diverse workgroups.* Academy of Management Review, 21, 463- 491.

Lovelace, K. , Shapiro, D. L. , Weingart, L. R. , Woodman, R. W , Cameron, K. S., Ibarra, H., et al. (2001). *Maximizing Cross-Functional New Product Teams' Innovativeness and Constraint Adherence: A Conflict Communications Perspective.* Academy of Management Journal, 44, 779-794.

McGrath, J. E. (1991). *Time, interaction and performance: A theory of small groups.* Small Group Research, 22, 147-174.

McGrath, J. E., Berdahl, J. L., & Arrow, H. (1995). *Traits, expectations, culture and clout: The dynamics of diversity in work groups.* In S. R. Jackson, Marian (Ed.), *Diversity in work teams: Research paradigms for a changing workplace* (pp. 17-45). Washington, DC: American Psychological Association.

McLeod, P. L., & Lobel, S. A. (1992). *The effects of ethnic diver sity on idea generation in small groups.* Paper presented at the Academy of Management Best Paper Proceedings, Columbia.

Pelled, L. H., Eisenhardt, K. M. , & Xin, K. R. (1999). *Exploring the black box: An analysis of work group diversity, conflict and performance.* Administrative Science Quarterly, 44(1), 1-28.

Rosen, N. (1989). *Teamwork and the bottom line.* Hillsdale: Lawerence.

Shaw, J. B. , & Barrett-Power, E. (1998). *The Effects of Diversity on Small Work Group Processes and Performance.* Human Relations, 51, 1307-1325.

Swanger, C. C. (1994). *Perspectives on the history of ameliorating oppression and supporting diversity in United States organizations.* In E. Y. Cross (Ed.), *The promise of diversity : over 40 voices discuss strategies for eliminating discrimination in organizations* (pp. 3-24). Burr Ridge: Irwin.

Tuckman, B. W. (1965). *Developmental sequence in small groups.* Psychological Bulletin, 63, 384-399.

Wagner, L. (1995). *Does teamwork buck America's tradition of individual achievement?* Retrieved 9/4/02, 2002, from http://www.prep.mcneese.edu/engr/engr431/TQM/tqm_html.htm

Chapter VIII

Diversity: A Strategy for Organizational Change and Success

Beverly R. Fletcher

Leading change in organizations involves understanding how to successfully influence others. Competent change agents know how to work with and through people who are different from themselves and each other. Change leadership necessitates understanding the multiple differences that exist in organizations, and requires the ability to harness the creative potential of those differences. The most effective leaders value diversity as a business strategy rather than merely employing minorities and women because they fear negative repercussions. They understand that it takes the input and energies of many different people to successfully shape and implement the organization's vision, to inspire its diverse workforce and meet the demands of its varied client/customer base, and the global society in which the organization exists. There are two terms used consistently throughout this chapter that need defining because although they are commonly used words, they are largely misunderstood: *leadership* and *diversity*.

A Core Leadership Competency

Leadership implies change, and effectively utilizing diversity is a core leadership competency. Leadership is defined as *an ongoing interactive process that occurs in the context of ambiguity or paradox, involving intentional influencing that causes an individual, a group, or an entire organizations to change direction, focus, approach, process, procedure, or even beliefs and values.* It is clear that if one adopts this definition of leadership, there is no leadership without change, and one cannot be a leader without willing followers. The ability to influence and utilize diverse perspectives in the service of purposeful organizational change is a core leadership competency (see Table 1).

By examining the differences between managing through positional power and leading through personal power (see Chart 1.), one cannot help but understand the need for a well-developed proficiency at utilizing diversity. In today's constantly changing complex organizations the line between management and leadership increasingly blurs as managers are expected to lead as well as manage.

Diversity competency therefore requires integrated management and leadership skills that can be divided into four areas:

1. intra-personal (within the individual)
2. interpersonal (between the individual and others)
3. diagnosing and problem solving, and
4. planning, implementing, and evaluating

To further explore specific competencies needed, an assessment tool is provided at the end of this Chapter—*Diversity Competencies Inventory.* This instrument is designed as a tool for self-exploration and does not provide standardized interpretations or comparison data.

A Working Definition for Diversity

The topic of diversity is often approached by organizations with the mistaken premise that everyone has a common understanding of the term "diversity." Since the 1960's diversity in the U.S. has been primarily approached as a process of increasing the numbers of women and minorities in the workforce. It has been understood as a compliance issue and has focused on discrimination, equal employment opportunity (EEO), and affirmative action (AA). Unfortunately, viewed through the compliance prism, diversity has been seen as a corporate liability as depicted by the left side of the continuum illustrated by Table 2.

LEADERSHIP	
1. An ongoing interactive ***process*** that occurs in the context of ***ambiguity*** or ***paradox***. 2. Leadership involves intentional ***influencing*** that causes individuals, groups, or an entire organization to ***shift*** or entirely ***change*** direction, focus, approach, process, procedure, or even beliefs and values. 3. It is integrally tied to interpersonal influencing—one cannot lead without followers.	
Managers	***Leaders***
• Exercise authority through positional power	• Influence people through personal power
• Require compliance	• Inspire commitment
• Operate within prescribed boundaries	• Act "outside of the box"—take calculated risks
• Respond to uncertainty and complexity by creating processes to carry out pre-defined mission	• Respond to ambiguity and paradox by creating vision, establishing direction, and translating vision into localized action
• Plan, budget, organize & direct within the established mission	• Create new structures, processes, etc. through collaborative processes
• Staff, monitor, analyze, and control	• Mobilize support and align people for action
• Identify and solve problems	• Define opportunities
• Delegate and empower subordinates	• Motivate, inspire, energize, and empower others
• Managers evaluate subordinates	• Followers evaluate a leader

Table 1. Managing Through Positional Power and Personal Power

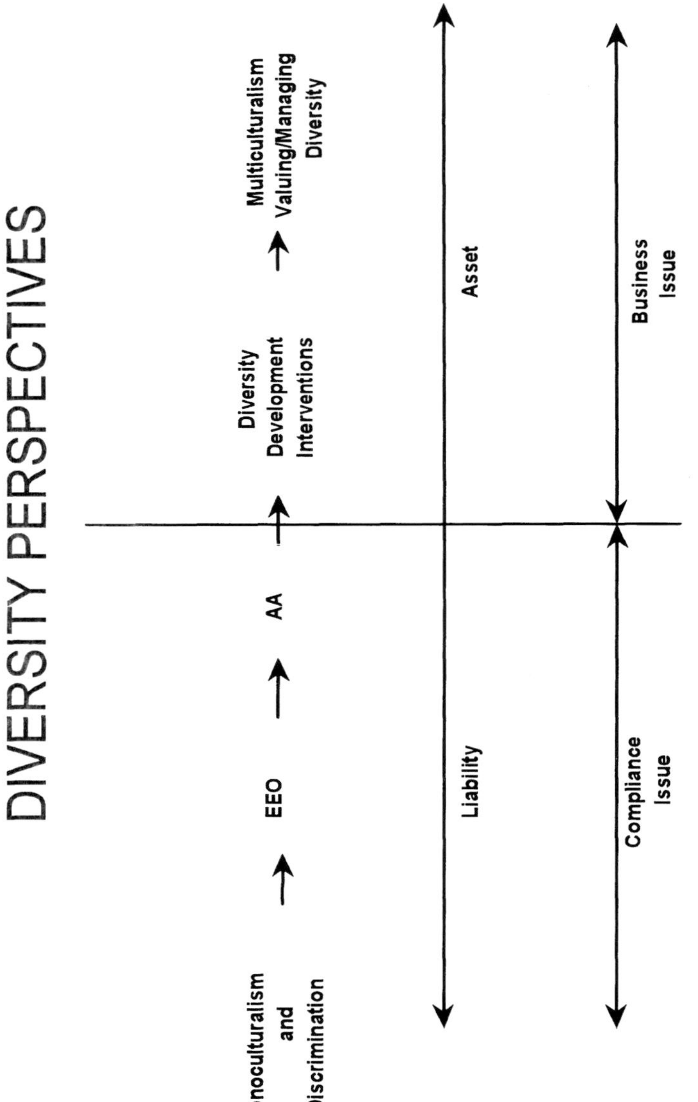

From: *Valuing and Managing Diversity in Business and Industry: Literature Review & Models.* Sandra J Johnson 1992, Minneapolis: University of Minnesota

Table 2. Diversity Perspectives Continuum

Diversity is all of the ways in which humans differ. Including primary dimensions such as gender, race, ethnicity, age, sexual orientation, and mental and physical challenges; as well as secondary dimensions such as geographic origins, education, economic status, religious affiliation, political affiliation, learning styles, personality types, communication styles, work styles, etc. The degree to which a variety of primary and secondary differences exist in a group is the degree to which the group is diverse.

Although numbers help us to evaluate goal achievement regarding the mix of certain primary differences such as gender and race, diversity involves more than just these limited numerical goals. A contemporary and more useful definition of diversity follows:

This definition includes everybody and does not focus exclusively on minorities and women. This broader definition of diversity has emerged partly as a response to mental and emotional blocks against diversity efforts in organizations. Change agents working in this area face negative attitudes, frustration, hostility, and arguments such as:

- ✦"When I heard the word *diversity*, I was immediately angry because it is a code word for *beat up on the white guy.*"
- ✦"We are tired of being made to feel guilty for something we did not create and cannot control—this diversity stuff only serves to make matters worse by creating bad feelings;"
- ✦"I am a good person who does not discriminate against women or minorities, so this diversity 'stuff' does not apply to me;"
- ✦"We've already tried that, and it didn't work;"
- ✦"We've already taken care of our diversity problem;"
- ✦"We've had training and know about (are fully aware of) all of that stuff;"
- ✦"Our problem has been solved—we've hired X number of women and X number of minorities;"

When change agents discuss diversity with organizational leaders, two common blocks to a meaningful dialogue may emerge:

1. Any positive statistical trends in the organization toward hiring women and minorities have caused leaders to believe that their job with respect to diversity is over or nearing completion.

2. Any negative experiences resulting from past diversity train ing is used as evidence that focusing on diversity is a use less and even dangerous process.

According to Roosevelt Thomas, the noted author, educator, and President of the American Institute for Managing Diversity, although many organizations have created a more diverse workforce, they must now ask themselves if they have the know-how to utilize the full potential of this entity that they have created. Thomas (1991) says that in the past organizations believed employees wanted to be assimilated into a homogeneous workforce (the *melting pot* metaphor). Now because people are increasingly celebrating the things that make them different, organizations must learn to lead people who value their differences rather than assimilation (the *salad bowl* or *stew pot* metaphor).

A Business Case

US Census estimates (1999) indicate that by the year 2050 the US population will increase by 50 percent. Minority groups will make up nearly half of the population; immigration will account for almost two-thirds of the nation's growth; and furthermore, our current workforce is aging, and we are being forced to learn the values and beliefs of the next generations of workers. At the same time, the up and coming generations must deal with the lessons and legacies of their elders. If organizations hope to maintain a competitive position in our global society, they must understand and value the differences among us.

Organizations are making a strong business case for diversity and many are taking the lead in demonstrating how diversity is becoming an important strategy for success. According to Bank of America: "Our markets demand that we be diverse because we serve such a diverse population. Diversity is more than the right thing to do—it's a business imperative." Charles R. Lee, Chairman and CEO of GTE notes, "From a business perspective, we believe a workforce that understands the diverse needs of customers and can successfully collaborate with all customers is necessary to achieve GTE's goals." In 1993, to achieve a number of diversity advancements, GTE launched a proactive diversity program called Breaking the Barriers which was tied to its business plan. Barbara Stern, Vice-President of diversity at Harvard Pilgrim Health Care explains, "Valuing diversity not only allows people to be more fully engaged and productive; we believe it enhances our ability to better service our patients." In its admissions processes, Harvard has begun to look for students who have the potential to contribute something distinctive and important to the business of learning, and considers these as factors among the many that go into assessing each potential student.

Given that diversity is an opportunity and business imperative, what does it take for an organization to succeed in a rapidly changing and increasingly diverse society? Certainly, producing effective, high quality outcomes that meet the needs of various stakeholders is essential. To achieve this, organizations must find ways to understand the needs of their diverse customers, clients, and constituents. As a first step toward that end, their workforce must reflect the diversity of the many people to whom they provide products, information, or services. But more important than statistics, workforce diversity represents a strategic opportunity to better serve these diverse constituents.

Former Vice President Al Gore's National Partnership for Reinventing Government (NPR) Diversity Task Force reports that the US Postal Service, the Defense Equal Opportunity Management Institute, and the US Coast Guard have progressed beyond mere EEO initiatives in the area of workforce diversity. The NPR Task Force recently conducted an organizational assessment of 160 federal entities, comprising all federal cabinet departments, major bureaus, high impact agencies, and training providers. According to the Task Force, "when diversity is recognized, valued and utilized, individual productivity, organizational effectiveness, and sustained competitiveness are enhanced."

The U.S. Postal Service (USPS), with its recent bad press and serious problems with violence in the workplace, has a labor force of over 850,000 people spread throughout the country. As a result of a major strategic change process, the USPS has developed integrated diversity initiatives that enjoy the full commitment of top leadership. These initiatives include strategic planning, policy integration, a diversity oversight committee, a diversity communications plan, management accountability, a recognition program, community outreach, and succession planning. According to USPS leaders, valuing diversity not only allows postal employees to be more fully engaged and productive; it enhances the ability of the Service to better meet the needs of its customers.

BankBoston CEO Charles Gifford agrees that, "Diversity is a strategic opportunity, if we understand how the work force is changing and its impact on the labor pool, new markets, and a growing global economy, we will be better able to capitalize on opportunities." According to *Business* Week, if diversity is seen as a strategic opportunity to increase organizational effectiveness by maximizing talent, fostering innovation, and tapping into the skills and creativity of an increasingly diverse labor pool, organizations can:

- Operate more effectively globally
- Create better organizational structures and policies
- Enhance recruitment, retention, and development efforts
- Move toward full-utilization of all employees
- Improve morale and commitment
- Smooth transitions during cuts and mergers, and
- Be more responsive to technological and organizational climate changes

The deceptively simple logic is that a diverse workforce will better understand how to serve a diverse customer base and that employees who are valued are more likely to value the customers they serve. It is clear that by valuing diversity, organizations can better meet their strategic goals: they can recruit more competitively for new talent; cultivate a high-quality work environment and positive staff morale; serve and satisfy their increasingly multicultural membership; minimize costs; maximize talents; and generate more perspectives, therefore, developing better ways to solve problems.

Building an Effective Workforce

Simply put, diverse work teams make good "business" sense. A study released in 1998 by the American Management Association reported that heterogeneous teams produce consistently better results. Years of academic studies demonstrate that heterogeneous groups out perform homogeneous groups, over time, in providing *more effective* problem solving and *more creative* solutions. The studies also demonstrate that homogeneous groups tend to be *faster* in the short-term. Hence, one of the challenges for change leaders is to invest now in fully utilizing the organization's diversity for long-term success.

Effective teamwork requires effective leadership skills. It is not just a matter of putting diverse people on teams, but drawing them out and utilizing their various talents and perspectives. Change leaders need superior facilitation skills and a thorough understanding of how diverse groups interact. To better understand why some teams are successful, Intel conducted research on their global team effectiveness in which they selected ten high-performing Intel teams—one of which designed the Pentium processor. The research results indicate a number of success components including respect among team members, trust, goals and focus, high motivation, listening skills, and diversity.

Organiation Change

During the past decade, change has become a way of life in all types of organizations, yet we continue to struggle with change and are perplexed by how to lead people through multiple transitions. If we as change leaders are to become effective agents of change, we must understand and grapple with fundamental phenomenon that consistently occur when organizations change, and we must be able to deal with them as a gestalt. Leading change requires diversity competencies inextricably related to all levels of organizational change efforts: Individual, group, organization-wide, and inter-organizational; and for all types of change: minor, major, and transformative. As the table below indicates, despite the *type* and *level* of change involved, a complete range of diversity competencies is needed to lead organizational change (see Table 3).

Types of Change	Diversity Competencies	Organizational Level			
		Individual	Group	Organization-wide	Inter-Oganizational
Minor	Intra personal Interpersonal Diagnosing & problem solving Planning, Implementing & Evaluating	X	X		
Major	Intra personal Interpersonal Diagnosing & problem solving Planning, Implementing & Evaluating	X	X	X	
Transformative	Intra personal Interpersonal Diagnosing & problem solving Planning, Implementing & Evaluating	X	X	X	X

Table 3. Type and Level of Change

Leading during conditions of constant change requires perhaps just one part science and two parts art. Along with the "science of change leadership," we must understand the part that requires some artistry: that is, a deep understanding of human responses to differences.

Levels of Response to Differences

It is clear that change leaders must effectively manage in several dimensions at once. To more successfully meet challenges posed by the dramatic societal changes profoundly modifying organizations, leaders must alter the view from diversity as inherently threatening to diversity as an opportunity to succeed. Diversity alone does not cause problems. Rather, our responses to difference either limit or expand our ability to lead effectively.

According to Carlos Cortes (1999) exercising the skills of leadership in a complex, diverse democracy involves the ability to do at least four things simultaneously:

1. Function in situations of dissonance and discomfort
2. Listen to conflicting voices—attempting to understand what is behind the words.
3. Mediate and find common ground; and
4. Chart new directions that build on diverse strengths, yet set limits.

Figure 1, *Responses to Differences,* is an "awareness" model that facilitates discussion and promotes dialogue about diversity. The model assumes that each person has different levels of response to various differences. It focuses primarily on *inherent* differences such as gender, age, physical and mental challenges, sexual orientation, race, and ethnicity, and also on certain secondary differences such as personality profiles, learning styles, and educational and economic background.

The model assumes that *valuing* these differences (at the top of the hierarchy) is a higher and more evolved level of consciousness than the desire to *annihilate* such differences (at the bottom of the hierarchy). It assumes that *realizing our connections and similarities* is a highly evolved level of consciousness and that, paradoxically, this level can only be achieved through a process of understanding and valuing these differences.

This model facilitates the process of developing the four critical skills outlined by Cortes (1999) by promoting discussion and dialogue about diversity. It provides a useful and easily understood conceptual structure that uses non-threatening language—it is a process tool for discussing diversity. It is also an awareness tool for enhancing individual understanding about various responses to differences, including those that may be problematic.

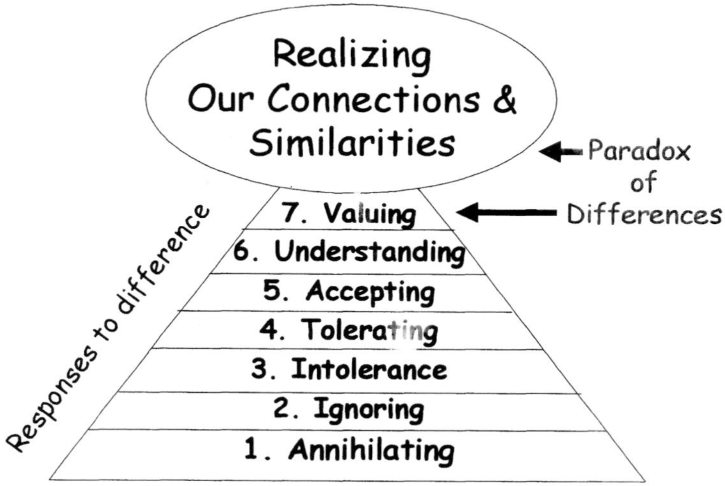

Figure 1. Responses to Differences

As we work on significant business issues like allocating scarce resources to various projects, deciding on a new business direction, or redefining the organization's core values, we can expect others to see the world differently than we do. These differences can be sources of strength because they open us up to new possibilities and to challenging our own assumptions. But this is only true if we can value the people who are different from ourselves as well as their differing views. It is predictable, and not surprising, that problem solving bogs down when we do not value differences. We confront each other and demand to be heard rather than hearing each other and searching for common ground.

Societal issues of diversity arise because part of each person's uniqueness is related to (although not necessarily determined by) the multiple societal groups to which each of us belongs. These groups may be based on such factors as race, ethnicity, gender, religion, age, ability/disability, sexual orientation, economic status, etc. Belonging to such groups may affect one's personal experiences, influence one's perspectives, or shape one's values. It may also have an impact on one's behavior and responses to others. It is this complex relationship between being an individual while simultaneously belonging to various groups that makes this model an important tool for sorting out individual and collective responses to difference. Because *Responses to Differences* is an "awareness" model, it may be used to understand how you approach others, how open you are to those who differ from you and how open you are to their ideas

To use the model in this way, it is important to understand the elements of the model. This involves first starting with the concept of *the Paradox of Differences.*

The Paradox of Differences

Paradoxically, we must value our ***differences*** before we can truly understand our ***similarities*** and ***connections***. In explaining the model (see Figure 1), it is effective to start at the bottom and move upward. It is also important to point out that as an awareness model, the primary purpose is to help individuals and groups to become more aware of or determine their own levels of response to various differences. One may conclude, in certain situations and environments, that a particular response (such as "tolerating") is "as good as it will get" with respect to that particular difference.

Level 1: ***Annihilating.*** At this level, difference is intolerable. The person not only "does not like" the difference, he/she actively seeks to destroy or annihilate it, or the person who embodies that difference. This is where acts of violence from gay-bashing to ethnic cleansing occur.

Level 2: ***Ignoring.*** Here the person does not want to talk about the difference. The claim is "I am blind to differences" or "Differences don't matter to me, I relate to people." In truth, this person tries to convince self and others that the difference does not exist. Refusing to acknowledge the difference is just another way of discounting and destroying that difference.

Level 3: Intolerance. While "ignoring" is an attempt to deny and thus destroy the difference, intolerance involves hostility towards the difference. It is placed above ignoring because the difference is at least recognized. At this level a person concludes that the difference is not benign and therefore actively strives to keep the difference away, thus segregating the difference from his or her daily interactions.

Level 4: Tolerating. Although tolerance is often touted as desirable, when in comes to dealing with differences. the implicit message goes something like: "I don't like your difference and would prefer not to have it in my life; however, for some unknown reason *the powers that be* made your difference, so who am I not to put up with it?" From the perspective of the person who is "different," this attitude is probably preferable to active aggression or overt hostility, but it still sends the message that the difference is negative, bad, or something the person really does not like or understand.

Level 5: Accepting. Accepting has a spiritual quality. The often, unarticulated expression of this position is: "I may not understand you or your difference, but I wholly accept you or your difference on the faith that it must be okay for you." The motivation may be an underlying affection for the particular individual. Yet, there is still an unwillingness to fully explore the scope and dimension of this difference. It is not uncommon for someone who believes themselves to be accepting to nonetheless become perturbed by certain situations. For example, when it is believed that the other person is "flaunting" his or her difference, the previous acceptance may then be withdrawn.

Level 6: Understanding. As a person moves beyond accepting to understanding, they also move beyond sympathy to empathy. Here the person is pro-active in seeking not just to accept but to know more about the difference. Judgment is suspended in favor of searching, seeking, inquiring and listening for answers to *What is it like to be you or to be this type of different?*

Level 7: Valuing. This is a form of embracing. After understanding, a person can make a conscious decision to *value* the difference. At this level, the focus shifts from the other person (the one who is different) to oneself. In other words, how do I benefit from having this difference in my life? Not until one reaches this level is one able to identify connections and explore similarities.

Realizing Our Connections & Similarities. Thus the paradox: until we have done the sometimes painful but sometimes exhilarating work of exploring and appreciating how we are different, we will not truly understand our connections or similarities.

It is clear in the context of leadership in a global society that diversity is an asset to be utilized, not a problem to be fixed. Furthermore, it is not just a "nice thing to do," it is a business imperative. Not only then is there a need for a broader more inclusive definition of diversity, but also we must understand the business case for diversity and realize that when effectively utilized, diversity produces better individual competencies, higher productivity, more innovation, and more effective change initiatives.

Engaging organizational leaders in meaningful dialogues about diversity may be difficult for change agents to do; and like other complex issues that change agents encounter, this one must be faced head on. Leaders increasingly call for bottom-line information that justifies diversity efforts as a part of their change initiatives. It is imperative that change agents respect this need by presenting organizational leaders with business case information. Moreover, the end result must promote valuing individual uniqueness, respecting cultural differences, and utilizing individual potential and collective talents for organizational success.

References

Business Week (1996, December 9). *Diversity—making the business case; Building upon work force capabilities and talents for innovation and global competition.*

Cortes, C.E. (1999). *Developing a multiculturally responsive agency (a case written for the FEI).* Charlottesville, VA: Federal Executive Institute.

Fletcher, B. R. (1999). *Levels of response to differences.* In Karp, M., & Fletcher, B. R. "*OHMYGOD," do I really have to deal with this issue?!*": *The gift of sexual orientation.* In A. Cooke, et al., *Reading book for human relations training* (8th Ed.) NTL Institute.

Fletcher, B. R. (Fall 1998). *Leadership definition.* Masters degree course: 54.650.01 *Leadership for Public Management.* Washington, DC: American University.

Hemisphere Inc. (1999). *Diversity: An inclusive approach.* http://www.diversityinc.com/Workforce/Research_Stats/wdn.html

Johnston, W. B. & Packer, A. E. (1987). *Workforce 2000: Work and workers for the twenty-first century.* Indianapolis, IN: Hudson Institute, June.

Johnson, S. J. (1992). *Perspectives on diversity in the workplace.* From *Valuing and managing diversity in business and industry: Literature review and models.* Minneapolis: University of Minnesota.

Thomas, R. R. (1991). *Beyond race and gender: Unleashing the power of your total work force by managing diversity.* NY: American Management Association.

U.S. Office of Personnel Management (FY 1997). *Annual report to Congress: Federal equal opportunity recruitment program, October 1, 1996 – September 30, 1997.* Washington, DC: U.S. Office of Personnel Management.

Wheeler, M. (1995). *Diversity: Business rationale and strategies; A research report.* NY: The Conference Board.

Diversity Competencies Inventory

The following inventory will help you to assess your diversity competencies in four important areas: intra-personal competencies; interpersonal and influencing competencies; diagnosing and problem solving competencies; and planning, implementing, and evaluating competencies. These behaviors, skills, abilities, and knowledge areas are necessary to effectively perform the key leadership role of "change agent" in diversity efforts. This useful self-assessment tool will help you with goal setting for professional growth and development.

Instructions

Read through the lists in each competency area and decide if you are ***highly competent***, at a ***satisfactory*** level of competence, or ***need some improvement***, making a check for each item in the appropriate place.

Some of the competencies important to your development as a change agent and leader may not be listed. Write those competencies on the blank lines.

After completing all areas of competence, review the entire inventory and circle one, two, or three competencies which you want to improve most. Develop a plan for your circled items, outlining specific goals for improvement and specific action plans. Identify a date and time for the first action you must take for each of the items identified.

Intra-personal Competencies	***Highly Skilled***	***Satis-factory***	***Need to Improve***
1. *Tolerating ambiguity and embracing paradox*	____	____	____
2. *Understanding my own motivations*	____	____	____
3. *Acknowledging and owning my emotions*	____	____	____
4. *Understanding my beliefs, values, and ethics*	____	____	____
5. *Understanding my biases and theoretical foundations*	____	____	____
6. *Having a clear understanding of the assumptions behind my behaviors*	____	____	____
7. *Separating my issues from group issues*	____	____	____
8. *Being aware of competitiveness in myself*	____	____	____
9. *Developing confidence in my own abilities*	____	____	____
10. *Managing my anxieties and stress while performing my tasks*	____	____	____
____________________	____	____	____
____________________	____	____	____

Interpersonal and Influencing Competencies	***Highly Skilled***	***Satis-factory***	***Need to Improve***
11. *Talking about my feelings as well as my thinking*	____	____	____
12. *Being authentic*	____	____	____
13. *Appropriately presenting myself (self disclosure)*	____	____	____
14. *Requesting feedback about the impact of my behaviors*	____	____	____
15. *Giving feedback on the impact of others' behaviors*	____	____	____
16. *Intervening without being a threat to others*	____	____	____
17. *Intervening at the appropriate time*	____	____	____
18. *Admitting and taking responsibility for my errors and mistakes*	____	____	____
19. *Inspiring others' confidence in my abilities*	____	____	____
20. *Inspiring others' confidence in their own abilities*	____	____	____
21. *Listening actively to others*	____	____	____
22. *Effectively selling my ideas (influencing without manipulating)*	____	____	____
23. *Appreciating the impact of my behavior on others*	____	____	____
24. *Helping others to discover their own issues and problems*	____	____	____
25. *Encouraging others to generate solutions to problems*	____	____	____
26. *Encouraging/acknowledging the creativity of others*	____	____	____
27. *Building an atmosphere of trust and openness*	____	____	____
28. *Understanding the motivations of others*	____	____	____
29. *Understanding group processes within the context of group development*	____	____	____
30. *Effectively dealing with group conflict*	____	____	____
31. *Negotiating "win-win" solutions*	____	____	____
32. *Drawing others out and giving them support*	____	____	____
33. *Openly acknowledging differences*	____	____	____
34. *Considering, discussing, and valuing the contributions of different perspectives*	____	____	____
35. *Pushing to understand others points of view*	____	____	____
36. *Helping the group to reach consensus*	____	____	____
37. *Attending to the group's process as well as its task*	____	____	____
38. *Treating others with respect regardless of their position*	____	____	____
39. *Having a "positive regard" for others*	____	____	____
40. *Understanding how "isms" such as racism, sexism, and homophobia are manifested in and affect groups*	____	____	____
41. *Working comfortably as a follower as well as a leader*	____	____	____
42. *Working effectively with people I do not like*	____	____	____
43. *Being able to say "no"*	____	____	____

Diagnosing and Problem Solving Competencies	*Highly Skilled*	*Satis-factory*	*Need to Improve*
44. *Creating and stating clear and "do-able" objectives*	____	____	____
45. *Actively listening and understanding others' ideas*	____	____	____
46. *Stating problems clearly and concisely*	____	____	____
47. *Summarizing discussions*	____	____	____
48. *Asking direct open-ended questions*	____	____	____
49. *Understanding what is happening in a group despite the complexity of the interactions*	____	____	____
50. *Looking beneath obvious symptoms to discover core problems*	____	____	____
51. *Giving in when others present a good case*	____	____	____
52. *Acknowledging and encouraging creativity in others*	____	____	____
53. *Teaching others to diagnose their own problems*	____	____	____
54. *Willingly being a student as well as a teacher when looking for underlying causes*	____	____	____
55. *Helping the group to maintain a logical sequence of problem solving*	____	____	____
56. *Describing how others have solved similar problems*	____	____	____
57. *Generating alternative solutions to problems*	____	____	____
58. *Encouraging others to generate alternative solutions to problems*	____	____	____
59. *Genuinely listening to others ideas even when they differ from mine*	____	____	____
60. *Pushing to understand others points of view*	____	____	____
61. *Critically evaluating possible solutions by examining consequences—without "put downs"*	____	____	____
62. *Challenging ineffective solutions without "put downs"*	____	____	____
63. *Helping others to evaluate proposed solutions critically*	____	____	____
64. *Asking for and graciously receiving feedback*	____	____	____
65. *Giving constructive, useful feedback*	____	____	____
66. *Reacting non-defensively when criticized*	____	____	____

Planning, Implementing, & Evaluating Competencies	*Highly Skilled*	*Satis-factory*	*Need to Improve*
67. *Valuing the abilities and knowledge of others*	____	____	____
68. *Being willing to delegate and not be needed*	____	____	____
69. *Asking for help from others*	____	____	____
70. *Starting my planning processes by clarifying vision and mission*	____	____	____
71. *Making values exploration a part of the process*	____	____	____
72. *Letting someone else take the glory*	____	____	____
73. *Promising only what I can deliver*	____	____	____
74. *Doing what I say I will do*	____	____	____
75. *Stating my commitments clearly and concisely*	____	____	____
76. *Communicating and negotiating expectations*	____	____	____
77. *Setting realistic goals for myself*	____	____	____
78. *Helping others to set realistic goals for themselves*	____	____	____
79. *Selecting appropriate interventions and knowing how to implement them*	____	____	____
80. *Attending to the details of planning action*	____	____	____

81. *Encouraging and helping others use their strengths and resources* ____ ____ ____
82. *Taking responsibility* ____ ____ ____
83. *Encouraging, empowering and allowing others to take responsibility* ____ ____ ____
84. *Developing contingency plans* ____ ____ ____
85. *Changing plans when emergencies come up* ____ ____ ____
86. *Assessing/evaluating my own contributions realistically* ____ ____ ____
87. *Realistically assessing/evaluating others' contributions* ____ ____ ____
88. *Acknowledging failure/accepting my part in outcomes* ____ ____ ____
89. *Helping others to acknowledge their part in outcomes* ____ ____ ____
90. *Feeling comfortable with others reviewing/critiquing my work* ____ ____ ____
91. *Evaluating and giving feedback on the work of others* ____ ____ ____
92. *Asking for and accepting feedback graciously* ____ ____ ____
93. *Dealing effectively with unpredicted changes* ____ ____ ____
94. *Demonstrating appropriate evaluation skills* ____ ____ ____
95. *Devising forms, inventories, etc. to aid evaluation* ____ ____ ____
96. *Sticking with the task until it is finished* ____ ____ ____
97. *Encouraging and helping others to finish their tasks* ____ ____ ____
98. *Keeping a journal and writing up what has been done* ____ ____ ____
99. *Letting go when the task is finished* ____ ____ ____
100. *Acknowledging/celebrating/rewarding the contributions of others* ____ ____ ____
101. *Sharing the credit with others when it is due* ____ ____ ____
102. *Celebrating my successes* ____ ____ ____
103. *Arranging follow-up steps* ____ ____ ____
104. *Writing summaries/reports of task/project outcomes* ____ ____ ____

____________________________________ ____ ____ ____

____________________________________ ____ ____ ____

Specific Goals for Improvement, Action Plans, and Timelines

____

____

____

____

____

Chapter IX

Diagnosing Diversity in Organizations

Deborah L. Plummer

Introduction

In the early 1990s, Pictionary, a popular board game, was introduced to America. The object of the game requires participants to identify, through clues sketched by their opponents, difficult words: verbs, persons, places, animals, or objects. Further challenge comes for the player who is sketching and must depict the word in just 60 seconds. As the game begins, the picturist has five seconds to examine the word before he or she begins to sketch. During those five seconds, the other players can clearly see the picturist struggling to take apart the word, in order to break it down into recognizable clues. The picturist may not speak or gesture to teammates and must rely solely on the sketch to put across the meaning of the word. Teammates strive to identify what the picturist is visualizing so clearly in his mind. Often, after the 60 seconds has elapsed, teammates berate the picturist for his or her poor representation of the word ("How did you get that from that word?" "What was that supposed to be?"), or they congratulate and high-five him for successfully depicting the word through his sketches. Many times, teammates are amazed that they were able to identify a word from a poor or limited sketch. The interplay of picturist and teammates in this game is what has made Pictionary a best-selling game and provided a great deal of fun for many families and friends.

All the aspects of the diversity diagnosis are contained in the game of Pictionary. The game employs *methods* of sketching clues for participants to *identify*. The picturist continues the *process* of sketching, and the players keep guessing, until the sketch has been correctly *interpreted*.

As with the game of Pictionary, approaching the process of diagnosing diversity in organizations is also a challenge. Unlike some other diagnostic procedures, diversity diagnosis requires a great deal of emotional preparedness on the parts of both the organization and the practitioner in order for such an assessment to begin. You probably can recall what it is like to be a student on the day that test results are given. I can certainly remember the butterflies in my stomach and the feeling of anxiety in my body as I listened to the instructor make general remarks about how the class as a whole performed on a test. The anxiety would be heightened even more if the professor chose to categorize the grading ("Only 2 people received As, and there were 3 Bs, 25 Cs, 5 Ds, and 2 Fs"). Suddenly, whatever confidence I'd had about how well I might have done on the test disappeared. In just a few minutes, waiting for test results, I had taken a roller-coaster ride with my emotions.

Similarly, approaching diversity diagnosis creates an emotional roller-coaster ride for organizations and for practitioners. Often considered to be a side issue for many organizations, diversity is only dealt with if there is a "problem". The "problem" may mean poor morale, team conflict, threat of a lawsuit, or a filed grievance. The diagnosis appears to be simple — diversity, or managing human differences in the workplace, creates problems that need to be solved, usually by personnel in human resources. It can be easy to understand why approaching diversity diagnosis is not at the top of interventions desirable to undertake in an organization. Yet without an accurate diagnosis, any diversity intervention initiated will be like a shot in the dark. Smart companies know that managing diversity well is one of a company's greatest assets, because managing diversity well leads to enhanced performance and greater productivity. Therefore it is necessary to assess and measure diversity in the organization's current state, if the desired state is to be achieved. Managing diversity well means beginning with an accurate diagnosis of exactly where the organization stands, in regard to managing human differences, and leveraging those differences for organizational effectiveness.

The aim of this chapter is to help you to understand the process of diagnosing diversity in organizations. It focuses on the process of identifying the current state of an organization and the methods for analysis. Topics to be explored include:

- ✦The process of making an organizational diagnosis using the lens of diversity
- ✦Diagnostic tools that support inclusion
- ✦Applying the process of data gathering and analysis to diversity issues
- ✦Feeding back diagnostic information about diversity
- ✦Challenges in diagnosing diversity

While it is arguably not so much fun as playing Pictionary, diagnosing diversity in an organization can be exciting to diversity professionals. It requires the use of a number of skills and competencies to achieve its goal, which many professionals find intellectually stimulating. The process can be quite rewarding — especially when the diagnosis is identified, and it guides the organization to organizational change and improvement.

Preparing to Undertake the Diagnostic Process

Because the diagnostic step is a critical one in the journey toward a diversity-proficient organization, it is important for a diversity professional to pay particular attention to the following conditions before starting a diversity diagnostic process:

✦**Timing:** Diversity initiatives require a great deal of valuable time and resources (financial as well as emotional) from an organization. Is this the right time to examine how differences are managed in the organization?

✦**Readiness:** How mature is this organization? Is the organization in a position to look at its internal operations, procedures, and policies? Will the present culture support this process?

✦**Intention:** Is the organization clear about its intention for diagnosing diversity? This does not mean that there are right or wrong reasons for undertaking this process; whatever the motivation, be it threat of lawsuit or moral integrity, the organization needs to be clear about its intention.

✦**Candidness:** The organization needs to be at a point where it can be honest about what it is and then be ready to hear the many voices that will need to be heard.

Similarly, the diversity professional must carefully consider certain processes when diagnosing diversity in organizations:

✦**Confidentiality:** To increase the effectiveness of the process, confidentiality must be managed in a professional manner. All data must be held confidential and revealed only to appropriate parties.

✦**Objectivity:** Although we know that it is a myth for any practitioner to be truly objective, the diversity diagnostic process particularly requires a balance of objectivity and sensitivity. The practitioner must conduct impartial representation of the data, yet be insightful enough to give meaning to the interplay of hard and soft data.

✦**Creativity:** The diversity diagnostic process requires creativity. The practitioner needs to rely on experience, intuition, and hunches as well as diversity theory, research, and scholarship when gathering and analyzing data, and formulating conclusions and recommendations.

Diversity Management Approaches

It is critical to understand the organization's approach to or understanding of diversity, as well as to know the approach of the diversity practitioner or consultant who will be guiding the diversity effort. The term "diversity" holds perhaps as many meanings as there are organizations, communities, and educational institutions that practice it. For a comprehensive understanding of the many dimensions of diversity and the frameworks that support them, refer to the chapters in the first section of this book. For purposes of diagnosis, differentiating between the three diversity frameworks described in the following section will aid in the initial steps of diagnosing. One or more of the following three frameworks do seem to operate in most businesses, communities, or educational settings:

Diversity as Social Justice: This approach grows out of diversity management's roots in the civil-rights movement. Eliminating oppression, or the ways in which inequitable practice of power is used, is the focus of this approach. Eradicating the "isms," or destructive beliefs and attitudes that individuals may have about race, gender, sexual orientation, or other human differences, is also a goal. Community-based and faith-based organizations often approach diversity from this perspective. Corporate organizations that concentrate on affirmative action and equal employment opportunity share this perspective, since these initiatives are designed to account for the wrongs of discriminatory employment practices in the past. "Leveling the playing field" is a phrase often used in organizations that reflects the notion of equitable use of power and equitable distribution of resources and opportunities. Group-membership identity factors — such as race, ethnicity, gender, class, sexual orientation, age, disability, and religion — become critical components for measuring diversity success.

Diversity as Economic Empowerment: This approach does not hold central the issues of oppression and "isms," but holds as its focus increasing the bottom line. Diversity from this perspective translates into practices that make good business sense — and cents! If a by-product of increasing the bottom line is better race and gender relations, then it is a bonus. If establishing better race and gender relations will increase the bottom line, then we need to have it as a critical part of the strategic plan. Diversity research helps to inform target markets and strategy. If Asians, African Americans, and Hispanics have a spending power of $700 billion dollars, then we need to know what to do to tap into this market. If recruiting information and technology talent is the goal, and the pool of talent includes younger people and people of color, then we need to go after them. If shareholders require the company to be socially responsive, then community partners in diverse neighborhoods will support our goal. Measurement of diversity is critical. Employment practices such as recruitment, retention, and promotion are analyzed from a dollar-amount perspective. Similarly, effective employee relations are measured by reduced employee complaints or grievances, and avoidance of lawsuits. Most for-profit organizations adopt this approach to diversity.

Diversity as Inclusion: This approach is born out of the human-resource frame that capitalizes on the interdependence of people and organizations. People are seen not only as the greatest asset of an organization, but also as key to its effectiveness. Thus, diversity means establishing an organizational culture that promotes inclusion of differences. This approach perceives diversity as a tool for growth and a means for assuring the organization's future. Diversity is an organizational asset, because differences enhance work practices by redefining markets, products, and strategies. From this perspective, organizations manage diversity in such a way as to enable all employees to be able to bring their full selves to the table, thereby enhancing creativity, morale, and productivity. Diversity success is measured by employee satisfaction, lower turnover rates, ability to recruit and retain the best talent, productivity, and an increased bottom line. Many organizations — profit and non-profit, community- and faith-based — operate from this approach.

In reading about these three approaches, you already may have positioned your organization in one of the three slots. Or, as a diversity practitioner, you already may have identified the approach that you lean on the most when approaching your work. Perhaps you are thinking that parts of your organization fit one approach and that others operate out of another framework. Similarly, you may work as a practitioner from one frame with certain organizations and from another frame with a different organization.

No one approach, in and of itself, holds precedent over another approach. Each approach is neutral. You may have had to read those two sentences again. Before you prepare for a debate on the topic, understand that it is not the approach, but the organizational fit (approach coupled with organizational culture and mission), that is the primary intent of the process of diagnosis. The meaning of diversity must work for the organization — if not, little will be achieved. Thus, it is important for the organization and the diversity practitioner to be clear on the meaning of diversity, for an accurate diagnosis to take place.

What is Diversity Diagnosis?

Consider the following case study:

Company Bigbucks, a moderate-sized insurance company, has

been in existence for close to 75 years. Originally a family-owned business, it prides itself on treating its 8,000 employees as its greatest asset. Demographics at each of its three sites have changed over the years, resulting in a considerably more diverse workforce. Because its reputation is a good one, the company continues to make a profit; however, profits have been slower as domestic competition and global markets have increased. The company is interested in being the premier insurance company, while maintaining the values that have been part of its tradition.

In the tradition of Mr. Bigbucks, the company holds to openly expressed values of hard work and excellence for all its employees, but particularly for managers and top leadership, these values are a requirement. Hard work translates into long workdays that extend into the evening and Saturday mornings spent in the office with coffee and doughnuts; a less formal atmosphere prevails, while the work is still accomplished. Managers and top-level leaders know each other and their families well. Most socialize together and even take vacations together. Discussion and evaluation of work projects often occurs at social gatherings, and vacations may incorporate "working lunches." Performance excellence means that one follows the prescribed methods and procedures for proven successful outcomes. Evaluations are based on how the work is done as well as on the outcome.

After a mailing of the company newsletter to its shareholders, a consumer called one of the men pictured in the brochure, requesting information about the company's diversity commitment. The picture of the company leaders displayed on the cover of the brochure showed a group of white males, and the consumer wondered whether the company reflected the client base that it served. The consumer was told that the company indeed employed some women and people of color, although the upper management (pictured in the newsletter) was composed entirely of white males. The consumer expressed dissatisfaction with this limited response, since the director had considered the subject of diversity only in relationship to group membership identity. In response to her dissatisfaction, he offered to send a representa-

tive to meet with her to address any further questions.

At the next leadership meeting, the director who received the call related the incident to his peers. After a brief discussion, they congratulated their colleague for dealing with the issue in a direct and courteous manner, especially because they perceived the consumer to be a complainer. The leadership team believed the incident was simply representative of the political correctness that was sweeping the country. The leadership team further determined that no other action was necessary.

Company Bigbucks is not an unusual case presentation for the 21st century. As a business, it is holding its own when it comes to reviewing the bottom line. The company also considers itself to be performing competitively and regards its organizational culture as healthy. Company norms are considered to be open, and the culture believes itself to be clear in its requirements for employment and promotion opportunities. Employees are prized and treated well, from a compensation standpoint. Yet would you vote this company one of the top organizations to work for, based on the information provided? How would you evaluate its relationship to diversity? What do you believe to be the working definition of diversity for Company Bigbucks?

While reading this case study, you may have already started the process of diversity diagnosis. Diversity diagnosis is the process that guides the development of diversity competencies in an organization. It is an assessment of how well the organization is doing with managing a diverse workforce and making use of its benefits to increase organizational effectiveness and learning. The process of diversity diagnosis is the initial step in developing interventions that will be linked to a diversity strategic plan for supporting organizational change and improvement.

What is diagnosed?

- ✦Organizational culture (values, traditions, norms, artifacts)
- ✦Business rationale (organizational history and mission)
- ✦Employee morale (work identity and spirit)
- ✦Physical space (decor, design)
- ✦Employee demographics (group membership identity of

employees)

- ✦Turnover patterns (reviewed according to group membership identity)
- ✦Promotion patterns (reviewed according to group membership identity)
- ✦Brochures (any written descriptions of company)
- ✦Organization's working definition of diversity
- ✦Board membership (reviewed according to group membership identity and leadership roles)
- ✦Mentoring practices (formal and informal)
- ✦Reward systems (reviewed for cultural flexibility)
- ✦Strategic plans (for inclusion issues)

Redirect your thinking to the case study of Company Bigbucks. As you consider the list of organizational aspects that are part of the diagnostic process, you may be acutely aware of the lack of information that you possess to support your initial assessment. You may have considered Company Bigbucks *not* to be diversity-affirming, but were unaware of a benchmark to support your claim. You may have considered Company Bigbucks to be diversity-affirming, but lacked a framework against which to defend your position. Whether you are a CEO, manager, supervisor, diversity-council member, consultant, or diversity practitioner, this chapter will help you to assess how well your organization is doing, in managing a diverse workforce and the related diversity issues.

Diversity Diagnosis Skills

Practitioners of diversity diagnosis are change agents of a special kind. Unlike diversity innovators, diversity champions, or diversity cheerleaders, professionals who engage in diagnosing diversity in organizations possess a distinctive set of skills and competencies:

- ✦Clarity about the meaning of diversity for the company, and about how diversity differs from the practice of affirmative action, equal opportunity employment, or social justice.
- ✦Ability to engage in dialogue as a communication structure that supports inclusion and objective research.

- Mastery of systems thinking — understanding the interrelationships that shape the dynamics of differences.
- Ability to hold multiple realities while still appreciating individual reality.
- Competent practice of qualitative research — a type of research that produces findings not arrived at by statistical procedures or other means of quantification.
- Competent practice of quantitative research — a type of research the produces findings based on statistical procedures.
- Use of the art of feedback.

Diversity Diagnostic Process

The steps of the diagnostic process are:

- Understanding the working definition of diversity for the organization
- Choosing the right method(s) for diagnosis
- Determining the level of analysis
- Applying frameworks for interpretation
- Developing appropriate reporting procedures

Although it would appear to be most logical to proceed in a step-by-step manner when diagnosing diversity, there are occasions when the level of analysis may precede the choice of method. Or the results from a previous questionnaire or focus-group study may be available for reinterpretation through a diversity lens. In the best conditions, however, fresh data, gathered with this particular diagnosis in mind, is recommended.

Understanding the Working Definition of Diversity

The process of diagnosing diversity in any organization begins with understanding the organization's approach to diversity management. If an organization does not have a working definition and is new to the area of diversity management, it may be necessary to develop a process that unveils their approach. An organization may be inexperienced in its formal management approach, but that does not mean that it does not have a definition of diversity informally operating within the system.

Because we are talking about what diversity means in an organization, it would be important to make sure that the definition is representative of the collective voice of the organization and that it does not come only from an assumed understanding of the term. If diversity means respecting one another in the workplace, the approach for managing it will be very different from that of an organization that holds, as its meaning of diversity, the enhancement of the bottom line through effective performance from all employees.

Start where the organization is. If your organization does not have a working definition, begin the process of defining what is already in existence in your system. This is different from a visioning process, whereby you work to determine your preferred future or desired state. You are simply labeling the "what is" of your organization, in order to accurately diagnose how well it is doing in achieving what it believes to be diversity. The process of identifying an organization's working definition of diversity uses methodology similar to the process of diagnosis — review of hard and soft data, interviews, questionnaires, and focus groups are appropriate choices. These methods will be discussed more fully later. However, the process of discovering the organization's working definition is clearly not so extensive or intense. A working definition is a dynamic entity. Thus, you merely want to ascertain what is already present rather than stir up the need to evaluate whether or not the present definition is a good fit. That information will clearly come out in the diagnostic process. The important aspect is to make sure the working definition is one that holds the collective voice and is not just one lifted from a book or video on diversity management. It needs to really work for your organization.

Once the definition is clearly in place, it is easy to understand that definition from the framework that it represents (see examples in Table 1).

Think for a moment about your own organization. What words or phrases characterize the meaning of diversity for your organization? Skim through your organization's promotional material, examine your mission statement, visually assess your company's decor, think about your organization's values and leadership. What does this information tell you about the meaning of diversity in your organization? Jot some of these phrases in the space provided. Next to each phrase in Table 2., put the basic approach from which the concept is born.

Definition of Diversity	**Diversity Management Approach**
Organizational effectiveness	Inclusion
Respect for and sensitivity to differences	Social justice/inclusion
Competitive advantage	Economic empowerment
Interrupting inequality	Social justice
Valuing difference	Inclusion
Creating an anti-racist, gender-fair, multicultural organization, community, or educational institution	Social justice
A business imperative for the 21st century	Economic empowerment

Table 1. Definition vs. Frameworks

Diversity Phrases	**Diversity Approach**
1.	
2.	
3.	
4.	

Table 2. The Meaning of Diversity for your Organization

What does this information tell you about your organization's basic approach to diversity?

The aim of diagnosis is not to change or influence an organization's approach, or where an organization should or could be, but simply to be able to lay out the data in a meaningful manner for the organization's development of diversity competencies. Building a credible database that includes quantitative and qualitative data, hard data (historical and present-day facts), and soft data (psychological facts) is the ground from which accurate diagnosis takes place.

Choosing the Right Methodology

How the data is collected will determine the *kind* of data that is available for interpretation. Thus, asking the right question and choosing the right method to support getting the appropriate framework is critical to obtaining the diagnosis that will lead to a measurable outcome. Get the sequence?

Right Question→Right Method→Appropriate Framework →Accurate Diagnosis→Measurable Outcome

Like a set of dominos arranged to stand one against the other, good positioning will allow the structure to stand erect. Poor positioning of any one of the dominos will collapse the entire setup!

Asking the Right Question

Asking the right question begins with being clear about the intended outcome. What do you want to see as different in the organization? How will you know when you have the answer? What is the desired goal? How will we know that we are successful after this intervention? These questions will lead to responses that will set the direction for the inquiry process. For example, if my desired outcome is to build an inclusive learning community for my educational institution, then I start by examining what is meant by "inclusive" and exploring what inclusive behaviors look like. From this dialogue, I can then get collaboration on what is meant by "a learning community" and how those inclusive behaviors might be practiced in that community.

With the specific understanding of what constitutes an inclusive learning community, I am now armed with a means by which to diagnose the culture under consideration. I can now choose the appropriate method for obtaining the answer to my question.

Choosing the Right Method

The methods for gathering data to support an accurate diagnosis are the practitioner's tools for success. Choosing the right tools will not only get the job done correctly, but will get the job done in an efficient manner. If you have ever watched a professional worker repair something in your home, you know the difference a correct tool can make to getting the job done efficiently and effectively. Similarly, in diagnosing diversity, the appropriate choice of methodology will assure the desired outcome. The data gathering tools most often used in diversity diagnosis are the following:

- Questionnaires and Surveys
- Individual Interviews
- Environmental/Cultural Scans
- Observation/Sponging/Scouting
- Focus Groups
- Historical Timeline Analysis
- Benchmarking
- Best Practices/Current Struggles Profiles
- Career-Path Process Mapping
- Diversity Dialogue Sessions
- Critical-Incident Interviewing
- Large-Group Interventions (Appreciative Inquiry, Whole-Scale Change, Future Search)

These methods are used most often in diversity diagnosis, because they tend to be inclusive in gathering data. Table 3.depicts the advantages and disadvantages of each method, considered from a diversity perspective.

METHOD	ADVANTAGES	DISADVANTAGES
Best Practices/Current Struggles Profile: An inventory process for cataloguing the organization's best diversity practices and its current struggles in diversity management.	Can involve the entire organization in the identification of the profile. A simple, inexpensive process that can yield rich data.	Only provides information on the current state of the organization; without careful analysis, does not support creating a meaningful organizational diagnosis or provide direction for future desired state.
Career-Path Process Mapping: Visual representation of the process for promotion and retention in an organization. Data is gathered from career-path interviews with leadership teams and key individuals.	Reveals the subtle and complex systems interactions of an organization. Identifies the soft data (psychological facts) that often lie behind the "glass ceiling," "race ceiling" or "pink ceiling" in organizations.	Requires senior-level diversity-consulting skills and deep understanding of both organizational culture and how institutional "isms" work.
Diversity Dialogue Sessions: An open but guided conversation on diversity issues in an organization.	A communication structure that supports the exploration of complex issues such as diversity. With the right groundwork and guidelines, can create a climate where rich data can surface.	Requires skillful facilitation. Not always a good method to use in early stages of an organization's diversity effort. Better for mid-stage diagnosis.
Critical-Incident Interviewing: Reports from employees of behavioral episodes observed in the organization that support or detract from inclusion efforts.	Reconstructs specific events or certain processes that create organizational culture. Can identify specific behaviors that support inclusive environments.	Requires good interviewing skills and careful analysis. Unless training is created that is directed toward development of identified behaviors, the data remains dormant.
Large-Group Interviews: Appreciative Inquiry, Future Search, Whole-Scale Change, Open Space. Group processes that can be used with the entire organization, and that can be specifically targeted to diversity issues in organizations.	Inclusive, engaging, and energizing interventions. Inherently diversity-affirming.	Requires long-term planning and skillful facilitation. Deceptively simple processes that can be a disaster if not well planned or executed by experienced facilitation.

Table 3. Advantages and Disadvantages of Data-Gathering Methods from a Diversity Perspective

METHOD	ADVANTAGES	DISADVANTAGES
Questionnaires/ Surveys/Rating Scales: Paper and pen measures, with questions focused on general diversity issues and topics.	Gathers information effectively and efficiently. Can be used with a very large to a very small employee base. Gives everyone an opportunity to have a voice in the process.	Not always sensitive to the affective realm, or to subtle complexities of diversity management. Often data is reduced to numbers that, in turn, do not influence organizational change.
Individual Interview: One-to-one responses to either open-ended or structured questions on diversity issues.	Can be sensitive to the complexities and affective realm of diversity. Interpretations can be checked.	Time-consuming; costly; interactive bias can occur; yields data that often gets lost, either because it is interpreted only on the individual level, or because of the data's expansiveness; does not influence organizational change.
Environmental/Cultural Scan: A process of exploring the physical and social context within which the organization functions. Its purpose is to discover the relationship of the organization to the external world.	Contextualizes diversity; yields information that provides direction for the organization's diversity mission and vision.	Big-picture emphasis does not attend to details. Presents only a theoretical framework. Data requires translation into action plans.

Historical Timeline Analysis: A process of reviewing the organization's history through the experience of its people. Participants create a dynamic history of the organization's life in relationship to external trends.	Identifies significant trends, rate, and rhythm of change, and impact of historical events on the organization's culture.	Requires strong identification with the organization, its culture, and its context. Also necessary are good facilitation and careful analysis, in order for identified trends, themes, and patterns to be used for future direction and strategic planning.
Benchmarking: A means of identifying the status of the organization in the progression of its diversity initiatives.	Lays the foundation for the change process to begin. Identifies organization's current state and allows the visioning process to begin.	Only limited frameworks for benchmarking and identification of diversity competencies are available, either for review or as prototypes. Consensus on necessary competencies for professional practice is still being established.
Observation/Sponging/Scouting: Watching individuals and experiencing the environment in its natural context.	Reality-based; enables observer to monitor how different groups interact. Provides rich data in initial stages of diversity change process. Allows soft data, or "psychological facts," to surface more readily.	Observer must be objective and consistent in documentation. "Hawthorne Effect," or influencing the behavior of people under observation, can occur.
Focus Groups: A group-interview process used for gathering data on general or specific diversity issues for an organization.	Identifies diversity opportunities and challenges. Provides a systematic process for recording, analyzing, and interpreting data. Representative sample of workforce allows organization to get a sense of organization's current reality. Values different points of view.	Requires development of meaningful questions, skillful moderation, and careful analysis and interpretation. Anecdotal responses reflecting systems-level impact require framework of higher-level analysis.

Table 3. Advantages and Disadvantages of Data-Gathering Methods from a Diversity Perspective Continued

Determining the Level of Analysis

You may have heard the phrase "If you only have a hammer, everything looks like a nail." For many organizations, the diversity toolbox only has a hammer in it. Thus, when diversity issues surface, the "fix" becomes training for the entire employee base. This often happens with minimal or no preparation for the employees and usually requires mandatory attendance. The workforce easily peers through this thin veil and wonders why the initiative is starting at this particular time. They quickly determine that the diversity effort is just the "flavor of the month," or a way for the organization to "cover its behind." With good facilitation and a stimulating training agenda, the sessions are not always a complete loss for the company. Often, these rollouts serve to get everyone on the same diversity page, as far as knowledge is concerned. However, this one-size-fits-all approach is not the ideal recommendation for diversity management. Based on both the definition of diversity and the organization's readiness, the level of system at which to intervene can be determined. The following table outlines the best diversity change effort in relation to levels of systems within the organization (see Table 4).

Level of System	Source/Catalyst for Change	Recommended Intervention
INDIVIDUAL	A personal diversity issue that does not reflect an organizational pattern but prevents individuals from fully tapping into their potential for the organization's benefit (e.g. religious affiliation, transgender, nationality differences).	• Coaching • Educational Inventories (workshops, classes)
INTERPERSONAL	Dyad has problems in teams or work groups (e.g., race- or gender-based conflict).	• Mediation • Team-Building Sessions
GROUP	Individuals who share the same group identity experience the same phenomena. Data identified through survey, rating, or anecdotal information.	• Network and Affiliation Groups • Focus-Group Evaluations • Career-Path Analysis • Diversity Dialogue Sessions
ORGANIZATIONAL	Norms, policies, and procedures systematically work against or underutilize differences in the work place (e.g., hiring and promotion practices).	• Leadership Briefings • Diversity Competency Training • Establishment of Diversity Councils

Table 4. Diversity Change and Levels of System

Applying Framework for the Interpretation

A limited number of theoretically based diversity frameworks are available for defining and measuring organizational effectiveness in diversity management. These models delineate the broad arena for guiding choices for diversity progression and change. Most practitioners find that the data-collection process generally yields a vast amount of data for interpretation — frequency charts, percentages, themes, anecdotes, case studies — all of which needs to be found useful for supporting the organization in moving toward diversity proficiency. Using any of these frameworks to express your diagnosis is one way of interpretating data. Two of the most frequently cited frameworks — "Continuum of Cultural Competence" (NIMH, 1989) and "Diversity Paradigms" (1996) — are summarized in Tables 5 and 6. Frameworks such as the "Continuum of Cultural Competence" and "Diversity Paradigms" can be used by organizations as external markers for charting diversity progression. Encouraging an organization to design its own continuum for charting its progression is perhaps the most meaningful way to support an organization in its effort to achieve diversity success. After a feedback session presenting the data, the leadership team or diversity council creates labels that mark the current status of the organization and labels for its future state. Descriptors of each marker can be gleaned from the data. An example of an internal marker for a fictitious company follows in Table 7.

Continuum of Cultural Competence

CULTURAL DESTRUCTIVENESS	CULTURAL INCAPACITY	CULTURAL BLINDNESS	CULTURAL PRE-COMPETENCE	BASIC COMPETENCE	CULTURAL PROFICIENCY
System holds attitudes, policies, and practices destructive to cultures and individuals.	System is biased. It supports segregation and displays ignorance and unrealistic fear of People of Color.	System has philosophy of being unbiased and well intentioned, but is ethnocentric. Ignores cultural strengths, encourages assimilation.	System realizes weakness and attempts to improve. Experiments. Displays false sense of accomplishment.	System shows acceptance and respect for differences. Continual self-assessment. Commitment to practices that flow from philosophy.	System holds culture in high esteem. Seeks to add to knowledge base of cultural competence. Advocates for cultural competence.

Source: National Institute of Mental Health (1989). "Towards a Culturally Competent System of Care" (CASSP Report). Washington, D.C.: CASSP Technical Assistance Center

Table 5. Frameworks for Interpreting Diversity Diagnostic Data--External Markers

Paradigms for Managing Diversity

The Discrimination-and-Fairness Paradigm
Focuses on equal opportunity, fair treatment, recruitment, and compliance with federal Equal Employment Opportunity requirements.

Key = assimilation

The Access-and-Legitimacy Paradigm
Focuses on a more diverse clientele, matching the demographics of the organization to those of critical consumer or constituent groups.

Key = differentiation

The Learning-and-Organizational-Effectiveness Paradigm
Focuses on incorporating employees' perspectives into the main work of the organization. Seeks to enhance work by rethinking primary tasks and redefining markets, products, strategies, missions, business practices, and even cultures.

Key = integration

Source: "Making Differences Matter: A New Paradigm for Managing Diversity," by David A. Thomas and Robin J. Ely. Harvard Business Review, September 1, 1996.

Table 6: Frameworks for Interpreting Diversity Diagnostic Data - External Markers

Exclusive/Perpetuating Organization	→	Engaging/Forming Organization	→	Inclusive/Transforming Organization
▪ Decisions are made by Dominant Group membership, without input from diverse membership and from those who lives will be most affected by those decisions. ▪ Dominant Group owns the property and makes the fiscal decisions. ▪ Financial gain, rather than organization vision, dictates behaviors. ▪ Public political affiliations are not representative of the whole or decided consensually. ▪ Unwritten rules and practices go unquestioned. ▪ Community contacts are limited to a select few. ▪ Mentoring practices are limited to Dominant Group. ▪ Conflict related to diversity is suppressed. ▪ Board memberships and governance exist to serve and support leadership.		▪ Analysis and implementation of diversity is superficial. ▪ Token recognition of People of Color and women is given for image or political reasons. ▪ People of Color are hired, but relegated to lower positions or culturally specific positions. ▪ Consensus is used for decision-making. ▪ Organization experiments with new initiatives and evaluates results in a positive manner. ▪ Community contacts are made for convenience and expediency. ▪ Conflict related to diversity is managed. ▪ Board membership includes demographic diversity, but not diversity of thought or expression.		▪ Policies and procedures are reviewed systematically for inclusion. ▪ Individual identity is appreciated as an organizational strength. ▪ People of Color and women are included outside of culture/gender-specific roles. ▪ Organizational effectiveness is the driving force for any business decision. ▪ Collaboration and dialogue are used for decision-making. ▪ Practices and procedures are clearly written and public. ▪ Organization is continually in a learning mode. ▪ Diversity-related conflict is viewed as an opportunity to enhance appreciation, support empowerment, and develop creative outcomes. ▪ Board membership exists to hold moral ownership on behalf of the community.

Table 7. An Example of a Customized Diversity Continuum Company XYZ Internal MarkerSystem Practices: A Continuum Toward Inclusion

Developing Appropriate Reporting Procedures

Most seasoned practitioners find that creating a picture — through words, symbols, and charts — that is customized for the organization is the best way to capture the diagnosis for an organization. The following "Benchmark Box" is an example of how a great deal of data was synthesized for an organization.

DIVERSITY BENCHMARK BOX

Name: Company XYZ

Location: 123 Diversity Highway

Type of Corporation: Service/Small Business

Services: Communications Delivery Systems

Number of Sites: 3

Number of Employees: 1,100

External Paradigm: Between "Discrimination and Fairness" and "Access and Legitimacy"

External Continuum: Between "Culturally Blind" and "Culturally Pre-competent" Organization

Diversity Report Card Rating: B- / C

Internal Benchmark: Between "Exclusive/Perpetrating" and "Engaging/Forming" Organization

Strengths: Long history of successful process and procedures for direct-service delivery. Integrated service-delivery system. Dedicated leadership and staff.

Improvement Agenda: Engaging the "whole system." Inclusion. Communications and measurement accountability for diversity. Enhancing the principle of full participation.

What is important in providing diversity diagnostic feedback to an organization is to make sure that the feedback is given in a collaborative manner. Presenting the data or findings in themes, or as growth opportunities, sets the stage for the cultural-change process to occur. Remember — unlike sales figures or stock-market results, diversity data are dynamic sets of energy that can position the organization for positive movement, leveraging all the human talent available.

Factors to Include in Reporting a Diversity Diagnosis

1. Identify the sources (hopefully, multiple) that contributed to the diagnosis.
2. Discern the organization's ability and readiness for change.
3. Provide snapshots of diversity competence already existing in the organization (most organizations are doing something right, even if it is just initiating the diversity diagnostic process).
4. Define where the organization is positioned, in terms of being fully functioning in regard to diversity. Frameworks help to clarify the progression.
5. Present a menu of interventions identifying those that are "quick fixes" — the easily attainable interventions that do not rely on a great deal of human or financial capital (e.g., removing the picture of the leadership team in the Company Bigbucks brochure and replacing it with pictures of the company's diverse workforce would get a lot of diversity mileage with consumers).

Challenges in Diversity Diagnosis

At the beginning of this chapter, we stated that other important ingredients for success include readiness for cultural change on the part of the organization and its drivers. In other chapters of this handbook, we have emphasized use-of-self as a tool in diversity management. Particularly in the diagnostic process, is it important for the diversity practitioner to be aware of his or her own personal interests, beliefs, and attitudes as they contribute to forming the lens through which the data is interpreted.

Many diversity practitioners who engage in this work are driven by a personal experience that has led them to a strong commitment of valuing human differences. Most diversity practitioners are passionate change agents. Using the energy of this passion in a way that first and foremost serves the client can prevent some diversity dilemmas.

In performing diagnostic work, it is critical to keep in mind a basic systems principle derived from Gestalt psychology — a system is always doing the best it can at any given moment. Only from that perspective can we, as diversity practitioners, effect positive change.

References

National Institute of Mental Health (1989). *Towards a culturally competent system of care* (CASSP Report). Washington, D.C.: CASSP Technical Center.

Thomas, D. & Ely R. J. (1996). *Making differences matter: A new paradigm for managing diversity.* Harvard Business Review. (September-October 50-61). Reprint No. 96510.

Chapter X

Assessing, Measuring, and Analyzing the Impact of Diversity Initiatives

Edward E. Hubbard

Introduction

If you were to analyze many organizational efforts to transition to a diverse work environment, a strange paradox would emerge: While a persuasive, measurable case can be made for the economic benefits of managing and leveraging diversity, this critical outcome is rarely emphasized in most strategic business initiatives.

In fact, in many organizations it appears that the business case for diversity is deliberately left out of the discussion. It almost seems counter-intuitive that this potentially powerful argument is omitted so often in organizations that have service, growth, profitability, and customer-focused marketing strategies at the top of their list of goals and objectives.

The purpose of this chapter is to identify a brief sample of tools, techniques, and procedures to assess, measure, and analyze diversity initiatives in quantitative and qualitative terms. It is designed to help outline methods to tie diversity to the organization's bottom line performance outcomes. Assessing, measuring, and analyzing the impact of diversity initiatives is a critical link for success in diversity management and organizational performance today, and in the future. "You can't manage what you don't measure" and managing and leveraging diversity is fast becoming a business imperative. If diversity initiatives are not approached in a systematic, logical, and planned way, calculating diversity return on investment (DROI) will not be possible and consequently, diversity will not become integrated into the fabric of the organization.

It is the job of diversity practitioners to make certain that the credibility of diversity efforts do not suffer. In order to be taken seriously, diversity practitioners must become adept at measuring diversity results that tie it to the organization's bottom-line. We must build a strong business practice reputation using effective diversity measurement and management techniques such that diversity is seen as an important driver of organizational performance!

Objectives

This chapter is designed to help you:

- ✦Dispel the myths related to diversity measurement
- ✦Identify at least four reasons why diversity measurement is not currently a common organizational practice beyond affirmative action statistics
- ✦Identify some common diversity measures and their potential profit impact
- ✦Learn methods to assess diversity initiatives
- ✦Describe the components of a "Diversity Value Chain"
- ✦Calculate Diversity Return on Investment (DROI) using the 7-step Hubbard Diversity ROI Model and a case study example
- ✦Describe why diversity measurement and management is critical to improved organizational performance

Is It All Subjective?

If you were to analyze many organizational efforts to transition to a diverse work environment, a strange paradox would emerge: While a persuasive, measurable case can be made for the economic benefits of managing and leveraging diversity, this critical outcome is rarely emphasized in most strategic business initiatives.

In fact, in many organizations it appears that the business case for diversity is deliberately left out of the discussion. It almost seems counter-intuitive that this potentially powerful argument is omitted so often in organizations that have service, growth, profitability, and customer-focused marketing strategies at the top of their list of goals and objectives.

There seems to be a myth operating within business, government and other communities which suggest that the outcomes or results created by a diversity implementation process defies measurement or can only be measured in the long-term. In a sense, it is presented with the fundamental belief that creating an effective diverse, inclusive work environment is something of a complex and mysterious art form. Allegedly, the real value of diversity work can only be judged by those who perform it, those who are truly committed to its purpose or value it as important, etc. Even then, the assessment of the results is saddled with subjectivity.

Some diversity specialists perceive that there is an inherent conflict between what is good for business and what is good for people. Some others believe, like truth, that the real reward is in the work itself. The words often used to describe the results include terms such as working better, appreciating differences, understanding each other better, less conflict, getting along, working as a team, and other similar non-measurement specific words. While these are admirable aims in themselves they are not enough. Especially when organizations are looking for strategies to deal with increased competition, options for reducing cost, adding value for stakeholders, adding dollars and increasing productivity to affect the bottom-line.

These notions seem to imply that quantifiable and quality-based measures cannot be applied to the diversity implementation process or a diverse work culture. Some people even believe that diversity is not a business focused activity, simply another form of affirmative action regulatory compliance, even though demographics, which are irrefutable, have been set in motion that make diversity not only a community, business and customer issue, but a global issue!

Whether the subjective position is valid or not is a key question to be sure. However, just the fact that it exists and that some diversity professionals and others support it creates major problems. It sets managing and leveraging diversity apart from the rest of the organization. While peers in other organizational areas are focusing on metrics which reflect their contribution such as sales, reduced costs, profits, income and expenses, service level to customers, etc., those implementing the diversity process may limit its contribution to increased awareness, improved feelings and increased satisfaction among groups. It is a real missed opportunity.

Some line managers quickly make judgments about diversity being a "soft", non-business-oriented endeavor that contributes little to bottom line performance. In addition, these managers may also assume that those involved in diversity neither understand or are interested in measuring diversity's contribution to the organization. As a result, diversity is not taken seriously, fewer managers support it in actual practice i.e., sending their workforce to be trained, structuring their workforce to leverage its richness through teaming, implementing strategic human resource advantages to penetrate key ethnic customer markets, etc. We know from current organizational practice that diversity initiatives experience less follow-through than other business initiatives. Many diversity managers resent this second-hand treatment, yet it is inevitable given the lack of a common connection and language which is fundamental to business. That language is numbers.

Reasons Why Not

There are a number of reasons why there is a lack of quantification in diversity. Probably the most prevalent is that diversity professionals simply do not know how to objectively measure diversity activities.

The focus on strategic diverse workforce management and development is still relatively new. In addition, there are many routes into diversity and the process of diverse workforce development. Until Dr. Edward E. Hubbard founded the Diversity Measurement and Productivity Institute, few, if any organizations offered public training in quantitative methods for diversity. Many diversity professionals are still trying to understand all of the implications of diverse workforce trends in the national and global arena. Since there were few predecessors, it is not surprising that many diversity professionals still rely on subjective measures.

There are some schools and individuals who have developed measures such as Dr. Taylor Cox Jr., at the University of Michigan in his book: "Cultural Diversity In Organizations: Theory, Research & Practice" (Cox, 1993). Or Lawrence M. Baytos, who co-published a book with the Society for Human Resources Management entitled:

"Designing & Implementing Successful Diversity Programs" in which he devotes a chapter on the subject of measuring diversity's benefits and maintaining momentum (Baytos, 1995). Dr Edward E. Hubbard's groundbreaking books: "Measuring Diversity Results" (Hubbard, 1997), "How to Calculate Diversity Return On Investment" (Hubbard, 1999), and "Building a Diversity Measurement Scorecard" (Hubbard, 2001) are changing the diversity measurement landscape. They outline step-by-step methods, processes, and procedures to measure the impact of diversity initiatives in infinite detail using both quantitative and qualitative measures. Dr. Hubbard's approach utilizes two systemic organizational change and analysis paradigms: the "Diversity 9-S Framework" and the "Diversity Return on Investment (DROI) Analysis Model. "All in all, for someone who wants to start a measurement system in their organization to change to a more inclusive, diverse workforce there is now more help available.

The second reason behind the subjectivity myth is the values conflict. Some believe that objective measurement is simply inappropriate for diversity work. In their eyes, diversity work is a function devoted to stimulating and supporting human development, and they see no reason to evaluate outcomes in other than humanitarian terms. This one-sided approach is prevalent in many occupations. Some managers believe, for example, the sole mission of training is to transfer technical information about work from one person's brain into the brains of the workers. This is the technical competency model of human development. They see no real responsibility to teach workers to think, evaluate, or form values. Some architects believe their job is to create a container within which some kind of activity can be efficiently carried out. They overlook the fact that human beings interact with the space and can be depressed or stimulated by it.

These perspectives ignore the holistic philosophies of systemic organizational views. Diversity is not done only for diversity sake. It is related to systemic organizational change. Like these examples, diversity measurement must be seen in an organizational context. One related to the improvement of organizational performance.

For those whose value system conflict with the notion of measuring diversity, there is little hope for change....unless they experience a "significant emotional event" like losing their diversity job, budget funding, and/or support because it is thought that very little value is derived from their diversity work. Even then some people still may not "get it".

Until they expand their outlook to include supporting the strategic purpose of the organization, there will be the perception that management should just see this as "a good thing" or the "right thing" to do.

Another very common reason why diversity organizations or diversity activities are not measured is that some diversity professionals fear measurement. Perhaps it is born out of a fear of knowing. However, if you don't know, you can almost guarantee that nothing will ever improve. But what if you're making terrific progress and don't know it? What if several organizations were doing a great job in leveraging the diverse talents of their workforce and are beginning to slip back into old, less effective habits? Key opportunities for adjustment and reinforcement would be missed. The implications of this can be mind-boggling. This brings us to the fourth and last reason for the subjectivity myth.

This reason relates to the fact that some members of top management have bought the myth of subjectivity (....but not for long)! Perhaps because for a long time, there has been little interest in human resource based issues. The early captains of industry simply never asked the question. As time progressed, the tradition of non-measurability went unchallenged. Few CEOs have taken more than a cursory tour in the human resources department during their careers. It was often just a quick stop along the way to the executive suite. Just about the time they were beginning to sink their teeth into what could be accomplished and what may need to be changed, they were off to another "developmental assignment". Many of these budding executives, knowing the assignment would be a brief 12-18 months, looked for quick projects with a lot of visibility. Very few embarked upon major, fundamental projects such as diversity that would touch all facets of the organization. However, today this is changing.

Actions Speak Louder Than Words

Rightsizing, downsizing, reengineering, reorganizations and other buzzwords depict widespread department cuts, sizable employee layoffs, and significant budget reductions without regards to the impact on workforce diversity.

The goal of these efforts? To eliminate functions that do not add value to the bottom line. Senior executives are examining all areas of the organization to determine contribution level and alignment with strategic and competitive goals of the organization. If organizational departments or efforts cannot demonstrate levels of contribution, they are considered suspect and potentially targets for elimination.

In an article in the Philadelphia Inquirer, this trend was confirmed with the headline: "As the year ends, companies step up the pace of lay-offs":

> It happens whenever new budgets are approved. But this year has brought more and bigger cuts. The list reads like a roster of blue-chip corporations: AT&T, IBM, 3M, Sprint, Fruit of the Loom, Bell South, and more. During the past month, companies at the heart of corporate America have announced plans to reduce their workforce's—in many cases, by the thousands.......AT&T Corp. dropped a blockbuster Wednesday with word it was offering severance packages to almost 78,000 managers to trim its payroll by a yet-to-be-disclosed number. Sprint announced 1,600 cuts the same day. Minnesota Mining & Manufacturing Co. (3M) said Tuesday it was cutting 5,000 positions in a restructuring......The reductions this fall come as companies struggle to increase profits in a slow growth economic climate. Some cutbacks are merger-related. Others are pure cost-cutting. For many companies, though, the job reductions are merely steps in an ongoing process.....Stephen S. Roach, chief economist at Morgan Stanley & Co., the Wall Street investment firm, says that by year-end the number of layoffs reported since March 1991, when the recovery from the 1990 recession began, will be 2.5 Million. "That's a carnage without precedent", he said.

Source: The Philadelphia Inquirer, November 18, 1995, p. D1

So, how does any organization's diversity efforts measure up? Does diversity bring value to the bottom line or strategic outcomes, or is it perceived as a luxury well suited for the ax? Diversity professionals have an opportunity to be a proactive force (rather than a reactive protector) in communicating the success and value of their diversity efforts. They can have positive, open discussions regarding the effects of the organization's diversity efforts on its financial, strategic, human capital development, and competitive goals. More and more, performance measures are being used to evaluate the effectiveness of every aspect of an organization; diversity is no exception.

The preceding discussion should not suggest that measurement is the panacea "cure-all" to diversity's acceptance into the corporate landscape. Measurement applied to diversity or any other human resource area is fraught with complexity among a cluttered canvass of contributors who claim to contribute to bottom-line outcomes of the organization. Remember, diversity activities are not conducted in a vacuum.

For organizations that are simultaneously going through activities such as terminating employees, major reorganizations and mergers, reengineering, etc., how do you separate the specific effects of the diversity programs with any degree of accuracy? It should be understood from the outset that the attribution of specific causes and effects will not be easy (Baytos, 1995). It's no surprise that measuring diversity results is beginning to surface more in corporate discussions, given the context of recent business trends and pressures for improved performance.

Watch Out for the Double Standard

"While the question of sincerity of interest in identifying the value of diversity interventions is not in question, one sometimes wonders if organizations are attempting to apply a tougher standard of evaluation for diversity processes than they do for other ongoing activities". (Baytos, 1995) This notion is an important consideration. There are numerous organizational activities that have little or no measurement support to justify their existence, yet they continue to be upheld vigorously by top management.

> For example, those who might be demanding some specific proofs for diversity programming, at the same time will be moving ahead on the following activities. A meeting costing $500,000 held for key managers and their significant others for "sharing the strategic plan and the chairman's vision, etc. The meeting is held at a posh resort during the workweek, and much of the time is spent on the golf course, cocktail parties and tennis courts. The activity is felt to be essential to "morale, commitment, communications" and so on, but there is no attempt to measure the specific impact of the meeting.
>
> Additions are made to the company jet fleet, and company limo service is expanded to enhance "executive productivity", without indicating how that productivity will specifically benefit shareholders, over and above the costs of the services. (Baytos, 1995)

The real question is should diversity activities (that potentially benefit so many employees as well as delivering business benefits to the organization) be held to a much tougher standard than other organization effort? And will the duality of this application of measurement standards in the workplace infer to employees an underlying bias or lack of commitment to diversity as the reason? It certainly raises the question!

Identifying Specific Program Elements Can Be Tricky Without the Right Approach

Broad-based diversity initiatives will proceed along several lines at the same time if they are systemic. Activities such as child-care services, flexi-time, flexi-place strategies, parental leave options, and others could be in action simultaneously. Let's suppose that at the end of a two-year period, management notes a 45 percent decrease in turnover among female managers. The impact of this decrease is an identifiable value to the organization in lower recruiting and training costs. However, which of the above programs caused the improvement during that period?

The reality is you may have difficulty and encounter complexity trying to unravel and isolate diversity's contribution without a systematic process to do so. But this scenario should not diminish the need or quest to locate effective processes to do just that. The Hubbard Diversity Return on Investment (DROI) process discussed later will outline a step-by-step process to use to successfully isolate diversity's contribution.

There are several measures that can be a part of the diversity toolkit for performance feedback. A sample list is shown in Table 1:

Activity Focus	Measurement	Potential Profit Impact
Affirmative Action Hiring & Retention	1. Numbers of females and minorities hired versus • previous years actual • percentage in the applicant flow • percentages of area availability as determined by EEOC data	Good results cut risk of costly compliance sanctions
	2. Turnover of females and minorities versus • % for white males • previous year's trend line • external benchmark	Lower turnover can • reduce costs of recruiting replacements • reduce training costs • reduce expenses and lost revenues due to inexperience of new employees in jobs
	3. Percentage of mothers who return from maternity leave.	Same as above

Table 1. Measures for Performance Feedback

Activity Focus	Measurement	Potential Profit Impact
Upward Mobility of target groups	Number of females and minorities in key management positions and on backup slates.	Reduced expenses for advertising, search and other employment costs to fill openings
Climate for Diversity	% of favorable responses to survey questions as compared with • previous survey • division within the company • external benchmarks	Early warning on developing issues can be used to avert high turnover, EEO charges, which in turn reduces costs (see above and below)
EEO Complaints	Number of AA/EEO related complaints per 1,000 employees as compared with • previous years • other parts of the company • community or industry benchmark	Reduced complaints lower cost of staff to investigate and defend company, and provide financial settlements
EEO Legal Action	Cost of settlement of EEO charges (see above)	Reduced legal and court costs, reduced costs of settling cases.

Table 1. Measures for Performance Feedback (Continued)

Activity Focus	Measurement	Potential Profit Impact
Community Outreach	Amount of business done with minority/female-owned organizations.	May not have direct dollar benefit for purchaser
Program Flexibility	% of employees at various levels, age/race/gender utilizing options in flexible compensation and benefit programs.	Satisfaction provided through more flexible use of current programs may forestall the need for costly enhancements, or make it possible to reduce other benefits with limited negative impact on employees
	Number of employees using flexible hours, job sharing, telecommuting	Same as above plus reduced turnover costs and reduced costs associated with unplanned absenteeism
Compensation Equity Analysis	Wage and salary adjustments in excess of guideline increases	Correction of pay inequities adds to expense, but may reduce future costs of excessive turnover and defense of EEO charges and suits
Training & Development	Increased numbers of females, minorities using development programs	Increased satisfaction reduces turnover and its associated costs and builds needed competencies within the organization

Table 1. Measures for Performance Feedback (Continued)

Activity Focus	Measurement	Potential Profit Impact
Productivity	Performance of homogeneous work groups versus diverse work teams • Output quantity • Quality • Time to complete	Greater output reduces cost per unit, increasing profits. Greater creativity produces new products, ideas.
Diversity Related Training, e.g., sexual harassment	Number of complaints, dollar value of settlements	Reduced legal fees and settlement costs increase profits
Marketing to Diverse Consumers	Sales and market share before and after programs generated by diverse marketing team	Sales dollar and profits from those sales Increased market share

Table 1. Measures for Performance Feedback (Continued)

As time goes on, more and more information demonstrating benefits will become available. Baytos (Baytos, 1995) also highlights examples of information now in the public domain that is summarized in Table 2:

Source / Organization	Program Type	Benefit Claimed
Business Week, American Airlines	"Supertrack" for female managers to provide more rapid advancement.	Increased women in upper levels from 12% to 21% in a five year period
Chicago Tribune Allstate Insurance	Work and family initiatives (broad)	The program saves money. It costs us $30-60,000 to train employees. Work and family programs help keep turnover low
OAG	On-site day care center	Post maternity turnover reduced from 44% to 22%
Wall Street Journal, Corning	Training in gender awareness ("Women as Colleagues")	Used to spend $4 Million per year recruiting and training women. Since the diversity training started the dropout rate and expense has been cut in half.
HR Magazine, Nynex	Mentoring circles for females and minorities	• Increase gender awareness by male mentors • Defuse potential serious sexual harassment situations • Provide visibility for upper level positions Builds support system to improve productivity on the job

Table 2. Demonstrated Benefits

Source / Organization	Program Type	Benefit Claimed
Wall Street Journal, Conference Board Survey	Flexible work programs-employer rationale e.g., Du Pont, Avon, Knight Ridder News, IBM	• Recruiting advantage • Increase productivity • Reduce turnover
Wall Street Journal	Understanding differences training	Improved understanding and reduced friction in working with non-U.S. employees
Avon	Employee advocacy groups	Provide solidarity and career help for members, tackle subconscious
Harvard Business Review, Digital	Training of thousands of employees in valuing or understanding differences	Help transform legal and social pressure into the competitive advantage of a more effective work force.
Wall Street Journal, Northern States Power, Helene Curtis, Household International	Mentoring & Networking programs	• Doubled the number of women officers/managers • Turnover of new mothers reduced from 31% to 7% • Cut new mother turnover from 40% to 25%

Source: Measuring Diversity Results, Dr. Edward E Hubbard, Global Insights Publishing, 1997

Table 2. Demonstrated Benefits (Continued)

What gets measured, gets managed—for diversity professionals to effectively understand and manage diversity's contribution to the organization's strategic business objectives, it has to be measured. As more diversity professionals begin cataloging and sharing their diversity measurement efforts, all facets of the diversity measurement process can be made more effective.

Assessing Diversity Initiatives

How Much Precision Is Really Required?

Any time the subject of measuring diversity work comes up, issues of accuracy and precision invariably arise. It has been argued that to measure diversity activities convincingly or with any high degree of confidence is difficult. Diversity measures based on "report cards" don't allow for competing hypotheses in assertions such as "managing diversity leads to increased profitability." (Some would argue that other efforts could just as easily have caused the profitability to increase). Another contention is that there is lack of control over thousands of factors that influence a large organization's profitability. That is, lack of control over factors like inflation, labor market conditions, and cost of money can make it virtually impossible to effectively measure diversity with accuracy.

In general, this argument is correct, though similar conditions prevail throughout the organization. Everyone knows certain factors are not controllable. The marketing department does not have control over the product or the customer; the finance department does not control the cost of money or inflation. Yet both departments are able to evaluate much of their work quantitatively. If we are willing, we might admit that there are more issues out of control than in the control of any organization. The task of management is to reduce the uncontrollable variables and to instill as much order as possible.

Management does not require accuracy at the .05 level of statistical significance. In research, precision is critical, obviously. In pharmaceuticals or medicine, extreme care must be taken with procedures and measurement. Results are often required to be statistically valid beyond the .001 level. That kind of measurement with a capital "M" is not required in operational measurement. We are operating not in a laboratory, but in the field, with all the problems inherent in field research and experimentation. Accuracy is necessary, but precision is naturally limited by internal and external conditions. Though we can't control the variables in the environment completely, we can still come up with usable numbers and "compelling evidence" of diversity's contribution to the bottom line.

It is not necessary to introduce heavy statistics to persuade management and employees of the need for progress and accountability in diversity change initiatives and to highlight their impact on profitability. This **does not** suggest that "control group", financial and "mental model" processes should be avoided. It suggests only that the optimum array of diversity measures should include a blend of data and levels of measurement. In many business situations, activity- and process-based (report card) diversity measures can play a vital role in the organization's leadership agenda.

Report card measures of diversity are like snapshots of the past. They can provide a historical reference to accomplishments or serve as milestones along the path to producing outcomes. Examples: the number of diversity training sessions completed, cost per diversity trainee-hour, and turnover by performance level by gender by length of service. These measures provide opportunities for personal feedback regarding achievement and measuring accountability for implementing new diverse workforce change or improvement activities and processes. These report card measures are a key part of a value chain for implementing change in an organization.

This value chain is comprised of four basic components:

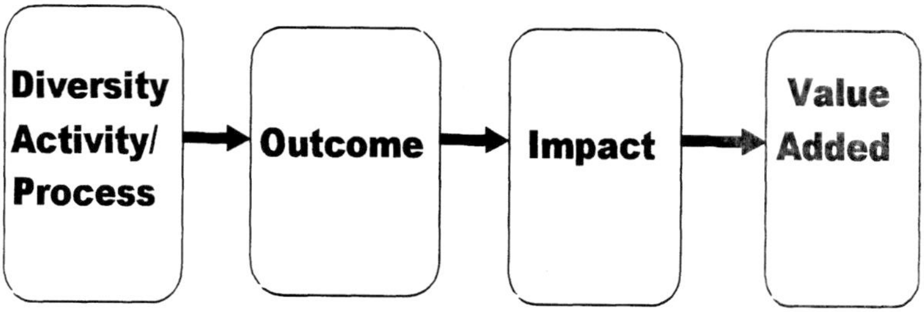

Figure 1. Value Chain

Generally speaking, all diversity processes are begun for the purpose of producing value. Any other purpose would be wasteful. One of our

Hubbard Diversity Return on Investment (DROI) Analysis Model

objectives should be to develop more effective ways to measure and evaluate changes made in the organization to improve performance based upon diversity improvement activities/processes, outcomes, impact, and resulting value.

Some typical value chain examples:

Activity/Process	Outcome	Impact	Value-Added
• Increase Diverse Talent Recruitment Sources	• Lower Agency Rates	• Lower Hiring Costs • Jobs Filled Faster (1) • Less Need to Use Temporary help (2)	• Reduced Operating Expense (1) • Faster Human Resource to Market (2)
• Improve Diverse Work Team Problem-Solving Processes	• Reduced Time to Solve	• Increase in Reason Given in Survey for Long Service by Diverse Member	• Retention Savings as Compared to Rolling Average of Previous Years
• Install Succession Planning for Diverse Workforce	• Fewer Emergency Minority Hires	• Less Recruitment Expense	• Lower Operating Expense

Table 3. Value Chain Examples

For every use of resources to improve an organization using a diversity activity/process, there should be an improvement in result. We call the result an "outcome". The difference between this outcome and the previous outcomes before the diversity process improvement was implemented is the "impact". The dollar improvement represented by the impact is the "value added". An example is to change the talent acquisition methods used to hire diverse workforce talent (activities/process), which shortens the time to fill jobs (outcome).

Time-to-Fill Formula: TF = RR - OD where:

TF = Time to have an offer accepted
RR = Date the requisition is received (e.g., January 4)
OD = Date the offer is accepted (e.g., February 20)
EXAMPLE
TF= January 4 - February 20
= 47 days

RR = Date the requisition is received (e.g., January 4)
OD = Date the offer is accepted (e.g., February 20)
EXAMPLE
TF = January 4 - February 20
= 47 days

As jobs are filled faster (see impact 1), there is less need to use temporary or contract workers (see impact 2). The cost avoidance can be calculated and a dollar savings computed (see value added 1). If, through the diversity department's effort to change acquisition methods, jobs are filled faster, not only does the organization reduce operating expense, but the cost of the human resource product is lowered and moved to market faster (see value added 2). Lower human resource (product) acquisition cost and shorter human resource asset delivery time to the organization can create a competitive advantage, especially in light of less successful competitors (based upon benchmarking analysis comparisons).

Thus, report card measures of diversity activities and/or processes are vital in order to gain feedback on staff accountability for generating solutions to address such key business issues as inadequate diverse talent acquisition. Without these activities or processes, we could not produce the accompanying outcomes, impacts and results. Even if these activities or processes produced poor results, the diversity department can gain by knowing what else doesn't work and then shift its efforts to more productive outcomes.

In addition to report card measures, it is critical to have "scorecard measures". A notion popularized by Harvard professors Robert Kaplan and David Norton in a book entitled: "The Balanced Scorecard" (Kaplan and Norton, 1996), the diversity scorecard, unlike the "report card", presents both lead and lag indicators of performance and profitability. Report card measures only tell of past performance (lag indicator). Scorecard measures, on the other hand, reflect both "lead" indicators (such as diversity climate survey ratings that indicate if an employee plans to leave within the next six months) and "lag" indicators of diversity performance (such as the number of people who are diversity competent or financial measures of profitability).

For the most part, any object, issue, act, process, or activity that can be described by observable variables is subject to measurement. The phenomenon can be evaluated in terms of cost, time, quantity, or quality. The central issue in applying measurement to the diversity change process is this: to decide what is worth measuring and to agree on the measure as a fair representation of progress and accountability (given field limitations). Often, management will accept progress over perfection.

Assessing Diversity's Value Goes Beyond Recording Activity

It's not about counting heads, it's about making heads count! Success is achieved through performance. Performance is more than activity. Each activity must be turned toward adding value. Most of those values must be measurable. In order to measure, it is vital to learn how to use simple arithmetic data to illustrate the value of the diversity effort.

The primary language of business is numbers, not feelings. Some people are afraid of numbers. They will use every excuse they can find to avoid having to deal numerically. People often fear the data will be used to hurt them. The irony is that numbers can be used very effectively to demonstrate how well the diversity effort is doing. Isn't it worth knowing before someone else tells you how well your diversity effort is doing with "their" numbers?

Though accuracy is imperative, precision is n
prise operates in an uncontrollable environment. E
not prove that it was their sales capabilities alon
(e.g., a major competitor leaving the market coul
sales to the organization). Statistical proof
Management often just wants to know: Are we moving in the right direction? Are the workforce diversity efforts we have in place helping us to meet key strategic workforce, quality of life, customer, and bottom-line organizational objectives? As Diversity professionals, we must provide the answers with appropriate quantitative and qualitative analysis to be credible.

Measuring the Impact of Diversity Initiatives: The DROI Analysis Process

Introduction to the Diversity ROI Process

For measurement purposes, when I use the term "*Diversity*", I define it as a collective mixture characterized by differences and similarities that are applied in pursuit of organizational objectives. I define *"Diversity Management"* as the process of planning for, organizing, directing, and supporting these collective mixtures in a way that adds a measurable difference to organizational performance.

Diversity and its mixtures can be organized into four interdependent and sometimes overlapping aspects: Workforce Diversity, Behavioral Diversity, Structural Diversity, and Business Diversity.

Workforce Diversity encompasses group and situational identities of the organization's employees (i.e., gender, race, ethnicity, religion, sexual orientation, physical ability, age, family status, economic background and status, and geographical background and status). It also includes changes in the labor market demographics.

Behavioral Diversity encompasses work styles, thinking styles, learning styles, communication styles, aspirations, beliefs/value system as well as changes in the attitudes and expectation on the part of employees.

Structural Diversity encompasses interactions across functions, across organizational levels in the hierarchy, across divisions and between parent companies and subsidiaries, across organizations engaged in strategic alliances and cooperative ventures. As organiza-

[illegible]s attempt to become more flexible, less layered, more team-based, and more multi- and cross-functional, measuring this type of diversity will require more attention.

Business Diversity encompasses the expansion and segmentation of customer markets, the diversification of products and services offered, and the variety of operating environments in which organizations work and compete (i.e., legal and regulatory context, labor market realities, community and societal expectations/relationships, business cultures and norms). Increasing competitive pressures, globalization, rapid advances in product technologies, changing demographics in the customer bases both within domestic markets and across borders, and shifts in business/government relationships all signal a need to measure an organization's response and impact on business diversity.

Hubbard Diversity Return on Investment (DROI) Analysis Model

Calculating diversity's return-on-investment requires asking key questions and performing key tasks along the way. To achieve a successful result, measuring diversity return-on-investment (DROI) requires a systematic approach that takes into account both costs and benefits. The Hubbard Diversity ROI Analysis Model provides a step-by-step approach that keeps the process manageable so users can tackle one issue at a time (see Figure 2).

The model emphasizes that this is a logical, systematic process, which flows from one step to another. Applying the model provides consistency from one DROI calculation to another. In essence, it suggests that the major aspects of diversity measurement you need to address include:

- ✦Knowing what you want to know
- ✦Collecting data and analyzing it
- ✦Isolating diversity's contribution
- ✦Converting the contribution to money
- ✦Calculating the costs and benefits
- ✦Reporting it to others
- ✦Tracking and assessing progress

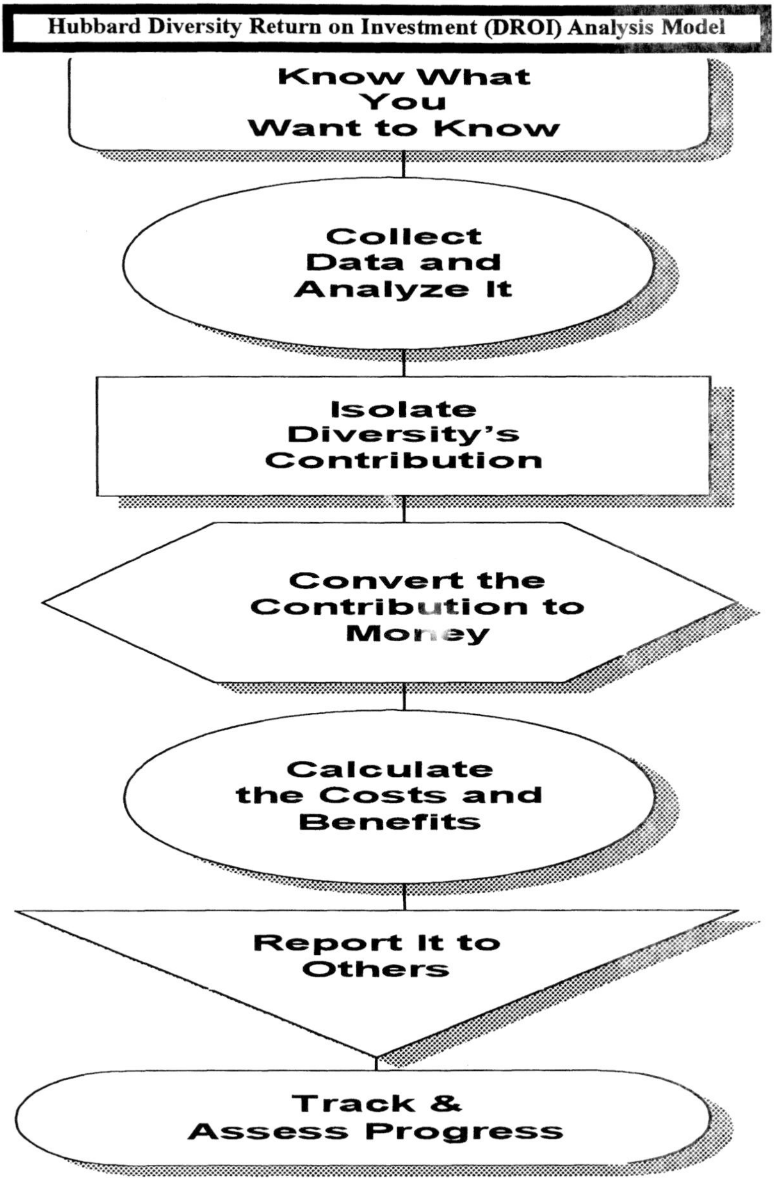

Figure 2. Diversity Return on Investment Analysis Model

Step 1: Know What You Want To Know

Conducting a diversity return-on-investment study requires that you clearly identify what you want to know as a result of implementing the study. This should be based upon, at bare minimum, the identification of a business problem or opportunity related to the organization's key business strategy. Second, you should be prepared to list a series of research questions you would like answered or hypotheses you would like to test. These questions may include things such as "In what racial categories do we have the most turnover?", "What diverse customer markets are not utilizing our products or services?", "How can we improve the idea and solution generation (creative) process using current cross-functional teams to improve operational performance?", etc.

While planning ways to address these research questions and ideas, it may be helpful to *begin with the end in mind.* That is, think of what will appear on your research report, create placeholders for them, and then generate the questions or hypotheses that must be answered in order for data to show up on the report as results. The final step in this phase is to summarize the questions you would like answered and formulate diversity measurement study objectives that will guide your work. Once this is done, you are ready to consider the appropriate data collection methods and develop your data collection plan.

Step 2: Collect Data And Analyze It

Data collection is central to the diversity return-on-investment (DROI) process. In some situations, post-DROI study data are collected and compared to pre-study situations, control group differences, and expectations. Both hard data, representing output, quality, cost, time and frequency; and soft data, including work habits, work climate, and attitudes are collected. Data are collected using a variety of methods including but not limited to:

- ✦Follow-up surveys
- ✦Post-study interviews
- ✦Focus groups
- ✦Etc.

The important challenge in the data collection phase is to select the method or methods appropriate for the organizational setting and within the time and budget constraints of the organization. During this phase, you will identify the data collection processes and specific metrics to use, create the appropriate evaluation instruments, and apply an organizational change methodology such as the Hubbard Diversity 9-S Framework (Shared Vision, Shared Values, Standards, Strategy, Structure, Systems, Style, Skills and Staff). It is used to guide the diversity measurement alignment process (see Figure 3).

Diversity 9-S Framework for Organizational Change

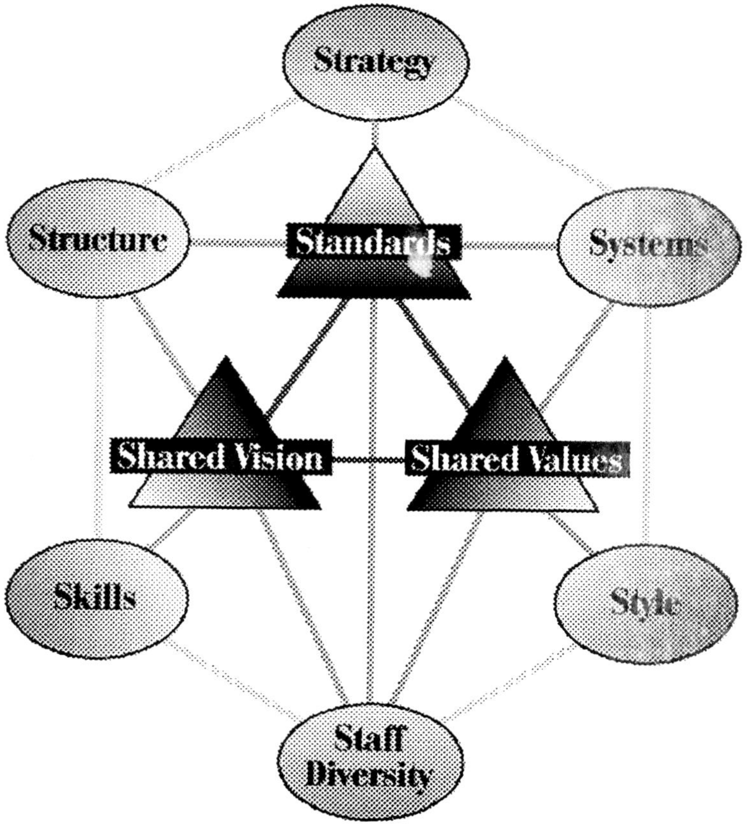

Figure 3. Diverstiy 9-S Framework

Step 3: Isolate Diversity's Contribution

An often-overlooked issue in most diversity assessments or evaluation studies is the process of isolating the effects of diversity. In this step of the process, specific strategies are explored, which determine the amount of output performance directly related to the diversity initiative. This step is essential because there are many factors that will influence performance data after the diversity initiative. The result is increased accuracy and credibility of the DROI calculation. The following strategies are an example of what has been utilized by organizations to tackle this important issue:

- ✦Control Groups
- ✦Trend Line Analysis
- ✦Forecasting Models
- ✦Etc.

Collectively, these strategies and others provide a comprehensive set of tools to tackle the important and critical issue of isolating the effects of diversity initiatives.

Calculating and isolating diversity's return-on-investment will require an analysis of operational and other business processes to isolate the specific areas where diversity can be applied to improve business performance. Once all contributing factors have been identified and their contributions calculated you would be ready to convert the contribution to money.

Step 4: Convert the Contribution to Money

To calculate the diversity return-on-investment, data collected in a DROI evaluation study are converted to monetary values and are compared to the diversity initiative costs. This requires a value to be placed on each unit of data connected with the initiative. There are at least ten different strategies available to convert data to monetary values. The specific strategy selected usually depends on the type of data and the initiative under analysis. Some examples of these strategies include:

- ✦***Output Data*** are converted to profit contribution or cost saving. In this strategy, output increases are converted to monetary value based on their unit contribution to profit or the unit of cost reduction.

✦The ***cost of quality*** is calculated and quality improvements are directly converted to cost savings.

✦For diversity initiatives where employee time is saved, the ***participant's wages and benefits*** are used for the value of time. Because a variety of programs focus on improving the time required to complete projects, processes, or daily activities, the value of time becomes an important and critical issue.

✦***Historical costs*** are used when they are available for a specific variable. In this case, organizational cost data are utilized to establish the specific value of an improvement.

✦When available, ***internal and external experts*** may be used to estimate a value for an improvement. In this situation, the credibility of the estimate hinges on the expertise and reputation of the individual.

✦Etc.

Step 4 in the Hubbard Diversity Return on Investment Analysis Model is very important and is absolutely necessary for determining the monetary benefits from a diversity initiative. The process is challenging, particularly with soft data, but can be methodologically accomplished using one or more of these strategies.

Step 5: Calculate the Costs and Benefits

Calculating the Diversity Initiative Costs

To successfully calculate DROI, both cost and benefits must be tracked and calculated in the process. The first part of the equation on a cost/benefit analysis is the diversity initiative costs. Tabulating the costs involves monitoring or developing all of the related costs of the diversity initiative targeted for the DROI calculation. Among the cost components that should be included are:

✦The cost to design and develop the diversity initiative, possibly prorated over the expected life of the initiative;

✦The cost of any materials and external staff resources utilized;

✦The costs of any facilities, travel, lodging, etc.

✦Salaries, plus employee benefits of the employee's involved;
✦Administrative and overhead costs allocated in some way.

Calculating the Diversity Return on Investment

The diversity return-on-investment is calculated using the initiative's benefits and costs. The benefit/cost ratio (BCR) is the initiative benefits divided by cost. In formula form it is:

BCR = Diversity Initiative Benefits / Diversity Initiative Costs

Sometimes the ratio is stated as a cost-to-benefit ratio, although the formula is the same as BCR.

The diversity return on investment calculation uses the net benefits of the diversity initiative divided by the initiative costs. The net benefits are the diversity initiative benefits minus the costs. As a formula, it is stated as:

DROI% = (Net Diversity Initiative Benefits / Initiative Costs)*100

In other words, the DROI formula is calculated as:

$$\frac{\text{Diversity Benefits} - \text{Initiative Costs}}{\text{Initiative Cost}} \times 100$$

This is the same basic formula used in evaluating other investments where the ROI is traditionally reported as earnings divided by investment. DROI from a diversity initiatives is often high. DROI figures above 450% are not uncommon.

Identifying Intangible Benefits

In addition to tangible, monetary benefits, most diversity initiatives will have intangible, non-monetary benefits. The DROI calculation is based on converting both hard and soft data to monetary values. Intangible benefits include items such as:

✦Increased job satisfaction

- ✦Increased organizational commitment
- ✦Improved teamwork
- ✦Reduced conflict
- ✦Etc.

During data analysis, every attempt is made to convert all data to monetary values. All hard data such as output, quality, and time are converted to monetary values. The conversion of soft data is attempted for each data item. However, if the process used for conversion is too subjective or inaccurate, the resulting values can lose credibility in the process. This data should be listed as an intangible benefit with the appropriate explanation. For some diversity initiatives, intangible, non-monetary benefits are extremely valuable, often carrying as much influence as the hard data items.

Step 6: Report It to Others

Next, it is critical that you have an organized communications plan to let others know the progress and challenges being addressed by diversity initiatives. During the development cycle of the communications plan, it is important to identify communication vehicles to use, how and when the report will be created, when it will be delivered and how to evaluate its implementation.

Step 7: Track and Assess Progress

Finally, in order to maintain any gains made or benefits from lessons learned during the process, you must make plans to track and assess the effectiveness of your diversity initiatives over time.

In order better understand how the diversity return on investment process works utilizing these concepts, lets examine an organization that would like to assess the impact of a diversity initiative.

Diversity Measurement Case Study: *TypiCo Insurance Company*

Background

Over the past several years, TypiCo Insurance Company, a medium-sized, full service insurance company in the Midwest, experienced a significant increase in the number of employees absent from work, especially among women and people of color. As a result of this problem, the organization found itself hiring more temporary workers, missing customer deadlines, handling more employee morale and discipline situations, answering more customer service complaint calls, losing market share, and the like. To combat this problem, the company implemented a diversity initiative with 15 Branch Managers.

Step 1: Know What You Want to Know:

The TypiCo Insurance senior management team noticed that absenteeism was down from its previous level and there were fewer complaints coming in from customers. They wondered whether what were some of the initiatives that paid off. The diversity organization wanted to know the impact of its efforts as well and asked the following questions (among others)...

- ✦What financial benefit did the diversity initiative contribute to the organization's strategic objectives?
- ✦What was the financial benefit of this effort?
- ✦What was the return on investment?
- ✦What was the overall percentage of reduction in absenteeism?
- ✦How do the results achieved compare with other organizations working on this type of effort?
- ✦What do the managers involved estimate as diversity's contribution to this reduction?

Step 2: Collect Data and Analyze It

To collect data from this initiative, a number of data collection strategies were used. Some of them included:

- ✦Interviews
- ✦Surveys
- ✦Workshop Group Discussions
- ✦Historical Review
- ✦Etc.

Among the objectives, a major objective of the program was to reduce the absenteeism in each work group using diverse work team relationship skills. Before the initiative was conducted, the average absenteeism rate for the employees in the branch was 7%. It was determined, in the follow-up evaluation, that the new average rate was 4%. A total of 120 employees work for the 15 branch managers and employees are expected to work 240 days per year. The fully loaded cost of this program for the 15 Branch Mangers totaled $7,565.23

Step 3: Isolate Diversity's Contribution

From a range of alternative diversity isolation methods, the process of using participant estimates was used to isolate diversity's contribution to this strategic business objective. In a post-initiative follow-up, managers estimate that 40% of the reduction was directly related to the diversity initiative.

Step 4: Convert the Contribution to Money

During the diversity learning intervention, managers (program participants) estimated the cost of a single absence to be $81. (This is the average value from all 15 managers.) External studies have shown that the cost of a single absence ranges from $60 to $70, depending on the industry and specific job.

Step 5: Calculate the Costs and Benefits

Based upon the information gathered, the diversity professionals were able to calculate the value-added from the diversity intervention. Their calculations were as follows:

- ✦Cost of the Diversity Initiative: $7,565.23
- ✦Pre-Initiative Absenteeism Rate: 7%
- ✦Post-Initiative Absenteeism Rate: 4%
- ✦Net Absenteeism Reduction: 3%
- ✦Isolation of Diversity's Contribution: 3% x 40% = 1.2%
- ✦Total Work Period Affected: 240days x 120 employees = 28,800 Employee Days
- ✦Adjusted Impact based upon Diversity Contribution: 28,800 x 1.2% = 345 employee days

✦Annual Savings from Improvement: 345 Employee Days x $60 = $20,700*

✦Note: A basic rule of diversity measurement is to use fully loaded costs and keep estimates of the benefits conservative. If the business case for diversity can be made at the lower cost level, it can certainly be made at levels that are higher.

✦Benefit-to-Cost Ratio for this Diversity Intervention: $20,700/$7,565.23 = $2.74:1**

** This means that for every dollar invested in this diversity effort, the benefit was $2.74

✦Diversity Return on Investment % : ($20,700 - $7,565.23)/7,565.23 = 174%***

*** This diversity represented a 174% return on the dollars the organization invested.

Step 6: Report It to Others

This information is then displayed in a set of charts and graphs that tell the story of diversity's contribution to the organization's bottom line using this initiative (see samples in Graphs 1and 2):

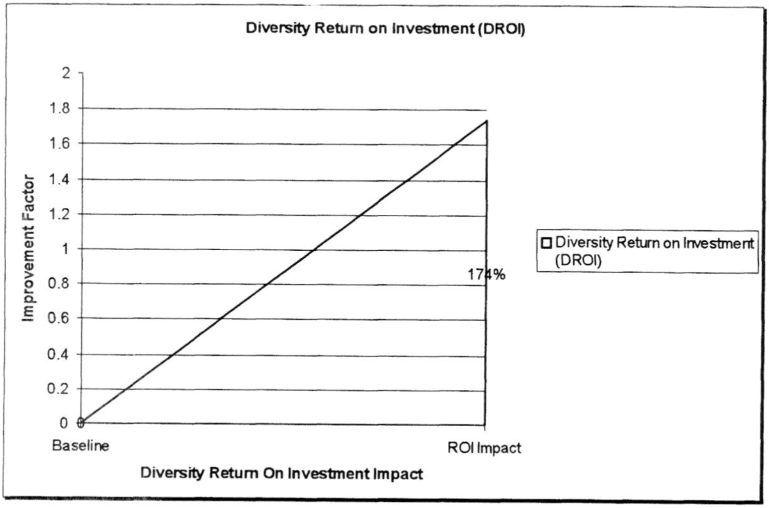

Graph 1. Diversity Return on Investment

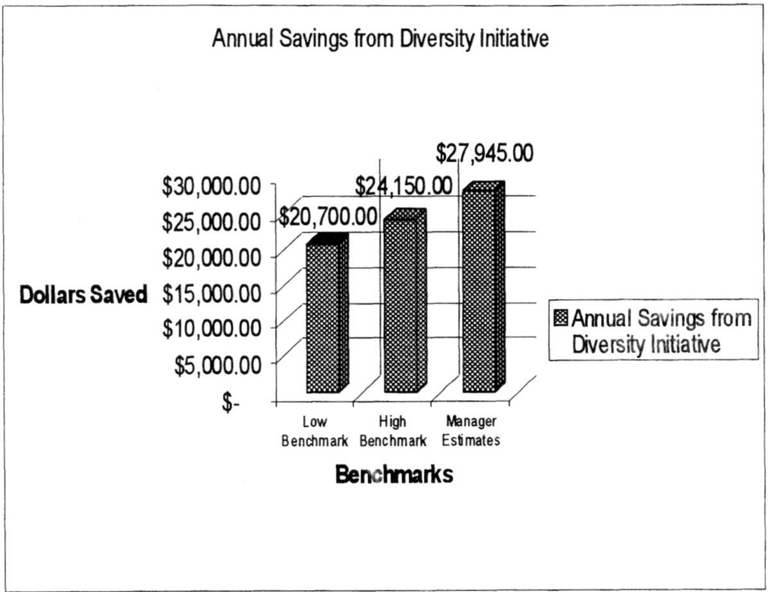

Graph 2. Annual Savings from Diversity Initiative

Step 7: Track and Assess Progress

The final step in the DROI process is to track this initiative over time as other programs are rolled out. Remember that the savings reported from this initiative are only for this initiative. That is, if other pilot sessions were conducted, it would be necessary to track the costs, benefits, isolation estimates, etc. that relate to that effort.

This example is just a sample application of the diversity measurement processes that can be used to demonstrate diversity's essential value and contribution to the strategic objectives of the organization. They can be applied to wide variety of industries such as government, education, non-profit, and a host of others.

Assessing, Measuring, and Analyzing DROI is a Critical Link for Success

Assessing, measuring, and analyzing the impact of diversity initiatives is a critical link for success in diversity management and organizational performance today, and in the future. "You can't manage what you don't measure" and managing and leveraging diversity is fast becoming a business imperative. If diversity initiatives are not approached in a systematic, logical, and planned way, DROI will not be possible and consequently, diversity will not become integrated into the fabric of the organization.

It is the job of diversity practitioners to make certain that the credibility of diversity efforts do not suffer. Assessing, measuring, and analyzing the impact of diversity initiatives is critical to the success of the organization and the credibility (and survival) of the diversity profession. In order to be taken seriously, diversity practitioners must become adept at measuring diversity results that tie it to the organization's bottom-line. We must build a strong business practice reputation using effective diversity measurement and management techniques such that diversity is seen as an important driver of organizational performance!

References

Baytos, Lawrence M. *Designing & Implementing Successful Diversity Programs*. New Jersey: Prentice Hall. 1995.

Cox, Taylor Jr. *Cultural Diversity In Organizations*. San Francisco, California: Berrett-Koehler Publishers. 1993.

Kaplan, Robert S., and David P. *The Balanced Scorecard: Translating Strategy into Action*. Boston: Harvard Business School Press. 1996.

Hubbard, Edward E. *Measuring Diversity Results*. Petaluma, California: Global Insights Publishing. 1997.

Hubbard, Edward E. *How to Calculate Diversity Return on Investment*. Petaluma, California: Global Insights Publishing. 1999.

Hubbard, Edward E. *Building a Diversity Measurement Scorecard*. Petaluma, California: Global Insights Publishing. Fall 2001.

Chapter XI

Facilitating Diversity Issues

Marilyn Loden

Introduction

In attempting to outline this Chapter, I found myself questioning what I could possibly say that has not been said already about this topic. Certainly, diversity as a focus for facilitators is not new. For the past twenty-five years, people have been facilitating discussions of diversity issues across the nation. Much of the discussion has occurred in workshops aimed at increasing participant awareness of diversity issues. Such programs have flourished in our public school systems, at many universities as well as in the public and private work sectors. Now, with the benefit of this accumulated experience to draw on, it seems timely to take stock of the impacts of this massive movement to educate and consider the path that we, as facilitators, will take into the future. This chapter, then, is an attempt to assess our accomplishments and outline where we, as a community of committed individuals, go from here.

Taking Stock: Our Past and the Present

At the heart of this assessment are several critical questions:

- What is our primary role in helping others manage the impact(s) of greater diversity in their lives?
- Do we achieve more by challenging the status quo and employ ing confrontational tactics?
- Or is the primary role of the diversity facilitator shifting from con frontation to mediation and conciliation?
- Finally, how can we as facilitators be ***most instrumental*** in help ing others build diversity-friendly workplaces and communities?

As we assess our society's progress to date in learning to leverage diversity, we see evidence that both facilitation based on confrontation *and* conciliation have served the greater good. But while the former can elicit a startling realization or "wake-up call" in some individuals, it is a method that also produces a significant amount of backlash and resistance in many others. Do the benefits outweigh the collateral damage? One can argue that society needed a loud wake-up call to become focused on overt discrimination and prejudice back in the 1960's and early '70's. But what about today? What is it that individuals and groups require from diversity facilitators at this point in our evolving history?

There are those who continue to believe that "more of the same" is required to deal with the persistence of institutional "isms." However, thirty years of legislation, litigation and consciousness raising have also helped to create a far more multi-ethnic and multi-cultural workforce – a workforce that includes many who embrace the principle of greater diversity. My experience suggests that the time has come to leverage this new, critical resource in a more focused, deliberate manner. *It is by focusing on this diversity-positive population that facilitators can effect the greatest productive change now.* Why? The answer is because *this group has the power to influence their peers and accelerate adoption of diversity as a core institutional and societal value.*

Enlisting Diversity Change Agents in the Work of Facilitation

I am speaking specifically about the small, yet extremely important segment of any organization know as early adopters or change agents for diversity. Historically, we as facilitators of diversity issues have taken this group for granted by and large–often assuming that it was more important to chip away at others' persistent resistance than to spend time and energy "preaching to the converted." Thus, we have typically provided little or no guidance to this grou] new skills to help them model different behavior for Instead, most facilitators of diversity issues have ch(needs of the change agents assuming that because the] say and "do the right things."

But by leaving the change agents to function on their own in most organizations, we have unwittingly minimized their ability to favorably impact the attitudes and behaviors of their peers. What's more, by focusing solely on the barriers to diversity and the resistance to change in organizations and individuals, we as facilitators have limited our own access to this powerful group as a source of creativity and support for the work that we do. While we take comfort in knowing that they are out there in the organizations we serve, they are seldom the people we spend our time working with. What a missed opportunity for building colleagueship and support!

To make matters worse, by focusing mostly on uncovering problems in individuals, groups and organizations, we have limited our own access to joy, optimism and seldom taken the time to celebrate the positive changes that are occurring. This focus on problems before opportunities has also lead to burn-out and frustration among many diversity facilitators and to a growing reluctance on the part of new trainers and organizational deveopment practitioners to get involved in this work.

Redefining Our Priorities

Fortunately, it is not too late to shift our focus from facilitating diversity *issues* to facilitating diversity *opportunities*.

> *By making this concious choice to place greater emphasis on building skills and competencies among committed individuals, we assure that leveraging diversity will become an institutional and societal reality.*

For taking this path will not burn us out. Instead, it allows us to transfer some of the skills of bridge-building and facilitating to a larger group of caring individuals–those change agents who want to play an active part in increasing inclusion, mutual respect and cooperation in their organizations and communities.

When I consider the excitement and optimism a facilitator derives om working with change agents and compare this to the popular alternative of challenging institutional "isms" and confronting the prejudices and privileges of institutionally powerful groups, I conclude that the first approach is an antidote to burn-out while the second assures that this is inevitable. Moreover, an enormous body of behavioral science research demonstrates that any change stands a greater chance of majority acceptance if those most committed to it use their actions and influence to help others see the benefits. Thus, our primary work should no longer be about waking society. Now it should become helping diversity change agents lead by example and providing them the tools and skills required to model inclusion, mutual respect and cooperation for others in their peer groups.

> *As such, the shift in consciousness that diversity facilitators helped to bring about over the last three decades and the emergence of a critical mass of diversity change agents, now demands a redefinition of our role and a new focus for the future.*

Redefining the Arena of the Work

Today, the work of building awareness and productive relationships across cultural boundaries is moving from the artificial setting of the workshop to the real-world setting of the workplace. As demographic diversity increases in organizations, it is change agents working as managers, supervisors and employees who now find themselves facilitating diversity issues in one-on-one discussions, during staff meetings, at sales calls, in classrooms and study groups – virtually anywhere that people gather to interact and do work. Here, then, is the growing opportunity for the facilitator: *empowering these committed individuals and diverse teams to build understanding, trust, rapport – and common ground.*

As support for diversity grows among U.S. workers, their need for relationship-building skills that respect differences is growing as well. *These are not the skills of challenging and confronting.* Instead, they are the interpersonal skills required to appreciate, understand, trust, model and respect oneself and others. At the grass roots level where most people interact with diversity on a daily basis, interpersonal skills *and facilitation skills* to enhance understanding and mutual respect are

needed as never before. With so much need, it
who call ourselves professional facilitators to re

Sharing The Tools of the Trade

The remainder of this chapter discusses concepts and tools that ca take the work of facilitation beyond where it often ends – with confrontation and conflict – to the next level of work – consolidating support and bridge building. It is divided into three sections including:

✦Roles & Goals. This section answers the questions: How should we position ourselves as facilitators of diversity issues now? What models and tools can be utilized to help others engage in meaningful discussion and exploration?

✦Building Diversity Competencies. This section describes communication techniques and principles that can be modeled and taught to enhance understanding of diversity issues, open up communication and build trust.

✦Bumps & Detours. This section outlines a few of the challenging issues that facilitators can face in their work with individuals and groups

While the information contained in each section applies to facilitation in formal workshop settings, it is as useful in one-on-one work and can be put into practice by both professional and non-professional facilitators alike.

Roles & Goals

To be effective facilitators of anything – including diversity issues, we must first be clear about our role and objective. At the very start of this clarification process, we must attempt to answer the question: "What is my expressed purpose and on whose behalf do I act?" All facilitation can be defined as *action in the service of others*. In the case of diversity issues, these actions should be aimed at helping individuals and groups recognize differing cultural perspectives, build trust and increase common ground.

Facilitator as Bridge-Builder

Through observation of interpersonal and group dynamics, diversity facilitators can help others become aware of identity issues, personal biases and cultural assumptions that may be invisible yet operative in their relationships and interactions. Once issues are identified, the facilitator then works with individuals to build the competencies and the personal comfort required to effectively cross cultural boundaries and work more easily and effectively with diverse others. To be experienced as truly helpful throughout this process, a facilitator's actions must reinforce the underlying purpose of the work, namely, helping others acquire the knowledge, insights and skills needed to build productive cross-cultural relationships. To the extent that she/he consistently models inclusive, respectful behaviors, these goals become more attainable for others involved in the discussion process.

While this may sound simple enough, it is not easy to accomplish. For there are always individuals who test the facilitator's patience, behave defensively, are insensitive to others and incite us to react in kind. These are the moments in which inclusion, mutual respect and cooperation become difficult words to live by. And it is at such moments that our actions as facilitators become live lessons for others. If we respond to challenges in a defensive or punishing manner, we weaken our own credibility and others' belief in the possibility of finding a better way. However, if we keep our goal in mind and practice generous listening, we have a much greater likelihood of creating to a more inclusive, respectful environment for discussion. It is during moments like this that the facilitator mantra "IMRC" (for Inclusion, Mutual Respect and Cooperation) can be helpful in guiding our behavior and showing us that better way.

Building Inclusion by Broadening the Frame of Reference

One important service a facilitator can perform at the start of any one-on-one or group discussion is providing a broad, inclusive yet specific definition of diversity for participants to reference. Introducing a broad frame of reference helps to set an inclusive tone, allowing all participants to explore issues of particular interest or concern to them – and ensuring that the conversation remains relevant for all involved. The dimensions of human diversity (see Figure 1.) illustrate one example of a broad definition of diversity that can be used to help focus and guide discussion. Using this frame of reference, a sample start-up activity for participants might be:

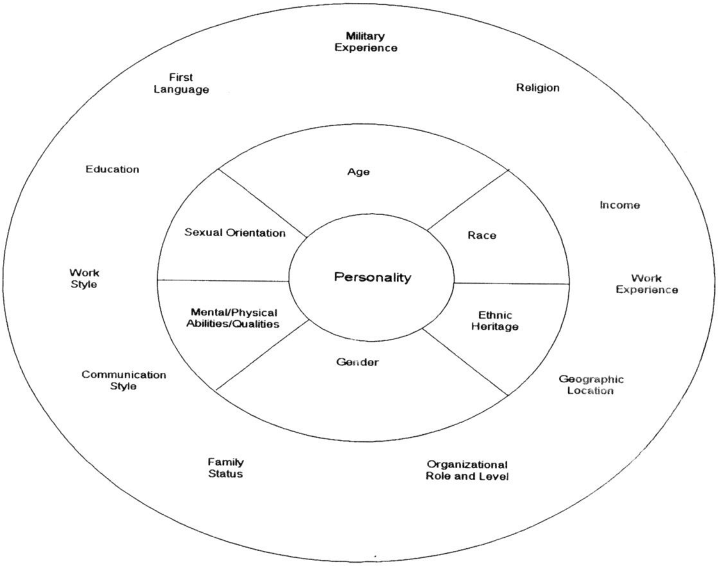

Figure 1. Dimensions of Human Diversity
Source: Implementing Diversity by Marilyn Loden © 1996, McGraw-Hill Publishing, Burr Ridge, IL

> ***Look at the diversity wheel. Which of the core dimensions (in the center circle) do you think have been particularly important in shaping your attitudes, behaviors and life experiences? Of all the dimensions listed, which ones do you find you are actively managing most in your current life situation? Be prepared to talk about why you chose these dimensions.***

Although everyone has a diversity profile, some individuals don't think of themselves as "diverse." By using a layered and inclusive model of diversity to start the exploration, the facilitator can help all individuals identify some powerful dimension(s) of diversity from their own profiles. More important, everyone can begin to tell her/his story through those diversity lenses deemed most relevant. As these stories unfold, it is the facilitator's role to help individuals recognize how multiple dimensions of diversity – not just a single dimension - inform our identities. In turn, participants can then consider how their diversity profiles influence their actions & reactions in diverse settings.

Establishing Ground Rules for Interaction

While effective diversity facilitation is more about mirroring and reflecting than about controlling the process, it is the responsibility of the facilitator to help the group organize itself for effective interaction. In order to do this, there are some agreements that facilitators can and should suggest participants consider adopting at the start of discussion. These agreements address unspoken fears about safety, inclusion and conflict – fears that people often bring to discussions of diversity issues. By framing some ground rules for discussion in *actionable language* and asking for everyone's commitment to honor them prior to the start of discussion, the facilitator can begin to set a positive, exploratory tone for what is to follow. A sample set of these agreements follows:

✦We Will Protect Confidences

✦We Will Provide Adequate Air Time for Participants to Tell Their Stories

✦We Will Allow Respectful Divergence

As discussion unfolds, these initial agreements become guidelines for interaction. They help establish a path for individuals to follow and serve as a reminder to all of their commitment to each other. While the facilitator can introduce these concepts, it is the participants who must endorse and put them into practice. To the extent that the facilitator helps participants recognize these agreements as a serious part of the exploratory process in the beginning, they will encounter less difficulty later managing their own behavior and accepting the diverse perspectives of others as discussion unfolds.

Building Diversity Competencies

As individuals begin to share their stories and react to each other, it is often apparent that some lack the interpersonal competencies required to build rapport and trust across differences. Such individuals may position themselves as evaluators of others' stories. They may dismiss what they hear from another person or insist "the same thing has also happened to me – even though I am not like you." Nothing can shut down conversation and diminish trust faster in diverse groups than this type of critical listening behavior.

To help participants avoid this trap, facilitators can suggest that individuals practice *generous listening*, as they share their stories.

The Art of Generous Listening

Generous listening means giving the benefit of the doubt to the story teller. It is *listening with unwavering belief in what is said and accepting that it is true and real for the storyteller*. This practice, originally developed for writer groups to critique each other's work is a powerful mechanism for building trust and increasing understanding through unchallenged disclosure (Elbow, 1999). Unfortunately, most people have had much more practice as critical or doubting listeners. As students and later as adults, we are conditioned and rewarded for finding the fallacy in other people's arguments, positions, logic, etc. This practice of judging information before accepting it can be a very useful tool. However, when our goal is to build rapport, trust and mutual respect, this approach can often backfire.

One powerful action that we can take as facilitators is modeling generous listening in our work. As generous listeners, we give each individual the benefit of any doubts we may personally hold; we respond to defensive behavior with flexibility and encourage others to consider the probability that multiple realities exist simultaneously. Through our support of *every* participant and curiosity about each person's story, we can demonstrate the benefits of "both/and" over "either/or."

Facilitators can also help others learn this important skill by suggesting ways to practice generous listening during discussion. For example, if a participant appears dismissive or critical, the facilitator can comment: "Your reactions suggest that you do not believe what you are hearing. I'd like to ask you to be more generous and assume that what you are hearing is really true for this other person. Will you do that?"

Becoming a more generous listener can be learned and used to enhance cross-cultural communication. Mastery of this technique requires a good deal of practice and feedback – but it is well worth the effort. In workshops where this technique is taught and practiced, participants are often surprised at the differences in outcomes that occur due to differences in their behavior as listeners. Once they have experienced the benefits that generous listening offers, e.g., greater disclosure, a more relaxed, open and candid exchange, increased information flow, many will express shock at how little is accomplished and how much time and energy is wasted in criticizing and disbelieving others. Because distrust and suspicion are always operative at the beginning of diversity discussions, the tone set by the facilitator and the skills he/she encourages participants to use will have a significant bearing on the long-term outcome. When facilitators rely primarily on challenge and confrontation to move the process along, they run the risk of intimidating some participants and inciting others. When they opt to be generous listeners and encourage others to do the same, they set a very different tone for group interaction.

By helping individuals hear others' stories without editing, the unfreezing of listeners' old attitudes and assumptions is gently begun. Faced with new and more in-depth information, the listener can then be invited to look inward in order to reexamine some personal values and beliefs. As the stories shared by others describe the multiple realities that co-exist in diverse groups, the listeners can modify old assumptions that no longer fit. Can individuals hone this skill and become generous listeners without support and guidance from a facilitator? Some do just fine without our help. But for many, particularly at the early stages of discussion, the facilitator as model represents a critical ingredient in the conversational mix – often determining whether the interactions will take a productive or destructive course.

Respectful Divergence

When there is no generous listening, many diversity interactions have the potential to erupt into argument or else to shut down as individuals with differing conflict management styles and contrary points of view give up on each other. Today, in many organizations, we see the results of this in the avoidance, prolonged silences, expressed frustration and sidebar conversations that occur when diversity conflicts surface.

Conflict is an inevitable part of the diversity conversation. Instead of letting it polarize sub-groups, diversity conflicts must be actively managed to achieve a productive outcome. One technique that aids in the facilitation process is the concept of *respectful divergence*. By providing individuals with a step-by-step process for voicing opposing opinions, one that assures all parties maintain self-esteem, diversity conflicts can be explored in more depth.

Respectful divergence requires that individuals acknowledge their assumptions and feelings as well as their opinions about an issue. It also encourages those in conflict to "try on" a contrary point of view and, essentially, see the situation from the opposite perspective. Finally, it is a process that encourages individuals to consider what needs to happen for all parties to maintain self-esteem and comfortably move on. Building on the practice of generous listening, respectful divergence allows for the airing and exploration of differences in opinion while minimizing hostility and withdrawal.

Time-Out Process Checks

Often in real-world settings, the "what" of the work that goes on serves to inhibit group conversation about the "hows" ¾ the way(s) in which people relate to and interact with each other as they perform their work. While individuals may notice team dynamics that need attention, there is seldom an agreed upon mechanism for stopping the "what" or action to discuss the "how" or group process. Such "time-outs" are particularly important in maintaining honesty and cohesion in a diverse group. While critical, they needn't be complicated to be effective.

A simple agreement to conclude each meeting with a brief (10-15 minute) process check is one standard way in which diverse groups can assure that process issues and observations get shared. By asking each member to comment on how the group is working from her/his perspective and allowing individuals to share views without challenge or interruption, the group can often learn more about itself and the needs of its members.

Acknowledging Intent & Impact

Years ago, at the dawn of diversity awareness training, facilitators often encouraged participants to pay close attention to the impact of their actions on others *without* examining or explaining their intentions. This was typically suggested to short-circuit the tendency of some participants to excuse the negative impact of their behavior by pointing to their good, honorable intentions. In essence, this was the "I didn't mean for it to turn out this way" defense.

Thanks to the vigilance of many facilitators over many years, this examination of impact without discussion of intent has become a valued norm in diversity issues discussions. Explaining one's intention is now widely seen as "denying" or "defending" and, therefore, seldom tolerated. I believe it is time to *put the intent back into our conversations* about diversity impact. While recognizing an individual's good intentions does not excuse destructive or insensitive behavior, it can help others appreciate that the actor is *more* than the sum of one action.

If as facilitators we want to increase candor, trust and deepen understanding among diverse individuals and groups, we must assure that there are opportunities for individuals to examine their behavior *and* express what is in their hearts. When we ignore what is in another's heart, we remain unaware of their higher aspirations. We can only form an opinion of the person based on an isolated and apparently negative action. I see this as a harsh and intolerant way to evaluate others' behavior – one that always puts the actor at an unfair disadvantage.

As facilitators and generous listeners we want to encourage everyone in the group to tell their whole story – not only the parts we can challenge and criticize. By inviting an exploration of intent and impact, we stand a better chance of understanding the complex nature of the actor and of finding a positive point on which to build self-insight and greater connection.

Music as a Medium and Metaphor for Understanding

Of the many devices available to facilitators that help individuals in groups comfortably cross cultural boundaries, none is more magical than the use of music. For many people from diverse cultures, music helps to create the context for their stories. Inviting participants to share a story about their ethnic history by sharing a favorite piece of music often frees people from the need to "say it" and allows many to be more creative and personally expressive in their story telling. Music is also a powerful metaphor in helping people consider how others experience them in conversation. As Brian McNaught, the renowned gay issues lecturer and facilitator often says: "We all give off some music in our interactions." Recognizing what that music is saying to others about our levels of comfort, acceptance, candor, etc. is an important part of the self-discovery process in diversity work. The musical metaphor itself is a very descriptive yet non-threatening way of inviting people to consider the subtle, often unspoken messages that their actions and reactions convey.

Bumps & Detours

A discussion of facilitation cannot conclude without some acknowledgement of the obstacles we frequently encounter along the way. Of the many that occur, there are two, in particular, that can pose significant problems for us and those with whom we work. Both have to do with initial expectations that individuals in our groups may have of us based on our core identities and our response to these expectations.

Group Presumptions based on Our Core Identities

While it is always useful to represent a broad range of visible and invisible diversity on the staff of a workshop, many of us facilitate in diverse settings where we are the only facilitator. At such times, participants who share our core identity may expect us to be strongly allied with their stated positions and feelings. If we remain interested but neutral, some may feel betrayed.

As tempting as it may be to offer (and receive) support by forming alliances with those of similar identity, such action serves to alter our role in the group. Once a special relationship is struck with an identity group, we are no longer perceived as equally interested in and supportive of other sub-groups. Now we are seen as the advocate and protector of people similar to ourselves.

Sub-Group Advocacy

Many facilitators believe that advocating on behalf of oppressed groups is a duty and obligation in guiding diversity discussions. Thirty years ago in workshop settings, this was definitely true. Today, however, individuals of all core identities are more experienced in the conversation and more capable of articulating their beliefs, and telling their own stories without special assistance. That does not mean we should not express empathy and support. On the contrary. We should make these available to everyone.

All individuals we work with need our help in expressing themselves, building understanding and increasing self-insight. The more we behave as advocates for any particular sub-group, the less likely it is that others involved in the conversation (both individuals and sub-groups) will feel as appreciated, included or empowered. In order to dispel fears that special alliances with the facilitator are inevitable in diversity work, we must *continuously cultivate a trusting, respectful relationship with all participants* – assuring everyone of our interest in and commitment to helping them learn and discover.

Conclusion

Today we have an opportunity to shift the primary focus of diversity facilitation from identifying issues to leveraging opportunities. As facilitators, our biggest and potentially most powerful opportunity now involves working with those already committed to diversity's value. By helping committed individuals master facilitations skills aimed at building relationships and common ground, we can assure that our vision of an inclusive, diversity-friendly workplace and society is realized.
Where we once relied on confrontation to motivate individuals and institutions to change, today we need to teach and model generous listening, respectful divergence, encourage understanding of others' intentions and equip individuals with the self-knowledge required to recognize their own music. By enlisting diversity change agents to adopt and model these skills, we can reinvigorate our efforts and accelerate majority acceptance of diversity as an institutional and societal value. These are the skills that must now be learned, integrated and passed on by us to our committed colleagues.

The glass is no longer empty in our organizations and our society. It now contains a critical mass of aware individuals who welcome diversity in their personal and work lives. It is this important group that will benefit most from our assistance now. With our help, it is these change agents who will become the stewards of diversity and productive change in the future.

Reference

Elbow, P. (1998). *Writing without teachers.* Oxford University Press, New York, NY: Oxford University Press.

Chapter XII

Momentum and Internal Organizational Relationship Building: On the Road from Exclusion to Inclusion

Leslie M. Saunders

Introduction

We know from our collective diversity management consulting experience over the past thirty or so years that an organization's movement from exclusion to inclusion is dependent upon a balanced combination of sanction by authority, shared vision and egalitarian environment. Muzafir Sherif's research focusing on the realistic conflict theory enlightened us in 1967. Unfortunately, organizational leaders and theorists of the time paid little attention to Sherif's learning points, thinking as Peter Drucker suggests, and too many still do, that it is safe to *pretend that tomorrow will be like yesterday, only more so* (Drucker, 1999). Nevertheless, time, shortsighted efforts, incremental improvements and multi-million dollar settlements to plaintiffs have taught us much about the process of transforming organizations from exclusive to inclusive and the various components that must be in place to ensure a successful transformation. However, in addition to leadership buy-in, a collective vision, and a democratic environment, we are beginning to appreciate how much relationship management increases or diminishes the pace at which an organization moves from exclusion to inclusion.

Recently, we have been introduced to some serious thinking and serious research about the power of social capital. But the importance of social capital is a consideration that trend analyst John Naisbitt (1982) attempted to get us to focus on more than twenty-five years ago in *Megatrends*. He warned us that in an age of rapid change, advanced technology and easily accessed information, people-to-people relationships would be an enterprise's most valuable commodity. Naisbitt told us that as our dependency on technology increased, we would have to become more adept at building and maintaining effective interdependent relationships with people from backgrounds other than our own. *The new source of power is not money in the hands of a few*, Naisbitt told us, *but information in the hands of many.* When Megatrends first hit the scene, I remember being involved in numerous management-centered learning opportunities at which the organization's capacity for technological transformation was assessed and the participants were required to plot high-T, low-R graphs in an effort to assess each participant's capacity for managing others.

But in all of the plotting and *Megatrends-mania* that followed, little to no attention was paid to the participating managers' ability to build and maintain effective interdependent relationships with people from backgrounds other than their own. At the time diversity management was considered to be a separate issue and in no way as critical as the issue of technological advancement to the future success of the organization. Nevertheless, in retrospect we probably overlooked Naisbitt's most important learning point ~ that being, all of the technological advancements, quality products, accessible information and competitive pricing on the planet are meaningless, if we do not have the relationships required to turn good intentions into desired results. Simply put, the relationships that exist or fail to exist between individuals and groups upon whom the organization's success depends, are critical and must be factored into the transformation strategy in order to gauge the organization's momentum or movement capacity.

Consider the organization whose governance body and senior management are gung-ho about moving from exclusion to inclusion and are sincerely committed to ensuring the necessary resources and time required to become an inclusively managed organization. "They get it at the top," is how this type of organization is often described by diversity management consultants. We do not have to convince them of the business case for managing diversity inclusively, as opposed to exclusively or passively. The organization's leadership is energized by the fact that as smart, forward-thinking, results-oriented leaders the desired transformation to the organization's new future should, can and will happen. Imagine how daunting it is when months and sometimes years later, this high-performance corps of can-do people must accept the fact that their rank and file constituents are not the least bit impressed or even aware of the organization's commitment to valuing diversity and maintaining an inclusive environment.

This moment of truth can have a devastating effect on the members of the leadership group, spurring some to adopt a more strident position regarding the nature of the problems and the strategies for working through said problems. For others, the realization may provide a reason to take a wait-and-see stance ~ doing little to help the organization move forward and generating just enough motion to give the appearance of strategically focused action. Meanwhile, members of the rank and file ~ who are already mired in various degrees of anxiety about the organization's future and their respective places in it ~ sense the pervasive leadership ambiguity and lack of esprit de corps and begin to start and stop relating to one another and the organization in a variety of ways, some of which can seriously temporarily deter ~ and in some cases permanently inhibit the organization's successful transformation to inclusion. The organization takes on a Tower of Babel like personality on the topics of diverse representation and inclusive environments.

Conversations about why the organization is getting no closer to its envisioned future run rampant and speculations range from *they (the rank and file) are too dysfunctional and incapable of dealing with change* to *they* (the leadership) *weren't really sincerely committed to change.* This state of confusion continues at both levels of the organization with leadership questioning rank and file employees' abilities and rank and file employees doubting leadership's integrity. Diversity becomes, as Tom Peter's describes, "a good word gone bad" *(Peters, 2001).* The notion of inclusion sounds as far fetched as The Emerald City. The momentum needed to move from exclusion to inclusion is stalled until a new relationship is established between the organization's leaders and its internal stakeholders.

Building New Internal Relationships

Like relationships between individuals, the relationships an organization builds with it internal constituents ~ or what the hip-hop generation refers to as its *peeps,* short for an entity's people ~ begins with an exchange of information and effective listening, especially on the part of leadership. And as unreasonable and risky as it may at first sound, the folks who are accountable for leading the organization have to remind their people where it is they are trying to take them and ask them *how do you like the trip so far?* If they are serious about getting back on course and gaining momentum along the way, they better brace themselves for what their people have to say and respond to their needs and interests, in a timely manner.

Ask Me No Questions...

Ask me no questions, I'll tell you no lies, we used to say as children, and we still say as employees of most organizations. And when the organization's leadership asks its people to evaluate the organization's capacity for inclusive management, the people can help pinpoint the barriers to progress and the organizational behaviors diminishing the momentum.

Several years ago, I was approached for help by the head of an organization who had invested an enormous amount of professional and personal leadership in an effort to move his manufacturing plant from exclusion to inclusion. He was committed to diverse representation at all levels of the organization, diverse vendor/supplier relationships that benefited his organization and the local communities, and to having his organization serve in the change leader role to help establish new standards of diversity management excellence. In short he wanted his organization to exhibit the characteristics of what Clifton & Maugham (2002) refer to as a 21st Century leader brand:

> *In the future, any brand looking to become one of the world's greatest will need to* ***think*** *and* ***act*** *like a* ***leader brand****... a brand that leads expectations, that leads people through an overloaded and complex future, and that leads standards ~ not just at the level of product, service and creative quality, but increasingly at the level of values and proactive social contribution."*

Nevertheless my client remained frustrated because his organization was not making any measurable progress. In fact, it had recently been served with a racial discrimination lawsuit and the threat of increasingly damaging negative publicity loomed heavily.

After hours of candid and relaxed conversation we agreed that the only way to find out what was and was not working was to ask his people to give him *the 411*. Yes, we actually referred to what he wanted to know as what the kids call *the 411* and we joked about the fact that that particular phrase worked so well because he wanted information, but he was also attempting to gauge the spirit of his people. We represented different races, genders, regional affiliations and professions but we shared a variety of common denominators of the rock and roll generation, so it was easy to liken his role to that as *the leader of the pack.*

A comprehensive listening-feedback-response strategy was designed and implemented. Innovative tools and methodologies were designed to ask the people carefully crafted questions regarding the organization's capacity for inclusive management. Once asked the right questions ~ the people who admitted to being caught off guard by both the novelty of the experience and the candor of the questions ~ *told no lies.* They said that they were proud of the product they made and, for the most part, liked the majority of the people with whom they worked. However they also said there were numerous internal relationship barriers and inconsistencies, including the fact that the organization's middle managers lacked the skills and the resources needed to facilitate the journey. Less than six months later, he knew exactly where the organization's transformation to inclusion effort was strong and where it seemed to be falling apart. Through the listening process, the organization began to build a new relationship with its people, which in turn had a profound effect on the momentum of the transformation process. This particular leader of the pack came to discover that there were three major levels of anxiety impacting the organization's diversity management strategy. At the very top of the organization, the people were frustrated by the fact that their efforts to communicate the organization's good intentions were unheard or considered less than genuine. Middle management level folks were upset by the fact that they did not know exactly where the organization was headed or what they were supposed to be doing, and non-management level people were wandering about in a maze asking, *Are we there yet? Are we there yet? Are we there yet?*

More recently, a similar strategy was designed and implemented by the Cleveland-based Rock and Roll Hall of Fame and Museum.

Motivated by a proactive desire to set new standards of diversity management excellence in the areas of talent recruitment and retention, vendor/supplier relationship management, corporate citizenship and consumer development (as opposed to any threats of litigation and/or diminished reputation), the organization's leadership decided to undertake an extensive listening process involving its internal constituents in an effort to pinpoint its diversity management strengths, weaknesses and opportunities to maintain its change leader status.

The most valiant aspect of the Rock Hall's endeavor was its leadership's decision to embark upon the process despite the current financial hard times that have befallen it and most museums immediately following the September 11, 2002 tragedies and the questionable state of the Nation's economy. The leaders of many organizations would have deferred the process and relegated its diversity management concerns to the better-times back burner. Nevertheless, the Rock Hall's leader of the pack, Terry Stewart, and the organization's board of trustees saw the process as an investment in the Rock and Roll Hall of Fame and Museum's future. Unfortunately most organizational leadership and governance bodies are not as courageous when it comes to doing what must be done to jump the curve and effectively drive the transformation bus into a new future.

Recognizing The "Are We There Yet?" Blues

I remember taking such a trip with one of my sisters and her two young daughters. We were driving from Silver Spring, Maryland to Los Angeles, California. Our plans called for stopping in several states along the way to visit family and college friends. We had our trusty AAA Travel Guide; my sister was beginning a new job and I was about to begin my pursuit of a graduate degree. My nieces, ages seven and nine, were as excited as we adults were about our pending vacation and about moving to their new future and new environment. As serious vacationers often do, we embarked upon our journey a few hours before dawn. My nieces were asleep in the back seat of the car before we got out of Silver Spring. About 50 miles into the trip, Arlene, my seven-year-old niece woke up, rubbed the sleep out of her eyes and inquired, "Are we there yet?" I remember my sister and I sharing a look with one another from our positions in the front seat. At that very moment, it dawned on both of us that we had given no consideration whatsoever to the fact that *"Are we there yet?"* was probably going to become one of the sub-themes of our loosely made travel plans. At that very moment we had no idea the many ways the *"Are we there yet?"* anxiety would impact the spirit and the momentum of the journey for everyone involved.

Throughout the next eight and a half days, Arlene asked whether or not we were *there yet* more times than I can or care to remember. By day four – Kansas – I had resorted to bribing her with quarters to not ask the dreaded question and my sister and I actually high-fived one another one evening when we realized we had driven two whole hours without having to respond to her on-going requests for a travel update. Thirty years later, that particular road trip comes to mind, when facilitating a client organization's effort to build inclusive relationship and reputation management skills. And as hokey as it may at first sound, I am convinced that diversity management consultants should give more serious consideration to the effect the *"Are we there yet?"* anxiety has on the transformations our respective clients have asked us to facilitate.

Organizations rely upon the expertise of internal and external diversity management consultants to facilitate the organization's transformation from its present state of being to its desired future state. In a nutshell, our work involves helping the organization transform the performance of both individuals and organizational systems. A portion of the consultant's responsibilities include helping the organization deal with the *Are we there yet?* anxieties that manifest themselves during the transformation process. It is no secret that all organizations do not embark upon the transformation process for the same reasons. Some do because they are convinced it is the smart and/or right thing to do. Others come aboard to comply with a court order that is the result of an employee or consumer-initiated litigation. Regardless of the reasons why organizations enter the process of transformation from exclusion to inclusion, each has to contend with a seemingly endless array of individuals and affinity groups who each have an assortment of personal, cultural and organizational anxieties regarding the transformation process, their roles in the process, and their respective place in the organization's new future, once transformed. Recognizing this, the role of the consultant becomes that of helping the organization determine the strategies needed to get the organization to its new future via effective organizational systems and appropriately skilled and engaged people. We also facilitate the organization's effort to respond to and manage the anxiety that is reflected in the various renditions of the "Are we there yet?" Blues. The support that the consultant provides in the handling of this, seemingly simple challenge can significantly impact the momentum needed to move the organization through the transformation process.

"Are We There Yet?" Variations On A Theme

Within the various levels of people in an organization, the *Are we there yet?* Blues manifests themselves in an assortment of ways. Too many middle managers are disturbed by the fact that although they are held accountable for serving in the role of cruise director for the adventure, most of the time they are unable to answer the *Are we there yet?* questions being asked by non-management constituents. They themselves are unsure as to exactly where *there* is, so they really are at a loss as to how to respond to *Are we there yet?* And the majority of non-management employees are frustrated because they have little to no confidence that their managers are sincerely committed and capable of helping the organization get to the envisioned *there.* So instead of a couple of small children in the back seat asking *Are we there yet?* throughout the duration of the meandering journey, these managers are trying to respond to – sometimes – thousands of employees acting like children in the back seat of a cross-country road trip. Imagine an enormous bus full of riders engaged in a continuous group whining session that is marked by repeated iterations of *Are we there yet? I'm bored. He's touching me. She keeps getting on my side. Are we there yet? I'm thirsty. My stomach hurts. It is my turn to sit next to the window. He said a bad word. Are we there yet? She's making fun of me. I'm tired of being in the car. I need to go to the bathroom. Are we there yet?* This is the situation the managers are asked to manage throughout the organization's journey to inclusion. And too often, in addition to not knowing where *there* is, they have no idea of the road signs to look out for to help them determine if the organization is getting closer to being *there.*

Two decades ago most organizations were convinced that it was in their respective best interests to focus their efforts on building relationships with whichever internal constituents seemed to pose the most immediate legal threats or whomever happens to be singing the blues the loudest. The leadership of the organization related to its people from a segmented point of view and its diversity management strategies centered on placating the needs and interests of various affinity groups within the organization. Some organizations adopted diversity management strategies that were basically adaptations of oiling the squeakiest wheels, i.e. the women, the non-whites, the non-heterosexuals, the persons with disabilities, the non-Christians, the non-English speakers, etc., only to discover that their segmented approaches to transformation management were not capable of crafting a set of solutions that addressed the needs and interests of most of their internal constituents, including the targeted population segments within the organization. These segmented diversity management strategies were founded on the assumption that diverse groups were monolithic in nature and that each group's issues could be addressed in a formulaic fashion. Nevertheless, in time, we eventually learned that there was no such entity as the all-encompassing or one-size-fits-all strategy for building and maintaining high performance relationships that met the needs and interests of all of the passengers making the trek to the organization's new future.

Identifying The People On The Bus

Not too long ago smart companies began doing everything they could think of to learn as much as they possibly could about the various racial and ethnic groups they hoped to attract as consumers, members and employees. More often than not they attempted to take what they perceived to be the easiest and quickest route, which amounted to picking the brains of internal and external demographers, known for their comprehensive understanding of individual population segments. In February of 1998, I was invited to New York to deliver the keynote address at the Annual Conference of the Direct Marketing Association. The address was entitled, *Diversity Management Issues Impacting upon the Future of Ethnic Marketing*. In attendance, were at least 300 folks, ninety-five percent of whom identified themselves as Asian, Black or Spanish-Speaking. These were the folks organizations were relying on to help develop and facilitate strategies capable of resolving challenges regarding how to attract and retain the non-traditional constituents needed to help organizations *win the war on competition* for talent, customers, members, investors, consumers, etc.

Embedded in the keynote address was a brief experiential learning activity during which all of the participants were asked to briefly study sketches of five individuals and then identify the race and ethnicity of each. The images had all been sketched by the same artist, and as they appeared on the screen, conference participants were instructed to correctly identify the following folks:

I

II

III

IV

V

The ten-minute identification exercise proved quite enlightening for all of the conferees. The room, full of racial and ethnic demography experts, had to laugh at the results of the experiment. When asked to share their individual responses to identify both the race and ethnicity of each of the individuals represented in the sketches, there was very little consensus as to the racial and or ethnic identification of any of the persons in the sketches. Provided below are the assorted responses that the groups of demographers gave for each of the sketches:

Iranian, Jewish, Middle Eastern, Muslim, Pakistani, Indian, Greek, European, Hindu, Vietnamese, " Indian" Indian (as opposed to American Indian) and White

Mongolian, Japanese, Alaskan, Eskimo, Russian and Asian

Cuban, African American, Bi-racial, Puerto Rican, Spanish, White, Black, Latino, Mexican, American and "Mixed"

American Indian, Native American, Mexican, Alaskan, Eskimo, Chinese, Japanese, Vietnamese, Cambodian, Navaho, Guatemalan, Peruvian and Spanish

Mexican, Alaskan, Eskimo, Chinese, Japanese, Vietnamese, Cambodian, American Indian, White, Caucasian, American and ~ my all time favorites ~ Charles Bronson, Jim Thorpe and John F. Kennedy

Imagine the conversation – not to mention the professional chagrin and laughter – that ensued as this group of racial and ethnic demographers shouted out their individual responses to the sketches. Not only did they realize that their answers were all over the place in terms of how to distinguish race and ethnicity, but all admitted being shocked to discover that each of the sketches represented people who were natives of Beijing, China.

The point of the exercise was not to embarrass or call into question the professionalism of the racial/ethnic demographers. Instead it was to help the audience understand that:

> 1). We have a lot to learn about the population segments organizations are attempting to recruit and retain, using monolithic strategies, methodologies and resources; and,
>
> 2). Even though we may succeed in correctly identifying an individual's race and ethnicity, it does not mean that we know a great deal about the other elements of said individual's diverse packaging.

In an article entitled, *Breaking Up America: The Dark Side of Target Marketing,* that appeared in the November 1997 issue of American Demographics Magazine, Joseph Turow predicted that:

> All signs point to a 21st Century in which media firms can efficiently attract all sorts of marketers by offering three things:
>
> ***Selectivity*** – the ability to reach an individual with entertainment, news,
> information, and advertising based on knowledge of the individual's
> background, interests and habits.
>
> ***Accountability*** – the ability to trace the individual's response to a particular ad and therefore a particular method of advertising.
>
> ***Interactivity*** – the ability to cultivate a rapport with, and loyalty of, individual consumers.

Turow further warned that while all of this increased segmentation and targeting "portends terrific things," the marketing strategies of the future promise to be increasingly more fragmented, with "hundreds of market-driven options targeted to carefully calibrated types." Turow cautioned that customized marketing and customized media "allow, even encourage, individuals to live in their own personally constructed world, separate from people and issues they do not care about and do not want to be bothered with." He suggested that this kind of cosial distancing ~ like gated communities ~ may further exacerbate social tensions and make it harder to carry our basic democratic processes.

This is not to insinuate that the business of target marketing will be responsible for the ultimate deterioration of democracy. Nevertheless, it highlights the fact that there are no easy or obvious solutions to satisfying the needs and interests of all of the individuals who represent the various population segments organizations are trying to attract and retain. At a minimum, it should make those of us in the diversity management consulting business help our clients understand that they are going to have to respond to even more segmentation, before they can build high performance environments in which inclusion ~ rather than segmented diversification ~ is the preferred way of work and life. For in the environments of choice that leading-edge corporations and communities are endeavoring to create and maintain for the 21st Century, relationships will have to be fostered with the whole individual as opposed to her/his race, ethnicity, gender and functional area of expertise.

Relating To The People On The Bus

In a much overlooked work published in 1999 entitled *The Dream Society*, Rolf Jensen, Director of The Copenhagen Institute for Future Studies challenged us to see additional groupings beyond the multiple dimensions of race, ethnicity, gender, ability, age, religion and sexuality that are thought to provide the foundation upon which individuals relate to an organization. Jensen suggests that in the post Information Age Society, organizations will need to pay attention to the manner in which people group themselves according to their respective emotional needs and interests. While focused primarily on understanding 21st Century market segments; Jensen's notions are to a degree quite similar to the ideas advanced by Don Beck and Christopher Cowan (1996), who advocate the notion that within any society or organization, people relate to one another and the organization at multiple levels of individual and groups sophistication.

Jensen (1999) sorts the people according to six distinct social capital markets that include the markets for:

1. Adventure (action seekers)
2. Togetherness (solidarity seekers)
3. Love (attachment seekers)
4. Who-Am-I (status seekers)
5. Peace of Mind (harmony and tranquility seekers)
6. Convictions (change seekers)

And Beck and Cowan (1996) categorize the people according to the spiraling mimetic hierarchy of:

1. Beige (Survival Sense) – staying alive through innate sen sory equipment
2. Purple (Tribal Order) – blood relationships and mysticism in a magical and scary world
3. Red (Powerful Self) – enforce power over self, others, and nature through exploitative independence
4. Blue (Absolute Order) – absolute belief in one right way and obedience to authority
5. Orange (Enterprising Self) – possibility thinking focused on making things better for self
6. Green (Egalitarian Order) – well-being of people and building consensus get highest priority
7. Yellow (Integrated Self) – flexible adaptation to change through connected, big-picture views
8. Turquoise (Global Order) – attention to whole-Earth dynamics and macro-level actions

Regardless of the sorting rationale, the fact remains that in the past two decades, we have come to understand that in addition to the various traditionally accepted affinities groupings of race, ethnicity and gender that people bring to the workplace, the needs and interests relating to said affinities and affiliations are not always in sync with those needs and interests corresponding to the other dimensions of the individual's diverse packaging. For instance, an organization's attempt to address racial and ethnic challenges can have a detrimental effect on the organization's effort to address challenges caused by an employee's gender, sexuality, ability and religious differences.

Jensen suggests reminds us that well educated people do not trust authority to make her/his decisions and that well-educated people reserve the right to make independent choices about everything, including about which diversity issues are most relevant in particular situations. So, while an individual's race may be the most significant diversity factor in some situations; in other situations, gender, sexuality, age, ability or other factors may have greater significance than race. Categorizing people according to what we assume to be their most pressing diversity issues goes against the ever-increasing trend of individuals making individualized choices based upon their personal beliefs, emotions, interests and values. .

Jensen (1999) continues to remind us that:

> *This has not always been so; previously, you shared your convictions with the social group to which you belonged, depending on whether you were a worker, a farmer, or a white-collar employee. And you placed your trust in authority, in the powers that be, in ideologies, in a certain set of values. The emancipation from the fixed menu has a clear corollary: it has become absolutely necessary to make independent, individual choices. (The Dream Society, p.108)*

In his *TREND LETTER (JULY 18, 1996), John Naisbitt provided documentation to substantiate the fact that " in households with incomes above $50,000 USD, the percentage of consumers willing to switch brands because a company was associated with a cause they supported was 82%."* Brand loyalty being based upon individual beliefs that are consistent with an organization's stance on said beliefs was a trend that Naisbitt (1982) originally told us was worth watching, twenty-five years ago. Today, increasing numbers of people subscribe to what I believe is a new consumer pledge of allegiance. Simply put, this new consumer pledge of allegiance says:

> *If I look into your organization, and do not see anyone who looks like me at all levels of you organization (including your trustees), and I see that your organization has no*

vendor/supplier relationships with anyone who looks like me, and I see that your organization is not investing in any communities that look like me, please do not expect me to share any of mydiscretionary funds, relationships or spheres of influence with yourorganization. Furthermore, be advised that if your organization values my diversity but devalues that of others, I will choose to align myself with one of your competitors that values the diversity of people I value.

Think about the growing number of heterosexual people who choose to disassociate themselves with organizations in which homophobia is tolerated or even encouraged because they have a gay relative or close friend. Think about the parents (of all races and ethnicities) who choose certain school districts or neighborhoods because they offer a broad, rather than limited, range of diversity. Think about the seemingly able-bodied employees who express dissatisfaction with an organization that does not make reasonable accommodations for persons with disabilities. In a nutshell, they are choosing to distance themselves from organizations that do not value everyone's diversity. Instead, they choose to pledge their allegiance to organizations that demonstrate a commitment to valuing not just the dimensions of their own diversity, but to that of others as well

This is why it is defensible to argue that the people on the organizational bus to the new future relate to one another and to the organization according to multiple cultural, emotional and social sorting classifications, making it virtually impossible for even the most seasoned diversity management consultant to design a flat or formulaic strategy for helping said organization relate to its people. As a result, the smartest diversity management strategies will be those that are based on helping transforming organizations establish and maintain new and improved internal relationship building skills. This means that organizations can no longer attempt to fix themselves by involving senior management and human resources professionals only.

Successfully Managing the Transformation Pace

Considering the unreliability of assessing the needs and interests of the people on the transformation bus according to cultural, social or emotional factors, it makes sense to propose we diversity management consultants help organizational leaders engage in some unconventional and uncharted ways of thinking about and relating to the passengers on the transformation bus. For when the leaders of the pack/drivers of the transformation process review the manifold and attempt to design and implement strategies capable of diminishing the chaos that can develop amongst the people on the bus throughout the journey, it is critical that the leaders of the pack be able to see the correlations between the organization's transformation pace (or momentum) and the assorted levels of *"Are we there yet? Anxiety" among the passengers.*

In order to make the continuous and measurable progress required to move the organization to its new future, the leadership and strategists must comprehend what Randall Root, founder and CEO of Root Learning refers to as the learning pace of the organization. Root (1989) and his partner Jim Haudan advised organizational leadership that if they are serious about transformation, they will come to understand three significant facts about the momentum of their respective entities:

I. **To learn is to think.**
II. **Before you learn, unlearn.**
III. **To win organizations must learn big and learn fast.**

In the same article, Haudan (1999) challenged us to think about the fact that "Companies will never have a truly sustainable advantage that based on product or prices," instead they "need to focus on the rate at which people learn. It is the learning speed of the slowest many, not the learning speed of the brightest few, that will set the pace…"

Understanding the pace of the organization is neither easy or something the leaders of the organization can accomplish without obtaining *the 411* from the people on the bus. It involves leadership's comprehension of elements such as *organizational time,* which is usually slower than *real time.* It requires organizational leaders to accept the fact that most organizations have varying degrees of fast-pace, medium-pace and slow-pace individuals and work groups, and that individuals of one pace group are usually members of mixed-pace groups. And the leadership has to understand that the momentum of the organization's transformation to inclusion is dependent upon the leaderships willingness and ability to develop the high performance relationships with members of each of the pace groups.

Amongst various pace groups within the organization, anxiety regarding *Are we there yet?* can lead to assorted back-seat behavioral manifestations. The fast-pace groups become fidgety because they see transformation as happening much too slowly, or not at all. They want to push the organization forward without waiting for the slower pace groups to get on board. The medium-pace groups become annoyed with those employees who want to speed up the process and frustrated by the pace group that complains the bus is exceeding the speed limit. And the slow-pace groups within the organization are convinced that taking the longest route and driving below the suggested minimum speed limit is in the organization's best interest.

The mistake many organizations make is assuming that the pace setters and organizational leaders are one in the same. That is to say, organizational transformation pace setters can be members of the organization's leadership, management and non-management groups. The key to maintaining steady momentum and forward movement in transformation to inclusion lies in crafting solutions to the following challenges:

> **I.** How to leverage the enthusiasm of the organization's pace setters regardless of whether they are members of the organization's leadership, management or non-management groups;
>
> **II.** What to do when the organization does not have enough fast-pace setters to keep the organization on the cutting edge or even to stay engaged in the transformation process; and, How to keep the slow-pace people from blocking the organization's transformation, obscuring the strategic vision of the organization; and/
>
> **III.** How to keep the slow-pace people from blocking the organization's transformation, obscuring the strategic vision of the organization; and/or diminishing the energy and momentum of those hoping to get to the organization's new future some time in the near future, in organizations where the slow-pace people are concentrated in mid-level management positions or in which they outnumber everyone else.

It is reasonable to expect that most organizations are comprised of mixed-paced groups, all struggling to relate to one another throughout the transformation process. Determining how to keep people in various pace groups effectively involved in the process, and appropriately focused throughout the trip, represents a critical component of the diversity management strategy. There are smart solutions to these three momentum-blocking dilemmas. Smart diversity management consultants and smart organizations have worked together to design and implement some innovative approaches for managing the people on the bus.

Leveraging Pace Setters' Enthusiasm

An organization pace setters can be found at all levels of the transforming organization. At the leadership level, pace setters are the champions of change or what Drucker (1999) calls *change leaders*. At the middle management level, pace setters are the pathfinders and performers who, if given the space, take on the task of handling the high performing as well as the less productive passengers on the bus. At the non-management level of the organization, pace setters are the CEOs of the underground, who ~ if appropriately focused ~ can and do use their considerable spheres of influence to convince the potential fence-sitters and nay-sayers from cutting up and acting out in the back of the bus. So leveraging the enthusiasm of the organization's pace setters regardless of whether they are members of the organization's leadership, management or non-management groups is a key factor of building and/or maintaining momentum throughout the transformation process.

While it is a multiple organization entity as opposed to a single organization, the City of Memphis, Tennessee comes to mind as an example of leveraging pace setter enthusiasm. In 1993, the change leading organizations in the Greater Memphis Area pooled their financial and relationship resources to establish the Memphis Race Relations and Diversity Institute – later re-named The Memphis Diversity Institute – to facilitate the community's move into a new and more inclusive future. This action was taken following an extensive disparity study, several missed opportunities to attract and/or retain major organizational relationships that were critical to the City's economic future and a variety of other indicators signaling a need for a comprehensive diversity management strategy. While not all of the City's major employers agreed to participate in the journey, the impressive list of change leaders was comprised some fifty-one organizations including Federal Express, Jimmy Dean Foods, The City of Memphis, AutoZone, the MidSouth Division of Coca-Cola Enterprises, the Methodist Hospital System, Baptist Hospitals, the Sara Lee Corporation, Delta Beverages (PepsiCo), Nike, Memphis Light, Gas and Water, Time Warner Corporation, the Tennessee Valley Authority, Coors Brewery, the Memphis Area Chamber of Commerce, Harrah's Entertainment, and a host of others.

The founding organizations provided more than $1.3 million dollars to fund the not-for-profit organization and purchased custom-designed consultative and education diversity management services for their respective organizations, throughout the next seven years. As more organizations experienced varying degrees of success in their respective transformation efforts, more organizations volunteered to come on-board. Added to the Institute's growing list of client/partner organizations were the U.S. Postal Service Bulk Mail Center, the Millington Naval Base, The University of Tennessee Medical School, The Memphis City School System, several religious institutions and parochial schools, the Federal Corrections Bureau, the Memphis Fire Department, and the Memphis Chapter of the Junior League, just to name a few. Organizational affiliates and individual graduates of the Institute were eager to share their diversity management successes, best practices and ever-evolving capacity for transformation with their industry peers, professional associates and neighbors. Individual graduates began to use their knowledge and influence to set new standards of excellence in diversity management for organizations on whose boards of directors they sat, their children's schools, professional, social and civic organizations in which they held memberships and their places of worship. By 1999, the Institute had delivered diversity management educational services to more than 6,000 senior and mid-level managers in the MidSouth Region, and provided comprehensive consultative services to more than 200 for profit and not-for-profit organizations in the MidSouth area.

Is this not to suggest that the Greater Memphis Area was successful in resolving all of its diversity management challenges during the seven-year tenure of the Memphis Diversity Institute? No not at all. Nevertheless, the momentum needed to build and maintain the City's transformation to inclusion was fueled by three significant factors:

Encouraging the change leaders to get the ball rolling regardless of who else initially agrees to get on-board;Assigning the pace setters to the role of designated driver of the transformation to inclusion bus; and,Nurturing the relationship management skills of the leaders of the pack and the pace setters to continuously widen their respective spheres of influence, thereby increasing the momentum of the transformation process.

Perhaps the most remarkable aspect of the Greater Memphis transformation story is the fact that the community's ever-increasing momentum and continuously heightening performance expectations amongst participating organizations and individuals were the result of people-to-people relationships. As a result, The Memphis Diversity Institute did not use any of its financial resources to advertise or market its services to prospective organizational clients.

Managing The Pace Setters Void

Determining what to do when the organization does not have enough fast-pace setters to keep the organization on the leading edge, or even to stay engaged in the transformation process, can be nerve-racking. Without a critical mass of pace setters, momentum can get stalled and seem, at times, to be at a complete standstill. However, an organization that seems to be addressing this particular challenge in an impressive manner is the U.S. Department of Transportation's Federal Aviation Administration (FAA).

In the early stages of transformation, this change leading organization realized that increasing the organization's capacity for effective diversity management was dependent on the establishment of individual and organizational performance expectations and accountabilities. They began designing and disseminating consistent messages regarding the individual and organizational behaviors that were characteristic of the desired future state of the organization.

The FAA's Administrator's Policy Statement On Model Work Environments, established in 1997 reads as follows:

The Federal Aviation Administration is committed to a com-

prehensive approach of managing diversity, practicing equal employment opportunity, and engaging in affirmative efforts to create and maintain an environment that supports and encourages the contribution of all employees and is free of inappropriate and unlawful behavior. In recognizing the importance of different viewpoints, perspectives, and experiences to problem solving, decision-making, responsiveness, and overall effectiveness, we pledge to have a productive and hospitable environment with a work force reflective of the Nation's diversity. In furtherance of our goal to create a work environment that supports and encourages the contributions of all employees, those occupying leadership positions must demonstrate an absolute commitment to actively engage in practices that facilitate a model work environment. This commitment will be manifested through the decisions we as an agency make, actions we take, and the results we achieve. Every employee has a shared responsibility to treateach other with dignity and respect, work together harmoniously and effectively, and take responsibility for our actions.

We must not discriminate on the basis of political affiliation, race, color, religion, national origin, sex, sexual orientation, marital status, age, disability, or any other characteristics not bearing on job performance.

By working together, we can maintain our commitment to keep the flying public safe.

By working together, we can focus the agency resources on business issues and work environment improvements, rather than on the manifestations of workplace discontent such as complaints, grievances, and malaise.

By working together, we can celebrate our successes and welcome the challenges the new millennium will present.

I look forward to working with you in our Model Work Environment.

The FAA's thorough Policy Statement clearly outlines the organization's envisioned future state, the market-driven business case for moving to the new future, the means of achieving said vision, the required behavioral accountabilities for both individuals and sub-groups within the organization, and the measurable performance expectations at all levels of the organizations. It leaves no room for misunderstanding or misinterpretation. And regardless of one's designated seating area on the transformation bus, it spells out where the bus is headed, how the organization plans to get *there* and how the passengers will be able to discern if the organizations is close to being *there* yet.

Has the FAA's Policy Statement On Model Work Environments enabled the organization to resolve all of its diversity management challenges? No, it has not. However, it did establish the individual and organizational behavioral expectations needed to build momentum while continuing to grow pace setter constituents at all levels of the organization.

Momentum Boosters To Counter, Especially those concentrated in mid-level management, Momentum Inhibitors

Ensuring that the slow-pace people do not inhibit the organization's transformation, is a challenge that most organizations are afraid to tackle. It involves determining where the momentum is slowest and the blockage is heaviest, providing consistent and continuous information to all internal constituents of the organization, and simultaneously building the individual and organizational skills-sets required to move the transformation process forward. It also requires providing an assortment of subtle and not-so-subtle reminders that every well-managed organization needs an array of well-lit exit signs.

This last challenge is especially taxing because addressing it involves engaging in what Drucker refers to as *organized abandonment,* that is "freeing resources (especially human resources) from being committed to maintaining what no longer contributes to performance, and no longer produces results (Drucker, 1999)". And often it requires dissolving some relationships to make room for others to grow. Leaders of the pack and pace setters at all levels of the organization are faced with the responsibility of telling their peers, well-liked subordinates and functional experts that, unfortunately, they no longer have a seat on the bus that is heading to the organization's new future.

Two scenes from the movie *Remember The Titans*, come to mind as experiential examples of this moment of truth. The movie is based on the true story of the relationship ending and relationship building that was required of the Alexandria, Virginia coaches, players and community when T.S. Williams High School was undergoing court-ordered integration. In one scene, the white former head coach tells his long-time friend and assistant coach (who is also white) that despite their, heretofore, enduring personal friendship and professional relationship, he has decided to help the new black head coach drive the bus to the Titan's few future, without the support of his long-time friend and co-worker. Later in the story, a popular player – All-American Gary Bertier is forced to make a similar decision when he asks Coach Boone to cut Ray, one of his life-long friends from the team, because of Ray's refusal to get with the program and his efforts to sabotage the efforts of the people on the Titan's transformation to inclusion bus. In both instances time-honored relationships were dissolved so that new and more inclusive ones could be established and nurtured. The difficult decisions that both the coach and the team captain had to make and stand by are the same difficult decisions that organizations and individuals have to make and honor when their friends and associates choose to disrupt, diminish, mar or otherwise interfere with the organization's transformation to inclusion.

In 1998, DuPont set new standards of excellence in diversity management by reforming its diversity vendor/supplier relationships. The corporation was out-pacing other companies by setting, meeting and – in some instances – exceeding local and federal compliance requirements regarding minority vendor/supplier percentages. Their efforts to meet the legislated standards reflected its commitment to diverse representation. Their willingness to surpass said standards was a reflection of the company's determination to be a change leader. Still, DuPont's leadership said, *we can do better.* And they did. By mid-1999, DuPont set new precedents when it rolled out its new outsourcing policy. It was one of the major points featured in its 5-point *Legal Model Alignment* strategy. In a nutshell, DuPont said to its current and future vendors and suppliers that it was not in DuPont's best interest to do business with companies whose commitment to ensuring diverse representations and to building and maintaining inclusive environments and relationships in their own organizations was in contradiction with DuPont's.

To make sure individuals had a clear understanding of DuPont's new expectations the company hosted groups of vendor/ supplier representatives at a lavish learning retreat, at a plush Sun Valley resort. Enthusiastic DuPont executives presented the organization's new relationship expectations to the invited guests and their presentations were supported not by a few handouts or a brochure but an explanatory book. The consulting entity I represented had been contracted to deliver a custom-designed diversity management educational opportunity to the invitees, in order that they had an even clearer understanding about what DuPont meant about diverse representation and inclusive environments and relationships. However the most impressive aspect of DuPont's precedent-setting commitment to change was the fact that by strategic design, because DuPont outsourced the majority of its vast legal work, the first group of service providers to get the news was DuPont's massive cadre of legal representatives. This type of change leadership was revolutionary and three years later it remains so. It reflected the seriousness of DuPont's commitment to valuing diversity and inclusion and it showed the organization's willingness to dissolve what were once thought to be time-honored relationships in order to build new relationships that were capable of helping the company to its new future.

Although different types of entities, what The City of Memphis, The Federal Aviation Administration and DuPont— all have in common is the fact that once they decided to get serious about undertaking a transformation from exclusion to inclusion, they took serious measures to boost rather than inhibit the momentum of the change process. Momentum boosters included providing encouragement and resources to the self-identified change leaders assigning significant leadership roles to organizational pace setters developing the relationship management skills of those people who were the most enthusiastic champions of the transformation from exclusion to inclusion.

Involving Everyone in the Transformation Process

If you want to identify those organizations that are genuinely committed to closing the gap between where they want to be and where they are, on the road to inclusion, look for those organizations that dedicate serious resources to involving all of its people in the organization's problem identification and resolution efforts. Is it a one-time activity or project? No. Can it be accomplished using a one-size-fits-all methodology? No. Is it without risks? No. Does it increase an organization's legal exposure? Yes, especially if the organization is unprepared or unwilling to respond appropriately to the solicited information and recommendations in a timely manner. Are the payoffs worth the effort? You bet they are. Because involving everyone can help the organization pinpoint the perceptual misalignments that exist between senior leadership's, middle management's and non-management's understanding about where the organization is heading and how close it is to being there. This type of total involvement effort will help the organization communicate the seriousness of its intentions to all of its stakeholders. It can also help the organization recognize its own transformation pace.

While the results of said efforts can boost the momentum for transformation to inclusion by leaps and bounds, the decision to get on this highway must be supported by an unwavering commitment to change and an even stronger organizational ego. After focusing immeasurable personal and professional attention on valuing diversity and inclusion, many a pack leader has had her/his feeling hurt upon discovering the gaps between organizational rhetoric and organizational reality, as told to them by mid-level managers and non-management employees. The non-management folks have been known to say: *We didn't know this bus was headed there!* and *You sure couldn't tell by the way our managers act!* And management folks say things like *We didn't know we were supposed to be doing those things on a regular basis!* and *You never helped us to develop the skills to achieve those goals and objectives!* It is what my mother used to call "an unmitigated rude awakening."

I am currently working with an organization that is nearing completion of this type of strategic listening and response endeavor. The entity in question has asked to remain anonymous until the project is finished and it is ready to publicize the results of its hard work to get the *411* from its people. Nevertheless, most exciting is the fact that although this company was, at first, taken aback by the idea talking to all 70,000$^+$ passengers on its transformation bus, just two years later the organization has experienced benefits and gained momentum of untold proportions. Some of the senior and mid-level managers who weren't even sure if they wanted to go on this particular bus trip are now acting as cruise directors par excellence and complaining about the fact that they have yet to be allowed to help drive the bus.

In this particular organization, the momentum for moving into a new, inclusive future is at an all-time high. Everyone is not exactly sure what is going to happen next. But now that the organization has made the effort to get the *411*, folks at all levels of the organization are excited about the fact that the changes that are occurring are based on the needs and interests identified by all of the people rather than by a few people at the top of the organization. They are also excited about the fact that ~ based on what has happened thus far – it is safe to assume that future decisions concerning the next leg of the organization's journey into the unknown will be made with their input and involvement.

Understanding the organization's transformation pace can strategically inform the organization's succession planning, training and development planning, communications, performance management, and internal relationship and reputation management efforts. But identifying the transformation pace is not a responsibility that should be delegated to the human resource department. Instead it should remain one of the key accountabilities of the organization's senior leadership team. Human resource personnel should be invited and encourage to participate in the organization's problem identification and resolution activities. For human resource personnel usually suffer the same anxieties and relationship management challenges as everyone else in the organization. However, they are not the guardians or stewards of the organization's environment, nor should they be required to bear such responsibility.

Recognizing & Rewarding The Indicators of Change

For the last year and a half, I have had the pleasure of facilitating a client's development of and move through a rapidly paced transformation to inclusion process that has involved increasing the diverse representation of its board of directors, as well as its senior and middle management level personnel. This ambitious, forward-thinking corporation is the embodiment of Randall Root's (1999) notions about winning big and winning fast. Without missing a beat in its endeavor to maintain high organizational performance while managing continuous acquisitions and growing national in scope, Charter One Bank has simultaneously taken on multiple tasks that most companies handle as serial activities. The task areas have included the following:

- ✦Revising its core values and thoroughly communicating how said values support the organization's commitment to valuing diversity and inclusion;

- Evaluating and addressing the diversity management skills-building needs of its managers;

- Increasing both the number and quality of its relationships with diverse vendors and suppliers;

- Requiring its external search engines to present balanced candidate pools or risk losing time-honored relationships to competitors

- Providing resources, opportunities and events regarding the value of diversity and inclusive environments to its non-management employees and their families via an assortment of communication strategies and initiatives; and,

- Playing a lead role in community-based organizations and strategic alliances that attest to the company's commitment to set new standards of excellence for diversity management in communities in which they do business.

For the past eighteen months, I have listened to the company's senior-most leaders wonder aloud as to whether or not their organization is getting any closer to being *there yet* and what all has to be done in order for them to arrive at the seeming illusive state of *there.* It was not until quite recently, while enjoying a casual lunch with the client's leader of the pack and Larry Hollins, president of The Hollins Group of executive recruiting consultants, that the client began to better appreciate how its efforts were being perceived by influential members of the population groups with whom they have been trying to build and maintain inclusive relations. The informal conversation turned to Charter One's endeavors to ensure diverse representation at senior management levels, and the six-month strategic planning process they had just conducted to assess senior management's current diversity management capacity. We laughingly reminisced about the making of the company's video, a few months earlier, in which Charles "Bud" Koch, Charter One's president and chief executive officer explains the Bank's business case for valuing diversity and inclusion and for establishing individual and organizational goals and accountabilities for effective diversity management both internal and external constituents. And, as colleagues often do, we reminded each other about all of challenges that seemed so insurmountable just a few months prior.

The Hollins Group's relationship with Charter One Bank was focused on diverse executive recruitment as opposed to all of the components of the organization's comprehensive plan for transformation. So prior to this particular conversation, Larry Hollins was not aware of the fact that in most of the cities it conducted business, Charter One exceeded local expectations regarding quantitatively and qualitatively meaningful minority vendor/supplier relationships by more than 5% - 10%. He had no way of knowing of Charter One Bank's many levels of involvement in various community transformation initiatives. After hearing more about some of the work our mutual client had accomplished during a exceptionally short time span, Larry leaned forward with a look of pleasant surprise and admiration and said to Charter One's senior vice president, Mike Bourgon, *You may not realize it, but you all are about 18 months or less from being the national model for corporate diversity management!*

This was a rewarding moment for Charter One, because it made their leadership team feel good about their efforts made to prepare the Bank for a high performance future. Several weeks later, when a potentially damaging story attempted to cast unwarranted aspersions on the organization's reputation lending practices within African American and Latino communities, Charter One officials were able to counter the criticisms and innuendos by telling and validating the true story regarding its relationships with its real and prospective non-white internal and external constituents and of their ongoing transformation to inclusion. Nevertheless, the series of events amplified a critical learning lesson for the leadership of Charter One Bank — the simple fact that no one is going to know the details of your organization's new story, if you do not help folks recognize and celebrate the indicators of organizational change.

Some organizations are reluctant to share the highlights of their transformation story, lest someone interpret their efforts to inform as attempts to proclaim themselves the paragons of virtue or to suggest to internal constituents that the organization is attempting to rest on its laurels. Others entertain hopes that the media will cast its spotlight on the organization's endeavors to value diversity and inclusion, especially after having been the center of widespread media attention when the same organization was wallowing in litigation during its pre-transformation days. However it is in the organization's best interests to become adept at telling its own transformation story both internally and externally. Dr. Bryan Gingrich, friend and colleague, advises all of our clients "organizational story-telling can be leveraged as a great organizational asset". And he's right. Because as Roy Harris, (2001) senior editor at CFO Magazine suggests, "while media outlets regularly examine the best workplaces for various non-whites and women, most coverage focuses on corporate missteps" such as those experienced by companies such as Georgia Pacific, Texaco and Denny's.

We can all recall the numerous times Denny's diversity mismanagement story was mentioned in both print and broadcast media. The same media outlets that focused our attention on Denny's diversity management shortcomings have done little to keep us informed about how Denny's is transforming itself to move into a new and more inclusive future. Therefore, it makes sense to encourage organizations to tell their transformation stories in an appropriate manner as a means of keeping the people on the transformation bus and any prospective riders informed about the progress of the journey. Regular and consistent internal and external messaging, recognition and rewards for individuals and work groups that are serving as transformation pace setters, and multiple channeled feedback opportunities to ask the passengers, *How do you like the trip so far?* are momentum boosters capable of lessening the effects of the *When are we going to be there?* anxiety bus passengers are known to experience.

Let's Give 'Em Something To Talk About

In 1994, Girl Scouts of the USA (GSUSA) developed and disseminated a management tool that helped its local boards of directors, executive staff and volunteer managers determine when various aspects of organizational behavior was characteristic of exclusive clubs, passive groups or inclusive teams. GSUSA's *Continuum for Institutionalizing Pluralism,* inspired by The Kaleel Jamison Consulting Group's *Building High-Performing Culturally Diverse Organizations* came to be affectionately known throughout the organization as *The Continuum.* Eight years later *The Continuum* continues to have numerous practical applications for Girl Scouts of the USA and for the hundreds of not-for-profit and for-profit organizations that have used it since. The user-friendly tool provided national and local Girl Scout entities with a get of guidelines delineating exclusive, passive and inclusive group behavior in each of the organization's major systems areas, i.e., governance, membership, program delivery, financial resource management and human resource management. It described behaviors, activities and language that served as indicators as to whether the group in question was functioning exclusively, passively or inclusively. For some it represented consistent messages regarding organizational guidelines and served as a behavior modification resource. For others it was a best-in-class checklist of sorts and was referred to as a routine part of any decision-making activities. Left with only sparse information and to their own devises, most well-intended managers do what we all do when venturing into the unknown ~ they make the plan up as they go along and in a crunch lean in the direction of the familiar regardless of whether or not it is the smart thing to do. A relatively simple tool for most users, *The Continuum* resolved the dilemma of: *How are we going to know what to do, once the consultant goes home?*

Other resources that do a good job of keeping the transformation to inclusion passengers appropriately focused throughout the journey are those that provide some basic guidelines regarding a) missteps to avoid, b) strategic action steps that have help others in transformation and c) special tips for leaders of the pack, regarding how to deal with adverse road conditions and disgruntled passengers.

During my twenty-eight years in the field as a diversity management consultant, I have pulled together a collection of empirical notions regarding best and worst practices in diversity management. Provided below are what I keep as my most significant learning points featured in *The Best and Worst in Diversity Management,* a resource most frequently requested by relatively new leaders of the pack, middle management pace setters and aspiring diversity management consultants:

TOP 10 WORST-IN-CLASS DIVERSITY MANAGEMENT PRACTICES

I. Unshared accountability *(placing the success of the organization's diversity management achievement on the shoulders of a single individual or groups of individuals such as the diversity manager, the human resources department or the diversity council ~ who generally lack both the authority and the resources to change the organizational environment) as opposed to holding everyone accountable for success ~ especially executive, senior and middle managers, regardless of their functional areas of expertise)*

II. Diversity-related gestures *(4Fs – one-shot program events involving ethnic* ***food****, ethnic* ***festivals****,* ***famous dead people*** *or* ***famous living people*** *as substitutes for effective diversity management strategies and processes).*

III. Not ensuring the necessary organizational resources *(including sanction and role-modeling by authority within the organization ~ required to realize vision and achieve goals related to effective diversity management).*

IV. Limited relationship building/management competencies *(exemplified by the organization and in various leadership positions within the organization).*

V. Compensating and rewarding internal adversaries of effective diversity management *(often better than the organization compensates and rewards internal advocates).*

VI. Failure to understand the organization's learning pace *(no educational programs beyond diversity awareness, trying to institute cultural change for the organization without providing competency-building opportunities and/or requirements).*

VII. Not involving all of the organization's constituents, *(i.e.*

employees, governance bodies, vendors/suppliers, consumers (real and potential) in processes designed to identify the organization's diversity-related strengths and weaknesses).

VIII. Identifying solutions to diversity management challenges prior to identifying the organization's diversity-related strengths and weaknesses *(usually without the expertise required to identify either the challenges or the solutions).*

IX. Counting people demographic statistics in organizations in which people do not really *count (gender, racial and ethnic headcounts that often do not tell the real story of whether or not said diversity is valued.*

X. Use of inconsistent organizational language and behavior regarding diversity and diversity management *(especially by organizational leadership and human resource professionals).*

10 BEST-IN-CLASS DIVERSITY MANAGEMENT PRACTICES

I. Clearly stated organizational vision for effective, inclusive diversity management, re-enforced by a supportive mission statement, consistent messaging, rewards and recognition systems, organizational and individual performance management systems, and governance oversight systems.

II. Sanction by authority – top down leadership, role modeling and accountability.

III. Holistic organizational change and management process oriented strategies rather than serial programs, episodic projects and segmented diversity priorities *(let's work on racial problems, then we'll resolve women's issues, then we'll take of disability challenges, then we'll work on problems related to sexuality, etc.).*

IV. Continuous measurement strategies that involve formal

assessment practices (surveys, focus groups, management systems) and ongoing, informal feedback opportunities for all constituency groups – even the most disgruntled.

V. Comprehensive competency building programs that provide educational opportunities in diversity awareness, conflict resolution, marketing, strategic planning and management and strategic measurement.

VI. Multiple programs and practices to ensure effective management of the multiple dimensions of diversity each employee or consumer brings to the organization as opposed to inflexible, one-way solutions.

VII. Meaningful consequences for managers who are unable or unwilling to help the organization achieve its vision for inclusive management of diversity – every well managed organization needs a well-lit exit sign.

VIII. Comprehensive communication systems to ensure internal and external awareness about the organization's diversity management vision, challenges, behavioral expectations and successes.

IX. Seeking external diversity management expertise with demonstrated results, when said expertise is not available within the organization.

X. Ensuring the resources necessary to support the organizational and individual transformations that are required to achieve the organization's vision and goals for effective and inclusive diversity management.

XI. Reputation and relationship management strategies that support the organization's diversity management vision and behavioral expectations in its internal and external relationships – not retaining legal, accounting firms, advertising, equipment supply firms that do not practice inclusive diversity management.

DIVERSITY MANAGEMENT PRACTITIONERS' CODE OF ETHICS

As does your organization, you too must have a code of ethics that guides your work as a diversity management practitioner. If you plan to be successful, make sure that yours incorporates the following:

Avoid leading with personal agendas and biases…just because you know a lot about diversity and diversity management it does not mean you are without bias and above stereotypic assumptions

Do not leave anybody out of the transformation process and stay clear of segmented diversity-related problem-solving…you know…I'll appease this group first, then that group over there, then whatever group represents the diversity flavor of the moments, as prescribed by media and political pundits

Own your limitations…if you do not possess the expertise to create and/or manage the entire transformation process, seek the assistance of others who do, be they internal or external

Recognize your organization's limitations…if you are serious and committed to excellence in diversity management and your organization is not (which can be discerned by assessing the organization's willingness to commit to best-in-class as opposed to worst in class strategies) invest your commitment and your sincerity in an organization of like values

Last, but certainly not least, do not allow this line of work and the numerous challenges associated with it to make you lose your sense of humor…believe me, if you intend to succeed in this field of endeavor, you are definitely going to need it.

Assigned Seating on the Transformation Bus

Providing information via user-friendly resources and communication opportunities canhelp keep the *Are we there yet?* Anxiety to a minimum while the organization focuses its energies on building inclusive environments and effective relationships needed to ensure high performance in the new future. It is critical that while remaining serious about its transformation to inclusion, the organization understand the importance of flexible and even regularly revised seating arrangements on the transformation bus. This means steering clear of relationship rigidities that can inhibit creative thinking and innovative behavior amongst the passengers on the transformation bus. Recent research provides us with new ideas about the best environmental conditions for growing innovative problem solving and decision-making. Whereas just a decade ago, we were fairly convinced that social capital promotes innovation and creativity. Research underway by Florida, Cushing & Gates (2002)suggest that environments achieving high scores on social capital – such as Birmingham, Alabama, Bismark, North Dakota and Cleveland, Ohio – score below-average scores in the area of innovative thinking and behavior. Why? this researcher team asserts that:

> *Weighing against the benefits that strong ties create is another dynamic. Relationships can get too strong that the community becomes complacent and insulated from outside information and challenges.*

They continue to suggest:

> *Strong ties can also promote the sort of conformity that undermines innovation. Weak ties, on the other hand, allow a basic level of information sharing and Collaboration while permitting newcomers with different ideas to be Accepted quickly into the social network.*

If Florida, Cushing and Gates (2002) are correct, further consideration and attention must be focused on the opportunities provided for passengers on the bus to interact with one another – especially with people to who they have had little previous exposure. In the case of most organizations attempting to create and move into an inclusive future, the people who most build and maintain the new relationships know very little about one another apart from an assortment of personal, cultural and organizational stereotypes. If permitted to select their own seating arrangements, many will try to stay within their individual comfort zones, which can mean segregating themselves and/or limiting their relationship building with others in an effort to retain membership in restricted connection groups and exclusive information networks.

This is reminiscent of Forrest Gump's first ride on the school bus on his very first day of school. As a newcomer and new passenger, he had no idea where to sit. So upon first boarding the bus, he attempted to sit in the first few vacant seats he saw. The bus driver had no policy regarding who was assigned to sit where. There was nothing preventing the other riders from telling Forrest he did not have permission to sit with them, or that the obviously empty seats were not "taken." All of the passengers were headed for the same destination. But Forrest ~ having no prior or positive relationships with any of the other passengers ~ was forced to sit by Jenny, the only rider who was not afraid to interact with the unknown and unfamiliar passenger. The seating arrangements on the transformation to inclusion bus can take on a Forrest Gump-like flavor, if the drivers of the bus only pay attention to road conditions, as opposed to the relationship dynamics unfolding on the inside of the vehicle. In an age where innovation and creativity can be the determining factor as to whether an organization dies, barely survives, or thrives, smart organizations will pay close attention to whether their internal relationships are inhibiting or promoting forward progress in the transformation process.

Conclusion

Some organizations take on diversity management with the idea of doing just enough to settle or avoid legal complications. Others agree to take on whatever tasks might be required to realize the surface benefits of diversity management, i.e. increased representation, flattering external reputation with targeted population segments, contracts awarded as a result of compliance fulfillment, etc. Nevertheless, organizations that genuinely wish to move from exclusion to inclusion, internally and externally, appreciate the fact that new results and a new organizational way of work and life require new strategies, imbued and fortified by new relationships with people who – although they may begin the trip as strangers ~ are all trying to get to the same new future.

Driving the organization's transformation to the inclusive new future can be a nightmare or it can turn out to be a thought-provoking, educationally enlightening adventure for everyone involved. Either way it is not risk or challenge free. It is not painless and – like most change processes it requires multi-level relationship management skills. When an organization that intentionally, effectively, inclusively and ethically, manages the diversity of its human resources - both internal and external - it stands to gain efficiency in its operations, advantages in the marketplace, and high performance relationships that can catapult the organization into its desired future. The essential factors for ensuring the road trip is as trouble-free as possible are:

- maintaining a clear understanding of the desired destination (inclusive vision),
- a well-mapped route with alternate driving instructions (flexible, effective strategies),
- carefully-selected designated drivers (visionary organizational leadership),
- skilled shotgun riders (managerial and non-managerial pace setters),
- informed and comfortable passengers (candid and continuous communications to stay on top of *the 411)*
- a properly maintained vehicle (consistent messages and continuous relationship building efforts),
- responsible speed adherence (responsive organizational pace),
- a resource to turn to when the trip gets complicated (professional consultative assistance),
- and – by all means – a plan to celebrate the organization's arrival to its new, inclusive future.

References

Beck, D.E. & Cowan, C. C. (1996). *Spiral Dynamics,* Cambridge, Massachusetts: Blackwell Business.

Clifton, R. & Maugham, E. (2002). *The future of brands: Twenty-five visions.* New York: University Press.

Dahle, C. (June 1999). *"Big learning, fast futures,"* Fast Company, 25.

Drucker, P. F. (1999), *Managerment Challenges for the 21st Century,* N.Y., New York:Harper Business: Harper Collins Publishers.

The FAA Administration Policy Statement on Model Work Environment (used with permission)

Florida, R., Cushing, R., & Gates, G. (July 2002) *"When Social Capital Stifles Innovation"* Harvard Business Review 80 (8) p.26.

Harris, R. (May 6, 1999) "The Illusion of Inclusion: Why Most Corporate Diversity Efforts Fail," CFO, May 6, p. 44.

Naisbitt, J. (1982). *Megatrends,* New York: Warner Books

Peters, T. (March 2001), *"Rule #3 leadership is confusing as hell,"* Fast Company.

Chapter XIII

Diversity Conflict & Diversity Conflict Management

Michael Brazzel

While the literature on conflict and conflict management has grown rapidly in recent years, little is included in the literature about conflict that results from diversity. This article provides a description of diversity conflict and diversity conflict management.

Diversity Conflict

Diversity conflict can be defined as:
In this definition, key aspects of diversity conflict are:

> **Exchanges of incompatible actions, behaviors or practices among two or more interdependent individuals, groups, or organizations with conflicting interests resulting from group-identity-based differences** (Adapted from Brown, 1983, pp. 4-5).

Multiple parties from different groups. Diversity conflict involves parties with group identities based in race, gender, sexual orientation, age, class, spiritual practice, ability and other human differences.

Interdependent parties. Diversity conflict involves interdependent parties. The greater the interdependence, the greater is the potential for conflict. Diversity conflict occurs at the contact point or boundary between parties, where they come face-to-face and interact. Diversity conflict can be interpersonal, inter-group and inter-organizational. It can also be between two or more parties who are a mix of individuals, groups, or organizations.

Conflicting interests. The parties to diversity conflict have different and conflicting interests / concerns / needs. Different interests result from group-identity-based differences in areas such as: facts, methods, goals, values, experiences, ideas, behaviors, language, physical appearance, emotions, spiritual practices, cultural backgrounds, world views, personalities, styles, expectations, performance, power, authority, and resources.

Incompatible actions, behaviors and practices. Diversity conflict results from actions, behaviors or practices by one of the parties that oppose, frustrate, or do violence to the other parties, that impacts their ability to work together effectively, that detrimentally affects their relationship, and that creates a hostile work environment (Brown, 1983, p. 5; Jameson, 2001, p.189). Behaviors can range from passivity, withdrawal, disagreement and debate to sabotage, violence and warfare. Violence involves actions, behaviors, and practices that are life-diminishing, life-deadening, life-threatening and life-ending experiences, rather than being life-enhancing, life-enriching and life-giving.

Normal and natural human experience. Diversity conflict is an inevitable, normal and natural response by individuals, groups, or organizations to differences experienced in "the other" in order to maintain boundaries, integrity and well-being. In this case, the other is experienced as a "force for change" or as a force keeping things the same. The parties to the conflict are neither good nor bad, right nor wrong. Diversity conflict itself can be both productive and harmful.

Positive and negative impacts on individuals, groups and organizations. Diversity conflict can be beneficial and it can be destructive. It can enhance performance and be a barrier to performance. Diversity conflict can be growth and creativity producing — and destructive and chaotic for organizational performance.

Conflict events / situations and systemic conflict. Diversity conflict is often written about and experienced as an event or situation which is related to overt diversity issues that are observable over a specific period of time and labeled as diversity conflict by the parties. Conflict is less often understood as a systemic process in which conflict results from the norms, values, customs, laws, behaviors, policies, structures, practices and other aspects of the cultures of groups, organizations and society. With systemic conflict, specific conflict situations may get resolved, only to have new conflict situations arise that affect the same and other parties.

The focus on conflict as a situation can be reinforced by the distinction that some authors make between conflict and a dispute. For example, Costantino and Merchant define conflict as a process of expressing disagreement and a dispute as one of a number of products of conflict, which is "tangible and concrete" (1996, pp. 4-7). They list other products of conflict as competition, sabotage, inefficiency, low morale and withholding knowledge (pp. 6-7). Alternatively, Jameson distinguishes between formal and informal conflict situations, with formal conflict occurring when there are policy, human rights or other violations that can lead to litigation (Jameson, 2001, p. 189). Other authors use the term "conflict" interchangeably with terms like dispute, disagreement, problem, struggle, tension, contention, and difference (for example, Singer, 1990; Isenhart and Spangle, 2000; Landau, Landau and Landau, 2001). In most cases "conflict" is applied to separate events and situations. The distinction between conflict events and situations and systemic conflict has important implications for methods used to address diversity conflict.

Two Sides of Diversity Conflict

Diversity conflict has two sides. It can be based in human differences and it can be based in actions, behaviors and practices of oppression. These two sides are described in Table 1.

Diversity Conflict Based in Human Differences

Human-differences-based diversity conflict is disagreement and conflict that results from the different interests, skills, backgrounds, perspectives, values, experiences, abilities and contributions of members of all groups. It is conflict based in the merits of difference, rather than in prejudice and power differences among groups. The resolution of human-differences-based diversity conflict provides opportunities for breakthrough and enhanced creativity, innovation, product-development, market-development, problem-solving, decision-making and

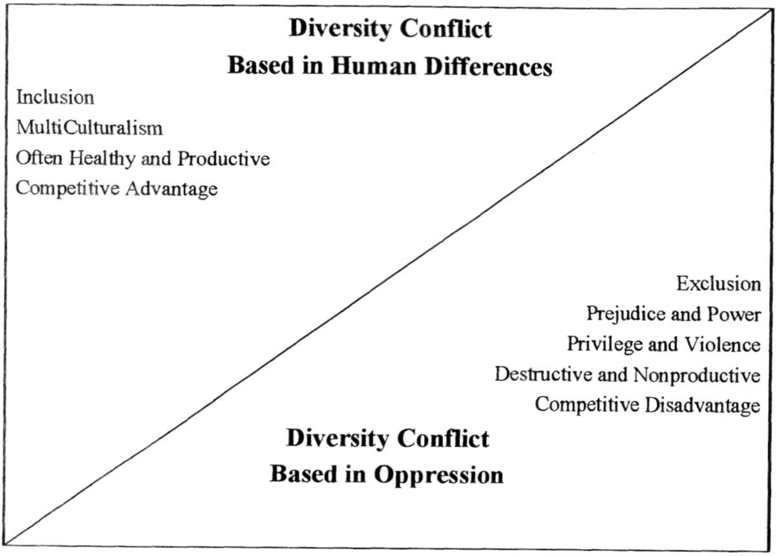

Table 1. Two Sides of Diversity Conflict.

competitive advantage (Landau, Landau and Landau, 2001; Caudron, 1999). Sy, Barbara and Daryl Landau write that the conflict which results from human differences and interdependence is "the oxygen of creativity" (2001, pp. x-xi). Diversity conflict based in human differences results from an organizational strategy of inclusion and multiculturalism: embracing and fully involving all people and their differences in the work, fabric and life of the organization in a way that makes use of their differences to enhance organizational effectiveness and performance.

Human-differences-based conflict is productive conflict when it enhances individual, group and organizational performance. This form of diversity conflict is healthy and needs to be supported and nurtured when it is productive and managed so that it does not get out of hand. Human-differences-based conflict can be nonproductive when there is too much or too little conflict.

Diversity Conflict Based in Oppression

Oppression-based diversity conflict is conflict between dominant and marginalized groups and group members that results from racism, sexism, heterosexism and other forms of oppression.

Oppression is a system of inequality, privilege, and violent actions, behaviors, and practices that benefit dominant group members and harm members of marginalized groups. Oppression is:

- ✦based in a combination of prejudice and power exercised by dominant groups over marginalized groups,
- ✦institutionalized in the norms, values, customs, laws, behaviors, policies, structures, and practices of groups, organizations and society and internalized in the values, beliefs and actions of individuals.
- ✦kept in place by the interdependent actions and collusion of members of both dominant and marginalized groups,
- ✦composed of the "isms" which are based in social identity group membership: racism, sexism, heterosexism and other forms of oppression.

Oppression, and the diversity conflict from it, is nonproductive. Oppression-based diversity conflict has negative impacts on the performance of individuals, groups and organizations. To resolve this form of diversity conflict, an organization must follow a conflict management strategy that addresses its basis in oppression.

Dominant and marginalized group memberships. Social identity groups — for example, men and women — are based in corresponding areas of human differences — for example, gender. Social identity group membership can mean dominant group membership for some individuals (men) and marginalized group membership for others (women). Dominant groups are groups with the power in organizations and society to influence and control resources and establish sanctions, rules, laws, policies, standards, values, and expectations that, intentionally or unintentionally, confer or deny privilege, power, recognition, and opportunity to individuals and groups. Marginalized groups do not have that power. When there is conflict between dominant and marginalized groups, this difference in societal-and group-based power gives dominant groups and dominant group members an ability to influence the outcomes of conflict that is not shared by marginalized group members.

The concept of dominant and marginalized groups relates to group identity and not individual identity. An individual dominant group member may hold little or no power over organizational and societal resources, sanctions, rules, and policies. Their dominant group identity confers privilege, however, whether chosen or not. In contrast, an individual marginalized group member may have substantial power, and because of marginalized group identity be denied privilege and subjected to harm, without recourse.

Dominant group privilege. Dominant group privilege results from oppression. Privilege is the rights, rewards, benefits, access, opportunities, advantages, and goods and services received by dominant group members because of their group membership. They receive these benefits without regard to individual achievements, performance, contributions and accomplishments (McIntosh, 1989; Kivel, 1996, pp. 30-32). Dominant group privilege is an unearned, unacknowledged, and often-unrecognized form of "affirmative action" for dominant group members that can become internalized and experienced as an entitlement.

Actions, behaviors and practices of oppression. Oppression results in a system of actions, behaviors, and practices of oppression directed at marginalized group members because of their group membership, without regard to individual performance and behavior. These actions, behaviors and practices of oppression experienced by marginalized group members can be conscious and unconscious, intentional and unintentional, and overt and covert. They are all forms of violence, regardless of consciousness, intention or visibility. They are life-diminishing, life-deadening, life-threatening, or life-ending. Examples of conscious and unconscious actions, behaviors and practices of oppression can be classified into intentional/unintentional and overt/covert categories seen in Table 2. (adapted from Plummer, 1999). These categories can be further defined as:

- Conscious oppression: Entitled oppression, Consciously-hidden oppression, and "Reasonable" oppression, and
- Unconscious oppression.

Entitled oppression involves conscious actions, behaviors and practices by organizations and society toward marginalized group members that are intentional and highly visible. These acts are justified from a dominant group perspective of righteousness and entitlement and the conviction that marginalized group members are abnormal, inferior and, even, less than human. Examples include: the Holocaust; genocide;

Conscious and Unconscious Actions, Behaviors And Practices of Oppression

	Overt	Covert
Intentional	Entitled Oppression	Consciously-Hidden Oppression
Unintentional	"Reasonable" Oppression	Unconscious Oppression

Table 2. Conscious and Unconscious Actions Behaviors and Practices of Oppression

slavery; ethnic cleansing; cross burnings; breaking car windows and slashing tires; burning, shooting and bombing homes, places of work and worship.....and marking/painting them with human waste and threatening and violent words and symbols; denying marginalized group members the ability to have children or taking them away; changing, distorting, obliterating the history of a people or group of people; subjecting marginalized group members to medical experiments and germ warfare; threatening, taunting, shunning, stalking, fondling, raping, sterilizing, castrating, beating, whipping, starving, torturing, detaining, imprisoning, putting them into work camps, concentration camps and reservations, buying and selling, enslaving, banishing, colonializing, mutilating, poisoning, torching, lynching, and killing them.

Consciously-hidden oppression involves actions, behaviors and practices by organizations and society toward marginalized group members that are conscious and intentional. They are hidden and denied because they are in violation of civil rights laws and/or the values of organizations and society. Examples include: red-lining; steering; profiling (group-identity-based stops, searches, arrests, prosecutions); paying marginalized group members lower salaries and charging them higher prices, interest, rent, and taxes; limiting the quantity and quality of their access to jobs, mentoring, information, feedback, recognition, promotions....and land, insurance, credit, phone service, houses, utilities, health and medical care, rest rooms, apartments, hotel rooms, restaurant food; limiting their access to marriage, business, professional and other licenses; limiting their access to professions, education, voting, recreation, entertainment, transportation, police and fire protection, religious services, family care, media; and polluting the water, air, and land of their communities with discarded and stockpiled hazardous materials and waste.

"Reasonable" oppression is conscious actions, behaviors and practices by organizations and society toward marginalized group members that are explained and justified on religious, statistical, legal/constitutional, scientific, cultural, values, beliefs, or other grounds (Armour,1997). In this category of oppression, the focus is on justification and the lack of intention. Impact is ignored. The actions, behaviors and practices of "reasonable" oppression are seen by dominant group members as unfortunate, unintentional acts that just happen. Examples include: subjecting marginalized group members to demeaning, disrespectful, abusive jokes, slurs, innuendoes, language and gestures; identifying them as the exception; not acknowledging them; questioning, checking, testing, watching, suspecting, ignoring, rejecting, avoiding, excluding, patronizing, undermining, interrupting, scolding, criticizing, berating, mocking, ridiculing, deceiving, slandering, badgering, isolating, censoring, expelling, exiling, shunning, castigating, following, searching, and stopping them; belittling and/or sexualizing their intelligence, spirituality, emotionality, sexuality, language, physical appearance and ability. Some of the hate crimes of entitled oppression and the discrimination of consciously-hidden oppression are included in the "reasonable" oppression category under some circumstances.

Unconscious oppression includes actions, behaviors and practices by organizations and society toward marginalized group members that are unintentional and unconscious. Examples include: attributing the ideas and accomplishments of marginalized group members to others; prejudging them as incompetent; telling them what to do and how to think; saying these actions, behaviors, and practices of oppression are a surprise, are a thing of the past and do not happen here or now, are not intended or conscious, are good for them, are not that bad, are the fault of marginalized group members because of their behavior, are the individual, personal baggage or problems of marginalized group members; saying these actions, behaviors, and practices of oppression just do not happen except in rare and unusual circumstances, and are one-time experiences unconnected to a pattern of actions, behaviors, and practices that have cumulative impacts; saying these actions, behaviors, and practices do not really happen and they happen to dominant group members as well; and being silent about these actions, behaviors, and practices of oppression.

The actions, behaviors and practices of oppression are all forms of violence, regardless of consciousness, intention or visibility. They are life-diminishing, life-deadening, life- threatening, or life-ending experiences, rather than life-enhancing, life-enriching an life-giving experiences. The unintentional, overt/covert acts are sometimes labeled "workplace incivility" to distinguish them from the more aggressive and violent forms of mistreatment involved in the intentional, overt/covert categories. Workplace incivility is interaction among parties in which there is violation of workplace norms and values about mutual respect and there is ambiguous intention to harm and injure another (Andersson and Pearson, 1999, pp. 457; Pearson, Andersson and Porath, 2000, pp.124-125).

Diversity conflict can be generated without conscious and intentional actions by dominant and marginalized group members. Because oppression is institutionalized in organizational policies and structure, oppression-based diversity conflict is generated on auto-pilot. It results from oppression's privilege, violence, and dominant-marginalized-group dynamics at the boundaries between different social identity groups, between dominant and marginalized groups, and within and among specific dominant or marginalized groups.

Parallel Experiences and Perspectives of Dominant and Marginalized Groups

Diversity conflict, like other forms of conflict, results from the interdependent behaviors of two or more parties. Dominant and marginalized group members have very different experiences and perspectives about diversity conflict.

When individuals operate from the perspective of dominant group memberships (for example, senior leaders and managers, white people, men, heterosexuals) they are likely to view and experience diversity conflict as an unexpected, undeserved, and often threatening event or challenge initiated by marginalized group members. Dominant group members see themselves as targeted by marginalized group members, who are being disloyal and disrespectful of organizational rules and are troublemakers.

Individuals operating from marginalized group memberships (for example, employees, people of color, women, gay, lesbian, bisexual, transgendered people) are likely to have very different experiences and perspectives with diversity conflict. When viewed and experienced from a marginalized group perspective, diversity conflict is likely to be seen and experienced as a process of disregarding unfair dominant-group-imposed organizational rules and conventions; acting to resist implementation of violent actions, behaviors and practices of racism, sexism and other forms of oppression; not colluding with oppression; or taking the steps necessary to survive ongoing, undeserved consequences of racism, sexism or other forms of oppression.

Patterns of Conflict

Levels of System

Diversity conflict is an interaction between two or more interdependent parties that involves exchanges of actions and reactions. Because of the exchanges of actions and reactions involved in diversity conflict, participants are both instigators and targets. If the conflict broadens in scope, bystanders and witnesses to initial conflict, within and outside the workplace, can be swept up as participants.

Conflict parties can be individuals, groups and organizations. Diversity conflict occurs at interpersonal, inter-group and inter-organizational levels of system. It can also exist across levels of system: for example, between an individual and a group or organization and between a group and an organization.

Conflict Spirals, Cascades and Other Diversity Conflict Patterns

Diversity conflict can include very complex combinations of intensity, breadth and power involving non-escalating, escalating, de-escalating, cascading, hidden, suppressed, and reoccurring conflict. Diversity conflict can vary in:

Escalating conflict. Escalating diversity conflict is a spiraling cycle of conflict between the parties that increases in intensity. For example, an exchange of avoidance, interruptions and name calling could lead to retaliatory ridicule, castigation and revengeful shunning or exile. Pruitt and Rubin identify five ways in which conflict escalates (1984, pp. 64-65):

- ✦Conflict behaviors or tactics increase in the level of aggressiveness and coercion.
- ✦Issues proliferate and increasing resources are devoted to winning.
- ✦There is a shift from specific issues to general, overarching issues and the relationship between the parties deteriorates.
- ✦Desired outcomes shift from doing well, to winning, to hurting the other party.
- ✦The number of conflict participants increases as the parties seek allies.

The potential for escalating diversity conflict is magnified by the backdrop of oppression in organizations and society. Dominant group members are blind to or in denial of their privilege and of the cumulative impacts on marginalized group members of ongoing negative experiences in the workplace and society. In conflict situations, organizations are likely to act more aggressively toward marginalized groups and group members than their dominant group counterparts.

Non-escalating conflict / stalemate. Diversity conflict can cycle between parties in an ongoing exchange of actions and reactions where the intensity of conflict is sustained.....neither escalating nor de-escalating. An example is a kind of "cold war" of criticizing, ridiculing and name-calling between the parties. Persistence of non-escalating conflict can lead to cumulative intolerance between the parties and escalating conflict or it can lead to fatigue and de-escalation. Pruitt and Rubin describe stalemate as an intermediate stage between escalating conflict and de-escalating conflict resulting from "failure of contentious tactics, exhaustion of resources, loss of social support, and unacceptable costs" (1984, pp. 126-127).

Cascading conflict. Escalating diversity conflict between two parties can spread to other individuals, groups and departments inside an organization and to employee families, customers, suppliers and other entities in the organization's environment. Pearson, Andersson and Porath identify ways initial escalating conflict can cascade within and outside an organization through secondary conflict spirals:

- ✦Modeling of the conflict behaviors with and enactment by witnesses and bystanders to the original conflict,
- ✦Displacement or retaliation toward new parties, and
- ✦Cumulative impacts of secondary conflict spirals and word-of-mouth descriptions of the conflict resulting in an organizational culture of disrespect and conflict (2000, pp. 132-133; also Andersson and Pearson, 1999, pp. 465-466).

Cascading conflict is often directed toward marginalized group members through the actions and behaviors of both dominant and marginalized group members.

- ✦Intensity: the level of aggressiveness/coercion in the parties' behaviors,
- ✦Breadth: the number of parties involved in the conflict, and
- ✦Power differences: power differences that result from group membership and oppression, with dominant group members obtaining benefits and privilege from their group memberships and marginalized group members being targeted for their group memberships.

Workplace mobbing. Workplace mobbing is a form of escalating and cascading conflict focused on one individual or group. Its purpose is to force them out of the workplace. It is a form of group violence. Colleagues, peers, superiors and subordinates attack the integrity, competence, dignity and self-esteem of an individual through psychological, emotional and physical abuse over a sufficient period of time to isolate and force them out of the workplace (Davenport, Schwartz and Elliott, 1999). Workplace mobbing is a form of scapegoating in which the target is held responsible for organizational ills and then sacrificed. The targets of workplace mobbing are often marginalized group members, who are branded as difficult, incompetent and mentally ill workers, who have brought about their own downfall. The parties to mobbing can be both dominant and marginalized group members and they may be participating voluntarily and involuntarily.

De-escalating conflict. De-escalating conflict is a cycle of action and reaction between the parties that decreases in intensity. The de-escalation can result from actions by one or both parties. Parties may react with inaction, behaviors of lesser aggression, apology, denying intent to harm, yielding to the other, withdrawal, or mutual problem solving (Pruitt and Rubin, 1986, pp. 130-132; Pearson, Andersson and Porath, 2000, p. 133). While dominant groups are best positioned to initiate de-escalation, marginalized groups and group members may have more limited conflict options that favor their strategic use of de-escalating behaviors and actions.

Reoccurring conflict. The absence of diversity conflict behaviors in an organization does not necessarily mean that conflict no longer exists in the organization. Parties to escalating diversity conflict may withdraw into inaction, take time to reorganize and gather resources, and then reenter the cycle of action and reaction. For example, resignations of employees who are marginalized group members can represent a form of reoccurring conflict for organizations. Pearson, Andersson and Porath report that employees who decide to leave their jobs after experiencing an incident of incivility often spend a year or more looking for a new job before they leave their organization (2000, p. 130).

Hidden conflict. Diversity conflict in organizations is often hidden, denied, suppressed, dismissed as an interpersonal dispute, or attributed to the individual, personal problems of marginalized group members who are labeled as difficult, often incompetent, employees (Kolb and Putnam, 1992). Organizations are most likely to notice and address diversity conflict when it in the interest of dominant group members to do so. Diversity conflict may be ignored when it is generated within and among dominant or marginalized groups or is the result of institutionalized privilege and oppression, unless there is strong and visible resistance from marginalized group members or the threat of litigation. Diversity conflict based in oppression is often unseen, denied, unnamed and/or not acted on by organizations that operate out of dominant group perspectives.

Suppressed conflict. Organizations can attempt to serve the interests of dominant groups by suppressing actions and reactions of marginalized groups and members through implied and actual threats, exclusion, co-optation, isolation, exile, and expulsion. Inaction, withdrawal, assimilation, and submission can create the appearance of the absence of conflict.....when, in actuality, the conflict continues unseen and underground as withdrawn energy, resistance, and sabotage or is delayed and re-emerges at a later time.

Impacts of Diversity Conflict

Diversity conflict has positive and negative impacts on individuals, groups and organizations. The pattern of impacts depends on whether the diversity conflict is based in human differences or oppression.

Impacts of human-differences-based conflict. Diversity conflict based in human differences can be productive for performance at various levels of system. If there is too little conflict or too much, diversity conflict based in human differences can act as a barrier to performance. Diversity conflict can be growth and creativity producing — and destructive and chaotic for organizational performance.

- ✦*Positive conflict outcomes* can include: increased involvement and motivation, improved mastery and retention of material, spontaneity in communications and relationships, growth and development, strengthened relationships, creativity and innovation, greater cohesion and increased productivity.
- ✦*Negative conflict outcomes* can involve: less energy available for tasks, destruction of morale and relationships, polarization of individuals and groups, reduced cooperation, dysfunctional behavior, suspicion and mistrust and diminished productivity.

Impacts of oppression-based conflict. Oppression, and the diversity conflict from it, have negative impacts on the performance of individuals, groups and organizations. The actions, behaviors and practices of oppression that are a part of this form of diversity conflict can harm employees, the organization, as well as family members, friends, customers and other stakeholders in what results from diversity conflict. Following are some examples of the impacts of oppression-based conflict.

Pearson, Andersson and Porath have collected information about the impacts of incidents of workplace incivility from interviews and questionnaires of workers, managers and professionals in a wide range of U.S. profit, non-profit and government organizations (2000, p. 124). Workplace incivility involves the unintentional, overt/covert actions, behaviors and practices of oppression described above. Pearson, Andersson and Porath defined workplace incivility as interaction among parties in which there is violation of workplace norms and values about mutual respect and ambiguous intention to harm and injure another. They differentiated workplace incivility from the more aggressive and violent forms of mistreatment involved in the intentional, overt/covert categories.

Pearson, Andersson and Porath found lasting, negative emotional and psychological effects of workplace incivility on employee attendance, commitment, performance and turnover because the workplace was unpleasant, or even hostile. Their findings include (2000, pp. 129-131):

- ✦Effects that last a decade or more.
- ✦Fear, confusion, panic, hopelessness that anything will change.
- ✦Reduced commitment to the job and organization: disengagement from tasks beyond job specifications, reduced efforts to meet work responsibilities, no longer doing their best work, decreased time spent at work, quitting their job or thinking about changing jobs.
- ✦Reduced workplace contributions: lost work time spent worrying about incivility incidents or avoiding perpetrators, no longer making voluntary efforts to help newcomers and assist colleagues, dropping off committees and task forces, reduced time generating and facilitating innovations.
- ✦Stealing property in retaliation toward perpetrators or the organization.

Davenport, Schwartz and Elliott report on the effects of workplace mobbing based on research from Europe, Asia and North American and their own interviews in the U.S. (1999). Workplace mobbing is group violence by colleagues, peers, superiors and subordinates that attacks the integrity, competence, dignity and self-esteem of an individual through psychological, emotional and physical abuse over a sufficient period of time to isolate and force them out of the workplace. (Davenport, Schwartz and Elliott, 1999). Davenport, Schwartz and Elliott define first, second and third degree mobbing in terms of duration, psychological, emotional and physical effects and the resulting ability of individuals to function in the workplace (1999, pp. 39, 89-92):

- ✦*First-degree mobbing*: individuals experience mobbing for a relatively short time, are functional in the workplace and experience anger, distress, confusion, irritability, crying, some sleep difficulties and lack of concentration.
- ✦*Second-degree mobbing:* individuals experience mobbing for a longer time, have health problems that begin to affect performance in the workplace, and experience high-blood pressure, gastro-intestinal illness, persistent sleep problems, depression, weight gain/loss, alcohol/drug problems, avoidance of the workplace, and unusual fearfulness.
- ✦*Third-degree mobbing:* individuals experience mobbing for a protracted period. They are not functional and may be unable to remain in the workplace. They experience severe physical and emotional difficulties that impact on work and family, including: depression, despair, rage, panic attacks, heart attacks and other severe illness, accidents, suicide attempts and violence directed at self and others.

Second- and third-degree mobbing can lead to post-traumatic stress disorder (Davenport, Schwartz and Elliott, 1999, pp. 94-95).

Measures of Diversity Conflict Impacts

Positive and negative impacts of diversity conflict can be defined and measured in some of the following dimensions (Cox, 1994; White, 1998a & 1998b):

- ✦*Outcomes:* profit, return on investment, revenue, cost, achievement of organizational goals and specific diversity initiatives, productivity; satisfaction of customers, vendors, community organizations, and specific group-oriented charities and organizations; market share; shareholder satisfaction and share price; representation of groups of people in customer sales and purchases from vendors; being listed / not listed by the media as employer of choice for women, people of color and specific other groups and being benchmarked / not benchmarked for diversity practices by other organizations.

- *Organization climate:* employee satisfaction and commitment, employee motivation, complaints / grievances, litigation, turnover rate, hiring and retention rate, offer-to-acceptance rate, job involvement and identification with work, job motivation, promotability ratings, job performance ratings, attendance and absence rates, employee perceptions about organization and leadership commitment and accountability.
- *Workplace management:* recruitment and retention of the most talented people, salary levels and parity, creativity, innovation, problem-solving and decision-making, organizational flexibility and tolerance of ambiguity, effectiveness of marketing strategies, communication efficiency, and representation of groups of people across organizational levels, salary bands, units, managerial, technical and professional jobs, customers, and vendors.

Diveristy Conflict Management

Diversity is woven into the fabric of organizations. Diversity conflict, as well, is an integral part of the life of organizations. Diversity conflict management addresses specific diversity conflict situations and the systemic causes of diversity conflict based in oppression. It involves:

- Identifying and addressing specific diversity conflict situations by maintaining and supporting productive conflict based in human differences and resolving nonproductive diversity conflict and
- Eliminating the systemic causes of diversity conflict based in oppression.

From the perspectives of this article, the purpose of diversity conflict management is to enhance individual, group and organizational performance.

Diversity conflict management in organizations is often linked with the concepts of diversity conflict settlement and resolution. Diversity conflict management, settlement or resolution are viewed in many ways:

- ✦ *Closure:* that the conflict is ended.....or that it appears to go away because it is hidden or suppressed.
- ✦ *Winning and losing:* that some parties win and the others lose, that all parties lose, that each party wins something and loses something, or that all parties win.
- ✦ *Achievement of a desired outcome:* that a particular outcome is forced or imposed on some of the parties, that parties go along with an outcome with which they do not agree, that they withdraw from the conflict into silence, inaction and denial, that they leave the organization, or that all the parties agree to an outcome.
- ✦ *Mutual agreement:* that a satisfactory solution to the conflict is agreed to by all parties.
- ✦ *Enhanced individual, group and organizational performance:* that productive diversity conflict is provided to enhance performance at different levels of system or that non-productive diversity conflict that reduces performance is eliminated.

Dominant groups are likely to define conflict management, settlement and resolution in terms of closure, winning / not losing, and achieving desired objectives. These are perspectives that manifest the power differences between dominant and marginalized groups. Marginalized groups may prefer that conflict management, resolution and settlement be viewed in terms of mutual agreement and enhanced individual, group and organizational performance.

Diversity conflict management is complex because diversity conflict is based both in human differences and in oppression and because diversity conflict management processes can be used as a means for supporting oppression. Parties to conflict bring incompatible actions, behaviors and practices and conflicting interests. The parties can also bring prejudice and the power differences of dominant and marginalized groups that result from oppression. Diversity conflict management can incorporate and extend the power differences of dominant and marginalized groups and support and extend oppression as a system of privilege and violence.

Specific Diversity Conflict Situations

Organizations can address specific diversity conflict situations by changing the nature of the conflict situation, by pursuing power-over and power-with conflict strategies, and by using conflict management processes involving negotiation, arbitration and adjudication. Specific conflict situations can be based either in human differences or in oppression. Many of the conflict management approaches used by organizations are appropriate for human-differences-based conflict, rather than oppression-based conflict. They do not address the systemic causes of oppression and can, in fact, be conflict management processes and systems that maintain and extend oppression.

Change the Nature of the Conflict Situation

Diversity conflict situations based in human differences provide opportunities for breakthrough and enhanced creativity, innovation, product-development, market-development, problem-solving, decision-making and competitive advantage. Too much or too little conflict can hinder performance. Organizations benefit by adopting a stance toward human-differences-based diversity conflict which supports productive conflict and discourages too little or too much conflict that reduces organizational performance. Too little conflict generates low levels of energy for challenging traditional patterns and methods of operation, resulting in lower performance levels. Too much conflict mobilizes high levels of energy and disrupts information flow and decision-making, resulting again in lower levels of performance.

David Brown suggests a number of actions organizations can take to increase or to lower conflict by changing the nature and intensity of specific conflict situations involving: interests / issues, boundaries, extent of interdependence, sources and distribution of power, perceptions and values, resources, and organizational rules and processes (1983, pp. 51-80). They are listed in Table 3. Brown identifies some actions that can either increase or reduce conflict depending on the conflict situation. They include:

- ✦Organize parties to cope with conflict.
- ✦Define and clarify alternatives, choices, and trade-offs.

ACTIONS THAT CHANGE THE NATURE AND INTENSITY OF SPECIFIC CONFLICT SITUATIONS

--Brown, 1983, pp. 51-80

Areas For Changing the Nature of the Conflict	Actions that Increase Conflict	Actions that Reduce Conflict
Issues	fractionate	consolidate
Critical personnel, information or other resources that change relationships among the parties	expand, diversify	contract, consolidate
Superordinate goals	---	focus on
Diversity of interests	focus on	---
Perspectives	reconceptualize to differentiate	reconceptualize to include
Forces that promote conflict	clarify	reduce
Perceptions, communications, and tactics	raise awareness of those that escalate conflict	raise awareness of those that reduce conflict
Boundaries among parties	create, clarify	de-emphasize
New, provocative, or disruptive parties	include	remove
Relationship between parties	reduce distance	reduce overlap
Parties= boundaries to information, personnel, inputs and outputs	open	close
Rules and procedures	loosen	tighten
Shared norms, standards of behavior, and values	loosen	tighten

Table 3. Actions that Change the Nature and Intensity of Specific Conflict Situations

✦ Provide trustworthy, less distorted communication and information exchange and flow.

✦ Define and clarify optional tactics for initial presentations, initiatives and self- defense.

✦ Involve upper management, key stakeholders, or outside mediators.

✦ Clarify incentives and costs of continued / more / less conflict.

✦ Reduce stereotypes of parties' innocence, victimization, helplessness, villainy, dangerousness, or similarity (pp. 51-80).

Other actions suggested by Brown change the nature and intensity of conflict situations and specifically increase conflict or reduce conflict (pp. 51-80). They are listed in Table 3.

These actions change the nature of specific diversity conflict situations and are an effective means to encourage and discourage conflict based in human differences to enhance performance and support productive outcomes. They can also be used to enhance the power of dominant groups and dominant organizational cultures by resolving diversity conflict situations to the benefit of dominant groups and the disadvantage of marginalized groups. These actions then would reinforce oppression and diversity conflict based in oppression.

Conflict Strategies

Actions to address specific conflict situations can also be viewed in terms of strategies for handling conflict that are used by individuals, groups and organizations when involved in conflict. They can be grouped according to (1) the degree of assertiveness the strategies represent for satisfying one's own needs, concerns and interests and (2) the degree of cooperativeness with satisfying the other's needs, concerns and interests (Thomas and Kilmann, 1974; Leas, 1984). Some are strategies that seldom work to provide productive diversity conflict and enhance performance. Others are strategies that sometimes work.

Some are conflict strategies that give further privilege to dominant groups and harm marginalized groups. These strategies are shown in Table 4.

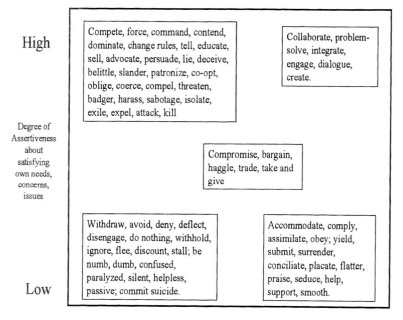

Degree of Assertiveness about satisfying own needs, concerns, issues	Low		High
High	Compete, force, command, contend, dominate, change rules, tell, educate, sell, advocate, persuade, lie, deceive, belittle, slander, patronize, co-opt, oblige, coerce, compel, threaten, badger, harass, sabotage, isolate, exile, expel, attack, kill		Collaborate, problem-solve, integrate, engage, dialogue, create.
		Compromise, bargain, haggle, trade, take and give	
Low	Withdraw, avoid, deny, deflect, disengage, do nothing, withhold, ignore, flee, discount, stall; be numb, dumb, confused, paralyzed, silent, helpless, passive; commit suicide.		Accommodate, comply, assimilate, obey; yield, submit, surrender, conciliate, placate, flatter, praise, seduce, help, support, smooth.

Table 4. Conflict Strategies

These conflict strategies can also be categorized in relation to their stance toward the use of power, where power is a party's ability to influence the outcome of a conflict situation. The strategies can be power-over and power-with strategies.

1. Power-Over Strategies

High assertiveness, low cooperativeness strategies. The purpose of these strategies is to prevail or win over the other conflict parties, achieve a desired outcome, insure that other parties lose, and force timely closure to conflict. They include the following strategies: compete, force, dominate, tell, educate, oblige, compel, sell, exile, co-opt, persuade, isolate, threaten, and kill. Killing the other party — emotionally, physically or figuratively — is a high aggression, high coercion example of this group of win-lose strategies. These strategies are often preferred by dominant groups and group members. The conscious actions, behaviors and practices of oppression — the entitled, consciously-hidden, and "reasonable" oppression categories — listed earlier in this

article are high assertiveness, low cooperativeness diversity conflict strategies. They create too much conflict and reduce organizational performance. . . and often lead to escalation and retaliation. These strategies range from using power to get rid of the other party, to making the other party do what you wish, and to convincing the other party to agree with your perspective about what needs to happen.

Low assertiveness, low cooperativeness strategies. These strategies are a means for a conflict party to attempt to moderate or bring timely closure to conflict. They can permit the other party to achieve their desired outcome. They can be a covert, interim strategy to gather and conserve resources for a high assertiveness strategy at a later time.....a kind of "rope-a-dope" strategy. These strategies include: withdraw, avoid, deflect, deny, ignore, flee, discount, do nothing, delay. Committing suicide — emotionally, physically or figuratively — is an extreme example of this group of win-lose strategies. Low assertiveness, low cooperativeness strategies result in too little conflict and low energy that leads to reduced organizational performance and can be a means for de-escalation. The unconscious actions, behaviors and practices of oppression listed above are low assertiveness, low cooperativeness strategies.

Low assertiveness, high cooperativeness strategies. These strategies permit a conflict party to escape diversity conflict or bring timely closure to conflict, by accommodating or yielding to the desired outcome of the other party. These strategies can be means for de-escalation or a covert, interim strategy to buy the time needed to gather and conserve resources for a high assertiveness strategy at a later time. They include: accommodate, comply, assimilate, obey, yield, submit, surrender, conciliate, flatter, praise, seduce, help, support, smooth. They result in too little conflict and low energy that leads to reduced organizational performance and can be a means for de-escalation. They are adversarial, win-lose strategies.

The three groups of conflict strategies discussed above — high assertiveness/low cooperativeness, low assertiveness/low cooperativeness, low assertiveness/high cooperativeness — are power-over conflict strategies that seldom work to provide productive diversity conflict and enhance performance. They:

- ✦ are adversarial, "win-lose" approaches where one party wins and the other loses.
- ✦ make conflict resolution the work of one party.
- ✦ can make the other party wrong, blame and demonize them and create "power- over" systems of oppression based in prejudice, superiority, and power.
- ✦ lead to escalation, polarization, retaliation, litigation or forcing conflict underground where it cannot be addressed or is not addressed.
- ✦ are unstable and cannot be sustained. One of the parties is likely to be dissatisfied with the outcome and with the lack of resolution of the conflict.

Medium assertiveness, medium cooperativeness strategies. These strategies include: compromise, bargain, haggle, trade, take and give. They are transitional or intermediate strategies between power-over and power-with conflict strategies in which both parties give up something to reach agreement. The conflict parties all win something and all lose something in the compromise process. These strategies can have even more unstable consequences than the three win-lose strategies described above. Compromise can lead all parties to be dissatisfied with the outcome and with the lack of resolution of the conflict.

The compromise strategies can bring closure to diversity conflict, though they are likely to require more time than the power-over strategies discussed above. In the compromise strategies, conflict interests and behaviors can become part of the negotiation process and so are available to be addressed by the parties. The compromise strategies can lead to productive conflict and increased organizational performance.....though they can also escalate into too much conflict. Power differences between the parties can impact results from the process. Dominant groups are likely to find compromise strategies more advantageous than marginalized groups as a means of resolving diversity conflict.

Power-over conflict strategies include compete, withdraw, accommodate and compromise strategies. They are adversarial, win-lose approaches in which one party wins and the others lose, or in the case of the compromise strategies where all parties give up something in trade for something else. Some or all parties are left dissatisfied with the win-lose outcomes of the resolution process. These strategies seldom work to enhance performance. They are often destructive of relationships among the parties. Where the parties include dominant and marginalized groups, the power-over strategies maintain or extend the power differences that result from the systems of inequality. Even when the diversity conflict situation is based in human differences, rather than oppression, the power-over conflict approaches can make some parties wrong, blame and demonize them and create "power-over" systems of oppression based in prejudice, superiority, and power.

2. *Power-With Strategies*

High assertiveness, high cooperativeness strategies. The purpose of these strategies is to find a mutually-agreed and satisfactory solution to conflict. The parties choose to address the conflict directly in ways that protect and enhance the relationship among the parties. Conflict interests and behaviors are available to be addressed by the parties. These strategies — collaborate, integrate, engage, problem-solve, dialogue — are win-win strategies. They are power-with, rather than power-over, conflict management strategies. Because the parties seek all-benefit solutions there is a greater likelihood they will result in productive diversity conflict and enhanced performance.

Power-with conflict strategies are collaborative approaches to conflict in which the parties seek mutually-agreed and satisfactory outcomes that represent gains for all the parties. This approach sometimes, but not always, yields productive conflict that enhances individual and organizational performance. The collaborative conflict strategies do not change already existing power differences among dominant and marginalized groups. Where those power differences exist in specific diversity conflict situations, collaborative strategies are likely to result in solutions that favor dominant groups over marginalized groups.

CONFLICT MANAGEMENT PROCESSES Singer, 1990, p. 116; Isenhardt and Spangle, 2000, p. 25.			
Negotiation	**Assisted Collaborative Negotiation**	**Arbitration**	**Adjudication**
Collaborative Competitive Compromise Avoidance Conciliatory	Mediation Facilitation	Non-binding Binding	Judicial Processes

Table 5. Conflict Management Processes

Conflict Management Processes

Conflict management processes include negotiation, assisted collaborative negotiation, arbitration and adjudication (see Table 5.)

Negotiation. Our work and personal lives are filled with negotiation. In negotiation the parties involved in conflict discuss, confer, or bargain with each other to reach agreement. Negotiation processes take a number of forms that mirror the above conflict strategies.

The most mentioned forms of negotiation are competitive negotiation and collaborative negotiation. In *competitive or "thrust and parry" negotiation* (Adler, Rosen and Silverstein, 1996), the parties seek to gain at the expense of the other parties. Alternatively, in *collaborative — or mutual-gain, integrative or problem-solving — negotiation* the parties work to satisfy all the parties' interests. Collaborative negotiation will be discussed in more detail below.

There are less mentioned forms of negotiation. *Evasive or avoidance negotiation* is a form of negotiation in which the parties do what they can to escape conflict. In *conciliatory negotiation*, the parties accommodate the interests and outcomes of other parties, but not their own. The term "negotiation," itself, is sometimes used for *compromising or bargaining negotiation* in which the parties give up something in trade for something they want.

Organizations are a complex web of relationships among board members, managers, employees and others both inside and outside the organization, that take the form of contracts, arrangements, partnerships, alliances. Those relationships are tested and forged through negotiations that address conflict and provide agreement. The point of negotiation is to settle conflict. Negotiations are a conflict management process that is often viewed as a series of single, separate, unique events that are the responsibility of the parties involved. Negotiations in organizations can also be viewed systemically. The many ongoing negotiations in organizations have major interrelated impacts. Some organizations are beginning to think systemically about the organization's capability and responsibility for negotiations and conflict management processes (Ertel, 1999).

Collaborative negotiation. The definition and understanding of collaborative negotiation has grown out of the efforts of Roger Fisher, William Ury and the Harvard Negotiation Project to define key steps or principles for negotiations that meet the interests of all parties and maintain ongoing relationships (Fisher and Ury, 1981). Collaborative negotiation has many names (Fisher and Ury, 1981, pp. xi-xii; Bizony, 1999; Isenhart and Spangle, 2000, pp. 46-51; Jameson, 2001, p. 167):

- ✦*Principled negotiation* that follows the core principles identified by the Harvard Negotiation Project,
- ✦*Problem-solving negotiation* that focuses on a mutually-agreed problem separate from the relationships among the parties involved in the conflict situation,
- ✦*Interest-based negotiation* that focuses on the underlying interests, needs and concerns of the parties, rather than positions or solutions advocated by the parties,
- ✦*Integrative negotiation* that identifies a solution that integrates and addresses the interests, needs, and concerns of all parties,
- ✦*Mutual-gain, win-win negotiation* that provides an outcome that is mutually agreeable to all parties and that gives the parties control over outcomes.

The core principles and steps of collaborative negotiation identified by Fisher and Ury and others are:

- ✦Separate the people from the problem.
- ✦Define issues so they are acceptable to all parties.

- ✦Separate issues from solutions and outcomes.
- ✦Focus on underlying interests, rather than positions.
- ✦Develop options to meet the interests of all parties.
- ✦Identify mutually-agreed standards or criteria for selecting among options.
- ✦Resolve issues based on their merits, rather than on power differences among the parties, that is, level the playing field.
- ✦Define and understand what would happen if the parties fail to reach agreement, that is, the parties' best alternatives to negotiated agreement.

Assisted Collaborative Negotiation. When negotiations bog down, a third party can be invited to assist the parties break the negotiation impasse. There are two forms of assisted collaborative negotiation: mediation and facilitation.

Mediation. Mediation is assisted collaborative negotiation supported by a third-party outsider to a conflict situation, who has no power to impose a resolution and who meets with the parties to the conflict, together and separately, to help them reach their desired outcomes in an all-win manner for the good of all the parties.

Conflict mediation approaches range from problem-solving, settlement-focused mediation (see e.g., Singer, 1990) to mediation focused on empowerment and recognition or "transformative" mediation (see e.g., Broderick, 1999 and Bush and Folger, 1994). The core elements of mediation are the same in both approaches. The key differences between the approaches are the mediation outcomes. Mediation outcomes for the parties can include one-some-all of the following: empowerment, building capacity and skills, recognition and acceptance, building and rebuilding relationships, coalitions and community, agreement, settlement, resolution of differences, and closure.

The mediator provides a container for the mediation process to support all-win outcomes that are good for all the parties to the conflict. Mediator roles include: resource provider, teacher, referee, bridge-builder, advocate, healer, witness, and peacemaker. Mediators carry out the following functions:

- ✦Provide information, resources and knowledge,
- ✦Teach conflict management and problem-solving skills,
- ✦Establish limits and guidelines,

- ✦Strengthen defenses,
- ✦Foster relationships and dialogue among parties,
- ✦Inquire about, listen to, acknowledge and affirm multiple truths,
- ✦Help to create a climate of safety and trust,
- ✦Foster communication,
- ✦Advocate for the interests, needs and concerns of the parties to the conflict,
- ✦Bring all parties to sit together at the table ,
- ✦Promote justice and fairness,
- ✦Support healing and reconciliation,
- ✦Encourage apologies and forgiveness,
- ✦Attend to and raises awareness of signs of conflict and of resolution,
- ✦Provide protection,
- ✦Support non-violent action, and
- ✦Intervene to preempt violence and support peace (Adapted from Ury,1999, pp.114-195; Singer, 1990. p. 20).

The mediation process includes the following steps:

1. Opening: Introductions, ground rules, roles, processes.
2. Conflict Assessment: The determination of the current conflict situation, including:

   - ✦Individuals, groups, and organizations who are direct parties or co- creators of the conflict and key spokespersons, are indirectly impacted by the conflict and key spokespersons, and can maintain or change the current conflict situation and key spokespersons,
   - ✦Major and secondary interests of the parties,
   - ✦Actions, behaviors, attitudes, beliefs, and norms of the parties that keep the conflict in place,
   - ✦Sources and distribution of power among the parties,
   - ✦Desired and minimally-acceptable outcomes for each of the parties,
   - ✦Expectations of what will happen if the parties fail to reach agreement and incentives and costs for continued / more /

less conflict,

- ✦ Impacts of the conflict on the parties and whether there is too much or too little conflict in relation to the conflict impacts, and
- ✦ Conflict strategies being used by each party.

3. Collaborative decision-making about the mediation outcomes:

- ✦ Define the issue(s) in a way that is acceptable to all parties.
- ✦ Identify resources and the interests, needs, wants and concerns related to the issue(s), rather than positions of the parties about solutions to the conflict.
- ✦ Develop options for meeting the interests of all parties and criteria for selecting among the options.
- ✦ Reach mutual agreement about the preferred option for addressing the issue(s) and the mediation outcomes.

4. Closure, celebration, provision for evaluation and accomplishment of the mediation outcomes.

Facilitation. Facilitation is a collaborative negotiation process, assisted by a third-party facilitator, who helps a group accomplish a task, purpose or goal by providing group process leadership and expertise (Fleischer and Zumeta, 2000). In contrast, mediation involves third-party assistance for two or more parties, who may be individuals, groups or organizations. The facilitator provides a container for the work of the group and follows a low assertiveness, high cooperativeness conflict strategy as a facilitator that involves helping the parties meet their interests without interjecting the facilitator's interests.

Facilitation addresses how group members work together, group tasks and work content, and group maintenance processes. Facilitation is a collaborative negotiation process and the facilitator helps the group address the core principles of collaborative negotiation processes identified by the Harvard Negotiation Project. Emphasis is given to group processes that provide consensus. Facilitator roles involve assisting the group to:

- ✦ Satisfy the physical and logistical requirements for the group to work effectively, including support needed from others, room size, seating arrangements, water and food, and other facilities, equipment and environmental needs of the group.

- ✦ Accomplish the group tasks, including establishing ground rules, clarifying purpose, assisting with idea-generation, prioritizing, problem-solving and decision-making processes, balancing time spent on task and process, identifying outcomes, and reaching closure.
- ✦ Establish and maintain collaborative relationships, including surfacing and addressing conflict, maintaining effective communication, listening, feedback and disclosure processes, and balancing participation opportunities (Isenhardt and Spangler, 2000, pp. 110-113).

Arbitration

When collaboration is not possible and negotiation fails, the parties to a conflict situation may turn to binding or non-binding arbitration, in which a third party hears all sides of the conflict and makes a decision for the parties (Isenhardt and Spangler, 2000, pp. 129-136; Singer, 1990, pp. 27-29). Arbitration is a contractual, win-lose process. The parties agree on an arbitrator, whether the arbitrator's decision is binding or non-binding, and any other aspects of the arbitration process. If the decision is non-binding and one of the parties rejects the decision, then the arbitrator's decision does not apply.

Adjudication

When negotiation, third-party collaborative processes, or arbitration fail or are not available, the parties may end in litigation. Adjudication is a binding, third-party decision-making process by the courts or administrative agencies (Singer, 1990, p. 29). The third-parties can include administrative and court judges, juries and other third parties appointed by the courts to encourage settlement prior to legal decision making (Isenhardt and Spangle, 2000, pp. 147-152; Singer, 1990, p. 29). Adjudication is an adversarial, win-lose process.

Some companies have viewed lawsuits for employee discrimination and harassment as a insurable cost of doing business and as an alternative to diversity policies and programs that prevent the mistreatment of employees (Abelson, 2002; Bean, 2002). The dollar value of jury verdicts and settlements for discrimination and harassment has increased substantially since the early 1990s. Average jury awards increased from $236,232 in 1994 to $783,926 in 2000, and 20 percent of jury verdicts were greater than $1 million in 2000 (Bean, 2002). Since 1990, the number of companies providing employee practices liability insurance has fallen and there have been substantial increases in premiums and deductibles, lower levels of coverage and greater care about companies selected for insurance coverage (Abelson, 2002; Bean, 2002).

Uneven Tables: The Issue of Power Imbalance and Oppression

When the negotiating table is uneven and power imbalance and oppression are an issue, the conflict management processes available to organizations and nations are poorly suited for addressing diversity conflict situations. In Morgan Llwelyn's novel, 1921, about Ireland's struggle for freedom and independence from England, one of the main characters asks, "What good is political negotiation when one side has all the power?" (2001, p. 87). Llwelyn describes the negotiating process between Ireland and England during the early 1900s which incorporated the results of 700 years of English colonialism, nation-state oppression, and the perception of Irish people as inferior humans deserving of their fate.

Specific diversity conflict situations seldom involve balanced power among the parties and oppression is too often the source of the imbalance of power. Phyllis Beck Kriteck writes in Negotiating at an Uneven Table, "I have never negotiated at a table I believed to be even, whether as a party involved in a conflict or as a negotiator attempting to resolve one" (2002, p.54). The effectiveness of the conflict management processes of negotiation, assisted collaborative negotiation, arbitration and adjudication for addressing and resolving specific diversity conflict situations are seriously limited by power imbalances among conflict parties.

The balance of power among individual parties in a diversity conflict situation depends on:

- the power of individual parties,
- the relationships among the parties and
- the organizational and societal environment.

Power is the ability of each of the parties to accomplish their desired outcomes. Sources of power imbalance in conflict negotiation and decision-making are explored below.

Individual Parties. Power imbalances result because of differences in power among parties, that can be individuals, groups, or organizations. Power differences among the parties result from:

✦*Individual resources:* The unique individual attributes and traits that are part of the makeup of the parties and can support or hinder them in the conflict negotiation and decision-making process. Individual resources are a form of social capital or goodwill (Adler and Kwon, 2002; Sobel, 2002) that can include for example: attractiveness, charisma, integrity, eloquence, trustworthiness, confidence, physical presence, willingness to take risks, and patience (Kipnis, 1976, p. 22; Gewurz, 2001, p. 148; Bacharach and Lawler,1980, p. 35). Individual resources may also include tangible commodities like monetary and other material assets. For individuals these resources are personal resources. They apply to groups and organizations as well. Consider the ways that individual resources have changed for Arthur Anderson because of the Enron scandal and for the Roman Catholic Church because of the pattern of sexual abuse by priests. For groups and organizations, individual resources are the assets and liabilities which are integral parts of their identity, image and reputation.

✦*Institutional resources:* Resources derived from position and participation in organizations and society. Individuals acquire decision-making control over tangible and intangible resources, such as information, monetary and other material resources, technology, networks, opportunity and access, from participation in organizations and society. These resources can include the opportunity and ability to establish or change rules, sanctions, values, laws, policies, structures and practices. Kipnis writes that "...access to institutional powers transforms insignificant men and women into giants" (1976, p. 23). The more significant the position and the larger the organization, the greater the institutional power and resources that are available. Institutional resources are associated with the institution and stay with the institution when the individual leaves. Groups and organizations also have institutional resources, which they gain from participation in societal, national, international and global affairs.

✦*Internalized oppression:* Racism, sexism, heterosexism and other forms of oppression that are internalized in individuals and institutionalized in groups and organizations. They are internalized systems of inequality that prescribe dominant group members as "better than,"normal, and superior and marginalized group members as "less than," abnormal, deficient, inferior, and less than human. Internalized oppression can inappropriately impact a party's sense of self and, depending on group membership, lead to self-aggrandizing or self-denigrating expectations and behavior.

✦A*lternative to a negotiated solution:* A party's expectations about what will happen if the negotiation does not produce an agreement and they chose to walk away from the negotiation. The parties can differ in the extent to which they are each dependent on the success of the negotiation and how much of their interests they are willing to forego to prevent failure of the negotiation process (Gewurz, 2001, p. 149).

Relationships among the Parties. The history and nature of the relationships among individuals, groups and organizations who are conflict parties also impact the balance of power among the parties and the extent of power imbalances in negotiating and decision-making processes.

✦Preferred negotiating style: The competitive negotiating style is an exercise of power. When one of the conflict parties pursues a competitive negotiating style, the purpose of negotiation for them is to win their desired outcome. If the other parties pursue a collaborative negotiating style designed to create a mutually-agreed, mutual-gain solution to the conflict, the competitive negotiator will always win (Gewurz, 2001, p. 148; Kritek, 2001, pp. 258-261, 324-325). Similarly, the competitive negotiator will win over avoidance and conciliatory negotiators. Negotiations between competitive and compromise negotiators are likely to end in stalemate or escalation, with compromise negotiators switching to a competitive style.

✦ Internalized oppression: Internalized racism, sexism, heterosexism and other internalized forms of oppression can also impact the relationships among individuals, groups and organizations. Conflict parties can internalize and embody systems of inequality in belief systems and behavior in ways that favor dominant group members and disfavor marginalized group members in negotiation processes.

French and Raven provide an often-cited description of power differences between parties in which the power base or resource of one party is used to accomplish desired outcomes in relation to the needs or motives of the other party (as cited in Kipnis, 1976, pp. 9-12 and Gewurz, 2001, pp. 137-138). Five sources of power identified by French and Raven are:

✦ *Reward power:* Ability to use tangible and symbolic rewards, or the promise of those rewards, to barter for the cooperation of another party. Rewards may include, for example, money, commodities, formal and informal recognition and promised new opportunities (Broom and Klein, 1995, pp. 63-64; Kipnis, 1976, p. 10; Gewurz, 2001, p. 149).

✦ *Coercive power:* Ability to get compliance from another party by withholding, or threatening to withhold, desired rewards or by administering, or threatening to administer, emotional, physical, financial psychological or legal punishment (Broom and Klein, 1995, pp. 64-66; Kipnis, 1976, p. 10; Gewurz, 2001, p. 149).

✦ *Legitimate power:* Ability to prescribe or ask for compliance, cooperation or agreement by a party because of one's position or role in an organization or society. This expectation by other parties of a powerholder's entitlement or legitimate "right" of compliance with the powerholder's wishes can also rest in areas, such as, family background, occupation, and academic degree (Broom and Klein, 1995, pp. 57-63; Kipnis, 1976, p. 11; Gewurz, 2001, p. 150).

✦*Expert power:* Ability of a party to influence the behavior of another party based on their belief that the powerholder has superior knowledge, experience or expertise (Broom and Klein, 1995, pp. 66-68; Kipnis, 1976, p. 11; Gewurz, 2001, p. 147). Examples of people with expert power are medical doctors and scientists. Expert power can also apply to organizations, for example, scientific institutes, universities, hospitals, and public utilities.

✦*Referent or attraction power:* A party's ability to influence the behavior of another party because of that party's personal identification with, attraction to, or admiration for the powerholder based on prestige, reputation, personal characteristics or valued group membership (Broom and Klein, 1995, pp. 68-70; Kipnis, 1976, p. 11; Gewurz, 2001, p. 148). Examples of people with referent power include celebrities, religious leaders, and political office holders.

Organizational and Societal Environment. Power derives from the organizational and societal environment in which conflict occurs and in which negotiation and decision-making takes place. Power imbalance can result from differential power conferred on individuals, groups, and organizations by the values, laws, rules, polices, structures, programs and processes that are a part of the cultures of organizations, society and nations.

There are many possible sources of power differences in specific diversity conflict situations. Some apply to diversity conflict based in human differences, where oppression does not apply. Others result from racism, sexism and other forms of oppression.

Collaborative negotiation, mediation and facilitation are mutual-gain conflict management processes that support joint problem solving. Concerns about power imbalance are sometimes addressed in mediation and facilitation by insuring that all parties to a conflict situation have a seat at the negotiation table and that the voices of less powerful parties are heard (Kritek, 2002, p. 39).

Institutionalized oppression: Race, gender, sexual orientation and other group- based prejudice is embedded and institutionalized in the beliefs, values, policies, laws, structures, practices, and behaviors of organizations and society. When embedded and institutionalized prejudice is enforced with dominant group power over marginalized group members, oppression manifests and is internalized as privilege and violence at societal, organizational, and group levels of system. This institutionalization process leads to actions, practices, and behaviors that support racism, sexism, and other forms of oppression for the benefit of dominant group members and the disadvantage and harm of marginalized group members.

Areas for changing the nature of specific conflict situations: Organizations can increase or lower conflict by changing the nature of specific conflict situations in the areas of: interests / issues, boundaries, extent of interdependence, sources and distribution of power, perceptions and values, resources, and organizational rules and processes (Brown, 1983, pp. 51-80). These actions also can generate power differences among the parties, directly and indirectly. They can enhance the power of dominant groups and dominant organizational cultures by resolving diversity conflict situations to the benefit of dominant groups and the disadvantage of marginalized groups. This reinforces oppression and diversity conflict based in oppression.

These steps do not change power imbalances that exist among the parties to a diversity conflict situation. When diversity conflict is based in human differences and oppression is not a factor, the outcomes of collaborative negotiation still reflect existing power imbalances and, as well, the possibility of dominant-party retribution after the negotiation process is completed. When racism, sexism or other forms of oppression are a factor in diversity conflict, collaborative negotiation can recreate and reinforce the outcomes of oppression that give advantage and privilege to dominant group members and disadvantage and harm to marginalized group members.

The central feature of competitive and other power-over negotiation processes is the desire of dominant conflict parties to achieve their desired outcomes at the expense of other parties. Arbitration and adjudication are also win-lose, adversarial processes for addressing conflict situations. High power parties have a greater likelihood of winning in these processes than parties with lesser power. When the source of power imbalances in specific diversity conflict situations is racism, sexism and other forms of oppression, arbitration and adjudication decision-making processes are likely to reflect the values, norms, structures and procedures of the dominant organizational and societal cultures in which they take place. Under these circumstances, arbitration and adjudication can maintain and reinforce oppression.

Negotiation, arbitration and adjudication are used by individuals, groups, and organizations to address specific diversity conflict situations. These conflict management processes are not effective when there are power imbalances. They are more appropriate for human-differences-based conflict than oppression-based conflict. They do not address systemic diversity conflict and the systemic causes of oppression. They can, in fact, maintain and extend oppression.

Sytemic Diversity Conflict

When diversity conflict is systemic and results from racism, sexism and other forms of oppression, it cannot be addressed with conflict management processes focused on specific conflict situations. Organizations must identify and implement ways to eliminate the systems of inequality that cause oppression-based diversity conflict. A range of organizational diversity programs, strategies, initiatives, and interventions are described in Baytos (1995), Cox (1993, 2001), Cross (2000), Hayles and Russell (1997), Jackson and Hardiman (1994), Katz and Miller (2001), Loden (1996), Miller and Katz (2002), and Thomas (1990). These approaches vary in the extent of their consideration of both human-differences and oppression issues, of diversity conflict, and of the relationship between interventions and the developmental phases of organizations related to diversity and oppression issues.

Some authors describe an early-phase, middle-phase and later-phase developmental process in which organizations grow and change from dominant culture organizations to integrated culture organizations.....as well as the interventions required to assist organizations to move from one phase to the next. See, for example, Cox (1993), Hayles and Russell (1997), Jackson and Hardiman (1981, 1994), Jackson and

Holvino (1986, 1988), Katz and Miller (2001), and Miller and Katz (1995). From this perspective the pattern of diversity conflict experienced by organizations depends on the developmental phase of an organization. Interventions and organizational change needed to address systemic diversity conflict based in oppression require time, conscious commitment of resources and energy and an understanding of the developmental phases of organizations.

The pattern and understanding of diversity conflict depend on where the organization is in its developmental process from dominant culture to integrated culture organization. The composition of diversity conflict changes from a preponderance of oppression-based conflict to human-resources-based diversity conflict as diversity intervention strategies are used to shift the organization toward being an integrated culture organization. The use of conflict management strategies to resolve specific diversity conflict situations does not address diversity conflict based in oppression. Oppression- based diversity conflict can only be addressed by eliminating oppression.

Concluding Comments

Many organizations today are looking to the advantages of the diversity of their employees — and the conflict inherent in that diversity — for competitive advantage in their networks of partners, allies, and competitors. To realize the advantages of diversity conflict, the destructive side of oppression-based diversity conflict must be addressed intentionally and consciously, not by stamping out all diversity conflict, but by eradicating racism, sexism, heterosexism and other forms of oppression.

Collaborative conflict management processes are useful for resolving specific diversity conflict situations based in human differences. They do not resolve systemic diversity conflict based in oppression. Collaborative conflict management processes maintain existing power imbalances and can maintain and extend oppression and diversity conflict based in oppression.

Organizations have a wide range of conflict management interventions to support productive diversity conflict:

- ✦Collaborative, power-with conflict management processes
- ✦Interventions to increase and reduce the level of conflict, and

- ✦ Interventions to move organizations from a dominant culture organization to an integrated culture organization and change the nature of diversity conflict experienced in organizations from diversity conflict based in oppression to a preponderance of human-differences-based diversity conflict.

The most effective approach for diversity conflict management is to support diversity and inclusion and to eliminate racism, sexism, heterosexism and other forms of oppression.

REFERENCES

Abelson, R. (2002, January 9). Surge in bias cases punishes insurers, and premiums rise. NYTimes.com. Retrieved January 9, 2002 from http://www.nytimes.com.

Adler, P. S. , and Kwon, S. (2002). Social capital: Prospects for a new concept. *Academy of Management Review, 27* (1), 17-40.

Adler, R. , Rosen, B. , and Silverstein, E. (1996, March). Thrust and parry: The art of tough negotiation. *Training & Development,* 43-48.

Andersson, l. M., and Pearson, C. M. (1999). Tit for tat?: The spiraling effect of incivility in the workplace. *Academy of Management Review,* 24 (3), 452-471.

Armour, J. D. (1997). *Negrophobia and reasonable racism: The costs of being black in America.* New York: New York University Press.

Bacharach, S. B. , and Lawler, E. J. (1980). *Power and politics in organizations: The social psychology of conflict, coalitions, and bargaining.* San Francisco. Jossey-Bass Publishers.

Baytos, L. M. (1995). *Designing & implementing successful diversity programs.* Englewood Cliffs, NJ: Prentice Hall and the Society for Human Resource Management.

Bean, L.. (2002, January 22). Bias insurance is harder to get, more costly, insurers scared by verdicts, numerous lawsuits. DiversityInc.com. Retrieved January 23, 2002 from http://www.DiversityInc.com.

Bizony, N. J. (1999). Interest-based negotiation: Beyond collective bargaining. OD Practitioner, 31 (3), 35-43.

Broderick, M. (1999, Fall). In people we trust: The essence of mediation. *SPIDR News*, Society of Professionals in Dispute Resolution, pp. 1, 3-4.

Broom, M. F , and Klein, D. C. (1995). *Power: The infinite game.* Amherst, MA: HRD Press.

Bush, R. A. B., and Folger, J. P. (1994). *The Promise of mediation: Responding to conflict through empowerment and recognition.* San Francisco: Jossey-Bass Publishers.

Brown, L. D. (1983). *Managing conflict at organizational interfaces.* Reading, MA: Addison-Wesley Publishing Company.

Caudron, S. (1999, September). Keeping team conflict alive. *Training & Development,* 48-52.

Conlon, D. E., and Sullivan, D. P. (1999). Examining the actions of organizations in Conflict: Evidence from the Delaware Court of Chancery. *Academy of Management Journal, 42* (3), 319-329.

Costantino, C. A. , and Merchant, C. S. (1996). *Designing conflict management systems: A guide to creating productive and healthy organizations.* San Francisco: Jossey-Bass Publishers.

Cox, T., Jr. (2001). *Creating the multicultural organization: A strategy for capturing the power of diversity.* San Francisco, CA: Jossey-Bass.

Cox, T., Jr. (1993). *Cultural diversity in organizations: Theory, research & practice.* San Francisco, CA: Berrett-Koehler Publishers.

Cox, T., Jr. (1994, Spring). The effects of diversity and its management on organizational performance. *The Diversity Factor,* 16-22.

Cross, E. Y. (2000). *Managing diversity: The courage to lead.* Westport, CT: Quorum Books.

Davenport, N. , Schwartz, R. D. , and Elliott, G. P. (1999). *Mobbing: Emotional abuse in the American workplace.* Ames, IA: Civil Society Publishing.

Ertel, D. (1999, May-June). Turning negotiation into corporate capability. *Harvard Business Review*, 55-70.

Fisher, R. , and Ury, W. (1981). *Getting to yes: Negotiating agreement without giving in.* New York: Penguin Books.

Fleischer, J. M. , and Zumeta, Z. D. (2000). Preventing conflict through facilitation. Retrieved August 1, 2000 from http://www.conflict-resolution.net/articles/zenandflei.cfm.

Gerwurz, I. G. (2001, Winter). (Re)Designing mediation to address the nuances of power imbalance. *Conflict Resolution Quarterly, 19* (2), 135-162.

Hayles, R. , & Russell, A. M. (1997). *The diversity directive: Why some initiatives fail & what to do about it.* New York, NY: McGraw-Hill and the American Society for Training and Development.

Isenhart, M. W. , and Spangle, M. (2000). *Collaborative*

approaches to resolving conflict. Thousand Oaks, CA: Sage Publications, Inc.

Jackson, B., & Hardiman, R. (1994). Multicultural organizational development. In E. Y. Cross, J. H. Katz, F. A. Miller, & E. W. Seashore (Eds.), *The promise of diversity: Over 40 voices discuss strategies for eliminating discrimination in organizations* (pp. 231-239). Burr Ridge, IL: Irwin Professional Publishing.

Jackson, B. W. , & Hardiman, R. (1981). *Organizational stages of multicultural awareness* (unpublished paper).

Jackson, B. W., & Holvino, E. (1988, Fall). Developing multicultural organizations. *Journal of Religion and the Applied Behavioral Sciences*, 14-19.

Jackson, B. W., & Holvino, E. (1986) Working with multicultural organizations: Matching theory and practice. In R. Donleavy (Ed.). *OD Network Conference Proceedings,* 84-96.

Jameson, J. K. (2001, Winter). Employee perceptions of the availability and use of interest-based, right-based, and power-based conflict management strategies. *Conflict Resolution Quarterly, 19* (2), 163-196.

Katz, J. H. and Miller, F. A. (2001). Diversity and inclusion as a major culture change intervention: A case study. *0D Practitioner, 33* (3), 30-36.

Kipnis, D. (1976). *The powerholders.* Chicago: University of Chicago Press.

Kivel, P. (1996). *Uprooting racism: How white people can work for racial justice.* Philadelphia, PA: New Society Publishers.

Kolb, D. M. , and Putnam, L. L. (1992). Introduction: The dialectics of disputing. In D. M. Kolb and J. M. Bartunek (Eds.), *Hidden conflict in organizations: Uncovering behind-the-scenes disputes* (pp. 1-31). Newbury Park, CA: Sage Publications.

Kritek, P. B. (2002). *Negotiating at an uneven table: Developing moral courage in resolving our conflicts* (2nd ed.). San Francisco, CA: Jossey-Bass.

Landau, S. , Landau, B. , and Landau, D. (2001). *From conflict to creativity: How resolving workplace disagreements can inspire innovation and productivity.* San Francisco: Jossey-Bass.

Leas, S. B. (1984). *Discover your conflict management style.* Washington, D.C.: Alban Institute.

Llywelyn, M. (2001). 1921. New York: Forge.

Loden, M. (1996). *Implementing Diversity.* Chicago, IL: Irwin Professional Publishing.

McIntosh, P. (1989, July/August). White privilege: Unpacking the invisible knapsack. *Peace and Freedom,* 1-4.

Miller, F. A., & Katz, J. H. (1995). Cultural diversity as a developmental process: The path from a monocultural club to an inclusive organization. *The 1995 Annual, Volume 2, Consulting.* J. Pfeiffer & Co.

Miller, F. A., & Katz, J. H. (2002). *The inclusion breakthrough: Unleashing the real power of diversity.* San Francisco: Barrett-Koehler Publishers, Inc.

Pearson, C. M. , Andersson, L. M. , and Porath, C. L. (2000). Assessing and attacking workplace incivility. *Organizational Dynamics, 29* (2), 123-137.

Plummer, D. (1999, September). Isms matrix presentation. Cleveland State University, Diversity Management Master's Program.

Pruitt, D. C. , and Rubin, J. Z. (1986). *Social conflict: Escalation, stalemate, and Settlement.* New York, NY: Random House.

Singer, L. R. (1990). *Settling disputes: Conflict resolution in business, families, and the legal system.* Boulder, CO: Westview Press.

Sobel, J. (2002, March). Can we trust social capital? *Journal of Economic Literature, XL,* 139-154.

Thomas, K. W. , and Kilmann, R. H. (1974). "The Thomas-Kilmann Conflict Mode Instrument." Palo Alto, CA: XICOM Inc.

Thomas, R. R., Jr. (1990). *Beyond race and gender: Unleashing the power of your total work force by managing diversity.* New York, NY: AMACOM.

Ury, W. (1999). *Getting to peace: Transforming conflict at home, at work, and in the world.* New York, NY: Viking.

White, M. B. (1998a, Fall). Measuring change. *The Diversity Factor,* 2-6.

White, M. B. (1998b, Fall). Work x shop=profit measuring change at Sears. *The Diversity Factor*, 7-10.

Chapter XIV

Conflict Resolution Systems for Diversity

Patricia Bidol-Padva

Introduction

One of the major opportunities for the American workplace arises from the increased diversity present within the workforce and marketplace (Judy and D'Amico, 1997). Diversity includes such dimensions as race, gender, ethnicity, sexual orientation, disability, religion, age, and education. For example, an individual's social identities may include being female, white, Jewish, and heterosexual.

Organizations with a diverse workforce are productive and motivated when employees are able to contribute fully to organizational goals, achieve their individual potential, and be rewarded for their work without being discriminated against because of their social-group identities (Cox & Beale, 1997). In response to these challenges, senior executives are creating diversity initiatives that support the contributions of all members of the diverse workforce. Successful diversity initiatives occur when organizational leaders and employees:

Acknowledge the broad range of cultural-group identities present within the organization.

Ensure that the appreciation of diversity is one of the key underlying premises used to create and implement the organization's policies and practices.

Jointly work to eliminate policies and practices (overt or covert) that maintain any forms of social oppression (e.g., racism, sexism, hetero-sexism, and ageism).

Inclusive diversity initiatives are perceived as having a positive impact on the organization. Successful diversity initiatives enhance corporate culture, employees' recruitment and retention, customer relations, and the capacity to move into emerging markets (SHRM, 2001).

One of the major challenges for diversity initiatives stems from the fact that most organizations have policies and practices (e.g., recruitment, promotion, and mentoring policies) that are derived from the current dominant social-identity group's behaviors and beliefs (white men). Members of a dominant group receive more benefits from these policies (e.g., promotions, raises, mentoring) than individuals who belong to social-identity groups that have been discriminated against by these policies (Greenhaus, 1990). Members of the dominant group who currently receive these benefits usually are not aware that they receive a disproportionate amount of benefits. They may perceive that a diversity initiative will hurt their careers. If the diversity initiative does not address institutional discrimination, it is likely to increase the marginalization of those who do not belong to the dominant group. The marginalization of members of the workforce results in decreased productivity and profits (SHMR, 2001).

It is inevitable that functional and dysfunctional conflicts will arise when executives and the workforce respond to the opportunities and challenges that they must address during the creation and implementation of diversity initiatives (Edley, 1996). Conflict resolution systems are being created to respond to these disputes. This chapter explores how conflict resolution systems support diversity initiatives.

Understanding Organizational Conflict

Organizational conflict occurs when one or more individuals are dissatisfied. The sources of the dissatisfaction in organizations with a diverse workforce often include such factors as unclear communications, the negative impact of policies and procedures, incompatible interests, cultural differences, power discrepancies, and perception that someone is not respected. Organizational conflicts occur at many levels, such as the interpersonal level, teams, functional departments, and social-identity groups, as well as between field offices and headquarters.

Conflict is expressed in many forms ranging from general discomfort to open disputes. Discomfort is a sign of a latent conflict, such as the perception that an individual's social-group identities are not appreciated. Latent conflicts are often the source of continued feelings of tension, mistrust, and frustration. A latent conflict that is not expressed usually grows into either an open dispute or a covert withdrawal of an employee's energy and willingness to share knowledge.

A dispute is a specific and tangible expression of a conflict. Disputes may be functional or dysfunctional. High-performance groups need to disagree while exploring divergent options, before they jointly decide on a solution. Spirited deliberations that produce quality decisions usually enhance relationships and improve productivity (Nemeth, C.J., 1985, Katzenbach & Smith, 1993).

Conflict Escalation Cycle

Disputes can be expressed from lower to higher levels of discontent, such as mild complaints, angry exchanges, increased absenteeism, complaints, work "slowdowns," grievances, and lawsuits. As the dispute escalates, the disputing parties and those that are impacted by the dispute usually change their perception of each other and of the issues. The phases of an escalating dispute (Carpenter & Kennedy, 1988) are:

The dispute emerges and a sense of crisis becomes manifest.

Perceptions become distorted, and the parties begin to believe that the other person's conflict-related behavior was deliberate. Viewpoints become fixed positions, and the parties become defensive.

The dispute moves beyond the original disputing parties when the disputants seek support from others.

Direct communication stops, and messages become distorted. In response, the disputants and their supporters attribute negative assumptions and motives to the other party. They begin to seek evidence that their negative perceptions are correct, and they feel righteous and blame the other for the conflict.

Positions harden, and the parties believe that they cannot collaborate because the other party is unwilling to dialogue.

The intense dispute fully emerges, and the organization's formal and informal systems are aware of it. External parties may know of the dispute and often enter into it. At this point, the dispute is now perceived to be a crisis.

Social Identity Disputes

Social identity-driven disputes often arise because of lack of appreciation of an employee's social-group identity (e.g., racism, sexism, anti-Semitism, or ageism), or as a result of policies that result in the unfair treatment of members of a social-identity group. Managers often misdiagnose, ignore, or suppress these disputes.

They are often ignored because managers are not aware that their organization is implementing discriminatory policies (e.g., pay, promotion, and performance evaluations) that benefit members of the organization's dominant social-identity group. When these discriminatory practices are not discussed and eliminated (if present), intense disputes often emerge. An example of a dispute that was not responded to when it arose is the Coca-Cola racial-bias class-action case. Two thousand current and former African American employees sued the company. Coca-Cola has agreed to pay close to $200 million in damages and to accept the recommendations of an independent task force that would monitor its employment practices for a four-year period (Stavraka, 2000).

As shown by the Coca-Cola example, it is dysfunctional to ignore the initial social-identity complaints. Initial complaints about discrimination or lack of appreciation of diversity are "gifts" for the organization. They provide an opportunity for members of the organization to enter into dialogue about their needs and values (Rothman, 1997). These dialogues are one aspect of the diversity initiative's conflict resolution system.

Definition of Diversity Initiatives

In order to understand the relationship between an organization's diversity initiative and the conflict resolution system that supports the initiative, it is essential to understand the nature of diversity initiatives. Effective diversity initiatives are inclusive and improve the organization for all of its internal and external stakeholders. They are customized to fulfill the needs of the total organization and individual employees. A successful diversity initiative has strategic goals whose accomplishment ensures its success (Gentile, 1994). These action goals usually are similar to the following:

- ✦Create an organizational culture in which the total workforce is appreciated.
- ✦Eliminate discriminatory policies and procedures for all employees.
- ✦Recruit and retain a diverse workforce.

In order for diversity goals to be fulfilled, all aspects of the organization must work together to accomplish them. An organization is an adaptive and open system composed of interrelated elements (e.g., formal workflow arrangements, informal networks, information and financial management, human-resource functions) that change in response to challenges and opportunities. The usual components of effective diversity initiatives (Thomas & Gabarro, 1999, and Morrison, 1996) are:

1. Senior executives who proactively support the initiative. They understand both the business case for the diversity initiative and the need for the organization to appreciate diversity and ensure that all employees are treated equitably. They often form an oversight body (e.g., diversity task force) and either are members of it or have it report to them. The executives openly support the task force's efforts to identify the organization's key cultural-diversity challenges and to develop a strategy to manage them.

2. Committees (e.g., affinity networks) that both address issues affecting a social-identity group (e.g., African Americans, Asian Americans, Hispanics, Gays and Lesbians, women, and those concerned with employee wellness) and support the implementation of all the diversity goals.

3. Outcomes that are clearly articulated and visibly supported by the executive, managers, and supervisors in their day-to-day interactions with their colleagues and staff.

4. Ongoing channels of communication with employees that are active throughout the initiative.

5. Interactive training that enables staff to appreciate all social-identity groups, develop mitigation measures for discriminatory practices in key areas (e.g., mentoring, recruitment, succession planning, and promotion) and create an inclusive organizational culture.

6. Conflict resolution mechanisms that support the initiative at all organizational levels (individual, interpersonal, team, group, department, and total organization).

7. Evaluation mechanisms that measure how well each component of the initiative (e.g., training, mitigation measures, taskforce, affinity networks) is meeting the initiative's action goals for key variables, such as pay equity, leadership commitment, recruitment, learning and development, mentoring and coaching, and external relations.

8. Accountability processes that ensure that managers be held accountable for the success of the diversity initiative. An example would be to link the size of the company's managers' bonuses to the amount of progress made on the diversity measures.

A Conflict Resolution System for Diversity Initiatives

An effective conflict resolution system (CRS) enables members of the organization to resolve conflicts that emerge during diversity initiatives. During the last decade, many organizational conflict resolution systems have been developed (Costantino, C. & Merchant, C.S., 1996, Walton, Cutcher-Gershenfeld & McKersie, 1994). The conflict management systems usually include a variety of interventions, such as prevention, collaboration, and an appeal to a higher authority to resolve conflict situations that range from latent conflicts to intense disputes.

Figure 1. illustrates a model of a conflict resolution system. The model describes a conflict resolution system that is flexible and enables decision-makers to refine their interventions as the conflict unfolds. The CRS has three components:

✦Assessment factors

✦Resolution interventions
✦Outcomes.

Conflict Assessment

Assessment of a conflict situation enables the disputants or the conflict intervenor (e.g., work unit manager, ombudsperson, or facilitator) to make informed decisions about conflict interventions. The conflict-assessment process includes data gathering and analysis of the five dimensions present in every conflict situation. These dimensions include the issues and interests, the parties, power and influence factors, relationships, and desirability of the proposed intervention (see Table 1.)

Figure 1. A Conflict Resolution System Model for a Diversity Initiative.

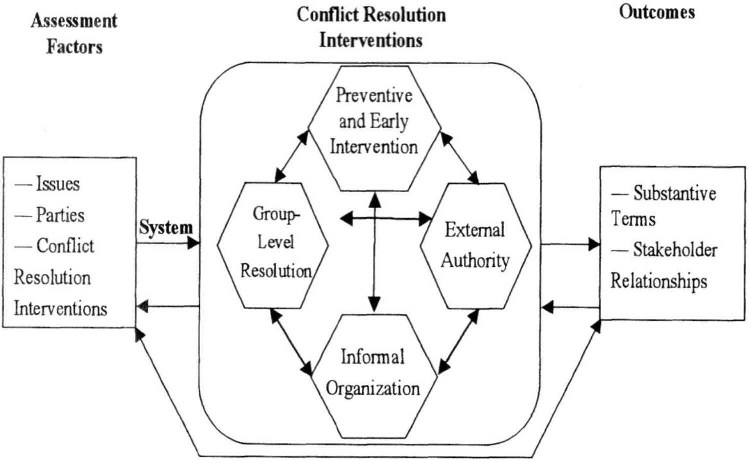

Assessment Factors	Interventions	Outcomes
Issues • Conflict characteristics • Central and secondary issues • Intensity level **Parties** • Main & secondary parties and their spokespersons • Impacted parties **Power and Influence Factors** **Relationships** **Feasibility** ▪ Value-added options ▪ Social justice	**Preventive and Early Intervention** ▪ Diversity task force ▪ Affinity groups ▪ Training ▪ Management practices ▪ Interpersonal relationships **Informal Organization** ▪ Leadership behavior ▪ Intragroup relations ▪ Communication processes ▪ Use of power and influence ▪ Interface with external stakeholders **Group-Level Resolution** ▪ Initiated by parties ▪ Collaboration when appropriate ▪ Use of internal & external facilitators **External Authority** ▪ Litigation ▪ Hearings	**Substantive Terms** • Appreciation of social-group identities • Elimination of discriminatory policies and practices • Support productivity **Stakeholder Relationships** • Positive feelings between involved parties • Perception by all impacted parties that intervention was fair and inclusive

Table 1. Conflict Assessment

DIMENSION	QUESTIONS
1. Issues (Substantive Terms)	♦ What are the issues for you and for the other parties? (Issues are behaviors or decisions that need to be addressed.) ♦ What are the needs for you and for the other parties? (Needs are requirements that must be fulfilled.) ♦ Is it possible that the solutions to the issues may cause negative or positive impacts on other factors (e.g., promotion opportunities, union contracts, personnel policies, and customer retention)? ♦ What needs do you and the other parties have in common? ♦ What is the major outcome you desire for each of the issues?
2. Parties	♦ What parties are directly involved in the conflict? ♦ What parties are indirectly impacted? ♦ What parties can hinder or enhance the implementation of the project? ♦ How do the social-group identities of the parties influence the creation and the management of the dispute?
3. Power and Influence	♦ What types of power and influence have each of the parties used (or are they likely to use) when they interact with the other parties? ♦ To what degree is oppression (e.g., racism, sexism, heterosexism, anti-Semitism, ageism) present, and what is the impact of the overt or covert oppression? ♦ Are multiple departments, divisions, and organizations with differing missions involved in the conflict?
4. Relationships (Social Contract)	♦ Do you and the other parties have to maintain an ongoing relationship? ♦ What is the level of interdependency between each of the primary parties? ♦ What is the level of interdependency between the other parties? ♦ What is the past history of interactions between you and the other parties? Are there strong emotions or values at play? ♦ Do you or any of the other parties belong to any groups that can consciously or unconsciously influence your management of the dispute?
5. Relevance of Collaboration (Value Added)	♦ What incentives exist to motivate the parties to use a collaborative approach? ♦ Will each of the parties obtain value-added benefits (substantive terms or social contract) if they participate in a collaborative approach? ♦ Is there a desire to establish or maintain cooperative and mutually beneficial relationships between the parties? ♦ What is the most collaborative way to resolve the problem? If collaborative negotiations are not feasible, what conflict management mode should be used?

Since all the actions taken during the conflict resolution process are interrelated, the resolution intervention should not be selected until the assessment data has been analyzed. For example, the process of gathering data about an intense dispute could result in the disputants deciding to engage in collaborative decision-making rather than referring the matter to litigation. The assessment process is repeated during a lengthy resolution process to determine whether or not the resolution strategy needs to be refined.

The disputing parties can jointly assess some conflict situations. The conscious and routine use of conflict-assessment processes by parties who are potentially involved in a dispute usually reduces the dysfunctional aspects of their communication patterns.

Identification of Issues

The issues and interests of the conflict need to be well defined and understood. The parties in most conflicts have many issues and needs. For example, the issue could be that members of a group perceive that they are not given prime assignments and thus are not promoted. Their interest (needs) could be to immediately rectify the unfair policies and procedures. They could also want the organization to appreciate their social-group identities.

In addition to identifying the current issues and interests of key parties, the assessment process needs to identify subsequent issues that could arise when an issue is resolved. For example, if unfair policies are changed, the parties that currently benefit from them may protest (i.e., charge reverse discrimination) if they perceive that their prime assignments would be reduced. On the other hand, the change in unfair policies could result in synergistic policies that create more opportunities for all involved parties. The new, mutually beneficial policies could then result in a positive substantive issue, such as how the new policies can be disseminated to other work units.

Parties, Relationships, and Power

The primary and secondary parties, who might be affected by the resolution of the conflict, and their spokespersons, also need to be identified. Most organizational disputes affect not only those who are directly involved but also other parties as well. For example, members of a group could assert their desire to have the performance-review process changed. If the review process is changed, it will affect all employees who use that process.

The number and types of parties will often determine what intervention process is used. For example, involving representatives of all affected parties in a collaborative decision-making might resolve the performance-review process. Instead of the collaborative meeting, the human resources staff could gather data about the process and design an inclusive review process, or the matter could be referred to litigation.

The assessment process also identifies how the parties currently relate to one another and the impact of these relationships on the resolution of the dispute. Relationships are complex and can be expressed in many ways, such as:

- ✦The parties respect each other but disagree about the disputed issues.
- ✦They are willing to collaborate to resolve the issues.
- ✦The parties interact to do their work but are moderately distrustful of each other. Each questions the motives and values of the other party.
- ✦The parties barely speak to each other, and each is sure that the other party cannot be trusted. Each is very suspicious of the motives, values, and statements of the other party.
- ✦The parties are hostile and vengeful. Not only do they want to win the dispute, they want the other party to experience a humiliating defeat.
- ✦The parties are so hurt and distrustful that they hide their anger, reduce the amount of work they do, and withdraw from the other parties.

The data on the relationships is interrelated with the other assessment data. Even if the parties are hostile, they can engage in collaborative decision-making, if this is the only way they can obtain the results that they want.

The assessment process identifies the power and influence factors that each party may use when they interact with each other and the rest of the organization to obtain the results they want. The way that parties use their power is often determined by the approaches (e.g., assimilation, mutual adaptation, separation) they use to manage the interaction of their main social-group identity with other members of the organization (Bidol-Padva & Jackson, 1999). Parties can use their power and influence by engaging in collaborative efforts, escalating the conflict, resorting to litigation, making administrative appeals, or staging community protests.

Feasibility Factors

During the feasibility phase of the assessment, the costs and value-added benefits of all the potential resolution interventions are assessed. Since collaborative interventions usually result in the resolution of the issues to the satisfaction of the parties and the enhancement of their relations, the underlying interests, needs, and values expressed by the parties are studied to determine whether or not a collaborative intervention can be used.

Many conflicts can only be resolved by the use of two or more interventions. Collaborative approaches are usually the prime intervention, unless the situation needs to be resolved by litigation or administrative hearings. Even when litigation or hearings are used, collaborative processes are often used to design follow-through remedies (e.g., replacing unfair practices with inclusive options).

Conflict Resolution Interventions

This CRS model includes four categories of conflict resolution interventions that can be applied at individual, work unit, and organizational levels. The categories are:

1. Prevention and early intervention
2. Informal organization interventions
3. Group-level interventions
4. External higher-authority interventions.

Prevention and Early Intervention

Preventive and early interventions include collaborative approaches that provide opportunities for dialogue and mutually acceptable decision-making on matters related to the diversity initiative. For the occasional conflicts in which the assessment indicates that the conflict situation is not likely to be positively managed by an active intervention, the disputants or the unit manager can respond by not taking action. Proactive preventive interventions include actions such as the following:

- ✦Formation of diversity-initiative task forces, whose members oversee the design and implementation of the diversity initiative, and of affinity groups (e.g., African American, women), whose members support the development and the implementation of the organization's diversity-action goals.

- ✦System-wide training in diversity management, collaborative decision-making, and negotiating that enhances the appreciation of diversity, the mitigation of organizational inequities, and the capacity for collaboration.

- ✦Consensus-based creation of diversity-initiative goals and action steps by all sectors of the organization, such as individual work units, the diversity task force, identity-based affinity groups, or system-wide planning sessions.

- ✦Opportunities for individuals and teams to engage in dialogue and create mutually beneficial options to resolve the conflict.

Large group interventions for organizational change involve a significant portion of the organization, internal and external, in the development and implementation of diversity initiatives. They use dialogue and collaborative decision-making tools that enable participants to appreciate their differences, work through conflicts, and produce mutually acceptable plans that result in an inclusive and fair organization (Bidol-Padva & Greenwood, G., 2000). Collaborative approaches that effectively involve the total system include Open Space Technology, Search Conferences, Whole-Scale Change, Preferred Futuring, Appreciative Inquiry, and SimuReal (Bunker & Alban, 1997; Holman, P. & Devine, T. 1999).

Large group interventions are collaborative interventions that reinforce the concept of a learning organization that channels the energy, wisdom and visions of the participants into the creation of options that allow the organization to grow and adapt (Senge, 1990). They provide opportunities for participants to explore feelings and assumptions, and to develop goals that support both the diversity-initiative goals and the functioning of the organization in the key areas of financial performance, customer outreach, and internal business processes (Kaplan & Norton, 1996).

Informal Organization Interventions

Organizational leaders can mobilize the energy and power of the informal organization to increase the support for the diversity initiative and to resolve any related conflict situations. The behavior of leaders influences the workforce at individual, interpersonal, and organizational levels. Employees constantly scan the words and actions of the leaders to determine whether they really support the diversity initiative. Since diversity initiatives change the status quo, and the changes may be perceived as "reverse discrimination," the leaders must proactively communicate that the diversity initiative is inclusive and will fairly benefit all employees.

The workforce needs opportunities to participate with members of the organization's groups in informal activities such as recreational events. The organization, through its formal and informal networks, can also communicate the positive impacts of the diversity-initiative strategy with its key external stakeholders such as customers, vendors, and the local community.

Group-Level Interventions

Group-level interventions occur within a work unit. A work unit can be a team, a department, a division, or an ad hoc unit (cross-departmental committee). Any impacted party can ask the unit manager to resolve the conflict. The impacted parties can include the individuals experiencing the discomfort, colleagues, work-unit manager, and other organizational stakeholders. The group-level intervention can resolve many conflicts, such as a specific complaint, a perception that the team needs to improve its interpersonal relationships, or a need to develop protocols (e.g., team assignments and mentoring) that are inclusive and fair.

Collaborative interventions are the primary conflict resolution tools used to resolve group-level conflicts (Isenhart & Spangle, 2000). In addition to being used for the prevention of conflicts and early intervention in an emerging dispute, they are used to resolve conflicts that have grown into an overt dispute.

One of the major collaborative approaches used to resolve internal organizational conflicts is that of team meetings, which uses consensus tools (e.g., brainstorming, active listening, and nominal) to create mutually beneficial options to resolve the conflict. Either the manager or a member of the group can facilitate the meetings. If the manager wishes to participate in the generation of the options, or if other situational factors warrant it, an internal or external intervener may facilitate the collaborative negotiations. Collaborative meetings between two individuals can also be held, and their manager or a neutral facilitator may conduct these meetings.

Collaborative meetings, occurring at either the interpersonal and group level, are designed to allow parties to share their needs, interests, and frustrations, so that they can jointly create options that meet their individual needs and those of the work unit. The following steps are usually followed during the collaborative meetings:

- ✦A climate is created in which the participants can safely share their story about the issues, the impact of the dispute on their work, and their feeling of self-worth.
- ✦Parties share their desired outcomes and educate each other about their needs.
- ✦Parties actively listen to each other, in order to understand what the other parties are saying and to be able to explore the meaning of what they hear.
- ✦Parties engage in a collaborative decision-making process that enables the disputants to concentrate on the interests of all parties, explore possibilities, formulate mutually beneficial options, develop criteria to evaluate the mutually beneficial options, and select preferred solutions.

Collaborative meetings usually produce such positive outcomes as:

- ✦Resolution of the conflict situation.
- ✦Increased interpersonal-communication and active-listening competencies.

- ✦Support for the relationships between the parties.
- ✦Support for the productivity of the impacted individuals, the work unit, and the total organization.
- ✦Increased appreciation of diversity.
- ✦Elimination of unfair practices and their replacement with inclusive practices.
- ✦Increased use by work units of collaborative decision-making tools that produce mutually acceptable options.

External Higher-Authority Interventions

External higher-authority interventions include such approaches as litigation, administrative hearings, arbitration, mini-trials, or fact-finding. They are used when the collaborative interventions do not work or cannot be used. . During the conflict-assessment process, if the conflict situation is a case of actual harassment or discrimination, it is an illegal action. The designated remedy (e.g., litigation or administrative hearings) must be used to resolve them.

Harassment and discrimination cases are governed by organizational personnel policies, union contracts, and federal, state, and local laws. In the United States, employees are protected by law from discrimination based on gender, race, religion, pregnancy, national origin, age, or physical ability. Harassment is a form of discrimination. Managers and leaders of diversity initiatives often do not understand harassment. They may mistakenly try to resolve a harassment case by the use of dialogue and coaching. During the conflict-assessment phase, the word "harassment" should not be used until an expert has determined that harassment has occurred. Until an expert has made that determination, the case can be defined as a conflict that has emerged due to inappropriate behavior.

In addition to litigation or administrative hearings, aggrieved parties may resort to community protests to ensure that the organization addresses their cause. Organizations may also resort to litigation or hearings when they perceive that they have been unfairly accused of not appreciating the workforce diversity or engaging in actual discriminatory acts.

Conflict Resolution Outcomes

Outcomes are the results of CRS interventions that have been used to resolve a conflict situation by preventing the emergence of a dispute, creating consensus options, communicating with formal and informal networks, or engaging in litigation. They are analyzed to determine whether or not the desired outcomes were achieved. The use of CRS in diversity initiatives produces two types of outcomes: substantive terms and stakeholder relationships.

Substantive terms are assessed to determine whether or not the intervention resulted in outcomes that resolved the issues of the dispute to the satisfaction of the impacted parties. In addition, the substantive terms are analyzed to determine the degree to which they contributed to the appreciation of the workforce's diversity and the development of inclusive and fair policies and practices. Stakeholder relationships are assessed to determine whether or not the impacted parties' relationships are the same as or better than before the intervention. The outcomes are also carefully studied to determine whether or not the parties perceived that the resolution processes were done in a fair and inclusive manner.

It should be noted that it is difficult for "higher-authority" interventions to make all the parties feel that the issues were resolved to their satisfaction. Litigation and administrative hearings produce outcomes that are based on objective criteria derived from laws, legislation, or regulations. These outcomes result in one side winning and the other side losing.

Designing a Conflict Resolution System for Diversity Initiatives

The conflict resolution system (CRS) needs to be customized to meet the needs of the individual organization. Although most organizational dispute-resolution systems are not designed just for diversity initiatives, the principles used to design generic corporate conflict resolution systems apply to those created for diversity initiatives. In fact, some elements of the conflict resolution system are part of an organization's generic system (e.g., routine human-resource processes), some of the preventive and early-intervention elements employ the approaches used in the initiative's joint decision-making, and some elements are outside of the diversity initiative (e.g., litigation).

When the CRS is designed, executives need to engage key stakeholders to gather information about such essential questions as:

- What do we need to do to create an organization that appreciates its diverse workforce and implements fair and inclusive policies and procedures?
- What types of conflicts (e.g., passive resistance, work-unit complaints, intense organization-wide disputes, external stakeholder protests) related to diversity matters are present in our organization?
- What conflict resolution processes (e.g., collaborative work-unit meetings, consensus tools, informal mediation, and whole-system forums) do we need to support our diversity initiative and the specific needs of individual employees, work units, and the total organization?

In summary, effective conflict resolution systems can analyze and resolve disruptive disputes that arise at interpersonal, group, and organizational levels. They enable diversity-based conflicts to be resolved, because organizational members have the capacity to identify key parties in a conflict situation, use consensus-building tools, create mutually beneficial settlement options, and build organizational support for the collaborative resolution of diversity conflict.

References

Bunker, B. B. & Alban, B. (1997). *Large group interventions ; Engaging the whole system for rapid change.* San Francisco: Jossey-Bass.

Bidol,P. & Crowfoot, J. (1991). Towards an interactive process for siting National parks in developing nations. *In resident peoples and national parks: social dilemmas and struggles in international conservation.* (pp. 283-300).Tuscon: University of Arizona Press.

Bidol-Padva, P. & Greenwood, B. 2000). Collaborative environmental and land use conflict management. Davis, CA: University of California, Davis.

Bidol-Padva, P. & Jackson, H.K. (1999). Diversity perspectives in human relations training. In *Readings Book for Human Relations Training* (8th ed., pp. 21-25).

Carpenter, S. L. & Kennedy, W.J.D. (1988). *Managing pubic disputes: A practical guide to handling conflict and reaching agreements.* San Francisco: Jossey-Bass.

Costantino, C.A. & Merchant, C.S. (1996) *Designing conflict management systems.* San Francisco: Jossey-Bass.

Cox, T.H., Jr., (1993). *Cultural diversity in organizations: Theory, research and practice.* San Francisco: Barrett-Koehler.

Cox, T.H., Jr. & Beale, R.L. (1997). *Developing competency to manage diversity.* San Francisco: Barrett-Koehler.

Edley, C., Jr. (1997) *Not all black and white: Affirmative action and American values.* New York: Hill and Wang.

Gentile, M. (1994). *Differences that work: Organizational excellence through diversity.* Boston: Harvard Business School Press.

Greenhaus, J.H., Parasuraman, S. & Wormely, W. (1990). Effects of race on organizational experiences, job performance and career outcomes. *Academy of Management Journal, 33*, 64-86.

Holman, P. & Devine, T. (1999). *The change handbook: group methods for shaping the future.* San Francisco: Berrett-Koehler Publishers.

Isenhart, M.W. & Spangle, M. (2000). *Collaborative approaches to resolving conflicts.* Thousand Oaks, CA: Sage Publications.

Judy, R. & D'Amico. (1997). *Workforce 2020.* Indianapolis: Hudson Institute.

Kaplan, R.S. , & Norton, D.P. (1996). *The balanced scorecard* . Boston: Harvard Business School Press.

Katzenbach, J. R. & Smith, D. K. (1993). *The wisdom of teams.* New York: Harper Collins.

Morrison, A. (1996). *The new leaders.* San Francisco: Jossey-Bass.

Nemeth, C. J. , (1985). Dissent, group process, and creativity. *Advances in Group Processes, 2,* 57-75.

Rothman, J. (1997). Resolving Identity-Based Conflict in Nations, Organizations and Communities. San Francisco: Jossey-Bass.

Senge, P. M. (1990). *The fifth discipline.* New York: Doubleday Currency.

Stavraka, C. (2000). Coca-Cola to pay nearly $200 million in race-discrimination settlement. DiversityInc.com. [On-line]. New York: Allegiant Media, Inc.

Society for Human Resources Management (SHRM). (2001). Impact of Diversity Initiatives on the Bottom Line. New York.

Thomas, D. & Gabarro, J. R. (1999). *Breaking through-the making of minority executives in corporate America. Boston:* Harvard Business School Press.

Thomas, R..R., Jr. (1990, March-April). From affirmative action to affirming diversity. *Harvard Business Review, 68 (2),* 107-117.

Walton, R.E., Cuther-Gershenfeld, J.E. & McKersie, R. B. (1994). *Strategic negotiation: a theory of change in labor-management relations.* Boston: Harvard Business School Press.

Chapter XV

Diversity Consultation Skills

Judith H. Katz
Frederick A. Miller

Introduction

The very term "diversity consultant" needs clarification. How one defines the work will define the approach. We define our work broadly because it has implications for all aspects of an organization's work, culture, and output. Consequently, we do not think of ourselves as diversity consultants but rather strategic culture change consultants. The focus of this chapter, therefore, is to outline the skills, competencies, and behaviors that are essential for individuals involved in strategic culture change work. Throughout, we use the terms "consultant" and "change agent" interchangeably, and though we acknowledge that both terms can be applied to people internal to the system, much of this chapter is reflective of our experience as external consultants.

In our earlier chapter, we map out a strategy and approach for creating higher performing organizations through building inclusion and leveraging diversity. Here we examine the competencies and skills that facilitate that work. There are several key assumptions that we make with respect to these skills:

You can not do this work alone. Working on strategic culture change—working to change the very fabric of an organization—is a major undertaking. No one individual has all the necessary skills and wisdom to transform an organization from being a passive club to an inclusive organization. In fact, the very nature of culture change calls upon us to implement the factors of diversity in our approach. Namely, we must bring together a diverse team of individuals to accomplish the kind of change that makes building inclusion and leveraging diversity a way of life within an organization.

Team members should model not only diversity of identity, but diversity of talent, focus, and expertise. Most importantly, the team must be comprised of individuals external to the system and key partners within the system. The team must model facilitation, the behaviors of inclusion, the effectiveness of being diverse, and the high performance that results.

In many ways the strongest message consultants send is the example of our own behavior—what we do, not what we say. How well we partner, leverage our own and others' own diverse talents, and how inclusive we are in our own approach will be telling to others. We must remember that as change agents, the system and individuals within it are watching our every move.

Individuals can not change a system. Systems can change a system. All too often, individual practitioners believe that with a good theoretical model, some great facilitation, a few tools, and the "right" client, they can change a system. As individuals we can have some impact on other individuals, but the real goal here is to create systemic change. Our challenge then is to find leverage points within the organization to change systems in addition to individuals. We must, therefore, not only focus on educating people within organizations, increasing their awareness, and developing new competencies, but also concentrate on systems and processes that will foster change. If we are to create an inclusive work environment, we need to focus on the human resource and management systems that help determine it. How are people being hired? Developed? Promoted? Coached? Praised? Rewarded? To what extent is the ability to leverage diverse talents and create a culture of inclusion seen as a vital and critical competency for being a manager and a leader? How is diversity represented on teams? How consciously does the organization link leveraging diversity and building inclusion to its business strategy? Are people within the organization being held accountable for delivering results in this arena, just as they are for other business objectives?

To change an organization you need to create alternative structures. One of the ways to "jump start" a change effort is to create alternative structures. Once you have leaders' buy-in and clear identification of the organizational and business strategy imperative, there need to be mechanisms that can help guide the effort and create momentum for change.

This includes creating, developing, and working with a Change or Strategy Council comprised of a diverse group of senior leaders who report to the CEO. They will work as a team to drive and align the change strategy across the organization and with their peers (other senior leaders). It also includes creating a leadership position (for 3-5 years) for Organizational Performance and Inclusion at the VP level or above. This individual and her or his staff will help drive the effort functionally and will be positioned to work with the CEO and the other senior leaders.

In addition to these new structures, there may be new networks, councils, action teams, policies, and other mechanisms that can help move the organization toward its goals. Consultants need to be able to assemble the right people and assist the client to create the structures they need to support the strategic change.

The Skills

The skills that a change agent needs are so interdependent and interwoven that dissecting them is not only difficult, but potentially misleading. Early on there needs to be a strong **Vision** and ability to **Find the Self-Interest** for the organization. **Positioning and Creating Alignment** are central to all phases of the intervention, especially **Getting Leader Buy-In.** Equally critical are **Partnering** and **Managing and Valuing Conflict,** two skills particularly influenced by the consultant's **Communication** skills. **Measuring Results** along the way is important for gauging the success of the initiative. It is also important to **Honor the System** and to **Support Leaders without Colluding**. Walking the line between resistance and acceptance of the change initiative creates subtleties of **Pacing,** a necessary skill since consultants need to **Accept a Continuous Change Process** that never reaches a definitive endpoint.

Skill: Vision

All change agents need to have a clear understanding of what they are working toward. If you can not imagine an inclusive organization, you cannot create it. If you think all organizations are inherently "bad," you cannot create a good one. And if you do not have an idea of what success looks like, you will never know if you have arrived, or even moved closer to it. Consultants must question their values and beliefs about organizations—their potential and their limitations.

The vision of success, however, cannot be created solely by the change agent. The goal is systems change and there is a team of people—change agents, leaders, stakeholders, members of the organization—who must all be involved in setting the goals and working toward them. Consultants can help steer the process and share expertise on what kind of change is possible and how it may be achieved. But consultants also must reconcile their ideas with the organization's own vision for its future.

In some ways, creating and collaborating on Vision is a matter of positioning: the change agent needs to orient the organization on what inclusion will look and feel like and provide compelling reasons for adopting this vision. Aligning vision also requires the change agent to become familiar with the work and needs of each particular organization. The approach and even the goals of building inclusion and leveraging diversity are not one-size-fits-all. Change agents need to tailor initiatives to individual organizations.

In some organizations—the ones most in need of diversity and inclusion efforts—envisioning success is not easy. The system may appear so broken or so steeped in privilege and oppression that the consultant despairs of ever making an impact. This again is why a strong sense of purpose and clear picture of the ultimate goal is vitally important. Change agents need some kind of focal point—no matter how distant—to be moving toward.

Skill: Find the Self-Interest

Most organizations have little understanding of how diversity can be a source of added strength, creativity, wisdom, and productivity, or how inclusive values and practices offer greater potential for achieving their strategic mission. To most, diversity remains a Human Resources issue unrelated to mainstream operations; a source of disruption to be neutralized; a problem area primarily related to lawsuits, morale, and public relations. Making the connection to the system's self-interest (often the organization's bottom line) is one of the most important skills a consultant needs. It amounts to framing the issues in a way that motivates and compels the organization to care about them and to act on them.

The connection is certainly there to be made. Technological advances and global competition are putting greater stress on organizations than ever before. Those that are not constantly innovating, continuously improving, and consistently increasing their productivity may cease to exist. It is becoming clear that to succeed, organizations need to have all of the people of the organization doing their best work. Every business can relate to the need for higher and higher performance, the ability to attract and retain top talent, the struggle for competitive edge, and the value of bottom-line benefits. Each may have its own unique opportunities. (For a more detailed analysis on creating the business case for change, see the next chapter in this book.)

The failure of organizations to recognize the bottom-line advantage that leveraging diversity and inclusion can offer them is often the fault of the consultant. Many change agents come from social justice backgrounds and bring with them an ingrained distrust of the profit motive. This can be a problem in working with businesses that need profit to survive. What good is a positive culture change if the organization goes out of business? (*The operation was successful but...*)

Only by connecting the change effort to the organization's bottom line (or for a non-profit organization, to its ability to accomplish its mission and goals) can you address the sustainability of both the organization and the change.

Skill: Positioning and Creating Alignment

To establish an atmosphere for a successful initiative, the consultant must do three things: position, position, position. We position the work itself as a valuable, attainable goal for the organization. We position the organization to accept and incorporate it. We position leaders to understand what inclusion is about and meaningfully enact it in their organizations. Other skills discussed in this chapter, including Finding the Self Interest, Managing and Valuing Conflict, Getting Leader Buy-In, Communication, and Pacing, are highly dependent on positioning in one form or another.

Positioning the effort for success requires not only a long-term strategy and an understanding of the internal "politics" of an organization, but also patience on the part of consultants. Many people want to jump in and start making changes. They have clear ideas about what is wrong in the organization and are eager to roll up their sleeves and put it right. They do not see that the system has to change itself, that people in the organization need to take ownership of the change effort, and that there are developmental phases of the initiative that need to be properly paced.

Positioning is crucial since we often only get one chance at doing this work: we can not fail and then expect leaders to let us try a different approach. We can not ask for people's trust and then fritter it away and expect to be given it again. We can not prepare the organization for a change effort and keep switching strategies along the way.

To orient the organization and create alignment within it requires learning about the system, meeting with key stakeholders, enrolling people in the effort, and getting support from leaders. Many consultants dislike managing the political aspects of change efforts, but without doing so, they cannot be successful. For us, positioning often takes months and involves multiple behind-the-scenes meetings. It is work that pays off when the initiative really starts to move. A change effort is like a rocket ship: when it first takes off, it may look like it's barely moving, but if the right combinations of chemicals are reacting in the ways they need to, there are propulsive explosions occurring that will ultimately carry you to the stars.

Positioning is also a means for creating alignment. In the early stages of an intervention, it is crucial that everyone in the organization be aligned on several key factors:

Goals. What exactly does the initiative aim to do? What does it mean to build inclusion and leverage diversity? There have to be clear goals at the outset so that people know what they are moving toward and can check their progress along the way. Many people have misconceptions about diversity—they think it's more of a social program than a business one, or that it's a new system of oppression to replace the old one. Only by articulating a vision of what the initiative intends to accomplish can the organization be clear and focused about why it is undergoing the changes it is undergoing and what each person's role in it must be.

Expectations. What is required of a leader in the new organizational culture? What is required of all associates? How long will the process take? What can you do—and *not* do—as a consultant to affect this process? Many well-intended initiatives are abandoned or labeled a failure because people were not aligned on what they could expect from the change effort. They thought they could leverage diversity by conducting senior staff education events, or that the initiative would take about six months and then be over. From the start they didn't appreciate the commitment of time and money resources that would be required for success. The consultant has to educate people up-front about what they can reasonably expect the effort to yield, what kind of resistance they are likely to see along the way, and what it will take to overcome that resistance.

Process. As Kaleel Jamison once said, "change in the middle looks like failure," and leaders do not like the appearance of failure. The consultant must prepare everyone in the organization for the pockets of resistance, episodes of backlash, and two-steps-forward, one-step-back nature of any change process. The goal is for the organization to get better and stronger. Everyone in the organization, and especially the leaders, must be clear from the start that success does not mean that every day sees incremental progress toward that goal. You can not start putting something entirely new in place and expect it to work perfectly. If people do expect that, they will be tempted to abandon the effort when the problems and challenges begin to arise.

Roles. There needs to be alignment around who does what...and who *can not* do what. Some organizations feel that in hiring a consultant, they have done their work. Now it's the consultant's job to come in, wave a magic wand and make everything better. Other organizations hire consultants for their expertise, but then demand that they adhere to the internal systems they were hired to change. Some rank-and-file members believe that responsibility for a diversity initiative lies with upper management and requires little or nothing from them. The consultant must align all people with what is expected of them. This is an important component of educating them about diversity in general and what it means for an organization to be inclusive.

Skill: Getting Leader Buy-In

Enrolling leaders at the start and keeping them on board is crucial. You cannot assume that by hiring you, leaders have tacitly understood and acknowledged what diversity is about and what the change effort will require of them. Most leaders start the process knowing only that change is needed and having some vague concept of what it is that a consultant does. In a lot of organizations, the decision to start the process comes from a smaller subset of the larger leadership group—which means there may be some powerful people in the upper echelons who do not even have that vague understanding or—worse yet—who oppose the idea. Your early work with leaders sets the tone and establishes what the partnership will be like. Your ability to be effective is a direct result of the partnership you build with the leaders.

Getting the leaders to buy into the process means getting them to buy into several main concepts:

Accepting that the organization must improve itself. Usually this is easy to accept *in theory*. No one thinks of the organization as perfect. When the exact nature and extent of the imperfections begin to surface, however, leaders' acceptance of this tenet sometimes wavers. They must be willing to hear how deep the issues are. Given that leaders are often insulated from the "true" voices of the organization by gatekeepers who ensure that bad news doesn't travel up, it may take some effort to open channels of communication. It is often shocking for leaders to see what is really going on.

Accepting that oppression and privilege are real and exist even in their organization, in both subtle and overt ways. This will be tested when the data starts to emerge and people's voices begin to be heard. But preparing leaders for it ahead of time can at least lay the groundwork for them understanding it so that they do not react defensively when dysfunctional and oppressive organizational and personal behaviors are brought to light.

Acknowledging that they may not fully realize what they have agreed to by starting this initiative. There is uncertainty and risk involved in tackling this work, though the work is essential and there are greater pitfalls for not addressing it. Culture change is a structured and purposeful process, but also an organic one. Consultants must help leaders get comfortable with the idea of following the process where it leads, trusting and adjusting along the way.

Being willing to step outside the blame game, including not blaming themselves. Most leaders are people of action who believe strongly in cause and effect. When they see a problem, they like to tackle it immediately. If Person A is being oppressed, it must be Person B's or Manager C's fault. They may feel compelled to call them on the carpet, or dismiss them immediately. They are not seeing the systemic nature of the problem. Consultants need to provide that perspective and vision.

Seeing the self-interest. If leaders are clear from the start that leveraging diversity and creating a culture of inclusion will not only result in a better work environment, but a more productive and profitable one, they may be more inclined to dedicate themselves to its success and to ride out the rough spots.

Understanding that the change is not going to be easy or quick. As much as people agree to this in theory, they usually still want a light switch—one magic button that will turn the organization from off to on. Leaders have to realize how unrealistic an expectation this is.

Mutually understanding the role of the change agent and what the leaders and the consultant need from each other. Establish expectations and limitations up front, so you do not set yourself up for failure or set the leaders up for disappointment. Of course, the relationship must be somewhat amorphous; you will define it as you go. But this very fact should be clear to everyone at the start. Change agents and leaders are in a partnership (see next section) and there needs to be support, trust, and clarity of roles.

Being open to where the process will lead. Leaders are much more used to contained, beginning and end projects than they are to open-ended initiatives. They need to understand that the change you are talking about goes to the very heart and identity of the organization and will affect everyone. They need to face the uncertainty of where exactly the process will lead and what steps it may require. You can only see so far down the road at any one time: you take a few steps, which let you see the next few steps, and so on.

Skill: Partnering

At its heart, leveraging diversity and creating a culture of inclusion is about people working together across differences. If consultants truly want to model the behavior they are endorsing, they need to work with partners and exhibit the kind of advantages and increased vision that other people can bring. You can not do this while working independently. What could be less diverse than a group of one? Working with partners also helps hone other critical skills: managing conflict, maximizing differences, taking advantage of your talents, and giving and receiving honest feedback.

PARTNERS GIVE YOU:

- ✦More wisdom to make better plans.
- ✦Someone to bounce ideas off and to brainstorm with.
- ✦Someone to watch your back
- ✦Someone to lean on when you get tired.
- ✦Another set of eyes and ears.
- ✦Someone to celebrate successes with.
- ✦Someone to confide in.
- ✦Someone to help you demonstrate new ways of interacting.
- ✦Confidence.
- ✦A different perspective.
- ✦The beginnings of a group that can grow toward critical mass.
- ✦Someone to challenge you.
- ✦Someone to support you.
- ✦Someone who can be honest with you.

Partnering with Other Consultants. Working with colleagues offers a great opportunity to model the partnership skills that the organization needs to adopt. It also provides many benefits and opportunities that are essential for culture change work.

We have been business partners for over 15 years: an African-American man and a Jewish woman who experiences white privilege. We have worked hard together, built a business together, played together, enjoyed our families together, fought over and celebrated our differences. Critical to our success has been building a strong safety net—knowing what we could and could not count on receiving from each other. We have learned to be clear about our needs and to be willing to raise tough issues with each other. Clients see our partnership and learn from our example.

Partnering with Allies in the System. In addition to other consultants, partnerships within the system are critical. No one can lead an organization through a culture change process without allies. Even a CEO needs partners, advocates, mentors, and a support system. If you are to be strategic about working for change, your first strategic action should be to forge key partnerships with leaders and other members of the organization. They can provide invaluable insight into the organization and how it works and also serve as a leverage point for enacting change. In working with them, you can teach, by example, the kind of partnership skills that they need to develop. Look for thought leaders—people who are influential in the organization because of their experience, respect, or personality. They are not always the titled, formal "leaders."

Eleven Behaviors for Inclusion

The Goal is to advocate and practice behaviors that:

- ✦ Facilitate the creation of a workplace environment that allows every team member to fully contribute.
- ✦ Promote effective teamwork among diverse team members.
- ✦ Create the opportunity for connection, understanding, partnership, and safety.

1. Greet others authentically.
2. Create a sense of "safety" for yourself and team members.
3. Address misunderstandings and resolve disagreements.
4. Listen carefully to the person speaking until she or he feels understood.
5. Communicate clearly, directly, and honestly.
6. Solidify the team's vision of its task, and its relationship to the organization's mission.
7. Hear all voices; allow for all options.
8. Ask others to share their thoughts and experiences, and accept their frame of reference.
9. Speak up when people are being excluded.
10. Make careful choices about group actions and schedules.
11. Be brave.

Observing certain ground rules can greatly enhance partnerships. (See "Eleven Behaviors for Inclusion.") These are the same ground rules that underlie inclusion itself—creating an environment in which all people can feel valued, respected, and are able to contribute as partners. They are behaviors the consultant needs to come in with and behaviors others in the organization need to learn.

Skill: Managing and Valuing Conflict

More participants, more diversity, and more inclusion will result in more conflict. It is important to realize that conflict in itself is not a negative; it can be positive propulsion for the organization if handled properly. A chorus of voices can be harmonious or chaotic, depending on how they are blended.

Managing conflict requires not only diplomacy, but an organizational perspective that doesn't indulge in binary thinking: this person is right, this person is wrong; this method is always best, this one always deficient. Many organizations have an environment in which people do not feel comfortable expressing themselves, one in which different points of view are seen as risky, contentious, and unwanted.

The consultant needs to model the kind of conflict management that the organization needs to practice. Consultants usually get plenty of opportunities to model it, since our work invariably creates conflict. Some leaders may not fully endorse our work. Some members of the organization will react against it. In other situations, we may witness disagreements between other members of the organization and be in a position to mediate. If we can show through our actions that conflict is propulsive and additive, that availing oneself of a multitude of perspectives and ideas creates greater vision, and that disagreements do not have to be destructive, we will have gone a long way toward laying the groundwork for a culture of inclusion that leverages diversity.

Skill: Communication

Valuing honesty is essential for change agents. If we do not speak the truth in an organization—especially the truths that those in the system can not speak—who will?

At the same time, how and when one chooses to speak those truths can make a big difference in how the message is received. Again, this is a matter of positioning. It is also a matter of modeling the kind of communication behaviors that the organization itself needs to be moving toward.

Straight Talk: A Norm-Changing Intervention. One of the most helpful interventions that can be made in a group or an organization is to change its norms of communication to Straight Talk.
Straight Talk is the practice of speaking clearly, directly, and honestly.

The foundations include:

- respecting others enough to be honest with them;
- sharing information in a way that produces an efficient, effective environment for communication;
- developing individuals by creating an environment in which it is okay to make mistakes, learn, and grow; and
- utilizing differences.

Straight Talk presumes that conflicting views, values, cultures, and styles are best addressed openly and that those differences—properly resolved—will enhance, rather than detract from, the human interactions and work of the group or organization. Straight Talk, therefore, is not a byproduct of a strong and inclusive organization; it's the prerequisite.

Few people, groups, or organizations practice clean, clear, straight, crisp communications. We often value politeness (no matter how thin or destructive) over conflict (no matter how necessary and additive) and our communication reflects this. We tend to use qualifying language (peppering sentences with "sometimes," "perhaps," "maybe," and other words that undercut the passion, authority, and precision of what we say) and diminishing language that subtly undercuts our own voice ("I could be wrong, but..." "You may not agree with this, but...").

Such linguistic habits detract from effective communication and undermine the essence of what we need to say. Straight Talk eliminates these barriers and has the added advantage of enabling individuals in a group or organization to grow as individuals. It is language that is empowering.

Straight Talk is not a license for rudeness, brutality, or disparagement. It should not be used to embarrass or humiliate, for public rebuke, or for a verbal "assassination." It is not a "hit and run" process and should always be conducted with respect for the listener.

When people learn to use Straight Talk, they enhance their collective efficiency and information is communicated clearly, without second-guessing and without hidden agendas. Thanks to an uncluttered information flow, work is accomplished in a more timely and efficient fashion.

Skill: Measuring Results

In many organizations, if you can not measure it, it is not real. Yet some consultants are very reluctant to use metrics in their work. This is probably the result of several factors: the misconception that culture change initiatives like building inclusion and leveraging diversity are resistant to measurement, the belief that it is too hard to attach numbers to initiatives like this (how can one quantify the degree to which people are accepted and allowed to bring themselves fully to their work?), and the legitimate concern that treating people as "numbers" is part of what the initiative is trying to discourage.

But if the impetus for doing this work is a bottom-line advantage, there ought to be some ways of seeing that. If people are to be held accountable for moving the organization forward, there needs to be some way of marking that progress. It is important to have some concepts of what success looks like. If no attempt is made to track certain aspects of the culture change effort, it is difficult to gauge its impact—or even be sure that it's having one.

What to measure and when. Many organizations already track certain statistics that can be of use here, such as information on hiring or employee retention. These metrics have obvious connections to the impact of efforts to build inclusion and leverage diversity.

There are many other opportunities for quantifying the effectiveness of a culture change initiative. Often they require being conscientious about what the goals of the initiative are and then checking to see if those goals are being met.

Conducting measurements at the start of the initiative is crucial. They will provide the basis for a clear diagnosis of the system as well as a benchmark against which future measurements may be compared to mark movement of the organization. An effort should be made to measure all aspects of the initiative, across the organization: the degree to which the culture change is being communicated to everyone, the commitment of leaders, the extent to which people are responding to the call for change in their own behaviors, the effect the effort is having on key partnerships, the impact on competitive edge and financial success, etc. Survey instruments and performance evaluations (and the ability to meet specific goals) are some effective methods for assessment.

Considering all these elements is crucial for right-sizing the issues: understanding what is key for the organization and then finding the strategic levers required to achieve change. Many consultants fail by merely going down the Best Practices track. They benchmark boilerplate approaches (e.g., mentoring, networks, training sessions) with the hope that something will resonate within the organization. The real skill here is to discern the relevant core issues for each individual organization and then find the best approaches and strategies for affecting them.

The limits of measurement. Measuring is both a science and an art, and the consultant needs to be skilled in both aspects of it. Measuring the effectiveness of a diversity initiative is not quite the same as measuring the success of a new vendor policy, or LAN, or payroll system. Culture change influences all areas of the organization and its impact on the overall environment can be difficult to quantify. What's more, the interrelationship of various components may be so dynamic and dependent that looking at only one metric at a time can be misleading.

As mentioned earlier, change in the middle looks like failure. It's important to remember this when looking at metrics that on the surface may seem discouraging. It is not uncommon, for instance, for the early stages of a culture change effort to result in some discomfort for people in the organization who do not fully understand the nature of the change effort or the need for it. This discomfort may be reflected in employee surveys and create the mistaken impression that the effort is failing. Keep this in mind when establishing accountability. Leaders and others can be held responsible for the results that fall under their purview. It is important, however, not to hold people accountable for behaviors they have not yet learned or pockets of resistance that may lie beyond their influence. This is particularly true at the early stages of the process.

In general, it is critical that consultants measure the organization's success, and equally critical that they recognize the challenges of such measurement.

Skill: Honor the System

As consultants become familiar with an organization and its culture, it is often easy to see what is broken and wrong about it. The more we meet people, hear stories, and observe first-hand the issues and challenges that are alive in the organization, the more dispirited we may become about the system itself.

A clear view of what is wrong with the system is, of course, essential for creating change. But a few other points are worth remembering too:

It is a privilege to be invited to work with an organization. The client organization has existed before our involvement and has probably had a good deal of success. It is composed of people, not merely policies. And it has reached out to us for guidance and help. No matter how discouraged we may become by the current state of the culture, or its resistance to change, we must remember that it is an honor to be in a position to learn about, observe, and ultimately affect the systems in which we work.

If the system knew better, it would do better. Malice and oppression are not often consciously embedded into the organizational cultures we are asked to assist; they come to accrue there, just as they do in the culture at large. We, as change agents, cannot blame and punish leaders and others in the organization for not knowing about issues that fall outside their expertise and experience. We are there to educate and share our own wisdom so that the organization will know better and can do better.

The answers are already inside the system. The essentials for a successful change initiative reside within the organization—in its people, its ideas, its opportunities, its business strategy. Consultants augment the system with "external" aids, such as benchmarking, models, and experience in other organizations, but we must remember that the solutions for each system lie within it.

Skill: Support Leaders without Colluding

The relationship between a consultant and an organization's leadership is a delicate one. Consultants—especially in their early work with a client—are sometimes the bearers of bad news; and how that news is broken can have a big impact on one's effectiveness. Obviously there is a constructive component to even the most discouraging of data gatherings and the long-term goal of improving the system has to be kept foremost in people's minds.

Consultants can not fear a "kill the messenger" response from top leaders and let that fear keep them from speaking the truths—no matter how ugly—that they discover about the organization. It is impossible to be an effective consultant and shield leaders—or, by extension, the organization itself—from what is going on in the organizational culture and what must be done about it.

At the same time, it is not wise to use such information in a way that harms or circumvents leaders. Remember, you're there to help the leaders. That means, among other things, letting them lead. If you blindside them in meetings or fail to work with them in a way where they can do their jobs effectively, you are not helping anyone.

When it's time to report our findings to leaders and their staffs, we try to be careful: we do not want to give them all the information before we walk into that meeting, nor do we want them to be so surprised by the data that they end up looking out of touch or lost. We'll often talk to them ahead of time—not to give them the full scoop before everybody else—but to give them a general indication of what they can expect and prepare for. They cannot lead their staff and deal with the material if they are sitting there stunned themselves.

Again, this is not done to "stack the deck" in favor of the organization's leadership, but rather to enable them to do their jobs. Remember that ultimately, the consultant will leave and the leaders will stay. The success of the enterprise can not be predicated on the consultant being there to do it all.

Another advantage to helping prepare leaders is that this enlists them as allies and advocates. The leader who stands before her staff ready for what they are hearing is able to function as a partner with the change agent. She is not distracted by her own knee-jerk reactions to what may be bad news, but is already onboard with the process. The staff sees this immediately.

Skill: Pacing

There is an initial start-up time where you need to build support and momentum for the change, and then a period toward the end where sustainability and long-term maintenance are the main thrust. The middle period, however, is in some ways the trickiest. Consultants often find themselves caught between resisters, for whom the change is moving too fast, and champions, for whom it's moving too slow.

Each group needs special attention. Resisters have a lot of fear about the new culture and what it will mean for them. They have either not heard the message communicated clearly enough, or their own insecurities and apprehensions about what change will really mean have not been overcome. Although a few resisters may in fact never be willing to align themselves with the new culture and may need to leave, the majority simply need more time, effort, and information.

Being patient with resisters, however, is sometimes perceived as a mixed message by those who have been enthusiastically supporting the effort and are eager to enact the new culture as soon as possible. These champions get impatient with a slow pace; they sometimes feel the brunt of the backlash that comes from resisters and they may resent the way in which such resisters are seemingly indulged by the organization. They may even accuse the organization and the change agent of not walking the talk.

This period of discomfort for both groups can be difficult to manage. One key to navigate this period successfully is to prepare people for it ahead of time. All parts of the change effort should be communicated early on. Once people recognize that what they are experiencing is a natural part of the process—that it actually indicates progress along some established continuum—they can see the larger picture and recognize that what may appear to be failure is actually part of the journey to success.

Managers need to be supported throughout this stage as well. They will feel the forces pulling them in opposing directions. They need to remain resolute about sticking with the change process as it has been established. Their actions and words must consistently say that the organization is moving forward and that everyone needs to get on board with the new culture. The discontent that accompanies change in the middle must be taken as a specific leadership challenge, and not as a failure of the initiative.

Skill: Accept a Continuous Process

There will always be new challenges, new issues, and new opportunities. This is why long-term, permanent processes need to be in place, such as accountability procedures and strategic planning for building inclusion and leveraging diversity.

The consultant's goal, therefore, is not to completely eradicate all the problems in the organization; no consultant could do that. You cannot eliminate conflict, but you can establish a process for conflict resolution that maximizes people's contributions and finds additive value in multiple points of view. The organization, too, needs to understand that building inclusion and leveraging diversity is not an isolated program or a discrete, finite effort with a clear endpoint. Ask them, when does an organization "stop" trying to be profitable or declare its drive for competitive edge to be "complete" and at an end? When does an organization determine that it has gotten sufficiently "smart" and doesn't need to learn any more?

It is the same with culture change work. Once the culture is aligned around the new goals, behaviors, and competencies, the emphasis moves from achieving the new environment to sustaining it. That is a change on the emphasis, but not an end to the effort.

At the same time, it is important to celebrate milestones along the way, to recognize the initiative's successes. This is another reason for setting specific goals; once they are reached, they provide snapshots of success. The successes create momentum for the rest of the initiative and help propel other areas of the culture change effort and they let people see that the organization is achieving something concrete as it walks along the path, even if that path has no final destination.

Conclusion

It is impossible to catalogue every skill that consultants need—each client, person, encounter, and system is different from all others—and the finesse required is resistant to easy formulas and broad generalizations. Nevertheless, the skills we have outlined here are called upon frequently and they support some of the hundreds of finer points associated with consulting work.

More than anything, consultants need to remain open to our own continuous learning and honing of skills. We need to be conscientious about what we do and the effect that it has on the organization. We need to make sure that the values we prize and espouse are the ones that we are living and modeling in all our interactions with the organizations we aim to help.

References

Jamison, Kaleel. "Straight Talk: A Norm-Changing Intervention." *OD Practitioner*, June 1985.
Jensen, Marjane. "Eleven Behaviors for Inclusion." The Kaleel Jamison Consulting Group, Inc., 1995.

Chapter XVI

Building Inclusion and Leveraging Diversity as a Way of Doing Business

Judith H. Katz
Frederick A. Miller

Introduction

Although there is much discussion today about the potential of a diverse workforce and how greater diversity can lead to enhanced innovation and creativity, few organizations have achieved this reality. Organizations often conduct isolated diversity training programs or focus their efforts on recruiting as the solution to a perceived diversity "problem." What is needed instead is to unleash the power of diversity in pursuit of the organization's overall business strategy. The key is to position diversity not as a problem but as a valuable resource waiting to be tapped.

Creating an organizational work culture that is inclusive, higher performing, and sustainable can be a formidable task. It requires changes to all the policies, practices, and programs that shape people's behavior within the organization. It requires additional skills for all leaders, managers, and associates. It requires new ways of defining and measuring success. It requires new ways of thinking about and working with people, individually and collectively, inside and outside the organization. In short, it requires a total system change. Unfortunately, most "diversity efforts" fall short of this kind of breadth of scope. Most efforts take the form of isolated programs that address individual awareness and possibly new behaviors. Rarely is diversity leveraged as an asset. More often, numbers are the goal and what is measured.

Engaging the Client

In most cases, the organization's "diversity problem" is actually a functional problem wherein the organizational culture and work-systems prevent utilization of the full range of skills, talents, and energies of the workforce. What is needed is a strategic culture change effort designed to create a culture of inclusion that leverages diversity, which will enable the organization to achieve its bottom-line objectives.

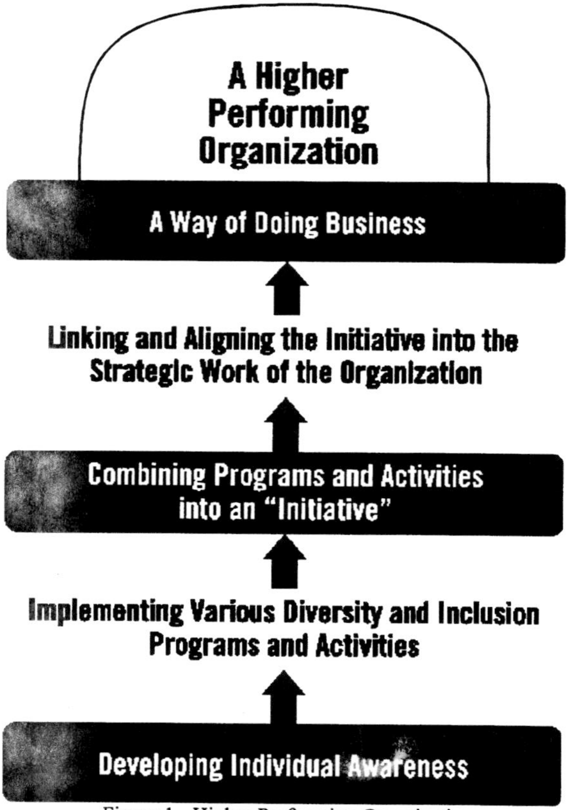

Figure 1. Higher Performing Organization

Diversity efforts are often spearheaded by mid-level managers, charged with initiating, or continuing, a diversity program. No matter who is responsible for the details, it is important to start by engaging the senior leaders of the organization as leaders in the change process. Although this may seem like a daunting task, failure to engage the senior leaders guarantees failure for any change effort. After more than 30 years working in this field, we have found that while change can start anywhere in an organization, it must be led from the top.

To engage senior leaders in the strategic culture change required to improve organizational performance, it is vital to create a framework from which they can see how the effort to create a culture of inclusion that leverages diversity fits with the organization's goals, direction, and strategies.

Making Diversity and Inclusion a Way of Life

Developing Individual Awareness

Most organizations involved in diversity-related activities begin by implementing diversity training sessions that relate primarily to differences among people. In these organizations, diversity work is seen as helping people from the dominant culture better understand people from other cultures or identity groups. The implied benefit and desired outcome is to change the way people see difference. To do this diversity work, organizations primarily use events designed to increase awareness: e.g., Ethnic Foods Lunches, Diversity Days, "Valuing..." or "Celebrating..." weeks. These programs are often successful in raising individual awareness and understanding of other cultures, but this is only a starting point.

Implementing Various Diversity and Inclusion Programs and Activities

In some organizations, the initial work on diversity leads to an awareness that more work is needed. This often occurs because the overall understanding about diversity issues has been raised, and people begin noticing and talking about inequitable experiences of different groups. To address these "new" issues, some organizations may institute programs such as: mentoring, support networks, career path development for high potential employees, targeted recruiting, and communication-skills enhancement.

Although these organizations may indeed research and select some of the best practices, they may not be the right practices for that organization. These programs may not even relate to the organization's strategy and mission, and because they are implemented as isolated programs and activities, the result is often that the effort is fragmented and the programs remain loosely related at best. This is why a strategic initiative is critical.

Combining Programs and Activities into an Initiative

At this point, many organizations realize that the programs and activities are not providing the hoped-for payoff. The next step is often to combine the programs in a way that leverages the activities. Recruiting alone, for example, is insufficient unless the culture supports individuals to do their best work and be retained once they are recruited and hired. Development and performance management must be a part of this, and education must be tailored to assure that individuals are learning a new set of skills to support the necessary behaviors. All of the activities can then become part of a larger strategic initiative.

Instead of pursuing these activities because they are "the right thing to do," the organization begins to pursue them because of a strategic intent. The various parts of the diversity work are evaluated, and those activities that fit with the strategic intent are knit together into a Diversity Initiative. The investment in this initiative is justified through the creation of a business case. The investment also includes changes in people-related systems, management practices, and accountabilities. The focus moves from the needs of individuals to the needs of the system and creating new competencies for a new culture and workplace.

Linking and Aligning the Initiative into the Strategic Work of the Organization

When an organization realizes that its future success hinges on its ability to link diversity to its core business results, the diversity work that had previously been given piecemeal attention as a "soft," people-related pursuit suddenly becomes an important business priority.

For the greatest effectiveness in changing people's behaviors and enhancing business outcomes, an organization must integrate the culture change effort into the strategic work and goals of the organization. This involves integrating the competencies and practices of creating a culture of inclusion that leverages diversity into all of the organization's major strategies and initiatives, e.g., Leadership, Quality, Mergers/Acquisitions, Strategic Alliances, Downsizing, and Becoming a Preferred Stock. For example, in establishing a leadership succession pipeline, candidates would be required to demonstrate competencies for creating an inclusive culture and leveraging diversity. Quality efforts would incorporate input from people from a variety of functions and levels to achieve a 360-degree perspective. Strategic alliances would be pursued only with organizations with inclusive practices.

A Way of Doing Business

As an organization unleashes the synergy gained from integrating its culture change effort with its business practices and strategic goals, the results include measurable benefits through new or improved processes and outcomes. In many cases, productivity rises, turnover drops, recruitment costs decrease, market penetration and new product introductions increase. Institutionalizing the change involves using these and other measurements to hold senior leaders, managers, and all members of the organization accountable for acquiring and practicing inclusive behaviors, and continually improving their performance, thereby continually enhancing the organization's skill-base, culture, overall performance, and business success.

To leverage the diversity that exists in every workforce to produce higher performance and more sustainable results, most organizations would need to achieve a breakthrough on both the conceptual and behavioral levels. To successfully leverage diversity, an organization needs to achieve an *Inclusion Breakthrough*.

Creating an Inclusion Breakthrough

A Methodology for Achieving Higher Performance Through Building Inclusion and Leveraging Diversity

The methodology starts with the premise that *all people are valuable and can add value*. The process engages the participants in identifying the needs of their organization for new competencies, behaviors, and practices, and in developing strategies to address those needs. The participants feel ownership of the process and therefore a strong commitment to the culture change effort. For them, this is not the latest training fad being imposed upon them by a distant administration; this is an educational and organizational change process that addresses their specific needs and concerns.

As people learn more about the experience of inclusion and the practices, competencies, and behaviors necessary to bring it about, they are able to develop more advanced and expanded strategies to integrate the Inclusion Breakthrough into more and more aspects of the day-to-day business of the organization.

Every organization is different, which is why this methodology provides tools for identifying actions and strategies that can enable the people of an organization to do their best work, and offers guidelines for addressing organizational issues in ways that will lead to sustainable success. It is designed to create an environment in which people are enabled to add value and enhance an organization's competitive advantage.

In creating an Inclusion Breakthrough, the return on investment comes from a greater ability to both (1) create more value by engaging a broader spectrum of talents and (2) deliver more value to a broader spectrum of customers. Organizations that have made long-term commitments to implementing this approach have seen substantive, measurable, positive results, including reduced employee turnover, improved customer satisfaction, faster and more effective customer service, increased market share, successful penetration into new markets, and increased productivity. From line workers to CEOs, people reported new levels of innovation, enthusiasm, commitment, job satisfaction, sense of belonging, and ability to contribute.

Four Cornerstones of Sustainable Change

The methodology that follows is predicated on these four essentials for an effective change process:

Leverage

Find and develop the most effective leverage points to gain the maximum payoff from each activity undertaken. Work to enhance strengths rather than attacking points of resistance.

Linkage

Coordinate and link all organizational initiatives and activities so they work together to create a sum that is greater than its parts. Avoid isolated, duplicated, and counterproductive efforts.

Leadership

Equip the leaders of the organization with the knowledge and skills needed to lead and model the change. Develop and support leaders of the change at all levels of the organization.

Learning

Understand that change is an act of continuous discovery and that making mistakes is part of the learning process. Forgive yourself for not having been as smart today as you will be tomorrow.

Four Phases of Change Strategies

The methodology is composed of four phases: Building a Platform for an Inclusion Breakthrough; Creating Momentum; Making the Inclusion Breakthrough a Way of Life; and Leveraging Learning to Challenge the New Status Quo.

The limitations of the printed page require us to present these phases sequentially, but in actuality the components are never implemented in a linear manner. While some actions and strategies may only be implemented after certain resources and competencies have been developed, others may be carried out simultaneously. In different organizations, different interventions may be required at different stages, and some parts of some organizations will move at a different pace from others. The methodology is flexible and adaptable to the needs of each organization; the individuals implementing the methodology must be flexible and adaptable as well.

Phase One of an Inclusion Breakthrough change effort is actually a time of preparation—of laying the foundation and gathering the resources for change. It is when the need for change is identified, the organizational commitment to change is sought, and the initial leadership of the effort is enrolled.

Following are key actions of Phase One:

Position the Effort as the New Way of Life

Change can *start* anywhere within an organization, but for any change effort to be effective and transformative it must be *led and modeled* from the top. Only the organization's senior leaders can provide the commitment, the resources, and the credibility required to convince the people of the organization to stop behaving in the ways they have always behaved (and been rewarded for) and start adopting new, unfamiliar ways that may initially feel awkward, embarrassing, and risky. Unless the senior leaders model the behaviors, values, and attitudes of the new culture as the organization's new way of doing business, the rest of the organization will continue to follow the old, safe ways.

A first step for an organization that is serious about undertaking an Inclusion Breakthrough is to take stock of how its leaders are positioning the change effort. Change efforts undertaken because they are "morally the right thing to do" can lose momentum in the face of more pressing, bottom-line business matters or shifts in the political winds. Moral imperatives and other non-essential expenses tend to be put on the back burner in times of crisis, and in most organizations, crises crop up with alarming regularity. The change effort must be described and modeled by the top leaders as *the* way the organization is going to conduct its business from now on. The leaders must understand why the Inclusion Breakthrough is *mission critical* and they must begin displaying behaviors that will engage and enroll others.

Establish the Organizational Imperative for an Inclusion Breakthrough

To engage senior leaders in the culture change strategy required for an Inclusion Breakthrough, it is vital to build a framework within which

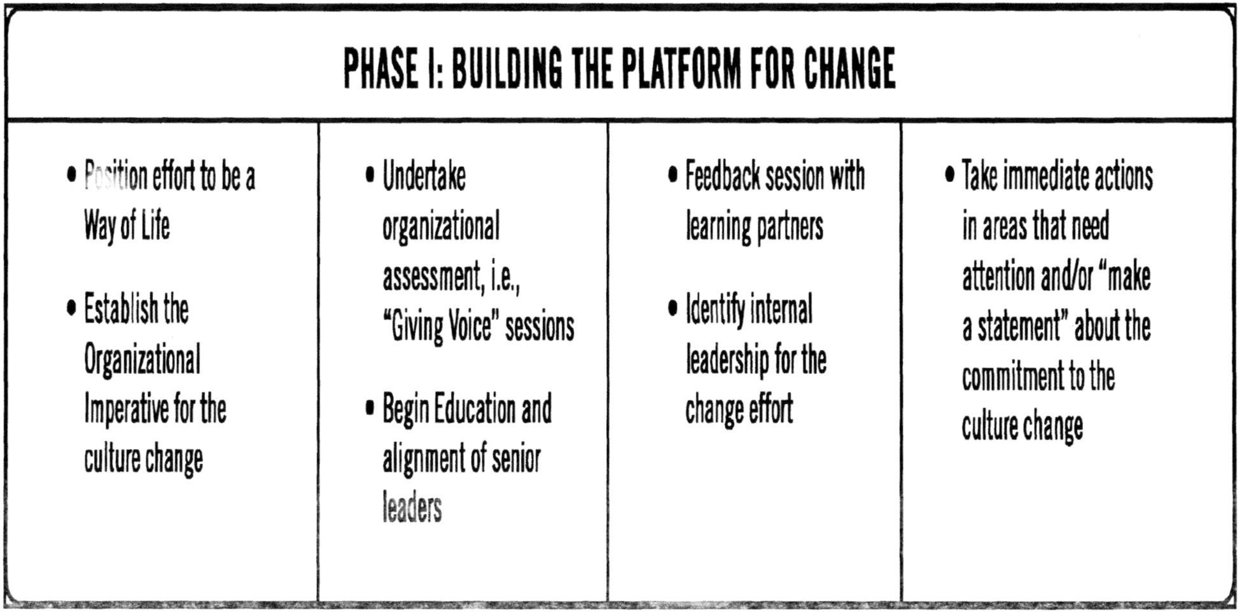

Figure 2. Phase I: Building the Platform for Change

everyone can see how the change effort will unleash the power of diversity and help realize the organization's goals and strategies.

This Organizational Imperative must state clearly how transforming the old culture and shifting to a new one will benefit each individual, including members of the traditional or original dominant social identity group. Three critical components of an effective Organizational Imperative include:

1. Telling the story of all the factors that have changed (i.e., the business environment, the marketplace, the needs and expectations of individuals and of the organization, the law, technology, etc.) to make an Inclusion Breakthrough necessary.
2. A clear statement of the Imperative (i.e., what is to be gained and why it is necessary for the organization's survival and success).
3. Examples of costs and missed opportunities incurred by operating under the old culture, contrasted with examples of expected organizational and personal successes likely to result from practicing the new culture.

In this stage of the work, to achieve "buy in" from the organization's senior leadership, it may be necessary to create a preliminary Organizational Imperative, based on external trends and a general knowledge of the organization. Later, after a thorough Organizational Assessment, this preliminary document can be revised for presentation to the organization as a whole, using the more specific information derived from the assessment.

Undertake an Organizational Assessment

The organizational assessment is a careful study of the organization and its current and future positioning—its culture, opportunities, challenges, long-term potential, and possibilities for maximizing performance. It also identifies what people need from the organization to contribute more effectively to its current and future success and what the organization needs from people. The assessment examines policies, practices, and interactions that support people in doing their best work or hinder them from doing so.

The purpose of the organizational assessment as an assessment tool is threefold:

1. To provide data about the current culture and capabilities of the organization.

2. To lay the groundwork for creating the comprehensive strategy required for an Inclusion Breakthrough (including the framing and/or refining of the Organizational Imperative for the change effort).

3. To establish a baseline for future measurements of the change effort's progress, and provide a benchmark for comparing the organization's practices with its competitors'.

The organizational assessment is much more than just a diagnostic tool. It is also a highly effective intervention for building a foundation for change. The interviewing and data gathering process focuses the attention of the organization's workforce on such issues as organizational performance, inclusion, diversity, and culture change. It starts people talking with each other, and sends a message that their voices and perspectives are important to the senior leaders and are a key resource in determining the organization's future.

In subsequent work with an organization, people who participate in the assessment often take an active role in the change process. Many feel a sense of responsibility and ownership for the changes they have helped shape, and they want to continue to be involved and work toward change.

Data Feedback: Report "The Voices of the People"

Collecting data is only one step of the assessment process; just as important is sharing that information with the senior leaders directly and candidly, conveying a vivid picture of peoples' actual experiences in the organization. Too often the senior leaders are sheltered from hearing critical information about what is really going on because no one wants to be the bearer of bad news.

Data feedback usually requires a day or day and a half with the leaders, during which the process is reviewed, the quantitative and qualitative data are presented, the themes and key findings are summarized and analyzed, and a path forward is recommended.

Educate and Align Leaders

To deepen the leaders' understandings of the data feedback and prepare them to lead the Inclusion Breakthrough process, it is most effective to engage them in an intensive education session. This session should include not only the senior leadership team but also a group of Learning Partners—people selected from different levels and functions who can provide a full range of perspectives about the organization and the experience of working within it.

Ideally, this education session is a multi-day, residential event during which the participants are removed from their everyday work environment. Since leadership education plays a major role in the culture change process, the longer and more intensive this session, the stronger the foundation of the change process will be.

Regardless of the length of the session, the priority is to provide the participants with an understanding of the characteristics and effects of organizational cultures, the differences between "exclusive" and "inclusive" work cultures, the nature and benefits of inclusive behaviors and attitudes, what it takes to leverage diversity for higher performance, and the nature of strategic culture change.

This initial education session also serves as a forum for practicing and experiencing the benefits of inclusive behaviors. It often becomes many participants' most significant experience of an inclusive, diverse culture. During this session, Learning Partners share their experiences in the organization, and the senior leaders have the opportunity to hear those true experiences and to speak about their own experiences as leaders of the organization.

Identify and Empower Internal Leadership for the Change Effort

Senior leaders alone cannot create an Inclusion Breakthrough. They must extend their leadership to others in the organization who can partner with them and support the effort, bringing more diverse skills, talents, and perspectives to its successful implementation. As a symbolic action, this demonstrates commitment to the culture change and belief in the values of the new culture. As a practical action, it creates an expanded leadership group with the broad vision and variety of perspectives needed to plan and implement a far-reaching, long-range process.

To reach these goals, the Inclusion Breakthrough leadership team must be both diverse and inclusive. That means people from the organization's dominant culture (usually the culture of the founders) must be represented, as well as people from other groups. If a diversity effort's leadership team is comprised exclusively of people whose social identities would be seen as representing the "newer" groups, it runs the danger of being perceived by the majority of the organization as a group of "them," severely hampering its credibility and effectiveness. This type of team also is not truly inclusive. Too many "Diversity Task Forces" are not actually diverse.

Take Immediate Actions that Make a Statement

To build a viable platform for change it is imperative to communicate the findings to the organization and to make a bold public statement, demonstrating that the change process is real and that the very top of the organization is committed to it. Examples of this kind of statement might be establishing a new senior-level position in charge of inclusion, enacting and enforcing a new people-development policy, or committing a significant amount of money to a budget for the culture change effort.

Phase One of mobilizing for an Inclusion Breakthrough can be a relatively quiet time of identifying, developing, and aligning resources. As the more action-oriented Phase Two gets underway, leaders of the effort must be prepared to be more visible. They must be ready to model the competencies and behaviors they wish to encourage in others, and they must be prepared for the feedback that comes to all pioneers and agents of change.

Following are key Phase Two strategies:

Develop an Initial Plan

In creating the initial 12- to 18-month plan for implementing organization-wide culture change, the Inclusion Breakthrough leadership team must focus on building and sustaining momentum for the effort. The strategies and actions that emerge from the data feedback process must be integrated into the action planning. In the initial planning stages of an Inclusion Breakthrough effort, it is important to realize that

PHASE II: CREATING MOMENTUM			
• Develop initial 12- to 18-month plan	• Implement aggressive efforts to engage, inform and enroll the people of the organization • Develop a critical mass of Agents of Change	• Begin education to create new competencies for senior leaders, managers, individual contributors • Create processes to address blatant or subtle discrimination/ barriers	• Support networks, mentoring, coaching and buddy systems • Identify and begin work in "Pockets of Readiness"

Figure 3. Phase II: Creating Momentum

the needs of the organization will become clearer in the future and the participants in the education processes will be better equipped for charting the course of the organization after they have had some time to integrate their new knowledge and skills into their day-to-day behaviors and tasks.

A change effort of this scale requires a great many actions, all of which seem critical, but not all of which are immediately practical or possible. Priorities must be determined. The organization may need to change to prevent an eventual demise; but it must also continue to conduct its day-to-day business or its demise will be immediate.

We recommend these priorities in planning and implementing the initial 12- to 18-month strategy of Phase Two: 1) develop resources, policies, and competencies that will support the Inclusion Breakthrough in the long term; and 2) connect the Inclusion Breakthrough to the bottom-line objectives, mission, and strategies of the organization. In implementing these priorities, there should be another, overriding priority: *Pursue the Inclusion Breakthrough in a manner that reflects and models the competencies and way of doing business the Inclusion Breakthrough is intended to create.*

Implement Aggressive Efforts to Engage, Inform, and Enroll the People of the Organization in the Change Effort

As the change initiative begins gaining momentum, the need to create realistic expectations also escalates. This is the time to make clear to everyone in the organization that there will be new expectations, new required competencies, new ways of behaving and working together. Aggressive, active communications are essential to ensure that everyone in the organization is well informed about the effort's goals, plans, and rationale. This should involve frequent and various communications from the senior leadership of the organization emphasizing the mission-critical nature of the process and the Organizational Imperative for the Inclusion Breakthrough.

Develop a Critical Mass of Agents of Change

To help build a critical mass of people who are actively living the new culture and utilizing inclusive behaviors in their work, a core group of Agents of Change should be selected for intensive education and skill-development training as leaders of change. They will be responsible for being role models and experts in the behaviors and business rationale for the new culture, to seed the organization with informal leaders who will demonstrate the new culture's behaviors and values in their day-to-day work interactions.

Begin Ongoing Education and Competency-Building for Senior Leaders, Managers, and Individual Contributors

The people of the organization should be involved in a rollout education process to increase knowledge and skills for creating a culture of inclusion that leverages diversity. Managers should receive special attention in developing skills for leading change and modeling inclusive behaviors. Managers (and all leaders) need to be coaches, mentors, facilitators, and partners, not just scorekeepers and attendance takers. Coaching, mentoring, and leading inclusive, diverse teams need to be formal, measured parts of leaders' job descriptions and accountabilities, with performance (or lack thereof) reflected in their compensation.

Create Processes to Support the New Culture and Address Blatant or Subtle Discrimination and Barriers to Inclusion

A diverse work-team should be assigned the task of assessing and enhancing the organization's recruitment, retention, career development, and other people-policies, based on the objectives of the culture change effort and best practices comparisons with other organizations.

Support Networks, Mentoring, Coaching, and Buddy Systems

For inclusion to take root, it cannot be manifested solely through passive policies. Too many people come from backgrounds, identity-group cultures, and work-life experiences in which exclusivity, "one-up/one-down" systems, and a status-based pecking order is the norm. New people need someone to reach out and show them the ways of a new organization and its organizational culture. Unless this is an established policy, some people will be overlooked—excluded—even if there is no active desire to exclude them.

Organization-sponsored identity-group (and interest-group) support networks can work to prevent isolation of individuals. To connect these groups to the Organizational Imperative and prevent them from being stigmatized or marginalized as non-essential social programs, their charters should tie their functions to furthering the organization's mission, goals, and strategies. Some networks have had great success in areas such as identity-group-focused recruitment, marketing, product development, and community outreach. To offer formal networking opportunities to all members of the organization and prevent them from being seen as "just for *those* people," network groups should also be available for white men, and membership in all groups should be open to all—not just to identity-group members but to allies and supporters. Buddy systems, coaching, and mentoring programs can provide needed supports for individuals' career and skills development. The key to making these processes work is to hold the buddies, mentors, and coaches accountable for the development and retention of each individual involved. One effective way to accomplish this is to tie bonus compensation to the retention, productivity, and progress of each individual. This ensures that all people have motivated allies they can look to for support and guidance.

Identify and Leverage Pockets of Readiness

Inevitably there are elements—business units or functions—that can move a lot faster than the rest of the organization. These *pockets of readiness* can be very advantageous to the change effort, because they can model the change and its benefits for the rest of the organization.
A mistake made in the course of many change efforts is an excessive focus of available energy and resources on the areas most resistant to change—a strategy analogous to attempting to storm a castle by attacking the most heavily defended parapet. It is far more practical and effective to start with the people and business units most willing to move forward and practice new, more inclusive behaviors and skills.
Initial and ongoing success is more likely once an organization has a successful unit to hold up as a model, so people can see that not only does a culture of inclusion work—it works *better*.

Key to developing an expanded and longer-term plan for achieving and sustaining the Inclusion Breakthrough is leveraging the new competencies, resources, and organizational capabilities that have been gained since Phase One. These new competencies, resources, and capabilities make a whole new realm of strategies possible. Even more significantly, they make a whole new realm of strategies *conceivable.* Before expanding the culture change effort, it is crucial that a critical mass of the organization's people gain new skills and share a comprehensive understanding of the nature of an inclusive culture and its ability to unleash the power of diversity. This new understanding will shape the next set of strategies and how they are implemented in ways that cannot be anticipated before the leaders (and others) experience the education process.

Following are key actions to undertake during Phase Three:

Expand the Initial Action Plan to a 3-year Strategic Plan that Integrates and Partners with Other Initiatives

Central to this phase of the change process is developing strategies that link the Inclusion Breakthrough to all the organization's operations and process-improvement initiatives. Such strategies might include applying inclusion-oriented competencies to achieve breakthrough transformations in customer service, product design, market development planning, and other aspects of doing business. The starting point may be a culture change effort, but the result is a repositioning of the organization's products and/or services for a more sustainable future.

Formalize Accountability for Acquiring New Competencies and Living the New Culture

A key to sustainable success for the change effort is the development of effective measurements for the new behaviors and the ability to hold people accountable for using them. This will require new tools for measuring individual and group behaviors, practices, and results related to inclusion and leveraging diversity, such as a "Diversity and Inclusion Index" and "Improvement Metrics." Managers must play a major role in the change effort, both in modeling the new behaviors and in holding people accountable for practicing them. Two of the keys to success for organizations involved in Inclusion Breakthrough efforts are (1) ensuring that managers possess the competence to practice, model, and foster the necessary behaviors for creating a culture of inclusion that leverages diversity, and (2) holding managers accountable for doing it.

PHASE III: MAKING DIVERSITY AND INCLUSION A WAY OF LIFE

• Expand the initial plan to a long-term strategic plan that integrates and partners with all change initiatives	• Formalize accountability for living the competencies in the new culture (scorecards & other tools) • Baseline leveraging diversity education into all training and programs	• Implement incentives and rewards to support the culture change and to create organizational pull • Enhance performance feedback systems to support the new culture	• Involve stakeholders (e.g., suppliers, joint ventures, acquisitions, community, board members)

Figure 4. Phase III: Making Diversity and Inclusion a Way of Life

Baseline Building Inclusion and Leveraging Diversity into all Education and Training Events

As the Inclusion Breakthrough becomes the everyday way of life in the organization, education and training on building inclusion and leveraging diversity must move from being "one-off" activities isolated from the organization's mainstream education and training programs to being fully integrated into all orientation, education, and training events. The skills, competencies, and talents the organization and its people need to succeed should be reflected in all people-development strategies, including retention, recruitment, technical training, and leadership development programs.

Implement Incentives and Rewards to Support the Culture Change and Create Organizational Pull

For the Inclusion Breakthrough to become everyone's standard business practice, it must be incorporated into everyone's most basic performance-feedback system—compensation. Effective strategies to gain people's attention and commitment would be to tie bonuses, pay raises, and promotions to learning and practicing inclusive behaviors, and to establish bonus pools and other reward mechanisms for successful partnership and team efforts.

Enhance Performance Feedback Systems to Support the New Culture

Performance feedback mechanisms must align with the new culture and fully support the new behaviors expected of each member of the organization, providing feedback on how to improve performance. To make sure managers' behaviors align with the new policies and performance objectives of the organization, it can be useful to engage in multi-directional evaluation of manager performance by those who report to them, their peers, HR, the "Inclusion" function, and their managers. "Forced Ranking" systems do not encourage teamwork or partnership and do not focus on job-skill improvement.

Involve the Organization's Stakeholders

Gaining the support of the people and entities that support the organization is a critical part of institutionalizing the change. Communicating the business gains (realized and projected) to the organization's stakeholders helps to enlist their support. Demonstrating and utilizing inclusive practices in interactions with suppliers and distributors—treating them like partners instead of vendors—helps develop more productive relationships. Developing and building on these partnerships is an ongoing part of the Inclusion Breakthrough, which requires greatly expanded levels of respect, inclusion, and mutuality in interactions. For example, some organizations require suppliers to sign agreements promising to treat their people in specific ways (e.g., no harassment, increasing their diversity, paying people a living wage, etc.).

The strategies of Phase Four leverage the learnings from Phases One through Three to evaluate progress-to-date and reassess the needs of the organization in light of the changes that have occurred since the start of the culture change effort. A key to the success of the continuing change effort is understanding that issues will arise that cannot be foreseen at the beginning. The organization's leaders must build in the flexibility and commitment to deal with these unexpected issues as they arise.

While the culture change effort should be viewed as a commitment to continuous (and therefore endless) improvement, the structures of the effort should not be viewed as endless or permanent. The Inclusion Breakthrough leadership team and other change leadership groups should have "sunset dates:" an agreement to end at a specific time within five to seven years. During those years, the groups' members should be rotated. New perspectives and fresh eyes will always be needed; they must always be included, even if they make the "old guard" uncomfortable (that is largely why they *must* be included).

Actions to take during Phase Four include:

Reassess the Organization

The only way to know if the process is working and serving the objectives of the organization is to conduct periodic re-surveys and comparisons. Revisiting and revising the Organizational Imperative for the Inclusion Breakthrough on a regular basis is an excellent exercise for renewing the organization's commitment to the culture change effort.

PHASE IV: LEVERAGING LEARNING AND CHALLENGING THE NEW STATUS QUO			
• Reassess organization to identify progress and gaps • Reassess how the work of the organization is done	• Communicate accomplishments and success practices internally and externally	• Identify and address areas that will support higher and higher performance	• Continuously improve the change process

Figure 5. Phase IV Leveraging Learning and Challenging the New Status Quo

Reassess How the Work of the Organization is Done

As an ongoing process, the organization should examine all its formal and informal work processes, internal and external. It is vital for individuals and workgroups to evaluate and re-evaluate their practices constantly to make sure they reflect the organization's values and serve the organization's mission and goals.

Communicate Accomplishments and Success Practices Internally and Externally

To gain the full benefits of an Inclusion Breakthrough it is absolutely necessary to communicate the organization's culture change efforts publicly. When an organization is known for its growth and success opportunities and establishes a reputation for having a culture that invites people's ideas and passions, it becomes a magnet for talented people from a wide array of backgrounds.

Identify and Address Areas that Support Higher Performance

To be successful in their culture change efforts as well as in their competition for talent, organizations working toward an Inclusion Breakthrough need to raise the bar, not just on themselves but on their competitors. They need to start announcing their success stories as well as their highest aspirations. They need to establish the standards to which they wish to be held accountable—and then make those standards public so they *will* be held accountable for them.

While this might seem risky, it is actually a clear strategy to take the lead across a range of key business fronts—from winning the competition for talent to becoming an industry's highest performing organization. By sharing its vision of change, the organization needs to be clear that it is working *toward* this aspiration. It needs to admit this is unfinished business without pretending that perfection has been attained so people who join the organization see themselves as having a role in creating a new company and a new vision and do not feel misled into thinking the work is already complete.

Continuously Improve the Change Process

For an Inclusion Breakthrough to succeed and continue over time, it must be treated as a process of continuous improvement. Ongoing benchmarking and internal surveys can provide the kind of feedback and analysis necessary for examining and enhancing all organizational processes and strategies. The primary assumption should be that strategies and policies *must* change over time, because the market, the environment, and the organization's needs *always* change.

After the Four Phases of Creating an Inclusion Breakthrough—Then What?

When the Inclusion Breakthrough begins to take hold throughout the organization, the leaders of the change process need to recognize that they served as catalysts and models for others. The process must continually evolve, with new sets of change leaders, new organizational assessments, and new examinations of the key questions: What have we learned? What opportunities are we missing? What do we need to do next in order to be more inclusive? How can we leverage a wider range of differences for even higher performance?

As long as the broader society remains a fundamentally exclusive culture in which differences are seen as deficits, the only way to sustain an Inclusion Breakthrough is to keep going back to Phase One. As long as an organization is committed to an Inclusion Breakthrough, there will be a need to return to the place where it started and experience it for the first time—but each time with greater wisdom and ability to adapt to these new learnings.

Once this process has taken on a life of its own, each round of self-examination and change will become less and less of a "starting-from-scratch" experience, as the organization is able to build upon the inclusive foundation that has already been established.

Few organizations have achieved an Inclusion Breakthrough throughout their entire operation. However, many have done so within small pockets: some as small as individual work groups, some as large as 10,000-person divisions.

The real breakthrough comes as a critical mass of individuals begin to operate in entirely new ways: thinking about people as partners and assets; solving problems by including all members who can bring different perspectives to key issues; enabling people from all levels and social identity groups to feel they belong and can add their value; and inviting newcomers to identify what others of longer tenure might not be able to see. The *breakthrough* comes from the inclusion (and all that goes with it) of *all* people. By unleashing the real power of human diversity and providing a beacon and a foundation for higher performance, for greater productivity, and for all to grow and develop, performance, productivity, and personal development can continue to grow limitlessly.

Chapter XVII

Diversity Management in Specialized Settings: Non-Profit, Faith-Based, and Social Organizations, Community and Government Agencies

Jim Henkelman-Bahn
Jacqueline Bahn-Henkelman

Introduction

Diversity Work Is Diversity Work: Diversity Issues Are Diversity Issues

This chapter, concentrating on the work of diversity practice in nonprofit, faith-based, and school organizations, community, and government agencies, will highlight both the uniqueness of these different agencies and organizations and their diversity issues. However, it is important to point out that, although there are differences between these organizations and the corporate world, the basic issues are the same. Diversity work is diversity work, regardless of whether it takes place in a corporation, a community, organization, or a school.

It is absolutely critical to bring these diversity issues to awareness, so that choices can be made and responsible efforts can be directed toward the creation of organizations and a society of social justice. There always has been, and will continue to be, misunderstanding, resistance, and denial where diversity issues are concerned. The work of the diversity professional is needed, both inside organizations and outside (provided by external consultants), to facilitate the development of organizations dedicated to the concepts of diversity. All the skills and approaches discussed in previous chapters of this book will be valuable and applicable to the work of the diversity professional dealing with nonprofit, faith based, and school organizations, community, and government agencies. Additional awareness of the uniqueness of these organizations and agencies will enable the diversity professional who works in this arena to be more effective.

Uniqueness of Organizations

The Bottom Line: A Mission to Achieve

Probably the first thing to note in the world of nonprofit organizations is that the bottom line is different. It is not as though there is no bottom line, but the bottom line is not based on financial profit. Nonprofit organizations are values-driven. They are motivated by a sense of mission. This sense of mission can be a compelling force for diversity, and it can just as easily create the conditions that make it difficult for the nonprofit to become an organization that is truly committed to diversity. Often, a nonprofit organization operates in the arena of social justice. On the surface, it should seem obvious that this would make the work of the diversity professional easier. However, this is not necessarily the case. The following example of a consultation with a nonprofit organization illustrates this phenomenon of an organization driven by values and a deep sense of mission, that is struggling to become more broadly based and diverse.

Several years ago, a coalition hired us as external consultants to help it become a more inclusive organization. The coalition was founded by the sex- or gender-equity education officers in the various states of the USA "to provide leadership in the identification and infusion of sex equity in all educational programs and processes." Later they added "and within parallel equity concerns, including, but not limited to, age, disability, national origin, race, religion, and sexual orientation." They had experienced success in achieving their original mission. However, they were unable to sustain a broadly based, diverse organization. Most of the membership in the organization was female and white. Despite efforts at programming and recruiting for a broader membership, people of color and males, after joining, often did not remain members of the organization. The coalition was interested in having us work with them to help them become more truly diverse.

Most of our consultation work has been with nonprofit organizations in this country and around the world, so this contract seemed like a good fit for us. Working together with the board of directors and the officers of the coalition, we developed a contract that called for the following elements:

Forming and guiding an internal team of members to do the following:

- ✦ Examine the basic culture, to determine what aspects of that culture encouraged diversity in the organization and what aspects of that culture were barriers to diversity,
- ✦ Operate as an internal organization-development team, approaching their work from a systemic perspective and operating basically as anthropologists, to uncover the true nature of the culture of the organization,
- ✦ Interview a sampling of members, with particular attention to current and past members who were male or people of color (as external consultants, we also participated in the interviewing, so that we would become familiar with the nature of the organization and its issues),
- ✦ Meet with us, the external consultants, to look for the themes we had uncovered about the culture that were conducive to and/or a barrier to diversity in the organization;
- ✦ Conducting interviews for several months prior to and during the annual meeting, to provide the basis for a presentation of results to the annual conference;
- ✦ Testing the themes in the data from the organization;
- ✦ Deciding on actions to propose that would enhance the diversity of the coalition.

In collaboration with the internal team, we developed a number of themes. One of the dominant themes that surfaced is appropriate for this discussion. The culture of the organization was seen by most as a dominant white females culture. Although there was no intention that the coalition be a "closed club," many individuals experienced themselves as being excluded or marginalized by the white-female dominant group. Several males reported that at conferences they had experienced what they perceived as male-bashing by some organization members as well as by some conference speakers and workshop presenters. This caused many men to pull back from the organization. In order to address these concerns, a male issues task force was formed to promote the inclusion of male equity issues at future conferences and to ensure that presentations did not denigrate males. The experiences of some women of color caused them to believe that their issues as people of color were not considered as important as the issues of white women. True to the nature of a voluntary organization, when the needs of the women of color and the males were not met, some of them took their membership, their passions, and their energy elsewhere.

Obviously, the dominant white-female culture of this organization had to change in order for a greater diversity to be developed. However, this brought into question the very mission of the organization. A basic question that the organization needed to address was whether emphasizing other aspects of diversity in programming would mean dilution of their central mission, which was gender equity in education. It is interesting to note that, as the organization began addressing this issue, the number of males and women of color participating at the coalition's latest conference increased. They were moving closer to their goal of being a truly diverse organization.

This consultation with the coalition is an example of how the very values-driven mission of the organization (i.e., addressing the gender issues in education) hindered it from becoming a fully diverse organization. The deeply held values that allowed them to do the work of gender equity were actually preventing them from seeing how some males and people of color were experiencing marginalization. This is one example of how the bottom-line mission of a nonprofit organization uniquely affects its culture and the work of the diversity professional.

Often Volunteer-Based

Most organizations in the nonprofit sector make use of large numbers of volunteers in order to carry out their mission. Often the number of volunteers far exceeds the number of paid staff, and organizations have to recruit and motivate these volunteers vigorously in order to succeed. One of the currencies of power that organizations have in relation to paid staff is the ability to give or take away the employee's current livelihood. The nonprofit organization does not have this same influence with volunteers and therefore lacks the same control over them.

Volunteers usually have very strong values related to the primary mission of the nonprofit organization, which is what attracted them to the organization in the first place. These strong values may or may not support the development of diversity in the organization. Volunteers who feel that their own perspectives are not supported may be quicker than paid staff would be to leave the organization and seek other organizations that support their views. Volunteers are more likely to vote with their feet — and to do it with less provocation than paid staff. So, once again, the passions brought to the organization may either support or become barriers to true diversity.

Perhaps an illustration of how strong the conflict can be between the values held by different members of a nonprofit organization will help to make clear the kind of effect such conflict can have on an organization. Recently, a small, nonprofit, community-leadership training program was initiated to provide training for grassroots leaders from various community groups. There was a basic commitment to diversity. In fact, the group of community members who had been meeting to initiate this work was clearly dedicated to creating a strong, multicultural leadership network in the community. The group that was meeting to form this organization included blacks, Hispanics, whites, and members of immigrant groups. Men and women of different ages were involved. The group had worked hard to develop their mission statement and a program to support that mission. However, when they were in the process of writing their nonprofit incorporation papers and bylaws, an interesting conflict developed.

The dispute arose around the wording of the non-discrimination clause in the coalition's bylaws. The model bylaws from which the group was working contained out-of-date language prohibiting discrimination based on "sexual preference." One of the members of the organizing group suggested changing the verbiage to "sexual orientation," in order to make the language consistent with current research and understanding. This brought the issue to the attention of a male African American participant, who held a strong religious belief that homosexuality is sinful. He immediately objected to including the language of sexual orientation in the bylaws. A debate ensued.

Although this was a group that was dedicated to creating a truly diverse organization, when sexual orientation became the focus, strong value differences surfaced. The African American male threatened to leave the organization if the wording were included. Some others were willing to let him leave, since they felt strongly about the inclusion of the revised wording. It was a test of the very values that were motivating the volunteers to form this organization. In this case, several members of the group took it upon themselves to work with the dissenting member in an effort to educate him about the issue of sexual orientation. In the final analysis, this effort was successful, allowing the group to continue its work and remain intact while including, in the articles of incorporation and bylaws, the language that prohibited discrimination based on "sexual orientation."

This is an example of how the strongly held views of a volunteer in a nonprofit organization may create unique issues that the organization must address. Although in this example the dispute was resolved, such conflicts can prevent nonprofit organizations from being able to model and fulfill their missions. When volunteers with strongly held values are unable to resolve their issues, they may leave the organization, or prevent it from fully embracing diversity.

Often Low-Paid

The pay scale in many nonprofit organizations is lower than the pay scale found in the corporate world. The effect on the diversity professional is the same, whether the professional is working inside or outside the organization. Although it is difficult to obtain accurate data on salaries or fees, we know that the diversity professional who chooses to work with a nonprofit organization often does so out of commitment to the organization's mission. These professionals can expect to be compensated at a considerably lower level, especially when working with very small nonprofit organizations. Some external diversity professionals provide their services as consultants *pro bono*, in order to ensure that the nonprofit organizations they value receive high-quality consultant services. One recent survey indicated that when fees were charged, the fees for consultants in nonprofit organizations ranged from $600 to $1200 per day.

The Role of the Board of Directors, the CEO, and the Staff

In nonprofit organizations, boards of directors often play a much more central role in the work of the organization than do board members in the for-profit world. Some boards of directors are considered to be working boards and take on certain responsibilities for making the organization run, such as recruiting and developing other board members and doing fund-raising. The board of directors also may become involved with the day-to-day operations of the nonprofit organization. Consultants need to help the organization monitor this day-to-day involvement to be sure that it does not lead to micro-management by the board, which could undermine the Chief Executive Officer (CEO) of the organization. Thus, an important consultant-facilitated intervention with nonprofits is board development.

When contracting with a nonprofit organization, the consultant needs to clearly determine who the primary client really is or should be. There have been times when members of boards of directors have asked us to work with them because of dissatisfaction with the CEO and times when staff members have asked us to work with the organization because they were having trouble with the CEO or a board member. Also, CEOs have warned us not to pay attention to certain board members or certain staff members. All these experiences have sharpened our antennae, so that we are always mindful of the need to sort out the relationship between the board, the CEO, and the staff, in order to maximize our effectiveness. The relationship itself may be creating serious issues for the organization.

Consultants should also know that nonprofit organizations tend to be legacy-based organizations. This legacy may take the form of the vision, beliefs, wishes, dreams, or practices of a person who founded the organization, or who has been with the organization and influencing it for a very long time. This person could be the CEO, a staff member, or a member of the board of directors. Consultants working with nonprofit organizations need to assess how much influence this person has in the organization and how effective or ineffective that influence might be. For example, a founder may continue to exert his or her influence long after the organization has grown beyond the need to receive it, as is illustrated by the following example.

When we were contracting with one nonprofit organization to conduct a strategic-planning process involving diversity issues, it became clear that the key issue in the organization was the organization's transition from one CEO to the next. After several decades of leadership, the founder and CEO of the organization was having difficulty letting go. He was caught in the dilemma of how to retire while he wanted to continue to influence the future of the organization. His legacy was at stake.

It was important for this organization to address the real issue — transition to a new CEO — as an initial part of the strategic-planning process. Consultants always need to be alert to the underlying issues in an organization, so that they can be addressed. It is important to remember that there is likely to be resistance in the organization to these underlying issues, yet the goal of the consultation often cannot be achieved unless the underlying issues are confronted.

Networks and Affiliation Important

Some nonprofit organizations are actually networks for other organizations, or they consist of affiliated member organizations. This networking is a strength of much of the nonprofit world. However, it also can work against the accomplishment of diversity goals. Each of these organizations is likely to be values-driven, and the values may conflict. In one case, an umbrella organization consisted of member organizations that strongly supported the issue of reproductive rights of women, while one member organization strongly opposed this issue. The strong, values-driven stance of one member organization meant that many of the issues of women's reproductive rights could not be addressed. This created significant values-driven conflict within the organization.

Uniqueness of Faith-Based Organizations

Faith based organizations are a special category of nonprofit organizations. Their bottom line is values-based, with the focus on worship and service. Volunteers do much of the work of these organizations. The pay scale for those involved in a consulting role is often even lower than in nonprofit organizations. Many local religious congregations expect *pro bono* consultant work, and they often get these services from their members. This often results in uneven quality of work, and it clearly undermines any external consultant wishing to work in faith-based organizations as a career.

Many local congregations also believe that they can solve their own problems simply by being faithful to their beliefs. This often means that churches and synagogues may be in deep conflict before they are willing to consider bringing in an external consultant. Some denominations do maintain networks of consultants, and sometimes the staff in denominational offices is trained to make organization development interventions. The situation is better at the denominational or judicatory level than in parishes. At that level, the work of a consultant is more clearly understood and valued. However, there are a couple of characteristics of faith-based organizations that deserve particular attention.

The Special Role of the Clergy

Clergy hold a very special role in faith-based organizations. It is important for diversity consultants to understand this distinction. In many cases, the clergy are in a role that, in other organizations, is equivalent to the CEO, but the way in which the membership relates to the clergy is quite different. Many members expect the clergy to have holy powers, and they project even more authority on them than they would on other CEOs. Some members in local parishes believe the clergy can do no wrong. When the clergy *are* perceived as being or doing wrong, the emotional issues raised can become highly exaggerated. The following example of an organization development consultation that we facilitated will illustrate the special role of the clergy as well as the way diversity issues become a part of the needed interventions — even when they are not are not presented as the initial issue.

This consultation took place in a local congregation of a main-line denomination over a period of approximately nine months. We were contacted by a member of the board of deacons, which was trying to resolve a conflict within the congregation. The presenting conflict was between the pastor and the minister of music. This is often a point of contention within Protestant congregations, since the music program and the pastoral program may not have the same aim, and each usually has a strong following. Being aware of this, and of the fact that all conflicts have multiple perspectives, we wanted to be sure that we had direct access to both the pastor and the minister of music. We talked with both of them before we entered into the contract.

We also needed to know which levels of the organization the contract included. Since this local church had a congregational form of government, we asked that our contract be with the church congregation. We wanted to be sure that we had the authorization of the church to carry on the work of facilitating transformation of the conflict. We used the term "conflict transformation" rather than "conflict resolution" or "conflict management" to enhance our desire to use the energy involved in the conflict for positive purposes.

There were multiple aspects of this consultation, and we will not describe all of them here. However, we will highlight the work that was done with the pastor and the specific diversity issues that were involved. The church was part of a denomination that welcomed gays and lesbians. The current pastor was homosexual, and the congregation was predominantly heterosexual. The people who contacted us indicated that issues related to heterosexism were not part of the conflict. We accepted this at face value, and we kept our eyes and ears open to test this assumption of the leaders of the church. The consultation consisted of several thrusts. First, we interviewed the pastor and the minister of music to determine their perspectives. Second, as the consultation proceeded, we interviewed selected members of the congregation and provided the opportunity for others to offer their perspective of the conflict. We met with groups, such as the choir and the Board of Deacons. We always remained alert to the various levels of the conflict that were likely to be present. We held educational meetings about conflict, to help the members become aware of their reaction to conflict. As we reported our findings, first to groups and finally to the whole congregation, our aim was to keep the intervention transparent and informative.

Early in the intervention, the minister of music decided to resign. It was clear that this resignation would not be helpful in facilitating the transformation of the conflict within the church. In fact, it made the problems more complicated and focused more attention on the pastor. We decided, and the congregation concurred, that it was important for the consultation to continue. The pastor had indeed functioned in a way that had created displeasure on the part of some members of the congregation. The pastor collected both realistic and unrealistic expectations from the congregation and became the lightning rod for anyone's dissatisfaction. Our way of working with the pastor was to provide coaching on the effect of the pastor's behavior. This was done with videotaped simulations conducted away from the church. The pastor's contributions to the conflict were eventually acknowledged, and more important, change in behavior began to occur. Although this conflict escalated for too long before the church decided to ask for outside help, the pastor was able to regain the confidence of the congregation and to continue with the work of pastoring.

The diversity concern that became clear as the consultation progressed was the depth of the issues related to sexual orientation. During the years before the current pastor came to serve at this church, the church had made a clear commitment to being open and affirming to gays and lesbians. There had been open conflict over this issue at an earlier time, when a homosexual pastor was invited for an interview without the congregation being informed of the pastor's sexual orientation. The search committee knew the pastor was homosexual, but it was not announced to the congregation before the pastoral role began. The pastor's existence in the broader community divided the community and led to violence, such as rocks thrown through the parsonage windows. There was also conflict within the congregation. This was finally resolved with a vote to support the pastor and to welcome gay and lesbians as a part of the congregation. Some members left the church. However, the solid majority stayed and openly welcomed gays and lesbians.

In recent years, more gays and lesbians had joined the church. When we were conducting the consultation, about the same number of heterosexual and homosexual new members were joining the church. In fact, a number of gays and lesbians were in responsible positions in the church. When we conducted our confidential interviews, we found that all members of the congregation were united in their stand of supporting a welcoming posture toward gays and lesbians. However, a deeper level of homophobia became apparent. It was not stated, but it was present. Some of the heterosexual members of the congregation were concerned not about being open and welcoming to gays and lesbians, but about seeing the congregation become a church in which they might soon be a minority. When this concern was publicly raised in open meetings with members of the church, all embraced the idea of an integrated church, although they had never openly addressed this. In fact, the gays and lesbians made it clear that they did not want the church to be all gay and lesbian. The real issue was the shift of power from mostly heterosexual leadership to a mixed leadership. The diversity issue was centered on how to make the transition from a church that was welcoming of others to one that was willing to be influenced by all, including the gays and lesbians. We believe that the congregation reached a new level of awareness of what it means to embrace an oppressed group and become more truly diverse, at least in connection with that social-identity group.

Strongly Held Values and Beliefs

Faith-based organizations are the organizations with the most strongly held values and beliefs. As was true for other nonprofit organizations, values and beliefs are a driving force toward creating a more truly diverse organization. Also, as was illustrated earlier, strongly held values and beliefs can prevent organizations from becoming empowering for all. It is important for diversity professionals working with faith-based organizations to be aware of the opportunities to capitalize on the diversity value that is held by the organization. The following intervention briefly illustrates an effort that capitalized on diversity values to truly bring a marginalized group into the mainstream. This intervention took place in a regional judicatory of a mainline Protestant denomination.

The regional judicatory had been actively involved in the civil-rights movement and had taken a strong stand on civil rights over a number of decades. The judicatory had a strong affirmative action program, but the number of black women in positions of power was small. There were many reasons for this. For one thing, there were a number of strong black pastors in the predominantly black churches in the judicatory who held a tight control of the leadership in those churches. Women were valued for their service, but they were not encouraged to become church leaders. Many of the women felt that their presence was a threat to the black male pastors. It was also true that the black women lacked the leadership training that might prepare them to move into positions of power and influence.

The intervention that was designed to address these issues was a program of leadership training and empowerment. A group of black women from different congregations was created to explore the formation of a yearlong empowerment program. A white consultant took a behind-the-scenes coaching role to help design the program and make the connections to obtain funding for the program. However, the leadership of the program came from one black woman, who provided the energy and focus for the program's success.

The program involved building a learning community that met once a month with a consultant. This learning community became the basis of support and empowerment for the women. In addition, four separate weeks of experiential training, at a training facility that specialized in the applied behavioral sciences, was required. Black females were chosen as the key leaders directly involved with the women in the program, in order to emphasize the empowerment possibilities of this identity group of black females, while most of the training was conducted with diverse teams of trainers. This highly successful program turned commitment into reality.

Throughout this intervention, the regional judicatory of the church was able to act on its strong values to reduce the racism and sexism in the church and to empower a group of black women to become important church leaders. Within a couple of years, several of the women moved into top leadership positions in both the regional and national church. It was clear that members of the group were empowered to take these roles. One region of this denomination had moved a step closer to becoming a truly diverse church.

Uniqueness of School Organizations

School organizations have some similarity to nonprofit organizations. The staffs of schools are generally motivated to do their job in difficult situations. The bottom line for schools is an "educated society." In order to achieve an educated society, schools employ paid professional staff and use volunteers to supplement the professionals. The customer or client for schools is not as clear as for many other organizations. The immediate customers are the students in the school. But the ultimate customers are the parents and the society. The pay scale for consultants in schools can be somewhat better than for nonprofit organizations, but it is ordinarily less than for the corporate world. One unique characteristic of schools is worthy of mention.

Multiple Constituencies or Stakeholders

In all organizations, it is important to consider all the stakeholders. However, when a diversity professional is working in schools, there are clearly multiple constituencies that are critical to consider. Schools are complex organizations that often can become highly bureaucratic — especially in large school systems. The various layers of the school system must all be considered when interventions are made. State and local school boards, central office staff, teachers and other professionals, and the students are all important stakeholders. However, any meaningful diversity work in schools must also involve the parents and the community. In addition, the staff, students, and community all belong to social-identity groups. Differences between these identity groups often become a point of contention. A micro-view of what it is like to work with these multiple constituencies is provided in the following example.

The setting for this example is a middle school in a large suburban school system. The school is located in what has been an affluent, primarily white neighborhood of highly educated and actively involved parents. As is typical, white parents who were most active and comfortable in this setting controlled the parent-teacher-student association (PTSA). As the demographics of the neighborhood changed, and more African American, Hispanic, and Asian American families settled in this area, the disparity between the racial and ethnic makeup of the parents involved with the school and the diversity of the neighborhood increased. In order to address this situation, a new African American principal at the middle school encouraged the formation and development of a separate parent's group for African American parents. This provided the opportunity for African American parents to join together in a comfortable way. This same opportunity was provided for Hispanics. The smaller number of Asian American families did not form a separate parents' group, and their lack of engagement was still at issue. In an attempt to create a more fully diverse school community, an intervention was designed to integrate these three groups. The first step of the intervention was to bring the leaders of the African American and Hispanic parents, called parent advocates for their social-identity groups, onto the executive committee of the PTSA. Then the PTSA executive committee, including the parent advocates for the African American and Hispanic parents, decided to conduct a joint meeting of their three groups in a diversity workshop. The diversity workshop was intended to begin the journey down the long road toward increased understanding, acceptance, and valuing of the diversity of the community. It is critical to work with all the diverse constituencies at their level of readiness for involvement. It is also important to remember that the process of differentiation must occur before integration is possible.

Uniqueness of Community Work

Diversity work in communities certainly involves all the same issues that are present anywhere in our society. Often the work in communities is done through nonprofit or faith-based organizations, such as we have already discussed. However, there are a few aspects of communities that are important considerations for the diversity professional working directly in communities. Perhaps the most important one is the fact that communities are much more amorphous than organizations. They lack the clear structure of an organization, with its clear roles and boundaries. With communities, the boundaries are loose, and the structure is often ill-defined. Also, within communities, there are very different concepts of leadership and of the source of authority. Both of these unique aspects are discussed in the following sections.

Loose Boundaries and Structure

In a community setting, it is often difficult to know where to begin diversity work. The loose boundaries and lack of clear structure make it very difficult, if not impossible, to work with an entire community of any size. Most often, diversity professionals work through community-based organizations, such as the local government, the schools or churches, or one of the many other civic organizations that comprise the civil society. However, whatever the choice, there is always the difficulty that working through one organization will shape whatever intervention or work is done in a way that rules out other groups, options, and opportunities.

A community-organizing approach can be used to raise issues in an attempt to develop a community that fully encompasses valuing diversity. The work of the community organizer is quite different from the usual role of the diversity consultant functioning within the framework of internal and external organization-development consultation. Community organizing is particularly effective in confronting specific issues of injustice to one segment of the community.

It is possible to use the skills of the organization-development diversity consultant to frame a diversity program and/or intervention in a community. The following description is instructive in indicating how one group of citizens working with diversity professionals addressed the issues in one community. This initiative occurred in Silver Spring, Maryland, an inner suburban area of Washington, DC, in the USA. Silver Spring is an unincorporated section of Montgomery County, Maryland. If it were incorporated, it would be the second largest city in Maryland. As happens in many inner suburbs, the downtown area had significantly declined during the previous several decades. After a number of years of false starts, an economic redevelopment plan was formulated, and by 1999, the process of renewal of the physical space downtown was underway.

The economic redevelopment had effectively made use of a citizens' advisory committee, and, as the work of that advisory committee was coming to a close, some of the members became concerned about how to develop the Silver Spring community as an empowered diverse community. One of the major issues was that different ethnic and racial groups, including new immigrants to the United States, were settling in Silver Spring, but the power structure remained mostly white. In addition, the separate racial and ethnic groups tended to be isolated from each other. Concerned citizens decided they would try to rectify this, but the question was how to proceed. They established an informal committee to decide how to shape Silver Spring in a way that would put a human face on the physical and economic redevelopment. The committee represented some of the diversity of Silver Spring, with white, African American, and Hispanic members. They collaborated with a diversity professional as they met, over weekly breakfasts for many months, to determine their direction. There were many ideas — and plenty of conflicts — about how to proceed. Following are some of the questions that were asked:

- ✦What is the vision of an empowered diverse Silver Spring?
- ✦What kind of intervention would be appropriate for addressing the issues involved?
- ✦What kind of structure or organization would be appropriate to carry out any intervention?
- ✦Should the group work through an existing organization, or establish a new separate nonprofit organization?
- ✦Should the work be primarily empowering or advocacy?

The informal committee decided to focus on creating the empowered diverse community through connecting the existing leadership and the emerging leadership of various specific ethnic and racial groups. It was decided that this would require leadership training. This raised a set of additional questions:

- ✦Who should be the target for the leadership training?
- ✦Should the focus for training be on the grassroots leadership

of specific ethnic or racial groups?
- Should whites be included in the training program?

Behind each question were differing, strongly held opinions and many pros and cons. When members of the group finally reached a consensus, they decided to form an independent nonprofit organization, originally called the Silver Spring Community Leadership Initiative (SSCLI), with the following mission statement:

> *Our mission is to provide training for community members of diverse backgrounds in order to develop skills and awareness needed to share power and build relationships that cross racial, class, and cultural lines.*

A pilot experiential training program was developed, in order to bring together leaders and potential leaders from all segments of the population. This pilot program tested both content and methodology for the training during four daylong Saturday sessions that took place over a two-month period. The participants in this training program represented many of the diverse segments of the community. It was decided that the trainers/facilitators for this pilot program would be selected to represent gender and racial diversity. The volunteer team of facilitators working with the pilot consisted of a black female, a white female, a white male, and a black male from the Caribbean.

Success of the pilot program led to the development of a nine-month leadership-training program designed to develop both the awareness and skills of participants seeking to make a difference as leaders in the Silver Spring community. This program involved three two-day retreats, monthly daylong Saturday meetings, and one evening meeting per month. In order to provide a basis for the training component, a supportive learning community was developed. In addition to the training component, community projects representing the passions of the participants were implemented. This program has had numerous successes on its way to achieving the vision of an empowered diverse Silver Spring.

Attitudes toward Leadership

During the development of the Silver Spring Community Leadership Initiative described in the preceding section, an interesting cultural difference in the way in which leadership is viewed was highlighted. When the leadership-training program was first announced, several Hispanics reacted very negatively to the word "leadership." As do many other group-oriented societies and cultures, some Hispanic societal groups see the words "leader" or "leadership" in terms of something that is imposed on them. The words belong to the oppressor. A true leader is not someone who sets out to be a leader; a true leader is one who arises from the group to carry out the will of the group. To this perspective, the source of authority for the leader lies in the group, not the individual, whereas in much of the United States' society, the leader is seen as the individual who is self-directed and seeks leadership. This represents a much more individual-oriented perspective. In the United States and Europe, a strong emphasis has been placed on individuation. This emphasis on individuation means that the word "leader" carries a more positive connotation.

In the end, the training program was not called a leadership-training program; it was called the Community Empowerment and Involvement Program, the better to reach Hispanic and other group-oriented segments of the society. It is important for diversity professionals to be aware of these differing views of leadership, held by different ethnic and racial groups, when working in a diverse community.

Uniqueness of Government Agencies

Public Service Organizations

Just as in the case of nonprofit organizations, government agencies also have a different kind of bottom line from that of the corporate world. Government agencies are service-oriented organizations. This service orientation means that most government workers care about their agencies. Although there are many denigrating jokes about government work, we have generally observed a dedication to the mission of the agencies that is similar to that found in nonprofit organizations.

Government, especially large federal agencies, tends to be slow to change. In the US federal government, there is an awareness that the persons at the top are subject to change every four years. However, there is a basic commitment to diversity that transcends political changes.

One does encounter the usual range of responses to diversity work. In one agency, we found a number of senior managers who prided themselves on being dinosaurs and unwilling to change. This group of white males created a very hostile environment for women attempting to move into management positions. However, we have observed that, overall, there is a dedication in government agencies to taking diversity work quite seriously.

Motivation in Government Organizations

Since many people in government agencies are drawn to the work because they want to make a contribution, generally the motivation is not only about salary. The reality is that government workers often are not paid as much as those in the private sector. Many of these people are altruistic and are motivated by doing something they consider worthwhile.

Diversity professionals also do not command the same pay in government organizations as they do in the private sector. This is true both for external consultants and for those diversity professionals who work inside an agency. In general, the pay scale for work with government agencies is somewhere between the corporate and the nonprofit worlds.

Federal Laws and Executive Orders

Federal law protects many groups that have experienced discrimination in the workplace. Equal Employment Opportunity (EEO) emanated from the 1964 Civil Rights Act, which prevents unlawful discrimination based on race, color, national origin, religion, and sex. Later, in 1990, the Americans with Disabilities Act (ADA) added protection for the disabled. The Civil Rights Act of 1991 provides further remedies to protect against and to deter intentional discrimination and unlawful harassment in employment. In the federal government, executive order makes it unlawful to discriminate based on sexual orientation. Affirmative Action (AA) was initiated as a national policy with a programmatic thrust; it takes proactive steps to make EEO law a reality. Recently, many programs designed to promulgate valuing and managing diversity have been initiated in government agencies. It is our experience that these laws, regulations, and programs are taken especially seriously in the federal government.

Over the years, the federal government has become a good place to work for many people who have experienced discrimination in the workplace. For instance, the federal government has been better than many other organizations in protecting the rights of gays and lesbians. Those with religious differences have been able to display symbols of their faith, as long as they refrain from proselytizing in the workplace. All this makes the federal government an employer of choice for many.

In working with the federal government, we have found it important to distinguish among the three different programs: EEO, Affirmative Action, and Diversity. People often misunderstand these three programs and confuse their missions. For instance, many believe that affirmative action programs involve quotas, even though this has not been the case in the government. As white males have lost some of their privileged status, resentments have developed. The competition for recognition and promotion has increased. This is illustrated by the following anecdote.

Recently, during diversity training in a government agency, a number of males, all of them white, were sitting together at lunch, talking about their experiences in the workplace. Although all the members of this group were committed to EEO and the goals of diversity, several of them were quite vocal about their sense that their own professional careers had nevertheless suffered. It is important to help white males see that their privileged status can no longer — and should no longer — be taken for granted. Should a white male truly experience discrimination, EEO law also protects him.

There is a common impression that government employees cannot be terminated. Although the processes for termination may be slow and tedious, they work. The government is not stuck with people just because they are there. If a person abuses another person, disciplinary action can be taken. If a person is incompetent, that person can be fired. However, in the end, it is important that compliance to EEO be seen as a tool rather than a weapon.

Norms and Culture of Nonprofit, Faith-Based, and School Organizations and Government Agencies

Much of the culture of nonprofit organizations of all types, and of government agencies, is based on interpersonal relationships. The values-driven basis and service orientation of these organizations mean that the interpersonal relationships can be used as an entrée to the diversity work. Just as the basic values and motivation of persons in these organizations can be either a barrier to diversity work or a contributing force, the culture of the organizations can also be either barrier or contributing force. Working with the relationships can often be a good basis for understanding others. Interventions around teamwork can be productive. On the other hand, the culture tends to reinforce behavior that is superficially nice. Therefore, conversations that are in persons' heads and not stated deprive these organizations of much of the data that is needed to function effectively. The diversity professional is challenged to help the organization move beyond being nice.

Contracting as a Diversity Consultant in Government and Nonprofits

Contracting and entry are always a critical part of the consultation process. This is true for both internal and external consultants. However, the external consultant needs to take particular care about having a clear contract. When conducting any organization development consultation with an organization, we believe it is important always to include diversity concerns in the contracting. This can take the form of something as simple as making sure that there is adequate representation of diverse populations involved in any intervention. Or it might involve raising the unstated issues of diversity that are present. Often it involves helping the client see how diversity issues are affecting the organization. An example comes to mind.

A few years ago, we were conducting a team-building retreat with a small nonprofit organization that had been a long-term client. In preparation for the retreat, we conducted interviews to determine what were the key issues for the retreat. Contrary to expectations, during the interviews we found that many of the participants were raising deep issues of racism. When we reflected these data back to the organization, it was unwilling to address the issues at that time. Our work as consultants with this organization did not continue. Essentially, we were fired for pointing out the truth. A short time later, another consultant was hired to come in and help them sort out the racism issues.

It is important for external consultants to raise the issues, even when the client doesn't want to hear them. The integrity of the work is more important than any particular client.

Responsibility for Diversity in Nonprofit Organizations and Government Agencies

Most government agencies and schools have well-developed offices for working with the issues of diversity — especially compliance. The EEO officers have extensive data and procedures. For instance, it is easy to make a case for promotion discrimination, because the data has already been gathered. This is particularly true in the USA federal government agencies. There are also organization development offices and training sections with diversity responsibilities.

On the other hand, in nonprofit organizations the situation is mixed. Large nonprofits sometimes have well-developed EEO offices. However, small nonprofits and faith-based organizations often have no processes in place and lack the resources for dealing with issues of compliance. And there will often be no one who is specifically responsible for diversity issues.

An increasing number of nonprofit organizations are beginning to take the need for increased emphasis on diversity more seriously. For instance, Outward Bound has hired an African American in one of its local offices to increase the preparation of people of color to be trainers. The clientele of Outward Bound increasingly involves people of color, and, traditionally, the trainers have been white.

Diversity Issues in Nonprofit, Faith-Based, and School Organizations, Community, and Government Agencies

Why Diversity Work Is Critical

In nonprofit, faith-based, school, community-based, and government organizations and agencies, it is important to make the business case for diversity work. As for the rest of society, the changing demographics of our society are a compelling reason to pursue diversity work. The people served by these organizations and agencies represent an increasingly diverse population. For example, organizations such as the Girl Scouts are serving more people of color, yet the leadership is still primarily white. They have concluded that they must address this issue in order to remain viable. Fortunately, the pool of applicants for jobs in all these organizations and agencies is more diverse.

These organizations and agencies have found that the cost of settling mediated discrimination suits is greater than the cost of investing in the creation of a workplace where each individual is fully valued and able to contribute to the maximum degree. It is clear that the business case for resources for diversity interventions is just as critical for nonprofits, churches, schools, community, and government as it is for the corporate world.

There are additional reasons for making the case for diversity, besides demographics and cost. There has been disappointment in the failure of EEO and Affirmative Action to solve such workplace problems as glass ceilings in promotions and other barriers to full use of a diverse workforce. And of course the demands for higher levels of productivity in all organizations have made it a requirement that all available resources be used to the fullest possible extent.

Moving Beyond a Culture of Niceness

One of the issues for nonprofits, churches, schools, community, and government is the culture of niceness that often prevails. This sometimes creates a climate where people are not addressed in a way that will allow the full development of each individual. For example, in order to avoid possible conflict, white male supervisors often do not provide people of color and women with the feedback from that is necessary for their growth. It is important to develop a culture of honest feedback. The skills of giving and receiving feedback can be taught in workshops. The culture of niceness can transform itself into a culture of growth and productivity.

Redefining Organizations for a New Age

It is clear that the agencies and organizations of the future will be diverse. Basically, the question is how this can be seen as positive. In order to be competitive, organizations must embrace the teamwork that will be necessary for meeting challenges. Diversity work may seem risky, but it is essential.

The example of our experience with the church, cited above in the section on faith-based organizations, illustrates what it means to move beyond mere tolerance and compliance. This church had demonstrated tolerance and even openness. However, the dominant group of heterosexuals was not ready to be influenced significantly by the group of gays and lesbians. Organizations of the future need to move beyond tolerance and acceptance to the point where they are open to the contributions of all the members of society, in all their forms of diversity.

Key Aspects of Effective Diversity Work

We have found that there are a number of aspects of diversity work that are important to keep in mind while one is doing the work. Probably it is most important to be sure that diversity-training work is done with sufficient depth to make a difference. It should be part of a larger organization development effort that is addressing the systemic issues. During training, it is important that the processing be in-depth processing, not just surface reflection or — worse yet — sugarcoating. There is a constant need for diversity professionals to advocate deeper, longer, and more systemic training. We believe that it is also critical to involve diversity in the selection of teams to work together as consultants or trainers. Many training organizations, such as the NTL Institute for Applied Behavioral Sciences, have standards requiring that all training work be done in cohorts that include men, women, people of color, and whites. Finally, it is important that sufficient support systems and follow-up accompany any diversity intervention, in any organization. In the final analysis, diversity work in any setting is hard work. There will always be conflict and emotional stress. However, the diversity professionals who immerse themselves in the work can find it very rewarding.

Chapter XVIII

Diversity Leadership

Ollie Malone

The Challenge of Diversity Leadership

As this chapter is being read, the dynamics of American organizations are changing dramatically. This fact should not come as new news to any individual who has been alive and engaged in organizational life for the past 15 years. Since 1985, the term Workforce 2000 has been on the lips of countless human resource executives, line managers, and organizational executives. Briefly put, the study entitled "Workforce 2000" told American leaders that the workers whom they would be leading in the year 2000 would bear little resemblance to those workers whom they were leading in 1985.

Additionally two major national organization, Texaco in 1996, and Coca Cola in 2000, have faced judgements of greater than $175 million for their organization's inability to create environments where individuals can grow and develop with the organization and without concern for bias based on race, gender, or any other non-performance-related factors. Companies are discovering that managing diversity is essential for corporate success, corporate reputation, and corporate conscience.

For some organizations, this information came quite a bit late. In the areas of customer service and telemarketing, women and people of color were already an overwhelming percentage of the workforce—percentages that, even in 1985, exceeded what had been stated as the percentages for the year 2000.

The fundamental challenge of diversity leadership, then, is multi-fold. Among the many factors to be considered are:

A. The executive's ability to examine his or her own organization in a manner that is as clear and as bias-free as possible. By this what is meant is that each person tends to approach life based on the lenses he or she has historically worn. For the larger majority of corporate executive, the "lens" is that of a middle-class, white, anglo-saxon male. This is not a criticism, merely a statement of fact. If this factor holds true, then other factors are likely to accompany this one:

1. He is likely to have always been in the majority.
2. He is likely to have limited experience in dealing with those who are not majority members.
3. He is likely to be mystified by those experiences, factors, and points of view that are so contrary to his own.
4. He is likely to have a network of colleagues, friends, and acquaintances whose backgrounds and experiences mirror his own.
5. He is likely to conduct his entire life dealing with persons like himself—particularly in the area of race.
6. He is likely to spend very little time in the organization with people whose backgrounds and orientations are different than his own.
7. He is likely to have no significant understanding of the company-related issues that affect persons who are different from him (by race, gender, or countless other factors), and as a result may miss the opportunity to address these issues effectively. By not addressing these issues effectively, he misses the opportunity to shape both the present and the future of the organization through individuals who occupy key roles.

B. The executive's ability to influence the behaviors and actions of those who are members of his or her group. Although this topic will be examined more fully shortly, a few key questions might help to illustrate the point:

1. To what degree are the groups in which the executive is a member seen as groups that are "part of the problem" or "part of the solution?"
2. To what degree is awareness and competence in the area of diversity important for members of the group?
3. To what degree do members of this group hold each other accountable for their behavior in this area—or does the group hold to a more "boys will be boys" attitude?

C. The executive's ability to influence the behaviors and actions of the entire organization in such a way that diversity competence is clearly "on the radar screen."

1. To what degree is "competence in diversity" seen as a factor essential for those who are in leadership or for those who would aspire to be in leadership? Are people who are in the organization expected to develop competence in diversity—or is the expectation that they merely be sufficient at dodging "diversity bullets?"
2. To what degree do company orientations/assimilations , training programs, practices, procedures, communication, and policies reflect an awareness of the need for diversity competence and reflect good models of those who have these skills?
3. To what degree does the mood of the organization reflect cooperation across levels of race, gender, and other forms of difference?
4. Who sits with whom in the cafeteria? Does the internal climate of the organization merely match or reflect the external climate—or is there drive and commitment to create an internal organizational environment that is far more cooperative, inclusive, and focused than its external counterpart?

Periodically, *Fortune* magazine prints information on those who are leading American corporations and those who are the leaders-in-waiting. The list is an impressive one. Most who occupy these lists are graduates of the most prestigious schools of business, with great grade point averages, and a history of leadership in their current corporations or some other corporation. To top it all off, most of them are good-looking. They seem to have it all—right? Well, no. You see, the majority of these individuals look like those whom they will replace—they are white, they are male, they are largely from middle class backgrounds, economically and, for the most part, they have had limited experience, exposure, or understanding of those who transact some of the most fundamental aspects of their businesses: *these people touch customers.* And, unfortunately, their leadership, largely, does not have a clue as to how to touch them.

The Leader's Personal Work

In responding to the challenge of diversity leadership, the astute leader, as a leader, needs to begin examination at home—with him or herself. Such a beginning may sound overly narcissistic, yet a good portion of the current literature on leadership suggests that executives succeed or fail not based on their ability to manage finance, sales, or technology, but on their ability to manage themselves. This "inability to manage themselves" is frequently captured in such descriptions as:

- ✦The ability to act and reflect on his or her action;
- ✦The ability to "learn;"
- ✦The ability to recognize and manage his or her emotions, i.e., "emotional intelligence;

He or she needs to ask him or herself:

1. Who am I, in terms of those demographic factors that are easily-identified: by race, gender, ethnicity, age, economic status, sexual orientation, and physical stature?
2. How do these factors shape my view of the world? To what degree do I believe that most people are like me—and to what degree do I *expect* them to be like me?
3. What do I know of those in the organization—particularly those who are on the "front lines" of the organization? How would they respond to the first question—and how would their responses differ from mine?
4. What are the points of overlap between me, as a leader, and

those whom I am here to lead?

As the leader responds to these four questions, a visual representation starts to occur, as is depicted in Figure 1.

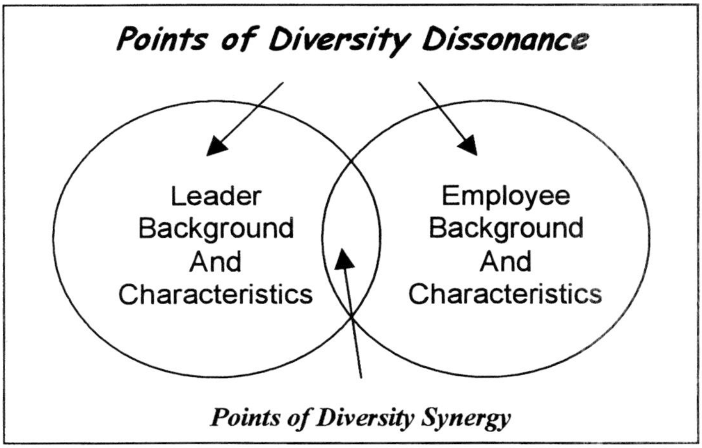

Figure 1. Leader-Employee Diversity Linkages.

After reviewing and responding to the questions listed previously, the leader might be saying, "So what, I tend to have that degree of disconnection between myself and any number of people in the organization—not just those who are different by certain demographic factors!" This is very true and it would be valid to assert that a similar disconnection exists with those individuals as it does with those who differ on these diversity-related factors. These diversity-related factors, however, are more problematic because:

1. Differences in race, gender, sexual orientation, or other demographic factors are seldom talked about in "polite" company.
2. When these topics are addressed, they are typically addressed at highly emotional levels, where little real dialogue occurs—only shouting.
3. When these topics are addressed, they are often addressed in "like" groupings: women talk with other women about men; men talk with other men about women; people with disabili-

ties talk with other persons with disabilities about those who have no obvious disabilities. The list goes on.

4. We have not learned how to hold meaningful exchanges with persons who are different from us.
5. When we have held exchanges with different others, we do so with great fear and trepidation, fearing our true incompetence will be revealed, and others will know how much of an imposter we really are.

These five areas are true for any individual who would endeavor to create a diversity-competent self. Contained in these five questions, in addition, are significant opportunities to succeed—or to fail. Just ask any number of companies who have labored or are laboring under consent decrees, significant lawsuits, impaired reputations, or all of the above. Diversity competence is costly, though largely invisible. For leaders, however, the complexity of diversity expands.

The Complexity of Diversity Leadership

To understand the complexity of diversity, it is important to create a framework. The essence of this framework is three-fold. Leadership in any organization occurs on three levels:

Level I: ***The level of self***. When asked about their leadership of diversity, many individuals respond with statements like, "I treat everyone in my organization fairly. I do not discriminate in selection, promotion, development, or affiliation decisions." In other words, "I am a good diversity do-bee." Others, who may be more self-critical, realize that they could do more, or do better in the areas where they are currently deficient. This is attention to the first level of change in the organization. This level of "self" corresponds to the questions that were asked earlier in this chapter.

Level II: ***The group level***. At the second level, the concern shifts from my individual behavior to the behavior of those who comprise a group with which I'm affiliated. If I am the head of engineering in this firm, my group might consist of "engineers." Or, If I think of my peer department heads, my "group" might be "department heads." Further, I might consider my group as being all of those individuals who are like me by race and/or gender. They might comprise my "group." Although I have only one "self," there are countless groups in which I hold membership. As a leader in the organization, my leadership is seen not only in what I do personally, but also in what I do as a member of a group. (This is where diversity leadership becomes much more difficult.)

Level III: ***The organizational level***. At the organizational level, a number of key actions occur: policies are made, practices are established, procedures are determined, and systems are put in place. These policies, practices, procedures, and systems are critical for the organization's successful operation. And they are key areas where those who would lead organizations must give attention. An example from a company that has wrestled with diversity for numerous years may help:

> During the mid-seventies, a *Fortune* 25 company maintained a policy that "in order to be promotable, you must be mobile." Translated, this meant that in order to move to the next level in the organization's hierarchy, an individual would have to be ready, upon brief notice, to pack up all of his or her worldly goods and move to another location. At first glance, such a policy seemed to make sense. By establishing this policy, the company was ensuring that it would have executives available for needed openings on short notice. This policy also was believed to be quite useful in "weeding out" those who although they were strong performers, were not true "company men or women." A closer examination of this policy, however, indicated some true unintended biases.
>
> During the period of the mid-seventies, it was quite rare to find women in key positions of leadership. Yet this company had done an excellent job of recruiting women from many of the top schools in the United States. These women were smart, they were campus leaders, they were appropriately aggressive, and they knew how to succeed in a male-dominated world. In many cases, they had also married individuals like themselves. Their spouses were doctors, lawyers, engineers, and other professionals who, like they, had careers and futures with their organizations. The problem is evident: in order for these high-potential women to advance with their organization, they would have to

commit their husbands (who were also high-potentials in their respective fields) to move wherever the company dictated. In relatively short order, many of the women were requesting to be removed from this high-potential program because of the associated policy requirement.

Was this company attempting to consciously eliminate women from its ranks of leadership? Most likely not—at least at a conscious level. This company had been quite up-front about its goals of moving women and people of color into leadership and believed that this high-potential program would be a great vehicle for doing so.

Effective diversity leadership at this third level examines the company's policies, practices, procedures and systems to ensure that they neither consciously nor unintentionally discriminate against any individual.

The Leader's Group Work

For most white males, the notion of "group membership" is a foreign one. Most white men do not see themselves as members of groups necessarily; more often than not, they consider themselves as individuals. Women and people of color, more often than not, tend to hold a greater understanding of what it means to be a member of a group. As one woman once stated, "When I apply for a position and I am turned down, I often wonder if the turn-down was as a result of not being suited for the position, not "hitting it off" with the interviewer, or my being a woman. I just don't know..."

As an elightened member of a group, however, the leader holds numerous opportunities to impact the organization and the people in it. By way of review, some of the groups to which the leader may be a member include those that are listed below. This list is not intended, by any means, to be an exhaustive one. Rather, it is an attempt to capture a sufficient number of groups so that the reader can better grasp the concept of "group membership." Some of these group memberships may include:

- The group of senior leaders of the company;
- The group of those who make over "X" thousands of dollars each year;

- ✦ The group of persons who enjoy a certain type of activity (i.e., going to the symphony, eating out at a certain restaurant).
- ✦ The group of those who live in a certain area of town;
- ✦ The group of those who worship at a particular place of worship;
- ✦ The group of those who play a particular sport (golf, tennis, etc.) at a particular location (country club, private club).

Again, these lists of groups are not exhaustive, but consideration of these groups may help the individual to see how narrowly defined his or her world is and how often his or her world excludes those who may be different by race and/or gender.

And in a manner similar to the leader's own work, the leader also encourages a climate where others who are members of his or her group also asks the types of individual questions that the leader has been asking him or herself. Competence at the level of the group is measured not only by the things that the group does at an overt, open, "available-to-the-public" level, but also at a level where the group member's action may not be as visible to those outside of the group (i.e., "locker room conversations").

The Leader's Organizational Work

At the level of the organization, the leader's work includes developing a panoramic view of the condition of the company. This panoramic view needs to be sufficiently slow and sufficiently in-depth so that the executive might be able to see things he or she previously was unable to see.

As an organizational leader, the individual must concern him or herself with the culture of the organization, particularly as it affects those who are "different." It is through the culture, that the executive is either going to succeed or is going to fail miserable because he or she has never addressed key issues to such a degree that a stake is placed in the ground and the organization knows that is expected of it.

Some of the key issues suitable for the executive's examination include:

- ✦ Who's "in" and who's "out" in this organization?
- ✦ To what degree is one's "in-ness" or "out-ness" based on race,

gender, or other non-performance-related factors.

- How do those leaders below me in the organization respond to issues that are diversity-related? Do they address issues quickly and definitively or do they wait and see what happens? If these individuals do not address diversity-related issues openly and honesty, is there a climate in the organization that would clearly make it "not OK" to say things that would be derogative toward one group or another?
- If an event occurs in the organization that is in clear violation of the principles that the company has determined it wants to live by, what is the result and what are the consequences? Do people (including the leaders) speak up for those things that are a part of who it says it wants to be? Are there consequences for violating a clear principle of the organization's existence?
- Do any of the current policies, practices, and procedures create hurdles and expectations that are more difficult for one group than another?

Dig Deep

In building diversity leadership competence, the executive needs to examine multiple factors before he or she is able to declare a victory. Often the executive assumes that because lawsuits have been reduced, or because there has been no significant upheaval, the organization is doing well. This is not necessarily the case. Often issues of diversity are not brought to the surface because the belief of the parties in question is that the executives neither understand nor care about their issues, consequently it is far easier to take their concerns to a lawyer (who makes his or her business being concerned), the EEOC (ditto the lawyer) or to the news media (three for three). But this need not be the case. By creating and managing systems for employee input, feedback, problem solving and action planning, the executive can lead his or her organization in such a way that the interventions of third parties can be dramatically reduced if not altogether eliminated.

Adopting a New View

The executive an build a greater level of organizational competence in diversity by concerning himself with multiple factors and, as a part of the diversity competence building system, ensuring that mechanisms are in place to monitor these factors. The factors include:

1. **Individual, group and organizational *behaviors*.** How do individuals who are different behave toward one another? In the organizational setting, is there healthy and productive exchange among those who may be different from one another? Or does the organization reflect predictable groupings based on race, gender, age, department, or other factors?

2. **Individual, group, and organizational *skills*.** Do people in this organization have the skills to work effectively across levels of difference? Some of the key skills include: skills of giving and receiving feedback, problem solving skills, skills of developing effective levels of dialogue on issues of difference, skills of recognizing, appreciating, and celebrating differences, and skills of leveraging differences in such a manner that the organization is better off as a result of these differences.

3. **Individual, group, and organizational *attitudes*.** How do people who are different from one another speak about one another? Is the tone used in reference to other groups an inclusive one? Do people see themselves as members of the same team, despite the fact that their roles, responsibilities, and compensation may be different?

4. **Individual, group, and organizational *beliefs*.** What seem to be the pre-verbal thoughts about other persons in the organization? Often the beliefs of one group toward another is not spoken. This becomes particularly true in the world of political correctness. Nevertheless, the real beliefs toward another group may be clearly observed. How do members of various groups look at one another? Do they greet one another in a friendly way, even though they may not be close working colleagues? How does the organization as a whole respond to those outside who may be different from the mainstream group?

5. **Individual, group, and organizational** ***core values***. At its heart of hearts, what does your organization believe? Does the organization's vision and mission stand as tributes to its creative writing ability—or are there "teeth" in these statements? Have the people of the organization taken these statements, and any others like them, to heart in such a way that there is an expectation that the organization will be come highly effective in living out these values?

Putting it All Together

Having examined the organization on the multiple levels listed above, executives should now concern themselves with creating, sponsoring, and implementing initiatives that weave diversity competence into the fiber of the organization's existence. This does not necessarily require millions of dollars in training or diversity consultation, but it will suggest that the company engage in some of the following activities:

At the organizational level:

- ✦ Reviewing the current vision and mission statements to determine the "goodness of fit" with a diversity competent culture. Do these statements capture an inclusive spirit of the organization? Is it clear that every individual, regardless of race, gender, age, organizational level, or ethnicity is an important contributor to the organization's overall success?
- ✦ Review of the organization's current communication tools (print, video, web) to examine whether or not the messages provided to the readers reflect an inclusive organization. This is not simply keeping tally on the number of non-white faces are included in the annual report, but in determining if the messages and images included reflect the whole organization, not just the "convenient" parts.
- ✦ Review of the organization's policies, practices, procedures, and systems, to determine if these are fair, unbiased, and equally accessible to all. If educational benefits are provide to employees, are they available to all employees? If they are not, are all employees equally disenfranchised, or do certain

groups suffer more at the lack of inclusion than do others?

At the group level:

- ✦ Reviewing "special project teams" or other high visibility groups to determine the makeup of these groups. Does the organization have a "go to" group that is always called upon for such opportunities? Or are these opportunities open to those who may be equally qualified but less known than others? This one arena, in particular, can help to not only identify new members of specialized teams, but also develop new talent for the organization.
- ✦ Similarly, reviewing those who are on "high-po" programs. Are the members of these groups all white men? All white women? All golfers? Are there others within the organization with similar levels of skills who never seem to make it to these lists?
- ✦ Reviewing the "informal" make up of the organization. In company gatherings, do participants have a level of comfort in mixing with others of other departments, or do there seem to be invisible walls around groups of participants? If there are such boundaries, there may be numerous opportunities to restructure these artificial boundaries so that there is the essential cross-pollination that will strengthen the organization and broaden organizational competence on multiple levels.

At the individual level:

- ✦ Reviewing individuals' performance and potential appraisals (assuming these are a part of the organization's human resource process) to determine if individuals are being provided feedback on their ability to address issues of diversity. If there is an expectation that leaders develop competence in diversity, then there must be also the associated coaching so that this competence can be internalized.
- ✦ Reviewing training programs to determine if issues of "difference" are included as a part of the focus. This is not to suggest that there must be countless courses in "managing diversity" but it does suggest that courses that look at such topics

as customer service, marketing, sales, and leadership, should also include attention to the issues of difference and how these issues affect success or lack thereof.

- Listening attentively in meetings or in other interactions to determine if issues of difference are spoken about and if individuals are coached in appropriate behaviors. This coaching does not necessarily require the leader to be the only coach, but that employees are coaching one another—and if there is a general expectation that persons will do those things that will result in an environment where every individual present is recognized, valued, and expected to contribute his or her best.

In Summary

The bottom line of all that has been discussed in this chapter comes back to the chapter's title—Diversity Leadership.

Diversity Leadership, in a manner similar to other forms of leadership, requires no special "silver bullet." It does require individuals—men, women, black, white, brown, yellow, red, short, tall, gay, straight, able-bodied, disabled, who will create an organization where others who are like them as well as those who are not, are welcomed, included, challenged, and rewarded.

This organization creation requires the willing to be able to ask tough questions—and to answer these questions honestly. Having gained greater levels of information and knowledge about the organization, the leader now must move forward with fearlessly addressing issues essential for success for all.

Such leadership will require a level of leadership courage that has not been widespread in organizations to date. This courage is not easily taught, but it is much more easily "caught" as the would-be courageous see the actions of those in the organization with the fortitude to do the right thing. Ultimately the cycle of diversity leadership and courage is self-reinforcing. It will create organizations that are stronger, more profitable, and better able to handle the challenges of an uncertain future.

Chapter XIX

Visioning for Inclusive Organizations

T. Herbert Stevenson

Defining The Vision

An organizational vision is a shared image or picture that represents what will happen or what will be different in the world just because the organization exists and is successful. These visions are worded in the present tense so that the future seems to be happening in the moment. They can overtly describe the emotional benefits of achieving the vision, but more often, the emotional benefits are left implicit to accommodate possible differing responses from each individual (Carver, 1997; Campbell, 1997).

Martin Johnson (1999) states that in a leadership context, a company's *vision* "is generally used to describe a form of organizational vision that wins the commitment and compliance of those people who are needed to implement it" (p. 336). Research indicates that to be effective, such a vision will incorporate "a visual image of a future state," a "concept of sharing in the creation and development of the vision," and the "personal values of the participants," altogether providing "beneficial effects" for everyone concerned. Johnson also maintains that the successful organizational vision is characterized by several particular qualities, listed below:

1. It shows a future achievement aim that can be readily visualized.
2. It receives contributions from a variety of sources.
3. It attracts the involvement of individuals with the specialist skills needed.
4. It can be communicated easily and in detail.
5. It is powerfully motivational in effect.
6. It intends to serve an important need for other people.
7. It is in accordance with the personal values of the prospective suporters. (p. 337)

Vision Components

Jones and Kahaner (1995) report that "mission statements—sometimes called value statements, credos, or principles—are the operational, ethical and financial guiding lights of companies. They are not simply mottoes or slogans; they articulate the goals, dreams, behavior, culture, and strategies of companies more than any other document" (p. ix). Organizations commonly also have a statement of vision that complements the mission statement, and that conveys how the organization will create and implement the vision. The vision statement is the formal document that includes the desired future explained in the mission statement, a glossary of key terms, and a set of guiding or core values that support the mission statement (Wall, Sobol, & Solum, 1992, pp. 32-33).

Symbolic Meaning

Symbolic representation of the vision's implicit values can be very powerful. Corporations invest heavily in the development of corporate symbols that convey the desired meaning of the corporate vision and mission. "The Rock," for example, exemplifies the strength and stability of the Prudential company. The symbol is peculiar to the organization; it both distinguishes the organization from all others (Abrahams, 1995), and establishes a shared base of special meanings throughout the organization. Even though the symbolic representation of the vision statement will have a certain power or attraction unique to the individual, every individual within the organization will nevertheless also have a shared or common understanding that may not be expressed in words beyond the vision statement itself. The people who share this understanding create a community comprised of many different individuals held together by common meaning (Lewis, 1997).

One of the most powerful "vision statements" in Native American lore is the story of the White Buffalo Calf Woman (see Appendix.) The Woman is an image representing transformation and living in balance with the laws of nature, and this image and its essential meaning have been shared among indigenous tribes and nations for many centuries. Although each storyteller of the White Buffalo Calf Woman will individualize the tale in small ways, the core story and symbolic essence is maintained, regardless of who tells it. Similarly, an organization's vision statement—composed of future vision, mission, and core values—is the primary source of and force for meaning-making throughout the organization—the "tribe," as it were. The vision statement creates simultaneously a special organizational identity and a common fund of shared meanings and understanding among the members.

Core Values

Over the last few decades, the characteristic of common meanings and understanding has become the touchstone for development of the organizational vision, leading to the conscious development of core values that support the organization's vision of how it hopes to be in the world. "Collectively," Kriger and Hanson (1999) explain, "value systems provide an inner, often invisible, governance system which can allow individuals and their organizations to stay on course in turbulent times" (p. 302). More basically, "[c]ommon values are the glue which binds an organization together; they motivate and create a sense of community" (Brytting & Trollestad, 2000, p. 55).

The current business climate of intense competition and rapid environmental changes generates a number of dilemmas for the creation of an inclusive and supportive vision statement for the organization at large. "No individual," assert Kriger and Hanson, "is in a job without conflicting demands—for innovation and stability, for quality and efficiency, for goal clarity and flexibility, for short-term results and long term effectiveness" (p. 302). At the same time, many organizations have concluded that if the organization doesn't "stand for something" as made evident through a coherent set of organizational values, the public image and internal assumption will be that it "stands for nothing." As the conditions that supported monolithic corporations in aggressive pursuit of single-market dominance and exclusive profits collapsed, the need for financially agile, structurally flexible, and employee-oriented organizations became clearer, as did the correlative concept that the "'right' human relationships are essential for effectiveness in our work systems" (Kriger & Hanson, p. 305). In other words, organizational success is dependent upon organizational values that reinforce the social meaning and purpose of the organization, and that convey a deep concern for the employees as individuals (Kouzes & Posner, 1995).

Visioning Processes

The visioning processes chosen tend to mirror internal structures in the organization. If the existing power structure is Active-Directed, the vision will be developed in detail and its implementation carefully controlled. If the power structure is open and undirected, the vision will be allowed to emerge from and be adapted during a number of open-ended procedures.

Methods of Awareness

Developing an organizational vision involves creating or surfacing an awareness of a new possibility for organizational existence. In terms of technique, the process typically entails either an *Active-Directed awareness* or an *Open-Undirected awareness.* Active-Directed awareness is a common vision development strategy that depends heavily on prescripted interview questions and protocols for selected individuals, aimed at crafting a vision statement that captures a consensus at the top. Open-Undirected awareness, in contrast, permits greater leeway in interview queries and styles, and favors delaying the formulation of a final "statement" in order to explore the client system as deeply and broadly as possible. Whereas Active-Directed awareness begins with an attachment to drafting and then steering the organization towards a particular outcome, Open-Undirected awareness seeks an outcome that arises "organically," so to speak, from within. Nevertheless, neither form of awareness is preferable over the other; rather, "good practice dictates moving back and forth..., keeping one's boundaries as open as possible to receive any and all data from self and other" (Nevis, 1987, pp. 110-111, 116). Table 1 presents a schematic comparison of these two approaches.

Awareness Process	
Active Directed Awareness	**Open-Undirected Awareness**
Goes to the world	Lets the World Come to you
Forces something to emerge	Waits for something to emerge
Uses Structures/frameworks to guide what you wish to see, hear etc.	Investigate without being organized or "prejudiced" in any way as to what you wish to see hear, etc.
Focuses questioning strives for a narrow, sharp field of vision	Is naive about how things work, hopes to find something new about how things work
Attends to things in terms of knowledge of how they work, what is present and missing in a normative sense	Is naive about how things work, hopes to find something new about how things work
Searching of sensory modalities	Receptive use of sensory modalities
Supports work by Content values and conceptual biases	Values process-oriented, tend to be content free

Table 1. Comparison of Awareness Processes
(From Nevis, P. 111)

Active-Directed Approach

Developing an organizational vision through an Active-Directed approach is a well established methodology. An individual or a team develops a vision statement, which usually includes a mission statement and/or a set of core values. This vision statement may be based primarily on intuition and personal knowledge of the organization and its external environment; or it may be derived from extensive research into organizational strengths and weaknesses, the competition (if applicable), and the external environment, including the economic, political, and social climates. Once the vision is developed, it is shared with other individuals for review, revision, and/or acceptance. In some organizations, this process may involve officers and directors; in other organizations, it may involve all levels of management; and in still others, it may involve representation from all ranks within the organization (Abrahams, 1995; Carver, 1997; Nanus, 1992; Wall, Sobol, & Solum, 1992). Generally, the Active-Directed approach is considered a top-down or management-first approach to visioning.

Open-Undirected Approach

Harrison Owen (1997a; 1997b) has brought the Open-Undirected form of the visioning process into modern organizational meetings through his conception of *Open Space Technology.* Owen has converted the creation of sacred space from spiritual traditions into an effective and innovative meeting format that can overcome conflict and systemic resistance. The format moves the focus of the meeting to the highest level of creativity by including the most lowest common denominators: people.

Similarly, David Cooperrider realized that the Active-Directed approach to organizational visioning was predisposed to focusing on "what is wrong" within the organization. He attributed this predisposition to the inculcated problem-solving mentality of the scientific method, which tends to ignore the "what is working," "what has gone well,", and the "what does not need to be fixed" components of the organization. In other words, the organization needs to be refocused from an analytic critique of organizational failures to a more supportive, more optimistic understanding of behaviors within the organization at large. Copperrider seeks to harness untapped creative energies by redirecting attention away from object-relations and problem-solving towards an *Appreciative Inquiry* into organizational stories of success. A sense of community is created through such an inquiry, as common themes and imaginative outlooks are discovered and put to positive use. The end result is a new perspective on the organization and of what is possible (Cooperrider & Dutton, 1999; Cooperrider & Whitney, 1999; Cooperrider, et al., 2000).

Tapping into the power of the possible is also Weisbord's aim in promoting common ground in his *Future Search.* Assuming that people want to feel good about what they do and that the real solutions lie within the individuals in the organization, Weisbord contends that behavioral and conceptual polarities and patterns are potent barriers to organizational growth. When people are encouraged and empowered to see beyond their old ways by assuming responsibility for their future, significant change occurs. Hence, the future search is a search for a common future (Weisbord, 1992; Weisbord & Janoff 2000).

Dannemiller Tyson Associates' (2000) *Whole Scale Change* brings together the heads and hearts of large numbers of people to engender change. The primary focus is to create a shared, compelling picture that is supported and preserved through individuals' commitment. People commit themselves to developing and nurturing an inspiring vision of *what could be.*

These applications of the Open-Undirected awareness model to develop an organizational vision statement share a notable readiness to discover and work with less overt or practical aspects of human behaviors, including spirituality and a sense of higher purpose. While practiced in present-day corporate America, Open-Undirected awareness applied in the service of an organization's serious search for a coherent, motivating vision bears strong resemblances to the centuries-old vision quests of indigenous peoples and religious leaders. As a process, Open-Undirected awareness relies on what is within people, seeking to develop the vision from internal resources, although it can also incorporate the findings of the various qualitative and quantitative—"scientific"—research methods. A Native American description of the relationship between awareness and scientific methods in seeking a vision suggests a deeper perspective, however:

> In the Turtle Mountains, North Dakota, Harry Boise...was with me eight months. At his request, I allowed him to teach the old Chippewa and Cree Indians there the modern scientific attitude with its view of things.... The chief among his pupils was old Sakan'ku Skonk (Rising Sun).... But Rising Sun, speaking the conclusion of all, pronounced "the scientific view" inadequate. Not bad, or untrue, but inadequate to explain, among many other things, how man is to find and know a road along which he wishes and chooses to make this said progress unless the Great Manitou by his spirit guides the mind of man, keeping human beings just and generous and hospitable. (Deloria, 1996, p. 38)

Vision Questing

Corporations and organizations generally follow an Active-Directed awareness model to develop vision statements, but it is a model that often excludes significant areas of human experience with regard to internal, informal organizational structures and behaviors. When an Open-Undirected awareness is employed, organizational visioning comes nearer to being what Native Americans understand to be vision questing, and certain important and suggestive human experiences converge in both these processes.

Riddington (1996) suggests that the Native American visioning tradition is part of a recognizable world view with relation to spiritual needs and communal harmony. Individuals, for example, may become aware of a loss of spiritual purpose or self-realization, and lose a sense of place in the family, the community, and the world. At the group (or organizational) level, the tribe seeking a vision acknowledges with humility that it lacks the clarity of purpose as a community that ensures a sound future for the next several generations. Whether within an individual or a community, the visioning process in the Native American tradition encompasses fourteen principles. These fourteen principles, furthermore, are implicit in organizational visioning processes that use the Open-Undirected approach, whether in the form of Open Space Technology, Appreciative Inquiry, Future Search, or Whole-Scale Change.

Fourteen Fundamental Principles

The fourteen fundamental principles below are Zen-like in their presentation in that they may seem enigmatic and filled with paradoxical riddles, but when assessed and practiced as a whole, the principles enable a quality of insight into self and other that is more than the sum of its parts. This broader and deeper sense of understanding begins the process of reawakening an awareness of relational perception that has been overshadowed by conventional analytic problem solving.

One: Visioning is a personal process that is begun in isolation; however, it is fundamentally conversational and social.

Implicit to this principle is that we are never truly alone. Even in isolation, we are accompanied by internal thoughts and compelling pictures of one's self. These thoughts and pictures lose their power to dictate how to see the world, however, when they are extracted from the social and cultural environments that initially gave them their authoritative meanings. Still, the individual's self-removal from the external environment is temporary; the intention is to return, to make the reverse transition that brings him or her once more into relatedness, but with deeper insights and new conceptions of possibilities. In corporate organizations, this transition could show itself as a shift from dictates to curiosity, from argumentative discussions to open dialogues.

Two: Even though it may seem that nothing is happening at the time, the experience itself changes the person, group, and/or organization.

The vision questing process encourages distancing oneself from "normal," everyday vision; it inspires a sense of having opened one's eyes for the first time. Initially, personal and social constructs of what constitute "reality" cloud the individual awareness of "what is." Yet as the questing principles disrupt these constructs by breaking perceptual mirrors of the past, a new, broader way of perceiving evolves. Often, this experience of moving beyond the mundane brings with it a deep, internal knowing that surfaces through the creation or emergence of compelling internal pictures, similar to the deep sense of self a child experiences when lucidly day-dreaming about his or her future—as a jet pilot, perhaps, or a champion of the community, or a time-traveler.

Three: The experience enables us to become more of who or what we are, and therefore changes how we are in the world.

Questing allows our innermost qualities to surface within our awareness, and therefore within our day-to-day world. This surfacing and embrace of the deepest and perhaps most hidden integral elements of personality and character correlates to the fundamental principle of the Paradoxical Theory of Change, which postulates that the more fully we are able to be who we already are, the more we will change.

Four: Visions come to children, and to adults who can make themselves like children.

This principle echoes Dannemiller's Whole-Scale Change premise to bring open-mindedness together with open-heartedness. This "child-like," passionate world is one wherein judgment is suspended and playfulness is possible, even necessary. It is that place where "what is" is defined through moment-by-moment experience instead of through various pre-existing internal constructs or through dictates from the outside and from the past.

Five: Vision comes when we are humble and pitiable.

Vision questing in its earliest form has been called "crying for a vision" and "lamentation." More recently, vision questing is described as being receptive and vulnerable, being at the boundary of oneself, or making contact with the Self or Other at the edge of discomfort. These characteristics mark a place where the veiled defenses of how *to be* in the world are lifted—like the moment just before one acknowledges that the emperor has no clothes.

Six: Vision's power comes as we listen to our own, internal stories.

We all carry within us domineering voices from the past as well as the unwritten yet indelibly known rules of being a member of a family, a community, or an organization. Gestalt theory refers to these internal constraints as *introjects*—image-creating and behavior-controlling concepts that we have "swallowed whole," that is, taken into ourselves on faith or demand without our conscious and/or reasoned input. These introjects are in many ways unconnected to the present, yet they are still impacting every moment of one's life. They are personal and/or social constructs that we have maintained as ways to "do" ourselves or ways "to be." Vision questing encourages these internal stories to surface, to come into awareness. As we give voice and ear to these internal stories, older and more deeply personal stories can begin to be told and, in the process, reborn.

Seven: Vision's power comes as we learn to communicate with our deepest selves.

Our deepest self is often the site of terrible fears and "unspeakables." By allowing these two negative aspects to fully and clearly emerge, we can decide upon and release what is no longer applicable. But old dreams and hopes may also surface from these deepest selves, reminding us of a forgotten self, of who and what we really are.

Eight: Vision's power comes when we can honor those dreams that energize the very essence of who we are and how we want to be in the world.

Forgetting or repressing one's heartfelt dreams in the interest of complying with social expectations banishes and damages the soul. Remembering the dreams of the soul soothes us deeply, and reminds us of our sense of purpose and of that which creates meaning in one's life.

Nine: Vision's power comes to us when we can be open to something greater than ourselves.

In religious and highly personal terms, what is greater than ourselves is the power of God, Spirit, Buddha, or any other worshiped or revered Being. In organizational terms, the essence of this feeling of the existence of something greater than oneself is tied also to a sense of relatedness with others. In the U.S. Marines, for example, this sense is named *Esprit de Corps:* the spirit of the body of individuals sharing membership in this social, purposeful organization. The complementary action of those who share an understanding of being in relation with, and dedicated to, something greater than themselves is known as *service*.

Ten: Vision's power comes as we listen to the stories around us.

Part of the success of most large-scale change is accomplished through storytelling. Listening to the stories of others begins to open our minds and hearts, if we will only sit with the story without judgment, allowing ourselves to be aware of how the story is affecting us physically, mentally, emotionally, and spiritually. Being eager to respond immediately with our own story can distance us from the storytelling other. The story we listen to well, without judging or forecasting, can touch our heads and our hearts in unforgettable ways.

Eleven: Vision's power comes when the story of a person's life joins the circle.

Building sufficient ground for a clear and compelling picture to surface enables the person to regain a sense of community with all of mankind and with nature, and to assume responsibility for one's place in the world. As the vision of the individual surfaces and joins with others', a deep sense of belonging is engendered. Such belonging becomes the "container" that holds and protects the shared vision.

Twelve: Vision's power comes when a person realizes a story that already exists.

Often, vision is experienced as a deep knowing, akin to double loop learning or the 100th Monkey phenomenon. Although the vision is inevitably something that already exists, the awareness of it as a deep knowing is new. Much of what makes a true vision so powerful and so compelling, then, is in fact its unfolding of an awareness of what has always existed.

Thirteen: Vision's power comes when we add a new episode to that story.

The personal vision illuminates how the world is different because of one's single self, and brings us to a realization that "fate" is not what happens to us, but is what we are when we are true to ourselves. Hence, the personal vision expresses a stage of "coming into one's own," wherein the individual has stepped fully into who he or she is as a mature and contributing member of a community. The organizational vision, similarly, kindles the awareness of how the world will be different because of the organization's existence in it. The organization's visioning experience is akin to coming to understand the fullness of its existence in very basic but powerful terms—in terms of the people who will be fed, not in terms of the number of jobs provided, or in organizational quality of life, or in amount of profit gained. Vision provides exquisitely human depth to the organization.

Fourteen: Vision's power comes when the story of a person's life becomes that of life as a whole.

The questing process results in a sense of interrelatedness, captured in the Lakota phrase *Mitakye Oyasin,* which means "all one tribe" or "all my relations." This interrelatedness comes as a sense of oneness or wholeness with all facets and beings of life. It is a deep knowing that each action of each individual or organization has significant consequences for the whole of life. Such understanding shifts the focus, of the individual or of the organization, to a truly world view.

Implementation of the Fourteen Principles

The fourteen vision questing principles as a model for organizational work were tested in an organizational setting. First, the principles were used as guidelines only. As a process that investigates the avenues and manifestations of awareness- building, the Open-Undirected approach forbade trying to solidify each of the fourteen points into an exact procedure in an ordered fashion. Rather, the fourteen principles functioned more as a set of guides superimposed over the visioning process as a whole. Second, beneath these superimposed questing guides, the actual process involved used open-ended questions, free association, and dialogue. Spread over six months and approximately 10 meetings, this visioning process proved to be both challenging and fruitful.

Awareness-Building Process

During an organizational intervention of a social service agency, using an Open-Undirected approach where open-ended questions functioned as the primary awareness-building process, we noted that no written materials existed that would indicate that the agency was an African-American organization serving a predominantly African-American community. This lack conflicted with the agency's physical appearance and with the focus of its service provisions. Ornate and rich cultural and ethnocentric artifacts covered the walls, for example, and the agency housed the National Rites of Passage program.

The intervention team reviewed the idea of including cultural values in the agency's vision, mission statement, operational values, and marketing materials. The agency's Board indicated agreement that cultural teachings were a critical part of the functioning of the organization. But the directors, officers, and managers had also stated that none of the consultants in the past had suggested directly integrating cultural values into the organization's presence, and the Board similarly remarked that it had never occurred to them that the organization could incorporate these cultural values in such a broad and manifest way. I asked the officers, managers, and directors to consider a different approach to the issue: Why had none of them suggested the inclusion themselves? The group became quiet, and then one of the directors said that most of the agency funding came from white sources; the leadership had assumed the agency would have difficulty getting funding (or perhaps even lose most funding) if they insisted on expressing cultural heritage. The entire group concurred with this assessment.

I offered the observation that the range of expression between perceived black radicalism and white racism was sufficiently wide to find an effective and appropriate way to bring the cultural heritage of the organization into their self-conceptions and public perceptions. In other words, rather than a problem to be solved, an "either/or" situation where there can be only one right way, this issue was a polarity to be managed, a "both/and" situation where both poles can be true at different times (Polster & Polster, 1973; Zinker, 1978; Latner, 1986; Johnson, 1992.; Weick, 1995). The leadership acknowledged that this was possible, and committed themselves to developing a more inclusive vision statement, expanded to cover the mission statement, operating values, and marketing materials.

Visioning Process

The next step, the visioning process, was a continuation of the awareness-building process. Open-ended questions concerning the organization were asked of the participating officers, managers, and directors. The questions prodded the participants to tell the others what excited them about the agency and what excited them about their job. Stories were strongly encouraged in order to enliven and support individuals' experiences of the organization. As the stories filled the room, themes began to surface from one person to the next.

Once the group had completed the sharing, two critical discoveries were made. First, the group realized that nearly everyone in the room had brought stories that were similar to the stories of others. Second, these stories often entailed similar dreams of how each individual hoped to make a difference in the local community. The combined discoveries—shared stories and shared dreams—revealed that the agency did have a common vision of how the world could be different because the agency existed. Moreover, this common vision became even more powerful when the group realized that even though none had ever discussed intimate hopes and dreams with each other, yet each participant had carried inside them similar hopes and dreams.

In subsequent meetings, the group collaboratively developed a vision statement of how the local community would be different because this agency exists, a shared mission statement of what the agency needed to support the vision, and a set of values based on the principles of Kwanza that would support the vision and the mission.

Further Thoughts

The use of the Open-Undirected approach to organizational visioning, and the adaption of vision questing to that approach, allows the spirits of the individual, the community, and the organization to find their voices and to surface not only compelling pictures of singular meaning and motivation, but also a spacious and inspiring vision of the place of the individual, the community, and the organization in the world: an awareness and an acknowledgment that the world will be impacted by the existence of this individual, this community, this organization, and an agreement that choices need to be made about the nature of that impact. This type of visioning and questing process is inclusive, drawing deeply personal voices and images out of the silence and the dark. On these occasions, exclusiveness falls away because commonality has been found between individuals in their stories, in their dreams, and in their hopes for themselves, their community, their organization, and for the world.

References

Abrahams, Jeffrey. (1995). *The mission statement book: 301 corporate mission statements from America's top companies.* Berkeley, CA: Ten Speed Press.

Brytting, Tomas , and Claes Trollestad. (2000). Managerial thinking in value-based management. *International Journal of Value-Based Management* 13: 55-77.

Campbell, Andrew. (1997). Brief case: Mission statements. *Long Range Planning* 30 (4): 931.

Carver, John. (1997). *Creating a mission that makes a difference.* San Francisco: Jossey-Bass.

Cooperrider, David L. , and Diana Whitney. (1999). *Appreciative Inquiry.* San Francisco: Berrettt-Koehler.

Cooperrider, David, and Jane E. Dutton, eds. (1999). *Organizational dimensions of global change: No limits to cooperation.* Thousand Oaks, CA: Sage.

Cooperrider, David, Peter F. Sorenson, Diana Whitney, and Therese F. Yaeger, eds. (2000). *Appreciative Inquiry.* Champaign, IL: Stipes Publishing.

Dannemiller Tyson Associates. (2000). *Whole-scale change: Unleashing the magic in organizations.* San Francisco: Berrett-Koehler.

Deloria, Vine, Jr. (1996). If you think about it, you will see that it is true. *ReVision* (Winter): 37-44.

Johnson, Barry. (1992). *Polarity management: Identifying and managing unsolvable problems.* Amherst, MA: HRD Press.

Johnson, Martin. (1999). A feasibility test for corporate vision. *Strategic Change* 8 (Sept.-Oct.): 335-348.

Jones, Patricia, and Larry Kahaner. (1995). *Say it and live it: 50 corporate mission statements that hit the mark.* New York: Currency Doubleday.

Kouzes, James M. , and Barry Z. Posner. (1995). *The leadership challenge: How to keep getting extraordinary things done in an organization.* San Francisco: Jossey-Bass.

Kriger, Mark P. , and Bruce J. Hanson. (1999). A value-based paradigm for creating truly healthy organizations. *Journal of Organizational Change* 12 (4): 302-317.

Latner, Joel. (1986). *The Gestalt therapy book.* Highland, NY:

Gestalt Journal Press.
Lewis, C. Patrick. (1997). *Building a shared vision: A leader's guide to aligning the organization.* Portland: Productivity Press.
Nevis, Edwin. (1987). *Organizational consulting: A Gestalt approach.* New York: Gardner Press.
Owen, Harrison. (1997a). *Expanding our now: The story of open space technology.* San Francisco: Berrett-Koehler.
——. (1997b). *Open space technology: A user's guide.* 2nd ed. San Francisco: Berrett-Koehler.
Polster, Erving, and Miriam Polster. (1973). *Gestalt therapy integrated: Contours of theory and practice.* New York: Brunner/Mazel.
Riddington, Robin. (1996). Voice, representation, and dialogue: The poetics of Native American spiritual traditions. *American Indian Quarterly* 20 : 467-489.
Stevenson, Thomas Herbert. (2001). Developing a vision for a non-profit social service agency. Unpublished thesis. Cleveland State University.
Wall, Bob, Mark R. Sobol, and Robert S. Solum. (1992). *The mission driven organization.* Roseville, CA: Prima Publishing.
Weick, Karl E. (1995). *Sensemaking in organizations.* Thousand Oaks, CA: Sage.
Weisbord, Marvin R. (1992). *Discovering common ground.* San Francisco: Berrett-Koehler.
Weibord, Marvin R. , and Sandra Janoff. (2000). *Future Search.* 2nd ed. San Francisco: Berrett-Koehler.
Zinker, Joseph. (1978). *Creative process in Gestalt therapy.* New York: Vintage Books.

Appendix

WHITE BUFFALO CALF WOMAN Brings The First Pipe
As told by: John Fire Lame Deer, in 1967

John Fire Lame Deer was a Lakota Holy man, and perhaps a Heyoka. His book Lame Deer, Seeker of Visions, (see book review) written with Richard Erdoes in 1972 . He died several years later on the Rosebud Lakota reservation in South Dakota; his son Archie carries on his spiritual work. This version of the Buffalo Calf Woman's bringing of the first sacred Pipe is from American Indian Myths and Legends, 1980, by Erdoes and Alfonso Ortiz

The Sioux are a warrior tribe, and one of their proverbs says, "Woman shall not walk before man." Yet White Buffalo Woman is the dominant figure of their most important legend. The medicine man Crow Dog explains, "This holy woman brought the sacred buffalo calf pipe to the Sioux. There could be no Indians without it. Before she came, people didn't know how to live. They knew nothing. The Buffalo Woman put her sacred mind into their minds." At the ritual of the sun dance one woman, usually a mature and universally respected member of the tribe, is given the honor of representing Buffalo Woman.

Though she first appeared to the Sioux in human form, White Buffalo Woman was also a buffalo---the Indians' brother, who gave its flesh so that the people might live. Albino buffalo were sacred to all Plains tribes; a white buffalo hide was a sacred talisman, a possession beyond price.

One summer so long ago that nobody knows how long, the Oceti-Shakowin, the seven sacred council fires of the Lakota Oyate, the nation, came together and camped. The sun shone all the time, but there was no game and the people were starving. Every day they sent scouts to look for game, but the scouts found nothing.

Among the bands assembled were the Itazipcho, the Without-Bows, who had their own camp circle under their chief, Standing Hollow Horn. Early one morning the chief sent two of his young men to hunt for game. They went on foot, because at that time the Sioux didn't yet have horses. They searched everywhere but could find nothing. Seeing a high hill, they decided to climb it in order to look over the whole country. Halfway up, they saw something coming toward them from far off, but the figure was floating instead of walking. From this they knew that the person was waken, holy.

At first they could make out only a small moving speck and had to squint to see that it was a human form. But as it came nearer, they realized that it was a beautiful young woman, more beautiful than any they had ever seen, with two round, red dots of face paint on her cheeks. She wore a wonderful white buckskin outfit, tanned until it shone a long way in the sun. It was embroidered with sacred and marvelous designs of porcupine quill, in radiant colors no ordinary woman could have made. This wakan stranger was Ptesan-Wi, White Buffalo Woman. In her hands she carried a large bundle and a fan of sage leaves. She wore her blue-black hair loose except for a strand at the left side, which was tied up with buffalo fur. Her eyes shone dark and sparkling, with great power in them.

The two young men looked at her open-mouthed. One was overawed, but the other desired her body and stretched his hand out to touch her. This woman was lila wakan, very sacred, and could not be treated with disrespect. Lightning instantly struck the brash young man and burned him up, so that only a small heap of blackened bones was left. Or as some say that he was suddenly covered by a cloud, and within it he was eaten up by snakes that left only his skeleton, just as a man can be eaten up by lust.

To the other scout who had behaved rightly, the White Buffalo Woman said: "Good things I am brining, something holy to your nation. A message I carry for your people from the buffalo nation. Go back to the camp and tell the people to prepare for my arrival. Tell your chief to put up a medicine lodge with twenty-four poles. Let it be made holy for my coming."

This young hunter returned to the camp. He told the chief, he told the people, what the sacred woman had commanded. The chief told the eyapaha, the crier, and the crier went through the camp circle calling: "Someone sacred is coming. A holy woman approaches. Make all things ready for her." So the people put up the big medicine tipi and waited. After four days they saw the White Buffalo Woman approaching, carrying her bundle before her. Her wonderful white buckskin dress shone from afar. The chief, Standing Hollow Horn, invited her to enter the medicine lodge. She went in and circled the interior sunwise. The chief addressed her respectfully, saying: "Sister, we are glad you have come to instruct us."

She told him what she wanted done. In the center of the tipi they were to put up an owanka wakan, a sacred altar, made of red earth, with a buffalo skull and a three-stick rack for a holy thing she was bringing. They did what she directed, and she traced a design with her finger on the smoothed earth of the altar. She show them how to do all this, then circled the lodge again sunwise. Halting before the chief, she now opened the bundle. the holy thing it contained was the chanunpa, the sacred pipe. She held it out to the people and let them look at it. She was grasping the stem with her right hand and the bowl with her left, and thus the pipe has been held ever since.

Again the chief spoke, saying: "Sister, we are glad. We have had no meat for some time. All we can give you is water." They dipped some wacanga, sweet grass, into a skin bag of water and gave it to her, and to this day the people dip sweet grass or an eagle wing in water and sprinkle it on a person to be purified.

The White Buffalo Woman showed the people how to use the pipe. She filled it with chan-shasha, red willow-bark tobacco. She walked around the lodge four times after the manner of Anpetu-Wi, the great sun. This represented the circle without end, the sacred hoop, the road of life. The woman placed a dry buffalo chip on the fire and lit the pipe with it. This was peta-owihankeshini, the fire without end, the flame to be passed on from generation to generation. She told them that the smoke rising from the bowl was Tunkashila's breath, the living breath of the great Grandfather Mystery.

The White Buffalo Woman showed the people the right way to pray, the right words and the right gestures. She taught them how to sing the pipe-filling song and how to lift the pipe up to the sky, toward Grandfather, and down toward Grandmother Earth, to Unci, and then to the four directions of the universe.

With this holy pipe," she said, "you will walk like a living prayer. With your feet resting upon the earth and the pipestem reaching into the sky, your body from a living bridge between the Sacred Beneath and the Sacred Above. Wakan Tanka smiles upon us, because now we are as one: earth, sky, all living things, the two-legged, the four-legged, the winged ones, the trees, the grasses. Together with the people, they are all related, one family. The pipe holds them all together."

"Look at this bowl," said the White Buffalo Woman. "Its stone represents the buffalo, but also the flesh and blood of the red man. The buffalo represents the universe and the four directions, because he stands on four legs, for the four ages of man. The buffalo was put in the west by Wakan Tanka at the making of the world, to hold back the waters. Every year he loses one hair, and in every one of the four ages he loses a leg. The Sacred Hoop will end when all the hair and legs of the great buffalo are gone, and the water comes back to cover the Earth.

The wooden stem of this chanunpa stands for all that grows on the earth. Twelve feathers hanging from where the stem- the backbone- joins the bowl- the skull- are from Wanblee Galeshka, the spotted eagle, the very sacred who is the Great Spirit's messenger and the wisest of all cry out to Tunkashila. Look at the bowl: engraved in it are seven circles of various sizes. They stand for the seven ceremonies you will practice with this pipe, and for the Ocheti Shakowin, the seven sacred campfires of our Lakota nation."

The White Buffalo Woman then spoke to the women, telling them that it was the work of their hands and the fruit of their bodies which kept the people alive. "You are from the mother earth," she told them. "What you are doing is as great as what warriors do."

And therefore the sacred pipe is also something that binds men and women together in a circle of love. It is the one holy object in the making of which both men and women have a hand. The men carve the bowl and make the stem; the women decorate it with bands of colored porcupine quills. When a man takes a wife, they both hold the pipe at the same time and red cloth is wound around their hands, thus tying them together for life.

The White Buffalo Woman had many things for her Lakota sisters in her sacred womb bag; corn, wasna (pemmican), wild turnip. She taught how to make the hearth fire. She filled a buffalo paunch with cold water and dropped a red-hot stone into it. "This way you shall cook the corn and the meat," she told them.

The White Buffalo Woman also talked to the children, because they have an understanding beyond their years. She told them that what their fathers and mothers did was for them, that their parents could remember being little once, and that they, the children, would grow up to have little ones of their own. She told them: "You are the coming generation, that's why you are the most important and precious ones. Some day you will hold this pipe and smoke it. Some day you will pray with it."

She spoke once more to all the people: "The pipe is alive; it is a red being showing you a red life and a red road. And this is the first ceremony for which you will use the pipe. You will use it to Wakan Tanka, the Great Mystery Spirit. The day a human dies is always a sacred day.

The day when the soul is released to the Great Spirit is another. Four women will become sacred on such a day. They will be the ones to cut the sacred tree, the can-wakan, for the sun dance."

She told the Lakota that they were the purest among the tribes, and for that reason Tunkashila had bestowed upon them the holy chanunpa. They had been chosen to take care of it for all the Indian people on this turtle continent.

She spoke one last time to Standing Hollow Horn, the chief, saying, "Remember: this pipe is very sacred. Respect it and it will take you to the end of the road. The four ages of creation are in me; I am the four ages. I will come to see you in every generation cycle. I shall come back to you."

The sacred woman then took leave of the people, saying: "Toksha ake wacinyanktin ktelo, I shall see you again."

The people saw her walking off in the same direction from which she had come, outlined against the red ball of the setting sun. As she went, she stopped and rolled over four times. The first time, she turned into a black buffalo; the second into a brown one; the third into a red one; and finally, the fourth time she rolled over, she turned into a white female buffalo calf. A white buffalo is the most sacred living thing you could ever encounter.

The White Buffalo Woman disappeared over the Horizon. Sometime she might come back. As soon as she had vanished, buffalo in great herds appeared, allowing themselves to be killed so that the people might survive. And from that day on, our relations, the buffalo, furnished the people with everything they needed, meat for their food, skins for their clothes and tipis, bones for their many tools.

Two very old tribal pipes are kept by the Looking Horse family at Eagle Butte in South Dakota. One of them is the Sacred Pipe brought to the people by White Buffalo Woman.

Chapter XX

A Framework for Diversity Ethics

Joan SalmonCampbell
Deborah L. Plummer

Introduction

This chapter addresses the importance for individuals, groups, and organizations (both for-profit and not-for-profit) of using diversity ethics. Diversity ethics, as a concept, implies an ideal perspective for the values of human differences and moral standards governing practitioners, groups, and organizations. Rooted in historical approaches to ethical discourse, this concept has specific application to the field of diversity management. In addition to this chapter exploring the concept of diversity ethics, it distinguishes between ethical principles and moral mandates and behavior, and identifies five ethical principles based on foundational work done by Jacques Thiroux (1998) that can be used as diagnostic, developmental, or assessment instruments.

A practitioner's personal clarity about the importance of diversity ethics is central to facilitating groups and diversity interventions within organizations. To promote deeper personal and collective understanding of this topic, examples of diversity dilemmas and trigger questions for discussion are presented throughout the chapter. Dilemmas of diversity ethics describe complex situations that arise for organizations undertaking diversity initiatives; they include the challenges diversity practitioners encounter in designing interventions.

The Importance of Diversity Ethics

Owing to the nature of human interaction, diversity dilemmas are common in every organization, corporation, and group experience. Dilemmas concerning diversity issues are particularly troublesome because of the lack of clear guidelines on how to process and manage them. These dilemmas may stem from dimensions of diversity as race, gender, sexual orientation, marital status, work location, personality, religion, or culture (to name only a few). Examples of diversity dilemmas include the following:

- ✦Intimate relationships develop among employees, both married and unmarried, across racial or cultural lines. What issues are apparent barriers to quality performance and work environment?
- ✦The organization sponsors a night at a sports event exclusively for Christian employees. When do the other religious groups get their exclusive night, and what religious groups does the organization recognize?
- ✦A conflict occurs between an employee's religious practice and company norms; it has an impact on the employee's performance, teamwork, and commitment. How could the employer have detected this possibility before the employee was hired?
- ✦The hierarchy of an organization shows an absence of diversity. How is this situation related to power? How is it addressed as a diversity dilemma? Within the organization, who would be the appropriate person to address it?

> ***Identify at least five diversity dilemmas. What is the ethical issue that makes each one a difficult situation?***

Diversity dilemmas inherently pose questions for the practitioner. Why do unethical attitudes exist toward diversity demographics in organizations, corporations, groups, and families? What is the value of the diversity effort? What do people of a distinctively diverse demographic background contribute to the moral mandate (accepted behavior) of the organization? How does an individual's self-efficacy, use of self, personality, and abilities contribute to positive or negative attitudes? How should individuals monitor their own behavior in the workplace, and how does the organization promote self-monitoring? Do moral mandates adapt or change in accordance with particular cultures?

Often, when a prevailing moral mandate seeks to influence their personal ethical standard, employers or employees are challenged to maintain or to compromise their core values. Consider the example of an employer who must decide whether to fire one of the organization's two employees of color and face charges of racial discrimination. Evidence may exist that this worker has not met production and attendance standards set for all employees, but is there also unexamined evidence to suggest that differential treatment has occurred?

Another example is the case of the human resources director who is told to interview all people who apply for work, but to limit actual hires of gay and lesbian individuals to zero percent of those hired. The director knows that the current corporate culture is not psychologically supportive to gays and lesbians; she rationalizes that by carrying out the directive, she has prevented the gay or lesbian job applicant from suffering considerable on-the-job stress.

In situations such as these, the practitioner/consultant is faced with making a distinction between personal ethics and moral mandate. An organization that perceives itself to be successful may logically ask, "Do we care whether the company's moral mandate [or socially sanctioned behavior] is in alignment with the personal ethic or core values of our employees?" In reality, most employees do not consciously associate their personal ethic with their job until a dilemma presents itself.

> ***—What are the benefits for organizations whose employees' base values are in alignment with the organization's core values?***
>
> ***—What are the dilemmas for organizations whose employees' values are not the same as the organization's expressed values?***

Unless the organization sets standards for corporate responsibility, the diversity practitioner will find it difficult to make authentic and credible assessments and recommendations. For the diversity practitioner, every contract is an opportunity to model the practice of value-behavior coherence. In matters of diversity initiatives and diversity management, leading from an internal core value is as important as the consultant's signature on the dotted line. Using this approach to leadership, the diversity practitioner embodies the integrity and authenticity of the assessments and recommendations that he or she is making to the client organization.

Practitioners can sharpen their awareness of the qualities of integrity and authenticity through the Use-of-Self Diversity Skills. Plummer (1998) outlines seven use-of-self diversity skills rooted in family therapy and systems thinking that increase the practitioner's clarity and ground his or her preparation for diversity effort. These skills, when practiced, support the organization in living out its core values.

Use-of-Self Diversity Skills

(1) **Self–Focus.** Becoming less of an expert on the other and more of an expert on the self. Requires an appreciation of the fact that we cannot change the other person and that doing so is not our job. We can, however, create climates in which people *want* to change.

(2) **Self-functioning.** Balancing the tendency to over-function or under-function in a situation. Over-functioners tend to know what is best for the situation and move quickly to fix it. Under-functioners become less competent as the complexity of the situation increases and do nothing.

(3) **Self-Disclosure.** Revealing aspects of "the self" to further movement in a cross-cultural interaction.

(4) **Grading.** Developing a concept or working on an issue in small steps. This process may incorporate the use of experimentation to discern what increases cultural understanding.

(5) **Principle of Staying Dumb.** Staying curious about the communication process and one's responsibility in a cultural clash.

(6) **Managing Process Loss.** Identification of the variables that cause efficiency to be lost in a communication process.

(7) **Figure Clarity.** Awareness that one is focusing on what is uppermost in one's mind and that others are doing the same. Thus, multiple realities are present and interacting.

Reflect on the following questions, and rate your understanding of Use of Self as a tool in your work:

(1) Self-Focusing

— Do I spend more energy on supporting other people's goals than they spend on their own goals?

or

— Do I keep clear boundaries between support and responsibility?

(2) Self-Functioning

— Do I try to fix situations quickly, without giving much thought to who owns the problem?

or

— Do I avoid situations that are complex and that require more personal input from me?

(3) Self-Disclosure

— Do I share personal information, when appropriate, to enhance teamwork?

or

— In the work place, do I consider my privacy as sacred?

(4) Grading

—Am I willing to take risks and change my behaviors to promote personal growth?

or

— Am I content with how I behave? Do I believe that people should accept me "just as I am"?

(5) Principal of Staying Dumb

— Do I listen for understanding and not rebuttal?

or

— Do I prepare my response while the other person is talking and then quickly defend my position?

(6) **Managing Process Loss**
— Do I pay attention and adapt my response to body language when I am communicating?
or
— Do I stay in my head, formulating my thoughts to make sure I am being clear?

(7) **Figure Clarity**
— Do I check to make sure I am clear on the topic for discussion?
or
— Do I presume that my lens for interpreting the world is the only reality?

> ***As a practitioner, how would you state your diversity ethics? How would you demonstrate it to a client? Is this statement of your diversity ethic something you might consider including as part of your bid, proposal, or contract?***

Where Do We Start?

The absence or lack of clarity of ethical guidelines creates confusion about acceptable behavior and organization. The terms "ethics" and "morals" are often used interchangeably and rarely defined by the speaker. The lack of clarity in the use of these terms is partially based on the fact that the culture of such individuals (the customs, relationships, dress, language, mission, goals, and survival practices shared by a group of people), rather than their personal ethical center, is informing their behavior.

Important research conducted by Lawrence Kohlberg and Carol Gilligan in the field of moral development has provided insight into the understanding of diversity ethics. Kohlberg (1958, 1981) examined whether a person's ability to deal with ethical issues can develop later in life and whether education can affect that development. He found that a person's ability to deal with moral issues is not formed all at once. Just as there are stages of growth in physical development, the ability to think morally also develops in stages.

Kohlberg regards each level of moral development as possessing two stages. The earliest level of development, that of a child between the ages of 4 to 10, he calls the *preconventional level*. At this level, a child determines right and wrong by what authority figures say is right and wrong, or by behavior that results in rewards or punishments. Here, the individual's moral judgment is motivated by a need to satisfy his or her own desires.

The second level of moral development occurs between the ages of 10 and 13. Termed the *conventional level*, it is the level reached by most adolescents. At this level, concepts of right and wrong are based on group loyalties — to family, friends, and nation. Moral values reside in performance of roles that are recognized as good or right, in maintaining the conventional order, and in pleasing others. Individual moral judgment is motivated by a need to avoid rejection or disapproval of others and by a need to avoid occasioning criticism from authority figures.

The third level is the *postconventional level*. At this level, which occurs from adolescence to adulthood, the individual stops defining right and wrong in terms of group loyalties and norms. The adult who is functioning at this level develops a viewpoint expressed from a universal point of view and holds principles that would appeal to any reasonable person because they take everyone's interest into account. Moral judgment is motivated by respect for all members of the community, respect for the social order, and willingness to live under legally determined laws. Such individuals are motivated by their own conscience.

Gilligan (1982) developed her theories about differences in ethical perspective in response to conclusions offered by Kohlberg. His findings suggested that men reached the higher levels of moral development more often than women. Challenging Kohlberg's findings, Gilligan's research, conducted over an 11-year period, suggests that women tend to be more concerned than men are with maintaining good relationships with family and friends, and with minimizing hurt to those they care about. These traits are characteristic of Kohlberg's second level of maturity. Men are more likely to look at moral issues from the standpoint of impartial and impersonal principles, a characteristic of

Kohlberg's third and highest maturity level. By implication, according to the standards developed by Kohlberg, women appear to reach the third and most mature level much less frequently than men, and they appear, therefore, to be less morally developed than men.

> ***—As you reflect on Kohlberg's perspective, what diversity dilemma do you see arising in an organization beginning to undertake diversity initiatives that has a top management that is 90% male and a workforce that is 50% female?***
> ***—Now consider Gilligan's perspective, and ask yourself the same question.***
> ***—How would you approach raising awareness of the diversity dilemmas you've identified?***

Gilligan's work challenges this interpretation. The problem, she claims, is not with women, but with the framework of moral development established by Kohlberg. Kohlberg's theory canonized the justice perspective, because he and most of his subjects were male. Males favor the justice perspective.

Females favor the care perspective. As Gilligan's research on women revealed, a care perspective could also be considered a morally mature stage of moral reasoning. Gilligan's research demonstrates that women, more than men, view themselves as part of a network of relationships and feel that sustaining these relationships is a moral imperative. Central to this "female ethic" are notions of care and responsibility for others. By contrast, Gilligan implies that the "male ethic" of Kohlberg's third level is one based on abstract, impersonal principles.

Gilligan argues that for most women, progress toward moral maturity is marked by changes in the focus of caring, not by the development of the abstract, impersonal principles that Kohlberg proposes.

In the care perspective, the earliest level of moral development, she claims, is one marked by a concern with caring only for oneself. At the second level, others become the focus of caring. At the third level of moral development, the morally mature person achieves a balance between caring for others and caring for oneself. Progress from stage to stage is motivated in part by the individual's increasing understanding of human relationships and in part by the attempt to maintain one's own integrity and to care for one's self without neglecting others. Throughout this process, women regard themselves as "selves-in-relation."

The various levels delineated by both Kohlberg and Gilligan imply that ethics (personal core values) are processes by which every individual forms standards and principles of right and wrong. Taylor, Gilligan and Sullivan (1997) expanded this research by adding the variables of differences. For example, if Gilligan's findings are true in an affluent suburban setting, what differences in moral development would be present for women from poor and working-class families? How would womanhood issues affect moral development?

> ***—What do you think some of the differences might be between the core values (ethics) and moral development of more affluent white men and women and those of low-income men and women of Color?***
> ***—Which perspective would be most valued — justice and fairness, or caring and responsibility?***
> ***—For what reasons?***

Definition of Ethics and Morals

We will use the following definition of **ethics** as a basis for building a working definition for diversity ethics:

Ethics is an intrinsic set of core values that every individual acquires through his or her cultural environment. It informs one's sense of right and wrong.

These core values provide the foundation for making decisions about acceptable conduct, which is called **moral behavior**. These core values, if compromised, affect the person's sense of meaning and identity. Core values constitute the ethical principles that inform the moral standards for how we live in society.

> ***—Identify two core values that you learned at the pre-conventional, conventional, and post-conventional levels of your development.***
> ***—Describe the standard of behavior expected from you by others at each level.***
> ***—What principle was established in light of this standard of behavior?***
> ***—If a core value states that one should always dress appropriately, how might individuals at differing levels of moral development interpret the principle of "Dress for Success"?***

The term "morals" is not synonymous with "ethics." **"Morals" refers to the standards that govern human behavior and that demonstrate the ethical principles of a person, group, or organization.** The understanding of standards that are deemed acceptable as guidelines for behavior by many people within society, culture, organizations, or family is known as the **"moral mandate." It dictates the expected behavior informed by agreed-upon moral standards.** Sometimes a moral mandate may be in contradiction to a personal ethic. For example, a generous donor to a nonprofit organization is also CEO of a company that intentionally excludes people of color from its leadership. The executive director of the nonprofit may struggle with this internally, because of her personal ethics, but may feel required by the moral mandate of her organization to accept the donation.

The Top Model for Diversity Ethics

Individuals who do not have clarity about their ethical center are vulnerable to confusion and uncertainty about what is appropriate behavior in various situations. This confusion and uncertainty greatly affect an individual's core realities — in the workplace as well as in other settings. Each person brings to the work environment a singular awareness of his or her ethical center that affects performance on the job, self-efficacy, and self-esteem as well as teamwork and effectiveness. The ethical center is the seat of being, where individuals begin to test the moral standards that have been shaped by their ethical principles.

Moral standards are constantly being tested and subject to development and change. The Top Model (see Figure 1) builds on the work of Loden and Rosen (1991) and expands the Four Layers model created by Gardenschwartz and Rowe (1994). Our values are the core and primary basis for the way we operate and function. In The Top Model, the core dimension considers six aspects of an individual's participation in an organization or group. Very often, one or more of these aspects is dysfunctional, and some aspect of the primary or secondary dimension bears the brunt of that dysfunction. For example, a female employee has the responsibility for generating proof-ready data, but does not have the computer skills to accomplish the task. When criticized for poor performance, the worker claims that the criticism is based in gender discrimination. Her immediate supervisor reacts to her charge without any attempt to assess aspects of her core dimension.

Without some mechanism to assess the core dimension, both employer and employee are at a disadvantage. Frequently, when employees are expected to perform a task, their lack of **ability** limits their **functionality** and **facility** to complete the task. When expectations and employee abilities do not match, dysfunctionality in performance occurs. Altered **personality**, defensive **sensibilities**, and lack of **agility** in responding to the expectation can be the germ for serious workforce diversity dilemmas. The task dilemma for both the employer and the employee clearly concerns the need to address differences in the core dimension. The situation becomes a more intense diversity dilemma when the reality (e.g., culture or race) of the employee also corresponds with any aspect of the primary and secondary dimensions, and this aspect is different from that of the employer or others in the work environment.

Six Aspects of The Core Dimension

The elements of the core dimension named above — **functionality, ability, agility, facility, personality, and sensibility** — are delicate aspects of every person's life (see Table 1). Challenges to the core dimension can make us feel exceptionally vulnerable, and this dimension can be easily damaged, disordered, and denied. This part of our

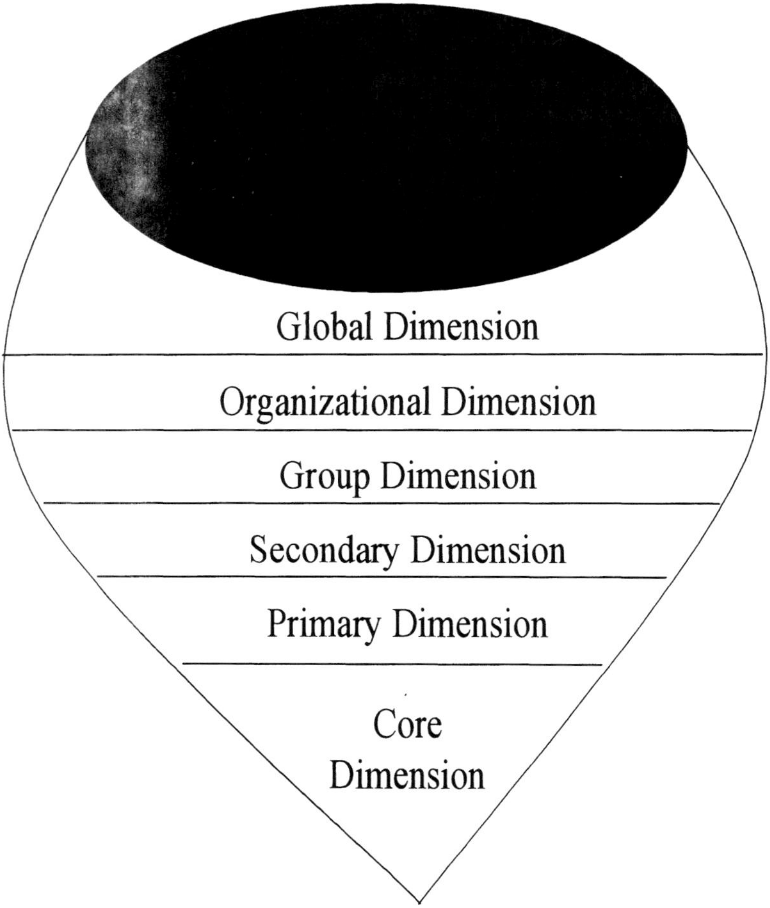

Figure 1. The Top Model of Diversity Ethics

*Diversity Ethics Formation
**Moral Mandate Formation

The Top Model of Diversity Ethics
For Individuals, Groups, Organizations

*Core Dimension	*Primary Dimension	Secondary Dimension	**Group Dimension	**Organizational Dimension	**Global Dimension
Ability	Age	Geographic Location	Leader	Classified Level	Culture
Personality	Gender	Income	Influence	Divisional Department Unit	Diversity Ethic
Functionality	Sexual Orientation	Personal Habits	Authority	Seniority	Communication
Sensibility	Physical Ability	Recreational Habits	Role	Environment	Development
Facility	Ethnicity	Religion	Responsibility	Work Location	Technology
Agility	Race	Educational Background	Diversity Ethic	Union Affiliation	Economic Status
		Work Experience	Representative	Management Status	Social Impact
		Appearance		Diversity Ethic	Services
		Parental Status			
		Marital Status			
		Language(s)			

Source: The Primary and Secondary Dimensions are Adapted from Loden, M. (1996). Implementing Diversity. Chicago, IL: Irwin Publishing

Table 1. Dimensions for Top Model of Diversity Ethics

being requires careful handling, tact, and consideration. Supervisors may or may not observe or know about these aspects of the core dimension of their employees, but they would readily admit that they definitely affect the work that is to be done. It is often the case that the individual worker may not even be aware of how these aspects of self affect job performance. To identify them is a starting place in considering ways to help workers and supervisors address the overall reality of the work arena.

Functionality — the capability of performing a function, of being useful, of contributing to the value added to a given situation.

> ***"What skill sets or competencies bring added value to this work situation?"***

Ability — the power to accomplish physical or mental tasks; it may include Intelligence Quotient (IQ) or educational achievement, Emotional Quotient (EQ) or emotional tolerance, and Adversity Quotient (AQ), or ability to persevere through adversity (Stoltz, 1997).

> ***"What level of knowledge do I bring to this situation?"***
> ***—"Do I respond to situations emotionally or rationally?"***
> ***—"Do I respond to situations willingly or reluctantly?"***
> ***—"Can I function in difficult situations and handle tension?"***
> ***—"Can I work under pressure?"***

Agility — the quickness or deftness of the body in the performance of an act; dexterity, rapidity and promptness; the tendencies or degrees of skillfulness.

> ***—"Do I have the physical stamina to type all day with arthritic hands?"***
> ***—"Can I gracefully get up those steps to make my presentation, knowing that my foot drags?" [from an employee whose multiple sclerosis has not been revealed to the employer]***

Facility — the ease of doing or making something, the absence of difficulty, the means by which something is done.

> ***—"Can I quickly and easily discern how to perform this task effectively?"***
> ***—"Can I think of more than one way to do the same thing?"***

Personality — the unique set of traits of an individual and how one chooses to express these traits in the world.

> ***—"How do I choose to interact with others in the world?***
> ***—"What do I need from others to enhance my strengths and complement my weaknesses?"***

Sensibility — the capacity for being affected, emotionally or intellectually, in either pleasant or unpleasant ways; the receptiveness to impression; the capacity to respond perceptively to intellectual, moral, or aesthetic values; delicate, sensitive awareness or responsiveness; the extent to which one is liable to be offended or repelled.

> ***—"Am I aware of what is going on around me?"***
> ***—"Do I respond sensitively to others around me?"***

These six aspects form the essence of the core dimension described in the Top Model for diversity ethics. Individuals in every organization could paint a verbal portrait of the various aspects of their own core dimension. How they live out this portrait, and how they are perceived at work, has significant impact on the entire work environment. Because each person's core dimension is unique, individuals and organizations must examine this most basic core dimension of diversity.

The Foundation For The Work Of Diversity Ethics: a Definition

Diversity ethics is an ideal perspective that overarches and saturates the field of diversity management and training. Arising from the Top Model, the definition of **diversity ethics** is presented below, followed by a discussion of the rationale for its component parts. Each phrase is used with the intention of carefully creating a word picture of diversity ethics in action. A consideration of the rationale behind the word picture will help you discern whether you can incorporate the definition into your own belief structure and behavior.

The Definition of Diversity Ethics

Diversity ethics defines the principles and establishes the standards for addressing every dimension of diversity. It acknowledges every person as gifted, unique, and deserving of respect, and further recognizes all of nature as a living and necessary part of the earth's ecological balance. Diversity ethics seeks to clarify the highest principles for the value of life and the acceptance of death, the value for good and right over evil and wrong, the value for justice and fairness, the value for truth telling or honesty, and the value for individual freedom in every situation. Leaders, facilitator/trainers, consultants — all those who presume to be proponents of diversity ethics — seek to demonstrate it through "use of self" rather than through empty rhetoric, ritualistic actions, or rigid, predetermined responses.

Diversity ethics is the mechanism used to fully explore and understand the value of diversity dimensions operating in a given situation. This mechanism helps to identify the ideals underlying the principles used by an organization to articulate its core values. Each principle has a complementary standard, used to guide behavior in the workplace, which ultimately shapes the culture of the organization. From this culture evolves an intrinsic set of core values and beliefs. Ideally, every individual and group within the organization begins to embrace these values and beliefs. These values inform the individual's sense of right and wrong as well as the rationale for best practices within the organization. This process cannot develop to its highest stage unless consideration is given to the impact of the organization on the environment that hosts the business endeavor. The mechanism of diversity ethics facilitates the assessment of various approaches to diversity dilemmas that the organization faces. Diversity ethics calls for accountability from managers and practitioners, requiring them to give evidence of how their behaviors are aligned with the diversity values expressed by the organization.

The Limits and Latitudes of Diversity Ethics

The work of diversity ethics occurs within a delimited space. It describes the basis for developing a principle-centered organization with principle-centered leadership. According to Covey (1990), the organizational leader of this millennium will be one who creates a culture or a value system centered upon principles. This is a tremendous challenge in this new era and can be achieved only by leaders who have the vision, the courage, and the humility to continuously learn and grow. Those organizations and persons who have a passion for learning through listening, seeing emerging trends, sensing and anticipating needs in the marketplace, evaluating past successes and mistakes, and absorbing the lessons that conscience and principles teach, will have enduring influence. This new era challenges leaders and organizations to matriculate in an environment rich with diverse cultures, ethnic groups, lifestyles, and issues of class. Leaders and organizations are expected to transform themselves in order to accommodate the increased demands of the global marketplace. Facilitating the groundwork for this transformation is the work of diversity ethics.

The core values of the system inform the stated principles that become the ethical center of life for the individual, group, or organization. The work of Jacques Thiroux (1998), professor emeritus at California State University, is especially helpful in understanding the use of ethics. According to Thiroux, ethics deals with what is right and wrong in human behavior and conduct. It asks what constitutes, in a person or act, the condition of being good, bad, right, or wrong, and how do we know? What theories of conduct are valid or invalid, and why? Should we use principles, rules, or laws, or should we let each situation determine our morality? In reality, each person, group, and organization has an intrinsic sense of right, wrong, good, or bad, which develops through accumulated experiences and impact from the environment. Over a period of time, this sense becomes the core, or central value system. These values are articulated in the form of principles (rules or laws) that offer guidance to the individual, group, or organization about appropriate or inappropriate behavior. It is around these issues that diversity dilemmas frequently occur.

> ***Be the practitioner: what is the dilemma of diversity ethics in the following situation?***
>
> ***With a past history for discrimination that was highly publicized, Company X is committed to becoming one of the top 10 companies for diversity management to be featured in a national business magazine within the next five years.***
>
> ***A young, bright, ambitious, and business-savvy professional has been hired as the diversity specialist. Chris's charge is to help the company accomplish its goal of reaching the top ten. The criteria for achieving this honor include evidence of employee satisfaction across the lines of race, gender, and age, as well as a commitment to community development. Chris feels that, with minimum reframing and sophisticated statistical analysis, the results of a recent employee survey can be used to earn points for the award.***
>
> ***—What are the dimensions of diversity involved in this situation?***
> ***—What core values or ethical principles are most likely to be called into question?***
> ***—Describe the dilemma of diversity ethics.***

"Ethics" comes from the Greek word *ethos,* which means character. Character is established from sorting out the impact of varied experiences and messages, and choosing what to believe. "Morality" comes from the Latin word *moralis,* which means customs and manners. Morals describe human behavior or conduct that flows from a person's ethical center. Diversity ethics uses two approaches to the study of morality in human systems (individuals, groups, and organizations). They are the scientific, or descriptive, approach and the philosophical approach.

In developing models to facilitate the work of diversity practitioners, the first approach of diversity ethics will use tools of social science by observing human beings in many situations, by collecting data about human behavior, by conducting analysis, and by drawing conclusions that give direction for transformation or change. No value judgment is made about what is right or wrong, nor are prescriptions given on how human beings ought to behave. This approach is a useful diagnostic tool, employing ethical frameworks as its basis.

The second approach is the philosophical approach, which has two parts. The first uses normative, or prescriptive, ethics and the second uses metaethics, or analytic ethics. The first deals with norms (or standards) and prescriptions. The second deals with analysis of ethical language (e.g., What do we mean when we say "good"?) The metaethicist is concerned indirectly with normative systems, concentrating on reasoning, logical structures, and language rather than content.

Diversity ethics seeks to synthesize these varying approaches in order to accommodate the rich diversity of ethical practices employed by the diverse groups that come together in the workplace or group, enabling the system to identify those principles and standards that best reflect the organization, nurture its learning posture, and facilitate its mission.

Ethics and Diversity Dimensions

Using The Top Model, the initial focus is upon the core dimension. Frequently, the varied aspects of how a person participates in the work arena affect every part of the task that is to be performed. When any one or more of these aspects is dysfunctional, individuals are hampered in their full participation in the work at hand. Some aspect of what is called "the other dimensions of diversity" bears the brunt of the dysfunction in the core dimension.

For example, if an employee can verbalize an understanding of the work to be done, but does not have the basic function of applying his or her words into assigned task; if an employee is able to do data entry, but has reduced facility due to arthritis; or if an employee does all the work effectively, but is an intense introvert and is unable to work well on a team effort, we have evidence of dysfunctions within the core dimension. Because the aspects of this dimension are not clear — even to the employee who displays the dysfunction — such matters are frequently overlooked, as they are difficult for supervisors to address for fear of the possibility of reprisal. Instead, the dysfunction may be tolerated or ignored, or another employee may assume the tasks of the worker who is dysfunctional.

Obviously, this works against value being added to the business endeavor. Diversity ethics holds leaders and supervisors, facilitators and managers accountable for helping the employee maintain a sense of dignity and uniqueness, as this is a vital part of what every employee brings to the workforce team. If such issues are not addressed, the common good of the organization, the dignity and potential of the employee, and the employee's right to social justice and fairness have been violated. Such a scene is likely to be found in an organization that is in a state of malaise and frustration.

Diversity Values

Principle-centered groups and organizations pay attention to the variety, diversity, and complexity of human beings within their system by discovering those principles that are truly basic and necessary to almost any moral set of standards. Thiroux notes that, historically, every ethical system has at least one principle, and some have more. For example, in ethical egoism, the basic principle is self-interest; in utilitarianism, it is the interest of all concerned. In Emmanuel Kant's system, it is the Categorical Imperative — the emphasis on duty rather than inclination and the principle that each person is an end and not a means. Principles are necessary in order to establish any kind of ethical system that applies to human morality (behavior).

Each group or organization must decide on how many principles the system will embrace. These principles can be found in what some companies call their code of ethics. One of the most popular principles people put forth, when asked what they base their ethics on, is the Golden Rule: "Do unto others as you would have others do unto you." While it is all right to put oneself in another's shoes, this precept is not adequate as the primary or sole principle upon which to base an ethical system (and for this reason alone, the discipline of diversity ethics is important for individuals, groups, and organization). First, in applying this rule, we assume that what the other person may want or need is the same as what we will want or need. This is not always true. Second, this rule does not really tell us what we should do. It only gives us a method for testing what we have chosen to do against how such an act would affect us, if we were on the receiving end of the action. Third, most often this rule becomes the official code of ethics solely on the basis of custom or tradition.

A more thoughtful approach requires us to ask ourselves — especially in diversity work — "What are the important things in life (for the individual, group, or organization), and which principles will protect and enhance them?" Answering this question will help us to construct a significant basis for moral behavior. The following five principles are based on the work of Thiroux (1998).

The value of life and the acceptance of death. Human beings revere life and accept death. This principle reflects a concern for the preservation and protection of human life. It is basic to ethics. There can be no ethics without living human beings. There can be no groups or organizations without human life. In addition to this, justification is provided by the fact that most systems of ethics include a statement prohibiting killing or the destruction of human life in general. Diversity ethics extends this ideal beyond human life to all living things.

Justification: This principle precedes all others, because without human life, there can be no good or evil (goodness or badness), justice or injustice, honesty or dishonesty, freedom or bondage. Life is a basic possession, the main possession of every human being. It is the one thing that we all have in common, yet we experience it uniquely. Therefore, persons (as Kant maintained) should never be treated merely as means, but rather as unique and individual ends in themselves. An individual's right to his or her own life and death is a basic concept. Decisions about whether a person should or should not live are to be made only with the person's informed consent.

> ***There are many ways that life and death occur in the workplace.***
> ***—With a partner, name as many ways possible that individuals experience life and death in the work arena.***
> ***—In light of the examples you chose, express at least three values for life, and make three statements about the acceptance of death.***
> ***—Give at least five expressions of the value for life and the acceptance of death, in the context of diversity ethics. (Example: "All employees will have maximum opportunity to make use of their full potential and talent in their assigned duties.")***

The value of life principle is held as a near absolute, because life is held both in common and uniquely by all human beings and constitutes the starting point for any moral system. The remaining four principles enforce the value of life principle.

The principle of goodness and right over evil and wrong. This principle is often stated as two separate principles:

1. We should always do what is good.
2. We should always try to prevent, and avoid committing, acts that are bad or harmful.

If morality means doing what is "good" or what is "right," then every system of morality must clearly imply the principle of goodness or rightness. We strive to be "good" human beings and to perform "right" action. This principle demands that we do three things:

1. Promote goodness over badness and do good (beneficence).
2. Cause no harm or badness (nonmaleficence).
3. Prevent badness or harm (nonmaleficence and beneficence).

Each individual, group, and organization must define in their ethical system what is meant by good and bad, and right and wrong, and thereby set the basis for moral standards to be articulated.

Justification: When we speak of an ethical person's life and moral action, we mean a good person, with a good life, who takes good action. Good and right involve happiness, pleasure, excellence, harmony, and creativity. All these are characteristics that a leading-edge organization can point to in its employee profile. However, the words take on different meanings according to the environment or culture wherein they are defined. There are some "goods" upon which individuals may or may not be able to agree. These include: life, consciousness, pleasure, happiness, truth, knowledge, beauty, love, friendship, self-expression, self-realization, freedom, honor, peace, and security.

> ***Think of your work arena and select five of the above descriptive words.***

—How does your employer define these words?
—How do you define these words?
—Find four other people and ask how they define these words.
—What is the same and what is different?
—What causes the differences?

Diversity ethics embraces the point of view that there are many "goods"; this is a part of the true meaning of multiculturalism in the context of diversity initiatives. The principle of goodness logically precedes all other principles, just as the value of life precedes them empirically.

The principle of justice and fairness. This principle concerns itself with the distribution of good and bad on a just and fair basis. It says that human beings should treat other human beings fairly and justly when distributing goodness and badness among them. It is not enough for people to be good and to do what is right; some attempt also must be made to distribute the benefits that ensue from being good and doing right. Examples of how established historical ethical systems have displayed concern for justice include the following.

- ✦**Ethical egoism**, which enjoins each person to act in his or her own best self-interest, also suggests that, while the promotion of one's own good is in accordance with morality, the cooperation of two individuals could result in mutual benefit. Extension of such cooperation to greater numbers could lead to just treatment for everyone.

✦**Kant's duty ethics**, known as the Categorical Imperative, concerns one's moral obligation to another, and has — along with regard for all human beings as ends rather than means — justice at its core.

✦**Utilitarianism** advocates a general concern for justice above the needs of self, deeming that right conduct supports the greatest happiness of the greatest number.

✦**Judaism and Christianity**, in the Ten Commandments, enjoin against such acts against other persons as killing, stealing, adultery, and the coveting of the possessions of others; Jesus' teachings to "love your neighbor as yourself" and "love even your enemies" emphasize justice and fairness.

Justification: If one accepts the concept that good should be shared, the next question to be considered is who should receive the benefits resulting from the good human action, and how should they be distributed? Reason dictates that there should be some order to any distribution of good and bad. All human beings have common characteristics, and each human being is unique; how do we distribute goodness and badness with these truths in mind? What facilitates and hinders equal opportunity for all? What criteria help to establish the basis for distribution of good and bad?

No one should be denied opportunity because of skin color, sexual orientation, religious belief, gender, age, or degree of beauty. No one should be denied the opportunity to earn as much money as anyone else, either for these reasons or for any others having nothing to do with one's qualifications. Herein we recognize the common equality of human beings, yet allow for individual differences, when attempting to distribute goodness and badness fairly. We must make use of the principle of justice in order to be moral toward others, because they are affected by our actions.

Organizations in the corporate world refer to and use this principle, incorporating into their code of ethics (sometimes called "code of conduct") ways in which they meet their social responsibility as a corporation. Errol P. Mendes, Director of The Human Rights Research and Education Centre at the University of Ottawa, and his colleague, Jeffrey

Clark, Senior Research Associate, have identified **five generations of corporate codes of conduct** and their impact on corporate social responsibility. Corporate social responsibility is the framework used by business to establish and clarify principles of justice and fairness.

According to research undertaken by Mendes and Clark, there are essentially four "generations" (later followed by a fifth) of issues of ethical and social responsibility for justice and fairness. Corporations use their code of conduct and corresponding management system as the mechanisms by which to implement their principles of justice and fairness. The focus of the **first** generation is on conflict of interest; the focus of the **second** generation is on commercial conduct; the focus of the **third** generation is on employee and other third-party concerns; and the focus of the **fourth** generation is on community and environmental concerns. Recently a **fifth** generation has emerged, which focuses on accountability and social justice. Generations might be defined as the various attitudes, values, and perspectives held by a corporation at a particular phase of its economic and cultural development.

Go to the website **www.uottawa.ca/hrrec/publicat/five** ***and detail the following:***

- ***—The meaning and primary focus of each generation.***
- ***—The justice and fairness issues that each generation of issues seeks to address.***

The principle of truth telling or honesty. This principle is a corollary to the principle of justice and fairness. It provides for meaningful communication, which is an absolute necessity in any ethical system or moral relationship between two or more human beings. Ethical theories cannot be communicated if no one can be sure whether the communicators are lying or telling the truth. All moral behavior depends upon agreements between human beings; some assurance is necessary that people are entering such agreements with honesty. Truth telling and honesty are basic cornerstones of ethics and moral behavior.

> ***Do you think that a company should integrate all five generations of issues into its activities? Why or why not? If such integration took place, what would be some of the barriers the company would face?***

Justification: A basic agreement to be truthful is necessary to the communication of an ethical theory. Such an agreement is also extremely important in establishing and maintaining vital and meaningful human relationships of any kind, moral and immoral. Human beings need to enter into relationship with each other with a sense of mutual trust, believing that whatever they say to one another will be as honest and open an expression of their thoughts and feelings as possible. Thiroux suggests that this may be the most difficult principle to try to live with, because human beings are essentially very vulnerable in the area of human relationships. In order to protect themselves, they may have built up defenses against exposing themselves to others. This is especially true in our contemporary workplace.

Lack of awareness of the employer's and other workers' principles regarding truth telling and honesty affect the core dimension of individuals in the workplace more than any other of the five principles. A strong attempt must be made to be truthful and honest in human relationships, because, in the final analysis, morality depends upon what people say and do. The basis of human relationships is communication. When communication is eroded by lying or dishonesty, that basis is destroyed and meaningful human relationships — especially those in the moral behavior sphere — become impossible. Truth telling and honesty are absolutely necessary, fundamental, and basic to any endeavor of diversity ethics to create moral standards.

Levi Strauss and Company prides itself on being a workplace where its employees aspire to be a part of a winning organization built on the strong foundation of accomplishments, traditions, and values that they have inherited and that continue to lead them to commercial success.

Go to the Levi Strauss and Company website (**www.levis-trauss.com/index-about*****).***   ***—Read the statements of mission, vision, aspiration, and values.***   ***—What statements reflect this company's principle for truth telling and honesty?***

At the site for Social and Ethical Reporting (**http://cet.sund.ac.uk/ethical/what*****), areas of corporate social-responsibility concerns include expressions of justice and fairness in environmental protection, philanthropy, urban investment, and employee schemes. For what reasons do you think truth telling and honesty are important in these areas?***

Another site to visit that underscores the need for principles and implementation strategies to address truth telling and honesty is: ***The Greenwash Award (*****www.corpwatch.org/trac/greenwash/ford*****)***

The principle of individual freedom. This principle is sometimes referred to as the principle of autonomy (the equality principle). It means that other people have rights equal to yours in moral matters, until they prove otherwise. People, being individuals with individual differences, must have the freedom to choose their own ways and means of being moral within the framework of the first four basic principles. Thiroux points out that this principle of moral freedom is limited by the other four principles.

In considering the tremendous variety of human desires, needs, and concerns, people must be allowed to follow the dictates of their own intelligence and conscience as much as possible. This principle is valid only as long as it does not interfere with someone else in any serious way. Because we each experience our own diverse cultural influences, there must be some leeway for people to deal with their difference in the manner that suits them best. One person should not condemn another for the way she or he lives, no matter how great the differences in lifestyles, as long as both people adhere to the principles of value of life, goodness, justice, and honesty.

Justification: Human beings have freedom — in a limited but real sense — of decisions and choices, including ethical decision and moral choices. The question is to what degree they should be allowed such freedom in their dealings with other human beings. The principle of individual freedom resolves the problem of instilling flexibility within the ethical system by taking into consideration the very real diversity that exists among human beings.

Many individuals have to be considered when an attempt is made to establish an ethical standard for them, and although they have common characteristics (bodies, minds, feelings, etc.), each person is unique. Human beings are at different stages of development; they have different talents and abilities and possess different feelings, wants, and needs. The ethical standards and moral mandate must allow for them to live out their lives in unique and different ways.

> ***For further illustration of the need for principles of individual freedom, go to the website*** **www.corpwatch.org/trac/greenwash*****, read the articles, and answer the following questions:***
>
> ***—What individual freedoms are being championed, jeopardized, or violated?***
> ***—From among the first four principles, which principles are not operative? What are your clues?***

Accepting a human being for the true individual that he or she is grants to all individuals the freedom to live their lives in ways best suited to them. This is a natural and empirical truth about human beings. They are in fact unique and different. Freedom, like life, is built into the human structure. The principle of individual freedom is extremely important to any ethical system, in that it can encourage the widest possible expression of moral preferences, choices, and decisions within the structure of the other four principles. This allows for the combination of flexibility and stability that diversity ethics needs to maximize its impact with individuals, groups, and organizations.

Individual freedom is at the core of every group, organization, and community, and must be guided by specific principles and standards. From the global perspective, the World Trade Organization is considered the world's policy maker for issues of trade. Policies that should be addressed by the principle of individual freedom are:

- ✦The impact of globalization on women workers in developing countries
- ✦The right of workers to organize and the right to collective bargaining
- ✦Child-labor issues
- ✦Sweat shops.

Closing Commentary

The challenge of diversity ethics is to help individuals, groups, organizations, and corporations at the most local level to grasp a framework for the work of diversity ethics. Each is ultimately a part of the global reality that nurtures the diverse challenges for economic and community development.

Many of today's corporations are invested in moving beyond affirmative action and hiring practices that provide face validity to consumers. In doing so, corporations are showing that they can take responsibility for their practices and their personnel as well as their products. Diversity practitioners foster corporate responsibility — especially by knowing, understanding, and modeling ethical behavior.

Reference

Covey, S. (1990). *Principle centered leadership.* New York, NY: Summit Books.

Gardenswartz, L. & Rowe, A. (1994) *Teams at work.* Burr Ridge, IL: Irwin Publishing, 1994.

Gilligan, C. (1982) *In a New Voice: Psychological theory and women's development.* Cambridge, MA: Harvard University Press.

Kohlberg, L. (1958) *Unpublished doctoral dissertation*, University of Chicago.

Kohlberg, L (1981). *The philosophy of moral development.* New York: Harper & Row.

Plummer, D.L. (1998). *Use of self diversity skills.* Lecture notes for Diversity Theories Workshop. Diversity Management Program.

Stoltz, P.G. (1997) *Adversity quotient: Turning obstacles into opportunities.* New York: John Wiley and Sons, Inc.

Taylor, J. M. , Gilligan, C. & Sullivan, A. (1997). *Between voice and silence: Women and girls,race and relationship.* Cambidge, MA: Harvard University Press.

Thiroux, J. (1998). *Ethics: theory and practice.* Upper Saddle River, N.J.: Prentice Hall.

Chapter XXI

Diversity Management: Its Future as a Profession

Sandra L. Shullman

Introduction

Many references in this text have made mention of diversity management as a field in its infancy stage. While most people trace its origins to the late 1950's and early 1960's and the Civil Rights movement, they acknowledge that actual practice termed "diversity management" came into its own in the late 1980's and 1990's. During that time, the realities of changing demographics and economics, described in *Workforce 2000* (Johnson & Packer, 1987), rose to conscious levels in some spheres of institutional and corporate America, while finding much resistance in others. Thus, diversity management, over the past ten years or so, has alternately been characterized as a consultant fad and an emerging field of practice. There have, however, been recent signs of infant growth in the direction of professionalism. Examples include the following:

1. Increasing numbers of people and organizations are using the term "diversity management" to refer to a field of endeavor.

2. At least one nationally focused professional organization has been

established. The Diversity Leadership Forum (referred to as the DLF) approved its name in 1998 and included in its mission "to develop the field of Diversity" (DLF, 2000, p.5).

3. At least one formal academic program has been established which focuses specifically on diversity management. In 1997, Cleveland State University, in conjunction with NTL, began a psychology masters degree program in diversity management as an off shoot of the Greater Cleveland Roundtable's Diversity Institute. Other schools and disciplines are beginning to offer diversity management interest tracks.

4. The Diversity Leadership Forum has developed a code of ethics, espoused by members of its association.

5. There has been proliferation of discourse and documentation about professional competencies for diversity management professionals. For example, as part of multi-year group interaction, the Diversity Collegium from the American Institute for Managing Diversity (Bentley College) developed and presented a conceptual framework for the practice of diversity (Diversity Collegium, 2001). Further, Halverson and DiTomaso (2001) have presented a competencies model for organizational diversity professionals.

Diversity management itself is a product of disciplinary diversity, establishing its foundation in applied behavioral science theory and methods. Such theory and methods include anthropology, economics, education, human resource management, organizational behavior, organizational development, political science, psychology and sociology.

Hence the questions arise: Could diversity management become a profession? Is it already moving in that direction? Should it do so? What are the possible consequences of moving in the direction of a profession? What does it mean to be a diversity professional versus a diversity practitioner? How will people prepare themselves to work in diversity management? In this chapter, the author, as a psychologist, provides some perspectives about these questions, recognizing that what is presented here is speculation at best about a future with a lot of unknown variables.

What is a profession?

Before answering the question of whether diversity management is gravitating toward a professional model, it is important to step back and look briefly at that model itself. The concept of a profession is clearly steeped in traditions and foundations of Western culture and plays a significant role in understanding the dynamics of modern Western society (Rice, 1997).

There are many views about both the origins and definition of profession (Cogan, 1953). One school of thought traces the idea of profession back to pre-Christian times, from the Greeks and the academies which flourished with the teachings of Plato, Aristotle, the Stoics in Greece and in studies undertaken in Alexandria's great library (Whitehead, 1935). An opposing view finds no roots for professions in the ancient world but rather in the medieval guilds (Carr-Saunders & Wilson (1933). This view describes occupational roles in both Greece and Rome, now considered as professions, as decidedly non-professional. Accordingly, Greek and Roman lawyers were described as friends pleading causes on behalf of litigants; accountants, architects and engineers were classified as salaried state technical workers; and Roman physicians were often slaves (Cogan, 1953).

It is clear, however, from all perspectives, that exclusive learning societies, which later formed the basis for universities and more modern forms of professions, were fully active by the eleventh century in Europe. The Catholic Church took control of the universities shortly after this time. Surgeons had formed a secular guild structure by the fourteenth century. In the fifteenth century, those who specialized in common law practice broke off from the Catholic Church. Two centuries later, English universities became secular rather than religious institutions. With the decline of feudalism and the rise of individualism, the emergence of science in the eighteenth and nineteenth centuries prompted scientific collegial association.

Thus, Whitehead (1935) viewed the notion of profession as emanating from the Greek schools while Carr-Saunders and Wilson (1933) viewed it as coming from the medieval guilds and the growth of science. Perhaps, of most significance, Whitehead (1935) finally concluded that, despite numerous differences in definitions of profession, focus on theory was the foundation of a profession.

No matter which of these (or other) constructions of profession are chosen, the notion of a profession itself is distinctively Western, steeped in a higher learning and higher education tradition and presented as theory based rather than technique driven. We will return to this in the discussion of scientist versus scientist-practitioner versus applied practitioner later in this chapter.

Lacking a consensus upon a definition of profession, Greenwood (1957) describes five attributes, held in common by all professions, which can serve as preliminary criteria for looking at the development of diversity management as a profession:

(1) A systematic body of theory.

> Currently, while many professions require a high level of skill, so do many other occupations that are not considered professions. For example, according to Greenwood (1957), it requires a high level of skill to do the work of a precision tool-and-die maker or a gem cutter, but they are not considered professions as such. First proposed by Whitehead (1935), professions seem most distinguished by "a fund of knowledge that has been organized into an internally consistent system, called a body of theory" (Greenwood, 1957, p.46).

(2) Professional authority.

> One aspect of a profession is the idea that a member brings a level of judgment to the work, based on advanced theoretically based knowledge, which surpasses the level of judgment of the recipient of the services. Professionals provide services to their clients; they resist thinking of them as customers. In the commercial model (an egoistic model) customers are expected to have much more leeway and responsibility to choose and criticize services as they see fit. When buying a used car, the notion is "buyer beware" and the buyer is expected to kick the tires. If a consumer buys a toaster and changes his/her mind, it can be taken back, whether there is anything wrong with it or not. The emphasis on customer service in the commercial model is based on the idea that "the customer is always right."

A professional model assumes that clients may not always be in the best position to even understand their service needs or have the ability to evaluate the nature of services provided. The emphasis in the professional model is based on the idea that the professional brings authority of action, based on public endorsement of superior expertise, to the client relationship, as long as the professional stays within the confines of areas addressed by that specialized knowledge.

(3) Community sanction.

According to Greenwood (1957), professions derive the power and authority to perform their services from the community at large. The community, for example, sanctions professions through licensing, certification, or accreditation activities. Along with such recognition and public trust comes the power and responsibility of a profession to regulate itself and its members. Often, confidentiality is a privilege granted by the community to the profession so that transactions between professionals and their clients can be viewed as private interactions. Such privilege allows the profession to develop and maintain its own professional standards and to evaluate the work of its members.

(4) Code of ethics.

By virtue of their unique roles in our society, professions do indeed garner a great deal of power, granted by the society. In return for the public trust, professions develop self-regulatory mechanisms to make sure services are appropriate, supply of professionals is accessible and adequate, and pricing is relevant to service. Professions develop formal codes of ethics to impel compliance within a range of behavior. See, for example, the American Psychological Association's *Ethical Principles for Psychologists and Code of Conduct* (APA, 1992). These formal codes of behavior and the informal, unwritten norms related to the code of behavior serve to keep professions focused on the public welfare, thereby protecting the public from egoistic transactions, such as those that underlie the commercial model. Professional behavior is thus comprised of private duties (individual transactions with client population members) and public duties to protect the general public.

(5) Professional culture.

Professions distinguish themselves by the nature and type of formal and informal organizations created to bring together members. Formal organizational settings include work settings, where professionals interact with clients, educational and training settings where professionals aggregate to acquire knowledge, and professional membership organizations where professionals gather on the basis of interest areas or other such variables. These formal and informal groupings, supported by organizational structures form professional cultures, where values, norms, symbols and rituals pull together members and transmit values and beliefs statements about the profession to the public. This public image in turn attracts new members to the profession, pursuing value-based careers rather than self-serving jobs. In fact, one of the vital functions served by professional schools and structures is to ensure that only those who are fit to serve and who are willing to behave consistently with the profession's norms are accepted into the profession.

Recent developments: Is diversity management moving towards a profession?

Looking at Greenwood's five core characteristics of a profession, it is clear that there has been movement towards professionalization in the diversity management community over the past few years. It is likely that momentum for such movement has come from both the public arena and from within the diversity community itself. Embedded in a culture of professionalism in America, potential organizational clients are more frequently looking for distinguishing characteristics of persons to whom they entrust high risk organizational strategies. Some of this pressure likely comes from the need to use resources in diversity management which can be portrayed as superlative, thereby meeting demands coming from potential or real legal challenges—a professional confrontation of the highest degree. Part of this movement toward professionalization may also be due to more widely heightened public awareness of the true complexity of diversity, resulting in the presumption of extensive knowledge and skill required to achieve desired results.

From another perspective on momentum, we see increasing numbers of practitioners in diversity, attempting to distinguish themselves in the marketplace by emphasizing superior knowledge, skills, degrees and certifications, based on formal existing disciplines such as law, psychology, anthropology, economics, etc. Increasing numbers of workshops are given on topics such as how to distinguish oneself in the marketplace and how to provide value added services to clients. Obvious momentum comes from hopes of rising fee structures, consistent with increasing perceptions of uniquely held expertise. In essence, professionalism represents both a desire for higher levels of practice and a branding strategy for practice survival.

Thus, in looking at the five core characteristics of professions, it clearly appears that diversity management is gravitating toward a professional model. Conferences, web sites, organizational functions and initiatives have all used diversity management as central to the nomenclature. Diversity management has in large part in some organizations taken the focus off of affirmative action, a legally embedded professional function. Diversity management as a term blends concepts from behavioral sciences with those from business, bureaucracy and the military and moves away from a legal focus.

We see the proliferation of theory seeking professional gatherings, formal and informal organizational structures, and increasing emphasis on codes of conduct as clear signs of movement. For example, In its 2nd Annual Membership Forum, the Diversity Leadership Forum (2001) sponsored presentations entitled "A Conceptual Framework for the Practice of Diversity", "Not By Chance! Ethical Practice in Diversity," and "Raising the Bar: Professional Standards and Competencies in Diversity Practice." Increasingly the phrase "diversity management professional" is seen in conjunction with diversity management practice.

Is movement toward a profession a good idea? What are the consequences?

Given what professions offer in this culture, it would appear on the face of value that movement toward professionalism by those working in diversity is a beneficial path. First, professionalization would emphasize the reliance on theory building and formal analysis and elevate the need for scientific underpinnings and processes in diversity management work. Under such a model, all work could be systematically questioned and examined. Second, it would help distinguish diversity as a vital unique field, attracting the attention of our best societal talent. Third, it would help to codify and organize societal support for values and concepts embedded in diversity work and move them toward full integration in organizational life. Fourth, it would help protect the public and its client organizations from some truly horrible, irrevocably damaging experiences, created in the name of diversity management initiatives, thereby bringing some consistency and predictability to the work itself. Finally, a profession of diversity management would create more and higher level career paths for those seeking to make diversity their vocational calling and higher compensation for designing and conducting diversity initiatives.

There could also be some unintended consequences of moving diversity work into the professional realm. First, professionalization of diversity may give the work more prestige, power and public authority at the cost of substantially narrowing the range of accepted practices, both positively and negatively. The movement toward consistency and consolidation that comes with early professionalization may tend, at least in the short run, to stifle some potentially creative and useful approaches, especially those based in non-Western cultural traditions. Such approaches could then be alternately viewed as either nonprofessional or unprofessional.

Second, the movement toward a systematic body of theory is likely to gravitate toward multicultural approaches to diversity rather than social justice methods. The building of a systematic body of theory will pull diversity work toward more objective, rational, analytic paradigms as the foundation of practice. The passions often freely expressed in the diversity community about oppression and social justice may find reduced space for expression in the traditionally cognitively based arena of theory building. Professional behavioral constraints may increasingly require all diversity professionals to be and act like all professionals in general—a distinctively white Western male behavioral paradigm.

Third, a likely byproduct of an increasing emphasis on multicultural approaches could be the increasing disenfranchisement and marginalization of social justice and social action agents in diversity. Such agents could run the risk of being increasingly viewed by their own profession as emotional, overly political, theoretically ungrounded, undisciplined, less committed to formal education, less accepting of normative interventions and outcomes, and less willing to conform to behavioral requirements of anointing training institutions. They could eventually even be viewed as a possible risk to the established public good. With formal professionalization, one could easily envision a more formal splitting of the multiculturalists and the social activists, resulting in increasing segregation of the diversity community.

Varieties of Professionalization: Scientist vs Scientist-Practitioner vs Applied Practitioner Models (A Psychologist's Perspective)

No discussion on the future of professionalization in diversity would be complete without some discussion of the relationship among pure scientists, scientist-practitioners and what I have termed "applied practitioners." (For purposes of this discussion and given the author's background, I will use psychology as the source of examples and basis of discussion.) Numbers of persons currently working in diversity are coming from a variety of applied behavioral sciences and have been formally trained at the masters or doctoral levels (and perhaps licensed or certified in some way). They present themselves to organizations as consulting or counseling or organizational psychologists, counselors, consultants, organizational development specialists, adult educators and many other designations. Some people with either terminal masters or doctoral degrees will have been trained largely in specific techniques and procedures consistent with their named field. For example, in the clinical area, some individuals are trained to be hypnotherapists and focus specifically on that area. For other individuals, however, at the Ph.D. or Ed.D. level, they may bring the core grounding of their behavioral science degrees plus the distinct perspectives and formal training of their respective specialties that enable them to call themselves general practice professionals.

For example, a doctoral degree per se in psychology does not presume readiness for professional practice. Professional practice designation requires another level of specificity about professional preparation. Specialty for the purposes of professional practice is defined only at the doctoral level in psychology (masters degrees in psychology are not considered terminal professional degrees) and is described as follows:

> "A specialty in professional practice is a definedarea of practice that connotes special competencybeyond that which is required of all practicingpsychologists. The defined additional competencyis secured through an organized sequence of formall education, training, and experience. It requires knowledge and skills acquired through a broad foundation of scientific and professional education and training in psychology and the knowledge and skills specific to the competency area defined." (CRSPPP, APA, 2002, p.2)

Currently, in psychology, most practicing, licensed psychologists have been trained within the specialties of clinical, counseling, school, or industrial/organizational psychology. (Several other specialty areas have been recently designated but would not yet have many graduates from programs designated by these specialties.)

Much of this complexity arises from adoption of the scientist-practitioner model by the American Psychological Association. By selecting this model, organized psychology has taken the position that those applying scientific psychology to real health and human services problems should be grounded in a core scientific foundation, in addition to using techniques and approaches based on sound scientific bases. (As mentioned previously, some other professions, for example, will designate members as prepared for professional practice with preparation only in applied procedures at both the masters and doctoral levels.)

The scientist-practitioner model is presumed to be more closely tied to a scientific foundation and hence better linked to the pure scientists whose primary goal is the generation of new knowledge. It also presumes a year or two of supervised formal training beyond the doctoral level. Hence, from a general professional practice perspective, the scientist-practitioner model can be considered within the profession of psychology to be at a higher level of professional preparedness required to do the full range of design, development, implementation and evaluation of complex organizational interventions in organizational diversity initiatives. Members of traditional specialties can add proficiencies to their professional training to prepare them with extended expertise for specific human issues, delineated populations, in-depth application of certain intervention techniques, or mastery of a specifiable set of interrelated techniques (CRSSP, American Psychological Association, 2002). In essence, proficiency preparation for a psychologist in professional practice represents a third layer of training beyond core scientific psychology and the specialty levels. For some other professions the proficiency level may be the sole focus for many shorter-term terminal degrees leading to some sort of licensed or certified professional practice.

What could the professional future hold for the diversity community: A view of the possibilities using a psychologist's lens

Taking some cues from the evolution of other fields such as education, social work, and psychology, there are a number of possible and even likely scenarios for the evolution of diversity work. While they are described here somewhat independently, the future is more likely to witness the blending of these approaches. The foreseeable future direction of diversity work will be much more a question of degree of turn than of exclusive selection of one pathway.

(1) Increasing influence of multi-disciplinary, multicultural scientists and scientist-practitioners.

These persons may well form the core of the current momentum for professionalization of diversity work. Rather than forming its own unique body of theory, diversity work is likely to continue to be viewed as a multi-disciplinary, multicultural application of the social and behavioral sciences. In this direction, senior scientists and scientist-practitioners (provided they do not split with each other) from a number of fields could define the core values, knowledge, and scientifically-based applications most relevant to diversity work. They would likely select their colleagues from others with similar credentials and backgrounds. As the marketplace, defined by client organizations, increases the variety of needs for diversity efforts, the scientists, in conjunction with the scientist- practitioners, may be the group asked to work at the highest organizational levels. Under such a scenario, national professional diversity organizations could structure multi-disciplinary dialogues about diversity issues, designed to serve as incubators for new ideas at both the theoretical and practice levels. As multicultural scientists and scientist-practitioners gain ascendance, this may accelerate a split with the social activists in diversity.

*(2) **Proliferation of applied practitioners**.*

In the rush to keep up with increasing demand, there could be an increase in applied masters level programs, where practitioners could be prepared and certified in shorter periods of time to do a variety of specific diversity techniques and procedures. Such practitioners could be used frequently in areas such as awareness building diversity initiatives. If these practitioners are highly successful, they could significantly reduce the demand for those representing higher order training models and create some momentum back toward diffusion of the diversity field. The proliferation of applied practitioners may keep social activists jointly engaged in formal diversity work and slow down momentum toward their separation. Some risk, however, may come from client organizations, who may not be satisfied with the level of progress made by less comprehensive or unproven diversity initiatives. Other risk could occur if multicultural scientists and scientist-practitioners also distance themselves somewhat from the applied practitioner community.

*(3) **Fuller integration of diversity within existing disciplines**.*

While albeit slow, many of the traditional social and behavioral sciences disciplines have begun making some movement to incorporate diversity knowledge into the core of their training programs. This could eventually result in the presumed full integration of diversity into all behavioral functions in the workplace, eventually leading to a de-emphasis on diversity as a vocational focus. Traditional professions in consulting firms would manage issues formerly targeted for diversity specialists.

(4) Separate and equal.

If more objective, scientifically derived interventions do not result in quick or comprehensive enough results in the multinational marketplace, the multicultural scientists and scientist-practitioners may actively work to incorporate social justice and social action approaches into formal intervention strategies. Social action and social justice approaches might be reframed under the rubric of geopolitical or global intervention strategies, especially in work with cultures with distinctively different norms than the U.S. (This skill may be interpreted as really persuading dominant cultures to apply key lessons to their own systems.)

(5) Professionalization slows down as diversity dissolves into something else.

As diversity focuses inward to organize its own growth, the dominant culture of the marketplace may move to different concepts involving diversity (e.g., inclusiveness as the multinational perspective). Such concepts may enable client organizations to go back to "business as usual" under a reformulated melting pot approach. A reconceptualization such as inclusiveness could become the domain of all organizational functions causing diversity to be diluted as an area of professional focus—at least for now.

(6) Many of the above will take wing at the same time.

It is most likely that a number of the scenarios described previously will take place simultaneously. With so much of our organizational and cultural life unsettled both internationally and domestically at this time, diversity challenges will keep emerging. There will be an increasing need for theory and examination of diversity management effectiveness. There will also be a need for more people with at least some level of professional training to do diversity work. The multicultural scientists and scientist-practitioners will have a major role to play in advancing new applications of knowledge. Applied practitioners will find new roles and new markets. Social justice and social action practitioners may find fertile area from which to leverage influence. Globalization in business will expand concepts of diversity and make them less U.S. centered for diversity practice. Some emphasis away from diversity as an organizing principle is also likely to occur. No one truly knows the impact that rapidly changing demographics and business patterns will have on organizational needs. It is clearly time for many things to occur.

In Conclusion...

Diversity will likely struggle with a number of challenges from within its community as differences in models of practice emerge as significant issues. It would appear to be a truly exciting time to be working within diversity management. The field is still being crafted, and professional roles and paths are still emerging. It promises to be a bumpy, thrilling and rewarding ride.

References

American Psychological Association. (2002). *Draft revision: Policy for theRecognition of Specialties and Practice Emphases (Proficiencies) in Professional Psychology).* Washington, DC: Commission for the Recognition of Specialties and Proficiencies in Professional Psychology. (This draft revision has not been formally approved as of August 20, 2002.)

American Psychological Association. (1992). Ethical principles of psychologists and code of conduct. *American Psychologist, 47,* 1597-1611

Brotherton, S. (2001). *Not by chance! Ethical Practice in Diversity.* Presented at the Second Annual Membership Forum, Diversity Leadership Forum.

Carr-Saunders, A. M. , & Wilson, P. A. (1933). *The professions.* Oxford Clarendon Press.

Cogan, M. L. (1953). Toward a definition of profession. *Harvard Education Review, 23,* 33-50.

Diversity Collegium for Collegial Review. (2001). *Exploring a conceptual framework for the practice of diversity.* Presented at the Diversity Symposium, Waltham, Massachusetts.

Diversity Leadership Forum. (2000). *By-laws.* Washington, DC.

Greenwood, E. G. (1957). Attributes of a profession. *Social Work. July,* 45-55.

Halverson, C. , & DiTomaso, N. (2001). *Raising the bar: Benchmarking professional standards and competencies.* Panel presented at the Second Annual Membership Forum, Diversity Leadership Forum. Washington, DC.

Johnston, W. B. (1987). *Workforce 2000: Work and workers for the 21st century.* Indianapolis, IN: Hudson Institute.

Rice, E. R. (1997). The scientist-practitioner split and the future of psychology. *American Psychologist, 52,* 1173-1181

Whitehead, A. N. (1935). *Adventures of Ideas.* New York: The Macmillan Co.

Subject Index

Name Index

About the Editor

Deborah L. Plummer, Ph. D. brings to each diversity and organizational development initiative over 20 years of training and consulting experience and a great deal of enthusiasm. In addition to being a psychologist and a Professor at Cleveland State University where she is the Director of the Diversity Management Program, she is President and Principal Consultant of D.L. Plummer & Associates. She has successfully delivered a variety of diversity training and consulting services for over 50 organizations: including corporations, nonprofit agencies, educational facilities, health care organizations and public agencies.

As a researcher and author, Deborah has published numerous articles and written several book chapters on managing diversity and currently serves on the editorial review board for *The Journal of Black Psychology* and *Gestalt Review*. She has written a non-fiction book on communicating and socializing across racial lines titled *Racing With Friends*. Deborah is a noted speaker of numerous formal paper presentations and invited presentations to the professional community and a regular guest psychologist for Cleveland News Channel 5. She maintains a small private practice counseling individuals, couples and families and has been appointed by the governor to the State of Ohio Board of Psychology.

Dr. Plummer received her Ph.D. from Kent State University in Counseling Psychology. She is also a graduate of the Post-Graduate Training Program at the Gestalt Institute of Cleveland with a specialization in working with groups and holds a Diversity Management Certificate from NTL Institute and a Change Leadership Certificate from Linkage, Inc. Her M.Ed. in Community Counseling is also from Kent State University. She received her B.A. from Notre Dame College of Ohio and has been awarded their Outstanding Alumni Award.

About the Contributors

Jim Henkelman-Bahn and Jacqueline Bahn-Henkelman are principals in BahnHenkelman Consultants. They practice as independent consultants in organization development and diversity management. Much of their work in recent years has been in developing countries working through United Nations agencies. While their practice includes both the non-profit as well as for-profit organizations and agencies, more focus has been with non-profitorganizations including faith based organizations.

Jim has his doctorate from Harvard University and a Master's Degree in Applied Behavioral Sciences from Whitworth College. During his career on the faculty of the University of Maryland College Park, he initiated and directed an experiential doctoral program in Human Resource Development. He is currently an Emeritus Associate Professor in the College of Education at the University of Maryland. and graduate faculty of the Cleveland State University. He is a member of the NTL Institute, the OD Network and the Diversity Leadership Forum.

Jackie earned her doctorate from the University of Maryland College Park and a Master's Degree in Applied Behavioral Sciences from Whitworth College. She is a graduate of the Cleveland Gestalt Institute's Organization and Systems Development Program. Jackie has applied her extensive human resources skills and experience as a therapist, coach, trainer and consultant in over twenty-four different countries.

Philip R. Belzunce, Ph.D., D.A.P.A., SMFT, RPP has extensive experience working with people of diverse nationalities and backgrounds in areas of management and psychology. He runs an organization consulting and psychological firm, Philip R. Belzunce, Ph.D. Inc., since its founding in Cleveland in 1982, and currently renamed, BELLATIERRA, INC. His consulting practice have included leading and facilitating a variety of human relations laboratories and inter-racial relations groups, multicultural and diversity consultation, leadership development and training for board members, couples/families, clergy, government, health agencies, civic and business groups in Asia, Europe, the Mid East, and the United States.

His psychological practice includes a specialty in working with executives, clergy, family business organizations, mixed race couples/groups, Asian-American families, new immigrants, around issues of difference, conflict, culture shock and cultural adjustment, transgenerational conflict, mental health and stress, gender and role difficulties in work-life interfaces, and life/system transition.

Raised in the Philippines and naturalized in the United States, Dr. Belzunce completed a doctorate in Psychology from Kent State University, and is a licensed psychologist in Ohio. He is professional faculty of the Couple and Family Therapy Training Program at the Gestalt Institute of Cleveland. He is adjunct faculty at the Diversity Management Institute of Cleveland State University and an approved supervisor for the AAMFT (American Association of Marriage and Family Therapy). He is affiliated with the American Psychological Association, the Ohio Psychological Association, CORPUS (Corps of Reserved Priest United Service) and the Philippine Institute of Applied Behavioral Sciences. As a certified Healing Tao instructor with the Universal Healing Tao Institute based in Thailand, Dr. Belzunce leads classes in Chi-kung and Tai Chi in Cleveland, Ohio, and incorporates Taoist principles in his teachings.

He is a published author of books entitled, *"What Really Matters is the Heart"*, and *"Heart Shadows"* where his rich cultural background, his training as a Psychologist, Catholic Priest, Taoist, Systems Consultant, and his worldview of Holism and Diversity, serve as a contextual thread.

Patricia Bidol-Padva Ph.D. has worked in the fields of organizational change, complex conflict management and diversity initiatives for more than twenty years. She is an internationally known consultant, mediator and facilitator for the private, public and non-governmental sectors with clients such as Nortel, Bell Atlantic, National Education Association, Florida Department of Transportation, Florida Atlantic University, Shell Canada, Miami-Dade County. She has served as core faculty for graduate programs such as Cleveland State University's Diversity Management Program and the University of Michigan's School of Natural Resources' Environmental Collaborative Conflict Management Program. She has conducted research and written on organizational development and conflict management initiatives. She is a member of the National Training Institute and the Association for Conflict Resolution.

She has worked with client systems to create implementable organization-wide diversity initiatives, form viable community partnerships composed of businesses, schools, special interest groups and other impacted parties and implement inclusive organizational change initiatives that enhance productivy and morale, and craft mutually-beneficial strategic plans.

She facilitated and mediated complex mutli-party conflicts for areas such as the creation of synergistic mergers, resolving tension between social identity affiliate groups and their managers and the creation of master plans for community development that do not displace traditional residents and design of large-scale environmental restoration projects.

Michael Brazzel, Ph.D. is an organization development consultant, economist, former manager in U.S. government agencies and university educator-researcher with consulting, university, and government experience in the areas of: organization development, evaluation, policy analysis, and university teaching and research. He provides organization development services to businesses, government agencies, universities, professional associations, foundations, and other non-profit organizations, in the following areas: strategic organizational change, team development, diversity and social justice, strategic planning, conflict mediation, mission/vision/values work, executive coaching, and organization assessment and design. Dr. Brazzel has held teaching and/or research positions with the American University, Cleveland State University, Harvard-MIT Joint Center for Urban Studies, Newton College, University of North Carolina, University of Missouri, and U.S. Air Force Academy. Dr. Brazzel holds a masters degree in human resource development from American University/NTL Institute and a Ph.D. in economics from Tulane University. He completed post-graduate certificate programs from the Gestalt Institute of Cleveland in the areas of Organization and System Development and Working with Groups. He is a professional member and trainer of the NTL Institute for Applied Behavioral Science, consultant with Elsie Y. Cross Associates and Kaleel Jamison Consulting Group, and member of the Organization Development Network, Diversity Leadership Forum, Association for Conflict Resolution, American Economics Association and Association for Social Economics. His life's work is based in the values: respect for human differences, social justice, and life-long learning.

Veronica Cook-Euell, M.A., P.H.R., served as managing editor, desktop publisher, and indexer for the Handbook. Veronica brought to this endeavor her background of over 20 years with the Postal Service in customer service, technical operations, sales and human resource (Diversity) functions. She has been responsible for over 400 Post Offices providing support and expertise as the Manager, Business Mail Entry. Her last positions include Diversity Development Specialist for the United States Postal Service and Executive Director for the Mayor of Toledo, Ohio. She also has studied extensively in desktop publishing and other technical areas. Currently, Veronica is C.E.O. of Euell Consulting Group which specializes in diversity training, career development facilitation, size acceptance, desktop publishing, indexing and camera ready copy. Veronica holds a Masters Degree in Psychology, Diversity Management Specialization from Cleveland State University and is a Certified Professional in Human Resources (PHR) and she works with organizations, schools and non-profit agencies designing creative solutions that positively impact the bottom-line. Her paramount area of expertise is size acceptance, which she promotes as "the other diversity."

Taylor Cox Jr., is Associate Professor of Organization Behavior and Human Resource Management at the University of Michigan School of Business where he teaches courses on organizational diagnosis and consulting, cultural diversity in organizations and human resources as a competitive advantage. He is also founder and president of Taylor Cox & Associates, Inc., a research and consulting firm specializing in organization change and development work for clients with culturally diverse workforces and markets.

He is author or co-author of more than thirty published articles and cases. His recent work has focused on the link between managing diversity and organizational performance, defining multicultural organizations and developing competency to manage in settings which are culturally diverse. He has authored two books, *Cultural Diversity in Organizations: Theory, Research and Practice* and *Developing Competency to Manage Diversity* (co-authored with Dr. Ruby Beale).

His book, *Cultural Diversity in Organizations: Theory, Research and Practice,* was the 1994 co-winner of the prestigious George R. Terry Book Award given by The National Academy of Management to the book contributing the most to the advancement of the state of knowledge in management during the previous two years.

He has served as senior consultant for the formation of a strategy for managing diversity for many Fortune 500 firms including, Eli Lilly, Ford Motor Company, Phelps Dodge, Exxon and Alcoa.

His consulting group has been working with Alcoa since 1996 and has done work with 10 different Business Units to date.

Beverly R. Fletcher, ED.D. is a consultant, educator, researcher, and manager, whose work focuses on organization development and transformation concepts/applications and issues of social justice. Dr. Fletcher has authored several books, one of which, *Organization transformation theorists and practitioners: Profiles and themes,* deals with how organizations are facing dynamic forces in the social environment that require them to either transform or cease to exist.

As an independent consultant and member of NTL Institute for Applied Behavioral Science, since 1989, Dr. Fletcher has worked with organizations both nationally and internationally in the areas of strategic planning, team development, diversity management, executive coaching, and large-scale change and has consulted with public, nonprofit, and business organizations. She brings to her work the grounding gained from years of experience as a manager, educator, and consultant.

Dr. Fletcher was Principal Investigator for a multi-disciplinary research project for the Oklahoma Department of Corrections on female offenders. The accumulated data resulted in two books *Women prisoners: A forgotten population* (Praeger, 1993) and *Female offenders: An annotated bibliography* (Greenwood Press, 1997). In addition, she has written several articles on the topic of diversity.

Dr. Fletcher received her doctorate in OD from the School of Education at the University of Massachusetts, Amherst. She holds an MBA degree from Pepperdine University in California; has earned a bachelor of science degree from the University of Southern California's School of Business Administration; and has done post doctoral work in Sociology-Justice at American University.

Lalei E. Gutierrez, Ph.D., SMFT, RPP, is a holistic psychologist, polarity therapist, diversity management , and organization development consultant in private practice for the last 19 years. She has extensive experience working with organizations, groups, families in family business, couples/partners/dyads, and individuals along issues of diversity, whole health and stress management, life/work/career transitions, inter-racial relations, leadership development, cross-cultural relations, team building, managing work-life interfaces, culture and gender roles, personal growth, communications and humans relations, executive coaching, professional/clinical consultation, wholeness and well-being.

As Adjunct Faculty with the Department of Psychology of Cleveland State University, she functioned as clinical faculty to the Diversity Management Program, and has taught Group Process and Development, and Applications of Diversity. She facilitates a yearly 9-month diversity leadership/personal and professional growth group for the Masters level students.

As Professional Faculty with the Couples and Family Training Program and the Physical Process Program at the Gestalt Institute of Cleveland, Dr. Gutierrez developed the Ground Sequences model from which she teaches, trains, supervises, and mentors postgraduate students. She is an approved supervisor of the American Association of Marriage and Family Therapy and member of the United States Association of Body Psychotherapy, the Ohio Psychological Association, and the Philippine Institute of Applied Behavioral Sciences.

Born and raised in the Philippines, Dr. Gutierrez completed her Masters in Clinical-Social Psychology at the Ateneo de Manila University. She completed her doctorate in Counseling Psychology at Kent State University and was naturalized citizen of the USA.

On a personal/professional-level, Dr. Gutierrez' life-career journey can be summed as a spiritual Journey that integrates and brings to balance mind-body-spirit to be a healing presence in her life, work and relations. As an energy medicine practitioner and polarity therapist, Reiki Master, and certified Healing Tao instructor with the Universal Healing Tao Institute of Thailand, Dr. Gutierrez teaches and integrates Healing Tao practices, energy and healing in her work. She is consulting author to the book, "Heart Shadows" and is currently co-authoring a book with her husband and colleague, Dr. Philip Belzunce, JOURNEY INTO THE THOU/ "TAO": BE-ING in RELATIONSHIP.

Evangelina Holvino, ED.D. is the Director and Senior Research Faculty at the Center for Gender in Organizations at the Simmons School of Management in Boston. Her research and writing focuses on the intersection of race, gender, and class in organizations. She is also President of Chaos Management, Ltd., an organizational consulting and research partnership. Evangelina has worked in the USA, Europe, Asia, Africa, Latin America and the Caribbean since 1979 specializing in collaborative approaches to organization change and social justice. She has consulted to a wide range of for-profit and non-profit organizations in areas such as: designing and implementing global diversity strategies, developing a nation-wide network of health change consultants in Nigeria, developing and conducting managing differences and conflict management educational programs, facilitating strategic planning processes and future search conferences, designing and implementing Latino leadership workshops, and helping leaders and managers increase awareness of and develop group process and intervention skills. Some of her clients include the Woodrow Wilson Center, Verizon, Kraft Foods, Lucent Technologies, The Latino Institute, Chiquita Brands, the World Bank, the Colombia Ministry of the Environment, and the Consultative Group on International Agricultural Research.

Evangelina served as faculty at the School for International Training in Vermont, the American University/NTL Master's Program in human resource management, and has designed and co-taught courses at the University of Massachusetts in multicultural organization development and organization development in alternative settings. Evangelina has a doctorate in organization development from the University of Massachusetts and is a member and former board member of the NTL Institute for Applied Behavioral Science and the Boston Center of the A.K. Rice Institute.

Evangelina was born in Puerto Rico and lives now in Vermont. In addition to her professional writing on topics such as multicultural organization development, class in organizations, Latinos in the workplace, and the simultaneity of race, gender, and class, she is authoring a book of short stories about her life growing up in Puerto Rico.

Edward E. Hubbard, Ph.D. is President and CEO of Hubbard & Hubbard, Inc., Petaluma, CA, an international organization and human performance-consulting corporation that specializes in techniques for applied business performance improvement, workforce diversity measurement, instructional design and organizational development.

He is the founder of the *Hubbard Diversity Measurement and Productivity Institute* and is also author of the groundbreaking books: *"Measuring Diversity Results", "How to Calculate Diversity Return-on-Investment" and his soon to be released book: "Building a Diversity Measurement Scorecard".*

Dr. Hubbard is one of the first metrics authors in the field of diversity. As a result of his extensive research in the area of diversity measurement and expertise in computer programming, he is one of the first to develop automated software technologies for measuring diversity return-on-investment and performance improvements.

He has performed client work in organizational change and diverse workforce integration for private companies, the U.S. Government, and corporate clients in the Far East and Pacific Rim. His work includes assisting organizations with staff development, quality improvement, performance improvement strategies, and restructuring work teams to utilize the strengths of a multiethnic workforce and handling diverse work group consolidations using self-directed work team and diversity return-on-investment measures and methods.

Dr. Hubbard is an internationally respected business consultant, trainer, former professor and Director at Ohio State University, a business professional at several Fortune 100 corporations, such as Computer Systems Analyst, Informatics Corporation, Computer Room Operations Manager, Battelle Memorial Institute, Internal Consultant, Mead Corporation, and Director, Training and Organization Development for the 17 billion dollar McKesson Corporation.

Recently, Dr. Hubbard received double honors being named to the prestigious Who's Who in Leading American Executives and Who's Who Worldwide of Global Business Leaders. Author of more than 37 books, some of his other book titles include: The Hidden Side of

Employee Resistance To Change, Managing Customer Service on the Frontline, Managing Your Business For Profitable Growth, Hiring Strategies For Long-Term Success, How To Start Your Own Business With Empty Pockets, Managing Organizational Change: Strategies For Building Commitment.

Articles by Dr. Hubbard have appeared in magazines and newspapers such as Inc., Fortune, Cultural Diversity at Work, Next Step Magazine, Forbes, American Society for Training and Development Journal, Sonoma Business Magazine, Organization Development Network Journal, The Cleveland Plain Dealer, The Press Democrat, The Diversity Factor Magazine, and many others. He has also been featured in several films and management development videos, on radio programs, and is a regularly featured speaker, and keynote for national and international conferences, tele-conferences, seminars, and workshops.

Dr. Hubbard is an expert in Organizational Behavior, Organizational Analysis, Applied Performance Improvement and Measurement Strategies, Strategic Planning, Diversity Measurement, and Organizational Change Methodologies.

Dr. Hubbard earned Bachelors and Masters Degrees from Ohio State University and earned a Ph.D. with **Honors** in Business Administration.

Judith H. Katz, ED.D. is Executive Vice President of The Kaleel Jamison Consulting Group, Inc. Drawing on more than twenty years of experience in strategic culture change work, Judith helps clients achieve long-term, sustainable change by connecting business strategies (including initiatives for quality, leadership, empowerment, and teamwork) to efforts that leverage diversity and create cultures of inclusion. She serves on the Boards of Directors for Social Venture Network and The Group for Cultural Documentation. She is also a member of the Diversity Collegium, a think tank of renowned diversity professionals in the United States. Judith has written over forty articles on issues related to change management, the development of high-performing organizations, and issues of oppression and diversity. She is the author of White Awareness: Handbook for Anti-Racism Training (University of Oklahoma Press, 1978) and co-author, with Frederick A. Miller, of The Inclusion Breakthrough: Unleashing the Real Power of Diversity (Berrett-Koehler, 2002).

Marilyn Loden is a leading authority on leveraging diversity in the workplace. For over 20 years, she has consulted to corporations, government agencies, universities, law and management consulting firms coaching executives, conducting research, designing and implementing comprehensive programs to align organization systems and people management practices in support of employee diversity. Her clients have included many of America's most successful organizations such as the Federal Reserve Bank of San Francisco, Genentech, Harcourt General, Johnson & johnson, NASA Procter & Gamble, Rohm & Haas, Salomon Brothers, Shell Oil, the University of California and the U.S. Treasury Department. Throughout her consulting career, Ms. Loden has combined her knowledge of organization and group development, her prior experiences as a corporate manager in the telecommunications industry and her life-long interest in diversity to help clients build work environments based on the principles of inclusion, respect, cooperation and personal responsibility. Her work and writings have been featured in national U.S. media such as the Chicago Tribune, New York Times, Newsweek, the Wall Street Journal, Washington Post, Working Woman and on the Today Show.

Ms Loden has also contributed to the literature on diversity with three ground-breaking books. Her most recent book, Implementing Diversity (McGraw Hill Irwin Publishing, 1996) discusses the importance of change management principles in orchestrating diversity efforts and candidly describes major obstacles that often derail well-intentioned initiatives. Marilyn was also the lead author of Workforce America! Managing Employee diversity As A Vital Resource (irwin Professional Publishing, 1991), the first comprehensive text about U.S. workforce diversity written for managers and human resource specialists.

Ms. Loden's first book, feminine Leadership or How to Succeed in Business Without Being One of the boys (Times Books, 1985) broke new ground in addressing the glass ceiling issues women managers face when moving up the career ladder into visible leadership roles. Selected as one of the 50 best business books of the year by The Library Journal, Feminine Leadership has been published in six languages.

Ms. Loden received her B.S. in Journalism from Syracuse University and did graduate work in Psychology at New York University. She is a fellow of NTL Institute for Applied Behavioral Science and served as an adjunct member of the graduate faculty at American University in Washington, D.C. In the 1990's, she was named Joyce Barnes Farmer Distinguished Guest Professor at Miami

University in Oxford, Ohio for her work and research on gender, leadership, and diversity. Marilyn is Married and divides her time between Tiburon, California and New York City.

Dr. Ollie Malone, Ph. D. has worked with organizations of various sizes for more than 25 years to improve their overall effectiveness and ability to compete in increasingly competitive environments. He was most recently Vice President, Organization Development and Training with Pennzoil-Quaker State Company in Houston, TX, and is president and principal consultant of Olive Tree Associates, a Dayton, OH-based consulting firm.

His previous professional experience includes working as a coach and teacher of the hearing-impaired at the Kansas School for the Deaf in Olathe, KS. Within the business world, he has held management and executive positions with A T & T, Sprint, The Mead Corporation, and Pennzoil-Quaker State in areas of marketing, finance, human resources, and operations.

Dr. Malone has consulted with numerous Fortune 500 companies in areas of diversity and human capital strategies development and is a published author of articles, exercises, and frameworks that deal with these and other areas of human performance.

His areas of academic focus have included business, communication, psychology and music. An accomplished pianist, vocalist, and flutist, Dr. Malone finds numerous parallels between his passions for classical music and jazz and his work in creating flexible and responsive organizations. He holds degrees from William Jewell College, the University of Kansas, and Texas A & M University.

Married for over 27 years, Dr. Malone and his wife, Christal, make their home in Dayton, OH. They have one son, Nathan, a daughter-in-law, Kelly, and a new granddaughter, Isabelle.

Jacqueline McLemore, Ph.D. has over twenty years experience as a coach, consultant and facilitator of change processes. For the last twelve years, she has been president of Brinegar+McLemore Consulting Associates. Jacquie coaches senior managers and executives as they work to change their organizations and themselves. Additionally she collaborates with teams and organizations to explore, effect and support change. Past roles include: a manufacturing human resources vice president, a senior organization development consultant in a Fortune 50 firm, and a university administrator. The impact of this breadth of experience is deeper understanding of the impact of planned changes and expanded resources for initiating and supporting change processes at individual, group and organization levels.

Jacquie consults with Fortune 500 companies, Professional service firms, Faith based organizations, Independent and public schools, Small to mid-sized companies, and Organizations in the non-profit and governmental arenas.

Examples of recent coaching and consulting engagements include: Collaboration with a global consulting firm on shifting to a more dynamic and inclusive culture; coaching and consulting work with independent school heads, faculty, trustees and staff to increase and strengthen individual, team and institutional strategies for planning and managing change and; designing and facilitating leadership development for emerging leaders under the age of forty.

Jacquie earned a Ph.D. in Organizational Behavior from Case Western Reserve University's Weatherhead School of Management and a Master's of Science Degree in Social Work from the University of Wisconsin-Madison. She is a member of the professional faculty at the Gestalt Institute of Cleveland, and NTL Institute. She has completed post-graduate training at The Gestalt Institute of Cleveland and she holds certification for the Myers-Briggs Type Indicatorâ, the KEYS Creativity Instrument and the Intercultural Development Inventory, and the Achieving Styles Instrument.

Frederick A. Miller has been President and CEO of The Kaleel Jamison Consulting Group, Inc., (KJCG) since 1985. Under his leadership, KJCG has grown from a two-person partnership to a firm of 100 people. A pioneer and renowned authority on issues and opportunities related to creating cultures of inclusion that leverage diversity, he was noted in *The Age of Heretics* (Currency Doubleday, 1996) as one of the forerunners of corporate change. In addition to being a former Board member of Ben and Jerry's Homemade, Inc., he served on the Boards of Directors of the NTL Institute, the Organization Development Network, and American Society for Training and Development. He served as managing editor of *The Promise of Diversity* (McGraw Hill, 1994), regularly publishes articles and speaks on topics related to leveraging diversity and inclusive cultures, and is co-author, with Judith H. Katz, of *The Inclusion Breakthrough: Unleashing the Real Power of Diversity* (Berrett-Koehler, 2002).

Joan SalmonCampbell, D.D. is the lead pastor of Christ's Church (United Church of Christ) in Cleveland, Ohio. Rev. Joan has been a spiritual and Civic leader preaching domestically and internationally--Switzerland, Italy, Nairobi, Kenya, Cuba, ethiopia and South Africa. She is founder and director of Spirit Associates which offers a Spiritural Spa--a virtual space which allows persons in need of strengthening their spiritual muscles to engage in spiritual calisthenics. In addition to diversity management and organizational development, they offer executive coaching tht integrates consulting, personal ethis with daily activies and relationships, spirtual guidance, reike and seichim and courses in Attitudinal Healing, Miracles, bible Discovery, Spiritual Anatomy, Meditation and Personal Mastery. Rev. Joan received her degree from University of rocherster's Eastern School of Music (B.A. in Music); Intermet Seminary (M.A. in Divinity; and Cleveland State University (M.A. in Psychology, Diversity Management Specialization). She has received two honorary doctorates and numerous awards for community and civic contributions. Rev. Joan is married to James Campbell and have seven sons, three daughters, and five grandchildren.

Leslie Meacham Saunders joined the Roundtable Staff in the Spring of 2000. In her role as Vice President of Diversity Management Services, Leslie oversees the work of the Greater Cleveland Roundtable's Center for Diversity Management and Education. Prior to coming to Cleveland, she served as President and Chief Executive Officer of the Memphis Diversity Institute and served in several senior-level management positions with the Girl Scouts of the United States of America (GSUSA), including director of pluralism strategy, director of quality recognition, director of mid-size cities management services and associate director of Girl Scouts National Field Center located in Dallas. Leslie's professional background also includes having served as Assistant Director of Admissions and Coordinator of Special Alumni Projects for the University of Kansas, and as a staff consultant for the State of Kansas' Department of Social Services.

Leslie's leadership, innovation and results in the area of diversity management have received recognition from the President's Commission on Race, the White House, the National Conference Board and the International Labor Organization (a division of the United Nations). Leslie serves on the board of directors of the National Civil

Rights Museum, and the nominating committee of the National Mental Health Association, she is a professional member of the World Future Society, the International Women's Forum, The Links, Incorporated and the City Club of Cleveland.

Leslie's innovative work has received several recognitions during the past two decades. In 1974 she developed one of the nation's first outreach programs for single-parent adolescents. In 1983, Leslie was recognized as being in the top one percent of not-for-profit managers in the nation. Since then, her innovative approaches to organizational development have received numerous recognitions within the for-profit and not-for-profit sectors. In 1999 she was selected as one of 50 Women Making a Difference in the South and one of 20 Southern Women to Watch in the in new millennium. And in November 2001, she was recognized as one of Northern Ohio Live Magazine's 2001 Rainmakers.

Donald J. Seyler, M. A. received his Bachelor of Arts in Anthropology from Washington State University, and holds a Master of Arts in Experimental Cognitive Psychology from Cleveland State University. Donald has presented and published in the area of mathematical cognition and working memory, and received a 2002 American Psychological Foundation/Chairs Of Graduate Departments Of Psychology scholarship award for continued research. He has worked as statistical consult for national corporations. Currently, Donald is continuing the investigation of the relationship between working memory resources and the cognitive processes of basic arithmetic.

Sandra L. Shullman, Ph.D. is Managing Director of the Columbus office of the Executive Development Group, LLC, an international leadership development and consulting firm. She received her undergraduate and master degrees from Dickinson College and Harvard University, and her Ph.D. in counseling psychology from The Ohio State University, where she previously served as part of the University administration. She was formerly co-founder and senior partner of Organizational Horizons, Inc., a regionally based firm providing behavioral healthcare and consulting services. Sandy has also directed Managerial Effectiveness Programs at the Center for Creative Leadership in Greensboro, North Carolina, and served as Senior Consultant and Director of Research for a management consulting organization in Charlotte, North Carolina. In addition, she was Program Director of the Ph.D. training program in Counseling Psychology at Kent State University.

Dr. Shullman is a nationally known practitioner and organizational consultant and serves as an associate for both Lominger, Inc. and the Fort Hill Company. She has written and presented extensively on the topics of performance appraisal, performance management, strategic succession planning, career development, management of self-esteem and motivation, team building, diversity management, sexual harassment, AIDS, and the management of individual, organizational and systems change strategies. She is well known for her work related to executive assessment and development and women's leadership issues. Sandy is Past President of the Ohio Psychological Association and a Fellow of the American Psychological Association, where she chairs the APA Work Group on Executive Coaching. She is also 2002 Chair of the Board of Professional Affairs for the American Psychological Association.

Dr. Shullman currently serves on the graduate faculty for the Diversity Management Program in the Psychology Department at Cleveland State University. She has been involved in assessment-for-development work since 1976 and has worked with managers and leaders from many parts of the world in both the U.S. and abroad.

Steve Slane, Ph.D. is the Director of the Clinical/Counseling MA Program at Cleveland State University. He has written and published extensively in the areas of stress and coping and impression formation. He is co-author of the text, *Statistics in the Behavioral Sciences*, 2nd edition. He is a former partner in Northcoast Behavioral Research Group, is a Senior Analyst for Tactical Decisions Groups, and is currently a partner in the Center for Effective Education. He has consulted for a variety of national and local firms including Smuckers, TRW, GenCorp, Wyse Advertising, Land of Lakes, and KeyCorp. A former chair of the Department of Psychology at Cleveland State University, Steve holds a Master's degree in Experimental Psychology from Idaho State University and a Ph.D. in Social-Personality Psychology from the University of Nebraska-Lincoln. He is editor of the *Journal of Psychology Practice* and is active in state and national organizations directing graduate training in Psychology.

T. Herbert Stevenson, M.A. has been a management consultant for twenty years. He specializes in executive coaching and diversity training. He has published 26 books and is listed in seven Who's Who lists including Who's Who in Finance and Industry and Who's Who in American Law. Herb facilitates mens' circles designed to address the issues of being a man, including increasing personal awareness of self for each member of the circle. Herb is a member of the faculty at the Gestalt Institute of Cleveland and founder of the Medicine of Men program that explores being a man in today's world. As part of his Native American Indian heritage, he has been exploring indigenous healing practices for trauma related incidents. He teaches shamanic healing practices in workshops around the country.

R. Roosevelt Thomas, Jr., Ph.D. has been at the forefront of developing and implementing innovative concepts and strategies for maximizing organizational and individual potential through Diversity Management for the past 15 years. He currently serves as CEO of R. Thomas Consulting & Training, Inc., and President of The American Institute for Managing Diversity (AIMD), and is the author of five published books: *Giraffe and Elephant: A Diversity Fable; Building a House for Diversity: How a Fable About a Giraffe and an Elephant Offers New Strategies for Today's Workforce; Redefining Diversity; Differences Do Make a Difference*; and *Beyond Race and Gender: Unleashing the Power of Your Total Workforce by Managing Diversity.* In 1998, the ***National Academy of Human Resources*** elected and installed Dr. Thomas as a Fellow. He has also been recognized by ***The Wall Street Journal*** as one of the top ten consultants in the country, and cited by ***Human Resource Executive*** as one of HR's Most Influential People. Dr. Thomas has been active for more than 20 years as a consultant to numerous Fortune 500 companies, corporations, professional firms, government entities, non-profit organizations and academic institutions, and he has served as a frequent speaker at national conferences and industry seminars.

Victoria R. Winbush, MSSA, MPH, LISW is the Administrator for Multicultural Concerns for the Cuyahoga County Community Mental Health Board. She previously served as the Director of the Multicultural Training Institute, which was responsible for developing and delivering multicultural training for the public mental health system in Cuyahoga County.

With over 15 years experience, Ms. Winbush has consulted to numerous organizations in the fields of education, human services and health care. Her areas of interest include the development of culturally competent organizations and professionals, and the impact of diversity on group and organizational change processes. She has also served as a department administrative director at a major teaching hospital, and an operations manager for a group practice HMO (health maintenance organization).

Ms. Winbush received her undergraduate degree in Social Services from Barnard College in New York City. She received her Masters Degree in Social Science Administration from the Mandel School of Applied Social Sciences at Case Western Reserve University, and her Masters in Public Health Degree from the University of Michigan. She has completed postgraduate training at the Gestalt Institute of Cleveland in both clinical practice and organization and system development. She is a member of the Professional Staff of the Gestalt Institute of Cleveland.